THE WAR THAT
NEVER WAS

THE WAR THAT NEVER WAS

The Fall of the Soviet Empire

1985–1991

David Pryce-Jones

WEIDENFELD & NICOLSON

London

First published in Great Britain in 1995 by
Weidenfeld & Nicolson

The Orion Publishing Group Ltd
Orion House
5 Upper Saint Martin's Lane
London WC2H 9EA

ISBN 0 297 81320 X

A catalogue record for this book is available
from the British Library

Filmset by Selwood Systems, Midsomer Norton
Printed in Great Britain by Butler & Tanner Ltd, Frome and London

CONTENTS

CONTENTS

PREFACE

As the crisis of communism mounted in the years leading to a peak in 1991, I was anticipating repression on the largest scale. In the light of Marxism–Leninism and past Soviet practice of this doctrine, nothing else was to be expected. Why did it not materialize? I set out to ask those who could provide the insider's answers to this question. I am grateful to everyone who consented to be interviewed.

Interviewing involves striking up a relationship, which may mean a tentative approach, and then the emergence of unsuspected information, leading to impromptu reactions. All the interviews were taped, and for narrative purposes I have often rearranged the sequence of the contents. Everything within inverted commas naturally remains as spoken. National Communist Parties had a General Secretary or sometimes a Secretary General, whom for the sake of clarity I refer to as a First Secretary, to leave the title of General Secretary exclusively to Gorbachev or his predecessors in that post in Moscow.

I should like to single out for their encouraging response, or help, Mark Almond, Shlomo Avineri, George Bailey, Natalie Benckendorff, Janusz Bugajski, Jessica Douglas-Home, Ian Elliott of Radio Free Europe in Munich, Beth Elon, Leonid Finkelstein, Gerald Frost, Paul Goble, Vartan Gregorian, Philip Hanson, Rikke Helms of the Danish Institute in Riga, Alexandra Henderson, Tanya Illingworth, Taras Kuzio, Walter Laqueur, Richard Layard, Nikita Lobanov, Katya Mitova, Bohdan Nayahlo, Herbert Pundik, Alexander Rahr, James Sherr, Nils Taube, Françoise Thom, Vera Tolz, George Urban, Philip Uzzielli, Sonia Westerholt, Dieter Wild and Frank Wisner.

Heartfelt thanks also go to Ben Barkow and Chris Charlesworth for the transcription of tapes from German; to Steven Daley for translation from Czech; to Helen Szamuely for translation from Hungarian; and to Judy Mooney and Emma Rogers and Katie Sutton for professionalism with the word processor.

In Bulgaria I was particularly helped by Filip Dimitrov, Aglika Markova, Miroslav Nankov, Elena Poptodorova, Miroslav Sevlievsky and Ivan Stancioff;

in Czechoslovakia by James de Candole and Martin Weiss; in Estonia by Endel Lippmaa, Hagi Sein and Hennig von Wistinghausen; in Germany by Brigitta Leitner and Michael Naumann; in Hungary by Miklós Németh and Johnathan Sunley; in Latvia by Imants Berzins, Dace Bula and Alexei Grigorievs; in Lithuania by Luba Chornay, Vilius Kavaliauskas, Audra Sabaliuskienė and Regina Stadalnikaitė; in Poland by Jakub Borowski and his wife Tessa Capponi, Marek Matraszek and Piotr Mrozovsky; in Romania by Sergiu Celac, Virginia Gheorghiu, André Pippidi and Christina Trepţa; in Russia by Lucy Ash, Mark Frankland, Misha Smetnik, Arkady Vaksberg, and above all Rachel Osorio, an invaluable guide and fixer.

INTRODUCTION

What the whole world used to know as the Soviet Union died in 1991, and the fears and hopes of mankind accordingly shifted. The Soviet Union was Russia on the march, the last great empire with several hundred nationalities and a dozen once independent states in its grip. It was also a dictatorship, a secret police state, and finally an ideological construct as convinced of its truth as any religion. Communism, in the view of those who promoted it, was destined by nothing less than history to remodel human society everywhere in its image.

Moral absolutes collided here. Reconciliation was impossible between those who believed in this ideological construct, and those who rejected it. How was the ominous reality of Soviet practice at home and abroad to be explained in the light of its messianic doctrine? This was a question about human nature, its ideals and limitations; and the record of the twentieth century in large part consists of the answers which governments and individuals everywhere gave to it.

Force and will had combined here on a scale without precedent. Right up to its deathbed, the Soviet Union was a superpower, with over 4 million men under arms, vast garrisons stationed from East Germany to the China frontier, a thousand warships in commission, and the largest and most lethal arsenal ever assembled, capable of destroying the globe many times over. In the crunch, such military might was none the less powerless to protect the ideological construct of communism, or even to deflect changes of historic magnitude – the sort of change normally resulting from war. Events in the Soviet Union from 1985 to 1991 amounted to The War That Never Was.

Russia recovered a national identity, and so did each of the conquered countries of Eastern Europe. The Baltic republics regained the independence robbed from them as a result of the Second World War. Another post-war anomaly, the creation of two Germanys, disappeared, and those involved in German reunification speak of a 'miracle'. The Russian–German relationship has once more returned to the core of European and indeed world politics.

I

Georgia and Armenia, first conquered in the name of Tsarist imperialism and then again by Lenin, emerged from the Soviet wreckage as states in their own right. So did Ukraine, whose population of 50 million and more had the unenviable distinction of being the world's largest nation not to have a state of their own. Centuries of oppression have to be undone in order for their independence to acquire reality. Belarussians, customarily patronized as a backward variety of Russians, have never known independence or statehood, any more than have Moldavians. The Muslim populations of central Asia are hardly incorporated as national states, but Azerbaijan, Uzbekistan, Tajikistan, Kazakhstan, Kirghyzia and Turkmenistan have sprung straight into the United Nations with all the associated trappings. As befits this explosion which has almost the force of war, there is also territory which nobody knows what to do with: the former East Prussia, now known as Kaliningrad, an enclave cut off from Russia proper.

It was exceptional, not to concede 'miraculous', that events of this historic order should occur so peacefully − as if mankind had learned at last how preferable are political means to the use of force in obtaining desired ends, and so curbed the resort to violence which has been natural down the ages. It was not a foregone conclusion. Although a political process destroyed the Soviet Communist Party, along with the dictatorship and police state which it embodied, aggression of the old unregenerate type was present. Its ructions were soon visible. As the Communist Party took the empire down with it, constituent countries, republics and hitherto suppressed ethnic groupings sought self-expression. 'Small peoples' used to be a typical condescending Soviet phrase to describe such as the Chuvash, Udmurts, Ostyaks, Ingrians, Mordvins, Buryats and dozens of others, altogether an ethnographer's delight. In the Russian Federation, over three hundred declarations of independence have been made, some in the name of peoples, others in the name of districts or even towns. The wish for independence may or may not have political validity. Perhaps the United Nations will receive Tatarstan, Bashkortistan, Chechnya, Yakutya (five times the size of France, with only two hundred thousand Yakuts) among its next petitioners for admission. Meanwhile Azerbaijan and Armenia dispute the territory of Nagorny-Karabakh; Christian Georgians attempt to assert supremacy over the Muslim Abkhaz minority; and Tajik clans do the same among themselves; the Russian general commanding in Moldavia resorted to traditional Soviet strong-arm methods to bring the Romanian population to heel. The final relationship between a nuclear-armed Russia and a nuclear-disarmed Ukraine is unforeseeable.

In numbers of victims, in its idiosyncratic mixture of brutality and refined cruelty, sentimentality and hypocrisy, the Soviet world was a tyranny the like of which had never before been experienced. Its shadow will not easily be lifted. No clear line exists between liberation and danger, hope and confusion.

The Soviet Union should have been able to guarantee a life of exemplary prosperity for its inhabitants. In addition to the famous 'black earth' agricultural belt and plentiful water, it possessed diamonds, gold and other metals in profusion, massive timber forests, and a quarter of the total world energy reserves, including almost half of all natural gas. Yet already by the 1970s growth rates and living standards alike were falling, leading to impoverishment for the mass of the population.

Central planning, the very core of the communist economy, was supposed to introduce a rational system of production and distribution. Loss of liberty, it was usually argued, was a small price to pay for satisfying basic aspirations to a decent life. Central planning in fact erected a producer's monopoly, with resulting shortages and queuing. The obstacles to invention were virtually insuperable. There was no incentive towards maintenance. Most destructively, the entire line from raw material to finished product was at the mercy of anyone who was in a position to interfere. Far from being rational, central planning was subjective and unpredictable, a tangle of the ambitions and greed of those with influence and the power to take decisions. Incompetence and waste and profiteering became the primary characteristics of the economy, and so of the state itself.

Doctored or suppressed outright, statistics are unreliable. Officially the national income had increased ninety-fold from 1928 to 1985, the period of the vaunted Five-Year Plans. In reality, the increase was more like six or seven times. The Soviet Union had only 2 per cent of world trade, less than the Russian share before 1914. Only about 7 or 8 per cent of its industrial production met world standards. One rouble of production in the extractive industries which provided the basic national income, it has been calculated, required two roubles of investment in the 1960s, and by the 1980s as many as seven roubles. What might have seemed like impressive production figures was actually pure squandering of wealth. Twenty-four thousand enterprises, or 15 per cent of the total, were run at a loss, the Prime Minister, Nikolai Ryzhkov, admitted in January 1989, in what was certainly an understatement. Nobody knew the size of the real deficit.

By the 1980s Soviet per capita consumption was somewhat below half that of Western European levels. At the end of that decade, sugar was rationed throughout the country; meat, sausage and animal fats were rationed in roughly one in every five of the 445 cities surveyed by the planning authorities. Three hundred large towns were without central sewage systems, and even in a city like Odessa water was cut off between midnight and five o'clock in the morning, so that lavatories could not be flushed. Rolling stock on the railways could meet about half the national requirements. Only a fifth of the roads were all-weather, and the climate was eroding asphalt surfaces faster than they could be relaid. Public health had collapsed to the extent that in September 1989 the Russian Minister of Health, I. A. Potopov, could without irony offer some general advice: 'To live longer you must breathe less.' Mothers in the Soviet Asian republics were forbidden to breast-feed their babies owing to the chemical pesticides in their milk. In 1988 over 50 million people still lived in communal apartments, and another 100 million had less than nine square metres per person.

In the end the Soviet Union presented the novel spectacle of a country of gigantic potential wealth, organized deliberately in such a way that there was little or nothing to show for it. Such was communism.

Early in the 1980s, a few observers of the Soviet scene began to report on the behaviour of an up-and-coming man, Mikhail Sergeyevich Gorbachev. With unusual self-confidence, he was positioning himself to make a bid for supreme power, photographed at the right hand of the incumbent General Secretary, chosen to make the keynote speech, a frequent traveller abroad and therefore presumed to be a man of the world.

From the party point of view, his was a virtually perfect biography. Born in 1930 in the village of Privalnoye, near Stavropol, about 500 miles from Moscow, he came of peasant stock. A conscientious student, he had risen in strictly orthodox style through the ranks of Komsomol, the youth organization, and joined the party in 1952, carrying on upwards in its ranks to become First Secretary in the Stavropol district. Ever since collectivization, the Soviet Union had been unable to feed itself, and, specializing in agronomy, Gorbachev knew at first hand this disaster zone. Once elected to the Politburo, he was years younger than his colleagues. The advanced age of these leading political elders used to be treated as evidence of the rigidity of the system, but it was also an insurance against a man who through inexperience and over-confidence might be tempted to make an ill-judged bid for power.

By the time that the incumbent General Secretary Konstantin Chernenko died early in March 1985, Gorbachev's succession had become a formality. Healthy, active, industrious, presentable, with an attractive wife, he was only fifty-five. The party leadership was satisfied with its promotion of someone with star quality. His chief sponsor had been the long-standing Foreign Minister, Andrei Gromyko, a thorough Stalinist who was supposed to have said of his protégé, 'This man has a nice smile, but he has iron teeth.' Nobody was left in doubt that like all his six predecessors in the post of General Secretary, Gorbachev would use force if exhortation was not enough. That the seventh General Secretary would also be the last was unimaginable.

Throughout the six years of his rule, Gorbachev insisted that he was a communist, and that the Soviet Union would remain true to its ideological self. To him, Lenin was still the founding father to to be admired and emulated. The party existed to build the 'new society'. Private property was unacceptable: 'Do with me what you will. I cannot accept it.' Communism was also an international reality, and 'to try to undermine it from the outside and wrench a country away from the socialist community means to encroach not only on the will of the people, but also on the entire post-war arrangement, and, in the final analysis, on peace'. Returning to Moscow on the day after the coup in August 1991 which effectively marked the end of his rule, he told a press conference, 'I will struggle until the very end for the renewal of this party. I remain a committed socialist to the depths of my soul.'

Renewal lay in 'perestroika' and 'glasnost', yoked like Siamese twins, and respectively meaning restructuring and openness in public affairs. Day after day during his rule, Gorbachev hammered away at these words, and the entire Soviet hierarchy from marshals down to local party secretaries and obscure journalists repeated and applauded them with the unanimity which was only to be expected. Both concepts in reality contradicted the very basis of party rule. As a result Gorbachev and his renewal destabilized the party, the country, the satellite bloc, finally the whole Soviet edifice.

Looking back after the event, and reflecting on what he now admits were his mistakes, Gorbachev has been constructing a statesman-like persona which cannot be squared with the orthodox communist that he was to the bitter end. What he once did is no longer consonant with his explanations. Becoming General Secretary, as he was to write a year after he had been obliged to resign, 'I knew that an immense task of transformation awaited me. Engaged in the exhausting arms race, the country, it was evident, was at the end of its strength. Economic mechanisms were functioning more and more poorly. Production figures were slumping. Scientific and technical conclusions were cancelled out by an economy totally in the hands of bureaucracy. The population's standard of living was clearly declining. Corruption was gaining ground ... Decomposition also affected the general spirit: the ideological monolith which apparently embraced society had more and more difficulty in preventing official lies, hypocrisy and cynicism from seeping in.'

To ask Gorbachev if at the time he knew where his decisions were leading him and the party is to receive the following answer (which I noted down as he spoke): 'We wanted to reform by launching a democratic process. It was similar to earlier reform attempts. By 1988 we saw that it was clear that the system could not be reformed, and we had to recognize that the economic model imposed in 1917, and based on party monopoly, that accepted the use of force to make it work, did not stand the test of history. We saw that a country and nation with our potential found itself in a historical impasse.'

If he had the opportunity to start all over again, he said, 'I would take the same road and the same strategy. But many things I'd do in a different order.'

Self-justification is only natural. No human being likes to conclude that his actions brought about the opposite effect from what was intended. In Gorbachev's case, a true believer has also been painfully disillusioned. In December 1990, by which time the party was in its death throes, Gorbachev was quoted in *Pravda* addressing his 'dear comrades': 'If Gorbachev was a man who lusts after absolute power, then why did he give it up when he had it? I did have it – the General Secretary in those days was a dictator, with powers unparalleled elsewhere in the world. Nobody had more power. Do you understand? Nobody.' Anger and bewilderment can be detected in Gorbachev's words. It is as though he himself cannot quite believe that his decisions and actions turned topsy-turvy everything he believed in and stood for.

If perestroika and glasnost were really as essential as Gorbachev had claimed, what could it mean except that the seventy Soviet years had led into this blind alley of waste and futile sacrifice? Who except the party and its leaders were to blame? Once out in the open, criticism of the kind could hardly be brought under control by the old repressive methods.

A tragic hero, in the classical definition, is one who causes his own undoing at the moment of his greatest potential. Inadequate information, lack of capacity to judge reality as it is, false preconceptions, can reduce the would-be hero to a fool. Gorbachev did not understand what he had set in motion. Was the nice smile misplaced, or the iron teeth?

In October 1987, in a speech commemorating the seventieth anniversary of the Revolution, Mikhail Gorbachev went much further than Nikita Khrushchev in 1956 by denouncing Stalin in public. This was a consequence of his campaign, then getting under way, in favour of glasnost or openness. 'Through mass repressions and lawlessness Stalin and his entourage have sinned before the party and the Nation. Their guilt is enormous and unforgivable.' In what was soon to be recognized as his habitual manner, he then retracted a good deal of the strength of this statement, by continuing, 'From the viewpoint of historical truth, it is indisputable that Stalin has contributed to the struggle for Socialism and to its defence in the ideological struggle.' Within a matter of weeks followed the foundation of the Memorial Society, whose purpose was to amass the historical record of Stalinism and its victims, to compile lists, and so bring the whole terrifying experience out of the realm of fear and mystification and into the living day. Branches of the Society were established in Karaganda, Potma, Vorkuta, Kolyma and elsewhere. Nobody knows how many people were the victims of communism. As Khrushchev put it, 'No one was keeping count'. Ten million killed in the civil war. Five million in the famine of 1921 and 1922. In the Great Terror perhaps 3 million were executed, 3 million more died in camps. Close to one in ten of the population was in a concentration camp in 1939. Soviet sources say that 10 million soldiers died in the Second World War, with another 10 million civilians. In 1990 the newspaper *Izvestia* calculated that 50 million Russians had died under Stalin. This approximates to the figures – recognized as conservative – of Robert Conquest, one of the foremost historians of the Soviet period, of 20 to 30 million dead during the 1930s. Sometimes it is claimed that as many as 100 million were killed from 1917 to the present.

Everybody was affected. Gorbachev's own grandfather was arrested. Boris Yeltsin writes in his first book, *Against the Grain*: 'I remember only too well when my father was taken away in the middle of the night, even though I was just six years old at the time.' Yeltsin's opponent and Gorbachev's uncertain ally was Yegor Ligachev, a man in the traditional Soviet mould. But his father-in-law, a general, was shot. 'One day my father disappeared,' writes Eduard Shevardnadze in his memoirs. 'My mother withdrew into herself, refusing to answer our anxious questions ... I felt as if the label "son of an enemy of the people" was already stamped on my chest.' The father of Elena Bonner, Andrei Sakharov's wife, was purged. One of Russia's most distinguished intellectuals, Academician Dimitri Likhachev, was due to be executed along with three hundred others one night in Solovki, a notorious camp in the Arctic Circle. He has described how he hid behind stacks of firewood while the shooting was in full swing. 'I was not found ... so they took somebody else instead of me and when I emerged from my hideout the next morning, I was a different man. So many years have passed since then ... and I still cannot forget it.' The executioner, he adds, is still alive.

Dieter Knötzsch was a sensitive German teaching in Moscow during the Gorbachev period and he noted in his diary the 'Week of Conscience' started by the Memorial Society on 25 November 1988. It was in Dom Kultury, or the House of Culture. Knötzsch went along with Valya, a friend who had just discovered from a journalist who had researched in the KGB archives that her father had been shot by the KGB. The queue outside in the street was 200 metres long. The visitors spoke to one another of camps, of dead or missing relations and acquaintances, and the possibility of rehabilitation. Everyone had a word to put in. After a short hour Knötzsch and his friend Valya were allowed in. Their eyes fell on a huge map of the Soviet Union on which the main camps and prisons were represented. On exhibit were photographs and documents of all kinds: objects retrieved from the camps and prisons, cross-examinations, lists of names and requests for searches. The room was full to the point of a crush, but instead of noise there was only a ghostly silence.

Writing in the well-known magazine *Ogonyok*, the journalist Olga Nemi-rovskaya picked out some of the details of this same exhibition. 'Ivan Mikhai-lovich Martemyanov, a poor peasant with nine children from the village of Blagoveshchensk. Arrested 1937. Fate unknown.' There was a photograph of this man and his family. Another photograph was accompanied by a note from K. A. Dudinskaya: 'None of my family came back'. This article recorded entire families destroyed at the time – thirteen from the Kiryanen family, ten from the Pyrstonen family.

This is a country built upon corpses. Alexander Milchakov is the chairman of the offshoot of Memorial known as the Foundation for the Search for the Secret Sites of Burial of Victims of Stalin's Purges. He has revealed sites near Moscow at Butovo and the Kommunarka collective village. Somewhere between 200,000 and 300,000 victims are buried here. 'They were turned to face the ditches and shot in the back', according to Milchakov who has interviewed some of the surviving executioners. Both sites were closed in the 1950s and homes were built over them to be given to the executioners or their descendants. Twenty-four KGB generals have dachas there, and 140 residents have acquired homes as a reward for their parents' involvement in the execution process, or as a reminder. Five mass graves have been revealed so far in the Moscow area alone. Ten victims were uncovered in the zoo.

Alexander Milchakov escorted the American journalist David Remnick to one of these mass graves in the Donskoi monastery, where there is a tomb for 'the grave of unidentified corpses'. In another of these dreadful burial grounds, the Kalitnikovsky cemetery, Milchakov explained that during the purges, 'Every dog in town came to this place. That smell you smell now was three times as bad; blood in the air. People would lean out of their windows and puke all night and the dogs howled till dawn. Sometimes they would find a dog with an arm or a leg walking through the graveyard.'

In Siberia there is a place called Butugychag where uranium used to be mined by slave prisoners. Their bones litter a whole valley. According to a Reuters report, 'So many prisoners died in such camps that skeletons seem to burst from the ground ... no one comes here ... some of the dead were simply thrown down unused mineshafts, others were left in shallow graves now laid bare by blizzards ... we step from the helicopter on to human bones, bleached an extraordinary white.' How is justice to be done in this vast concentration camp and graveyard of a country? And where is the beginning to be made to recover a sense of humanity? Horror springs out of the landscape. One day playwright Leonid Tanyuk was walking through the forest outside Kiev, to come upon a group of children playing football with a human skull. That was how the communal graves in the forest at Bikivnya were discovered, with perhaps another 200,000 bodies in them. Every one of the twenty-five districts of Ukraine is believed to hide at least one mass grave. 'Kurapaty, the Road of Death' was the title of an article in a Belarussian journal, *Literature and Art*, by three Belarussian intellectuals. According to the authors, excavations in May 1988 had revealed several hundred mass graves with thousands and thousands of corpses spread through different sites in the Kurapaty forest. Subsidence and buckling of the earth had finally located these graves. Right across the Soviet Union, it now transpires, local populations knew of these killings, and grave-robbing was frequent. Provincial newspapers have carried accounts of teams, including dentists, setting out at night to recover the gold teeth of the massed corpses.

Pilar Bolet, a Spanish correspondent in Moscow, described how in the spring of 1979 corpses were disinterred in Kolpashevo in the Siberian province of Tomsk. Melting snow and ice in the River Ob had eroded one of the banks, first to uncover a mass grave, and then to sweep the bodies downstream. The captain of a barge was ordered to chop up these bodies with his propeller, and to keep his mouth shut. The party First Secretary in Tomsk at that time was none other than Ligachev and he refers to this ghastly incident in his memoirs. In his account, 'Two dredgers raced up the Ob, quickly demolished the remains of the precipice, and washed the secret cemetery, the visible reminder of Stalin's victims, into the river'. The decision to hush up the whole event, he writes, 'corresponded to the mood of society'. A dismissive phrase like that may contain the most profound explanation of the failure of the Communist Party.

Deep in the collective memory are the degradations to which these unfortunate people have been driven. To be silent about them is by no means the same thing as forgetting. Galina Vishnevskaya, the great singer and wife of the cellist Rostropovich, has recorded how a girl in her class at school stole her ration card during the Leningrad siege: 'animal hunger had overcome reason'. That girl survived, however, because 'she ate human flesh'. Nikita Khrushchev himself in his memoirs quoted a letter sent to him by his subordinate A. I. Kirichenko, party First Secretary of the Odessa region, after a visit to a kolkhoz, or collective farm, in the winter of 1946. 'I found a scene of horror. The woman had the corpse of her own child on the table and was cutting it up. She was chattering away as she worked, "We have already eaten Manechka. Now we will salt down Vanechka. This will keep us for some time." Can you imagine? This woman had gone crazy with hunger and butchered her own children.'

One of the many millions whose lives were ruined was Evgenia Ginzburg, whose book *Within the Whirlwind* is not only a classic in itself but a monument to Soviet inhumanity. In a camp at Belichye near the Burkhala gold mine in

Kolyma, one morning she came face to face with three thugs 'holding a long Yakut sleigh laden with cuts of human flesh. Frozen, bluish hands stuck out obscenely from this heap. Chopped-off arms trailed in the snow. Now and then parts of the entrails spilt over on to the ground. The sacks in which the corpses of the prisoners were supposed to be buried were sensibly utilized by these riff-raff "anatomists" for various barter deals. So I beheld the Belichye funeral rights in their brutal glory.' Evgenia Ginzberg also recalled how a friend of hers, Polina Melikova, a Sinologist and translator, one day hanged herself in camp leaving a note, 'I've had enough', in three sprawling words.

The apparently indiscriminate and open-ended nature of this persecution endows it with that special chilling horror which in the end will be communism's only lasting legacy. Communists will survive in folk memory like the Vandals or the Mongols of old, the most savage of destroyers. It was as if Russians, political cannibals, had devoured themselves. No other nation has ever done such damage to itself, killing so many of its own people while also laying waste to so many other countries.

Yet terror had its rules and its logic, inherent in the theory and practice of communism. Here was a doctrine which claimed to have discovered the key to history, knowing beyond question the means whereby human society was advancing towards its predestined end of perfect justice and equality. Although secular in form, the doctrine had the appeal of religious belief, for whose sake people would willingly sacrifice themselves, as undoubtedly many did, in making the revolution which was the prelude to the new Jerusalem. The means by which equality and justice were to be realized were simple. The masses, the poor, the 'proletariat' in communist parlance, had only to acquire the means of production which were in the hands of the rich, or 'capitalists' – land, factories, banks. Since the capitalists were bound to defend their interests, class warfare was inevitable and therefore to be waged with expectation of certain victory. Since communists knew what was in the best interests of other people, what might look like confiscation and rule by force should really be perceived as utopian, akin to loving kindness. Busy constructing its heaven on earth, the party itself loftily theorized about confiscation and enforcement. From the revolution of 1917 onwards the party entrusted the secret police with the ugly administrative mechanics. The secret police was euphemistically described as 'the avenging sword of the proletariat' or 'the shield of the revolution' though nobody was in doubt about the nature of its activities. The pursuit of justice and equality, as already defined by the party, rendered superfluous all considerations of law. To the party, in any case, law was not some objective code or set of civic regulations agreed between rulers and ruled, but a mere expression of the will of whoever happened to be applying it. That was an elementary deduction for those who believed that ownership of the means of production determined the entire society. So the secret police was encouraged by doctrine and allowed in practice to be a law unto itself. From the outset the party and the secret police were interacting bodies, in which temporary conflicts of interests were secondary to the prime common purpose of compelling everyone to submit to the dictates of communism.

A recently declassified instruction from Lenin in August 1918 runs: 'Comrades! The rebellion of kulaks in five regions must lead to its merciless suppression. We must teach them a lesson. 1) Hang 100 inveterate kulaks publicly. 2) Publish their names. 3) Take away all their bread. 4) Take hostages. Make sure that the people for many miles around saw, trembled, knew and screamed.' After an interview with Lenin the philosopher Bertrand Russell commented, 'His guffaw at the thought of those massacred made my blood run cold.'

Under Stalin, terror and communism were revealed as synonyms. Nothing that Stalin said or did suggests that he ever had the least doubt or scruple about deploying terror as the means to fulfil communism. Pipe in mouth, he jotted 'Shoot' or 'Shoot at once' in red pencil on the margins of the innumerable lists placed on his desk. Whimsically, he was sometimes harsher to those whose names he recognized, though sometimes he might spare one or two. The instrumental view of terror has never been more inhumanly expressed.

With the benefit of hindsight, it is a riddle how anybody could ever have believed in such simplifications as 'proletarians' and 'capitalists'. Messianic doctrines need a division between the good and the bad, friend and foe, the chosen and the damned. Self-evidently, human beings are too various to be reduced to such catch-all categories. Class is a term too vague to have much application outside sociology departments and sloganizing; it has no functional meaning. The reduction, however, enabled the secret police and the party to eliminate by whatever means it chose the long and oppressive list of its enemies, the 'bourgeois', kulaks or those peasants of whom it disapproved, deviationists, Trotskyites, fascists, landlords, imperialists, and the equally long and oppressive list of its supporters who for one reason or another had failed the test, 'wreckers', 'saboteurs', 'enemies of the people', 'Titoists', 'parasites', Zionists, followers of the 'cult of personality' and all the rest of it.

The KGB, to use the acronym by which the secret police came to be known in its final stages, is thought to have employed some 400,000 officers and men, with another 200,000 border troops. Responsible for security, it also ran the operations of internal and foreign intelligence. It had branches in all Russian cities and towns, its own provincial organizations, and networks under its control in virtually every country in the world. KGB influence has been detected where no Soviet interest could possibly have been at stake, for instance, in the islands of Fiji, Vanuatu and Grenada. According to one specialist, John Barron, more than 250,000 KGB operatives were employed abroad. Nobody can guess how many informers, whether volunteers or recruited under some form of compulsion, were also employed, but probably millions all told. It could also call on infantry and armoured divisions nominally under the control of the Ministry of the Interior; it had its own special force known as the Dzerzhinsky Division for the protection of the communist élite, and numerous units with specialist roles of which OMON and Alpha were latterly the most notorious. KGB officers were seconded throughout the army and party to ensure reliability.

The relationship between the General Secretary of the party and the chairman of the KGB was always critical. It used to be said that the two men would communicate at least half a dozen times a day. Should they not reinforce one another, the resulting uncertainty was bound to be reflected down to every level in society. Should they disagree, then the prospects of a power rivalry appeared. Yuri Andropov was chairman of the KGB from 1967 to 1982, when he was elected General Secretary. This was an open acknowledgement of the obvious proposition that the KGB effectively ran the country. Whether Gorbachev was a hidden candidate of the KGB when he was elected General Secretary in 1985 is not known. This much can be stated, that whereas he set about reforming the entire political and economic existence of the Soviet Union, he left the KGB as he found it. It must have seemed to him, as it did to everyone else, that the KGB was the ultimate guarantee of stability, quite uncrackable, capable of keeping control where it mattered, on the streets, in mines and factories and collectives, irrespective of what anyone in the Soviet Union might do or say. Ultimately, Siberia was as cold as ever, the camps had not been dismantled, trains ran, and the apparatus for repression needed only the will to activate it.

Was it the arrogance of power? The KGB had been in absolute control for so long, had manipulated, organized and frightened everyone at home and abroad so thoroughly that its leadership could not conceive of anything else, nor imagine that they were vulnerable, or more accurately, loathed. Or did they set in motion a process of reform which was not intended to be genuine but only to provide the secret police and the party with some sort of legitimacy?

Gorbachev's reforms were in the direction of law and accountability. By that yardstick, the KGB would stand exposed as the criminal organization that it was, not only for its terrorization in the past but for its position above the law in the present. The last chairman of the KGB, Vladimir Kryuchkov, duly joined the other conspirators in the coup in August 1991 whose purpose was to restore the absolute power of the party and the secret police.

★   ★   ★

Nazism, the kindred totalitarian system of this century, was brought to destruction only by a world war. At Nuremberg, the surviving Nazi leaders were tried and those found guilty were hanged. Twelve subsidiary trials followed with numerous further judicial procedures through military or other special tribunals. Only a few of those judged *Hauptschuldige*, or top-category war criminals, escaped justice. Party members were screened, filling in some 13 million questionnaires. By 1 January 1947 there had been 64,500 arrests of Nazis in the British zone of occupation, 92,250 in the American zone, 18,963 in the French zone, and 67,179 in the Soviet zone. In the three Western zones, according to the researches of Wolfgang Benz, 5025 Nazis were accused and sentenced on the main charge of genocide, of whom 806 were sentenced to death, 406 of those sentences being executed. Anyone who had been a member of the Nazi Party prior to May 1937 was purged from public life. By 1948, in the DDR, over half a million people had been excluded from politics and the professions. There were exceptions in both East and West Germany, whereby some former Nazis slipped through the net or were actually promoted precisely because of that past. The East Germans were delighted to uncover an official with a Nazi past in the entourage of Chancellor Adenauer, while ignoring their own uses of a Nazi racist 'expert' like Professor Hans Günther to pen anti-Zionist diatribes. Otto John, the intelligence officer who was the victim of a spectacular kidnap to the DDR, has recorded how three former SS officers named Heinz Felfe, Hans Clemens and Erwin Tiebel were promised an amnesty from Nazi crimes on condition that they worked for the KGB.

No such house-cleaning has occurred to bring communists to justice. Tens of thousands of KGB criminals – camp commandants, torturers, guards, interrogators, trained killers – are living out their retirement on pensions. Not one single trial of secret policemen has been held in Russia to date and no KGB man need consider himself seriously bound by the law. One of the most cold-blooded mass murders ever performed was the butchering in 1940 of at least 15,000 Poles at Katyn (and the disappearance of many more). This murder had the objective of depriving Poland of what was likely to be its post-war élite. The commander of the murder squad was Dimitri Tokaryev, who has appeared on television to justify himself on the grounds that these Poles were class enemies. In another country, he might well have been arrested on leaving the studio. He told the author Nicholas Bethell, 'I am proud of the work that I did in defence of our revolution, I am only sorry that our country seems to have gone to the dogs.' Among other examples of such men left at large, Bethell mentions a Judge Zubiets, who had once sentenced the dissident Irena Ratushinskaya to prison for her poetry and religious faith. 'Times were different then,' says Zubiets, 'I did my duty.' He is now the president of the Kiev Supreme Court. Kryuchkov was brought to trial but only for his role in the August coup. When the trial was suspended he was released, and gave interviews to justify his lack of respect for the law. In Germany, the trial of Erich Honecker collapsed, and the trial of Erich Mielke, the head of the Stasi, or secret police, ended in farce. A few others – Hans Modrow the last communist Prime Minister of the DDR, General Markus Wolf the spymaster, Willi Stoph, Harry Tisch, Werner Krolikowski – were tried, but only one or two of them have been imprisoned. In Romania, Emil Bobu, General Iulian Vlad, General Tudor Postelnicu, Manea Manescu and Stefan Andrei were among the communist leaders imprisoned for crimes. So was Nicu Ceauşescu, playboy son of the late dictator, only to be released on grounds of ill-health. In Latvia, the last First Secretary of the party, Alfrēds Rubiks, was held in prison pending trial. The widow of the Albanian party leader, Enver Hoxha, received a sentence of nine years for embezzlement, which she is currently serving. Todor Zhivkov in Bulgaria has been tried and sentenced to house arrest. Never mind retribution, justice itself is not the order of the day. In Czechoslovakia, a process known as lustration is slowly removing from office known secret policemen and compromised party officials. Communist crime, it seems, is an enormity not to be brought within the law as Nazi crime was.

A vacuum now exists, a free-for-all with power lying in the streets as it did in 1917, so that anyone with the ambition to pick it up may try to do so. The end of the party-state has not coincided with the imposition of the rule of law. In 1917 V. V. Rozanov, a thoughtful and dismayed witness of the Revolution, wrote that Russia had wilted in two days, at the most three: 'It is amazing how she suddenly fell apart, all of her, down to the particles, in pieces.' And what remained? 'Strange to say, nothing, a base people remain.' Rozanov also wrote that 'an iron curtain has descended on Russian history. The show is over. The audience has risen from its seat, it is time for people to put on their coats and go home. They look around. There are no more coats and no more homes.'

As zero hour returns, it is no less baffling that once again there is nobody to blame, in the absence of any reckoning with the party and the KGB. Whose fault is all this? To whom is the credit due? Have cause and effect been suspended? Did Gorbachev bring this about? Or did Presidents Reagan and Bush, Star Wars, Nato, the CIA? It is the hoary conundrum about who influences what, and the role of the individual in the making of history. Perhaps television and Western broadcasting seeped in to arouse dissatisfaction and expectation, and maybe there were enough computers to break the party's stranglehold on information and its dissemination. The country could no longer pay its way and, bankrupt, it imploded. Perhaps Pope John Paul II provided a moral alternative in traditional religion, at least in his native

Poland – the KGB may have paid him that tribute in the failed attempt to assassinate him. Perhaps the refusal of the Baltic States to be absorbed was the bone in the throat which choked the Soviet body. Did the Israelis spread consternation in the Kremlin when, in 1982, over Syria they proved that Soviet anti-aircraft defences could be penetrated and destroyed, and the Soviets would lose a world war? Was it imperial overstretch, the invasions of Hungary in 1956, Czechoslovakia in 1968, Afghanistan in 1979, the $500 million paid annually to Nicaragua, the $4 or $5 billion paid to Cuba, and the same sum again to Vietnam? Could it be some supposed superiority acknowledged in Western democracy, although expressed through the cheap symbols of blue jeans and pop music? Something in the *Zeitgeist*, whereby there is neither moral belief nor any supreme authority, and even a secret policeman who insists on obedience is rather ridiculous, with his outlook and vocabulary inspiring pity rather than fear?

There rises up out of the ruined streets and cities of Russia, as out of this bloodstained century itself, the spectral procession of Lenin the archetypal schoolmaster, bald and bearded, Stalin for whom 'every killing was a treat' as Mandelstam wrote in lines that cost him his life, Yagoda and Yezhov and Beria, Bukharin, Lunacharsky, Castro and Guevara, Ulbricht, Thorez, Gramsci, the podgy Khrushchev and the phlegmatic Brezhnev, Kim Philby and Guy Burgess, the prosecutor Vyshinsky, Zhdanov, so many death-dealers, creators of nightmare and illusion and dread in our time. And it was all in vain.

In the old days it was impossible to go beyond formal contacts with Russians. Everyone behind the Iron Curtain was compelled by the KGB to live in an exclusive, frozen and stultified universe. A foreigner who was allowed to pass the time of day with the Russians, to eat or drink with them, perhaps to crack a careful joke, could be sure that he was in the company of secret policemen or their informers, and that anything that transpired in the course of such contacts found its way into the secret police records. The most passing acquaintance with a foreigner was therefore a dangerous liability for the ordinary Russian, and friendship inconceivable. A smile, after all, might lead to exchange of information, and that might lead to questioning, and so on to doubt, and finally to loss of control. One among many upsetting features of the old Soviet Union was the precautionary refusal of passers-by to look you in the eye on the streets. Fear and shame could be read in their expressions. It was a reminder of the Polish poet Adam Mickiewicz's observation about the Russian brutality of his day, 'Every face is a memorial to the nation.' I do not forget the first evening I spent in the company of Russians, in the sunken gloom of the Brezhnev era. A journalist on assignment, I was escorted by three or four 'guides', ostensibly from the Intourist Agency to see 'a typical family' in a highrise building. The plumbing had been installed so that the waste from above roared close to the sitting-room wall. An evening of tormented silence was broken either by the exchange of platitudes and lies, or the submerging swell of this noise.

A complex and protracted system of visas and prepaid vouchers for hotels and restaurants ensured that a foreigner could never escape supervision. Travel was regulated. The KGB operated or manipulated all likely contacts such as taxi-drivers, black-marketeers or dubious women in the hotel lobbies, indeed anyone who appeared to have something to buy or sell. City maps were unavailable. There were no telephone directories, no Yellow Pages, no gazette, no means of finding out addresses, no prospect for the most innocent initiatives to sightsee or to make friends. To make a move not planned in advance for you by the authorities at once acquired an overtone of illegality, of stepping out of line into subversion or espionage.

Some of the technical obstacles remain – there are still no telephone directories, so that shrewdness and success is often a matter of possessing the numbers where men of influence may be reached, whether in their offices or elsewhere. In many cases, the concept of an interview with a westerner is still an unwelcome invasion and you are likely to have your request turned down flat. You have to learn the custom of the country, and approach people through a whole range of intermediaries and fixers, who are either part of their loyal retinue or in a position to ask for a favour in return for something they have themselves performed. Negotiations ensue. 'And now we come to the delicate matter of an honorarium', as one of these fixers said to me. The highest in the land have no scruples about asking for fees in return for an interview. On a number of occasions in the course of preparing this book, I had no choice except to pay, usually about $100. In my mind this had been written off as a transit tax on the passage from communism to a market economy. Or you smash against the custom of the country. Yegor Ligachev agreed to meet me, for example, only to leave for a vacation from which he would not say when he might return. Agreeing to a second appointment, he told me to telephone once I was in Moscow. I flew there, to be informed that conditions had changed and he was not available.

In the ranks of the fixers are drivers with cars, preferably a shattered Moskvich with a windscreen as cracked as ice, blending into the landscape, no invitation to thieves. Often the drivers are exhausted by the search for fuel which has kept them up half the night, sometimes involving barter deals and special payments. Off you set in the morning, to the buildings in special brick reserved for the privileged. They have maintained their apartments there in spite of the collapse of the Communist Party to whose patronage they owe everything except gratitude. You sit in rooms of astonishing similarity, on more or less identical sofas upholstered in something tough and brown, with, in the background, a cupboard for the best china and glass, bookshelves overloaded with Soviet classics, perhaps an African mask or Afghan rug collected in the course of service to the party-state. The ultimate status symbol for these people is a Labrador or English terrier. In their offices, the central feature is usually a vast old-fashioned safe, with locking devices like steering wheels, the repository of secrets and spoils. These former communist dignitaries conform startlingly to a physical type. Broad-shouldered, bulky not to say beefy, swelling necks straining at collars, they give the impression of taking it for granted that nobody will stand in their way. Faces like soup plates. They speak with a menacingly blank politeness and the voice very rarely rises. Sometimes a story will substantiate some piece of villainy or double-dealing, and at its climax there breaks out humour, a grimly satisfied laugh at deceit understood and exposed. They have in common the gesture of wagging the index finger as heavily as a stick, and chopping the air with the hand extended like an axe, or hunching energetically forward with the shoulders, as Gorbachev does, daring anyone to contradict. Years of imposing their will on others have formed a mould.

And you set off to academic institutes, those think-tanks beloved of the Soviets, winding up desolate and draughty stairwells, along corridors that look half abandoned with perhaps a noticeboard or curling poster, to find specialists with national and even international reputations in cold and bare rooms. The typist or receptionist is more likely to have in front of her a wilting potted plant than a typewriter, let alone a computer terminal.

In these institutes are the few hundred men who seem to comprise national public opinion, to have some kind of special licence, whether granted by society or by each other, to talk freely: Yuri Afanasiev, Academician Bogomolov, Abalkin, Aganbegyan, Nikolai Shmelyev, Galina Staravoitova, Sergei Stankevich, Gyorgi Shakhnazarov and the others. These are the insiders of the Sadovy Ring, or central Moscow, and their names crop up in virtually all Western books and articles, setting a line quite as firmly as once their party predecessors did. Nobody is controlling them, to be sure, and the interviews are conducted in private, affably, with a range of emotion from idealism to cynicism. Just one more interview, you think, and the truth must become evident about why communism collapsed.

And you set off too in search of outsiders, who will not repeat the truisms of the Sadovy Ring. Just a couple of kilometres away from the centre of Moscow the roads may turn almost unnavigable. The Moskvich begins to shake like a little tram over gaping potholes and ruts, past dislodged paving blocks and cobbles, past rubbish and detritus, coming to a stop where the road itself may peter out into mud, puddles and broken hulks of cars. Here you see lonely drunks swaying or being helped home by a concerned friend. Addresses seem movable. A building or *Dom* may have a sub-unit or *Korpus*, even a dozen sub-units. Each *Korpus* may have a score of entrances, some impenetrable, others like public lavatories in every sense. Press the button of a Russian elevator and it stops and makes a report like a revolver shot. How, you wonder for the umpteenth time, is it possible for people to live like this? Yet you come away from interviews impressed by the unflinching determination of these people to discover the world they could never enter and the stock of human ideas which they were never allowed to explore officially. Where did they find the courage to educate themselves and how did they manage to persist?

'Everything is negotiable,' the driver says. To illustrate this, he roars out of the car park without paying and the attendant merely shrugs. Like everyone, he secretes somewhere inside his clothes dollars and packets of inflating roubles, in a sheet of newspaper cut and folded elaborately into the form of a wallet.

This is a country in which the shopper is expected to provide his own containers for purchases. There is a way of folding newspaper sheets into the shape of a cornet to be filled by street vendors with billberries, cranberries and the like. In Cairo, in the bazaar, I once encountered second-hand plastic-spoon sellers, and never thought to find a comparable expression of poverty. In Moscow, there are people who make a living selling second-hand plastic bags. Others stand in line in the street, many hundreds of them all together in a straggling snake, offering for sale a piece of used clothing, a single egg, a block of paper, some item of household equipment like a tap. Outside the churches, elderly men and women beg in a manner which is patient but ferocious under the surface. I felt that I had been caught in some time-warp from a Russian novel when I gave a small sum to a blind woman outside the Danilevsky monastery, only to observe more able-bodied beggars moving in to whip it off her the moment I was too far away to do anything – not that I would have dared.

This is a country in which drivers remove their windscreen wipers and disconnect their batteries the moment they park their cars. When I was staying in the Stalinist tower opposite the metro station known as Barricade, I used to have to make my way past a trench dug by some municipal workforce or other, and long since abandoned, with no precaution against accident, no markings of any kind. Old and young, bicyclists, porters from the nearby street-market would stumble in this trench. It is the same with the long grilles set into subway passages and underpasses; these apparently solid metal strips have been twisted up or broken, to create one little mantrap after another.

This is a country where the swimming-pool attendant requires proof of identity, for instance your passport which she will keep and return only after you have swum and conducted yourself according to the rules. She gives you a piece of paper and writes a number on it. This pool was built for the 1980 Olympic Games, but it exhibits many of those smashed iron grilles; ceramics have fallen off the walls; the concrete is stained and damp; electrical fittings are so many wires drooping in the air. Somehow a bird has entered in through the roof and flies beating its wings in panic until it drops dead. You return the piece of paper and request your passport. It is the same attendant, but now she yells '*Straf*', her face reddening. *Straf*, a German loan word, like *Lager*, which has made its way into Gulag. And '*Straf*' confirm two colleagues who suddenly appear in the booth alongside her. Slips of paper have no standing, and she flatly denies having given this one to you. No, that is not her handwriting. Where is the round tag of tin with the number on it which has to be exchanged for official identity cards, papers and passports? If you do not have this tag, then '*Straf*' and she will call the police. Her hand moves towards the telephone. Ah, you can pay a fine for losing the tag you never had, and so give her a trivial amount and the same again to the two colleagues. Everything is negotiable. The whole performance has lasted fifteen minutes, during which time an angry queue has built up with remarks flying about how westerners cheat and abuse others, cannot be trusted, and should stay at home anyhow rather than taking up space in our fine pool.

Here and there, critics used to maintain that communism could not endure in the long run but these were few and far between, dismissed as a rule as incorrigible optimists or self-deceivers. After his stint as a correspondent in Moscow at a time when Stalin was getting into full stride, Malcolm Muggeridge went against the grain. It was a conspicuous act of intellectual freedom and moral vision for him to write that 'the destructive force innate in Bolshevism cannot be carried through to the end'. He continued, 'No whole society can hate long enough to destroy itself; and self-destruction is the only conceivable end of Bolshevism.' So it proved, but the world had long accommodated the more familiar pessimism of George Orwell's resonant image of the future, as a jackboot stamping on the human face for ever.

During the years of Brezhnev's rule, the Soviet Union powered to parity with nuclear weapons with the United States, and huge superiority in conventional weapons. Pre-war aggressions, for instance a fomented revolution in Brazil or the attacks against Finland and the Baltic republics, appeared amateurish in comparison to modern techniques which blended utter brutality with sophisticated deception, perfected in such outrages as the invasion of Czechoslovakia in 1968. In Eastern Europe, what the long serving Foreign Minister Gromyko was pleased to call 'international relations of a new type'

19

had been established once and for all. Under Brezhnev, communist moves in Portugal and Chile threatened the balance of power. The Sandinistas of Nicaragua destabilized Central America after 1979. That same year Brezhnev, seemingly in a fit of pique, sent troops into Afghanistan. There the communist leader Hafizullah Amin had just murdered his predecessor, which Brezhnev found presumptuous. Hafizullah Amin was therefore declared to have invited the Russians in (which, needless to say, was not the case). Within hours he was murdered by those purporting to rescue him and replaced by a Brezhnev stooge, Babrak Karmal. Centuries of feuding in the style of the Great Game had been summarily resolved, and the only repercussion was President Carter's lament that he had suddenly learned more about the nature of communism than in the whole of his previous life. In Africa, a historical process of gaining independence from the colonial powers was reversed as the People's Republic of Congo, Benin, Ethiopia, Mozambique and Angola became Soviet clients. Laos, the Cambodia of the Khmer Rouge and Vietnam, announced that they were 'proletarian dictatorships'.

Between thirty and forty regimes in the world were Marxist–Leninist, in other words tributaries of the Soviet Union. Receiving subsidies from Moscow, a score of National Liberation movements were embryos for the next even larger generation of Marxist–Leninist regimes. One such was the African National Congress and another the Palestinian Liberation Organization. Documents captured from the PLO give the flavour of this type of sponsorship in a résumé of talks held in Moscow in November 1979 between Yasser Arafat, Foreign Minister Gromyko and his deputy Boris Ponomarev. 'Lately we established a committee for friendship and solidarity with the Palestinian people. When the Vietnamese people struggled with the US, we established a similar solidarity committee,' said Ponomarev, adding, 'Vietnam, as we know, later won and we hope that this victory will be achieved too.' Arafat's reply was typical: 'For our part we set up a committee for solidarity with you.' The PLO were ready to do whatever was required of them. At the core of the 'socialist camp' were such institutions as the Council for Mutual Economic Assistance (known as Comecon) and the Warsaw Treaty Organization established in 1955 to protect the Soviet Union and its satellites including Mongolia, Cuba and even Vietnam. In support, too, was a network of some hundred Communist Parties in the enemy or 'capitalist' camp with a total of 80 million members. These parties and their members were also preparing their next Marxist–Leninist generation, destined to enlarge into the permanent progressive future.

In 1973 Alexander Solzhenitsyn took what seemed a leap into the dark when he published an address to the leaders of the Soviet Union. The party would keep its political monopoly, he supposed, but its totalitarian ideology was already void and it might therefore shift to nationalism to sustain any legitimacy it might claim. Four years after this, the dissident Andrei Amalrik published a book with the astonishing title *Will the Soviet Union Survive Until 1984?* In a comment on Amalrik's book the French historian Alain Besançon noted that the Soviet regime in its Leninist form was incapable of evolution. 'If it takes a single step beyond itself, it will burst, volatize and disappear', as indeed happened. Another French writer Emmanuel Todd was reaching the same unusual conclusions at that time. 'The tensions within the Soviet system are approaching the point of rupture. In ten, twenty or thirty years, a surprised world will partake in the withering or the collapse of the first of the communist systems. The Soviet regime is hateful but not stable.' In London in August 1976, the journalist Bernard Levin wrote in *The Times* that he believed a new Russian revolution to be inevitable. The thirst for freedom and decency could not remain much longer unslaked. More or less accurately he predicted, 'There will be no gunfire in the street, no barricades, no general strikes, no hanging of oppressors from lampposts, no sacking and burning of government offices and no seizure of radio stations or mass defections among the Military.' Instead, new faces would appear in the Politburo and he supposed, with a flourish in the direction of an earlier revolution, that this would happen on 14 July 1989.

Opinion along these lines was seeping into some academic circles. Peter Wiles, an economist, for instance wrote in 1982 about Eastern European countries that they displayed a *'fin de siècle'* feeling. Disappointments were cumulative. 'Not just the economy but the whole of the theocratic system is no good, it perpetuates itself just by its own inertia.' Serious reform had to come, he concluded, in the direction of the market and decentralization. The doyen of Russian historians, Richard Pipes, wrote in 1984, 'A deeper insight into internal conditions of Communist countries, the Soviet Union included, indicates they are in the throes of a serious systemic crisis which sooner or later will require action of a decisive kind.'

Such voices had little public influence. Presidents and politicians everywhere, academics, journalists, almost everyone who fancied himself an opinion-maker, believed that the Soviet Union was here to stay, if not by right then by might. Nothing could change what they would have called the facts of life, 'Realpolitik'. The best that could be expected, so ran conventional wisdom, was that the US–Soviet rivalry could be regulated through contractual agreements, for instance over arms control and disarmament. That there was no means of enforcing any agreement which the Soviets might make was no apparent obstacle. Europe would remain divided, there would be two Germanys, two Koreas, and every so often another National Liberation movement would succeed in enlarging the 'socialist camp'. The world might be running out of countries, as Solzhenitsyn said, but the Soviet Union would have its way for as long as it wished.

Almost nothing in the mental awareness either of Soviet Russians or westerners had prepared them for the events leading to the end of communism. On 1 May 1989 the traditional communist parade unrolled in front of the Kremlin with its grandstand on which the dignitaries took the review, Gorbachev centre-stage. Exactly one year later he was booed off that very same platform, and scuttled away from it in ignominy. Yet one more year again and there was no parade and no President Gorbachev, no Communist Party and no Soviet Union. The hammer and sickle had disappeared. It was proposed that Lenin should be removed from his memorial and decently buried next to his mother in St Petersburg. In contrast, the Tsar was to be sanctified as a martyr, and Moscow Cathedral, pulled down by Stalin, rebuilt. In this short span, the familiar communist world was turned upside down. And suddenly that army which had been so frightening was converted into a source of cap badges and fur hats and medals, to be sold everywhere in those glum lines of street vendors. Suddenly those endless socialist-realist books, commissioned to stir the proletariat in order to raise production on all fronts, were revealed as kitsch. Suddenly what had appeared unmitigated power was revealed as pitiful, not frightening at all, but sad and lost in illusion. The recovery of old place-names throughout the empire was symbolism of a dramatic kind. Cities named after Kirov, Kuibyshev, Zagorsk, the ineffable Italian communist Togliatti, reverted to Guenja, Samara, Sergeyev Possad, and Stavropol and Volga. Mount Stalin disappeared from the Tajikistan map. In Hungary, Leninvaros was renamed Tizaujváros, and in Czechoslovakia Gottwaldow reverted to Zlin. In Montenegro, Titograd became Podgorica. Communist stars such as Gheorghiu-Dej, Ulbricht, Zhdanov, Suslov, Kalinin lost their commemoration in the geography of what was no longer the socialist camp. Even Gorky Street in central Moscow recovered its original name of Tverskaia. Statues of Marx and Lenin were cleared away by the thousand. Squares all over the empire from Estonia to the Pamirs have nothing but holes and perhaps a few rivets and stanchions to show where heroic statues of the founders of Marxism–Leninism were once rising larger than life. In the centre of Moscow, a gigantic head of Marx in stone which must weigh hundreds of tons was to be observed with the attachment of a balloon publicizing a credit card. In Warsaw, Communist Party headquarters have been given over to the trading rooms of a Western bank. The Scinteia building in Bucharest, a Stalinist monster, is now the Romanian Stock Exchange. Most striking of all, perhaps, in front of the Lubyanka, the most notorious of prisons, the statue of Felix Dzerzhinsky, founder of the secret police and its archetypal monster, has been removed. On the surviving plinth is a cross with the inscription 'With this we have won' in Old Church Slavonic.

'Homo sovieticus' was a frightening concept, dating from the Brezhnev era. Its presupposition was that communism claimed to have changed human nature, and actually had done so in Russia, and possibly in the Soviet satellites as well. Conditioning is everything. Like Pavlov's dogs, human beings can be taught according to a system of ideology, supported by carefully measured punishments and rewards, to become units, performing like so many social parts of an engine rather than individuals. Some higher mechanic has only to tinker in order to tune these parts as he wishes. In the depths of this concept is fear: the most primitive animal fear that each one of us, when confronted with our totalitarian jailer or torturer, will sacrifice every value and moral standard to save his skin. This is the lesson of twentieth-century literature, never expressed more lucidly or shatteringly than in George Orwell's *1984*. That novel's famous and archetypal character Winston Smith is terrorized into abdicating his very self. Big Brother does nothing less than steal his personality, after which, the tears pouring down his cheeks, Winston realizes that 'He loved Big Brother'.

Could it happen? Is human nature malleable in this way? In the 1960s as Brezhnev and the party succeeded in suffocating their own people and advancing communism abroad, a number of Russians began to ask these questions. Dissidents, as they came to be called, were to provide headline news for the next twenty years. As yet no book does full justice to the dissidents, and their achievements cannot be properly evaluated. At the time, it was not possible to decide if they were the last of a species of individual now facing extinction or, on the contrary, the first spokesmen to assert that human nature is, and always stays, triumphantly itself.

In the late 1960s, wrote the Russian historian Alexander Yanev, now living in the West, 'it was as though "from under the rubble" of moss-covered official ideology, fresh new voices suddenly started to force their way through, proclaiming the need for a single "national rebirth". This new spirit arose from below and swept like a whirlwind.' Solzhenitsyn (who was still writing *The Gulag Archipelago*), Yanev thought, summed up the current mood when he described Russians not as a ruling class but as the state's slaves. They were going under: 'The Russian people are emaciated and biologically degenerating, their national consciousness is humiliated and suppressed.'

Dissidents in general agreed with this judgement of Solzhenitsyn's. Among them, Alexander Zinoviev and Vladimir Bukovsky stood out for the range, brilliance and courage of their opinions. Both were soon to be catapulted out of the Soviet Union into the West. Prolific writers, they naturally were not always consistent in their observations and their conclusions, and in any case their own personal examples proved that communist ideology could not be as inhumanly unstoppable as the party claimed.

Although scattering his shot very widely, Zinoviev may have done more than anyone else to establish that Homo sovieticus had indeed been born and was reaching adulthood. At least one part of Zinoviev evidently believed that the Russian people had degenerated intellectually beyond repair; the truth was so cunningly concealed from them that they simply had no access to it and so could never acquire perspective on their wretchedness. 'Our norm,' Zinoviev wrote, 'comprises the most repugnant qualities of human nature without which it is impossible to survive in Soviet social conditions. And all this filth is veiled by the most grandiose and the most mendacious of ideologies.' Life at the frontier of social possibility 'engenders social bugs, social worms, social rats, social snakes, lizards, scorpions', and these types had 'a better chance of survival here than the species which emerge in the favourable social conditions of Western civilization'. The country's social system, Zinoviev concluded, had become by this means 'essentially unshakeable'. Homo sovieticus was in the ascendant. 'The Soviet Union as a whole behaves like the average Soviet citizen: It is unreliable, mendacious, hypocritical, it is boorish when it is in a position of strength, cringes in the face of superior strength, and in addition is absolutely sincere.'

Bukovsky was dismayed to discover that others did not share his magnificent combativeness. 'It is said that for twenty years an eccentric Englishman cut the tails off rats in the expectation that they would produce tail-less offspring, but nothing came of it and he gave up. What can you expect of an Englishman? No, that's no way to build socialism. He lacked sufficient passion, a healthy faith in the radiant future. It was quite different in our country. They cut off people's heads for decades, and at least saw the birth of a new type of headless people.' Witheringly, he could go further: 'Our Soviet life was actually nothing more than an imaginary schizophrenic world populated with invented Soviet men building a mythical communism. Weren't we all living double or even treble lives?'

Other commentators and observers often emphasized that a dual nature was central to communist society. Another early dissident, Konstantin Simis (also a refugee in the West), put it well in a book published in 1982 when he wrote that 'Homo sovieticus simply has two separate systems of morality'. Breaking the law, he did not consider himself immoral. Lying to representatives from authority and the party was compatible with honesty to friends.

In that case, Homo sovieticus was not quite as alarming as he appeared.

One took precautions outwardly, while inwardly keeping reservations and setting oneself standards of behaviour in areas where such standards mattered. The double and treble lives were safeguards rather than degenerations.

Westerners had little evidence to go on, and they are hardly to be blamed for taking at face value what they were told by Russians. Few books by westerners were more influential in forming attitudes towards Soviet Russia than Hedrick Smith's *The Russians*, published in 1976. Smith had been the *New York Times* correspondent in Moscow. On one page he could spot 'ideological dry rot', only to continue a few pages later, 'Russians retain a basic unquestioning confidence in their way of life' – a judgement which can be seen today to have had no foundation.

David Satter of the *Financial Times* may be thought to have summed up what was the collective wisdom of correspondents observing Moscow at first hand when he wrote in 1982, 'The Soviet Union claims to have created a new man and, I believe, unfortunately, that there is truth in their claim'. This new man believed in the validity of his own spiritual suffering and his powers of endurance, and to this he brought instinctive respect for authority as well as deeply ingrained fear. Such reporters and correspondents were doing no more than pass on what they heard from Russians themselves. Here is Anatoly Koryagin speaking in May 1987 – he was a doctor who protested against the imprisonment of dissidents in mental hospitals, for which he was himself arrested. 'Oh yes, there is undoubtedly a psychological type we can call Homo sovieticus. When I was in the Gulag the camp commander said to me one day: "Come on, Koryagin, after all you and I are both people. You are a man and I am a man; so come on, let's try and find some common ground, let's try to make some compromises." What he had in mind is that I should meet his demands halfway. So I answered: "Yes, we are both human beings, but I am Homo sapiens while you are Homo sovieticus. You and I cannot possibly find any common language."' To Koryagin, this new man had inwardly accepted the stereotypes foisted upon him and to various degrees was willingly controlled from above. 'He is a programmed being, a psychological robot, putty in the hands of Soviet ideologues.'

Such harsh descriptions were true as far as they went, but the defensive mechanisms of human nature were too strong to give them any lasting significance. In the aftermath of collapse, it has become obvious that even dissidents and informed westerners internalized the communist self-portrayal. In this image of Homo sovieticus, they were coming to believe what the communists wished them to believe. Their very gloom was itself magnification and flattery of communism and its consequences. They had to take evasive action for fear of coming into the ken, or reach, of those masters; they had also to live with their families or neighbours. Clearly innumerable strategies were possible, some of them offensive, some of them defensive.

Russian history, with its unbroken succession of despots, had prepared many such mechanisms, honing them to fine arts. Yuri Afanasiev has described an immemorial attitude persisting in the mass of people, who in his view could not be considered either pro-communist or anti-communist. 'They are simply indifferent to what goes on. In villages and distant little towns, people drink and let the world go by. They work a bit, from time to time, for form's sake, they steal regularly any collective property', but not in excess and not enough to be caught at it. Afanasiev further certified the proposition that everything is negotiable, nobody is punished: 'You use state transportation or kolkhoz tractors to go and buy vodka from the next village.'

'A passion for self-dramatization' is a Russian trait, according to Ronald Hingley. His study *The Russian Mind* thoroughly explores national character, that subject too fluid to be properly defined. Hingley quotes a pre-revolutionary writer Leonid Andreyev to the effect that 'the Russian is incapable of telling downright lies; but he seems equally incapable of telling the truth. The intermediate phenomenon for which he feels the utmost love and tenderness . . . is vranyo.'

'Vranyo', in Hingley's definition, is a key concept, a particular 'national brand of leg-pulling, ribbing or blarney'. Not outright falsification, it is a dissemination of untruths, for purposes of self-protection and hiding. This has emerged since Stalin's death, Hingley explains, at the centre of the public posture under Soviet totalitarianism. Dispensers of vranyo may or may not believe a word of what they are saying. The object is solely to impress their own essentially sound and correct behaviour and opinion upon their interlocutors. The consequences will be to spare them from any punishment for their actions. Khrushchev banging his shoe on the table at the United Nations, several thousand members of the USSR Supreme Soviet raising their hands together in unanimous voting, the May Day parade of the uniformed hundreds and thousands with their supporting tanks and missiles, 'democratization' as introduced by Gorbachev, are examples of the self-dramatizing vranyo induced by communism. In the ruins of today, communism itself is coming to look like some gigantic example of vranyo which the Russians projected on the whole unsuspecting world.

In his *Memoirs of Shostakovich* Solomon Volkov gives another example of inherited attitudes surviving to circumvent and obstruct the demands of communist ideology. Like virtually everyone else, the composer Shostakovich had no wish to enter into open conflict with the authorities. He chose to become a 'yurodivy', another untranslatable term, meaning someone who plays the fool, under cover of which he is really drawing attention to the injustices and evils which are obliging him to play the fool. The yurodivy behaves within the conventional limits required of him – but his behaviour is itself a screen erected with mockery, sarcasm and false stupidity. Knowing his own limits, he makes sure that others are puzzled about him. That huge, dreary and downtrodden mass so contemptuously reduced under the phrase Homo sovieticus, in fact consisted of millions of individuals, yurodivy and masters of vranyo negotiating as their forebears had, through an infinite variety of strategems, dodges and evasions, calling upon cultural memories to help them survive commissars as once they had survived Khans and Tsars and other assorted despots.

I

'NO ONE WAS HAPPY'

'If you like the Soviet Union so much, why don't you go and live there?'
Everyday arguments about communism and capitalism often concluded
with this retort. It was not at a high intellectual level, but it none the less
contained its truth. Communism had transformed what ought to have been
the simplest and most routine matters of daily life into a variety of hardships
and obstacles. The penury was deliberate, the product of bureaucratic sadism,
whose purpose was to control the entire population. Natalia Perova has literary
tastes and has become a publisher. The communal flat in which she grew up
in Moscow was shared by many people. The floor was common to everyone
and what had once been open space had been partitioned or sectioned into
rooms. The result was that whoever walked in these rooms caused the whole
floor to creak. Everyone shared a kitchen and a single lavatory. One of the
inhabitants was an exhibitionist who would position himself in the lavatory
with his trousers down. Another would bring several prostitutes into his room
at once. There was an old woman who enjoyed making life impossible by
tampering with the washing line, turning up the kerosene, even dropping a
rat into the soup. People would cook for two to three days at a time, once
their turn had arrived to use the stove. There was a weekly visit to a bath-
house. Marriage for Natalia Perova eventually brought the inestimable bonus
of moving into a communal flat with only one neighbour to share it.

There was a general social atmosphere to which one became used, she says.
It was difficult to be registered with the university without a bribe, so she
enrolled for night classes and attended by day. She could afford only the night
classes, where the students were notably less motivated, but sympathetic
teachers saw her ambition and admitted her to day classes. In her first year at
university a group of Americans came from the Russian department at Yale
and it was permitted to practise the English language with them. These
Americans sang Russian songs and said they were going south to Yalta,
suggesting that Russian students should accompany them. So they did. It was
highly innocent. A boat took them from the Crimea to the Caucasus coast.

29

To meet Americans was excitement in itself. Back in Moscow, the KGB summoned Natalia, explaining that they had kept this party under surveillance. At the end of the second day of interrogation a KGB man said, 'How could you, a Komsomol member, become friendly with enemies of our state?' As a graduate in English, she obtained a job at an agency called Progress, concerned with translation. Once again she was summoned to the KGB to be told that she had a talent for working with foreigners and would have to report on their activities. It was obvious to her that someone had tipped them off. She suspected a colleague, and warned others in the office against this person. Moving later to Intourist, the agency handling all visitors to the Soviet Union, she was routinely required to fill in reports on foreigners, in particular any anti–Soviet reactions. Growing up, her daughter worked in the same way with the same people in the same room, a striking example of the pervasive sense of fate inculcated by the party into ordinary people, that there was nothing they could do to take charge of their own lives.

Discovery of the society in which he was expected to live, and the subsequent disillusionment, was no less painful for Yuri Mityunov. He was born into a Stalinist family. His father was a border guard, and his mother a party member for thirty-five years. They lived in Arkhangelsk, in the region of concentration camps. Prisoners were part of the landscape, hardly to be considered human beings. As a boy, the aim of his life was to study Marxist–Leninist theory and propagandize it so that the whole world would understand it. Studying Latin American languages at a specialist institute, he met foreigners. One day in 1974 the dean of the faculty invited him into his office. A stranger there produced in identity card and proposed that he work for the KGB. For Yuri Mityunov, it was a dream come true, he saw himself as a secret knight for the party. Whenever he had heard that KGB personnel had special privileges and access to goods and services denied to other people, he had thought this was Western calumny. Now he discovered KGB agents paying for him to eat expensive meals in restaurants. It was the first blow to his convictions. The KGB found him work in the Council of Religions, in the department of analysis and statistics. Then came the next blow, because he saw how the law was being broken not by religious believers but by the state. The institute, he discovered, was a KGB structure, designed to keep in check any sign of free expression in the name of religion.

The decisive incident concerned his apartment. Important people connected with the Bolshoi Theatre wished to obtain it and began harassing him. When he complained to the Moscow city council, one of the officials there punched him in the face. This was unusual even in the Brezhnev years, so he took the man to court. Friends began to explain to him that he was opening himself to accusations of being a dissident. A long story unwound, involving all sorts of pressures upon him. Although his sponsors in the KGB felt that they could not abandon him he was also aware of being shadowed. Dismissed from his job on indefinite leave, he was threatened with a spell in a psychiatric hospital. With a group of friends he occupied the office of the Council of Religions and demanded a hearing. The KGB officer who supervised the Council of Religions was a Colonel Valentin Timoshev, and he agreed that there would be an investigation, the question of the flat would be sorted out, and the occupation of the office would have no repercussions. Three days later he was allowed his flat. None the less the man who had punched him in the face had been promoted. It is his belief that Andropov himself had heard of the affair and in 1982 arranged for him to work at Gosteleradio, the official radio station, as a translator.

To Mityunov and his friends the election of Gorbachev in 1985 meant nothing. They had no information about the man. The first Gorbachev slogans concerned acceleration and cleaning up corruption, which sounded like similar campaigns for discipline under Andropov. A moment of open break came in March 1986 when he was ill. Instead of a doctor, a committee of psychiatrists arrived, wanting to certify him insane. He decided it was better to be anti-Soviet than mad. So he resigned from the party as did his mother. Immediately he was sacked from Gosteleradio. A course was set whereby he joined the Helsinki Group in defence of human rights and soon became a Moscow correspondent for Radio Liberty. From the authorities' point of view, Radio Liberty was the voice of the enemy. This was open confrontation. This was also how the scales were pulled off the eyes of true believers.

'In 1987 we still could not see what was coming,' says Mityunov, and it was only two years later that people began to believe in Gorbachev's reforms. Perestroika, as Gorbachev called his restructuring, had got into gear as another phase in the non-productivity of the economy. Communism had proved itself a parasite, and everyone understood that there was nothing more left to steal. The collapse of communism was a process with a dynamics of its own, Mityunov thinks, and not the work of any one individual. The process involved everyone, picking them out in turn, from the highest to the lowest. It is not worthwhile to distinguish between the contributions of Yeltsin, Sakharov, Afanasiev, or anyone. As a journalist, he used to attend the Congress of People's Deputies, the parliament created by Gorbachev in 1989. Both Gorbachev and Yeltsin exploited the desire of the masses for the rule of law and a fairer system, in which, Mityunov says, 'their psychological symmetry was startling. Yeltsin really does not understand democracy. It is a power urge. His relish in the public humiliation of Gorbachev lacked all taste. In this country, the lowest priority is that of human rights. It is futile to look for honourable people in politics here. Even those who may have started out in

31

politics with sincere ideals are caught lying several times a day. You have to look on Russia as the sick man of the world, it can't help itself.'

Few Moscow intellectuals have a higher reputation than Alla Latynina. For someone like her to have survived at all, with her freedom of expression and independence of mind, seems a triumph of the human will. She remembers an occasion when people were sitting in her Moscow apartment, in the Andropov days, discussing different possible scenarios for the future. They concluded that there was no way out: totalitarianism such as communism could not be destroyed from inside. External forces would have to overpower it, and the Soviet Union was too strong, too powerful for any such event. The only possible conclusion was that the situation would extend into the future, without hope. History in fact found an irrational way out of an impasse.

Communism as such was not susceptible to reform. The attempt at reform was destruction enough. If you pull out a single brick, then the whole edifice collapses. Western political scientists and historians had special difficulty perceiving this. 'The Communist Party for a long time had had little or nothing to do with ideology, it had become the party of state management. The vast majority who joined the party did so for some kind of state career. In another country they would have been administrators pure and simple. Had these bureaucrats been able to maintain the power structure without the ideological foundation, then they would have been quite willing to do so. Actually we know very little about the life and ideas and habits of this ruling class, but whenever anything about them emerges it is plain that the ideological trappings were simply so many justifications of power.' During the Brezhnev period, in any circle including party bureaucrats it was considered to be appropriate and *bon ton* to start telling anti-Soviet and anti-communist jokes. 'I had some contact with these people in spite of their two-faced behaviour, and it was plain that they could discuss things quite freely among themselves. They reminded you of Dostoievsky's grand inquisitor in that they believed in the empire but you could not say that they believed in communism.'

Looking back, what was the effect of the dissident movement?

'Dissidents enjoyed the totally silent but strong sympathy of most of the intelligentsia in the country.' There was a network of support, and even if people did not want to participate actively in the movement, they felt obliged to give money and help. There were many intellectuals who did not want to turn themselves into dissidents — not out of cowardice but because they felt it was more useful to use their strength for something more positive, changing society gradually rather than destroying it. 'I was one who believed that it was more useful not to be a dissident but to participate in the most honest and political way I could. It was absolutely essential to find legal forms of acceptable activity, to print articles in the official press where several million people could read them. It was essential to find ways of deceiving and tricking the official ideology.'

Massive efforts were made on those lines and Alla Latynina is convinced that what was done legally did more to change society from the 1960s onwards than the confrontational activities of dissidents. The regime did soften considerably. Besides, enormous pressure was coming from within it, through the thousands of intellectuals and millions of ordinary people who had completely lost belief in communist ideology. This explains why the whole thing collapsed so quickly and why the masses were so indifferent to it.

Soviet life, then, was an abyss of limitless degradation, creating in each individual a sense of his own helplessness. The failure to experience this at first hand accounts for much of the astonishment abroad generated by the system's abrupt ending. The distinguishing mark of non-Russians, soviet-ologists above all, in their confrontation of Soviet reality, was absence of imagination; they could not believe that underneath the ideological surface there really was a life quite different in kind and quality from anything experienced in the West. In communal flats, wrote Vladimir Bukovsky, there was a daily struggle for room to breathe. Life demanded aggression. 'Cultivation and courtesy have turned out to be impossible when confronted with uncouthness, baseness and brute force. How can one oppose these things? By using the same methods? But this leads to spiritual degeneration, the two sides become indistinguishable from one another. By remaining the same? But then you face physical extermination.'

Anatoly Marchenko came to fame as a dissident so revolted by communism that he mutilated himself in protest at what he was made to suffer. His home town was Barabinsk, far away in the provinces. 'Our two-storey wooden barrack had twenty-four rooms inhabited by twenty-four families. There was a kitchen for every three families. Thank God there were only four of us. Some of our neighbours had seven or eight people to a 16-square-metre room. There were times when Father returned from a trip and we had a visitor, say a neighbour or a relative from the village. He'd have to wash up right there, in the room, by the stove. And when he needed to change, Mother took a blanket off the bed and, standing in front of him, blocked him from the visitor's view.' When eventually Marchenko left home it was to find a job in a brickworks in Kursk. He thought himself lucky to scrounge a bed in a room to share with others. Many of the brickworkers appeared to live at the plant, on top of the brick ovens. At first Marchenko thought he was the victim of a practical joke, but during a smoking break he climbed on top of the ovens and, sure enough, discovered the living quarters, littered with empty food cans, food scraps, and vodka and wine bottles everywhere. Marchenko's fate was ultimately tragic, for he died in a concentration camp. Before then, however, he had returned to Barabinsk and this is how he describes what had happened to the friends of his youth. 'Nikolai, Vasily's elder brother, was doing another turn in the camps. Also in the camps were Romka Vodopyanov, Nikolai Katyushin, Petro Pervukhin, Shurka Tsygankov, Vitka Chernov, Zhenka Glinsky, and our "chieftain" Yurka Akimov. Ivan Sorokin, who went in for robbery . . . died of tuberculosis in the camps.'

Nor was there anything particular about the small town of Barabinsk. Chuna, the Siberian settlement where he lived next, provided a hair-raising inventory of crime. 'There were murders: a man shot his grown son with a hunting rifle and the dead man's mother testified for the defence; in another family, a teenage son shot his drunk father; a woman, aided by her mother and brother-in-law, inflicted knife-wounds on her husband, then left the man by the neighbours' fence, where he froze to death; a couple killed their two-year-old daughter (she had made their lives difficult); a single mother doused her newborn with dimethyl and burned the body (or, possibly, the live child) in a stove; a man from Odessa was killed for money; a soldier from a construction battalion raped and murdered an old woman; another soldier raped a six-year-old girl.' This was a reflection, in Marchenko's view, of 'the peculiarities of our era' as well as the level of development of mankind. And no wonder officials did not dare publish crime statistics.

Marat Akcharin is a sensitive writer who in May and June 1990 travelled through the Soviet Union in its final stages of disintegration, publishing his account, under the title *Red Odyssey*. Originally from Tatarstan, he is a Muslim. In the early stages of his journey, he was in Cheboksary. There, in the Palace of Culture, he met a gang headed by Vityok and Lyokha who had given themselves the task of making sure that all girls entering the building removed their knickers. In disgust, Marat Akcharin hit Lyokha with a lead knuckle-duster. Someone called Igoryosha then offered him 'a small moon-faced girl with craters of squeezed pimples on her chin'. This girl was about to comply obediently, when Marat Akcharin hit Igoryosha in turn. Whereupon the girl looked down at Igoryosha on the floor, stood over him with her legs apart and urinated all over him. Next, at the crossing of the Volga, Akcharin picked up a drunk who gambled his wife at cards and lost. In a train going on towards the Aral Sea a student was about to be beaten up by four drunk Kazakhs. In a taxi from Chimkent to Alma-Ata, Akcharin was told by the driver that previous clients had pulled a gun on him and shot him twice, stolen his car and then had killed themselves in a smash with a truck. In Byshkek (which used to be Frunze, so named after a Soviet general), the capital of Kirghyzia, Akcharin was assaulted by Kirghyz who were looking for Uzbeks to kill. For a week Akcharin walked around Dushanbe, meeting people and asking them about life in the age of perestroika and glasnost. 'I met no one who was happy with his life.' Everything that he saw, heard and learned in Azerbaijan weighed like a stone on his soul. 'I think that responsibility for the eruption of national intolerance lies mainly with the pre-breakup Kremlin itself.' An image of despair came to haunt him, remembered from a Moscow market, 'when I caught sight of an armless, drunken man with a cigarette, trying to light a match with his stumps in the wind'. Akcharin was reduced to sitting on a bed, 'crying over my miserable country and her humiliated citizens'.

Far from being neurotic or a misfit, Akcharin is an energetic and creative man refusing to submit to the conditions to which communism has reduced everybody. His book, he says, was a death mask of the former Soviet Union. Evidently there was also a death wish.

2

'I WOULD PREFER NOT TO'

In dangerous times, people seek safety, and exiles and refugees have left the Soviet Union by the million. The communist regime deliberately deprived the country of an extraordinary range of talented men and women in all walks of life. Stravinsky, Chaliapin, Diaghilev and all the stars of the Russian ballet, Berdyayev, Bunin, Vladimir Nabokov have been followed down the years by Rudolf Nureyev, Joseph Brodsky, Solzhenitsyn, Vladimir Bukovsky, Vladimir Voinovich, Rostropovich, with the result that the contribution of these and thousands more to Western culture has been inestimable. But has any other country ever devised techniques of depriving its own people of citizenship and driving them abroad as the Soviet Union did?

The purpose behind the hounding of gifted individuals was the simple one of pretending to unity as decreed by communist doctrine. *Bartleby* is a story by Herman Melville in which the hero, a clerk, says to his employer, 'I would prefer not to'. Challenging the party's monopoly of truth, defiance of the sort had to be suppressed. Nobody could prefer to be his own master. The monolithic façade presented by the Soviet Union was one of its most horrifying characteristics.

The façade was completely false. An unbroken history of dissent, strikes, uprisings and armed rebellions was ruthlessly suppressed from the rest of the world in order to pretend to communist unity and solidarity. Throughout the 1920s, and beyond the period of compulsive collectivization starting in 1929, peasants in Russia, Belarussia and Ukraine forcibly resisted deportation and the break-up of their inherited way of life. In the Muslim republics, *Basmachis* or rebels fought for independence. In a popular uprising in Georgia in 1924, 4000 people were executed. Yakuts revolted in 1928 and Buryats the following year, with 35,000 dead, according to Solzhenitsyn. A Kazakh revolt was crushed in 1930. The German invasion in 1941 provided an opportunity for Ukrainians, the inhabitants of the Baltic republics, Georgians, Cossacks and many ordinary Russians, to welcome what was imagined to be their liberation: a mistake about Nazi intentions for which they were to pay dearly afterwards.

After 1945 Ukrainians for many years engaged in armed resistance to further subjugation by the Russians as well as maintaining contact with émigré Ukrainian organizations in Germany and Canada. In the Baltic republics at the end of the war, the so-called 'forest Brotherhoods' sprang up, consisting of perhaps 30,000 armed men in Lithuania under a unified command, and another 10,000 or more in both Latvia and Estonia. Guerrilla warfare lasted in these republics until 1952 or 1953. Riots broke out in Tbilisi in 1956 and in the Kazakhstan city of Temirtau in 1959, and in the south Russian city of Novocherkassk in 1962, while the December 1970 riots in Gdansk marked the moment when Polish continuation in the Soviet Empire could no longer be taken for granted. Nobody knows the extent of resistance and rebellion in the concentration camps.

Solzhenitsyn's *Gulag Archipelago* documents innumerable such instances, as do the memoirs of survivors. In his book *My Testimony*, Anatoly Marchenko describes a typical break-out. At the time he was a free worker on assignment at the Bukhtarma power station, living close to a camp with the usual barbed wire and control towers. 'One summer day one of these watchtowers started firing in the direction of the nearby River Irtysh.' He could see a swimmer more than halfway across. A guard launch was in pursuit, and in it an officer with a pistol in his hand. When the swimmer reached the far shore this officer leapt out and shot the escaper in full view of the watching crowd. Andrei Sakharov, the famous scientist, tells a story of the place simply called 'the installation' where he was posted to work in 1949. The camp there contained a small group of prisoners, some political and others criminal, who had been digging a pit. These prisoners grabbed one of the jailer's sub-machine-guns, hijacked a truck, and then shot up other prison warders. Some fifty prisoners fled the camp. The secret police cordoned off the area and closed in with artillery and mortar fire until every last escaper was slaughtered. Sakharov adds that many who did not join the fugitives were probably executed as well. *Kolyma Tales* by Varlam Shalamov is one of the greatest books to have come out of the Soviet period. Shalamov himself has written that these concentration-camp stories are based on his own experiences. One of the most dramatic of them, 'Major Pugachov's Last Battle', is an account of a dozen men breaking out of their camp, holing up in a cave and shooting it out with the secret police. 'These men who had died in battle were the best men he had known in his life' were Major Pugachov's last thoughts before he shot himself to avoid recapture.

When General Grigorenko publicly criticized the Brezhnev regime for its disregard of human rights, he knew that the secret police would make an example of him. For a Soviet general with a distinguished war record to turn dissident was an unheard-of challenge to the party. Shut up in a mental asylum, he was further abused through injections of dangerous drugs. In his writings he showed himself not prepared to compromise in any respect. Among similar-minded people whom he recorded was Sergei Pisaryev, an idealist like himself. This man had been expelled eight times from the party, always on the charge of 'lack of confidence in the ruling party organs'. During his first imprisonment, Pisaryev was subjected to forty-three interrogations, thirty-eight of them with torture. The ligaments of his spine had been torn. And still he found the endurance to write in 1953 to Stalin that the sensational 'Doctors' Plot' of that time was an obvious absurdity.

What might be called a civilian example of such defiance is given by the Ukrainian dissident Leonid Plyushch. In 1967, it seems, the workers rebelled in Pryluka, a factory town of 60,000 not far from Kiev. A young man at a dance had tried to protect some girls from drunken teenagers. The militia arrested this young man, dragged him in a car to the police station and beat him to death there. The militia doctor reported this death as a heart attack. The entire factory turned out for the young man's funeral, and as the mourners passed the place where the young man had been beaten to death, the militia captain appeared. A woman cried, 'Down with the Soviet SS!' The crowd then smashed the militia station and all factories went on strike. A general had to be flown in from Moscow to restore order.

In the eyes of the whole world, Alexander Solzhenitsyn was pre-eminently a man who, in the manner of Melville's hero, asserted his individuality rather than do as he was told. Perhaps no other literary document has ever had the impact of his *Gulag Archipelago*. Its publication smashed the communist façade of unity. Even the most gullible westerners had to take account of his careful research into the atrocities of the entire Soviet period. In a response unique to Soviet society, he was dumped in the West in 1974, as Trotsky had been dumped over thirty years before. Three years later, Vladimir Bukovsky was no less bizarrely exchanged for the head of the Chilean Communist Party. Whereas Solzhenitsyn was first and foremost a writer, Bukovsky was a politician, potentially a member of a Russian social democratic cabinet, on the day such a thing should come into existence. It so happened that I met him in 1980 soon after his arrival in England. His forecast at that time seemed too good to be true. There now existed a basis to challenge the Soviet Union according to its own laws, however imperfect and misapplied. This legalistic and non-violent dissent, he believed, doomed the Soviet Union and he was sure that by 1990 at the latest the whole repressive mechanism would have ceased to function and a democracy would take its place. Since that time he has been one of the best informed and persistent advocates of this view, a one-man band of opposition from his home in Cambridge, where I interviewed him.

'The regime was obviously in crisis by the early 1980s. You can imagine that it was obvious to the Politburo sitting there and receiving all the reports about politics and economics. They knew the contempt for them of the entire country, they knew they were in trouble. They would receive reports no matter how distorted by what we call in Russian *pripiska*, doctoring, improving figures. From the standpoint of cybernetics the system was very foolishly organized, it did not have a feedback. You had the single instrument, the party, and it was enforcer as well as controller. Since their feedback was inaccurate, they waited for too long, by which time there was no cure.' In Bukovsky's opinion, the disease was not diagnosed early enough. Had it been, Gorbachev might have been able to find resources to restore productivity in oil and gas and other primary products. Even so, the whole enterprise was senseless, doomed through its inherent lack of productivity. No enterprise was profitable. Instead of a budget, there was only the organized distribution of stolen resources so that work itself acquired something of the character of stealing rather than producing. If dissidents like Solzhenitsyn or himself had any real effect, Bukovsky believed it was in delegitimizing the party and taking away any glamour that the ideology of communism still held in the West. The last glow of such glamour had been seen in 1983, in demonstrations a quarter of a million strong in West Germany and Britain against the introduction of the Cruise and Pershing missiles in Nato. At the time, Bukovsky had exposed how these demonstrations were instigated from Moscow. With hindsight, those demonstrations were not as harmful as had been expected. In part this was because they were shown every day on Soviet television and had the contrary effect of generating inside Russia an independent peace movement into which the Western peace movement was also caught.

The whole external machinery of the Soviet Union was brilliant, 'unmatched in history'. In Bukovsky's opinion, there has never been a machine for conquest of such vitality. Internally, however, it was already obeying the laws of nature, growing old and senile, in the preliminary stages of dying. The whole idea of communism was aggression. Communism contained the false premises that people would work better collectively than individually, and that social circumstances would perfect the human being. All these things are biologically wrong and unscientific. Destroying the nation, communism has left Russia with no spiritual resources, which is why the transition to something more modern is so fraught.

'Gorbachev and his Politburo weren't thinkers or philosophers, just party apparatchiks who had come to the top of the promotion ladder.' In the early 1920s Lenin had already faced the failure of communism and instituted what he called his New Economic Policy, or NEP. Gorbachev's intention was to return to this example. This had the further advantage of allowing him to claim that the whole experience of Stalin and Stalinism had been a distortion, a historic mistake, and the regime was now returning to the path that it should never have left. Reforms along NEP lines had been tried in Hungary, Yugoslavia and even China. Since these reforms seemed to work, Gorbachev said to himself, Russia should emulate them. This was to overlook a significant difference, that these countries had come to communism much later than Russia, and consequently have an older generation that remembers how to live productively. In Russia, that generation was dead, leaving behind the trauma of collectivization and the stamping out of all productive patterns from the past. The moment that the individual depends upon himself for his skills and productivity and not on his connections with the party, the party must lose its prestige and power. As the party goes down, everything in communism goes down with it.

'Gorbachev's trouble was that he weakened his own system. His only instrument of power was the Communist Party, but his reforms weakened precisely that instrument. He was like the proverbial man sawing off the branch on which he was sitting. There could be no other outcome except what happened. I knew Ligachev, and the interesting thing about him is that he is at least honest, he is a true believer in socialism. Gorbachev was just a confidence trickster, he knew how to deceive people, that's all. Ligachev was not against reform but he was always anxious not to undermine the party. Since he was not very clever, he could not understand that these two conditions were irreconcilable. On the one hand he would be voting for reform every time the question came up on the floor or in the Politburo, but on the other hand he would always caution against going too fast and too far because it would undermine the party. He was quite right except for one thing, that he shouldn't have voted for reform. But that was their dilemma, very dialectic, and there was no way out of that tangle in logic or in theory.' The moment a new NEP-type reform began, the party started to disintegrate and lose control.

That brought up the nagging question of what used to be called the 'internal empire'. Acting on Leninist ideas, Gorbachev created the Popular Fronts in the numerous republics. Aware that he was broadening the social basis of running the country, he expected to control these new forces through the KGB, forgetting that you might not be able to control whatever it is that you create. In that predicament, Gorbachev then tried to instigate expatriate or minority groups to struggle against the majority he had himself unleashed and that is how he came to have these hot spots of ethnic conflict. He was responsible, however much he might deny it. The irony is that the game of divide-and-rule was an instrument in his downfall, not his salvation. That is a genie which cannot be put back into the bottle. The same result occurred wherever Gorbachev tried to legitimize the role of the party by changing direct appointment of officials at all levels into processes of election. In founding his new Congress of People's Deputies, he had also believed that he would be able to maintain control. In conducting those relations he was very skilful, arranging that 80 per cent of the deputies were members of the Communist Party where the old Soviet only had 75 per cent. But times had changed, people were different, and it was a further mistake to televise the proceedings of this newly elected Congress. Although Gorbachev had premonitions of the destructive power of television, he found in practice that he could not stop deputies playing their games on television for the public. For several weeks almost everyone in the country stayed away from work, and the more they watched television the more impressed they were at the images of their leaders, their incompetence and dishonesty. For the first time in the history of the Communist Party people could see their leaders as they were. Once they felt that the centralized power had weakened, they perceived that there was no very great risk any longer in demanding higher standards of confidence and honesty. Such was Gorbachev's approach. Feeling that he was not in control of the country, he would always create additional forces. Glasnost was devised to keep the party obedient by unleashing criticism of it from outside. The Congress of People's Deputies was similarly intended as a kind of counterbalance to the party. Gorbachev constantly fought to create these manipulative forces but the approach showed only the limits of his mind: there was no way in between. Either you have a party-controlled centralized regime or you have a democracy.

Do you give him any credit personally for what he did?

'Whatever he did was not for the purpose of reform but to retain power and salvage socialism and the Communist Party. He was a skilful commander of an army in retreat. He knew from the start that he had to find a way to make the retreat more orderly. You have to allow that he was ingenious but also he was profoundly dishonest. They needed credits from the West, and could not hope to obtain them until they had stopped the arms race. A new period of détente was therefore inevitable. The mere impression of becoming a democracy was enough to fool the West completely into believing that this was more than just a repeat of the NEP. Gorbachev was much more successful outside the country than inside. His purposes had nothing in common with the purposes that the Russian people had.'

3

'INFANTILE RUSES'

Lying and corruption are endemic in all societies. How each particular society sets about placing these naturally self-serving human traits under acceptable restraint is the test of its success. Depotisms are here at a systemic disadvantage. Claims of the despot to be ruling legitimately but without popular consent must sound hollow and contrived.

Scholars like to split hairs concerning certain unique collective forms of administration and ownership which traditionally prevailed in Russia. The bleak fact remains that down the centuries one-man rule was the norm. Genuine forms of representation were never created. The Tsars justified their rule on a basis of religious aspirations and divine right, or else through imperial and national aggrandizement. If these failed, they resorted to the knout, the firing squad and exile in Siberia. Until this century, Russia remained exceptional in Europe as the one country where the ruler was unaccountable to any parliamentary or popular institution. Attempts to install such institutions were eventually driven by fear of revolution on the part of successive Tsars. Never wholehearted reformers, the Tsars delayed until it was too late for the remedy of turning subjects into citizens by means of voluntary and agreed arrangements for election and representation. By definition, despots do not have the character to introduce measures to curtail their absolute power.

The despot's possession or control of all national property gives rise to the endemic flaw of corruption. Asked about the state of his country, the great historian Nikolai Karamzin early in the nineteenth century replied that he could sum it up in a word: 'thieving'. It was not that Russians had some inborn moral defect; they were responding to the system under which they were obliged to live. One of the first American journalists to visit Russia, J. A. MacGahern in the middle of the nineteenth century, spoke for almost all foreign observers when he said that the 'lower classes of the Russian people' might be ignorant and superstitious to the last degree, but they were 'not by nature either cruel or brutal'. Corruption for them was a matter of getting their hands, by whatever means were required, on enough property to be able to look after themselves and their families. Karamzin's thieving was the product of circumstances.

Similarly with lying. In a situation in which the individual cannot count on the support of law in his dealings with others, especially his superiors, it is only prudent to conceal true responses, for fear of provoking a more powerful counter-response against which there is no defence. Along with verbal lies come all manner of physical deceptions, such as an expressionless face, or gestures containing irony and resignation, postures of subservience, and so on. Quite soon, anyone outside these prudential lies and codes of conduct will be at a loss, as well as at a disadvantage to those who have grown up familiar with these subtle procedures.

The 'Potemkin village' is perhaps the most lasting metaphor for the deception and lying inherited with Russian despotism – at any rate it is the one which has most caught the imagination of the world. Façades were erected by Count Potemkin along the shores of the Volga down which Catherine the Great was sailing, in order to give her the impression that she was passing through prosperous and settled countryside. Informed about the true state of the country, Catherine the Great in fact realized that a constitutional regime was necessary if Russia were to enjoy the standing in the world which was its due. For this purpose she called on French philosophers such as Voltaire and Diderot, much as Gorbachev and Yeltsin in their day were to call on Harvard professors. Nothing resulted. In the 1830s Michael Speransky, the most far-sighted of Russian reformers, codified the law, defining rights and duties as they then existed, and introducing notions of contract and private property. Speransky's aspiration to a law-based society offered an escape from traditional despotism, and if it had been put into practice, Russia might have been spared the horrors to come.

In 1839 the French Marquis de Custine visited Russia. A few weeks were enough for him to gather observations and judgements still relevant today. Custine saw that Russia was a civilization in its own right with much to be admired, but fatally burdened by despotism. The dominant trait in the conduct of their lives was guile. 'Russians have a dexterity in lying and a natural talent in falsehood.' Daily conduct was reduced to 'infantile ruses'. It shocked him that people could be killed without hatred. 'Here, a calculated murder is carried out like a drill movement.' The police could deny all knowledge of the disappearance of a woman when they had themselves retrieved her corpse and sold it for anatomical dissection. The news that a boatload of people had drowned in the bay of St Petersburg was suppressed for fear of spoiling a celebration of the Tsar's. Custine was far ahead of his time in perceiving that incidents of this sort were primarily responses to despotism. More than that, he grasped an essential: 'Everyone here thinks what no one says.' It was wrong

43

of him, however, to go on to blame Russians for allowing themselves to be 'accomplices and victims'. What in fact could they have done? The means for articulate protest did not exist. Even the attempt to protest was unthinkable because it was akin to self-destruction. So there could only be more of the same.

Perhaps as a result of his own experience of the French Revolution, Custine understood the dire consequences. This despotism must expand or burst apart. The idea of conquest was 'the secret life of Russia'. He was ready to prophesy: 'Within the next fifty years, the civilized world will either pass once more under the yolk of the barbarians, or Russia will suffer a revolution more terrible than that.' In the event of this revolution, 'you will see the villages changed into barricades and organized murder spring fully armed from the cottages'.

Custine's prediction became an orthodoxy. Throughout the nineteenth century, Russian absolutism was an object of loathing on the part of those in direct contact with it, just as communism was to be in this century. The Revolution was anticipated by almost everyone who thought about politics, but the sudden and absolute collapse of despotism still proved a surprise. In a famous phrase, Lenin and the Bolsheviks had found power lying in the streets in 1917. An event of such historic magnitude can obviously be considered in several perspectives. Was it a coup or a revolution? Was it the response of a country which felt itself left behind in the Industrial Revolution, and in need of catching up with Western inventiveness, and modernizing? A gigantic literature around these questions found its second wind when history seemed to be repeating itself in the Gorbachev era.

The constitutional regime, however imperfect and approximate, set up in February 1917 lasted until 5 January 1918, when the Bolsheviks turned machine guns on the crowd coming to the Tauride Palace where the Assembly was sitting. In the early hours of the next morning, bored soldiers pushed the deputies out into the street and told them to go home. 'A Party of a new type' was what Lenin claimed the Bolsheviks to be. No such thing; it was the oldest form of political association known to man, a raiding party out to seize all the spoils. From the first moment, Lenin employed terror to secure his ends. Whoever was not with him was against him, and was eliminated accordingly. Like any Tsar, Lenin and his successors could not conceive of power-sharing which would make their despotism less absolute. The despots had changed, but the essential fact of despotism was continuous.

4

SEIZING THE SPOILS

Article Six of the Soviet Constitution declared that the party was 'the leading and guiding force of the Soviet society and the nucleus of its political system, of all state and public organizations'. Comprehensively and cunningly, the party had set about implementing this overriding intention. An enormous apparatus was constructed to contain in its grip a country second in size only to China, with immense variations of climate and geography, population and culture. According to Yeltsin, the party finally had 1,115,000 organizations, from the level of the federal Soviet Union at the centre, inner Russia and the fourteen other constituent republics, Autonomous Republics, provinces, cities and towns, down to districts. The whole was a conveyor belt, designed to transmit orders and decrees from the top to the bottom, receiving in return information concerning performance and morale.

The General Secretary of the party at the top; the dozen or so Politburo members who met with him every Thursday in a panelled room in the Kremlin to publicize what were by then prearranged decisions; the several hundred members of the Central Committee of the party, out of which the Politburo and the General Secretary had been selected; the thousand members of the full-time Central Committee secretariat with its departments for international relations, party matters, personnel and ideology, working in concert to transform decisions into reality; and then 100 all-union Ministries and the 800 republic Ministries; the Supreme Soviet in which 2250 nominated deputies met for five days a year, and raised their right hands simultaneously in unforgettable displays of discipline; the Prosecutor General and his staff; the KGB and the army, the unions of 'creative workers' or intellectuals, all interlocked into a party-state, that hybrid brought into being by and for communism as defined long ago by Marx and Lenin.

To the victor the spoils. Never before had that most time-honoured of war cries been realized on such a scale. Bewildering in number and ramification, the bureaucratic institutions of the party-state might look as if designed for varying purposes, but those were Potemkin perspectives. The party-state had the monopoly of power and organization, money and finance, land and agriculture, and not least of all, information. A massive administrative machine, the party-state rolled together the legislative and the executive and the judiciary. The concept of formal checks and balances could not apply. Civil or human rights were intolerable impediments to the party. 'Who's the boss: we or the law?' Khrushchev once exploded to a Prosecutor General, who was objecting to shooting some alleged speculators, a word reserved for some-one who had tried to make money on his own. 'We are the masters over the law; we have to see to it that it *is* possible to execute these speculators!' What was a Prosecutor General except someone with his party duty to perform?

Assuming responsibility for all welfare and behaviour, the party-state elim-inated competition, primarily all values and features associated with the market or deriving from it. The 'command economy' involved overall control and planning, intended to achieve economic prosperity undreamed-of by the benighted capitalists, doomed to chaotic free enterprise. To ensure that it always had its own way, the party-state relied on the KGB and terror. In order to define what that way was, the party-state resorted to Gosplan, a specialist planning agency with the herculean task of elaborating year by year, and in the celebrated Five-Year Plans as well, production norms and quotas for the entire spectrum of industry. From intercontinental missiles and MIG fighters to pins and needles, Gosplan had to specify every detail in the output of at least 25 million items, taking into consideration extraction of raw materials, delivery and distribution, factory capacity, labour availability and so on. Costs, or any form of benefit analysis, were as necessarily excluded as checks and balances were from politics. If anything in the Soviet Union was equivalent to law, it was Gosplan's yearly projection of what would be mined, manu-factured and finished. Whatever was not foreseen in the plan could not in theory exist. In everything that they were to produce and consume, people were regulated by this single agency over which they could have no influence, any more than they could over the KGB.

So there were no clearing banks and no private accounts or chequebooks, no tax structure, no insurance policies, neither credit nor mortgages nor housing agencies, neither employment agencies nor accountancy nor business studies, no opinion polls or even anything that could be considered public opinion, no criteria of profit and loss, no clear definition of ownership and no law-backed contract, no wholesale or retail distribution, no corner shops, and no advertising or promotions or window displays or discounts or pack-aging, no suburbs but only 'labour storage facilities' (in a phrase of Jillian Becker's), no charities or clubs, no homes for stray animals, no tabloids or beauty contests, nowhere to play golf or polo or other sports deemed unproletarian, no philosophy or history written according to the dictates of scholarship rather than the party-state.

In contrast, there were party congresses, conferences, presidiums, plenums, and all the gatherings and activities of the collectivity and its command economy, such as enforced demonstrations and parades, compulsory enrolment in youth organizations, the Komsomol especially, work quotas to be fulfilled month after month, with bonuses for doing so, titles and decorations including Hero of Soviet Labour and the Orders of Lenin and Stalin, cheap housing and heating, cash but little to spend it on, food and goods sold far below cost-price thanks to subsidies, and shortages of food and goods for the selfsame reason or else due to the vagaries of Gosplan, unavailability of anything outside the purview of the planners, approved books published in vast runs costing a few kopecks, free local telephoning (if the instrument worked), hundreds of press publications with indistinguishable contents.

To envisage an alternative to all this was vain, absurd. Everyday conduct had to be tailored to the demands of the party-state and the command economy, at least in make-believe. One of the dissidents deported from Brezhnev's Russia was Alexander Ginsburg, and on his arrival in New York he stated the demoralizing truth that the party-state's monopoly denied democracy and democrats any point of entry. 'None of us is capable of running a country or even of taking part in governing it. There is no one to elect.'

Like all societies, the party-state needed managers. Plenty of people were quick to perceive that the monopoly of power and a command economy opened vistas of advancement to those with the character for it. The path to the top was open. In the first flush of the Revolution, the élite had chosen itself through dedication to communist ideals. As early as 1931 Stalin had decided that equality was not in itself desirable. Since terror was the principal administrative instrument, terrorists had to be rewarded for efficiency.

Milovan Djilas, at one time Tito's leading apologist and even heir apparent, had been a firm believer in terror and its institutionalization until he saw the consequences in his native Yugoslavia. In the early 1950s he published an influential book, *The New Class*, the first to expose how party-state managers had established themselves as a new ruling class. Power and advantage came to whoever could manoeuvre himself into the position of operating monopoly.

In a Darwinian process of survival of the fittest, a large group of such operators emerged, generically known in a Latino-Slav compound as the 'Nomenklatura'. Mikhail Voslensky, another dissident in the West, published a pioneering book with that title in 1984, in which he calculated that the Nomenklatura was about 750,000 strong. Writing after Voslensky, a Western expert, Gordon B. Smith, considered that there were 300,000 Nomenklatura positions at the disposition of the Central Committee in Moscow, another

47

260,000 in the republics, and at the regional level 76,000 more. The Nomen-klatura was the collective owner of the 'property of the state'. Its sole activity was the parasitical one of sharing out among its members property which it had not produced, otherwise the spoils. Public ownership of property in practice meant the private enjoyment of it by the managers. To Arkady Vaksberg, a respected commentator from *Literaturnaya Gazeta* as well as an author, the Nomenklatura was akin to a mafia. Their schemes to gratify the wish for increasing power and wealth were not really obscured by ideological dressing-up. In his view, the Nomenklatura consisted almost entirely of 'little-educated, wholly uncultured and, most often of all, simply ignorant people, from the most humble, narrow-minded, limited background, nou-veaux riches in the literal sense'.

Arkady Shevchenko was a Soviet diplomat, eventually posted to the United Nations in New York, where he was to defect and publish his memoirs. Promoted adviser to the then Foreign Minister, Andrei Gromyko, he found that he had a post qualifying him to belong to the Nomenklatura. This was a caste system, he wrote, with its many levels enjoying various degrees of privilege according to rank. For Politburo members at the top there was no limit. The Central Committee established the hierarchy of those eligible for inclusion. Unlike ordinary mortals, Shevchenko went on, Nomenklatura members received 'high salaries, good apartments, dachas, government cars with chauffeurs, special railway cars and accommodation, VIP treatment at airports, resorts and hospitals off-limits to outsiders, special schools for their children, access to stores where consumer goods and food are available at reduced prices and in plentiful quantities'. As the 'backbone of the status quo', this élite was certain to obstruct anything that might affect their privileges.

Evidence of this privilege was everywhere. Right there, on the open street, were special shops restricted to the Nomenklatura, in which they had to pay with foreign currency which only they could acquire. Through those windows, crowds of people used to gaze at goods forever beyond their reach. Determination to pay whatever price was necessary to become a customer in such a shop was selfish, but also a perverted version of enterprise and liberation. Georgi Markov, the brilliant Bulgarian writer who was murdered in London by the KGB, had once worked in a factory. He left a characteristic account of it, describing how an electrical fitter one day had arrived to announce that he had joined the party and wanted different tasks now. 'I didn't become a party member in order to work. Find me an administrative job. I, too, want to walk round the factory twirling my watch-chain ... When you are in the party, you're in power. If you are in power, you don't have to struggle so hard! Let the others struggle!'

Galina Vishnevskaya has described how her title of People's Artist of the

USSR brought with it a good rent-free apartment, permission to make trips abroad and have vacations in government sanatoria. An illness was treated in a private room in the Kremlin hospital, where across the street stood an anonymous pharmacy offering every Western medication for the privileged few. Special institutions taught and trained Nomenklatura children or potential recruits: the Higher Party School, the Diplomatic Academy, the Academy of the Ministry of Foreign Affairs, and the Higher Schools of the KGB, the Institute of International Relations, the Institute of Foreign Trade. Anyone with ambition and talent would be tempted to seek enrolment. To refuse to do so required a moral decision of a high order, because it was self-injuring and without benefit to anyone else.

Virtually everyone who has had to live under communism has complained of the deadening effect of the Nomenklatura and the cumbersome and nasty patterns of behaviour imposed by it. The Polish historian, Krystyna Kirsten, typified thoughtful criticism when she wrote that the Nomenklatura stifled initiative and the spirit of enterprise thanks to 'the leading role given to mediocrity, to conformism, to abject incompetence'. To take the initiative, to express a creative or original idea, paid off only if you were also able to push past all obstacles, an action which was far more likely to rebound through its exploitation by others who were out to climb at your expense. Better therefore to stay quiet.

It is a comment on human nature that the individual fought for himself under communism with a selfishness and fierceness in complete opposition to the self-sacrifice theoretically resulting from collective doctrine. Only a great novelist could do justice to the calculations and self-serving intrigues underlying all transactions between Soviet people, down to the most fleeting exchanges and meetings. Bukovsky dramatized it with the observation, 'When you met a person for the first time, you invariably thought of him as a witness in your future trial.' Therefore your neighbour should not be placed in a position which later will prompt a guilty conscience. It was as though everyone had to negotiate his own crossing through a swamp, in which there were no firm footholds, and the choice was either to drown or to save oneself by pushing others down first.

You would have to advance, taking care never to say or do anything which might be turned against you; attending the innumerable party meetings and plenums and committees, approving and aping the words and attitudes of the leaders, while also taking care to discover that those leaders were not about to be purged; never backward but never forward either; cultivating influential friends while realizing that these too might be disgraced suddenly and so keeping an eye out for whoever might cause that disgrace, or happen to replace them; estimating then whether those influential friends had best be kept in reserve to protect you against others, or on the contrary might be best manoeuvred to promote you; concealing intentions even, or especially, from close friends and colleagues; warding off suspected rivals while not appearing to be doing so and finding a way to circumvent obstacles put in your own path by rivals; hardly daring to confide in your wife or husband or children – 'infantile ruses' in which the tiniest slip or accident might land you in an interrogation by the KGB which could spell ruin and worse.

For those with the nerve for it, a 'provocation' was likely to be the most rewarding of strategies. In Soviet parlance, a provocation meant tempting someone with whom you were in conflict into making a step he judged proper, but which you had anticipated would in fact destroy him. Khrushchev defined it: 'One of Stalin's favourite tricks was to provoke you into making a statement – or even agreeing with a statement – which showed your true feelings about someone else.' So you put a loaded question, you told a deliberate lie in praise of an enemy or in condemnation of an ally, in order to smoke out some opinion which damned whoever uttered it. As the stakes rose and clashes of interest became matters of life and death, you could hope to force a rival into making his bid for power prematurely, checkmating him, and best of all, allowing the blame for his ruin to be placed squarely on himself.

To get a piece of work done, in the words of Zinoviev, an engineer by training, involved months and years of tension, 'of meetings of sections, the department, the management, groups, sub-groups, teams, the party bureaux of the sections, of the department, and of the Institute ... so many meetings, speeches, notes, reports, accounts, plans, individual and collective commitments, denunciations, anonymous letters ... add to all this changes in foreign and domestic policy, changes in the leadership, sessions of the Secretariat and the Politburo, plenums of the Central Committee, meetings within the Central Committee, in the City Committee, in the department, in the Presidium ...'

These myriad and convoluted personal advances and retreats were miserable substitutes for the formal checks and balances of constitutional society. No laws of ownership and contract defined obligations or responsibilities, and so nobody knew how far he could proceed except by testing it out. Everyone, everywhere, continuously, was engaged in a test of strength with everyone else. Where other people's tests of strength might emerge, and how they might involve you, was haphazard and unpredictable. If you were to survive in such constant uncertainty, the whole trick was to assess correctly when you were the stronger and would have your way, and when you were the weaker and had to surrender with as little damage as possible. On the one hand ruthlessness was at a premium, at least towards inferiors, and on the other hand servility, at least towards superiors. Trust was excluded. Communism destroyed the ties and habits and common assumptions that bind people together. In the name of the collective, Soviet people were desocialized.

Whoever was in a position to offer goods and services had the upper hand in transactions with anyone in need of them. What ought to have been plain commercial issues of obtaining sausages, installing a telephone, arranging medical treatment, buying a pair of decent children's shoes, fixing house repairs, turned into tests of strength. Even in shops where an inspector might visit, declared prices were not respected, and available goods were withdrawn in order for privileged buyers to make deals favourable to them and to the seller. The scarcer a commodity or a service, the higher the bribe to be paid, by whoever was in need of it. That person either had to find the cash or defend himself by having something of his own to barter. Daily life in the Soviet Union was a vortex of bribery and bartering, in which everyone was whirled all the time. The practical matter of shopping and working wiped out what ought to have been moral considerations about dubious conduct.

Those empowered to authorize permissions and licences could name their price. Among personal documents, everybody was obliged to have an internal passport without which travel inside the country was forbidden, and a set of papers registering domicile, and a workbook logging a lifetime's employment. Evidence of the number of square metres of an apartment, of attendance at party meetings, of satisfactory performance in one or another sphere, determined who got what of the spoils. *Spravka*, the word covering these certificates and testimonials, was a daily preoccupation. Huge numbers of people were either unable to satisfy *spravka* demands, or were in breach of them; they therefore forged their papers and bribed officials to cut through the web of queuing and red tape. Priority on a list was a question of cash. For their part, officials had every inducement to be as obstructive as possible, raising the price for buying them off. Extreme regulation found its consummation in a black parody of the free market, whereby those with cash pushed past those without.

From time to time, someone particularly corrupt was arrested, or on orders from above against 'racketeers' or 'speculators' the KGB might open a campaign and carry out some exemplary death sentences, but in fact there was little the party-state could do to rectify an inherent flaw. However damaging in itself, corruption may even have made bearable and human the tests of strength which could not otherwise have been regulated.

While he was *Washington Post* correspondent in Moscow, David Remnick employed Irina to look after his children. One day Irina had to arrange her mother's funeral. The attendants at the morgue, the undertakers, the coffin maker, the grave-diggers, were paid by the state but all invented some excuse why they could not do their jobs. By reason of the indispensable service they had to offer, these men were bound to win this test of strength; they knew that Irina had no choice but to bribe them.

In Maurice Friedberg's *How Things Were Done in Odessa*, a metallurgist described favouritism and corruption in that city. A common practice for gaining admission to the Institute of Metallurgy was to buy someone else's high-school diploma and substitute the name. Such doctored diplomas were sold by the admission officers themselves. Members of the entrance examination committee took paying pupils whom they admitted after an oral examination only. Committee members rotated, and in an off-year had to rely on friends to admit their pupils, extending the corruption. A student might be examined by a single teacher with no witness present. 'Corruption in university admissions has remained rampant.'

Extortion, false charges, trumped-up denunciations, forgery, were routine procedures in establishing the hierarchy of the strong. A woman who managed a restaurant (in another typical example, from Jeffrey Klugmann's book *The New Soviet Elite*) had a history of good relations with the party First Secretary, but bad relations with the Komsomol First Secretary. Who was the stronger was uncertain. The Komsomol secretary put it to the test by complaining to the party secretary that the manager would not accept staff he had recommended, and had excluded another Komsomol committee member from her nightclub because it was supposedly sold out. Reprimanded, the manager discovered that the Komsomol secretary was actually the stronger, and all she could do in future was admit him and his friends free to the nightclub. The party secretary had simply refused to back her.

Soviet literature comprises a shattering record of incidents of this type. Nobody and nothing were safe when the victors were out to enjoy the spoils. General Grigorenko found himself one day with another general in the Arkhangelskoye military sanatorium. This general told Grigorenko that a colonel in the room was the son of a highly placed official. The colonel had raped a nine-year-old girl, an offence carrying the death penalty. Instead of punishment, a special psychiatric hospital 'cured' him in a matter of months.

After his experiences as a political prisoner, Bukovsky plumbed the tragicomic realities. He described what he called 'the fantastic cases' he had come across, including that of a whole factory arrested for stealing diamonds. Iosif Lvovich Klempert, the director of a dye factory, had remained untouched while filling his own pockets corruptly. Then he decided out of altruism to build a block of flats for his workers. This led to investigation, and he was finally shot for what he had done on behalf of his workers. Bukovsky wrote, 'Whole enterprises would be beavering away – helped by party committees and socialist competition – while the profits were siphoned off into the private pockets of deputy ministers and management chiefs. And the opposite also occurred. Entire industrial complexes existed only on paper, appeared in the plans and were allocated funds by the state – even the Section for Preventing the Embezzlement of Socialist Property was on their payroll – whereas in actual fact their sites were occupied by virgin Russian forest or an expanse of steppe.' And he concluded, 'Khrushchev wasn't very far from the truth when he said in one of his speeches: "If people in our country would cease stealing for even a single day, communism would have been built long ago."' Here was Karamzin all over again. Without this stealing, though, the economy would not function at all.

'You don't know life. No one lives on wages alone,' Brezhnev said. 'I remember in my youth we earned money by unloading railroad freight cars. So, what did we do? Three crates or bags unloaded and one for ourselves. That is how everybody lives.' Yeltsin had also got the point: 'Each salesperson was obliged to overcharge the customer and hand a certain sum each day to his or her supervisor, who kept part of it for himself and gave part to the general manager of the store. Then the money was shared out among the management, from top to bottom.'

Rackets might cut horizontally right across a republic, or vertically through Ministries and the party. In the Muslim republics the towns are isolated, and communications poor. Officials therefore cornered the ticket sales on buses, price-gouging the customers while claiming subsidies for many who had never travelled at all. In Azerbaijan, a special racket was in caviar; in Georgia, in wines and precious stones; in the Baltic republics, in the fishing fleet. At the same time, the Ministry of Fishing sold the catch through its shops, with ministers conniving that the whole supply sometimes disappeared into the black market. The military–industrial complex, through an institute called Aftomatika-Nauka-Tekhnicka, sold railroad cars loaded with Soviet military equipment for dollars to Nato countries. Kirghyzia specialized in meat fraud.

Dinmukhamad Kunayev, once First Secretary of Kazakhstan, used to send Brezhnev 'whole wagonloads of gifts', according to General Liatchenko who observed it. Brezhnev's son and his son-in-law made illegal fortunes on such a scale that they could not escape prosecution. By the time of Brezhnev's death, the First Secretaries of Kazakhstan, Uzbekistan, Tajikistan and Kirgyhzia had been in office for over twenty years, and most of the other First Secretaries over ten years. All of them embezzled money from Moscow. Since none of it had to be accounted for, nobody can be sure where it went. Sharif Rashidov, the Uzbek First Secretary, became legendary by promising to deliver five million tons of cotton from his republic. 'Make it six million, my little Sharif!' exclaimed Brezhnev, to which Rashidov replied, 'As you wish, Leonid Ilyich.' Neither of them could have believed such vranyo. State bonuses, investments in farming and irrigation, subsidies, wages, poured into Uzbekistan, but the cotton did not exist in such quantities, and the workers were mere names on lists, the money filtered away into the pockets of Rashidov and his cronies. When he died suddenly in 1983, Rashidov was buried in state in a gold-domed mausoleum in Tashkent.

Nikolai Shchelokov, the Minister of the Interior, stole 700,000 roubles from state funds, and the most luxurious trappings he could lay hands on for himself and his family. When his Ministry took delivery of nine German cars, he appropriated five of them for himself, his wife, his son, daughter and daughter-in-law. In Georgia, the First Secretary Vasily Mzhavanadze auctioned jobs, and pocketed the bids. His wife Tamara was a byword for her jewellery and antiques.

Inefficiency and corruption might seem to be evidence of bad character, but usually they derived from the precariousness of all except the more humdrum tests of strength. One party might be a KGB agent, or have backers who cannot be gainsaid, but he might also be so greedy or arrogant that he would bring about his own undoing if exposed by denunciation or an appeal to superiors. Standoffs might follow, with feuding and plays of revenge having unforeseeable consequences.

Konstantin Simis, for instance, once had to travel to Salekhad in the Arctic Circle to look into the case of a man called Berlin, the director of a telegraph department there. The local prosecutor had imprisoned Berlin for alleged misuse of office. What had actually happened was that the First Secretary of the local party had ordered Berlin to supply workmen and materials to build him a private house. Berlin was in a dilemma. Either he could comply, becoming an accomplice to stealing state property and diverting it to private ends, perhaps asking for a suitable bribe for himself, or he could refuse; in which case he had to be sure that those to whom he would appeal for help would prove more powerful than the First Secretary, his patrons and his clique. Whether out of miscalculation, or obstinacy and pride, Berlin refused. In retaliation, the First Secretary fabricated a report against him. The judge, prosecutor and accounting experts were all anxious to propitiate the First Secretary, and so they lied. Berlin was therefore victimized and imprisoned.

At the very top, a test of strength would determine a career and even a fate. When Ligachev was First Secretary of Tomsk Province Party Committee, so he relates in his autobiography, a major in charge of a military construction unit from the Ministry of Medium Machine-Building was posted to the region. Ligachev invited this man's general to second the unit to build roads. The general replied, 'The homeland has given us different tasks.' Ligachev threatened to call a meeting of the party which had the power to strip the general of his party card, after which he would lose his command. The general,

Ligachev says, 'turned out to be tough. He jumped up and barked: "It wasn't you who gave me my party card, and you don't have the right to take it away!"' The general had no means of predicting that this bolt would fall on him out of a blue sky, or of fending off the next move against him. Ligachev resorted to higher authority, in this case Yefim Slavsky, the USSR Minister of Medium Machine-Building. 'Slavsky apparently weighed all the circumstances,' Ligachev writes slyly, meaning that Slavsky had decided that Ligachev was stronger than the general and had to win this test. The general was replaced by someone who consented to build everything Ligachev wanted, from poultry farms to a scientific centre. 'They made a capital investment of hundreds of millions of roubles,' boasts Ligachev. Whether or not these works were in themselves justified, the episode reveals the negative consequences of administration by test of strength: abuse of office, lack of accountability, diversion of resources and funds, and ill treatment of a general with a sense of duty.

The embodiment of despotism, the General Secretary was the supreme arbiter of everything, and in fulfilment of that role, nothing was too trivial to escape his attention. Hence the ubiquitous KGB; and also the practice, much encouraged, of writing to him. From the lower depths, people posted their humble petitions for redress of wrongs. Up in party circles, personal intervention and access counted. Exactly as Ligachev described how he won supremacy through the aid of a minister, so a range of Politburo and Central Committee colleagues, mediators and hopeful wheeler-dealers were knocking on the General Secretary's door, picking up the secret Kremlin telephones and begging for a private meeting, even past midnight and into the small hours. Stamina was indispensable.

A General Secretary who plumped one way or another made enemies as well as friends. Postponement, prevarication, split decisions which must evolve into further tests of strength, were virtues. What might look like incompetence, some sort of inherited Russian fecklessness, was usually a deliberate circumventing of a dangerous test of strength by blocking all the moves the contestants might make. The matching of men to party-state tasks demanded precise and delicate balancing. A thrusting careerist might be stopped by a difficult assignment, while something easy might be given to a dimwit whose bungling would be reason enough to be rid of him. Management was an art of arranging equilibrium. Here were checks and balances indeed, but they were informal, at the mercy of caprice and accident.

As issues rose in significance, corruption at some indefinable point lost its capacity to influence: members of the Politburo and Central Committee already possessed privileges enough to satisfy their every wish. The resort to violence was not different in kind to the use of corruption, but marked that what was at stake had reached a degree of importance compelling those involved to do whatever they could to win.

No example is more extreme than the lengths to which Stalin went to kill Trotsky and all his supporters, real or imaginary. Millions were to die before Stalin rested assured of victory. Once Stalin himself had died, a similar test of strength faced Beria and Khrushchev, the two contenders to succeed him. The latter's description in his memoirs of how he went about winning is a classic of its genre. As an experienced KGB leader, Beria could contrive circumstances in which to arrest anyone he liked, Khrushchev included. For Khrushchev, it was a matter of isolating Beria, but not too much in case he became suspicious, and of enrolling his other Politburo colleagues in a con-spiracy, but one by one, gingerly, in case they saw advantage in defecting to Beria. Only if confronted suddenly with the *fait accompli* that the whole Politburo was against him could Beria be prevented from striking first. Khrush-chev duly enlisted the members one by one, but with setbacks. The rather dull-witted Voroshilov got the wrong end of the stick, and said, using Beria's first name and patronymic, 'What a remarkable man we have in Lavrenty Pavlovich, Comrade Khrushchev!' To which Khrushchev could only reply, 'Maybe not. Maybe you are overestimating him.' The more cold-blooded Molotov rightly asked, 'Where is all this leading?' and answered the question even more rightly, 'We must, so to say, resort to more extreme measures.'

When Lazar Kaganovich was approached he craftily inquired whom Khrushchev meant by 'we', quickly covering his tracks with, 'Of course I am with you, I was only asking.' Relating this, Khrushchev came clean: 'But I knew what he was thinking, and he knew what I was thinking.' Enrolling eleven marshals and generals, Khrushchev was acquiring a makeweight to the KGB, if need arose. These do-or-die rivalries contained the germ of civil war. A fatally overconfident Beria was to attend a Politburo meeting into which burst Marshal Zhukov, the most famous of Soviet commanders from World War II, to shout at him, 'Hands up!' Imprisonment and execution were mere formalities.

Public figures ranging from Stalin's friend and potential rival, Sergei Kirov, to Jan Masaryk, Foreign Minister of Czechoslovakia when it was taken over in 1948 by the communists, were the victims of arranged accidents and 'suicides'. By then the millions murdered in Gulag had also been haplessly caught in tests of strength fought out over their heads. For them, after the event, the party-state introduced 'rehabilitation', as weird an administrative practice as any ever invented. The dead could not be restored to life, of course, and there was never any question of paying compensation to surviving family members. A certificate simply declared that so-and-so had been murdered, for no good reason. Here was open recognition of the consequences of the tests of strength out of which the whole turbulent history of the Soviet Union had been spun.

'In no other State,' wrote Speransky, the frustrated reformer of Tsarist despotism, 'do political words stand in such contrast to reality as in Russia.' Solzhenitsyn put it with contemporary bluntness: 'It has always been impossible to learn the truth about anything in our country – now, and always, and from the beginning.'

The population learned soon enough of decisions taken against it, such as collectivization and industrialization through terror, but in general terms the entire decision-making process was irrational and invisible. No one has ever properly described how successful party careerists were selected for the Central Committee and Politburo. Nobody really knows how tests of strength within the party and its agencies came to be decided one way rather than another. In his memoirs, Ligachev makes some disclosures about the process. 'There were times when we could not say some things aloud, but wrote to each other on scraps of paper.' According to him, Politburo sessions were quiet and polite because by that stage it was a question of ratifying what had already been agreed behind closed doors in one little conspiracy after another.

A leader expressing readiness to be violent could expect not only to be feared but admired for his will. The urge to resort to force was best restrained by the threat of superior force. 'We'll break their skulls in,' as Kaganovich said of class enemies. 'In a revolution, victory belongs to whoever splits open his adversary's skull,' was Bukharin's version of it. Shevchenko quotes Khrushchev cursing Dag Hammarskjöld, the Secretary General of the United Nations: 'He has seized authority that does not belong to him. He must pay for that. We have to get rid of him by any means. We'll really make it hot for him' (and Hammarskjöld was the victim of a mysterious air crash). Sakharov reports a typical story of the bitter enmity between more or less comparable rivals, Marshal Zhukov and Vyacheslav Malyshev. 'Gavrilov told me he was present at a meeting when they clashed publicly: cursing loudly, they threatened to shoot each other. During the exchange their subordinates sat there petrified.'

The party-state was at great pains to suppress information leaking out about such regular and unavoidable conflicts of interest, clashes of opinion, and challenges for personal power. Censorship was absolute. The list of topics which journalists were forbidden to air covered five printed pages. Information about the Nomenklatura was a state secret. Statistics were not objective measurements but a tool in the hands of those planning their own advancement; the figures were suppressed or invented accordingly. Year after year the Soviet budget was shown to be balanced down to the last rouble, a fact which should have been enough to discredit it. Nobody knew what the money supply was. Since the rouble was not convertible, nobody had any idea of its real worth. Nobody knew the real expenditure on defence or the KGB.

In the words of Tatyana Zaslavsky, a well-known academic, 'Data are not published on the prevalence of crime, the frequency of suicide, the level of alcohol and drug abuse, or the ecological situation in various cities and regions.' Nor were data on population movements or disease distribution published. She concluded that it was difficult to name a simple administrative decision affecting vital interests that had been based on a reliable study.

The whole country, not just the people in it, became a gladiatorial arena in which the manifold tests of strength were fought out with utter disregard for the consequences. Over the years the army had taken over something like 2500 sites, the core of the military–industrial complex. These towns and surrounding areas, almost half the country, were closed to foreigners, deemed potential spies of the arms factories. No restrictions were placed on these or any other factories in the pursuit of production, what was called 'production for its own sake'. Like Rashidov with his cotton, a factory manager would stop at nothing. Air and water pollution were worse in the Soviet Union than anywhere else in the world, from ten to twenty-five times above permitted levels. According to Georgi Golitsyn, vice-president of the Russian Academy of Sciences and a specialist in ecology, techniques of farming have led to deforestation, the spread of desert, erosion and poisoning of the land. Out of 1.5 billion acres of cultivated land, nearly half has been seriously damaged. The world's greatest ecological disaster is the drying up of the Aral Sea, drained for irrigation in the great cotton scams (which have also led to the draining of the Amu-Darya and Syr-Darya rivers in a way which is a threat to the climate of Central Asia). Murray Feshbach is an American authority who first drew attention to the destruction of the Soviet countryside, and in a book which he wrote with Alfred Friendly, *Ecocide in the USSR*, summed up: 'No other great industrial civilization so systematically and so long poisoned its land, air, water and people. None so loudly proclaiming its efforts to improve public health and protect nature so degraded both ... it beggared itself by endangering the health of its population.'

To put it another way, the lack of objective and legal accountability at all levels meant that communism was practised as a process of uninhibited plundering and destruction; the party-state encouraged the role of profiteer. If this were ever to be substantiated in public, and the lying and cheating and corruption were acknowledged, the party-state would forfeit its claim to be the leading and guiding force in Soviet society. Since Lenin's day, every party leader had emphasized that party unity had to be maintained at all costs, no matter the mystification and falsification involved. Otherwise there would be factionalism. This was communist parlance for a test of strength so deadly that the parties to it would stop at nothing. That, the leaders always understood, was the only way in which the party-state monopoly could be broken.

5

THE MAN ALLOWED TO LEAVE

In the Gorbachev era, Gennady Zotayev was appointed chief economic adviser to the European Economic Commission in Geneva. 'For one week in the year, we would get together to explain what is going on in our corresponding countries,' he says. 'I was the man allowed to leave – a very Soviet expression – meaning that I was the man the system trusted.' Fantasies or what he calls 'devil's thoughts' then entered his mind unbidden: that with his wife and daughters he would unexpectedly vanish for ever from the Soviet Union. That was when he realized that finally he had understood how the system worked. By then he had seen at close quarters those who personified the system, how cynical they were, and he wanted no more of it.

The Soviet Union in the 1950s had been at the level of development of present-day China and structural reform should have been undertaken then. The creation of the huge military–industrial complex prevented the party-state from taking the Chinese route. The arms race ultimately excluded what might have been a gradual evolution of normality. Sooner or later the system created by Stalin would have collapsed, but its existence could have been prolonged further. 'We have huge resources, and the people are obedient. The system also had its internal logic which made us all players of the same game.'

Zotayev joined Gosplan in 1981, on the day before Brezhnev's funeral. Looking back, he finds it astonishing that many officials in Gosplan, the Central Committee, the Ministries, did not understand the reality of Soviet society and the command economy. Some Gosplan officials saw that the economy was not competing with developed countries and would have to be changed. 'At the same time we had no idea how to do that.' Cynicism, the communist type of cynicism, was revealed when the deputy chairman of Gosplan referring to the West habitually used the term 'rotting capitalism'.

'I would like to stress that people in this well-regulated mechanism were playing the role of little bits and pieces. I was active only when I was asked to be. I started thinking only when someone told me to, or when I felt a threat to my personal wellbeing and position. One would think one thing and actually do the complete opposite. That accounts for the comprehensive cynicism.'

At Gosplan, Zotayev had access to what was known as the 'cradle', a special shop on Granovsky Street supplying quality products including caviar and good meat. 'We could put on our table quite a variety of things. My family got used to it very quickly.' People may not have hated his family as a result, but his feelings were confused. Standing in line once behind a marshal with three stars and the title of Hero of the Soviet Union, he had watched him fill his shopping bag as he himself was doing. 'I was ashamed of him. I didn't see why such a distinguished serviceman should be standing in this quiet little queue in this backyard and bringing all this stuff secretly to his family.' It dawned upon him that this was a distribution system of a feudal character and he had been admitted into the circle of nobility serving the monarch or ruler. In that sense he was the marshal's equal. This thought served to rationalize privilege.

The most powerful departments of Gosplan were the so-called 'branches of industry' departments, which had equivalents in the similar departments of the Central Committee and the Council of Ministers. The party-state set its priorities, first the military–industrial complex, then the energy-producing complex, agriculture, and so on. Tests of strength arose between them. In a dispute with the Prime Minister, the chairman of Gosplan appealed to the General Secretary of the party. But basically Gosplan was following the system of priorities that had been defined previously elsewhere. The Central Committee and the Council of Ministers had statistical bodies of their own upon which to base planning. Production figures, overall rates of growth and macroeconomic numbers were exaggerated. What with predetermined political priorities, untrustworthy figures and tests of strength deriving from rigid hierarchical organization, planning had almost nothing scientific or rational about it. The survival for so long of the Soviet Union is a tribute to its natural resources and mineral reserves.

In Moscow, in the Central Committee and its circle, it was possible to inhabit a fictional world in which plans were drafted, reports circulated, figures agreed, and tests of strength settled. A rising Nomenklatura man like Zotayev had before him an enticing vista of party-state career opportunities and proconsular postings. The same combination of character traits and political manoeuvrings could be brought to bear in every situation throughout the empire. There was none of the bewildering variety of civil and military services, governerships and colonial offices with which the French and British had run their empires. Party-state centralization theoretically made all the pieces interchangeable in the machine. Unlike the French and British in their empires, the Soviet administration took no notice of regional and cultural differences.

Imperial assignments outside Moscow opened Zotayev's eyes. For three months he was a member of a small team sent by the chairman of Gosplan to elaborate a Ten-Year Plan for Ethiopia, which had been brought into the empire in 1974 by the coup of the communist Colonel Mengistu. The Ethiopian regime had asked for help to raise the economic growth rate from 3 to 6.5 per cent. It was clear that the Soviet Union did not have the money to meet Ethiopian demands. Over bottles of vodka, Zotayev's colleagues said that it was not their task to persuade the Ethiopians that the command economy was no good. The advice was simply to buy presents in the market for their families, go home to Moscow, and let events take their course. As a propagandist and adviser, he also visited Poland, East Germany, and Tajikistan. 'We understood only later that the real purpose of being in Tajikistan was to prepare a report showing that the First Secretary there was unsuitable.' Someone superior was manipulating this Gosplan delegation into being his instrument in an otherwise invisible test of strength.

By 1988 he saw that collapse was imminent. To begin with, he had been an ardent supporter of Gorbachev. But then 'Gorbachev grew extremely afraid of what he himself had done', so that support and faith in him were no longer possible.

Did Gorbachev understand economics?

'Absolutely not', but Gorbachev could have gone on 'thinking communist'. Instead, he removed the element of fear which released everyone's ambitions. There was no law or tax enforcement or anything to check them. Decision-making in Stalin's day had been so very 'concrete' that incompetence was detected fast. In Khrushchev's time the sense of fear started to subside, and competence with it. The alternative to fear, in this view, was anarchy and chaos.

6

'TOMORROW THE WHOLE WORLD'

European empires had conjured up abstract arguments in defence of expansion, such as 'the white man's burden' or '*la mission civilisatrice*'. Realistic profit-and-loss calculations in this century led to decolonization and the end of empires. Whether any country derived material, strategic or other benefits from imperialism is open to question.

Had the 1917 revolution not occurred, Russian imperialism would no doubt have been obliged to make a similar profit-and-loss calculation. As it was, communism renewed the imperial drive through its fundamental doctrine of 'world revolution', a concept quite as abstract, convenient and compelling as any devised by the British or French. Here was an example of vranyo, for in reality those who might have objected to being conquered by a Russian army had to applaud their 'liberation' by a Soviet army. Anyone who still objected was counter-revolutionary. Statesmen, political parties, whole countries were personalized as counter-revolutionary, class enemies, and therefore marked for rightful destruction.

Absence of institutional constraint upon power secured the Soviet Union its great advantage in foreign relations. The process whereby the strong gained supremacy at everyone else's expense generated criminal and wasteful rivalries within the Soviet Union, but once operating beyond its borders, that selfsame process converted into a formidable and purposeful national expansion and empire-building. On its own terms, this kind of absolutism is completely consistent.

The moment a Soviet foreign policy objective had been identified, every single means of pursuing it was appropriate, without respect for morality, diplomatic convention or the law. For the Soviet Union, foreign relations were so many tests of strength at the international level, crude in themselves but sophisticated in the evaluation of the balance of forces. Terror had to be minutely calibrated, for fear of being detected and arousing a backlash. The techniques applied were those already refined in habitual party conduct, now projected all over the world: bribery and espionage, denunciation and threats, subversion through secret agents and Communist Parties, contrived appeals for help in the name of solidarity, sometimes 'international' and sometimes 'proletarian', with the final resort to outright violence through invasion and occupation.

'We have no stake in your capitalist state, we would be ashamed if we had … We are the party of the Czech proletariat and our supreme revolutionary headquarters are in Moscow. And we go to Moscow to learn, you know what? We go there to learn from the Russian Bolsheviks how to twist your necks. And as you know, the Russian Bolsheviks are masters of that.' Klement Gottwald's rhetoric to the Czech parliament in 1929 was duplicated in exactly that tone of jeering violence by Soviet spokesmen in international forums, and by communists in every Western country. As so often, Khrushchev hit upon the simplest formula, with his resounding threat to the entire West, 'We will bury you.' As nothing less than a doctrine, Brezhnev stated that a communist victory in any country was irreversible. Gorbachev's speeches displayed the schematic view of the world which he had inherited. At a party congress in 1986 he could describe 'the worsening of capitalism's social problems' and the militarism which he claimed was cultivated to hide those problems, while brushing aside Stalinism as 'a concept thought up by the enemies of communism and widely used to discredit the Soviet Union'.

By the time that the democracies had realized how the Soviet Union had treated the Second World War as a colossal test of strength which it had won, it was too late to do anything about it. Either the Western Allies were supine or they had deceived themselves about the dynamics of communism. Soviet undertakings at the summit conferences of Tehran, Yalta and Potsdam, to introduce and respect power-sharing, were ignored, waved away by *force majeure*. The Red Army stayed in the positions it had occupied in 1945, while the Allies demobilized.

Bulgaria and Romania were monarchies established in the previous century. In the Baltic republics and Poland, the Soviets were reasserting an imperial presence dating from Tsarist days. Hungary, Czechoslovakia and Yugoslavia, and Albania, were also creations of the settlement after the First World War. These countries had only embryonic democratic traditions. Their populations, involving the many minorities among them, were competitively nationalistic in culture, language and religion. On the grounds that communist doctrine overrode all such retrograde sentiments or pieties, the newly arrived Soviet troops and authorities set about obtaining absolute power, and with it the immense expansion of their empire. Once more, power equated to looting. According to reliable estimates, the Soviet Union transferred to itself from the occupied countries various forms of wealth worth about $14 billion, a sum of the same order of magnitude as the aid which the United States was currently giving under the Marshall Plan to Western Europe.

At the time, the Soviet Union could count on support only in Czecho-slovakia. By September 1945, the Czech Communist Party had 700,000 members, the one and only mass movement of the kind in the region. In the other countries put together there were probably hardly 50,000 communists. Known to have been infiltrated by spies and agents, the Polish party had been virtually wiped out by Stalin. Bulgaria had about 15,000 communists, Hungary 3000, Romania 800, and the East German party even fewer. Throughout the war, indigenous communist leaders had been kept in reserve in Moscow for the day when the Red Army could install them in their own countries – for example, Mátyás Rakosi and Imre Nagy in Hungary, Vasile Luca and Valter Roman and the once notorious Ana Pauker in Romania, Walter Ulbricht and Wilhelm Pieck and Otto Grotewohl in East Germany. Years of persecution in their own countries, followed in their Russian emigration by the experience of 1930s terror, had bred in these people a devotion to party demands which amounted to a negation of their independent selves. Lenin had been despatched eastward in 1917 in a sealed train by the Germans to undermine Russia through revolution; now these conspirators were despatched westward by the Russians for a reverse of this performance.

Democratic parties stood no chance against these armed plotters. Demo-cratic leaders like Stanislaw Mikolajczyk in Poland, Iuliu Maniu in Romania, Nikola Petkov in Bulgaria, the Czech President Edvard Beneš, the Yugoslav Colonel Mihailović, had expected Western support but instead they were abandoned to a fate of death or exile. Communist takeover in Greece seemed a possibility but the West made an exception and intervened there militarily and decisively. A characteristic atrocity was the kidnapping of perhaps as many as 40,000 Greek children, who were then force-marched over the mountains into Bulgaria and on to the Soviet Union for indoctrination. Clandestine sections of the local Communist Parties prepared revolutions in Italy and France. Soviet archives have yet to reveal Stalin's true attitude to these plans.

In Hungary between 1948 and 1954 more than 300,000 families of busi-nessmen, farmers and professionals were deprived of their property and jobs. The historian Rudolf Tökes writes that 'the regime deliberately handicapped the life prospects of at least 750,000 middle-class Hungarians'. Up to 200,000 Czechs were condemned on political grounds to mine uranium or coal, and there were perhaps 500 victims of judicial murder, including the socialist deputy Milada Horáková, and finally party leaders themselves, like Rudolf Slánský. In Bulgaria, the post-war communist bloodbath and purging, in the words of R. J. Crampton, a Western authority, 'per head of population claimed more victims than any other in Eastern Europe'. According to official figures there were 11,667 trials after the arrival of the Red Army; according to unofficial figures possibly as many as 100,000. For a population of some 8 million, there were a hundred concentration camps. In 1952, 7000 prisoners were held in one camp alone, Belene, on an island in the Danube. In his book *Romania in Turmoil*, Martyn Rady writes that 60,000 Romanians were executed in 1946 and 1947. The Association of Former Political Prisoners of Romania has estimated that another 300,000 people died in labour camps under the regime of Gheorghe Gheorghiu-Dej. In addition to camps like Lugoj, Dumbraveni and Vaslui, a huge complex grew up along the Danube canal which was dug by slave labour in true Stalinist style. In 1992, 300 corpses were discovered at Caciulata, twenty-five miles outside Bucharest, believed to be early victims of the communist seizure of power.

Forcible conversion from Nazi enemy into communist satellite made East Germany a special case. The historian Hermann Weber has quoted a Soviet document from the Ministry of the Interior concerning the ten camps that existed in the Soviet-occupied zone, some of them taken straight over from the Nazis. Buchenwald, Sachsenhausen and Bautzen, for example, functioned until 1950. This Soviet source reveals that between 1945 and 1950 122,671 Germans were imprisoned, of whom 45,262 were eventually freed, 14,202 were handed to the East German authorities, 12,770 were deported to the Soviet Union (this is almost certainly an understatement), 6680 were treated as prisoners of war, 212 escaped, 42,889 died for one reason or another, and 756 were condemned to death by military tribunal. Mass graves of communist victims have been found in proximity to the mass graves of Nazi victims.

One of the German communists who returned from Moscow was Fritz Löwenthal, to be placed in charge of a department of Legal Administration in 1946 in the Soviet zone. In no time he understood how he had been duped by his beliefs. His book, *News from Soviet Germany*, published a few years later, was, he hoped, 'a passionate protest against the injustice and oppression being committed today by those very people who, when they were not in power, cried out so loudly against injustice and oppression'. He described the looting of whole streets and towns, blackmailing, pressuring of honest officials, all the conniving tricks and bodyblows of despotism. 'From time to time, particularly when troops were withdrawn and relieved by others, violence, robbery, murder and rapes flared up again to new heights. A wave of suicides bore witness to the despair and desperation of the local inhabitants. In Rostock alone there were 400 suicides, and 300 even in a small town like Waren.'

Lali Horstmann's *Nothing for Tears* is a small masterpiece from this grisly period. Her husband Freddy, a newspaper magnate and landowner, insisted on staying in his house at Kerzendorf, close to Berlin. 'Women were particularly insistent and repetitive in telling exactly when, how and how often they had been raped,' she wrote. The last in the series of outrages she experienced was the arrest of Freddy by the secret police. Only eighteen months later was she able to discover that he had died of starvation, and been buried along with other victims in a concentration camp.

Wolfgang Leonhard was another of those returning from Moscow, where he had been educated for a leading position in the Nomenklatura. He too could not stifle his conscience and so defected, but not before having heard Walter Ulbricht, the first General Secretary of the SED or East German Communist Party, issue a directive: 'It's quite clear – it's got to look democratic, but we must have everything in our control.' Potemkin himself could not have been more to the point.

The People's Democracies, as these occupied territories were misleadingly labelled, were dependencies under Soviet control. The same imposed party structure of General Secretary, Politburo, Central Committee and secretariat, Council of Ministers, a non-representational parliament, Komsomol or youth organization, served the double purpose of centralizing power in each country while also attaching it to the Soviet centre. Politics reproduced the Soviet model of settling issues and conflicts of interest in favour of the most powerful. Key figures in these satellites had Soviet counterparts or correspondents at their own level of the party hierarchy, whom they consulted and visited regularly to obtain instructions and backing. In each People's Democracy the single most powerful man was the local KGB representative, accountable only to his KGB superiors in Moscow, where his word would carry more weight than anyone else's. Soviet garrison generals, ambassadors, trade representatives, visiting dignitaries and delegations, could also be appealed to in an emergency. In any serious test of strength, especially involving promotion or demotion of top personnel, the interested parties and their rivals and supporters alike flew straight to Moscow, where decisions were taken behind closed doors.

Economic and military planning, espionage against the West, propaganda, repression of dissidents, were all activities co-ordinated in advance in Moscow and then relayed outward. What might look like a local political line, local speeches and newspapers articles, books and films, architecture, even food supplies, had originated in plans in Moscow. To cause even the least surprise to the Soviet authorities had unforeseeable and therefore dangerous consequences. The secret police in every People's Democracy had the task of anticipating and eliminating any likelihood of it. All available human and material resources were at their disposal. In East Germany and Romania, the Stasi and the Securitate, the respective secret police forces, always remained agencies like the KGB, accountable to nobody except the General Secretary. In recent years the secret police in the other countries were placed under the Ministry of the Interior. The effect was not to spare the population from totalitarian measures, but to put another link into the chains running from KGB headquarters in Moscow.

The immediate aftermath of Soviet colonization was a rash of show trials throughout the People's Democracies. About 1000 leading personalities were purged, and a number of them judicially murdered. All were veteran communists. The Bulgarian Traicho Kostov had had his life spared before the war by King Boris: now he was hanged. Wladyslaw Gomulka, First Secretary of the Polish party, was imprisoned. The Hungarian Minister of the Interior, László Rajk, told colleagues that 'one must have a compass and my compass is the Soviet Union'. Tortured, he confessed instead to 'deviationism' and was hanged. In Czechoslovakia, Rudolf Slánský was executed with ten other party leaders. As in the Soviet Union, terror of this sort carried exemplary warning.

Until then, these countries had been largely peasant societies. Czechoslovakia alone had advanced industrialization. As in the Soviet Union, collectivization of agriculture was introduced to satisfy doctrinal demands for central control, but it had the secondary aim of breaking the old tradition of sturdy survival through self-reliance. Poland along refused to collectivize. Mindful of the Polish will to oppose Russian oppression down the centuries, Moscow did not insist, a concession to peasants which it came to regret. Another unusual feature of Poland was that its landowners, now dispossessed, tended to remain in the country, in spite of certain persecution for having been born who they were. The Czech, Hungarian and Romanian aristocracies could not be blamed for preferring exile. Prosperous Bulgarians also left. Emigration levelled East Germany. Between August 1949 and August 1961 when the Berlin Wall was built, 2.7 million East Germans, or 15 per cent of the population, fled to the West. Thousands of country houses, medieval in style as well as baroque and neoclassical, were abandoned or placed under collective ownership. Everywhere these relics with their derelict parks and gardens were visible reminders of a heritage arbitrarily repudiated.

As a potential focus of anti-communism and nationalist rallying, religion had to be uprooted. In the wake of the Red Army's advance of 1944, persecution of all religious denominations started. The Uniate or Catholic Church of Ukraine was forcibly merged with the Russian Orthodox, and its head, Cardinal Josif Slipyi, imprisoned for seventeen years, then exiled to Rome. In Lithuania, Bishop Vincentas Borisevičius was executed; Bishop Julijonas Steponavičius of Vilnius and Cardinal Vincentas Sladkevičius were both exiled for over twenty years; a third of the clergy were deported. Father Tiso, the wartime leader of Slovakia and a Nazi collaborator, was hanged, and Slovak priests deported *en masse*. Hundreds of Croat priests were killed as alleged collaborators in Tito's Yugoslavia. Put on trial on a similar charge of collaboration, Cardinal Aloysius Stepinac was sentenced to hard labour.

Cardinal József Mindszenty in Hungary was imprisoned as an alleged spy, and Cardinal Joseph Beran of Prague served sixteen years in prison. Two Albanian archbishops were murdered in prison and four bishops were shot. Polish bishops were sent to prison. Cardinal Stefan Wyszyński, the Polish primate, was arrested. The reading list which he presented to his jailer gave a measure of the man: Dobraczyński's *The Letters of Nicodemus*, Manzoni's *Promessi Sposi*, *War and Peace* in Russian, St Thomas à Kempis's *Imitation of Christ*.

A proportion of the clergy was unwilling to be persecuted, let alone martyred. 'We do not wish to be a Church alongside Socialism, nor a Church against Socialism: we wish to be a Church within Socialism.' When the Lutheran Bishop Albrecht Schönherr of Berlin said this, in 1971, he revealed how successful the party had been in closing off opposition on moral or religious grounds. Near the ruined country houses in the landscape stood the padlocked churches, gothic pinnacles and gilded onion-domes alike in decay.

Jan Šejna, a member of the Czech Central Committee and Chief of Staff to the Minister of Defence until 1968, was one of the highest-ranking communists ever to defect. In his book *We Will Bury You*, he has described how one night in 1949 two policemen visited Colonel Vasek, an officer of the General Staff. His is only one of countless such fates in this period of sovietization. The two policemen accused him of being a spy, beat him senseless, threw him down an airshaft and drove the corpse away for incineration. They then informed his wife that he had defected. What she said in her distress was used in evidence against Vasek at a tribunal convened that afternoon. Vasek was declared guilty of treason and condemned to death when he was already dead. Šejna concludes, 'The murder was legalized in just eighteen hours.'

Handing their zone of occupation over in 1949 to the SED to run as the new German Democratic Republic, the Soviets had something like 3500 people still awaiting trial. Less than half were Nazis or war criminals, though all were framed on such charges. Transported to a camp at Waldheim, they were tried in batches. According to Hans Eisert, the historian of these proceedings, among them were 90 publishers and editors, 130 judges and lawyers, and 160 people accused of sabotage such as tearing down posters. Another was Margaret Bechler, whose mere presence there was an embarrassment to her husband, already Minister of the Interior of Brandenburg and groomed for even higher rank in the Nomenklatura. He declared that she had died in September 1946. To hide her out of sight, Margaret Bechler was sentenced to life imprisonment. Doctor H. Brandt from the Ministry of Justice visited Waldheim in 1950, and complained about these tribunals. Arrested for it, he was himself imprisoned until 1964.

Once installed in power, the SED, like other parties in the People's

Democracies, held show trials. Purging the leadership proved a continuous process: Paul Merkur and his group in 1949; Politburo members Zaisser and Herrnstadt in 1953; Franz Dahlem, the leading contender for Ulbricht's post, also that year; George Dertinger, and Max Fechner, the Minister of Justice, in 1954; Wollweber and others in 1956; Wolfgang Harich and others in 1957; and Schirdewan a year later. In 1958 a third of the leading party workers in local offices were replaced. No other party so faithfully reproduced the systemic Soviet lawlessness. The veneer of efficiency and self-righteousness, however, was its own special contribution.

Starting at the Baltic Sea, and running down the western perimeter of the Soviet Empire, was an Iron Curtain of high barbed-wire, watchtowers with searchlights and mounted machine guns and minefields. The sole loophole was through Berlin, until this was closed by the building of the Berlin Wall, referred to by Ulbricht, an excellent pupil in the art of vranyo, as 'the anti-fascist wall of protection'. From then until 1989, desperate people attempted to escape across, under or over the wall, and some 600 of them were shot dead as they did so. A border guard who killed a would-be escaper received a bonus and a decoration.

The empire had the aspect of an extended concentration camp, inside which terror had degraded everyone including the warders, and standardized everything so that nothing wrought by the hand of man was worth doing. So starkly symbolized by the Iron Curtain and the Berlin Wall, the essential divide was between absolute despotism and a law-based society. The incompatibility is as old as civilization. Law-based societies suffer from a disadvantage in that they mobilize for defence only with the consent of the majority, and that consent is likely to materialize only at the last moment in the face of present danger. In the event of invading across the Iron Curtain, Stalin and his successors could count logistically on occupying the rest of Europe in a matter of days.

Archives may one day reveal the extent to which Soviet leaders con-templated pre-emptive strikes to extend their empire. The habitual Soviet discourse of fronts and trenches and blocs and hegemony, 'leading Nato circles', and 'sinister heralds of the camp of war and death', tended to warmongering and paranoia. As late as 1983, apparently, the Kremlin talked itself into a belief that a nuclear attack was about to be launched against the Soviet Union. Agents were busy detecting such telltale indications as the number of lights blazing late in Western Ministries of Defence. The East German army had the task of driving towards Brest and the Atlantic coast of France. After 1989, warehouses were discovered in East Germany crammed with road signs to guide the columns across France, as well as stacks of occupation currency.

The development of nuclear weapons after 1945 froze the confrontation into a stalemate, the forty-year-long Cold War. To communists, the Cold War had nothing to do with Russian expansion or the challenge of absolutism to law-based societies. Ideology dictated that the Cold War was a necessary showdown between communism and capitalism.

Development and installation on the ground of nuclear weapons stabilized an armed peace. As soon as an armoured attack across the Iron Curtain implied suicide, the Soviet Union devised an alternative strategy. The detachment of Germany from the Western alliance became a long-term, not to say obsessive, aim of foreign policy, whether pursued openly or clandestinely. The condition for reunification was neutrality, whereby Germany would become another Austria, harmless to the Soviet Union. In that event, American bases in Germany with their nuclear arsenal would have been closed and Nato would have fallen apart. How German statesmen from Adenauer to Brandt and Kohl responded to this Soviet bait became the measure of their moral fibre and political capacity. Had any German Chancellor surrendered to the temptation of unification on Soviet terms, the rest of Europe was certain to have been neutralized and sovietized in due course. Conversely, the Soviet Union emphasized that incorporation of East Germany into West Germany on Nato terms would lead to a nuclear exchange. '*Ce n'est que le provisoire qui dure.*' Voltaire might have had the peculiar status quo of Germany in mind.

The Cold War, in the words of the playwright Julius Hay, another who had returned in 1945 from Moscow only to be disillusioned with communism in his native Budapest, was 'this dreadful and indefatigable Punch and Judy show of international dimensions'. Paul Warnke, President Carter's adviser on disarmament, could speak of 'two apes on a treadmill'. Such equivalence between the two sides acquired the ring of a truism, but it was misleading. To suppose that here were two of a kind was itself evidence of how widely the communist world-view had been absorbed.

The 1930s phenomenon of fellow-travelling was a complex psychological response to the Soviet Union and its rise to power. Some fellow-travellers were deceived; many more deceived themselves. All of them were seeking to appease an absolute despotism whose projection of power threatened them and the law-based societies in which they lived. In this respect they were no different from those appeasing Nazi despotism in the same period.

Nazi military success in the opening campaigns of the war put an end to short-term prospects of resistance. Those who had hitherto tended to appeasement now favoured its next step, collaboration. Collaborators everywhere justified themselves as making the best of a bad job. If they were injuring their conscience, they argued, it was for the sake of the national interest. In every country which they occupied, the Nazis were to install

71

quislings, whose function was to do as they were told with a sincerity which everyone else was expected to imitate. Italy and France were the outstanding collaborationist countries. Italy under Mussolini was a case on its own. After the rout of the French army, Marshal Pétain met Hitler in October 1940 and declared that 'today I am embarking on the path of collaboration'. A wave of relief swept France. 'To come to terms with yesterday's enemy is not cowardice but wisdom.' In this judgement André Gide might have been speaking for all Frenchmen. One of the most conspicuous of fellow-travellers, Gide had visited the Soviet Union in 1936 and his unexpected denunciation of what he had then seen for himself was an intellectual sensation at the time. But here was an articulate representative of the very many who in the short space of a few years could think that collaboration with despotism, Soviet or Nazi, was wisdom.

Soviet military successes after 1945 posed a similar choice between resistance and collaboration, between what was cowardice and what was wisdom. Dependent upon Soviet forces to support them unconditionally, the new local communist regimes were quislings in their turn. Exactly as many French, Italian and other intellectuals had justified Nazi occupation as heralding a new order, so now the next generation – sometimes, actually, the very same people – justified Soviet occupation as another new order to be welcomed. Fellow-travelling reached what might be called its mature stage of mis-representation, whereby reality was stood on its head. It is still hard to decide whether this was the cause or the effect of moral and intellectual degeneration.

For some, Soviet imperial power was evidently attractive. Kim Philby, the arch-spy, for example, explained that when the Soviets asked him to place his talents at their service, 'I did not hesitate. One does not look twice at an offer of enrolment in an élite force.' For him, the transfer of allegiance seemed natural. The twilight of the British Empire had no scope for élite forces. For others like Bertolt Brecht, Pablo Neruda, Jean-Paul Sartre or Graham Greene, it was a question of being on the side of the winners, and enjoying the self-esteem which derived from that. Louis Aragon, Paul Eluard, Sean O'Casey, the historian A. J. P. Taylor who thought that 'In the end, Stalin was a rather endearing character', Louis Althusser, Michel Foucault, Ernst Bloch, György Lukacs, Herbert Marcuse and thousands more men of letters, academics and opinion-makers had a brutal and manic streak in their characters which found its correspondence in this collaboration with similar sadists. Hatred of one's own country, as well as its cognate, a hatred of America, were also powerful impulses. In France, a non-existent but allegedly despicable entity, 'les Anglo-Saxons', was used to foster the illusion that the Soviet Union was always in the right. After 1966, French governments stood their distance from Nato. In the event of the withdrawal of American bases, French collaboration with the victorious Soviets would have been the repetition of Marshal Pétain's collaboration with the Nazis. Slogans like 'US Go Home!' and 'Nixon' with the central letter in the form of a swastika, strengthened a misrepresentation of reality arising from alienation. An enemy who promised an end to this alienation was worthy of admiration. Absurdities were coined to justify the enemy, on the lines of Susan Sontag's 'America is a cancerous country', Mary McCarthy's statement that capitalist alternatives to communism were 'all ugly in their own ways and getting uglier', or the influential sociologist C. Wright Mills's defence of Castro's killings as 'just and necessary'.

The Polish intellectual Alexander Wat had insights based on personal experience of communism, and he wrote, 'It is impossible to overestimate dandyism as a motive for embracing communism.' For the run-of-the-mill writer, artist, journalist and film-maker, identification with the Soviet cause and apologetics for the Soviet conquest of the People's Democracies was often unreflective chic, to do with the bright figure which they hoped to cut in the world.

'Social realism' and 'commitment' in the arts were matched by the policies of Western governments to accommodate to the Cold War threat through their own measures of central planning. Although the welfare state was designed to pre-empt communism, much of its conception and execution derived from Marxism–Leninism as interpreted and absorbed by Western governments, by no means all socialist. For democracies and democrats it was as unwelcome as it was bewildering to be caught in this all–embracing test of strength thus imposed on them by Soviet might. Values and practices which seemed to resist and defy the Soviet Union were accordingly weakened and dispensed with. Those who defended them – Raymond Aron, Arthur Koestler, George Orwell – were sneered at as 'Cold Warriors'.

The more unyielding the Soviet Union, the more inventive were the attempts to duck out of this test of strength, pretending ostrich-like that it would vanish of its own accord. Détente, 'the spirit of Camp David' (where President Eisenhower met Khrushchev), the Campaign for Nuclear Disarmament advocating surrender under the childishly oversimplified slogan 'Better red than dead', peaceful co-existence, the liberation theology of some priests, Euro-Communism, Ostpolitik, SALT I, the so-called Sonnenfeldt doctrine that the United States had to agree to Soviet dominance of Eastern and Central Europe, were so many milestones on the road to wishful collaboration. At the end of that road, we were supposed to find 'convergence', meaning that the law-based society and absolute despotism had somehow become one and the same, and moral equivalence was true after all.

During the final phase of its expansion under Brezhnev, the Soviet Union was able to exploit collaboration in a way which surpassed its expectations.

At Helsinki in August 1975, the Soviet Union, the United States and thirty-three European states signed what was known, with a rather sinister ring, as the 'Final Act'. The frontiers of Europe, 'the territorial integrity of states', were thereby guaranteed. An international act of law confirmed the Soviet Union in its invasion and occupation of Eastern and Central Europe. For the Soviet Union the Helsinki Final Act was what the Munich Agreement of 1938 had been for Hitler's Germany. In effect, the Soviet Union had won that stage of the Cold War, and was poised to move to complete supremacy over the remaining European democracies.

Among those who recognized where collaboration was leading was General Grigorenko, trapped like all Russians, so he believed, in an absolutism which the law-based societies now accepted could never be changed. Here was a great victory of Soviet diplomacy, he wrote, and conversely, 'the most shameful page in the history of Western diplomacy'. In the so-called 'third basket' of the Final Act the Soviet Union consented to respect human rights. This had little significance. The West had no means of obliging the Soviets to distinguish between infringements of a legal code and political activity of which it disapproved: both were crimes of equal standing as defined by the party and punished by the KGB.

The quislings of the satellite countries now consigned for ever to the Soviet empire were cock-a-hoop. For Erich Honecker, General Secretary of the SED, the Helsinki Final Act was a peak of his career, according to Egon Krenz, who was destined to succeed him fourteen years later. To Honecker, East Germany was no longer a Soviet zone masquerading as independent, but a recognized state. If unification with West Germany was ever to come, it could now only be on Soviet terms. General Jaruzelski in Poland concurred. Confronted by a weakened West, he was to write in his memoirs, 'The socialist community seemed to be at the height of its power and cohesion.' Recognition of the 'immutability of frontiers in Europe' meant that people like him could settle back, glad that their decision to collaborate was now beyond questioning.

The Helsinki Final Act confirmed in many, if not most, westerners, attitudes which by then they were ceasing to recognize as appeasement or collaboration. Once more, some were deceiving themselves and others were being deceived. The well-known economist Paul Samuelson wrote in 1976 that it was 'a vulgar mistake to think that most people in Eastern Europe are miserable'. J. K. Galbraith, also a well-known economist and pundit, could write in 1984 that the Soviet Union had made great material progress in recent years, and this was evident from the statistics and from the general urban scene. 'One sees it in the appearance of the solid wellbeing of the people on the streets ... and the general aspect of restaurants, theatres and shops ... Partly, the Russian system succeeds because in contrast with the western and industrial economies, it makes full use of its manpower.'

Psychologists have to explain such suspension of critical faculties. Normal powers of observation should have dispelled fancies of this kind. A consensus had arisen by then in Western intellectual and political circles that Soviet achievements were genuine, and to be respected as such. Gorbachev was elected to the Politburo in 1981. He and his colleagues were immersed in what was a two-way traffic of illusion, whereby what they did and said was accepted at face value in the West, and Western appeasement and collaboration were accepted at face value in return. When in 1983 President Reagan suddenly blurted out that the Soviet Union was 'the Evil Empire', he could be treated by the Kremlin as a throwback, a political freak, an American vranyo-monger, and in the West as a Cold Warrior, a cowboy, or worse, an actor. But it was the reality, and the victims of that Empire recognized it.

7

'WE CAN'T GO ON LIKE THIS'

On the evening of 10 March 1985, at 10 p.m., the Politburo convened a special meeting. Gorbachev returned home from it very late, and took his wife Raisa out into the garden. Even they had to be at a distance from KGB bugging devices. Gorbachev told Raisa, according to her memoirs, that the question had arisen of his taking over the leadership of the party. Next morning he would be confirmed as General Secretary. But 'It is impossible to achieve anything substantial, anything on a large scale, the things the country is waiting for.' She quotes his glum observation, 'We just can't go on like this.' It had become, and was to remain, a refrain. What exactly was the country waiting for? The vagueness was glib: it could be interpreted as a return to communist orthodoxy, or alternatively, reform.

A General Secretary arriving in office had the overriding consideration of securing his absolute power. Everything else could wait. The purging of rivals and their placemen and nepotistic appointees was akin to change of government through elections in a democracy. Immediately Gorbachev eliminated those Politburo members who had opposed him, or from whom he could expect nothing – they were nonentities, as luck would have it, and notoriously corrupt. Gromyko, who might have wanted to be rewarded for having sponsored him, was instead kicked upstairs. About one in five in the party organization was dismissed; 500 in Kazakhstan alone, 50 in Moldavia for 'immoderate style of living, extravagant spending and abuse of power for self-interest'. By the beginning of 1986 Gorbachev had purged almost half the holders of Nomenklatura posts. By then only 172 out of 307 members of the Central Committee had survived from five years earlier. He was attempting to fashion the party in his own image.

Picking and choosing reliable men was a skill indispensable for a General Secretary. He had to assess character accurately but could never be sure what was really happening down among the party cadres. Relying on advice and KGB files, he was at the mercy of anyone who had access to him and could plead a convincing case for himself or for someone who might well be a relation, a client or a crook, or all at once.

Eduard Shevardnadze, Boris Yeltsin and Yegor Ligachev had been respectively First Secretary of Georgia, First Secretary of the Sverdlovsk district, and the Central Committee Secretary for Party Matters. Like Gorbachev, all three had a reputation as hard drivers of men, as movers and shakers. Appointed at first to head the Moscow City Party, and then to join the Politburo, Yeltsin, like everyone else coming into power, set about establishing absolute authority in his realm. He began by purging 20,000 party members, 30,000 'research assistants' and arresting 800 on corruption charges. 'We dig further and further down,' Yeltsin said, 'but can never find the bottom of this cesspool.' Gorbachev also appointed to the Politburo the Chairman of the KGB, Viktor Chebrikov, and Nikolai Ryzhkov. In early 1986 Alexander Yakovlev became the Central Committee secretary in charge of party work, and soon afterwards a Politburo member too. Anatoly Lukyanov took over the General Department of the Central Committee, which made him the senior party-state bureaucrat. Personal advisers with more or less open access to Gorbachev included Anatoly Chernyayev, Gyorgi Shakhnazarov, Nikolai Petrakov, Vadim Zagladin, and his *chef de cabinet* Valery Boldin.

In a despotism, loyalty is withheld except on the part of those whose servility makes it worthless. In democracies, politicians represent parties, and parties represent defined interests. Voters and the press are able to see to it that what politicians do and what they say are not so very far apart. Ryzhkov was a manager of heavy industry, and Chebrikov had the KGB behind him; there was a sense in which they could appeal to what might be called retinues, but in their own cause. In a similar sense, Shevardnadze, Yeltsin and Ligachev could appeal to retinues in their home-based territories. But each one of them finally represented nobody and nothing but himself. The only certain deduction was that each would act to his own advantage as he saw it. How was Gorbachev then to make a reasonable choice of colleagues and advisers? How could he trust those he promoted not to engage in tests of strength against him? Men like these had been careful all their lives to keep their KGB dossiers clean. They were all feared. All paid lip service to party doctrine. Yakovlev and Lukyanov had reputations as good haters of the West and capitalism. In the course of party-state duty, Gorbachev had crossed these men's paths, and he promoted them now out of hearsay and some instinct that they were to be trusted. Everything is negotiable; but to have to advance the very men whom the system is pushing to destroy you also has a ring of classical tragedy.

Coming to power, a General Secretary needed some slogan which was easy to grasp and enforce as policy. Behind slogans like 'Proletarians of all lands, unite!' or 'Socialism is order', Soviet armies had invaded and camps filled with prisoners. Glasnost and perestroika were vranyo-like terms waiting to be used – the former had a history going back to 1861, when the Tsar used it in connection with his proposed measure to abolish serfdom. The intention at any rate was to restore party discipline; that was what the country would receive, whether it was waiting for it or not.

A typical campaign of repression opened. Almost everybody with a plot or a garden, sometimes only a window-box, was in the habit of growing fresh vegetables and fruit otherwise unobtainable. Sold on the black market, such produce is sometimes estimated to have provided between a fifth and a quarter of the entire food supply. In May 1986 a Law Against Unearned Income was passed with the aim of closing down this entrepreneurial activity – the wording of the law was a characteristic reversal of truth, since such income was hard-earned. Everywhere police set about smashing greenhouses, garden frames and the like, and confiscating flowers and vegetables. 'The Criminal Tomato' was the title of an article in the *Literaturnaya Gazeta* on 12 August 1987, in which the author described the destruction of greenhouses near Volgograd, directed by a 'commission for the struggle against negative phenomena' and consisting of prosecutors and militia who had conscripted hoodlums and students for the rough work. An author summed up the campaign in the journal *Novy Mir*: 'The country was swamped by an avalanche of persecution against people who tried not to sit down at the dominoes table after the plant whistle had blown but to work a little more at their own responsibility and risk.'

Similar campaigns were launched against the poor quality of industrial goods, with inspectors given the power to return such goods to the factories, thus depriving workers of bonuses. One authority, Françoise Thom, gives the figure of ten million so-called 'people's controllers'. Corruption was attacked. Tens of thousands of people were sentenced for embezzling state property. Where trade and catering were concerned, the Prosecutor's Office reported, 'Theft and bribery, poor management, and over-reporting, extortion, and concealment of goods are as widespread in the industry as before. Large-scale thefts in particular are increasing.' The cure reproduced the disease.

'In the eyes of the Russian the principle support of civilization is vodka.' This well-known crack of Hitler's glossed over the part played by alcohol as an escape from misery. For most people there was no other recourse. In her memoirs, Raisa Gorbachev gives the information that in 1985 Gorbachev received 412,500 letters addressed to him personally, not including those reaching him through the Central Committee. In 1986, the volume increased to 60,000 a month. Unread and unanswered, these humble petitions were the underside of public frustration, along with mass drunkenness by way of compensation. The country had 40 million officially acknowledged alcoholics. In his first hundred days in power, Gorbachev raised the price of vodka 200 per cent and cut production by 60 per cent. Over eighteen months, the militia confiscated 900,000 distilleries. Famous vineyards in Georgia were uprooted.

By the time repression had worked through the country, the Nomenklatura and the rest of the party could take the measure of Gorbachev's public pronouncements in the manner to which the past had accustomed them. While greenhouses and distilleries were being vandalized, Gorbachev was boasting that 'national oppression and inequality of all types and forms have been done away with once and for all. The indissoluble friendship among nations and respect for national cultures and for the dignity of all people have been established and have taken firm root in the minds of tens of millions of people. The Soviet people is a qualitatively new social and international community, cemented by the same economic interests, ideology and political goals.' Gorbachev saw no contradiction between what he was saying and what he was doing. Evidently he believed in the figment of Homo sovieticus.

Disciplinarian measures from the top spread through the country down the party-state organizations, disintegrating into the very assertions of power and privilege which they were designed to prevent. Party members and militia and the KGB saw themselves authorized to exercise arbitrary power, in this case pilfering fruit and vegetables, confiscating vodka which they then drank or sold on the black market, and accepting bribes to turn a blind eye to manufactured goods whose quality could not conceivably be raised within the limitations set by Gosplan.

For Gorbachev and those whom he had just established in the leadership, it would have required a tremendous effort of intellect and imagination to be able to separate cause from effect in an outcome like this. Everything in their upbringing and practical experience led to the conviction that undesirable results had derived from human failings, not from the structure of the party-state. The search to find people free from human failings fuelled perpetual purging.

Guile was the alternative to violence. Corruption and sleaze would have to be exposed in public. This meant widening glasnost for purposes of control, enrolling newspapers and journalists. By the end of 1986, Gorbachev was summoning select gatherings of editors and writers whom he addressed as though they were natural colleagues in a great enterprise. They were to be free to write about abuses of power. Fear of exposure, and shame, were to restore discipline. Not that there was anything unusual in directions from above of this kind. Publication was propaganda. Still, here was the General Secretary saying that taboo subjects for once ought to be revealed rather than concealed. Items were to be removed from the censorship's five printed pages.

Gorbachev said that there were to be no 'blank spots' in Soviet history. Invited to act like inspectors and controllers and militiamen, journalists had a special role. They were flattered.

There is no sign that Gorbachev or his advisers had any inkling that this might lead to contrary results. A printed revelation does more to shift the collective memory than any amount of spoken rumour. Besides, journalists would know how far they could go only by testing it out, a process certain to align them against the authorities. Glasnost, wrote Alexander Zinoviev in his book *Katastroika*, was 'an occasional means of disinformation and the manipulation of public opinion' by a General Secretary who was a run-of-the-mill careerist. To James Billington, the Librarian of Congress in Washington and a historian of Russia, Gorbachev was a pure child of the party élite, 'the Russian equivalent of a chief lifeguard in Palm Springs'. At a state dinner in 1987 he asked Gorbachev what word he would like for an epitaph. 'Dynamism,' Gorbachev replied. This was the party virtue above all others. Dynamism meant that if glasnost did not work as an instrument of repression then it was easily stopped in its tracks, to leave no more trace in public than any other mobilizing slogan of the past.

Argumenti y Fakti began in the Brezhnev era as a specialist publication for planners and statisticians. The print run was 10,000 in 1979 and by 1990 the editor, Vladimir Starkov, had increased this to 33 million. It was a monument to glasnost. In Starkov's opinion the party had functioned as a military structure with extremely severe discipline. But history was beginning to show that in practice the slogans always on the lips of party officials could not be realized. An objective process of collapse within was under way. The importance of Gorbachev should not be exaggerated: he was 'totally a creature of the party'. The party wanted to keep power and saw in Gorbachev its last best hope to do so. Gromyko and Ligachev and others like them had supported him in order to have a progressive evolution, but within communism. 'I used to meet him and ask, Mikhail Sergeyevich, why don't you ally yourself firmly with democrats and democratic forces? But he hadn't got it in him to do that.'

The Soviet press had paid no attention to the interest of readers. Everybody was functioning in the real world but journalists were in a construct dreamed up by themselves. Television was so much more popular in the Soviet Union because the picture formed some sort of objectivity.

'Discipline and violence had already proved useless': hence glasnost. In the preceding decade the authorities had crushed open dissidents but not underground or *samizdat* publications. A desire for free speech on the part of journalists took hold of Gorbachev's glasnost and ran away with it. Throughout the Gorbachev period the circulation of *Argumenti y Fakti* more than tripled every single year.

'We had no influential patron. Our development went unnoticed by politicians. I am always being asked who let you write such and such an article, was it Yakolev or who? Absolutely nothing of the sort.' Layout was sober and old-fashioned. The paper rose to sensational popularity because it printed articles reporting on day-to-day problems truthfully. Nothing like it had appeared in Soviet history.

'I have no messianic aims. Publishing from a position of common sense, *Argumenti y Fakti* never functioned under the slogan "Down with communism". We did it a different way. We published tables of statistical information – for instance comparing the performance of the Soviet Union with that of other countries. If the thrust of Soviet propaganda said, This is the best country, our paper showed that it was actually thirty-third in the table. Of course this got us into trouble with the authorities. We delved into the history of Stalin and Trotsky and Bukharin, and this influenced public opinion, which was more or less non-existent when we started. When I started at *Argumenti y Fakti*, I was not an ignoramus, but still I knew nothing about the country. There were plenty of people like Sakharov and Bukovsky who could see that the country was being run by incompetent old men and that it was being robbed, but the development of a public arena in which to say so out loud dates from the past few years. There used to be total unanimity. It was put about, for instance, that Gorbachev and Ligachev were the dearest of friends. Only recently we had an interview with Ligachev, and he spoke of his personal conflicts with Gorbachev. I asked why then he had always claimed this wonderful relationship, and he answered, "That was party discipline, I could not have done anything else." ' To Starkov, Gorbachev appeared a man pleased to be General Secretary, and enjoying the good things of life. 'They were in cloud-cuckoo-land about the strength of the system they belonged to. They were getting misinformation. I do not think Gorbachev really understood the consequences of his actions. If he had, he would have put the brakes on.'

With the spectre of factionalism in their minds, delegates at communist mass meetings did and said the same things, seemingly so many partakers in a priestly spectacle. If the party were to speak with more than one voice, it could evidently not be the repository of truth. Only when differences of opinion had been sorted out in private could a speaker mount the rostrum in front of hundreds and even thousands whole sole function was to applaud at appropriate moments. On the surface dull, but with an ominous undertow, the organization was faultless. Khrushchev's partial revelations of Stalin's criminality, at the Twentieth Party Congress, were made in a secret session. It was exceptional. The intention was probably to inform the world of a new line by means of a drama which could be deliberately leaked.

Gorbachev was to preside over three of these ritual or semi-druidical occasions: the Twenty-seventh Party Congress in February 1986, a specially summoned Nineteenth Conference (as opposed to a Congress) in June 1988, and the Twenty-eighth Party Congress in July 1990. With cumulative effect, he was informing the party that he was not satisfied with its performance. General Secretaries had been in the habit of complaining in that manner of the party's human failings. The man at the microphone had no need to raise his voice, but this was deceptive too. Tortured polysyllabically and jargonistically almost beyond meaning, party parlance in fact concealed a blunt instrument for selecting who would fall and who would survive.

There was need for a more effective political system, Gorbachev told the Twenty-seventh Party Congress, and perestroika would deliver it. Nobody was to escape their party duty. For a number of years, Gorbachev said, 'The practical action of party and state agencies lagged behind the demands of the times and life itself. Problems in the country's development grew faster than they were resolved. Sluggishness, ossification of the forms of management, decreased dynamism in work, growth of bureaucracy – all these things did considerable damage to the cause.' Chebrikov confirmed the KGB's support for perestroika, because it had the aim of 'cleansing society of all its negative phenomena'.

Everybody in the Kremlin Great Hall had heard this sort of barrage all their lives. Listening impassively, each was calculating whether he now faced improved or diminished chances in the tests of strength and conflicts of interest engaging him. The practices and slogans remained much as usual: 'Forward in the rhythm of acceleration!' or 'To work – in a new way!'

On 26 April 1986 the Chernobyl nuclear reactor exploded in a combination of faulty design and human error. Glasnost or not, the censor instructed that news of this catastrophe was to be restricted: 'It is forbidden to publish anything except this Tass bulletin.' (Tass was the official party news agency.) The May Day celebrations in nearby Kiev were allowed to unfold without regard to nuclear fallout. The inhabitants of Ukraine and Belarus were left to suffer radiation. Not until 14 May did Gorbachev appear on television. His statement was guarded and probably he would never have spoken at all if levels of radiation had not been monitored in the West. In Reykjavik, Iceland, Gorbachev had tried every means of maintaining Soviet parity with America by pressing Reagan to abandon Star Wars. In Afghanistan the Soviet military had been reinforced for large-scale offensives. An American journalist was snatched off the streets of Moscow by the KGB. On hunger strike in the punishment cell of a concentration camp, Anatoly Marchenko died.

Yet perestroika, Gorbachev was repeating in ever-rising tones at every opportunity, was 'urgent, it affects everyone and everything'. There could not be the slightest relaxation in concentrating upon it. By 1987 he was defining it as 'the determined overcoming of stagnation, and the destruction of braking mechanisms'. The year 1988 was a critical one for perestroika. 'The basic task,' Gorbachev told the special conference that June, 'will not only *not* undermine discipline and order' but on the contrary would take place on 'the basis of awareness. This is how we will rectify our shortcomings.' In plain or non-party language, people would obey without having to be ordered to do so. That had been the ideal of communism's founding fathers.

One of those purged by perestroika was Richard Kosolapov. Since 1978 he had been a staff member and then editor of *Kommunist*, the main theoretical journal of the party and the most influential publication after the daily *Pravda*. The Central Committee had control over all the mass media, and *Kommunist* was its particular mouthpiece. Only a small proportion of the material, according to Kosolapov, was placed in the journal without prior consultation, notably speeches by the General Secretary and articles by the party leadership. Documents of this type could not be edited.

In the 1970s, he says, he was a widely published writer. After 1985 publication of his work in journals of mass circulation was prohibited. In the run-up to the Twenty-seventh Party Congress he was pushed out of *Kommunist*, to become a professor at Moscow University. Purging was done 'in a subtle way'. Orthodox communists like him none the less feel that they were victims, and resent Gorbachev for it.

'I feel no responsibility for what is known as perestroika and I am very glad about that. It was an aphoristic expression for what happened, it should be called destructuring. Look at the slogans Gorbachev was advancing, rally clichés, aphoristic emblems whose meaning Gorbachev and his closest advisers were unable to explain. As an academic I had a clear understanding of the state of the economy and knew that none of the proposed measures would accelerate anything. In those early years I suggested that Gorbachev was setting out on the path to nowhere. All those slogans indicated that he was playing political games, for example, the idea of returning to true Leninist forms of socialism. One slogan we had was "More democracy, more socialism", as if such things could be measured in kilograms.'

The leadership never paid attention to Marxism–Leninism. 'It is merely amusing to talk about Brezhnev or some of those advisers like Arbatov and Petrakov as Marxist. Bureaucracy was the cancer killing the system. Once entrenched, the Nomenklatura worked solely to its own benefit.'

In January 1986 Kosolapov wrote a letter to Gorbachev. 'I forecast the future course of events, saying in an acceptable form that I believed that Gorbachev was an ill-educated communist. I couldn't describe him as anti-communist because I couldn't assume that he was about to dismantle his own state. I had a clear idea of what kind of major overhauls would repair the social structure. It is inaccurate, though now popular, to say there was no alternative. Removing people like me from positions of influence left Gorbachev free to say that there was no alternative.'

Why were demonstrations in favour of perestroika so large?

'The big so-called popular demonstrations were organized by the party. You needn't delude yourself that Yuri Afanasiev or some other reformer roaring and ranting on Manezh Square really enjoyed support. People do not know who they are. As official leader of the party, Gorbachev was exploiting party structures to reinforce his own position.'

8

ELECTIONS

Like most books by political leaders, Boris Yeltsin's memoir *Against the Grain* was drafted by advisers with short-term objectives. Yet it seems truthful as far as it goes. Born in 1931, an almost exact contemporary of Gorbachev's, Yeltsin looks back on his childhood as a fairly joyless time. The family lived in a communal barracks, where the aim was merely to survive. 'My father's chief instrument for teaching good behaviour was the strap.' One day when his father reached for his strap, the teenage Yeltsin gripped him by the arm and said, 'That's enough!' Describing himself by nature as an optimist and fairly extrovert, he concedes that his character is difficult, awkward, obstinate, prickly. He is, he says, constantly having a fight with someone.

'I was brought up in the system; everyone was steeped in the methods of the "command" system and I, too, acted accordingly' and he added with his familiar gruffness that no one used to reveal the workings of that system. Style, dress, speech and even physical appearance, marked him as a successful manager of the command-administrative system. To an interviewer in 1990 he said, 'I am primarily a man from the productive sector. I understand the people and the common man.' There is no evidence that he had given thought to ideological, intellectual or even social aspects of this system.

In their days as First Secretaries, he says, he and Gorbachev used to extend a helping hand to one another. You gave a favour, you claimed one in return. Although Yeltsin has several times wondered why Gorbachev had come to choose him, he knew that further mutual favours were expected. In the name of perestroika and glasnost, Yeltsin was to throw his weight around, in his words 'to clear away the old debris, to fight the mafia' and Gorbachev was to earn credit. Hearing a progress report, Gorbachev commended Yeltsin in February 1986: 'You have brought in a strong and welcome gust of fresh air.' In the manner of any caliph or Tsar, Yeltsin had taken to inspecting factories and stores, to dispense praise and blame. He travelled on the Moscow metro. In October that year, the German schoolmaster Dieter Knötzsch happened to catch sight of him emerging from a shop and climbing into a car without the expected status symbols. 'An impressive appearance, large and broad, white-haired and vital.' Here, in his opinion, was a tribune of the people.

A year later, Gorbachev was to force Yeltsin out of his position in the Moscow City Party and the Politburo. It was a personality clash. Yeltsin has described how at a Politburo session he suggested changes to a draft speech of Gorbachev's. A furious Gorbachev stormed out of the room and for the next thirty minutes the membership of the Politburo and the secretaries sat there not knowing what to do or how to react. When Gorbachev returned, he let fly at Yeltsin personally with all the complaints and resentments that had been building up.

Soon after this, in the company of his peers from the Politburo and Central Committee, Yeltsin repeated this tactic, declaring that perestroika was not working. The party, and Ligachev in particular, was impeding it. The convention was always to give due warning of any criticism which might be levelled, in order to minimize personal clashes of opinion which could get out of hand, with prospects of split votes and standoffs leading to the forming of factions. Probably Gorbachev saw his chance to suppress a tribune of the people who was growing unruly. But Yeltsin may have believed himself to be saying what Gorbachev wanted to hear, or he may have been set up in a classic provocation. Here was 'a mysterious affair', in Yeltsin's words, and much remains invisible about the origins of this test of strength.

Brutal in manner, the twin dismissals frightened Yeltsin. The humiliation of the experience inspired revenge. Ill in hospital with a temperature, he had been summoned to the Kremlin as though by Stalin himself to hear his fate. Barely conscious, he says, he was obliged to appear in front of the Politburo and the Moscow City Committee whose leaders were like a row of waxwork dummies. It was inhuman and immoral, it was a civil execution, 'like a real murder . . . A rusty nail is still lodged in my heart and I have not pulled it out.' Russian sources quote Gorbachev as saying to Yeltsin, 'I will never let you back into politics!' These actual words may be dramatized but the logic of the system dictated the sentiment.

For someone in Gorbachev's position, the prudent course of action was to be rid of Yeltsin once and for all; his predecessors would have arranged a show trial or a fatal accident. The cunning alternative was to offer a sop, some post with Nomenklatura privileges to ease hardship, but without possibility of a comeback. It speaks well of Gorbachev's character that he made Yeltsin First Deputy Commissioner for the State Committee for Construction. Not even exile to the provinces. Either Gorbachev felt fully self-confident or he underrated what could by now only be an implacable foe. This leniency freed Yeltsin to pick the fight of his life. Single-mindedly, he consolidated when he could and gambled when there was no other choice, taking advantage of

Gorbachev's moves and forcing him into error, inexorably and punishingly pushing his rival to the wall.

In their determination to plot and kill fifty years earlier, Stalin and Trotsky had been unequally matched, but the country could have split into armed camps. The reprise between Gorbachev and Yeltsin also contained the seeds of civil war. Enough of a political process had started to check their rivalry just short of civil war, but as Lenin had foreseen, factionalism was lethal. The price for it was the destruction of the party and the Soviet Union.

Enunciating a policy of renewal, Gorbachev heedlessly fashioned weapons which would be stolen by others and turned against him. Tacitly, and then on every public platform, he was conceding that the past had been malign. This defined the party as the originator of self-serving lies and corruption. But the party had chosen him as its leader. He was never able to draw a convincing line between the admitted deficiencies of the party and his own virtues of leadership.

Thoughtful Soviet people had long appreciated that Gorbachev's criticisms were true in a general sense, though his exhortatory formulas were too unspecific to have much practical application. The reforms such people advocated were in the direction of civil and human rights, but discussions along those lines had been repressed or driven underground as dissidence by the time Gorbachev came to power. Andrei Sakharov was the spokesman of those who hoped to see restructuring begin with some establishment of guaranteed rights. An Academician much rewarded and respected for his contribution to developing the Soviet hydrogen bomb, Sakharov began in the 1960s to reflect on the nature of this totalitarian state which he had done so much to make invulnerable. By his own account he had tolerated the use of slave labour to realize his own bomb projects, and had chosen to remain ignorant of the crimes of Stalin's era. At first following the practice of writing letters to the leadership, he later began to publish his thoughts in the West, evolving into a dissident as famous in his way as Solzhenitsyn. For this, he was stripped of privileges and exiled to the provinces for almost seven years, twice going on hunger strikes, and steadily refusing to recant. Nobody did as much as he to introduce into Soviet debate the concept of a law-based state in which the party was to be held accountable for its actions.

In February 1986, in an interview with the French communist newspaper *L'Humanité*, Gorbachev had called Sakharov a criminal. Ten months later a telephone was installed in Sakharov's place of exile and Gorbachev himself then rang up to announce that Sakharov could return home to Moscow. Through this traditional gesture of clemency on the part of a despot, Gorbachev was recruiting on his own behalf a figure of world renown, expecting thereby to win over the rest of the intelligentsia. This did not prove difficult.

During the course of 1987, through skilful purgings of opponents and promotion of loyalists, the entire press was refashioned in Gorbachev's image. Taking glasnost to the next stage, the press boosted the formation of voluntary associations, or discussion forums for cultural and educational and ecological topics. A few hundred such groups became a few thousand by September, and 30,000 by the middle of 1988. People meeting in a public hall or cinema to make spontaneous pronouncements on whatever concerned them were escaping party supervision. Gorbachev apparently approved. He also favoured televised walkabouts as a way of putting across himself and perestroika. On a tour of Siberia in August 1988, he was confronted by a barrage of complaints from bystanders, and he answered, 'You should give your leaders a good shake-up!' Here spoke the benevolent Tsar; he did not include himself in those leaders. A heckler took him up. 'It's useless! Just look at the brand-new houses here, Mikhail Sergeyevich, it's impossible to live in them. Within a month there are huge cracks in the floor and the doors don't shut ... and that's not the end of the story.'

Perhaps with his conjuror's mastery Gorbachev could have kept in the air all the different balls – baleful and brooding Yeltsin, Ligachev and the Central Committee resentful of criticisms from above which were felt to be unjustified, the earnest and even ponderously academic Sakharov, the informal discussion groups. The first Soviet polling organization, the Institute for the Study of Public Opinion, opened in 1988, and nine in ten of those polled at 120 enterprises were in favour of perestroika.

Instead Gorbachev convened the Nineteenth Party Conference, in itself an emergency measure. There he spoke in the idiom of Sakharov on the need for accountability via secret ballots, multiple candidates, limited terms of office. Outwardly obedient, the party apparatus of Ligachev and his men concluded that however many had already been purged, the General Secretary was still not satisfied with the party. Yeltsin had contrived to become a delegate at this conference, and when he spoke, his voice trembled with emotion. Repeating what had already caused him so much trouble, he said that perestroika would proceed faster and better without the obstructions of Ligachev and his like. But he concluded with a public and abject request to be rehabilitated. This was not granted. In a mood of arrogance Gorbachev closed the conference with a call to establish a new Congress of People's Deputies. The old rubber-stamp Soviet was to be refashioned as this Congress, which would give Gorbachev the party that he wanted, putting perestroika into place, and revitalizing the party-state for the coming century.

Nobody really knows where the idea behind the Congress of People's Duputies originated. It was dreamed up by Gorbachev himself, it is said, or by Lukyanov who had been active in the old Soviet. Or else by Alexander

Yakovlev. Of all the men prominent in the Gorbachev entourage, he is the most unfathomable. His real character cannot be deciphered from what he said and did, so inscrutable are his workings, so hidden the wheels within wheels. Older than his colleagues, he had been wounded in the war and walks with a stiff limp. A strictly orthodox Nomenklatura man, he had been the loser in a test of strength in the 1970s and was swept out of the way as ambassador to Canada. His speciality was party propaganda. He is a notable polemicist. Placed by Gorbachev in the Politburo in charge of agitation and the press, he found himself in conflict with Ligachev who had a similar responsibility within the Central Committee's secretariat. Since the division of powers was never defined, the two men almost automatically clashed. The most famous episode was in March 1988, when Ligachev planted in the press a lengthy article by a teacher called Nina Andreyeva. This was a strident demand to put a stop to perestroika and glasnost and return to communist values. This particular test of strength lasted three critical weeks, ending in Yakovlev's favour when he arranged for the publication of an article he had written under a pseudonym entirely repudiating Nina Andreyeva and all she stood for.

Time and again, in spite of his communist past, Yakovlev was to use his influence, stealthily and deviously, to push forward reform that extra inch. A man for a private gathering, exercising his influence in the corridors of power, he preferred invisibility. Travelling busily around the republics and the satellite states of Eastern and Central Europe, he was in the habit of holding tête-à-tête sessions with First Secretaries to impart confidentially the latest instructions, though nobody could tell whether these were really Gorbachev's or his own. The political system of the satellites was, in his words, 'parasite socialism'. The political system of the Soviet Union was no better, and whoever wished to change it could be sure that an appeal to Yakovlev would be supported. By 1987 he was repeating the Sakharov themes of the need for morality and accountability, upping the stakes to introduce the idea of a market, missing no opportunity to criticize lawlessness and the KGB. His was the grave-digger's role. To Yeltsin, Yakovlev was 'a most intelligent, sensible, and far-seeing politician', whose prime failure lay in being soft on Ligachev, their common enemy. According to Sakharov, Yakovlev was intelligent and well-versed in domestic and foreign policy. But he sensed in this enigmatic man 'an indelible residue of Leninist dogma'. When finally a constitutional court was set up after the collapse of 1991 to inquire into the Communist Party and its activities, the attorney briefed to defend communism began his cross-examination of Yakovlev with the remark: 'Please explain what you did to destroy the Soviet Union.' It was a well-directed shaft.

Again it speaks well for Gorbachev that he decided to build his new party by means of a structure like the Congress of People's Deputies, rather than simply murdering off those associated with the former party and its structures, in the manner of Stalin or Mao-Zedong. By means of this Congress, corrupt and obstructive Nomenklatura veterans were to be bypassed and affirmative Gorbachev supporters would have an alternative conduit of power.

The secret lay in the nomination of deputies. One-third of the 2250 deputies were to be selected directly by party organizations and the other two-thirds allotted on a basis of territory and population to Union republics and regions. Minorities like the Balts were certain to be over-represented but at that stage this was judged sensible and conciliatory. A complicated process was laid down for preselection of candidates, in which at all levels the First Secretary had the final say. On paper, this process could produce a contest only between the old type of communist and the new Gorbachev men. On paper again, nobody could enter this Congress without the party's approval. Once in the Congress, moreover, the deputies were not responsible for the business of legislation; they still had to approve programmes placed before them from above. On the surface, but not in substance, the Congress was to have Sakharov's account-ability. But there were no legislators to elect, no constitutional lawyers to consult, no debates about the separation of powers or the limits of the party-state. This Potemkin improvization would allow the same absolutism as before, under different management.

As garlic to a vampire, so elections to a despotism. Any element of rep-resentation is enough to crack the monolithic front. Gorbachev announced at the Nineteenth Party Conference in June 1988 that elections would take place on 25 March 1989. Even at the end of 1988, neither he nor anybody else imagined that Yeltsin would skilfully manipulate his own election as a deputy; as would Sakharov, and between 250 and 400 others prepared to join them in a block. Unexpectedly Yeltsin had a forum in which to probe at the rusty nail in his heart. Quite unintentionally – suicidally, as it turned out – Gorbachev had let him back into politics.

Language in which to do justice to the careerism of these politics is inadequate. Western commentators, and above all professional sovietologists, were in the habit of listening to the interminable proceedings of conferences and congresses, minutely dissecting precedence given to speakers or decon-structing press articles. What was often great expertise was vitiated through frequent failure to perceive the careerist character of those proceedings and the multi-layered tests of strength that drove them. Instead, Soviet politics were reduced according to the organizing principles of democracy, so that reactionaries were said to be opposing reformers, or with even more childish simplicity, hawks were at odds with doves. It was inapposite to fit to the Soviet Union any political categorizations of left and right, conservative or radical.

It is hard to avoid the blanket phraseology of 'certain forces' and 'elements in the party' and 'leading circles' and 'taking necessary measures' and 'emerging cadres' but such parlance was also taking the system at face value, obscuring the very direct and personal rivalries actually under way. Habitual Western categorization was laughably confusing once the tests of strength could be publicly observed in the Congress of People's Deputies. Those who fought to save their privileges were employing the same methods as those determined to wrest them away. The so-called conservatives and reformers were equal as wreckers.

Gorbachev, Yeltsin, Yakovlev, Ligachev and Lukyanov were all cut of the same cloth and all engaged in the selfsame struggle to maximize their power through the elimination of other contenders. Their moves against each other were all of a piece, each containing a semblance of advance into an area deemed to bring them support, with an escape route left for any necessary withdrawal. In theory Gorbachev held supremacy through the army and the KGB. Any day he liked, he could order a crackdown, mass arrests and a reversion to Stalinism and barbarity, and in their inner selves everybody anticipated this likelihood. But in that case he had to be able to count on party support. His constant carping at the party and the whittling down of Nomenklatura privileges were alienating. Why stay loyal to a General Secretary who was always tongue-lashing and finger-wagging? Let him dig himself out of his own hole. Weakening his natural power base, Gorbachev exposed and isolated himself. Perestroika could make little headway against the party and so it withered. The public became disenchanted with Gorbachev and his ceaseless rhetoric which was leading to austerity and rationing hardly ever experienced in times of peace. Gorbachev then had nowhere to turn except abroad, to foreign leaders, and mobs in the streets of Germany and France, mindlessly shrieking 'Gorbi!', unaware of how they were mere popularity-fodder in his tests of strength at home. From televised scenes of Gorbimania, Russians were invited to consider that Gorbachev was a world statesman who should be allowed to proceed as he liked. Meanwhile Ligachev stepped towards the void now at the centre of a demoralized party. Rallying the faithful he could hope for power.

Sakharov died suddenly in 1989. In his last book *Moscow and Beyond*, written in the course of that year, he said that he did not idolize Gorbachev or believe that he was doing all that was needed, but still he had altered the country and people's psychology. As for Yeltsin, he was a person of a different calibre, whose popularity was to some extent dependent on Gorbachev's unpopularity. Yeltsin's highly original and startling perception was that he could steal Sakharov's thunder; he could call for accountability and the rule of law. Truthfully he could tub-thump that the quality of life was not improving but on the contrary deteriorating and that a flagging perestroika had to be stepped up. The more Gorbachev criticized the party and blustered about restructuring, the more he handed the initiative to Yeltsin. Gorbachev found himself in a vicious circle of his own making. Where Gorbachev mobilized westerners, Yeltsin could call Russians out on to the streets and tell them what they wanted to hear. What these rivals did and said were not functions of ideology, as they might appear to be, but of power.

9

THE RIBBENTROP–MOLOTOV PACT

Lev Besimensky is a historian specializing in Nazi Germany, and he works for the newspaper *Novoye Vremya*. In his office there is a photograph of him in a circle of Soviet officers standing with Field Marshal von Paulus on the day of the German surrender at Stalingrad. In 1988, in response to glasnost and perestroika, a commission was established under the chairmanship of Alexander Yakovlev to inquire into the Ribbentrop–Molotov Pact of 1939, and Besimensky was a member of it. Among the results of this pact, serving the interests of both Hitler and Stalin, was the partition of Poland which started the war, and the consigning of the Baltic republics in secret protocols to the Soviet sphere of influence. Then and afterwards, the Soviet line was that the Baltic republics had not been occupied but liberated, and communism had been a free choice, not a military imposition. This vied with the massacre of captive Poles at Katyn as the most wicked of the 'blank spots' in history.

'Glasnost revealed many new things about the Soviet period and its mechanism,' Besimensky said. 'When you live inside a system like that, some of its co-ordinates appear to have a natural existence of their own. Much seemed natural that wasn't, such as the ideals of communism, which were used to justify a whole range of policies and actions, the Ribbentrop–Molotov Pact in particular. In the 1930s we all believed that repression was unavoidable and justifiable. With glasnost, the moral foundations for previous convictions ceased to apply. This forced me to discuss things previously not considered. In my books I had avoided consciously the issue of the 1939 Pact because I guessed the existence of secret protocols and in order to avoid lying simply chose not to discuss the topic. Bear in mind Soviet psychology. If you find lots of people who now say they protested against the system, don't believe them.'

As a historian, Besimensky had far more information than was available to the man on the street. Western historians had long since published the truth about the 1939 Pact, but he did not believe them. 'I had been educated to mistrust. Historians in this country have had the rug pulled away from under their feet. All of a sudden we had to accept that Western assessments of our society were more accurate than our own.'

Glasnost opened archives concerning the party, as well as foreign policy, until the mid-1950s. The KGB archive remains largely closed. So does the presidential archive which is properly the Kremlin archive, and more specifically the sixth sector of general affairs of the Communist Party of the Soviet Union, containing all the documents of the General Secretaries, the Politburo and the Central Committee and its secretariat. Valery Boldin was the last person in charge of this material. In 1989, as Gorbachev's *chef de cabinet*, he transferred the entire sixth sector to the Kremlin and made it inaccessible. 'Boldin was one of the experts on Yakovlev's commission and they could get nothing out of him. So I have reason to think that the originals of the secret protocols are there.' The highest level of security are the so-called Special Folders of the Politburo, whose existence was known only to an inner circle. These Special Folders remain closed.

Quite what, and quite when, Gorbachev and then Yeltsin knew either about the Katyn massacre or the secret protocols of the 1939 Pact is contentious. 'I can't believe Boldin would have familiarized himself with the Katyn dossier and not told Gorbachev. People close to Gorbachev say that he did not like looking at documents, he always procrastinated over unpleasant things until it was too late; that was Gorbachev's whole mentality. Chernyayev says that Gorbachev had almost an allergic aversion to documents, and this affected perestroika.'

Besimensky's account of the Yakovlev commission and its proceedings show how even matters critical to the future of the Soviet Union were decided not on intrinsic merit but through the subterfuges of personal tests of strength which themselves would be irrelevant in more rational politics. Although glasnost and perestroika may well have been rational concepts, they could not be realized except within the existing context, thus adding to the motives for pitting people against each other in desperate and finally chaotic conditions.

At a Politburo meeting in late 1988, Besimensky said, Yakovlev and Shevardnadze and Vadim Medvedev (responsible for ideology at the time) proposed that the 1939 Pact be condemned. Ligachev and Chebrikov and Marshal Yazov were opposed. If the Baltic republics had been incorporated by force against their wishes then clearly their claims to independence would have to be viewed favourably. Gorbachev closed the discussion. 'You cannot say that it is a credit to glasnost or to historians that the Pact was finally condemned. Only external pressure from the Balts achieved it.'

At the first Congress of People's Deputies, Gorbachev managed to avoid the question. The Balts then demanded a commission. 'At first Gorbachev tried to talk them out of it. Then he did something clever: he agreed, throwing responsibility for the whole *démarche* on to Yakovlev by appointing him to head it. A disproportionate number of the members were from the Baltic States, so the work was less a proper investigation than a struggle for independence. The Balts were supported by some like Yuri Afanasiev, but others like Valentin Falin of the International Department of the Central Committee did not want to hear of it.'

They could agree that the secret protocols existed. On the question of whether to condemn the protocols, opinion was so split that the commission became unworkable. Yakovlev stated that the secret protocols existed, but as a member of the Politburo he needed permission from his colleagues to condemn them. The fiftieth anniversary of the Pact was 23 August 1989. As that date approached, mass demonstrations began in the Baltic republics. The members of the commission therefore agreed that it would be better to get the issue out of the way, and admit the secret protocols and their criminality. Yakovlev could not persuade the Politburo, Gorbachev vacillated, and so the commission did not report.

'Cleverly Yakovlev said to the members of the commission that he would pretend that nothing had happened, and he would still report to the Congress of People's Deputies but as though he were a private individual. The huge majority of deputies then declared that the existence of the secret protocols was a bourgeois *canard* and that the Pact had been necessary. When a vote was taken, Yakovlev failed to get a majority. It was threatening the whole foundation of glasnost and perestroika to have a Congress of Deputies refusing to accept a proven truth.'

What the deputies did not know was that a document had come to light. A clerk in 1946 had been ordered to transfer some of Molotov's papers from one archive to another. Conscientiously, this man noted what he had done, and copied the original of the secret protocols as well. Somebody in the archives handed this to Shevardnadze, who handed it to Yakovlev. That night the commission met and it was agreed to reveal this document. Yakovlev did so in the Congress of Deputies the following day.

As Speaker, Lukyanov was in charge of proceedings in the Congress. 'Lukyanov did everything in his power to stop this. Gorbachev had a stony expression. The vote was taken again, Yakovlev got his majority. It demonstrates the extent to which people do not want to believe the facts placed before them. Homo sovieticus. We always underestimated our psychological problems.'

10

FIRST STEPS IN REFORM

A Russianized Latvian, Otto Latsis is a foremost economic and political commentator. He became an adviser to Yakovlev, whose role he judges to have been 'absolutely decisive'. Several simultaneous power struggles centred on Yakovlev. He and Vadim Medvedev swapped jobs; when one became Ideological Secretary, the other became Secretary for International Affairs, and vice versa. Gorbachev had 'this transcendent admiration for Medvedev who was rather boring and mediocre; much more restrained and cautious than Yakovlev'.

In charge of the Central Committee secretariat, Ligachev was regarded as the second man in the party after the General Secretary. Latsis says, 'Even people working in that field were not clear in their understanding of how the duties between Yakovlev and Ligachev were carved up. They were caught in an even more bitter struggle. Yakovlev was far closer to Gorbachev personally. Especially with regard to a big issue like the Nina Andreyeva letter. That was published on Ligachev's initiative, whatever he likes to say. At a time when Gorbachev and Yakovlev were both abroad, Ligachev stood up three times at an editorial meeting to recommend publication. Subsequently a directive went out from the Central Committee to instruct regional newspapers to publish the letter. For several days there was as much ideological confusion as if a coup had taken place. Nobody had a clear idea of which direction the country would take. Gorbachev was horrified.

'After his pseudonymous article rebutting the Nina Andreyeva letter, Yakovlev was made head of the Committee for Rehabilitation of Stalin's victims. Then he was put in charge of a commission whose chairman in theory was Gorbachev, with responsibility for writing the new edition of the party's history. That was a canonical work.'

Among the main developments of 1988 was the formation in each republic of Popular Fronts. This phrase had a hardened communist echo. From the outset the Popular Fronts appeared suspiciously like KGB structures to channel and divert local nationalisms.

'Yakovlev played a very public role in supporting the Popular Fronts, especially in the Baltic republics. I travelled with him when he went in 1988 to Lithuania and Latvia at the point when the Popular Fronts were growing in importance. There was discussion about whether they should be repressed or allowed to carry on their work. Yakovlev was crucial in deciding that administrative repression was out. Shortly afterwards, the Popular Fronts began to open out into independent movements. At which point some people began to turn fiercely against Yakovlev for his attitudes, particularly at the Twenty-seventh Party Congress. Gorbachev did not want these attacks, so he manoeuvred to get rid of Yakovlev. One step was to put him in charge of the commission to reassess the Ribbentrop–Molotov Pact. That commission became one of the main planks justifying the independence of the Baltic republics. Briefly, he was in charge of the Secretariat of International Affairs, and he and Shevardnadze infuriated the military by proposing tactical withdrawal from Eastern Europe. In discussion about what should be done about the party, Yakovlev once more took the lead. A split loomed, and Gorbachev was desperately trying to avoid that until the very last moment. Right from the Twenty-eighth Party Congress Yakovlev was very determinedly leading the faction insisting on a formal split within the party. Gorbachev should just write it off, follow Yakovlev and separate himself entirely from Ligachev. But Gorbachev was tending more and more to ally himself with the hardliners.'

But to be rid of Yakovlev could not imply Ligachev's victory. 'Gorbachev did not do anything so silly as to take Ligachev's job away. He made a brilliant tactical move. Under the guise of reorganizing the party he dismantled much of its structure. There was no longer to be a secretariat, but instead a number of separate commissions, outside the control of the apparatchiks. Suddenly Ligachev discovered that despite the fact that he still had a job, a big car and a grand title, he was no longer in charge of the whole apparatus as before.'

During the two years between the Nineteenth Party Conference in 1988 and the Twenty-eighth Party Congress in 1990, the whole party–state apparatus was dismantled. It was only around the middle of 1989 that the party–state managers realized that perestroika and restructuring were not empty words to lull the public into a state of acquiescence. Through party discipline, they had always been accustomed to taking on trust what the General Secretary said and did. Trying to regain power, they discovered that the party apparatus, their sole avenue, was no longer effective.

Gorbachev underwent a process of education in office. He came to understand the inadequacies of the command–administrative system but then had no model with which to replace it. His political convictions hampered him.

He saw himself as having to build consensus. After the 1989 elections, he was as slow as other apparatchiks to realize that the principal seat of power was no longer concentrated in the party but had moved to the revamped Soviet, the Congress.

Economic policy exemplified the mistaken attempt to build consensus. In the summer of 1987, for example, two completely independent parallel teams were set to work in a dacha on the outskirts of Moscow which once had belonged to Andrei Zhdanov, Stalin's ideological hatchet man. They were to prepare economic policy planning. The Central Committee group, headed by Yakovlev, contained Abalkin, Abel Aganbegyan, Valentin Pavlov, Latsis himself and others. The other group, headed by the Prime Minister, Nikolai Ryzhkov, came from the Council of Ministers. Once presented and compared, their policy documents had nothing in common.

'Starting in 1988, supposedly on the basis of these documents, the reform programme was formalized in all its contradictions under Ryzhkov. He started working on the basis of a projected budget deficit of 100 billion roubles, a fantastic sum, with catastrophic inflationary prospects. Ours is the only country in the world where the State Bank is directly controlled by the Ministry of Finance, and it can grant as much credit as is demanded of it, not backed by anything. 1989 was the first time they admitted they had a budget deficit, of 36 billion roubles. Yegor Gaidar, the economist (later Yeltsin's Prime Minister) and I pointed out in an article that a deficit on that scale would lead to collapse. Nobody objected. Then Yuri Maslyukov, the head of Gosplan, did a clever trick, announcing that a deficit for the current year of 127 billion roubles had been anticipated, so one of "only" 100 billion would be an improvement. It was still equal to 12 per cent of GNP. Ryzhkov did not want to confront the powerful military–industrial lobby or to cut back on state spending in prestige projects like railways and dams. He knew how to run a factory but never had to deal with demand or supply, nor was obliged to cover a deficit. That was as far as his economic understanding went. As late as 1990, the economy could have been saved. After that it was too late.'

In 1990 Gorbachev was still employing rival teams of economists. One set advocated a drastic move towards the free market. The other, still under Ryzhkov, rejected private ownership in favour of more centralization. These incompatibilities were cobbled together in the Shatalin Plan, named after one of the experts pushing market concepts. This plan was to be implemented in 400 and then – for the sake of a still rounder number – 500 days. In the circumstances, consensus meant collapse. Postponing a hard choice by means of artificial reconciliation, Gorbachev had locked the economy, and with it the future of the party and the Soviet Union, into tests of strength which could have no outcome except contradiction and paralysis.

Did Gorbachev not anticipate that in the Congress of People's Deputies power might escape from his hands?

'Maybe he did, maybe he didn't. The decision to have the Congress was part of the internal manoeuvring whereby Gorbachev was trying to distance himself from Yeltsin. The hardliners assumed that all talk of election was just fine speech and they would take control, which they did in about half the territory of Russia. Only at the last moment did they see they might lose in the large cities. Then the regional party committees talked of betrayal in Moscow. By means of that election Yeltsin levered himself to head the democratic movement. What he meant by democracy is extremely difficult to assess, and rather unimportant. Expulsion from the Politburo had made him a hero. He represented a timely and elemental protest.

'I worked as campaign manager for Academician Bogomolov, who was standing against a factory manager and old apparatchik called Bryanchin. He ran a depressing campaign on the basis that the party should be trusted. It was very close until two days before the election, when Bogomolov came out strongly against the unfair attacks on Yeltsin. He won by over 50 per cent. It had become possible to read and to see for yourself, to vote out some party boss and elect an unknown candidate.'

To Professor Jerry Hough, an American sovietologist and a prolific writer, it seemed wildly optimistic in 1988 to think that the Soviet system would shatter over the coming five to ten years. Two years later, he considered that Gorbachev 'had manoeuvred the situation to precisely where he wanted it', and was sure to remain in power at least until 1995. With similar fantasy, the CIA had enormously overestimated Soviet growth rates, to conclude that the Soviet economy was not of a very different order of magnitude from the American. Following the rises in the oil price in the 1970s, the Soviet Union had earned over 170 billion dollars from oil exports alone. That wealth has been dissipated, nobody can say quite how. On a table of living standards of all countries, the Soviet Union was around the position of sixtieth.

Vassily Selyunin did more than most Soviet economists to dig out the true state of affairs. He was employed on a specialist journal. With a colleague, Gregory Khanin, in 1979 he used methods not based on phoney official statistics to project a model of the Soviet economy. They reached the conclusion that without change the economy would collapse by the mid-1990s. As a result of glasnost, a challenging exposition of industrial and economic failure could be published in 1987, in *Novy Mir*, by which time it was clear that the economy was moving as they had predicted, and not according to the projections of either Soviet or American officialdom. In Selyunin's opinion, someone other than Gorbachev might have tried by force to stave off impending collapse, but in that case the outcome would have been terrible indeed.

In 1986 Selyunin published the first of many articles to advocate the opposite of Gorbachev's programme. 'To his credit, Gorbachev was not offended by them. He said something rather incomprehensible to me, that I was an extremist but none the less right.

'His reforms were to be means to an end. The country had fallen behind the West by a whole epoch in scientific and technical spheres, as reflected primarily in the machine-tool industry. Our machinery was extremely poor, which accounted for the lag. Gorbachev argued that the entire five-year period of the Twelfth Plan – from 1986 to 1990 – should be devoted to the production of modern machinery. In the Thirteenth, Fourteenth and Fifteenth Five-Year Plans it would be possible to consider raising the general standard of living. That meant leaving centralized planning intact. The population was to tighten its belt and catch up yet again with the West. Gorbachev even proposed a measure not employed since Stalin's day, to increase investment in machine-building at the expense of consumption. Through Gulag and repression, the party-state used to compel people to accept declining living standards, but neither a Five-Year Plan nor a single year's target were ever fulfilled. Force was no longer practised either. In other words, the command-administrative system had reached an absolute crisis point, and the programme of accelerating progress through machine-tool building was doomed from the beginning.' Four-fifths of the machine-tool industry consisted of weaponry and the equipment for producing it. Half the industrial labour force was employed in the machine-tool sector. No other economy had ever been so militarized. Restructuring without diminishing the proportion of four-fifths only meant more equipment for arms.

The military–industrial complex was efficient, perhaps more so than in the West, producing more types of weapons such as tanks and missiles and nuclear submarines than all the Nato countries put together. 'But we were utterly defeated in the production of more sophisticated weapons. The American Star Wars programme created a major panic here, as Soviet industry could produce nothing of the sort. Gorbachev's reforming plan for machine tools essentially meant that we would be able to re-establish our previous military supremacy and so militarize further the Soviet economy. In fact, it needed to be directed away from superpower ambitions towards human beings, and this could be done only by the introduction of the market. To start a transition towards the market, the command-administrative system should have been completely dismantled.' Selyunin pointed to the two Germanys, the two Koreas and the three Chinas (with Taiwan and Hong Kong) as instances where for historic reasons the very same peoples had different systems. Economic comparisons between the separate entities need no comment.

'Gorbachev never accepted that you won't have a market unless first you privatize property. The essence of communism is the elimination of private property. In 1988 at a students' congress in Moscow, Gorbachev was asked what his attitude was towards private property. My position is that of the *Communist Manifesto*, he answered, which was mystifying, but I am sure he meant it. He never changed his outlook.'

The Law on State Enterprises came into force on 1 January 1988. The gigantic industrial monopolies were to continue as before, but with a measure of freedom in running their affairs. 'It's rare when you can date a mistake so precisely. Independence should never have been given to state enterprises. They had all the rights of a proprietor but none of the responsibilities. They could never go bankrupt. They raised salaries as a priority, without connection to production or costs. Our group of economists recommended that this law would be disastrous but Gorbachev and his team simply did not understand. It did the greatest damage to our economy. We had empty shops. Trade was only in the streets, in the black market. Between 1988 and 1991 there was a drop of over 25 per cent in production. They printed money. Investment here is done entirely by the state through the budget. Defence spending also. That is why we had a budget deficit of more than 20 per cent. If you look at the point where military coups are carried out in Latin America, you will find that they coincide with a budget deficit of 20 per cent. That is when a country becomes ungovernable.

'In June 1990 I was invited with other economists to meet Gorbachev. He started the meeting by mentioning that he had had a telephone call from General Jaruzelski about unemployment and price-rises in Poland. How was this to be avoided if we were to reform, Gorbachev asked. The economist Larisa Piyaseva and I had just returned from Poland and we told him that nothing terrible was happening there. He was a good listener, nodding his head. That was a five-hour conversation. When we were leaving he almost started hugging us all, and said he would finally decide to introduce shock therapy. That was how we understood him. Two days later he gave a speech in Odessa, a military district, and said the absolute opposite. Without giving names, he said that "certain elements" were trying to push us into "shock therapy" and we were not going to adopt it. He was not the man for that.'

For most of 1990 Nikolai Petrakov was Gorbachev's principal economic adviser. Like Selyunin, he is familiar with Western economic theory, to which he had access in his academic institute. Sooner or later, he believed, communism would inevitably collapse. That it occurred so fast was due to Gorbachev. Someone else might not have taken measures so certain to lead to that result. Revival, mere continuity even, proved impossible for the simple reason that the communist system generated no internal stimuli. In the absence of motivation to improve production in industry, people function solely on the basis of compulsion. The bonanza to the Soviet Union of the OPEC-manufactured energy crises had dragged out illusions of a functioning economy.

Gorbachev and the leadership realized that the unbridled expenditure on arms for parity with the United States was dislocating, but they believed that additional investment in technology and industry would avert the crisis without remodelling the economy. That was Aganbegyan's initial advice. 'I do not agree that the situation in 1990 was more acute than it had been five years before. Gorbachev's determination to maintain the Soviet Union intact and the hyper-atrophied military–industrial complex swallowed resources. One of the key points was the restoration of private property. Plenty of totalitarian countries – Germany, Japan, Spain – have been able to restore democratic norms and ways of life, once the dictator had disappeared. The dogma of proletarian dictatorship had frozen the Soviet economy.'

Did Gorbachev link private property and freedom?

'I spent a whole year trying to explain that, and having failed singularly, I was forced to resign. I talked about it first to him nine years earlier. Recently I talked to him, and I am convinced that he still does not think that privatization of property is the essential motor of social change. He remains a convinced reformer of the socialist system.'

Two months after Petrakov was appointed economic adviser, the Shatalin Plan was formulated. Might this have worked? In the eyes of Yakovlev, it was a last chance and its rejection was Gorbachev's worst mistake.

'As an historical sidelight, Shatalin's name was associated with the Plan only as a political expedient. The whole time the Plan was being prepared, Shatalin was in hospital and did not write a single word of it. The Plan was prepared principally by Yavlinsky and me. At the time it stood a chance of success. While it was under discussion, Gorbachev came under heavy pressure from the party bureaucrats who could not abide me. He surrendered. Here is an interesting point about the political games that were being played at a time when they were trying to mediate the direct confrontation between Gorbachev and Yeltsin. Yeltsin still had a weak political platform and was sincerely keen to perform the job Gorbachev wanted. Gorbachev allowed the hardliners to destroy the move. His lack of boldness was a political weakness. But I feel his individual role should not be underestimated. In discussing whether it was accidental or deliberate, I draw a parallel with Columbus who discovered America but to the end of his days believed it was India. Like Columbus,

Gorbachev did something marvellous but only found out afterwards what it was.'

More succinctly than any other Western economist, Anders Åslund of the Stockholm Institute of International Economic Studies has analysed the disaster of economic policies contrived in so slapdash a manner. His book, *Gorbachev's Struggle for Economic Reform*, documents the ignorance and illusion in which the Soviet Union floundered. After 1991 Åslund was to become an economic adviser to Yeltsin.

For Åslund, the essential fact was that the Nomenklatura dictatorship ruled in its own interest. They subordinated national interest to their privileges. Unable to provide economic dynamism, the Nomenklatura one day was certain to be dispossessed.

'A substantial part of the leadership realized that this society was not viable in the long term. At the same time they did not see any solutions. They supported Gorbachev unhappily and only because he, at least, wanted to do something. The rest wanted to stay with the old system as long as possible.'

Between 1985 and 1991 the leading members of the Soviet Politburo put forward at least five different economic programmes. The thrust towards acceptance of the market and free enterprise met the brake of the command-administrative system. Unable to be a supreme arbiter, Gorbachev was helplessly tossed to and fro by these tests of strength around him, now swayed here, now swayed there. Decrees and regulations and laws and rhetoric spouted from his office in contradictory and self-denying bursts. Nobody in the leadership seems to have thought through how to lay foundations for the constitutional and legal infrastructures without which the market cannot operate: laws of contract, definitions of property rights and ownership, civil codes and an independent judiciary capable of interpreting and enforcing them. The concept of the market seemed something of a fetish, to be borrowed from the West where its magic powers had been proven.

'You have improvisation in Russian politics because there is always this process of contest, and in order to win you have to throw a surprise on your opponents, and in order to be able to do that, you have to be able to improvise. In order to change the economic system, you have to work in accordance with an archaic and decayed procedure but if you do, you will never get the opportunity to reform. The ensuing contradiction of policy is an ideal way to change the entire economic system. I would say that potentially none of the Soviet economists had a good understanding of macroeconomics. There were younger people Gorbachev could have called upon and it is striking that he did not. The Shatalin Plan could not really have worked but it was the first reasonable plan for stabilization of the economy and for far-reaching privatization. It was important as a big qualitative step for all sectors because Gorbachev supported it, or seemed to support it when he was politically weak. Some days after it had been discarded altogether, he said that we have just thrown out a plan that looked like a train timetable. But that was how Gorbachev moved ahead. He would never have reached the position that he had if he had not compromised. While you can say that Yeltsin would never have reached the position he did if he had not been the opposite – a man who takes his stand. In order to break down the system, a compromiser who wanted to do something different was really needed. The advantage of Gorbachev was that he managed to carry out the breakdown of the system fast and in a reasonably orderly fashion at a relatively small human cost, given the enormous task that he performed. The only problem was that he mistook construction for destruction. If he had not believed in the reformability of socialism he would never have been able to destroy it. That is the ironic side of it. Gorbachev could only succeed in destroying socialism because he did not want to do any such thing.'

WAR AS CLASS STRUGGLE

The two sides of the Cold War were at cross-purposes over détente. To the West, détente signified a relaxation of tension, leading to reduction of arms levels. If the Soviet Union were then to normalize trading, cultural and military relationships, so the argument ran for many years in Western capitals, it might disengage from the dreadful and even apocalyptic tests of strength it was inflicting on the rest of the world. For over four hundred years imperial Russia, and then the Soviet Union, had been expanding territorially but even responsible Western statesmen used to plead that allowance be made for contemporary fears of encirclement. Here was the nub of the fallacy that collaboration with the Soviet Union could replace the costs of resistance to it. To the Soviet Union, in Brezhnev's definition of 1976, 'Détente does not in any way rescind, nor can it rescind or alter, the laws of class struggle. We do not conceal the fact that we see in détente a path towards the creation of more favourable conditions for the peaceful construction of socialism and communism.'

Under cover of détente, and its twin brother, peaceful coexistence, the Soviet Union achieved military parity with the United States and Nato. As Arkady Shevchenko, the Under-Secretary at the United Nations who defected, expressed it, 'The Soviet Union has never contemplated agreeing to arrangements that could in any way tie its hands in pursuit of what it wanted.'

Arcane, fatiguing in detail, couched in a horrible jargon of first-strike capacity and kill-ratio, disarmament talks tended to be boring and alarming in equal proportions. The Heads of State often appeared willing to leave complexities in the hands of experts and military officers, as though they themselves had neither a proper grasp of the technicalities nor full control over ultimate decisions. Brezhnev and his successors introduced the last serious Cold War crisis by installing the SS-20, a missile which for the first time held the whole of Western Europe at its mercy. One successful aggression led to another: the invasion of Afghanistan, the crushing of the Solidarity mass movement in Poland, Soviet intervention in Central America. In response, the West counter-deployed the Pershing II and Cruise missiles. On the grounds that Germany might be both the firing-ground and target of future missile exchanges, the German Social Democrats voted against Nato plans. 'I believed there was a shorter way to achieving arms reduction and control,' the former Chancellor, Willy Brandt, was to say. That was not the point. Between the Helsinki Final Act and Gorbachev's assumption of office, a sense of fear in Germany encouraged the Soviet Union to hope that the prize of German neutrality lay in its grasp.

Four of the fourteen post-war American–Soviet summit conferences took place between Gorbachev and Reagan. Presidents Bush and Gorbachev were to meet in a weatherbeaten Malta in December 1989, and again in Washington six months later. Reagan had never hidden his aversion to nuclear weapons. Scientists debated the merits or otherwise of Star Wars, but he clung to his conviction that his space-based programme would diminish and possibly nullify the nuclear threat through its capacity to destroy nuclear-armed missiles before they reached their target. A perception had also arisen that the United States could force the Soviet Union into an arms race which its economy could not sustain.

Like his predecessors, Gorbachev hoped to manoeuvre the West into voluntary limitation of its powers of resistance and defence, while also agreeing to treaties whereby the Brezhnev Doctrine flourished. Perestroika, Gorbachev's internal version of détente, appeared to be the kind of normalization for which the West had hoped for so long. Gorbachev's standing in the West soared – he was the politician of the year in Germany, and Man of the Decade for *Time* magazine, recipient of many honours including the Nobel Prize for Peace.

Restricted to the Soviet Union, perestroika over a lengthy period might conceivably have led to the kind of renewal which Gorbachev pleaded for, securing the base for further superpower activity. Gorbachev need only have utilized Reagan's 'Evil Empire' speech as a pretext to stall summits, and cut military expenditure until such time as the extra resources could be provided. Nobody in the West could reliably penetrate Soviet secrecy. Disinformation to the effect that spending was actually rising was likely to have been believed. Nobody has yet explained why Gorbachev instead insisted on simultaneously extending perestroika to his foreign policies.

Soviet supremacy had always rested on the unmistakable will to use force as the final and determining instrument of policy. The imaginary worldwide class struggle between communism and capitalism had served to place a mask of ideology over plain brutality. Now Soviet foreign policy, in the footsteps of domestic perestroika, was to respond to real and acknowledged hopes and fears. Momentous consequences followed. The nature of the Cold War was called into question. The division of Germany, the occupation of the People's Democracies and the Baltic republics had been justified by ideology now undergoing redefinition. Numerous conflicting national interests within the Soviet Union had been repressed by the same ideology-inspired use of force. To cast any shadow of doubt on the ideological justification of communist conquest was certain to release grievances and outright hatred from the past. The peoples of these victim nations knew that they had been sovietized at gunpoint against their will. They were certain to test out how far their various nationalisms could now rebound. Repudiation of force was a complete misunderstanding of the essential character of communism.

Gorbachev, to be sure, was never to do so. On the contrary, Soviet troops were to shoot and kill demonstrators over much of the empire, in Tbilisi, in Nagorny-Karabakh, in Baku, in the Ferghana Valley of Uzbekistan, in Riga and Vilnius. Horrible as these scenes were, they could not to be compared to the atrocities of the previous seventy years. The difference of intention was striking. Former Soviet leaders had gloried in bloodshed as a virtuous extension of the communist monopoly of power. Gorbachev was embarrassed by it and sometimes shifty; he liked to deny responsibility for it while also calling nationalists or other demonstrators hooligans, who had to expect a response of this kind if they took to the streets.

The more he urged the therapeutic values of perestroika everywhere, the more he was untying the bond of force which alone maintained his own and his empire's standing. The paradox was of his own making.

In summit talks and elsewhere, Gorbachev made dramatic offers to cut the Soviet military as well as future arms development. Round about 1987 he started the hare of a 'Common European Home', a phrase from the discourse of national rather than ideological interests. In a speech at the United Nations on 7 December 1988 he made a statement which resounded round the world and perhaps more than anything else cemented his statesmanlike image. 'Force and the threat of force can no longer be, and should not be, instruments of foreign policy. This applies in the first instance to nuclear weapons, but it goes further than that. Everyone, and the strongest in the first instance, is required to restrict himself, and to exclude totally the use of external force.' Regularly he repeated this message. Ten months later, for example, in Helsinki where Finlandization had long been a synonym for the desire to collaborate with the Soviet Union, he said, 'There can be no justification for any use of force: whether by one military–political alliance against another, or within such alliance, or against neutral countries by any side.'

For the post of Foreign Minister in the forefront of the changes to come, he chose Eduard Shevardnadze. Born in 1928 in a village of his native Georgia,

Shevardnadze had had an orthodox career, first in the Komsomol, then in the party. He rose through his connections with the police force of the Ministry of the Interior, and perhaps the KGB. In 1976 at a Georgian party conference he speechified in the accepted style. 'Georgia is called the country of the sun. But for us the true sun rose not in the East but in the North, in Russia – the sun of Lenin's ideas.'

Corruption in Georgia was a way of life. Konstantin Simis has described how Shevardnadze set about documenting its extent, for the purpose of pressuring the corrupt either to promote him or to get out of his way. Nobody was more corrupt than Vasily Mzhavanadze, the long-term First Secretary of Georgia. 'He proved to be exceptionally mild and trusting,' Shevardnadze writes innocently of his local mentor. 'But I could not close my eyes to certain traits in his character ... when I had the opportunity to tell him this, I did. As a result, a little while later, I was offered the post of First Deputy Minister of Public Order in Georgia.' Only those involved in this particular test of strength could do justice to a process of implicit blackmail and threat of denunciation on the one side, with fear and calculation of how to buy off a dangerous rival on the other. Soon Shevardnadze was First Secretary of Georgia in place of Mzhavanadze. 'I had no other choice than to play by the rules', as Shevardnadze demurely puts it.

As Foreign Minister he soon purged seven of the nine deputy Foreign Ministers, and seven of the ten ambassadors at large, half of the sixteen chiefs of the regional departments, and sixty-eight ambassadors. Few were so devoted to Gorbachev, so assiduous in repeating and stressing the General Secretary's line as it evolved. On his sixtieth birthday Shevardnadze wrote a letter to Gorbachev which Raisa Gorbachev has quoted in her memoirs. 'For a large part of my life I too served the Party's cause as well as I could ... My doubts ... were always kept down by my faith that the decisive and critical hour would strike for our Motherland. Now that it has struck I feel for the first time that my life is in complete accord with the life of the Party and the people.'

In February 1987, on an official visit to East Berlin, he repeated the tenets of the Helsinki Final Act. 'We believe that the stability and inviolability of existing borders, which have emerged after World War II and are enshrined in international law, provide the most reliable guarantee for the peaceful and tranquil development of Europe.' Two German states existed to demonstrate it. It was impossible to guess from this the imminent drama of reunification.

A year later, responding to Gorbachev, at the Nineteenth Party Conference Shevardnadze made the first public statement to the Nomenklatura that the whole ideological basis for their position of power and monopoly would be cut from under their feet. Foreign policy, he said, would no longer be conducted as the extension of the class war. 'We are building a foreign policy that will exclude for ever the discrepancy between our ideals and our behaviour ... The struggle between the two opposing systems no longer constitutes the determining tendency of the contemporary era.'

Ligachev for one was quick to see that this reversal spelled the end for the party and the Soviet Union. From then on, he gave regular warnings that the reunification of Germany loomed in sight, in which case the Soviet Union would have forfeited its principal gain from the Second World War. Class warfare and foreign policy, he counterattacked, remained identical. In his memoirs he writes scornfully, 'I was amazed at the elasticity of Shevardnadze's political views, his constant readiness to support the leaders in everything.'

'If we were to use force,' Shevardnadze told the American Secretary of State, James Baker, in July 1989, 'then it would be the end of perestroika. We would have failed. It would have been the end of any hope for the future, the end of everything we're trying to do, which is to create a new system based on humane values. We would be no better than the people who came before us. We cannot go back.'

As a Georgian he may have understood more clearly than Gorbachev that communism had been an armed imposition and never a voluntary choice. He found himself unable to reply to Ligachev and others except by raising spectres of worse alternatives. Not an orator, he sounded querulous. By the Twenty-eighth Party Congress in July 1990, the People's Democracies were already their own masters, and Germany was three months away from final reunification. Shevardnadze was asked whether he and Gorbachev had appreciated that their activities would lead to the end of communism and the empire. 'Is the collapse of socialism in Eastern Europe a failure of Soviet diplomacy?' he answered rhetorically. 'It would have been, if our diplomacy had tried to prevent changes in the neighbouring countries. Soviet diplomacy did not and could not set out to resist the liquidation of those imposed, alien and totalitarian regimes.' *Pravda* quoted him at that time. 'In principle, we sensed this, we knew this. We felt that if serious changes did not take place, then tragic events would result.'

Communist hardliners in his own Ministry were to criticize him in 1990, a few months before his resignation. The Soviet Union had lost the world's respect. It was a great country, Shevardnadze replied to this accusation, 'but great in what? Territory? Population? Quantity of arms? Or the people's troubles? The individual's lack of rights? Life's disorderliness? In what do we, who have virtually the highest infant mortality rate on our planet, take pride? It is not easy answering the questions: who are you and who do you wish to be? A country which is feared or a country which is respected?'

Youthful and even sprightly in appearance when appointed, Shevardnadze aged in office; his face fattened and his hair whitened. He acquired a hunted look. In the party-state apparat, the Ministry of Foreign Affairs was relatively unimportant, a lesser cog, stymied by the International Department of the Central Committee which had overlapping but more invisible responsibilities. As Gorbachev's front man, he expertly made the best of an increasingly hopeless job, smiling at the photo-calls when the leaders of the world fore-gathered, throwing overboard the armour-plated dogmas on which he had thrived.

A Soviet expert with realistic and far-sighted political perceptions is Vyacheslav Dashichev, who has an international reputation. From 1982 to 1990 he was the head of a department of one of the more influential Moscow think-tanks, devoted to the World Socialist System. He was also head of an Academic Council for the Foreign Ministry.

The Helsinki Treaty, he argues, introduced a whole chain of events. The Soviet Union was allowed to expand into the Third World; this looked like strength but actually weakened the isolation in which the system alone could prosper. Advance into countries like Angola and Ethiopia killed off détente, and that in turn convinced the West that the Soviet leaders had no intention of relaxing tension. Some, like Mikhail Suslov, the veteran head of ideology, had wanted to destroy détente on the grounds that it was harmful. Not only did the standing of Soviet leaders suffer, but the American reaction under Reagan was to increase the arms burden on the Soviets through Star Wars – a strategy of exhaustion. Early in the 1980s Dashichev and others had con-cluded that this Stalinist–Brezhnevite policy of expansion had led into a blind alley. He began to prepare memorandums to that effect.

A position paper of his in November 1987 had the title *Some Aspects of the German Question*. 'This was the first time since the 1950s that the possibility of German reunification had been considered. There was a very negative reaction from the Defence Ministry, the Foreign Ministry and its Academic Council and other party institutions. I prepared these memos about our German policy for Shevardnadze and forwarded them to Gorbachev. Shev-ardnadze says that already in 1986 he had come to the conclusion that the German question would be on the agenda of European development. This was a taboo theme, and could not be stated openly. The division had main-tained our dominance over Eastern Europe. It was a Hitlerian policy in that it placed political goals above economic and spiritual ones. The Nomenklatura and the military justified themselves in this way. And while this occupation lasted we could not hope to reform.'

The military attacked his memorandums. So did the International Department of the Central Committee under Valentin Falin. In June 1988, at the Soviet Embassy in Bonn, Dashichev made a statement to the effect that the Berlin Wall was a relic of the Cold War and should disappear. This was a sensation. The next day, the SED paper *Neues Deutschland* carried a polemic against him, and against German imperialism for good measure. Honecker himself had ordered this article.

'We concluded that the policy of the Honecker regime would lead to political and economic crisis in the foreseeable future. In general, the division of Germany was no longer beneficial.'

The use of force, he says, 'is a delicate question'. If force had been used in the DDR in October 1989, it would have led to the fall of Gorbachev. Every attempt at repressing European uprisings, for instance in 1956 and 1968, had immediately had the contrary effect of strengthening those in the Politburo and Central Committee who wanted reform. Force might have blown up in Gorbachev's face, handing the military and the hardliners the argument that he was destroying socialism through bloodshed. 'One of the main reasons Gorbachev was not inclined to use force was from fear of playing into the hands of Marshal Yazov and Ustinov, Ligachev and Chebrikov. They and others demanded intervention to restore the Wall. We on the contrary proposed to abandon the Brezhnev Doctrine because the empire's costs were always high, and people who dominate others are themselves not free. To my regret, very few thought like me.'

Appointed Foreign Minister in April 1985, Shevardnadze soon met Secretary of State George Shultz in Helsinki, and he took with him Sergei Tarasenko. Under the different titles of Assistant, Adviser, Chief of Staff, Policy Planning Director, Tarasenko remained Shevardnadze's right-hand man. Born in 1937 in Lipetsk, Tarasenko is of Ukrainian origins. A steam-boiler operator in his youth, he heard from a Komsomol secretary who knew his mother that the Foreign Ministry maintained a highly secret college from which it recruited four-fifths of its staff. In 1956 this college had decided to diversify its enrolment. Qualifying through his background as a worker, he started his career as an American specialist. Anatoly Dobrynin, Soviet ambassador in Washington for many years, picked him out and by the time Shevardnadze became Minister, he was Number Two on the American desk.

Tarasenko makes the point, 'We all functioned in a certain setting.' Careerism was everything. Only those paid to preserve the ideological fabric ever gave a thought to Marxism–Leninism. That was incantatory. 'It was politically correct to have Lenin in your library. If you had to teach Marxism or write a speech, you were keen to find a Lenin quote, and there was a book of quotations, say Lenin on foreign policy, two volumes, you turned to the index.

On a human scale, let me speak of my father who was ten in 1917, took part in collectivization, and has witnessed the collapse of the system. Within one lifespan.'

Shevardnadze had not really been a policeman by training, according to Tarasenko. In Nomenklatura practice, you were ordered to take up this or that assignment, depending on the situation in the party and your own standing. A natural politician and diplomat, Shevardnadze in Georgia managed to maintain good relations with Moscow while taking steps which were not ideologically clear. 'He had to gather a certain number of chips to be cashed in Moscow. He praised Brezhnev or other leaders. You could not survive a week if you allowed yourself to say anything against Moscow. That was the centre. They all went to Georgia expecting to be wined and dined, and he made a good job of that, attentive to wives and families, making gifts, so in return they said to themselves, here is a smart guy. To get oil or some other necessity for the republic, it was common practice for the official from Georgia to take cases of premium cognac to Moscow, to give to the man with power to grant what you wanted. You had to live in this system. It made good diplomats. If I knew I had to do something for my boss, just to be comfortable, and everybody was doing it, it became acceptable and you thought no further. That was the custom, the Soviet way of doing things.' Shevardnadze's idea, which he had broached with Gorbachev, was that the party should lead the way in introducing democracy within its ranks. Otherwise the party would be the loser. The dream was to move the Soviet Union towards becoming a modern industrial society integrated into the world economy. 'We were not theoreticians, we just saw that things were bad and we would like to improve them. What was this backwardness? Why don't we have consumer goods? Why can't we travel round the world when everybody else can?' Somehow Shevardnadze had overcome the totalitarian legacy, Tarasenko thinks, to release inborn democratic instincts. 'He is warm and considerate. Maybe it was culture, it depends on family.'

Shevardnadze used to hold one- or two-hour sessions in private with Gorbachev twice a week. Early in the perestroika years Gorbachev asked him for specific comment on internal, constitutional and party matters. Shevardnadze's method was to talk to Gorbachev in advance, and persuade him. At inner-circle meetings he did not speak much. On foreign trips Gorbachev would gather all the staff around him, they'd compete in compliments while Shevardnadze would sit sipping his tea. One of his characteristics was never to give himself credit for a good idea.

'A quick learner with an extraordinary memory and capacity to grasp things, he was his own boss in at most two months. He related foreign policy issues to domestic issues. Foreign policy for him was a way of influencing internal developments. Before that, we had a distorted relation between foreign and internal policy. In the West foreign policy is determined by the possibilities of financing it, by resources and interests. We calculated the other way about. The country may be in ruins but the leadership says that money must be found to support the ends it wants.'

During his first December in office, Shevardnadze presented a policy report at a party conference within the Foreign Ministry. It was published for limited circulation. The following May, he engineered Gorbachev to give an address to the Ministry because he wanted by this means to have legitimacy for what he himself was doing. Sanctifying change, Gorbachev's speech opened the way for more of it. It was at the Nineteenth Party Conference that the concept of class war as the basis of foreign policy was scrapped. In December 1986 Shevardnadze had called the first of what were supposed to be annual meetings for Ministry officials and ambassadors to prepare the coming changes, but Gorbachev then postponed giving another address to the Foreign Ministry. 'Nobody would know what the decisions of these conferences and congresses really meant. You had plenty of latitude. Only a Politburo member had the right to interpret major party decisions and whoever did so first was also the one who laid down the interpretation. Lesser beings would not pick a fight. It took a lot of courage to go against a Politburo member. The General Secretary had the final ruling on whether to remove him. But if a Politburo member said what the line was, and he was not then removed, then that *was* the line. There was a gentleman's agreement about the division of turf. One Politburo member would not encroach upon another's responsibilities. Members would just sign a memorandum "in favour" without reading it. If you were to block it you would pay later. You interfered with Defence or the KGB and next time they would interfere in your field.

'The day after Shevardnadze annulled the class-warfare concept, we received a reaction from Ligachev on behalf of the Central Committee that Shevardnadze had overstepped the line. As actually delivered, the speech had been much more explicit than it appeared in the published version. We tried hard for damage control. Chernyayev, Gorbachev's assistant, telephoned me to say, Thank God, at last you have said it, you have opened the way for others to argue like that. Ligachev still took him up. A couple of weeks after that, Gorbachev went on vacation which gave Ligachev the chance to put things right ideologically. Speaking in the town of Elektrostal near Moscow, he was openly critical of those saying there was no class struggle in the international arena, that was only confusing people's minds and so on. At the time we were in Kabul, and we published an interview in a paper there to rebuff Ligachev, using the very same words, accusing him of confusing the minds of people. It was a game but a dangerous one. In the Ministry there was still a sizeable faction of hardliners, and considerable hostility. The odd school believed that before you talk to someone it is better to hit him and then he will understand your argument. We held lots of meetings with the Consular Corps, Ministers from the republics, the scientific community, so Shevardnadze could hammer away at the new ideas.'

Did he master details of the arms negotiations?

'Unbelievably. Nobody could advise or correct him. Following Secretary Shultz or Baker he might have trouble with an imperfect translation but he would get the sense, mark the passage and comment later to clarify it. Technically it was quite a feat.

'The agreements worked in the interests of the Soviet Union. The splitting of hairs and counting of missiles was pointless. We could not sustain the huge burden. The military lost because for a long time they could not believe that an agreement was obtainable. They thought they could block it. It slipped their attention that somehow we had crossed the line and agreement had become inevitable. Nobody except the Foreign Ministry was in favour of disarmament. The military played hard on Star Wars. We argued that the programme would never be realized, so that if we were to harp on about it we gave a higher profile which harmed us by arousing internal pressures.'

Shevardnadze seems to have decided very early on to relinquish the Soviet satellites.

'The practice was that if one of the satellites wanted to do something internationally, they would ask our advice. Our people prepared a reply, to the effect that this is a good idea but the timing must be thought through, or else that the idea should be scrapped. Soon after he became Minister, Shevardnadze was asked for such advice and he replied that we had none to give. Those were sovereign states with every right to do what they deemed necessary. He became emotional and I remember him saying, This practice should be stopped.'

Tarasenko was taken by Shevardnadze to Central Committee meetings. These were still well-orchestrated in 1986, when Gorbachev would deliver a speech, and speakers would support and praise him, with plenty of applause. 'Then it waned. The audience became cool. Whatever Gorbachev spoke about evoked no response from the hall. Just stony silence. People would leave or criticize him in subtle forms. He was afraid to put an issue to the vote because he would be defeated, so he would stall by referring it back to the Politburo. He manoeuvred a lot, he was quicker and cleverer than the average man in that hall – some could hardly spell. There were 700 of them, members, visiting members, candidate members, and maybe some 200 guests, media people and the military very visible in their uniforms. As the attacks became more hostile, Gorbachev lost interest in these endeavours.

'They felt he was leading them to ruin. They would lose their jobs. The policy of trying to preserve these people in their place and sacrificing the greater interest of the party and society was extremely damaging. On the eve of elections they were still arguing and bargaining about whether they would stay in power for ten or fifteen years, not realizing that their days were numbered. Gorbachev made the same mistake, believing in party support till the end. At the Nineteenth Party Conference Yeltsin tried to return to the party fold, asking for forgiveness. He would have remained a party functionary, collaborating with Gorbachev, but when that was impossible, by default he went to the people and called himself a democrat. Shevardnadze is not to be compared.'

At the Foreign Ministry, Tarasenko says, the current of opinion was against the use of force. But there could be no assurance that the military would not intervene. The possible reaction from the West had no influence at all. In Hungary in 1956, the costs had been tolerable, and the 1968 invasion of Czechoslovakia had been cost-effective. In the event of suppressing Solidarity in Poland, he takes it for granted, large-scale bloodshed would have marked a policy failure. The impossibility of subduing Afghanistan showed that a situation had arisen in which it was more profitable not to use force. From his first day in office, Shevardnadze made that the centrepiece of his policy.

To announce in advance that force is excluded is to tie one's hands.

'Some people fought Gorbachev on this. But the plight of the country meant that the use of force might have precipitated violent collapse. Far from maintaining the empire, it would have ended in blood.'

Did Gorbachev hand the issue of German reunification to Shevardnadze?

'I would rather say that Shevardnadze seized it. One of the things that went in his favour was the speed of the process. The International Department of the Central Committee was used to a long and slow discussion. Shevardnadze played it quick. He was clever enough to see it was going to happen in any case. For us the choice was either to become irrelevant or to race for a settlement in which to gain something for ourselves. Smoothly we extricated ourselves from a potentially dangerous, expensive and dead-end situation. We are better off with a buffer zone between us and Nato. Our allies in Eastern Europe were not reliable, they would have shot us in the back.'

If anyone can be said to have forged Soviet policy towards Africa and the Third World it is Vassili Solodovnikov. An official from the Ministry of

Defence, he took advantage of a long-term posting at the United Nations in New York to promote national liberation movements. As ambassador in Zambia, he was the senior Soviet official in Africa. In the light of history, he thinks, the Cold War was a natural consequence of great-power rivalry, and not altogether negative.

Sponsorship of liberation movements and terrorism gave the Soviet Union an edge in many parts of the world. The underlying interest was not material, but ideological. 'We were sure we were weakening the rich West whose economies were based on colonialism and cheap natural resources. The costs to us were less than might be thought. It was not big money. The military equipment was not first-class, and many people from those countries have now received their education in our institutions.'

The Cold War, Solodovnikov observes, was fought out through Africans, Arabs, Afghans, the people of Vietnam and Cambodia. In a sense they were victims, and he readily agrees that Ethiopia, Mozambique or Afghanistan are nightmares, and no longer functioning as countries. But tribalism, religious intolerance and local warlordism led to armed conflict in these areas as a matter of course; outside interference was an effect, not a cause. Superpower confrontation also provided some sort of overall stability, as well as opening up a competition whereby victims often became winners. They could play one side off against the other to obtain arms and aid. Whatever happened in distant corners of the globe was of far less significance than the continuation of stalemate – not exactly agreeable, but peaceful – in Europe.

'When I was the director of the Western Africa Department in the 1960s I received practically all the leaders of the African countries. Many came with the idea of imposing socialism and I would tell them it was impossible. The economy had first to develop a working class.' It was sometimes a shock when regimes declared themselves communist. Refusal to help in Mozambique or Afghanistan was an ideological impossibility, even though conditions for effective help did not exist.

'When class struggle ceased to be the basis of our foreign policy, I was very much against it, and I wrote two or three letters to Shevardnadze. Social division in Africa was a reality, there were poor and rich. Shevardnadze oriented our policy towards the West, practically ignoring developing countries. In my letters I told him this was a mistake and we should continue to support them.' The idea of separating foreign policy from ideology came from Gorbachev and his team, he says, and Yakovlev in particular. Yakovlev was director of another specialist institute, and he offered to employ Solodovnikov in 1984. At that time, he knew Yakovlev to be an orthodox communist. The change of mind in such a man is 'very surprising'.

12

'A MAN WITH WHOM WE CAN DO BUSINESS'

Unregenerate communists like to attribute the collapse of their party-state to the infernal machinations of the CIA and Wall Street. Some are eager to accuse their former leaders by name of venality, the possession of secret bank accounts abroad in which to squirrel away illicit gains and bribes, and downright treason. During the entire Gorbachev era, Soviet counter-intelligence at the CIA was in the hands of Aldrich Ames, subsequently tried and condemned to prison as a double agent in KGB pay. If there was CIA subversion, the KGB can only have known of it by this means well in advance. This irony does nothing to pull conspiracy theories up short.

President Reagan and Mrs Thatcher were unusual among world leaders in their genuine detestation of communism. It was a question of right and wrong. Moral outlook of the sort troubled neither post-war French Presidents nor German Chancellors. However clumsy or barbarous, to them the Soviet Union was preferable as an element inside a balance of power rather than as a fundamental opponent of the values of law-based societies, and to be resisted as such. Helmut Schmidt, former German Chancellor, spoke for the majority of post-war European policy-makers when he said in 1985 that he did not believe in the effectiveness of pressuring the Soviet Union.

The role of American policy, overt or clandestine, in toppling the party-state cannot yet be established. In the People's Democracies, American ambassadors more and more openly cultivated dissidents, sometimes subsidizing them in order to visit Washington to lobby. It was perhaps more symbolic than significant that Mrs Thatcher went out of her way to meet Lech Wałęsa in Poland or János Kádár in Hungary; and President Mitterrand also began travelling widely in Eastern Europe, sympathetic to incoming democrats.

During his second presidency, from 1984 to 1988, Reagan conspicuously changed the tone of his public statements about the Soviet Union. Achieving his purpose of rolling back the Evil Empire through concessions over arms control and reduction, Reagan shifted American public opinion in favour of Gorbachev. A Harris opinion poll in mid-1986 showed that over half the respondents had a favourable impression of Gorbachev, a proportion which had risen to three-quarters two years later. By that time, less than a third of the respondents still held the view that the Soviet Union was an enemy. Reagan and his European counterparts had begun actively to promote Gorbachev by means of repetitive meetings, after which they issued statements in praise of perestroika which might well have been drafted by Soviet spokesmen.

The dismantling of empires is a flash point of violence and from the middle of 1988 several civil wars were already shaping in embryo within the Soviet borders. Stability seemed to dictate support for Gorbachev, a point he himself stressed. If there was ever to be a likelihood of German unity, he repeated to all and sundry, a Soviet general would be found sitting at his desk. The German problem, in Mrs Thatcher's words, was something too delicate for well-brought-up politicians to discuss. In fact, none of the leaders, the German Chancellor Kohl included, anticipated either the break-up of the Soviet Empire or the reunification of Germany until these developments had almost overtaken them. Responding to Gorbachev's appeal, they damped down and dismissed speculation around such issues. The Soviet garrison – 300,000 strong – was present in the DDR as a piece of unfinished business dating from 1945. It seemed an insuperable and incalculable obstacle.

An instinctive defender of status quo everywhere, President Bush dispensed with even the residual moral opposition to communism lingering from the end of Reagan's presidency. Temperament or prudence – if this is what it was – dictated a reactive and conciliatory attitude. Almost nothing in his words or deeds provided evidence that the United States had a vital interest in the overthrow of this implacable ideological militarized enemy. The first summit meeting between Bush and Gorbachev was on warships anchored off Malta in December 1989. A well-placed journalist, Don Oberdorfer, has described how Bush opened the proceedings with unmitigated praise for perestroika. 'You are dealing with an administration that wants to see the success of what you are doing.' A delighted Gorbachev responded that the Soviet Union no longer visualized the United States as an enemy.

By the time of the Malta meeting, the People's Democracies with the exception of Romania had already crossed the threshold to independent statehood. The Berlin Wall had fallen in the previous month and demonstrations in favour of unity had been held in the DDR. Gorbachev had apparently not yet realized that the replacement of old party leaders in the People's Democracies was a step towards the emptiness of perestroika rather than its fulfilment. At the Malta summit he still emphasized that because the states of Eastern and Central Europe had become democratic did not mean that they had become Western politically. History had ruled that there were two Germanys with inviolable borders. From Malta, Gorbachev flew home to a Warsaw Pact meeting, the very last which would be held. It was somewhat surrealistic of him to say to this assembly of largely new leaders that Nato and the Warsaw Pact remained equally necessary to the security of Europe.

At Malta, conspiracy theorists in Russia like to say, Bush mastered Gorbachev. It was a carve-up, a reversal of what had been agreed in 1944 at Yalta – there is play upon the rhyming of the two place-names. After Malta, in sober fact, Bush went even further out of his way to accommodate and enhance Gorbachev, at the risk that the pair of them might be left equally high and dry by what was happening. The United States had always refused to recognize the incorporation of the Baltic republics into the Soviet Union. As Baltic independence movements precipitated a crisis for Gorbachev, Bush said in March 1990, 'I am not going to be a President who gives subject people the false impression that if they rebel, they are going to get help.' A month later Gorbachev blockaded these republics and Bush turned a blind eye. In a major speech while visiting Kiev as late as August 1991 when Gorbachev was clearly a spent force, Bush was to tell an audience of Ukrainians wholeheartedly hoping for independence that some nationalisms were 'unhelpful'. With a unanimity that the glasnost-minded Gorbachev might have envied, American politicians and commentators apologized for the Soviet Union to the end. In a poll of American historians, nearly two-thirds rated Reagan below average or even a failure as a President. Refusing to condemn Gorbachev even after the crackdown in the Baltic republics, Senator Lee Hamilton was typical of the prevailing attitudes in Washington when he said, 'We have to help them get through the immediate crisis.' To him, it was not in the American interest to see the Soviet Union break apart at the seams. Ronald Steel, a pundit who for many years had enjoyed access to the columns of leading newspapers, could judge that the collapse of Soviet power had removed a source of order in the world. Communism, in his view, had held in check the violent nationalisms of Eastern Europe and the Soviet republics. The opposite was more nearly the truth. Communism had entrenched and fostered nationalism as the only certain antidote to it.

Those from President Bush downwards in a position to influence American politics and public opinion appear with hindsight to have been dragged uncomprehending in Gorbachev's wake. Lack of active participation in the Soviet downfall had the one great merit of preventing the birth of legends of the stab-in-the-back variety, whereby communists could blame their own defects on the warmongering capitalists. American policy had on the contrary prolonged the political existence of Gorbachev and the party-state until both imploded through self-induced misfortune. Astonishment at victory in the Cold War was a function of parochiality and ignorance. Mere unfolding of events had brought this prize, but it was a matter of luck rather than judgement.

*　　*　　*

In an interview I asked James Baker, President Bush's Secretary of State, whether perestroika might not have made the Soviet Union successful, and therefore more aggressive.

The Soviets had begun to put into practice the principles which the United States had long been urging on them, he answered. Had these principles been applied, the Soviet Union might well have emerged stronger but that was not the same as belligerent. If one project did not work Gorbachev would pull another out of his hip-pocket. Confrontation became co-operation, and that became partnership. 'I think that they had come to the realization that they could not compete. SDI was important, and so was a commitment, or an important belief, that good arms-control agreement lessened the drain on their resources. That was Shevardnadze's view.' He gives Gorbachev and Shevardnadze credit for political courage, while at the same time pointing out that they ran risks because they had no alternative.

'We kept saying, The Baltics are a problem for you, why in the world don't you let them go? They kept saying, We can't do that because it would be the end of the Union.' In retrospect, if the Soviets had negotiated autonomy earlier, the Balts might have accepted something short of absolute freedom. At various stages, the administration was afraid that the Soviet leadership might use force to stop the process of change. But having concluded that they were not going to win the Cold War, the Soviets wanted to end it in a way that no longer left them outcasts. 'Over the unification of Germany I remember Shevardnadze telling me in my airplane on our way to Wyoming that they would never use force. I said, That's not what people believe. It won't happen, he said. Without Shevardnadze we would not have seen the unification of Germany within Nato.'

German unification had been a steadfast policy of the United States. At the end of 1989, Shevardnadze made a speech about peace and unification. He and Gorbachev liked to see it through a noble prism but what finally persuaded them was money. 'You could maybe say they sold out too cheaply.' Still, nobody could have fully foreseen events. 'If you find anyone on our side or theirs who tells you they knew what would happen, I think they are blowing smoke at you.'

From the beginning of the Reagan administration until the end of December 1989, Richard Perle was Assistant Secretary of Defense for International Security Policy, and therefore at the centre of the arms-control process.

The standard of Soviet weaponry was high, in his opinion. There was a period when the most accurate ballistic missile in the world was the Soviet SS-18. Where the Soviets were deficient in quality of equipment for ground forces, they made up for it in quantity – unbelievable numbers of everything. They also stole Western technology constantly and prodigiously. The civilian economy was subordinated to the military to a degree that official intelligence estimates never recognized. Dissident economists who said so were derided by the intelligence community. The percentage of Gross Domestic Product going into the military was underestimated by at least half, and maybe more. The lies of the Soviets in this respect were matched by acceptance of them in much of the intelligence community. To this day it has never been fully reported how far they had burrowed underground, in vast complexes which could house 30,000 to 40,000 people, to shield the leadership in the event of war. Some of these bunkers had underground railway lines. That was an example of massive spending never subjected to accounting.

'We now know from Russian testimony that we also seriously under-estimated the total number of nuclear weapons in the country.' Those who advocated disarmament, partial or total, were inviting a freezing of the situation based upon such imperfect information that they would have left the West in a position of inferiority. It is easy to say that the arms-control process came out all right in the end, but it had been a real menace through its constant pressure to conclude agreements that had the effect of legitimizing the size and rate of growth of the Soviet arsenal. It also led to pulling punches on ideological matters such as human rights. 'Naïve visitors would go to Moscow, discover that the plumbing didn't work and conclude that the Soviet Union was a Third World country bound to collapse. When you look in detail at what they were able to do militarily, it is pretty impressive. And one of the reasons the plumbing didn't work was because all the competent plumbers were busy fitting out nuclear submarines.

'There was a view, which I and some others held, that the principal benefit of certain programmes was the cost to the Soviets of countering them. Those highly leveraged investments seemed a very good idea. The deployment of relatively modest bomber forces on our side, for example, caused the Soviets to make a huge investment in bomber defence, vastly greater than our investment in bombers. Even if we never managed to deliver a single bomb, the programme would have paid for itself many times over by diverting resources from what could otherwise have been offensive capability on the Russian side.'

As for SDI, or colloquially Star Wars, it had the potential to deprive the Soviets of their ballistic missile force, the jewel in the crown of their defence. 'The warhead of the SS-18 was so large that it made no sense to use it against soft targets like a city in retaliation. It looked like a weapon intended to destroy our weaponry pre-emptively. SDI was a challenge to them to build more missiles to overcome the defence, or a way of persuading them that it was futile to go on building these missiles because we would deploy defences to neutralize them. Everything therefore depended on something called the cost-exchange ratio – how much did an increment of defence cost us and how much did an offsetting increment of offence cost them. Calculations showed that you could buy defence a lot more cheaply than you could overcome it. Also you could challenge them in the technological domain which played to our strength in computers, principally in data processing – there is no way round the fact that ballistic missile defence requires the ability to acquire, manipulate and disseminate vast quantities of information in real times. There was simply no way they could overcome their deficiencies. Their efforts to steal technology accelerated at this time.'

Perle thinks that there is merit in the view that SDI forced the Soviets to consider whether they could expect to hold on to the preponderance of their offensive military capacity. More realistic than Brezhnev, Gorbachev was prepared to take on generals who gave him unconvincing answers. He understood that their only recourse was further offensive development at a point when they were already operating near maximum capability. Here was a race which could not be won. In the eyes of the Soviet military, the Reykjavik and Geneva summits were a test of his diplomatic skills at bargaining the United States out of the programme.

'SDI said to the Soviets, We're not going to let you keep an offensive ballistic missile capability so formidable that we really worry what you might do with it. We are going to offset it, not with a hermetic seal from the United States, but a defence good enough so that any thoughts you might have about a pre-emptive blow will not be convincing. Strategic defences in that sense could contribute to deterrence rather than substitute for it.'

It was devastating of Reagan to challenge the Soviets on their most sensitive spot, the regime's lack of legitimacy. But he also understood better than almost anyone how burdensome military spending was for the Russians. On the subject of disarmament he was totally sincere; he held the utopian view that nuclear weapons could be eliminated by agreement. 'Reagan was a tough bargainer, and you could persuade him that we were right to insist on a deal that really did deprive them of weapons that they would otherwise have, not the kind of deals we had before, which essentially legitimized their building plans. But he was vulnerable to the view that the world would be better off without nuclear weapons, and that a technology was available to rid the world of them by giving us a defence against them. This was very stark at Reykjavik. To have pulled off a deal which killed Star Wars would have been a great triumph for Gorbachev.'

SDI had political importance because it persuaded Gorbachev and others to question whether continuing military competition with the United States was in the Soviet interest. It further drove home Soviet technological inferiority. In spite of, or because of, the persistent stealing, virtually all Soviet computers were inferior copies of IBM computers. It came as a shock, Perle thinks, to Gorbachev as to millions of Russians, to realize how far behind the West they actually were.

In her memoirs Mrs Thatcher pays tribute to Charles Powell as 'in all respects, simply outstanding'. As her Private Secretary from 1984 to 1991, he enjoyed a ringside seat for encounters with Gorbachev.

Early in 1984, three potential Soviet leaders of the future were invited to Britain; Gorbachev was the one who accepted. That December, when he turned up at Chequers, the Prime Minister's country house, he made an instant impression. 'There's a sort of great hall with a huge fire and the first moment he came in, you could see he was alive, not dead on his feet like Brezhnev nor stony-faced like Gromyko, but lively, with conversation and banter. He exuded power. Never still, his eyes darted round the room. I think Mrs Thatcher was immediately entranced, recognizing someone powerful and disputatious. There's nothing like a good argument to make her feel really toned up.'

Over lunch that day, Gorbachev developed ideas about decentralizing the Soviet economy. There followed a discussion lasting over four hours in the Hawtrey Room. 'Gorbachev had a few notes in his own hand in green ink in a little book, to which he occasionally referred. There were no prepared statements. He never showed the slightest interest in his advisers and paid no attention to them whatsoever. He was constantly after her assessment of the Americans. No sparer of persons, she told him that she thought communism was a rotten system and the sooner he got rid of it the better. Also that Chernenko, then General Secretary, made no sense at all, and that the Soviet Union was the cause of most of the world's problems and it should take a lead in disarming. Many would have got huffy or retreated into a shell, or terminated the conversation, but the good thing about Gorbachev was that he didn't – he hit back in similar terms.'

In a phrase that did much to launch 'Gorbimania', Mrs Thatcher announced that here was a man with whom we could do business. Discovering Gorbachev early on, she thought that she had scored a lucky strike and this was a relationship on which to build. For her visit to the Soviet Union in March 1987 she informed him that she wanted something different, for instance, the chance to see streets and shops for herself, to appear live on television, and to travel to Georgia. He agreed to arrange whatever she wanted. Her presence was to have an electrifying effect, especially in a famous television interview when she routed three Russian journalists put up to attack her. The Soviet audience heard from her that they had more weapons than any other country, and that the information they were fed was worthless.

'With Gorbachev the discussions were tough. She spoke of the damage that communism had done to the Soviet Union and the rest of the world. He replied about Northern Ireland. She went so far that I was beginning to pack up my briefcase, thinking we had better get out of here while still alive. Again to his credit, he was capable of breaking the tension; he would suddenly push back his chair and lean back and make a joke or laugh about something, or go out for a bit, and then they would start on another subject. An awful lot, I think, he was hearing for the first time, being exposed to the outside world in a crude and powerful form. Increasingly from 1987 onwards he found it useful to test out his views. But there was this strange phenomenon of attraction and repulsion which kept them together for thirteen hours. Reagan wasn't capable of discussions at this level of intensity.'

Mrs Thatcher read voraciously every speech of Gorbachev's. In them was hard evidence that he was listening and changing. In retrospect she would come to judge that he had shied away from difficult decisions that should have been taken. Although enthusiastic about perestroika, she saw it as transitional, a first step towards replacing communism with a market economy and the rule of law. A momentum had to be created. She would tell him that she had had a similar experience of trying to change Britain; his problems were far more extreme.

One effect, Powell says, was that she built up a strong stake in Gorbachev and his success. However much she might disapprove of actions such as his attempt to suppress the Baltic republics, she never abandoned belief in him. At private sessions, at lunches or dinners, in the Foreign Ministry guest house where she stayed in Moscow, they talked about everything under the sun: Gorbachev's early days, for example, or the nature of class. It made an impression on her to be the first to get on these terms with a Soviet leader. On his visits to London, in the atmosphere of the small dining room at Downing Street, he talked even more freely. To some extent she allowed herself to be used to carry the message for Gorbachev in the world, and he in turn skilfully exploited this promotion.

'He valued what she had to tell him about the Americans. Loyal to Reagan, she would say that he was a decent and honest man who could be relied on. You could negotiate with him and he would stick up for what you'd agreed. Of course much of the concern was with SDI. One knows from the amount of time spent discussing it with Gorbachev that it was a major preoccupation.'

'Her first session with the Soviet military was during the 1987 visit. We went down to the Ministry of Defence and found ourselves sitting on one side of the table with the whole Soviet General Staff under bulky old Yazov on the other side. She let fly at them in her usual outspoken terms and they sat there in amazement. They had never been spoken to like that before. The second session was in September 1989 in the same Chiefs of Staff room. It was exciting, and had influence internally and externally.'

The prospect of German reunification cast a late shadow over the relationship with Gorbachev. Powell was despatched several times to discuss this question with Horst Teltschik, his opposite number on Chancellor Kohl's staff. As late as December 1989 reunification was still regarded as unlikely within four or five years. 'The September 1989 meeting with Gorbachev sticks in my mind as they had a very frank discussion about the date of reunification. She believed that Gorbachev shared her assessment of the danger of German reunification and that he would help to slow it down, if not block it, and she was consequently deeply disillusioned when he went along with it early in 1990.

'Another crucial conversation about that time was with Mitterrand. He had come over in alarm at the prospect and in private was actually more outspoken than Mrs Thatcher ever was about Germany and that's saying something. In 1990 Mitterrand had a couple of private meetings with Mrs Thatcher where he again spoke of his misgivings, wondering how unification could be slowed down or even avoided. Of course he took an entirely different line in public, so that she who had been speaking out was left hideously over-exposed.'

Coloured by the wartime experience of her generation, Mrs Thatcher feared that German strength would lead to domination, possibly precipitating conflict. 'My impression is that the Soviets were seriously listening to her. But they got swept off their feet by the pace of events. It was clear that they couldn't and wouldn't – or wouldn't and couldn't, whichever way round it was – stop what was happening. Undoubtedly Gorbachev was never prepared to use force in Eastern Europe. It may seem a small thing but he was terribly proud of the fact that he was a lawyer. He wanted to be seen as somebody on a par with Western leaders and their attitudes. I think he understood that the success of the reforms on which he had embarked would cost him his political career. He didn't expect it to come out the way it did or at the time it did, but I think he knew that it would eventually happen. He wanted to be seen as a civilized leader of a civilized country and he knew that this was not possible while the situation lasted in Eastern Europe.'

13

NATIONAL IN FORM

The prison-house of nations – this description of Russia was one of the Marquis de Custine's unforgettable phrases. By the time Lenin borrowed it, the doctrine of self-determination had captured much of the world. Here was the key to release the prisoners of empire. Those peoples who thought they constituted a nation on lines of race or culture or historical experience had the right to set up as one. Every language was to have an army; every army was to speak only one language.

Self-determination is not democracy in spite of the common element of popular choice. In the case of the Soviet Union, the 400 constituent peoples, some large but others numerically insignificant, had a corresponding range of languages and religions. Heirs to historic rivalries, they were eager to promote their own national identity, and no less eager to reject their neighbours' national identity as mere say-so and pretension. The doctrinal tidiness of self-determination soon provided a new cutting edge to belligerence. Marx and his teachings were no help in this conundrum. An iron law of history justified stronger and more advanced nations having their way with the weaker. Genocide to Marx was not in the least shocking but evidence of progress. Ultimately the dictatorship of the proletariat was destined to extinguish all races and nations. Regret for what had to happen was foolish and indulgent.

Reconciliation of the very real aspirations behind self-determination with Marx's highly unreal and ugly fantasy caught the Soviet leadership in a permanent cleft stick. The dual track of violence and vranyo-mongering drove the problem of empire out of sight but not out of mind. From the centre in Moscow, the party built a pretence that its control was not absolute by means of a structure of fifteen constituent republics and twenty so-called Autonomous Republics, at each level complete with local party and First Secretary, Central Committee and Council of Ministers. Supposed to look like local independence, this was actually replication and extension of the centre. Article 72 of the Soviet Constitution even accorded republics the right to secede. Lip service of this kind, sheer make-believe, concealed the centre's grip. The appropriate party-state bodies in Moscow formed a Soviet core, deciding essentials such as the money supply, conscription into the armed forces, subsidies, contributions to the Soviet budget, investment policy. Republics were deemed to have no right of ownership to their own resources or productive capacities. By decree from Moscow, colour television sets were to be made in Lithuania, or tractor tyres in Armenia – and nowhere else. In a celebrated example, Estonian biscuit-making was regulated in Moscow. Lobbying for subsidies and investment between the centre and the republics was a primitive and corrupt substitution for market forces.

The system was further riddled with anomalies. Russia itself, far the largest republic with 135 million, almost half the population of the entire union, had a Council of Ministers but no Communist Party or First Secretary or Central Committee. By this peculiarity, the centre simply had the wealth of Russia paid straight to it. This appropriation was the real basis of party power. Hardly less significant, control from the centre appeared to emanate from Soviet bodies rather than the Russian bodies which they actually were. This was dust cast in the eyes of the peoples out in the republics.

Historical accident alone determined who was to be allowed nationhood. Ukraine therefore found itself on the same standing as each of the tiny Baltic republics. Some boundaries were based on nationality or ethnicity, others on geography or territory. Peoples with a strong sense of identity were persecuted for it. Chechens, Ingush, Balkars, Crimean Tatars and others had been deported in acts of genocide by Stalin. When the cattle-trains finally arrived at their destinations, as many as half the deportees were dragged out dead. The lowest Soviet common denominator tended to assimilate those with a weak sense of identity. Volga Germans were presumed guilty of ethnic association with the Nazis. At least half of them were murdered and the rest uprooted, so that today few have a German culture or even the language. Only surnames are reminders of their origins. Jews had been unique in welcoming almost unanimously communist ideals in the hope of emancipation from the world of ghettos and pogroms. The party and the secret police contained disproportionate numbers of Jews, some of whom clung to illusions of emancipation long after these had been exposed as empty. Whether to be rid of a resented minority or to gain credit with the United States, a decision was taken in the Brezhnev era to allow Jews to emigrate to Israel. Altogether exceptional in Soviet history, this concession singled out the Jews, and in turn aroused envy and resentment. The larger or more prominent nations can each make a convincing claim to have suffered the worst persecution.

Every religious confession was restricted to the point of virtual elimination. The Russian Orthodox Church was broken, its hierarchy enrolled into the KGB. The KGB ran a Society for the Promotion of Atheism, converting cathedrals and other places of worship into anti-God museums. Historic churches and monasteries were closed. Vladimir Soloukhin is one of many writers filled with nostalgia for what had been vandalized and lost. In one of several memoirs, he described the day when the decree to dismantle church bells reached his hamlet of Alepino. Shouting women blocked the path to the bell-tower, but in vain. The bells were not in fact recast as guns as promised, but smashed and discarded. Humiliation of the villagers was the purpose. 'The important thing had been to break their spirit once again, this time with the bells.' As a young engineer in 1934, General Grigorenko was given the task of blowing up the cathedral of Vitebsk. Passengers in ships sailing down the River Dvina had been in the habit of crossing themselves at the sight of its five great cupolas. This irritated the authorities. 'There was no explosion in the common sense of the term,' Grigorenko wrote. 'The church merely shook, let out a long groan, and settled into a pile of bricks.' Synagogues survived only in cities like Moscow, Kharkhov and Kiev. Of the 24,000 mosques operating in 1913, about 300 survived into the present.

A parallel assault on identity was mounted through language. As the obligatory state language, Russian relegated all other languages to secondary status. Kindergartens did not teach in the local language, and in Ukraine or Belarus and the Baltics a secondary school using the local language was a rarity. A book published in 1971 stated the official view: 'The study of Russian promotes the formation of the scientific world-view, aids the formation of the communist ideology, and broadens general culture and outlook. In the epoch of the extensive construction of communism the Russian language promotes further drawing together of nations and achieving by them of their complete unity – the unity of statehood, economy, ideology and culture.'

An extended campaign cut Muslims off from their heritage. As a first step the Arabic script of their literature and religion was forcibly latinized. With similar linguistic absurdity, this latinized alphabet was later transcribed into Cyrillic.

Russians were encouraged to settle as colonizers in other republics on collective farms or in factories, and 25 million have done so. In Kazakhstan there are almost as many Russians as Kazakhs. In Latvia, Russians outnumber the native people. Divide-and-rule was the centre's long-term strategy. In 1925 Moscow took the Don Basin and the Kuban from Ukraine; in 1954 it handed the Crimea to Ukraine. Moscow annexed a slice of Estonia, of Latvia, of Finland, as well as pre-war Ruthenia; and it incorporated the republic of Moldavia out of the left bank of the Dniester taken from Ukraine and southern Bessarabia taken from Romania. It presented Lithuania with the previously Polish city of Vilnius. Nagorny-Karabakh, an area inhabited by Christian Armenians but designated an Autonomous Republic, was handed to Azerbaijan whose inhabitants are Shia Muslims. The Uzbek region of Osh was transferred to Kirghyzia, and predominantly Tajik Samarkand and its surrounding region to Uzbekistan. Gorbachev himself was to say that only 30 per cent of the internal borders had been legally defined. Playing upon hate, implanting a future of revenge, these ploys maximized the centre's supremacy.

According to one of the hoariest of slogans, the resulting Union was 'national in form and socialist in content'. Nothing was left to be 'national in form' except folk-dancing troupes, and even they were standardized. Music and certain musical instruments aroused suspicions of nationalism not yet repressed. Native costume barely survived: the Uzbek *khalat* in its brilliant colours was mass-produced out of synthetic materials. Arts and crafts died.

Before the war, in their writings Beatrice and Sidney Webb made themselves a laughing stock for posterity by their literal acceptance of everything they were fed by the Soviet Union. Refusal to analyse or even to recognize vranyo was typical of intellectuals. No other area with such diversity of races and nationalities, in the opinion of the Webbs, could boast of such a complete absence of discrimination. To be so dismissive and patronizing was itself an example of outstanding arrogance. Repeated year after year by fellow-travellers and collaborators, this flight of nonsense about racial and national harmony came to acquire status as the finest apology of the Soviet Union. It may well be that Soviet leaders believed what they heard repeated on every side. Brezhnev took a leaf straight out of the Webbs' book: 'We have every reason to say that the nationalities question in the form in which it came down to us from the past, has been resolved completely.' Russians as the first among equals helped 'backward outlying national areas' and this in the proper parlance was a glorious contribution to internationalism. Gorbachev was of a similar mind: 'Into the consciousness and heart of every person there has deeply entered the feeling of belonging to a single family – the Soviet people, a new and historically unprecedented social and international community.' To Shevardnadze he was to say, 'Yes, you are a Georgian but you are a Soviet man after all.' To him, his country was the 'Great Union of friendly peoples'. In his book of 1987, *Perestroika*, in an echo of Brezhnev and the Webbs, Gorbachev wrote that the nationalities question had been resolved 'in principle'. The Union, he was still claiming the following year, was 'one of the greatest accomplishments of socialism'.

Only in September 1989 did the Central Committee at his instruction consider that the Union might have to be restructured to take account of the rising nationalism. The republics were already in ferment and nationalists were demanding a new relationship to the centre, but Gorbachev's reaction was to propose changes to the Constitution and Article 72 which would make secession an impossibly cumbersome business. In his usual homage to correct parlance, he repeated that the party was a 'consolidating and directing force of social development'. At that Central Committee meeting he declared that the full force of the law would be used to maintain the Union. He sounded as though he were reversing the condemnation of official violence which he had been making in the West.

To see ourselves as others see us requires rare imagination. To subject peoples, Soviet citizenship meant only Moscow-derived regulations, violently enforced, and nothing else. Soviet nationality was nonexistent. They cherished their own identity of race and religion all the more. The only recognizable member of the Soviet family so sentimentally evoked by the centre was Big Brother Russia, perceived as a hateful bully prepared to kill and afterwards shed crocodile tears over what he had done. Glasnost and perestroika were so many levers convenient for prising open this hypocrisy. Each and every republic could claim its particular 'blank spot'. To air grievances in the local press and at public meetings was the initial act of mobilization. Nobody in the leadership seems to have realized what a double-edged weapon a newly created public opinion would prove to be.

Voluntary association at the individual level immediately swelled during the course of 1987 and 1988 into nationalism, which is voluntary association at the collective level. *Pravda* estimated that by 1989 60,000 informal groups and movements were in existence. Far the most important of these associations or groups were the Popular Fronts which sprang into sudden life in the republics, Autonomous Republics and provinces, and even cities. In the Russian republic alone, 140 Popular Fronts were thought to exist.

Nobody now wishes to claim paternity for the Popular Fronts. Without the consent of the leadership, however, they could never have come into being. The idea behind them in all likelihood was to have an organizational structure within whose strictly controlled limits nationalism could be expressed, adjusted, and in an emergency switched off. The Popular Fronts would be safety valves. More positively they were originally designated as support groups for perestroika. But perestroika tended to affirm the Soviet Union, and nationalism to fragment it. Neither Gorbachev nor anyone else paused to explain this incompatibility of purpose.

The initial inflammatory step was taken in Armenia. For some time Armenia had been agitating and partitioning for the return of the Autonomous Republic of Nagorny-Karabakh. The Nagorny-Karabakh local Soviet voted on 20 February 1988 for a transfer to Armenia. Within days demonstrations in the streets of Erevan, the Armenian capital, were three-quarters of a million strong. The Azeri response was to fall on the Armenians. On 1 March, in the town of Sumgait, thirty-two Armenians were massacred and over a hundred injured. These officials figures are probably too low.

Hopes had been aroused by perestroika and glasnost which could not be fulfilled. In this dispute, either the Armenians or the Azeris were bound to be losers. A commission was set up to investigate and recommend action. Its report offers insights into the deviousness with which the system operated. 'The population must be calmed by concessions in cultural, social and daily matters, if need be by the sacrifice of a part of the leadership, and of course, by the discovery of guilty parties at a lower level. However, Nagorny-Karabakh should not be attached to Armenia. The impression should be created of a total glasnost, in distinction to the previous era, and then pinpoint as far as possible the smallest confrontations for which the blame is to be laid on the Armenians. Armenian society must be infiltrated to the maximum extent, notably through exploiting the Kurds who of all of those who inhabit Armenian territory are the most narrowly disposed in respect of Armenians, while trying at the same time to destroy such friendly relations.'

Awarding the disputed enclave to Azerbaijan that July, the centre precipitated civil war. If Armenians were going to fight for what they saw as redress of grievances, then every other people in the Soviet Union could draw the conclusion that they would have to follow this lead.

Redress of grievances in Estonia, Latvia and Lithuania was projected solely against the Russians. In the last century these republics had developed a contemporary westernized sense of nationhood through writers such as Friedrich Kreuzwald in Estonia or Jonas Basanavičius in Lithuania, as well as musicologists like Kristianis Barons who collected and published a dozen volumes of Latvian folksongs. None of the Western powers had accepted the incorporation of the Balts into the Soviet Union by means of the *force majeure* of the Ribbentrop–Molotov Pact and subsequent invasion. Having fled to the West, hundreds of thousands of Baltic exiles kept this issue alive through persistent publicity and lobbying. Internally as well as externally, an increasingly large and vociferous body of opinion maintained that the clock of history had to be returned to 1939, restoring sovereignty and independence to these republics.

One course of action open to Gorbachev was to clear up the most onerous of the 'blank spots', by going beyond denunciation of Stalin to undoing all his works. If carried out in time, the surrender of Moldavia, the Baltic republics and the Sakhalin Islands seized from Japan, might have lightened the historic burden. Gorbachev could then have stood his ground on everything inherited from 1917. Fearing that the least concession would trigger a chain reaction, he seems never to have seriously contemplated this. Consequently the Baltic republics were to remain a bone stuck chokingly in the Soviet craw. These apparently helpless and victimized peoples played a disproportionate role in destroying the empire.

Commuting in dismay to Moscow, hardline communists pleaded with whoever would listen for a resort to the old methods, declarations of a state of emergency, martial law, summary justice, shooting. Perestroikists were in a quandary. An open break with the hardliners led to certain factionalism. The Popular Fronts, though, dragged them away from party ideology in the direction of nationalism. By the summer of 1988, intelligent and ambitious communists in the republics had realized that sincere commitment to the party on the one hand and to the Popular Fronts on the other was no longer possible. It was time for a choice. In calculating which way to jump, they had to interpret signals from Moscow. In one republic after another Gorbachev purged hardliners and replaced them with men in his own image, who spoke of compromise rather than force. Encouraging Popular Fronts on his journeys to the republics, Yakovlev bestowed approval. Increasingly Yeltsin was arousing Russia itself in some form of informal mass Popular Front behind him. By the end of 1989 the victory of the Popular Fronts had become a self-fulfilling prophecy. The last Popular Front to be established was Rukh, in Ukraine, with former political prisoners and dissidents setting the pace. Ukrainian exiles in Germany, Canada and Australia pressured Rukh to push for independence. Whoever was responsible for dreaming up the Popular Fronts left the party with no middle way in the republics between repression and national self-determination.

When I interviewed Petru Lucinschi, he still spelled his name in the Russian manner, rather than as now in the Romanian of Moldavia, where he comes from. One of the younger members of the old Central Committee, he had once been party Second Secretary in Tajikistan. As chairman of the parliament in Moldavia, he has evolved into the foremost politician there. Algirdas Brazauskas and Leonid Kravchuk, respectively from Lithuania and Ukraine, are examples of others who have made a similar transition, in their cases from party First Secretary to national President. Moldavia consists of provinces truncated from Romania, with which it shares language and culture. On the lines of Germany, reunification might seem natural, were it not for overriding local impediments. About half a million of the population of 4 million are Russians settlers, concentrated in the city of Tiraspol, still defended by a Russian garrison army, an imperial relic. Independence for the republic instigated fighting between the Moldavian Popular Front and the Russian settlers on the one hand, and with a small national minority, the Gagauz, on the other. The Gagauz argued that sovereignty and independence were as good for them as for the Moldavians.

From a practical point of view, Lucinschi thought, the Soviet system had worked more or less well, although latterly local antagonisms had mushroomed. Republics which claimed to have been held back economically by the centre were being perverse; they took every advantage. In the republics, independent mafia networks had always carried out intrigues and machinations of their own accord. Second Secretaries posted from the centre always had to bear in mind that their appointments were temporary, and they tended to leave well alone. Usually a Russian, the Second Secretary had the delicate tasks of explaining the centre's policy to the local party, and facilitating contacts with those at the centre. Totalitarian control imposed from outside had functioned by maintaining a balance. As soon as the republics became independent, this balance was destroyed. In the case of Tajikistan, the Central Committee had always been aware of the potential of conflict of the different clans.

'Once you had clawed your way up the ladder to a certain level in your region or republic, then it would be automatic that you would get into the Central Committee at federal level. With one or two exceptions, the First and Second Secretaries, the chairman of the local Supreme Soviet and the chairman of the local Council of Ministers would be ex-officio Central Committee members. You were required to have a position corresponding to your standing in the party-state hierarchy. If you were outside the party but socially active, at some stage you would have to comply and do what everyone else was doing.'

Party apparatchiks lost no time transforming themselves into nationalists.

'You cannot look at the present generation of communists through the prism of 1917. We are capable of analysing the situation in terms of common sense rather than ideology. It is less a question of loss of ideology than a question of coming to power. I joined the Central Committee thirty years after Stalin's death, when we had no strong political faith but were united by a belief in moving society forward. Gorbachev's basic outlook was to seize every opportunity to push this huge country towards democracy, although his understanding of democracy was based on ideas current here, and very hazy. He operated on the principle that a republic's problems should be solved at the republic's level, whereas the republics had a view that the centre should solve them. There was a breakdown in communications here.'

In Lucinschi's view, the centre's most serious mistake concerning the republics was russification. This was actually a policy of national oppression. Forbidding the use of the Romanian language as well as the importation of books from Romania were deplorable aspects of the centre's ideological battle with Nicolae Ceauşescu, the Romanian party First Secretary. Moldavian was considered a language for peasants, and business was conducted in Russian. Now the Russian settlers are obliged to use Moldavian for official purposes,

133

which surprises and irritates them, but is hardly a violation of human rights. They drafted angry resolutions. The defensive reaction of the centre led to armed struggle and civil war. Gorbachev, says Lucinschi, 'has been turned into a saint with a halo by Western observers but his stature is actually quite small'. By 1987 at the latest, Gorbachev should have started work towards a meaningful federation of republics.

14

THE MUSLIM HERITAGE

Dushanbe, Alma-Ata, Tashkent, Ashkhabad and other main cities of Central Asia have a Soviet look about them. Huge central squares for the obligatory parades, boulevards on a grid pattern, a Central Committee headquarters in layered and discoloured cement, with an opera house and the local *Pravda* offices in close proximity, mass housing which provides ready-made slums. I first went there in the early 1970s when the accompanying KGB men took pains to ensure that it was impossible to learn anything about local life.

In Tashkent the Mufti for Central Asia received me. A young man in his thirties, very sharp, he had studied in Egypt and had lately been on the *hajj* to Mecca with twenty other pilgrims. Once the older generation had died off, he made me understand, Islam would be a matter of special study. But one Friday, shortly before noon prayers when the imam was already preparing to preach, my KGB escorts took me into the Shahr-i-Sabz mosque, where Tamerlane had prayed. If looks could kill: but the Russians were indifferent to this hostility.

Beyond the cities are thousands of square miles of majestic landscape under what seems the brightest and mightiest of skies, the black sands of Kara Kum, the now ruined Aral Sea, the snow-capped Pamirs, historic Khiva and Samarkand and Bokhara, Lake Issyk-Kul. The Golden Horde came to rest here as nomads and herdsmen. Up in the Alai mountains of Kirghyzia, in the aftermath of the Revolution, Gustav Krist, an adventurer and Austrian by birth, witnessed what he called the passing of Kirghyz freedom. The Kirghyz were escaping the Soviet census. 'To an enormous distance I could see camel train after camel train; the entire horde was on trek, flying from the officials of the Soviets.' In Turkestan, he described how the communists 'flooded the country with regulations, proclamations, and rallying cries. They formed a staff of professional agitators. Next, factories, co-operatives, peasant organ-izations, and workshops had to be created in the deserts and oases ... so as to conjure up class consciousness where none had been before.'

Kazakhstan alone is the size of India. Large numbers of Kazakhs followed the fleeing Kirghyz into China. One in three Kazakhs were killed under Stalin through terror, collectivization and starvation. 'Relative to the size of their population, the Kazakh holocaust exceeded that of any other nation', in the words of Bohdan Nahaylo and Victor Swoboda, authors of *Soviet Disunion*, a recent history of Soviet nationalities. Two particular horrors were inflicted on the Kazakhs: the Gulag camps of Karaganda, and the nuclear testing range of Semipalatinsk.

One of the millions of letters addressed to Gorbachev was signed by L. Boikova. Born in the village of Beskaragai, she lived two hundred miles from the nuclear testing zone. Something like five hundred nuclear tests have taken place there. On days of tests, she wrote, 'We were herded into a deep ravine and told to lie on the ground, face down, with the mouth wide open (the latter was supposed to protect our eardrums from bursting).' They would watch the aircraft circling, and the bomb dropping and igniting. Where the mushroom cloud billowed would depend on the wind. 'Sometimes, it would blow towards the Abolsk region, at other times towards us. There was also the sound wave. It would come more or less immediately, knocking people off their feet ... during one of the exercises the top storey (of our school) was sliced off, like with a knife. Many houses collapsed ... There were never any medical checkups, in spite of the radiation we were exposed to. People in our village began to die of leukaemia but for some reason it had to be kept quiet.'

The Kazakh Institute of Radiation in Semipalatinsk has preserved a few of the thousands of deformed stillborn or aborted foetuses. Max Easterman, reporting on this Institute, wrote of the thousands more who had been born alive with terrible abnormalities but survived, 'living proof of a defence policy rooted in an official disregard for human life'. To many Kazakhs, what had been done to them by Russian imperialism is genocide. In the 1989 census, two-thirds of the Kazakhs were bilingual but not even one per cent of the Russians spoke Kazakh.

Encounters at less horrific levels still generated prejudice on the part of Russians and nationalist resentment in Muslim minorities. Eighty-nine patients, who were Kalmyks and mostly single mothers, had a mysterious infection in a hospital in Elista, capital of Kalmykia. This was used to stir up racism against the Muslim Kalmyks, according to a newspaper report. ' "At the time Kalmyks were thrown out of hotels, kicked out of hostels, and buses from here were stoned as they travelled through neighbouring regions. Reading the press, you had the impression Kalmyks didn't wash," says Dr Badma Tachiev, current head doctor of the hospital. Investigation into the case has been closed. He had never seen a disposable syringe.'

With the advent of perestroika it became possible to speak without KGB listeners to the men of the older generation. Wearing a Tajik or Uzbek skullcap, or a round fur-trimmed Kirghyz hat, tribal elders are the keepers of public conscience, and to be found in tea-houses, *chai-khanas*, under trellises of vines and bougainvillea. Reaction to the Russians comprises hate and fear, to be sure, but it is compounded with the wariness and tragicomic humour which comes from long experience of surviving despotism.

Some of the peoples of Central Asia are Turkic and look to Turkey, others are Iranian and look to Persia. Chagatay has long since ceased to be a lingua franca, and most people have their own language. Sunnis outnumber Shia. Literature, poetry especially, in some cases goes back to the earliest Muslim centuries but in others is an innovation. What all these peoples share is an unbroken history of despotic one-man rule, which has preserved their identity but also prevented them from forming nation-states in any Western sense. Common to all is the tribal or clan structure, whereby primary loyalty is owed to those of one's own kind. Pluralism and power-sharing are concepts without a point of entry in this scheme of things. As yet there is neither statehood nor citizenship, neither rights nor responsibilities. Tolerance rests upon a strict do-as-you-would-be-done-by basis.

In their historic heyday Genghis Khan and Tamerlane left such a stamp of cruelty and despotism that the memory of it is still vivid. Their successors, local emirs and khans, were different not in outlook but in power and range. Unable to mount expeditions in search of wealth, they finally became incapable even of defending their own kind, and so were overpowered by the Russians.

To the peoples of Central Asia, Russian despotism is recognizably kindred to their own inheritance. It is familiar that the strong grab the spoils while the weak can only scheme to recapture them. But the centuries of Orthodox Christianity laid the foundation for something new, a national identity in whose pursuit the Russians had fought the Muslims and won. A religious rather than a national community, Islam in contrast had not succeeded in enlarging the tribal structure. Tribal and ethnic particularity, it was obvious to thoughtful Muslims, impeded the birth of a nationhood capable of withstanding Russia. Nineteenth-century Baku was at least the equal of Cairo in the intellectual attempt to define how to be both Muslim and modern. Without communism, the Muslims of Central Asia might well have developed secular nation-states on the model now found in the Muslim Middle East, though no doubt still with identity troubles.

Invaded and overpowered, the Central Asian peoples fell back upon remedies which had served to mitigate despotism in the past. Outward humility and compliance concealed the inner self. From time to time an imam or a mullah was arrested travelling incognito in these republics, and usually revealed to belong to a Sufi society like the Naqshbandi. The Soviets liked to pretend that their strong-arm methods alone contained an explosive Islamic fundamentalism, but this was probably a self-serving scare.

A despot too strong to be resisted militarily has to be approached with stealth and flattery, lulled, bought off with tributes, inveigled into what looks like co-operation but is actually nothing of the kind. Themselves skilled in these black arts by virtue of their own history, Russians had met their match in Central Asia. The first defence of the clan and the tribe was to select someone of its own to be its chosen representative in the party, where he duly mouthed the parlance and earned promotion to the top, danced attendance on the centre, all the while directing money and jobs to his own clan and tribe. As often as not, party leaders in the Muslim republics were only clan notables in another guise. Sovietized outwardly, these notables were brilliantly inverting the party into a source of money and patronage. First Secretaries were so many khans and emirs, with Soviet medals on their jackets instead of the jewelled embroidery on costumes of the past. Far from being considered corrupt petty tyrants, to their own peoples Sharif Rashidov as Uzbek First Secretary, or Dinmukhamad Kunayev who ran Kazakhstan almost uninterruptedly from 1954 to 1986, or Haidar Aliev in Azerbaijan, or Jaber Rasulov, the Tajik First Secretary from 1961 to 1983, or Saparmurad Nizayev arranging a 99 per cent vote in Turkmenistan, were admirable in what they could get away with, their fraudulence perceived as a grand and almost heroic trick on the Soviets.

Ayatollah Khomeini, overthrowing the Shah in 1979, was only the latest in a long line of Persian or Iranian neighbours deemed unsatisfactory in Moscow. In the Tsarist era such an upheaval would have been a pretext for another war of conquest. This time the Soviets invaded Afghanistan from where they hoped to be poised to pressure Khomeini. Muslims might have had to overlook the Soviet despot doing harm to them if the invasion had proved successful. Its failure put the Soviets to shame and galvanized a sense of gleeful pride in the Central Asian republics. Sounding off like any Russians with racist prejudices and a bottle of vodka to warm them up, Gorbachev fulminated against what he called 'parasite republics' who claimed money but earned none, and he warned whoever would listen about the danger of Islamic fundamentalism which was 'showing its sharp teeth', regardless that he was actually stimulating it.

With similar short-sightedness, attacking the effect but not the cause, he tried to clean up the Muslim republic parties. The Kirghyz First Secretary Turdakun Usbaliev was dismissed in 1985, and the Kazakh First Secretary Kunayev the following year. An article in *Izvestia* claimed that among other assets Kunayev had control of 247 hotels, 414 guest flats, 84 cottages, 22 hunting lodges and 350 hospital beds. The haul was not improbable.

Thousands were purged and imprisoned. The nationalist backlash was fierce. Sadiqjan Yigitaliev, chairman of the Supreme Court of Uzbekistan, for instance, accused Russian officials of systematically tampering with the scales of justice by imprisoning innocent people and pressuring the courts for convictions. He singled out the local party Second Secretary Vladimir Anishchev and two colleagues as the three Russians who actually controlled Uzbekistan. What began with the Russians as the imposition of justice ended in the Uzbek perspective as persecution. It seems to have astonished the centre that large-scale local rioting at once erupted.

Tribal politics, like communist politics, are careerist – you rise, in other words, insofar as you impose yourself on others. All methods of offence and defence are appropriate. What you say and do may have no relation to what you think, and only once you have reached the very summit are you able to reconcile these differences and to claim to be representative of your own kind. Trying to express their thoughts honestly, or at least to come to grips with reality, intellectuals are the outcasts of careerist politics.

Disaffected intellectuals were quick to perceive the opportunities offered by a Popular Front, the new political body which was beginning to sweep the European republics in the distant west of the empire. Some travelled to see for themselves how it worked; Baltic nationalists also arrived to spread the word in Central Asia. Sajudis, the Lithuanian Popular Front, was a model. Here was the instant westernizing through imitation which has been a feature of the Third World, an import which has probably done more to confuse than to construct.

Eighteen Uzbek writers and professors founded Birlik (meaning Unity), their Popular Front, in a private meeting in Tashkent in November 1988. The poets Muhammad Salih and Erkin Wahidov and an academic, Abdulrahman Pulatov, took the lead. Rastakhiz in Tajikistan, Agzybirlik in Turkmenistan, Adilet in Kazakhstan, Ashar in Kirghyzia, and so on for other peoples, completed the chain of Popular Fronts in Central Asia. Only a handful of prominent personalities were involved, virtually none of whom could claim to represent anything or anyone much more than himself.

One approach towards enlarging the tribal structure into nationhood was to attack Soviet imperialism. A well-known writer Olzhas Suleymenov was First Secretary of the Kazakh Writers' Union. Elected a deputy to the first Congress of People's Deputies, Suleymenov declared from the podium to Russians listening with reluctance, 'The principal aspect of perestroika for me is the continuation of the decolonization process which was suspended in the 1920s.' Another approach lay through Islam and its revival. Early in 1989 the weekly organ of the Uzbek Writers' Union and the Ministry of Culture published an article in which religion was still savaged as 'a means of cultural poisoning of the proletariat and all working people'. Only a week later, the former KGB Mufti for Central Asia was purged and his replacement, Muhammad Sadiq Muhammad Yusuf, then published an article in that same journal in praise of the traditional Muslim family.

The sole programme upon which everyone could agree was to restore the supremacy of the national language in each republic. With unexpected compliance, the First Secretaries of the parties caved in and passed a law to that effect. Achieving this goal, the Popular Fronts and the embryonic national movements then fragmented. Those who wanted either more democracy and power-sharing, or more Islam, quarrelled with those who wanted less of all these. As in the independent Arab or other Muslim countries, no unified vision of the future could be formulated. There was no mechanism for introducing the pluralism which alone keeps the peace. First Secretaries mobilized their tribes and ethnic groups, swiftly brushing aside and arresting and imprisoning well-meaning westernizing intellectuals. Respect for such intellectuals as individuals did not imply tribal support for them. Local civil wars burgeoning in the republics of Central Asia appeared to be struggles between die-hard communism, nationalism and Islamic fundamentalism, but these abstractions had little reality, merely being pressed into service for more profound tribal and ethnic identities. This was not a case of communism giving away to Third World anarchy but a reversion to the traditional past. Politics as the armed defence of one's own kind against everyone else seemed to leap once more out of the ground in all its destructive vitality as though Soviet occupation had been another passing interlude in history, leaving no social imprint, nothing except a few buildings in cheap and already deteriorating cement.

Emil Pein is an eminent ethnographer in Moscow who has studied the Muslim republics. He goes so far as to maintain that Soviet imperialism, or communism, actually preserved the old ways. Diverted from the idea of the nation-state, the peoples of Central Asia could not modernize. In Tajikistan and Turkmenistan the clans still compelled loyalties and social behaviour. Nationalism in the case of the mountain Kirghyz springs from opposition to ethnic groups who have settled in the rich valleys and lowlands. What with their Turkic ethnicity and Shia confession, the Azeris had no sense of national identity until it was fired in the conflict with Armenia over Nagorny-Karabakh.

The imposition of communism on these peoples, Pein argues, was a simple matter of a new vocabulary. Soviet words did not alter reality. In Tajikistan the northern clan had been supreme for centuries, and its emir evolved into the First Secretary. The social structure remained intact. An Uzbek kolkhoz with which he was familiar in the course of his academic work had up to 15,000 members. The chairman could not know the details concerning those who came to petition him, and he acquired the information necessary for taking decisions through the *makhalya* or old tribal council. In practice, those who ran other people's lives were the notables. Corruption alone developed new relationships, mafia-like. Much was common to traditional local custom and Soviet totalitarianism. 'Either new names were given to old roles, or old roles functioned as before under cover of the new names.'

A number of the élite were culturally russified through education, and to that extent westernized. In towns and cities, some Tajiks and Uzbeks have identity problems as a result. This Nomenklatura retains close links with Russians at the centre, for purposes of extracting more privileges especially when it comes to educating their children. Soviet socioeconomic organization has been a very limited modernization.

Anwar Usmanov is a westernized intellectual, an Uzbek who was in with the Popular Front, Birlik, from its inception in his home city of Tashkent. Its initial programme, he says, was limp and modest, offering future co-operation with the Soviet Union without a word about independence. 'We were under the influence of Eastern Europe. Groups had supported perestroika but they had disappeared. Raising the question of the state language gave them a great deal of popularity. According to the 1977 Constitution there was no state language. As a result the Uzbek language was being edged out into a kind of kitchen lingo. This was very convenient for the Nomenklatura, you had to know Russian if you wanted to get on. The powers reacted negatively to Birlik. The Central Committee of the Uzbek party argued that they were doing all this anyhow, so why was Birlik trying to be involved.'

As part of the struggle to establish Uzbek as the state language, Birlik organized a demonstration of 10,000 in Tashkent on 19 March 1989. This shook the whole republic. Then on 1 May 2000 delegates from eight of the twelve regions of the republic attended a conference of Birlik in Tashkent. They elected a committee of management with Abdulrahman Pulatov as chairman. His field is artificial intelligence and robotics. 'He was right for the post, midway between the writers and technicians.'

The new Birlik programme had the primary aim to 'awaken the Uzbek people from political slumber. We were far less politicized than Russians or Ukrainians. The second point was to form a democratic secular society. At that stage there were no Islamic activists. Others joined, and Birlik aimed to represent all the nationalities of Uzbekistan. The Communist Party was participating in these activities from the start, with the purpose of controlling it. So the Government promised to look into the language question. Via the

Central Committee, the Supreme Soviet officially favoured the supremacy of the Uzbek language.' But that June Uzbeks attacked and slaughtered Meshketian Turks, another Muslim people, in the Ferghana Valley. Quite how or why this happened is obscure. Usmanov is convinced that the massacre was provoked by groups from Moscow. 'At the time we held it was our personal mission to prove it was organized by Gorbachev, like the massacre of Armenians in Sumgait. This was a centralized campaign to prove that Uzbeks had no prospect of social organizing on their own. It actually awoke Uzbeks from apathy and sowed the seeds of national consciousness.' Some Uzbeks might therefore have an interest in attacking the Meshketian Turks but Usmanov rejects that possibility.

'In the autumn of 1989 a very large demonstration was held in Tashkent. The Central Committee began to manoeuvre, manipulating a split in Birlik. Muhammad Salih and other writers started to argue that it was time to suspend activism through demonstrations and to work for a compromise with the Government. Salih and his group left Birlik to start Erk (meaning Will). Birlik wanted democracy and independence in that order; Erk advocated independence first and then democracy. Islam Karimov, the First Secretary of the Uzbek party, saw his chance to crack down. Nineteen ninety was very complicated, as Birlik struggled to survive.'

The Osh region is populated by Uzbeks but had been arbitrarily allocated by Stalin to Kirghyzia. On 5 June 1990 15,000 armed Kirghyz stormed down from the mountains and started to kill Uzbeks in the town of Osh itself and in nearby Uzgen. Usmanov happened to be in Uzgen at that time, a witness of this event. Thirty thousand Uzbeks lived in Uzgen alongside four thousand Russians and three thousand Kirghyz. Researching the background of the massacre, Usmanov learned that Karimov had been forewarned on the eve of the massacre and had telephoned Gorbachev to request emergency powers. He offered to take responsibility for sending in troops. Gorbachev, says Usmanov, hesitated and then telephoned Marshal Yazov who did indeed order the crack Pskov division into Uzgen, but only once the massacre was in full swing.

On the back of this whole sequence of events, Karimov was able to bolster his position as First Secretary with a claim to being an Uzbek nationalist. Whether he liked to call himself a communist or a nationalist mattered less than the maintenance of his one-man despotism in Uzbekistan. He duly crystallized his supremacy by establishing himself as President. Birlik called him the Bolshevik Khan of Central Asia. It remained for him only to close down both Birlik and Erk, and persecute its leading lights. Pulatov and Muhammad Salih have been beaten up, and imprisoned. Anwar Usmanov's house in Tashkent was burnt to the ground.

15

THE BALTIC REPUBLICS

> I stand alone by the roadside
> Where there once used to be a village
> And write with a piece of charcoal
> On the gravestones of chimney stacks
> A song about long-cold ovens,
> And coals that have long since died out,
> A song about cats left homeless
> And children who keep on weeping
> By the bodies of their dead mothers.

The mood of this poem, written in 1964 by Imants Ziedonis, is one which pervades the Baltic republics, Estonia, Latvia and Lithuania; the elegy is authentic. Powerful and murderous neighbours almost succeeded in sweeping out of history these three peoples, each of whom has an identity that it values with passion, intensely aware of what has been lost and what is to be salvaged. White-haired, his face handsome and refined, Ziedonis himself is the very image of the poet as national bard. Listening to the exclusive way in which he spoke about his native Latvia, I asked him whether Shelley was spouting rubbish when he described the poet as a citizen of the world. Appealing for support to other Latvians round the table, Ziedonis replied that those who come from large countries can never understand those who come from small ones.

Thin straight roads cut through the Baltic landscape which is flat and unrelieved, except for spectral forests of birch or indigenous pines whose reddish bark turns grey towards the top of the trunk. Lakes spreckle everywhere, amongst lonely homesteads of clapboard or the rotting hulk of a Soviet kolkhoz. Driftwood along the sandy shore, wan seaborne light, and in winter, ice ridging the coast. Klaipeda, Liepāja, Ventspils were once Hanseatic ports with German names. In the old churches are monuments emblazoned with extravagant heraldry to the Baltic German aristocracy: Horn, Toll, Krusenstein, Üxküll, Pahlen. Prince Biron ruled what was then the Grand Duchy of Courland for Catherine the Great, and he commissioned Rastrelli, the architect of St Petersburg, to build him the palace at Rundāle. Empty, its magnificence battered and patched, it is now an object stranded in the way that the Sphinx is.

Cocooned inside the dim Soviet outskirts of Tallinn and Riga are the churches and palaces and merchant houses of the past, flaking and abused, though since independence scaffolding everywhere indicates the first repairs in decades. Near Šiauliai, in northern Lithuania, is a tump planted thickly with crosses of every size in iron or wood, draped with rosaries and pious messages in a cobweb effect. Every so often the Soviet authorities used to bulldoze this Golgotha of a site, but Catholic pilgrims then surreptitiously replanted their crucifixes. Pope John Paul II was one of them. With its vistas of baroque architecture and the university founded by the Jesuits, as well as an ancient Jewish quarter, the Lithuanian capital of Vilnius once had an intellectual and cultural reputation throughout Europe. At its heart what was called Lenin Street has recovered its rightful name of Gediminas. In the window of the main department store stood a child's bicycle, Soviet-made, spotted with rust even before it was sold. So many sights and experiences at all levels here arouse fear or shame. You cannot forget that you are on the scene of great crime.

'It is difficult today to imagine the simple mode of life of those days in that little corner of Europe,' writes Tania Alexander in *An Estonian Childhood*, a memoir of her pre-war upbringing in rural Kallijärv, with fruit-picking and walks in the woods and music-making. She was the daughter of Baroness Moura Budberg, a cosmopolitan lady, the mistress of H. G. Wells and Maxim Gorky, as well as a lifelong KGB informer. Moura Budberg arranged for Wells to interview Stalin in 1934. Wells was at the height of his fame as a thinker and writer. He could not wait to congratulate Stalin. 'Today the capitalists have to learn from you, to grasp the spirit of Socialism.' Only weeks later Stalin was to have his colleague Kirov murdered, and unleash the next wave of terror. Stalin replied that there were many wicked men in the world: 'I do not believe in the goodness of the bourgeoisie.' Returning with his scoop from the Kremlin to Kallijärv and Moura Budberg, Wells splashed about in the local lakes, unconscious that Stalin's crime was served by folly and double standards like his.

After the Ribbentrop–Molotov Pact, the Baltic Germans were advised, often by word of mouth, to leave. Submitting to a Nazi regime rather than a Soviet, some 60,000 did so. Successive Nazi and Soviet invasions killed at least a third of the Baltic populations. The Nazis deported about 150,000 Balts and singled out the Jews to be murdered almost to the last one. The ferocity was unique in Lithuania where anti-Semitism was even more vicious than in Poland or Ukraine. 'The intense involvement of the local population', as Dina Porat, the historian of the genocide of Lithuanian Jews obliquely expresses it, fatally combined with German thoroughness and organization. An American journalist, Genevieve Abel, published an account in the *Baltic Observer* of a tramride she had taken one autumn day in 1992 from the centre of Vilnius to the edge of the city. A local farmer took her out to a wood, which was Ponary, in Lithuanian Paneriai, one of the most dreadful killing-grounds. Jews had been shot down into pits, and buried where they lay fallen. Breaking through the earth, bones and teeth were now everywhere. 'The forest closed in around me,' she wrote. No effort had been made to give these victims a decent burial; there was not even a memorial.

Monstrous parallels arose from the Nazi and Soviet versions of totalitarianism. At the very moment when the German army was marching into Paris on 14 June 1940, the Red Army was occupying the Baltic republics. President Antanas Smetona of Lithuania fled to the United States but his Prime Minister and stand-in, Antanas Merkys, was deported. In Moscow at the time, the Lithuanian Foreign Minister, Jouzas Urbšys, was simply held captive. Kārlis Ulmanis and Konstantin Päts, respectively presidents of Latvia and Estonia, were deported and died in exile. Romuald Misiunas and Rein Taagepera are the authors of the definitive history of these republics under occupation, and in their restrained words, the arrest and deportation of leading statesmen of one state on the orders of another was 'perhaps an unprecedented event' in modern international relations.

Piotr Yakir was the son of an outstanding Soviet general, one among many others shot out of hand at Stalin's order in 1937 during the terror after Kirov's murder. As his father's son, Yakir found himself in 1941 in Gulag, in Camp 7 of a complex called Severallag. He watched the Balts arrive, sixty to a boxcar, in twelve trains from Riga and about the same number from Tallinn and Vilnius. Families had been split up. Men and women were deported separately. Their names had been on lists previously compiled by the secret police. When the trains were unloaded, Yakir wrote, people were scarcely able to walk out of the cars. Soon they were scavenging for something to eat among the rubbish. 'I remember the case of the secretary of the President of Lithuania who was so weak that he couldn't climb out of the dustbin into which he had clambered to get some rotten fish-heads.' They were not alone in their misery. Solzhenitsyn pinpoints the unloading in Solikamsk of a train from Leningrad at that same period when the entire embankment was covered with corpses. In the winters after 1944, he writes, prisoner-trains from the Baltic, Poland and Germany, used to arrive at the main rail junctions in the north with one or two carloads of corpses tacked on behind. The Balts were the first to die, Varlam Shalamov noticed in one of those observations which sear into the memory, because they were physically bigger than the Russians.

From 1945 to 1955 another 80,000 Estonians and 100,000 Latvians and 260,000 Lithuanians were deported. One from Estonia was Lagle Parek, 'a cheerful fair-haired woman', according to Irina Ratushinskaya who shared her prison hut. Lagle Parek was sentenced to six years of camp and three more of internal exile for issuing a *samizdat* journal. 'Her father was shot, her mother sent to a camp, Lagle and her grandmother and sister to Siberia. Her grandmother managed to get both girls to Siberia alive, where Estonians standing knee-high-deep in snow then told her they were destined to remain in eternal exile.' Only when Lagle Parek was arrested did she learn of her father's fate, seeing the order for his execution in her own file. She is now a Minister in the Estonian government.

A handful of dissidents were determined and secretive enough to survive the Brezhnev era. Others, like Johannes Hint, an Estonian mathematician, died in prison. A foreboding grew that the historic identities of the Balts were about to be lost for ever. *Cogito Ergo Sum* is the title of an Estonian documentary, a short but moving film about a very old man who had been overlooked when everyone else in his village had been collectivized or deported. Once he had taught philosophy and theology in Tartu University; now he decided to stay alone in the abandoned village. Over the years the place had virtually returned to the wild, but he gave himself the satisfaction of being a living defiance. Speaking to the camera at the end of the film, this indomitable figure said that each of us has the power to think out who he is, and this power, properly used, is the meaning of life. A well-known poet, Māra Zālīte, articulated in June 1988 to a gathering of Latvian intellectuals at the start of the national liberation movement, a general anxiety: 'The Latvians are on the verge of extinction.'

Russian was the official language for party business, bureaucracy and commerce. The Latvian Boriss Pugo, also a KGB general, was only one among party leaders so russified that he was unable to speak his native tongue. 'Speak a human language!' was how Russian shop assistants were known to address their Estonian customers.

Intellectuals and students were first to perceive and act upon the ambiguity of perestroika: party officials who encouraged them to take up revival and restructuring could not then order them to be insincere about it. Praising Gorbachev, they could hardly be accused of burying him. Experiment alone could reveal what exactly were the tolerated limits. A more sure-fire preparation for a test of strength would have been hard to devise. A timely article, lecture, or an outburst on television, tapped the pent-up and fearful frustration of decades, converting it straight into nationalism. Private resentments swelled into public opinion at one bound. Often unwittingly, the individual who struck the right note found himself immediately promoted into a spokesman with a microphone, addressing enthusiastic crowds in a park or stadium.

The first demonstrations were in the spring of 1988. That summer, within the space of a few days at the end of May and the beginning of June, leading intellectuals and personalities held meetings that were to lead to founding congresses of the Popular Fronts in all three republics. Hitherto possession of the national flag had been cause for imprisonment. Sported everywhere, flags now became emotional symbols, as did anthems and songs.

Karl Vaino, Boriss Pugo and Ringaudas Songaila were the First Secretaries of the parties of Estonia, Latvia and Lithuania respectively. Brought up in the old ways, long-serving, they were not well equipped to deal with organizations whose spontaneity and popularity so quickly escaped control. On the one hand, Gorbachev was known to reject force, and therefore was likely to disown and possibly punish them in the event of a crackdown; on the other hand, no promises or fine words could get the demonstrators off the streets or the flags out of their hands. The party was being openly defied. In this predicament, the First Secretaries sought for a middle course, ordering force insufficient to disperse demonstrations but quite enough to outrage the majority. Indignant in the aftermath, nearly everyone rallied to the Popular Fronts. The botch brought down the First Secretaries. Showing that he did not necessarily disapprove of them and their conduct, Gorbachev promoted Boriss Pugo to his inner circle in Moscow. The succeeding first secretaries in Estonia, Latvia and Lithuania were respectively Vaino Valyas, Jānis Vagris and Algirdas Brazauskas. Supposedly perestroikists, appointed by Gorbachev, they were instructed to work with the Popular Fronts.

The Popular Fronts began as ragged and improvised meetings of like-minded people. Bohemian by nature for the most part, unversed in administration, the organizers had no offices, staffs or facilities with which to compete against the party. The Latvian Popular Front newspaper *Atmoda* had an initial print run of 20,000, the Sajudis newspaper *Atgimimas* of 100,000. By 23 August 1989, the fiftieth anniversary of the Ribbentrop–Molotov Pact upon which the whole case for independence rested, the Popular Fronts were able to mobilize what must have been almost the whole of the three populations to form a chain holding hands over the hundreds of kilometres between Vilnius, Riga and Tallinn. More than a stunt, it was a folk-uprising for justice to be done, but almost pastoral in its gentleness. By processes of internal selection, the Popular Fronts chose as their presidents Dainis Ivāns, Vytautas Landsbergis and Edgar Savisaar in Latvia, Lithuania and Estonia respectively.

In general terms the Latvian Popular Front tended to follow the example of the other two. Anatolijs Gorbunovs, the chairman of the Latvian Supreme Soviet and other leading local communists, renegades so to speak, were extremely shrewd in promoting themselves by means of the Popular Front, smothering it with patronage and approval with a view to ultimate takeover.

Landsbergis and Savisaar were two of a kind, temperamentally narrow and disinclined to compromise even with friends and colleagues, almost unbearably confident in their own rectitude and sound judgement; in short, exactly suited to stand up to the Russians in a critical hour. Both men showed every sign of being willing to submit their nations to the ordeal of going down in blood under Soviet tanks.

The Popular Fronts and the party ran briefly in tandem. Brazauskas became First Secretary in Lithuania on 22 October 1988, and two days later Sajudis held its first congress in Vilnius. Addressing that congress, Brazauskas warned that the Soviets might use their military might, and he was well received. By the beginning of the New Year, this odd equilibrium was lost. The Popular Fronts set up a chain reaction. As in the Muslim republics, they forced the First Secretaries to concede the supremacy of the national language. Culture is also politics: promoting nationalism, the Popular Fronts inspired more of it. Fresh demands, especially for sovereignty, drew in more recruits and increased the nationalist power base. Popular Front strength forced the local party to take an attitude. Careerists made sure to end up on the winning side. The party split. The Popular Front was then powerful enough to take over the Government. The party became a fractious and dwindling opposition. *Quod erat demonstrandum*: it was as clean as a Euclidean proposition.

In the last analysis the weapons dealing communism its deathblows were the 1989 elections to what had been the Supreme Soviet of the Union, and then the corresponding elections to the local republican Supreme Soviets in March 1990. At both levels the novel appeal to public opinion swept reformers and the Popular Fronts to victory. It was another perfect symbol that Professor Viktor Palms, a radical and nationalist from Tartu University, defeated the chairman of the Estonian KGB, General Karl Kortelainen. In the belief that the built-in safeguards were enough to rig the results in favour of the party, Gorbachev and the centre had not anticipated that anyone else could run away with these elections. The Popular Fronts out in the Baltic republics replicated Yeltsin's challenge to Gorbachev at the centre.

The demand at the end of 1988 for sovereignty was the sole conceivable point at which Gorbachev might have interrupted the chain reaction and stabilized the Baltic question through a compromise. Distinctions between sovereignty, autonomy, confederation and independence were fluid. Untrammelled by any theory or practice of constitutional law, Gorbachev and the centre could have made up any definition or arrangement to defuse the crisis on the rise. A serious proposal for separate Baltic identity within the Soviet Union might at least have bought Gorbachev time.

Short-sightedness blossomed into indecision. Emissaries from Moscow arrived in the Baltics with opposing viewpoints. One day it was Yakovlev to make one of his cryptic interventions: 'We have let the genie out of the bottle.' Another day it was the browbeating Chebrikov, former head of the KGB. Brazauskas was summoned to a meeting in Moscow in November 1989. A special congress of the Lithuanian party was billed for early in December and Gorbachev tried to have it postponed. The congress took place, and at it the delegates voted by 855 against 160 that the party would now be quite separate from the overall Soviet party. The 160 hived themselves off as loyalists to Moscow. One of them told reporters, 'I never heard any mention that Lithuania was occupied.' Here was the party nightmare of factionalism. But Brazauskas and the majority were now able to face Sajudis as Lithuanians, not quislings.

'You have left the Communist Party of the Soviet Union,' Gorbachev was to tell Brazauskas at an embarrassing meeting of the Central Committee in Moscow on Christmas Day. 'Others will do the same. Let's think logically – what is left?' Ligachev was blunt. 'The last obstacle in the way of the separatists has been removed. What kind of perestroika is it, Comrade Brazauskas, if you announce that the main aim of your party is to set up an independent state?' It was a good question.

Gorbachev's last card was a regal tour of his own, and he arrived in Vilnius on 11 January 1990 with the Uzbek First Secretary Islam Karimov, of all people. In Gediminas Square stands the handsome neoclassical cathedral and Gorbachev was met there by 300,000 demonstrators. Among their placards was one reading, 'Gorbachev, Go Home and Take the Red Army with You.' No previous General Secretary had ever been subjected to anything of the kind. Gorbachev laid a wreath on the Lenin monument and he told the crowd, 'We have been tied together for these fifty years, whether we like it or not; moreover, we have not lived in a federation. We have lived in a unitary state with its own realities.' His attempt to appeal over the head of Sajudis to Soviet solidarity had its bravery but it was utterly misconceived. Evidently he too had never heard any mention that the Baltic republics had been occupied. The quip of a controversial journalist, Algimantas Čekuolis, caught the Lithuanian attitude: 'You cannot get a divorce unless you are married. We were never married, we were raped.'

Triumphant after the republic's election and now President of the Lithuanian Supreme Soviet, which was renamed the Supreme Council, Landsbergis on 11 March proposed a motion to declare the 'Restoration of the exercise of sovereign powers'. It was carried unanimously. The Soviet Constitution was no longer valid in Lithuania. Appointing Mrs Kazimiera Prunskienė Prime Minister, Landsbergis behaved as an unquestioned Head of State. Pernickety as only he could be, he rejected in spirit any least infringement of state sovereignty. Estonia and Latvia issued similar declarations of sovereignty, but with qualifications. The Latvian elections had not been so clear-cut. As President of the Latvian Supreme Soviet, Gorbunovs played a waiting game. It was opportunistic but the tactic in part stemmed from the presence in Riga of Colonel General Fyodor Kuzmin, commanding a Soviet army group in the Baltic, a man who made no secret of his belief that tanks were the be-all-and-end-all of politics. In all three republics the KGB formed so-called Interfronts intended to represent Russian settlers and their interests against the Popular Fronts.

Sovetskaya Rossiya was one of several Soviet newspapers to declare that a political coup had taken place in Lithuania. 'Reactionary forces have seized power with the principle aim of abolishing socialism.' Marshal Sergei Akhromeyev was openly to threaten force. The Soviet Congress of People's Deputies passed a resolution that the Lithuanian declaration of sovereignty had no validity. 'This means war!' in the words of one Russian deputy. Gorbachev said that he was 'alarmed'. He ordered KGB troops to take over buildings, including printworks, in Vilnius. There was an ultimatum: Lithuania had three days to recognize the illegality of its self-declared sovereignty. The ultimatum expired and Gorbachev then declared a blockade. This soon inflicted hardship.

Contrary to expectation, no Western government recognized the Baltic declarations of sovereignty. Protest about the blockade was a virtual formality. For almost half a century American policy had aimed to roll back Soviet imperialism and set free captured peoples. At the very moment when this guiding ideal for the first time had any chance of being realized, the Bush administration could only call for 'immediate constructive negotiations'. This hackneyed and fudging response made a mockery of Bush's subsequent claim to have won the Cold War, and it was one reason why he was not re-elected President. Landsbergis was not afraid to recognize betrayal for what it was. 'This is Munich. We feared that America might sell us.' It was his finest hour. There was about him an echo of General de Gaulle in 1940, as he held himself to represent his people. He asked whether it was possible to sell the freedom of one group of people for the freedom of another. 'If that is so, then of what value is the idea of freedom in itself?' Neither the blockade of Lithuania nor the KGB attack in January 1991 on the Vilnius television centre when fourteen people were killed, brought Landsbergis, Sajudis or the Lithuanians to their knees. But the defenceless Balts were still under the heel of the largest army ever known. The force which alone could resolve this unequal standoff was to come from an unexpected direction, in the form of the August 1991 coup.

16

THE WISH OF THE MAJORITY OF ESTONIANS

On several occasions violence was a real possibility in Estonia. 2 February is celebrated in the Estonian calendar because on that day in 1920 Lenin recognized the independence that the country had gained at the end of the First World War. On 2 February 1988 the militia used wolfhounds to attack a commemorative demonstration in Tartu. The selection of delegates to the Nineteenth Party Conference led to the next crisis, in June, when another demonstration gathered in Tallinn to protest that the delegates already chosen to go to Moscow did not represent public opinion. Karl Vaino, the First Secretary, proposed to break up this demonstration with force. Gorbachev instead dismissed him. Toompea is the hill in the centre of Tallinn at whose top is a historic medieval tower, and it also gives its name to the eighteenth-century parliament building next to it, crushed strawberry in colour. Supporters of Interfront, the Russian response to the Popular Front, crashed through the doors of parliament on 15 May 1990, and almost took it by storm. Finally, Soviet armoured columns drove into the city during the August 1991 coup.

Sovereignty was declared on 16 November 1988, and then independence on 2 February 1990, to be repeated at the end of that year. The seesaw between these national assertions on the one hand and party or Soviet violence on the other rose higher, with greater danger each time.

Someone with a claim to have triggered nationalist protest is Juhan Aare. Very much the young and thrusting media man, he introduced a television programme called *Panda* in September 1986 as part of glasnost. In Moscow the following February, he interviewed Yuri Yampol of the Fertilizer Ministry, an official who haplessly revealed plans to mine phosphates in a particularly scenic and unspoilt corner of Estonia. Here was a scoop. Estonians were to have no say in this egregious example of central planning at their expense. 'I received a lot of letters for the programme. At a press conference the Prime Minister at the time, Bruno Saul, launched a fierce attack on me for slander. Another hardliner, Rein Ristlaan, suggested opening an investigation into my background. I would probably have been arrested if I had not been able to count on the support of the Academy of Sciences and the public at large.'

Aare founded and led the Green Party. In March 1989 he was elected to the Congress of People's Deputies. In Moscow as a deputy he found that concepts like democratization and the market economy were not understood by scientists or generals, never mind the ordinary people. Well-educated as far as the system allowed, Gorbachev at least had a partial grasp of what was involved. The Baltic deputies often raised the question of independence with him. 'He used to reply to us, But when? If I concede to you, everyone will say they want independence too, it will lead to a generalized state of civil war.' Gorbachev listened and debated. Yakovlev, Aare says, could not say openly what he thought. In discussions Yakovlev explained that the Soviet Congress would never vote for Baltic independence. Another body would have to serve for that purpose, for instance, the new State Council instituted by Gorbachev. Marshal Akhromeyev at least was honest when he told Aare, 'I don't like your position, you are my enemy.' The removal of Karl Vaino in June 1988 came about when two members of the Estonian Politburo flew to Moscow to explain to Gorbachev and Ligachev how close bloodshed was. 'Some of the party leaders had been prepared in principle to send tanks out against the population. The Soviet military was on alert. It was possible that we could have had a drama like Baku or Tbilisi.'

Marju Lauristin is the daughter of the first chairman of the Council of People's Commissars in the newly sovietized Estonia of 1940, a key collaborator in Stalin's takeover of the country. He was killed soon afterwards. Her mother then married another of the handful of Estonians who had been communists before the war. But this stepfather was later sent to Siberia and her mother expelled from the party. Confusingly for someone born and brought up in the communist aristocracy, she had to think of herself as the child of 'an enemy of the people'. Tartu University was exceptional in the Soviet Union in experimenting with sociology between 1966 and 1975, and that is where she began her academic career. The Popular Front was to make her a well-known speaker and public figure. Energetic, disposing briskly of fools, she was to become a government minister after independence.

A veteran demonstrator, Marju Lauristin was present when wolfhounds were used by the militia in Tartu. 'Vaino was really hated,' she says, 'he felt the ground quaking under him.' Gorbachev looked to her like the Khrushchev of her generation. Never specific about his aims, his skill was at tightrope walking. 'He supposed we were supporting him and only became angry when he found out this was not so. We were insufficiently grateful.' As an artist discovers what is hidden in his material, she also says in a striking phrase, so

Gorbachev discovered what was hidden in history. Some sort of autonomy granted early would have slowed things down, she thinks, but not lastingly. 'We wanted IME, an acronym which stands for self-government but in Estonian is also the word for miracle. I wrote the letters on the blackboard in a seminar in Tartu University, and the audience grasped it at once.'

The Popular Front began on television. Hagi Sein (later head of Estonian television) was the anchor man of a phone-in talk show, *Let's Think It Over*. The topic on 13 April 1988 was 'How to Make Democracy'. Edgar Savisaar was to lead the discussion and he had invited Marju Lauristin to be an adviser. 'Preparing for this broadcast, we discussed whether the time was right for something more formal than spontaneous rallies and meetings. Grass-root movements were considered a type of democracy. Then and there, on the programme, Savisaar suggested the formation of something like a popular front. The phone calls to the studio were fantastic. Everyone was in agreement. It was a real public event. Those in the studio stayed to write a manifesto.

'One participant was Viktor Palms, professor of chemistry at Tartu. The next morning he arrived back in Tartu for a meeting of the so-called Heritage Society, another popular movement for restoring historical memory prohibited in the old days. Everybody was out on the streets. Everybody knows everybody else in Tartu. I remember Viktor Palms arriving, opening the car door and waving a paper, saying, I have copies of the appeal we wrote last night in the studio. He handed them out. We went into the university, and formed a Tartu support group for the Popular Front. Savisaar was doing the same in Tallinn. He favoured something hierarchical and party-like while we academics insisted on a real grass-root movement, no lists of members, no power structure. Our viewpoint prevailed. People were afraid of involvement in anything which might land them in the hands of the KGB. It was safer to belong anonymously to a movement. Anyone interested in democracy was invited to start a support group in his workplace or among friends and family. The group had to be registered with a contact person for those wishing to join.'

The Creative Unions, into which intellectuals were grouped by the party, held a meeting in Tallinn on 1 and 2 April. The first public appeal for Estonian sovereignty was formulated there, and forwarded to Gorbachev over the heads of the party. Marju Lauristin and Savisaar were speakers at the June rally protesting against the choice of delegates to the Nineteenth Party Conference. The run-up made it clear to the party leaders that inaction would turn this whole event into a mass protest against them. It was shrewd to sack Vaino at that point. But it was strange, she points out, to have been protesting and holding hands in this first demonstration of the strength of the national movement when the underlying issue was whom to send to a Moscow communist plenum.

Hardly less strange was the founding congress of the Popular Front, held that October in Tallinn. Valyas attended. A telegram of greetings was sent to Gorbachev. The contribution of the Popular Front was first to incorporate the general public into the political process and then to open opposition within the party. Western indifference to the fate of the Baltic republics was harmful, and Marju Lauristin still resents it. 'The day I arrived for my first visit to America, the *New York Times* had an editorial accusing the Balts of rocking the boat. I was furious. My friends arranged for me to meet the people there and we had an outright quarrel. They accused us of endangering Gorbachev and the whole West and one of them said, You will never have your independence.'

From the past she remembers Valyas as a 'severe ideological oppressor' who closed down her sociology department in the 1970s. As a result of losing a test of strength with Vaino, he had been posted as an ambassador in Latin America, returning home quite another person. 'As a character, he has some inner sense of religious devotion, his own code of honesty, and I think that is why he did not attempt to use force.' Arnold Rüütel, the chairman of the Supreme Soviet, kept his distance from other party leaders, playing the role of innocent patriotic leader, so to speak apolitical, while Valyas was, and remains, a communist.

Küllo Arjakas is a well-known Estonian historian of the younger generation. He worked in Moscow for the Yakovlev commission investigating the Rib-bentrop–Molotov Pact. Various models had existed for fighting the Soviet regime, he points out, guerrillas, dissidents, underground groups, religious organizations, but the Popular Front was the one producing the desired result. The national question proved to have priority over all others. Another way of putting it is that Homo sovieticus was far less a reality than they had imagined.

The party had been ambushed by Savisaar's television appearance on 13 April. Thanks to glasnost, they could no longer arrest him. Savisaar's other great moment was when the Interfront tried to storm Toompea in May 1990. Militia and troops from the Interior Ministry were there. The Interfront members prised open the main iron gates and swarmed into the inner court-yard from where they could have occupied parliament and government offices. Inside Toompea, Savisaar telephoned the radio station and kept the line open, broadcasting to everyone for help in what he called an attempted coup. In a few minutes thousands were running to Toompea, including housewives still in their slippers. At the sight of this huge crowd assembling, Interfront withdrew, down a human corridor which democratic Estonians opened up for them.

★   ★   ★

The Congress of Estonia was another mass movement which sometimes joined the Popular Front and sometimes opposed it. Lines between the two were not clear. In the end the Congress of Estonia proved to have been more in tune with public sentiment. Its policy was adopted officially and in independent Estonia its leaders have acquired more influence than Savisaar and others from the Popular Front. To the Congress of Estonia, perestroika was regarded as suspect and scarcely more than Gorbachev's rallying cry. Autonomous status within a reformed Soviet Union seemed to be its likeliest outcome but this was to be feared as another and rather more legitimate prolongation of Soviet occupation. Were the situation to change in favour of the perestroikists, a new republic might be proclaimed. That would have cast a cloak of legality over the years of Soviet occupation. The Congress of Estonia wanted to establish legal continuity between pre-war Estonia and the present. The surest protection for the future lay in exposing the Soviet invasion for what it was. Starting in February 1989, the Congress of Estonia set up citizens' committees, registering 900,000 people and then electing out of them a representative body which was nothing less than an alternative parliament.

Tunne Kelam was one of its leading lights, as he is today in the parliamentary party which has evolved out of it. He received me in his office in Toompea. He has that brand of toughness and humour common to hardened dissidents. In the old days he had been a lecturer on international affairs and a television commentator. Although he had always known about the Ribbentrop–Molotov Pact, he first saw the documents when they were published in 1968 in a Slovak cultural weekly.

He and other dissidents met in secret. In 1972 this group smuggled out to the United Nations a memorandum in English about violation of human rights, and asking for the withdrawal of Soviet troops and free elections. 'Of course we received no answer but it was played back through the Western media and I later heard from Estonian refugees that it had been vital to have this document. There had been talk only about peaceful co-existence, improving relations and disarmament. In practical terms the Baltic was considered part of the Soviet Union.'

Arrested, five of this group received prison sentences of either five or six years for 'slandering the Soviet Union'. Interrogated himself, and subjected to house searches for six months, Kelam managed to wriggle out. 'The KGB major spoke to me in sporting terms, that I had won this round, they were certain that I knew more than I had revealed but they could not nail me. I was dismissed and sent to work as nightwatchman on a chicken farm near Tallinn. I was there for ten years. It was the best place for someone like me, with plenty of free time for underground activities. I used to return from KGB headquarters in the evening, and go to a secret flat to prepare another memorandum. It was morally important that while they were investigating your past, you were preparing something new.'

The proclaimed objective of the Congress of Estonia was to convene a non-Soviet representative body of legal Estonian citizens. Political and psychological breakthrough was immediate when people realized that they did not have to be Soviet citizens but had the right to be Estonians. The elected representative body was to be temporary, co-operating with the official parliament, the Supreme Soviet. Party membership was no obstacle. 'We travelled throughout the country, creating these committees without the assistance of the press and distributing our own material. We also proceeded on the understanding that refugees living abroad continued to be Estonian citizens. Our example was followed later in Latvia and then Georgia, but it was the first example that a non-Soviet way could succeed.'

Savisaar and the Popular Front, in Kelam's opinion, were still acting through Soviet institutions. In turn, they accused the Congress of Estonia of endangering perestroika. 'This was also the message we received from the West: Gorbachev's position should not be undermined.' But the Popular Front finally joined in the Congress of Estonia elections and won about a quarter of the seats. Competition between the two popular movements was further complicated by the reaction of the Supreme Soviet, and its chairman Arnold Rüütel. 'We tried to convince Rüütel to stand as a candidate for the Congress and it appeared that he was trying to understand us,' Tunne Kelam says, 'at least he did not try to suppress us. But in March 1990, a week before the first session of the Congress, we published our first draft documents pointing out that all institutions introduced by the Soviets were basically illegal. It was a shock for Rüütel. He summoned us, and he was very angry, shouting, red-faced, claiming that we were liars who had betrayed him. We could distinguish between institutions and people, we replied, and we respected him as someone trying to do something for Estonia within a different framework. But obviously he felt insulted to be regarded as a representative of an illegal institution, a quisling.' Congress of Estonia elections were held in February 1990, and Supreme Soviet elections a month later. In almost comic confusion, people hardly knew whom or what to prefer, and several candidates were elected to both the Congress and the Supreme Soviet.

A compromise was made with Savisaar when he formed a Popular Front government after winning the Supreme Soviet elections. It did not stick. The coup in Moscow on 19 August 1991 brought a swift end to these rivalries. Occupation of the governing institutions or the television station by Russian troops would have been resisted by everyone. On the 20th, some fifteen politicians met in Tunne Kelam's office and agreed on terms for a new constitution establishing the continuity of Estonia as a state. In other republics, notably Lithuania, party leaders converted themselves into nationalists and stayed in power by adapting the high-handed methods they had always used. It is Tunne Kelam's conviction that the Congress of Estonia prevented that from happening in his country.

Arnold Rüütel has a clean-cut face, grey hair which can still be seen to have been blond, and he is an elegant dresser. I found myself sitting opposite him at a round table with perhaps thirty seats, and he addressed me as if I were an entire conference. It may have stood him in good stead that he is a man with whom you can hardly get a word in edgeways. A veterinary researcher by training, he was rector of the Estonian Agricultural Academy from 1969 to 1977. To listen to him, he was always a pragmatist and a nationalist, in the party only because it was obligatory for someone in his position. His power and influence in the final years of Estonian communism derive from the fact that as chairman of the Supreme Soviet, his signature had to be appended to all legislation. He was also a deputy in the Soviet Congress of People's Deputies.

He credits himself with a whole series of measures which progressively weakened the party. A law was proposed in January 1988 to introduce into the country OMON, the special forces of the Ministry of the Interior. The KGB had sensed the coming unrest. Until then, all laws passed in the Supreme Soviet of the Soviet Union had to be passed in identical form in the republics. With pride Rüütel says, 'They categorically demanded that I pass this law but I refused.' And so when Karl Vaino approved the use of the militia with their dogs in February 1988, he could not fall back on OMON troops. Similarly he legalized the national flag; and the sovereignty declaration of 16 November 1988, one clause of which specified that raw materials and natural resources were the property of the nation; as well as giving Estonian law priority over Soviet law. 'In January 1989 we forbade the activity of the Communist Party in all juridical bodies, and in the KGB and the militia. The party still existed but it was forbidden to operate through ministries or government bodies. This meant that the party could no longer dictate to the Presidium or the Council of Ministers.'

As a communist, I interject, he was working then to destroy the base of the party's power. Was he therefore more responsible than Savisaar or anyone else for the collapse of communism?

By way of a reply Rüütel gave me a short lecture on the history of the Estonian party. For the declaration of independence on 2 February 1990, he says, a meeting of 4500 delegates from all levels had been prepared in secrecy six months beforehand. 'To discuss such matters, we avoided offices and went outside. Ulo Nugis, the speaker of the Supreme Soviet, helped these preparations but Savisaar neither participated nor knew about them. When we convened the heads of the regional government to prepare for 2 February, Moscow did not know how to react. In the old days the Presidium or even the Supreme Soviet could have been exterminated but in the present-day world it is not so easy to wipe out 4500 legal delegates.'

Meetings and demonstrations did not destroy the party. The party was paralysed through deliberate foiling of its activities, and that was Rüütel's task. He paints a picture of himself taking the brunt of official Soviet criticism. After the first declaration of sovereignty on 16 November 1988, for instance, he had to defend himself for four hours and twenty-five minutes to the Soviet Presidium. He was ordered to apologize to the entire Supreme Soviet. 'They banged their fists on the table. Of course I already saw myself in the Lubyanka.' On the day when the vote on the Yakovlev commission failed to pass, he saw Gorbachev five or six times, finally at midnight persuading him to put it to the vote the next day.

'At Presidium and other joint meetings, Gorbachev attacked me viciously. But when we discussed privately, he was quite reasonable – at least he understood what was happening although he never said outright that he approved of what we were striving for. As a personality, he was able to make contact with all sorts of different people and perhaps this was the trait which prevented him from resorting to force in the complicated situation that he was in.'

The climax of Rüütel's relationship with Gorbachev came on 12 June 1990. 'The idea was to join the three Baltic republics in the struggle against the centre. Although we had applied to be received as a joint Baltic delegation, neither Moscow nor Gorbachev agreed. At midday on the previous day I telephoned Landsbergis and Gorbunovs to set up this meeting and at last we got Gorbachev's agreement to a State Council meeting with him, Ryzhkov and Yakovlev. At this meeting each of us presented his case why our state should finally be independent and how it should settle its future with the Soviet Union. When Gorbachev gave me the floor, I said that Estonia and the Soviet Union had to be on terms of equality. Since we had never agreed to enter the Soviet Union in the first place, we could not secede but only return to the status quo. Once this State Council was over, we returned to Gorbachev to emphasize that our country had been occupied. Yes, he said, he had heard us, but if he were to consent to that point of view he would be under pressure from revolutionaries from every other republic.'

Eyes with a twinkle in them make Vaino Valyas a slightly impish figure. He likes to say that he was born on the island of Hiiumaa and can trace seven generations of his family through the church records there. He learned to sail a ship and to fish before he knew the alphabet. Most of the inhabitants of Hiiumaa fled from the Soviets in 1944, and it is said of Valyas that he too would have fled if his mother had not sent him on an errand at the time. At the end of this interview, coming down the steps of the apartment house where he lives in Tallinn, he quoted a long-ago remark of Johannes Käbin who had been Estonian First Secretary for a quarter of a century: 'Valyas, the only thing you can do well is to fish.'

Through the Komsomol, he had known Gorbachev and Shevardnadze since 1956. They could talk with mutual confidence and trust. Soviet ambassador in Venezuela, he had been posted to Nicaragua in 1986. At one reception in his Embassy, Graham Greene was presented with the highest Sandinista decoration and made a grateful speech in praise of Moscow's policies.

Valyas's predecessor, Karl Vaino, subordinated Estonian interests to Moscow. The police action in February 1988 was a pretext to appoint in his stead a perestroikist. Straight from a vacation in the tropics, Vaino Valyas had returned to Estonia on 13 June 1988 to discover that Gorbachev was summoning him urgently. From Moscow airport he was taken the next day directly to Gorbachev, with no idea why. Their talk lasted three hours. 'Gorbachev said that he wanted me to accept the post of Estonian First Secretary. I had been absent for eight years and was not familiar with the situation. Refusing at first, I said that I would return to Estonia and if the party Central Committee then approved my appointment, I would accept. I put the precondition that I had to be the ultimate maker of policy. There was no objection.'

The cause of Estonian national independence, Valyas realized, had been clearly expressed at the conference of the Creative Unions that April. The political will of the Estonian people was embodied in the Popular Front and that was 'overriding'. That September he organized a plenary session of the Central Committee in which members of the Popular Front participated and he quotes a sentence from a report of that session: 'Taking into consideration the wish of the majority of Estonians we see that the future lies in the independence of the Estonian nation.'

You were First Secretary of a party perceived as an obstacle to independence.

'Of course. It was hard. The support of the huge majority for independence obliged us to align with the Popular Front, not against it. The question was not the destruction of the Communist Party but how to change its face, its activity, its ideology. Hardliners did not agree with this analysis. They wanted to suppress the Popular Front and restore the old order. We had battles in the most serious sense of the word. There could be no compromise. The result was a formal split. At the Twentieth Congress of the party, at the beginning of February 1990, the pro-Soviet faction split away. A unique situation arose whereby we had two Communist Parties, and in the Politburo there were two First Secretaries. It was analogous to the split in the Lithuanian party in December 1989. Brazauskas and I came into office as First Secretaries at more or less the same moment, in the same way, for the same ends.

'The mildest expressions used about me by hardliners were traitor, restorer of capitalism, dissolver of the Soviet Union. This battle was quite as intense in Moscow itself. If we had not had confidential relations with Gorbachev, Shevardnadze, Yakovlev and others, they would have ground us to powder. We could not rely on the army or the KGB, which was informing Moscow in the blackest colours of the events here. The Popular Fronts were not a construct of Moscow's foreign policy, but penetration of them by the KGB is something else, quite natural, an operational matter. The Congress of Estonia radicalized politics through insisting on Estonian continuity since 1938. The Popular Front had the opinion that fifty years had passed and this meant a transition period. We were that faction in the party which took the risk of throwing in our lot with the Popular Front and the people.'

Your old Komsomol friend must have said, Stop! to the more and more insistent declarations of sovereignty.

'Naturally. I had a number of talks with Gorbachev in Moscow. Rüütel and I had to stand together in the Presidium of the Supreme Soviet, listen and take it. I had a repeat performance in front of the Politburo and I do not recommend the experience. If subjective considerations can be allowed, then I would say that Gorbachev's humanist attitude was helpful. He didn't threaten force directly but I think he hinted at it, if you read between the lines. In passing judgement on Gorbachev, never forget that if I had my hardliners, he had his, and he was always fighting them.'

What do you suppose Gorbachev makes of it today?

'Not what he did in 1985 and 1986. He is a child of his times too. He wanted a more efficient Soviet Union but finished with no Soviet Union at all. That is his tragedy.'

17

'YOU HAVE KILLED SOVIET LATVIA'

With headquarters in Riga, General Kuzmin had something in the order of 150,000 troops under his command in the Baltic. In the course of half a century of occupation, the Red Army had acquired hundreds of barracks and installations, including airfields and ports. The most sophisticated space monitoring station is at Skrunda. Large-scale military housing drew many officers of all ranks, as well as career soldiers, to retire in Latvia. The republic was more russianized than any other. In Bolshevik lore, Latvian riflemen played a decisive part in 1917. Within a short walk of the cathedral in Riga is a statue in dark red granite of these riflemen, as gigantic and indestructible as it is embarrassing.

The Latvian Supreme Soviet declared sovereignty on 28 July 1989. Full independence was visibly the next goal. In response the Central Committee in Moscow put out its heavy-handed warning on 26 August, calling into question the very viability of the three Baltic republics if they continued on their course. Boriss Pugo, already Gorbachev's adviser, opposed Latvian independence. So did Alfrēds Rubiks, head of the Riga party and a local Ligachev, trying to incite the Popular Front to go too far. Co-ordinated with the attack on Toompea in Tallinn on 15 May 1990, Soviet army officers and cadets in Riga mounted their demonstration of Soviet loyalty. That September bombs exploded in various Soviet bases. An atmosphere of provocation and counter-provocation remained murky to the end. Paratroopers under General Kuzmin seized the Riga Press House and other buildings on 2 January 1991, and a number of people were injured in scuffles. A few days later, Soviet special forces attacked the Vilnius television centre. Fourteen people were killed. During the August 1991 coup, Kuzmin declared himself the supreme authority and sent out the tanks, threatening to arrest the Latvian leaders. Random shooting broke out in which there were several casualties – the various accounts have discrepancies. Latvians point out buildings in Riga whose façades are pocked with bullet-marks. In the fashionable Ridzene Hotel the marble staircase was chipped and holes have been left as reminders.

Edvards Berklavs interpreted the Central Committee's warning as a psychological preparation for the violent repression of the democratic movement. The grand old man of Latvian politics, he has a pugnacity and stubbornness bred first from communism, and then from resistance to it. Educated in the Stalinist era at the Party School in Moscow, he was hand-picked to be a future First Secretary. But by the time he had graduated, he says, he had realized that the party's ends were criminal and not political. Either he had to resign, which was the equivalent of despatching himself to Siberia, or use his position to stop occupation and russification. He chose the latter course.

Nationalist uprisings in the DDR and Hungary had alarmed Khrushchev and in 1959 he decided to stamp out Latvian nationalism of the Berklavs variety. About 1000 people were deported and many more purged from the party. For nine years Berklavs was in exile in Vladimir, with a job hiring out movies. He and Khrushchev had been friends. Whenever he appealed to be allowed to return home, Khrushchev's reply was that if Berklavs did not make a full confession of his mistakes he would be swept away. Still sometimes referred to as the Latvian Dubček, he admits that for a long time he thought socialism could have a human face. But after exile he had no party career and no illusions either.

'While Gorbachev was claiming democratization and glasnost, I was being called once a fortnight to the KGB in Riga, and so were all my friends from the 1950s. Our offices and apartments were searched. Pugo was responsible as head of the KGB. I knew his father better than him. If there can be such a thing as an honest communist, it was Pugo's father. I cannot say the same about the son.'

The Latvian National Independence Movement, the LNIM, was to Latvia what the Congress of Estonia was to that country. Berklavs was one of its three founders. On 10 July 1988 4000 supporters met in a park and adopted a programme in favour of Latvian democracy. Within six months, the movement had spread across the country. 'In obedience to glasnost, the party took its directions from Moscow and could not resort to outright violence. So they could not find any legal means to close us down.' Nevertheless he accuses Gorbunovs, then a member of the Latvian Politburo as well as chairman of the Supreme Soviet, of doing whatever he could against the movement, for the purpose of keeping Latvia within the Soviet Union.

'The Popular Front was founded in the autumn, soon after the LNIM. I was a member of the Popular Front, on its board. We were against the party, they had the support of the party. That was the great difference. The Popular Front was organized by Jānis Peters, at that time a member of the Central Committee, and Jānis Škapars, an active communist and editor-in-chief of a newspaper. Peters recommended Dainis Ivāns as first chairman, but he was a communist too. It was a trick to incorporate protest. I have just been checking up how Gorbunovs and these others were saying up until 1992 that we should not quit the Soviet Union. They were for the transformation of the Soviet Union into the Commonwealth of Independent States. We were in the Popular Front in order to prevent the party from taking it over completely but we did not succeed in writing into the programme that Latvia had to be out of the Soviet Union at the first possible moment. The Popular Fronts were organized in all the Baltic countries at the same period from Moscow, just as in 1940 all three were occupied simultaneously. Gorbachev promulgated glasnost, and the leaders in the republics jumped to it. But in essentials nothing changed. The army remained, the colonists and the kolkhoes. Democracy and the market economy was only talk.'

Gorbachev, in his view, never envisaged radical change. After the 1989 elections, the Baltic symbolized the launching point for democratic forces in Russia towards independence. Events then moved faster than Gorbachev intended. 'The ideology of the whole system proved a complete failure, that was the root of it. Thanks to that ideology, nobody was prepared to work, corruption spread. Institutionalized corruption destroyed the workers and the intelligentsia alike. To re-establish the human element will take years. Loss of self-confidence is the worst of the legacy.'

Mavriks Vulfsons has seen it all. When I asked him about his flight to the Soviet Union as the Nazis invaded Riga in 1941, he raised his eyebrows. 'I retreated. I had a rifle in my hands.' For nearly fifty years he was in the party, a self-described fanatic, by profession a journalist and commentator. He had joined Berklavs in 1959 in making a stand against russification and in favour of communism with a human face. Euro-Communism in France and Italy had influenced him. What was missing was some formula capable of restoring full independence. This emerged after the more-or-less free election. Part of the Russian population even voted for the Popular Front.

In two speeches Vulfsons made his mark on events. Seven hundred members of the Creative Unions met on 1 June 1988 in the Congress Hall in Riga, with among them Pugo and Gorbunovs and others from the Politburo. He had studied the documents of the Ribbentrop–Molotov Pact, including the secret protocols. 'I decided to speak out,' he says. The Soviets had not liberated the Baltic countries but occupied them. Nobody had dared say such a thing before. In the uproar afterwards, Pugo called him over and said, 'You have killed Soviet Latvia.' The next day the speech was published.

Appointed a member of the Yakovlev commission on the Pact, Vulfsons was called to speak in the Supreme Soviet on the day when the commission's findings were voted down. He repeated that occupation was not liberation.

Anatoly Lukyanov, the Speaker, asked him to leave the tribunal; Gorbachev recalled him. This speech influenced many deputies to change their opinion when the vote was taken again the following morning.

A young and successful artist, Sandra Kalniete was in at the start of the Popular Front. Her parents had spent fifteen years deported in Siberia, where she had been born. Independence became a cause which swept aside her previous conviction that nothing but evil came from politics.

The true beginning for the national liberation movement, she agrees, was the meeting of the Creative Unions on 1 June at which Vulfsons had spoken. Someone had written a memorandum that a Popular Front should be started. She asked the delegate reading aloud this memorandum to clarify it but he could not do so. 'At a party plenum they spoke about restoring order militarily. That was when we realized that we needed the Popular Front. Nobody knew exactly how to form it. We looked at the Estonian example. The two problems were how to explain what this was, and the lack of a leader. We turned to one of the most respected Latvians, Jānis Peters. Long and confidential negotiations took place between only six people, of whom I was one. Jānis Peters hesitated because he was a member of the Central Committee. Our movement's future was unpredictable. I believe he was pressured into nego- tiating by the liberal faction of the Central Committee, with Gorbunovs among them.'

The founding congress was in October 1988, in the building of the Artists' Union. Sandra Kalniete arranged for offices there, legalizing the movement, drawing up membership lists and fund-raising. 'Only later, when I look back, did I realize that we had worked under close supervision of the KGB and the Central Committee, but they were too arrogant to realize the true power of the people. A month before the founding congress they had signs that the movement would not be easily controlled, and so they started their Interfront, or Intermovement. We set a deadline for registration, as we had to know how many people would be represented at the congress. Three days before that deadline, a hundred telegrams arrived to confirm that support groups of the Popular Front had been established in all military districts and in the fleet and so on. But they were too late to receive instructions. A little earlier, and they would have been represented at the founding congress and could have smashed it to bits.'

What if you had all been arrested at that point?

'Maybe it would have stopped us for a while. But look at Ukraine. I took part in the first public meeting in Kiev, there were 3000 people and the Popular Front there, Rukh, was prohibited. It was only a matter of time, and probably of victims. We realized what we were facing. The night after the founding congress, I had gone to sleep totally exhausted. I suddenly woke up trembling at the thought of what we had launched. There was no way back for me or the others.'

Led by Rubiks, the hardliners worked from March 1989 to prepare another repression on the lines of 1959. Party officials from Vagris downwards were to be purged. The Ideological Secretary, Ivars Kezbers, had even written his letter of resignation. The Popular Front received the message that a large demonstration should be mounted in order to bolster and protect those destined to be purged. 'We arranged a truly impressive mass gathering for 12 March. We were prepared for the worst. I wrote instructions that people had to stay together in groups of fifteen, familiar with one another, in order to avoid provocation. We even managed to have it broadcast that nobody should shout slogans or do anything the party could exploit. I really admire how the Latvian people did it. Not a single casualty. When it was over, I addressed the crowd to say thank you and tell those to my right to go home one way and those to my left the other way. In twenty minutes they were all gone. High discipline like that was a threat to the party.'

As First Secretary, Pugo reacted calmly, never agreeing to proposals for force. His successor Vagris was the right person at the right time, proclaiming, 'We must take strong measures', but then not doing so. An explicitly liberal First Secretary would have pushed the hardliners to act against him and the Popular Front. Backed by Gorbachev, Vagris 'wriggled through the plenums'. Kezbers was the type of liberal who might have upset the balance between the unstated alliances and expediencies. As for Gorbunovs, his election as chairman of the Supreme Soviet had no significance at the time; it seemed like going into exile. 'Once reforms took place, he saw how to fill the post with new powers. A really successful man, with a true sense of how to act and retain power. He never let himself be associated with anything damaging, never made a step that could compromise him but always appeared to take credit when things had been decided appropriately. When our victory was inevitable, he turned to us, and saw that the law on the elections was adopted with all the Popular Front amendments except for limitation on voting rights for the Soviet army.'

Drawing the liberal wing of the party over to it, the Popular Front had hit upon the tactic to split it once and for all. Victory in the March 1990 elections legitimized the national movement and returned a representative parliament. The rest, as Sandra Kalniete says, was a formality. But Gorbunovs and like-minded colleagues had the last laugh. Their political skills were far superior. Relabelling themselves nationalists, democrats, free-marketeers and anything else, they in turn divided the Popular Front, made it redundant and kept a hold on power much as before.

Not quite three weeks after Latvia declared independence on 4 May 1990, Jānis Jurkāns became Foreign Minister, holding the post until October 1992. He had been the Popular Front specialist on foreign affairs. In his earlier career as a lecturer in English literature, he published a book on James Joyce.

Going further than Sandra Kalniete, Jurkāns says that the Popular Front was successful because it had been started by the party and the KGB. 'They knew the truth, that the state called the Soviet Union was going down the drain. They decided to open the door and let fresh air into the room, never realizing that this would cause a draught to blow the whole house down. They granted freedom to tell the truth, which was the main thing, and they were smart enough to push forward innocent people, themselves staying behind the scenes. Their representatives were in our midst. They created the instrument that destroyed them. It may be unusual but it revealed that they realized the truth about the situation and about themselves. We expected force. They did not use it because we had lots of sympathizers inside the Soviet Union. By the time the army saw that something had gone wrong, we had become contagious to our people and to theirs.'

The declaration of independence was drafted by lawyers in Latvia or overseas, after the Estonian example. That was not the point of no return, however. The declaration was a provocation. Gorbachev did not recognize it as such. First he was evidently dependent on the West where Latvia enjoyed sympathy too, and then he no longer had a local power base. He could not risk using force brutal enough to destroy the state-building process. 'From Yakovlev and Shevardnadze we could feel that we would obtain everything we wanted.'

Wide-eyed and curly-haired, in jeans and a sweater, Dainis Ivāns looks the perpetual student. A journalist, he and a colleague Artūrs Snips published an article in 1986 to object to the building of a hydroelectric dam on the River Daugava. In mythology, literature and art, he says, the Daugava is held to be the mother of the Latvian nation. 'This article pushed the right buttons at the right time.' Thousands of letters supporting the authors reached the Central Committee. Eighteen months later, the project for the dam was abandoned. Out of the ecological protest grew the nationalist movement. Condemned by the local party, Ivāns managed to publish in Moscow. In hands like his, glasnost was a loophole. To call for openness only to repress it made no sense.

'On 7 October 1989 the first really free demonstration in Latvia since the war was held in Meza Park. It was shown on television. In practice that was the day we felt we were free. It was like a holiday. I had written my speech that morning, it was an essay about Latvia and the power of its spirit. I spoke mainly in metaphors but I think that speech was the main reason why at the founding congress over the next two days I was elected president of the Popular Front.

'The idea came from Edgar Savisaar. He became a personal friend. It was his idea to organize legally and to support perestroika as a means to liberate our nations. This was the parliamentary step-by-step route to independence. At the foundation of the Popular Front we decided to participate in the elections for the Soviet and so destroy the system from within. Russians, Ukrainians, Moldavians, the people from the Transcaucasus, came to learn from our experience. Lawyers from our Popular Front went to Georgia to help them draft their programmes. I remember how in one meeting of the Congress of People's Deputies, Gorbachev said that the Baltic countries are an infection, exporting revolution. He was right.'

Although the Latvian Central Committee had formal power, its secretiveness worked against it. Openness gave the Popular Front practical power. People could listen and participate. The elimination of one individual from a collective leadership was pointless. 'During our telephone conversations we would stop to address the KGB, saying, Colonel, please listen to our plans. It paralysed the KGB that a few minutes after such a call between ourselves, we would appear in public and say the same things aloud. They could obtain no hold on us. A former KGB officer told me that their attitude was that I should be tolerated in case somebody more extreme were to replace me.'

The Swedish Social Democrats laid on a course about the organization of elections. Latvian émigrés donated cars and minibuses and computers. *Atmoda's* circulation rose after the founding congress to 100,000. It was paradoxical that the Popular Front candidates intended to destroy the Congress of People's Deputies to which they were striving so hard to be elected.

Before that Congress's first session Ivāns had a preliminary run-in with Gorbachev in an antechamber of the building. The Latvian delegation was proposing to ask Congress to stand in silence for one minute to honour those recently killed by the army in Tbilisi. Dainis Ivāns spoke out, only to be snubbed by Gorbachev, who replied that there was more serious business. When proceedings began, a member of the delegation, Vilen Tolpeznikov, a Russian from Latvia, took advantage of a brief pause to step to the tribune and propose a minute of commemorative silence. 'You should have seen the faces of the Politburo,' Ivāns recalled. 'All had to stand. It was the moment when first the democrats turned and started to destroy the planned Congress of People's Deputies.'

The first serious session with Gorbachev was on 14 March 1990. Three days earlier Landsbergis and Sajudis, winners in their republic's elections, had passed the Lithuanian declaration of independence. The Latvian elections were due on 18 March and Ivāns, accompanied by Gorbunovs, was to explain to Gorbachev the Latvian hope for a state. The Latvian declaration of independence was in fact passed shortly afterwards on 4 May. 'Gorbachev replied that people preferred to live in the Soviet Union and that we were negative politicians. I think he really believed it. He refused to listen to us, he raised his voice and did not permit others to speak. You see what is happening in Lithuania, he continued, and if you too announce independence – he used very vulgar expressions – we will block all the Latvian holes too. Russian regions would separate and organize their autonomy for themselves, and in my opinion he had already prepared for this sort of countermeasure. You will discover that Latvia is very small and powerless to deal with the free choice of your Russian inhabitants, he went on, because you are not democrats and ignore Russian interests and so on.'

'We did not mention Yeltsin but Gorbachev for some reason did, saying that he himself intended a peaceful resolution but if Yeltsin were to obtain power he would break our necks. It was the opposite of the truth. Yakovlev was present and wanted to soften the approach, I believe. Ryzhkov, also present, used a nice Russian expression that he could harpoon Lithuania. As a journalist I was interested to have the opportunity eventually to compare the language of Gorbachev and Yeltsin. Gorbachev's language was bureaucratic, Soviet, with phrases which had no content but consisted merely of verbalization. Yeltsin managed the language with meaning, free from Gorbachev's vulgarity and artifice.'

During these official proceedings, Ivāns and the Latvian delegation had been sitting opposite Gorbachev. Gorbachev said finally to him, 'I know all about your activities including what you have been doing in Western countries. You are a young man with the opportunity to make a good career but I don't like your way, you are choosing the wrong way.' Ivāns had indeed been abroad and given interviews to foreign correspondents but still it took him by surprise to be threatened personally. He also could not help noticing how short Gorbachev was, a head smaller than himself.

In effect Gorbachev was saying that the Latvians had a simple choice, to be with or against the Soviet Union. Violence seemed to be in preparation during the course of 1990. The Russian element of the population was being put up to demonstrate against the nationalist governments. 'We asked Gorbachev what it signified. You see the result of mistaken legislation, was his reply, that Latvian people are against you.' Gorbachev had real economic and military power, but in practice he could not influence Latvians in any legal way. The legislature and the judiciary were in the hands of the nationalist government. A rival system to the communists had developed.

OMON, the special forces at Gorbachev's disposal, staged a series of armed assaults. On 12 January Gorbunovs and Ivars Godmanis, the Prime Minister, met Gorbachev in Moscow and raised the question of OMON. As far as he knew, Gorbachev said, there was no cause for anxiety. At about eleven at night on the 13th, Gorbunovs and Godmanis returned to Riga where the Presidium of the Latvian Supreme Council was awaiting them. They reported what Gorbachev had said, as well as similar protestations of innocence from Pugo and Kryuchkov.

'I was then Gorbunovs' first deputy. My colleagues and I told him we had no confidence in Gorbachev, we believed that a Soviet attack on parliament or the Government was imminent, and we needed to organize resistance. We agreed to disagree. I went home to sleep and around midnight a colleague telephoned me to inform me that shooting had started outside the parliament in Vilnius. I called my colleagues of the Supreme Council and they were listening to the radio announcement of Soviet aggressions. It was not possible to call Gorbunovs or Godmanis, but around 3 a.m. we resolved to go to parliament and appeal to people to rally there. At 4.15 a.m. I spoke on the radio.

'Half an hour later people started to arrive, by 8 a.m. Doma Square was full. I spoke in Latvian and Russian on the radio and on television. At eleven o'clock we had a meeting of the Presidium and members of the Government. Gorbunovs came at midday, and the reason for his absence until then remains obscure. I still cannot comment on it.

'I had contacts with Western correspondents and a practically continuous open line to Radio Free Europe. Some of my colleagues called Yeltsin and woke him up in the middle of the night. We also called Pugo but he did not answer. A few days earlier I had received a decree from the Supreme Council that I was to represent the Latvian government in the West, and if necessary form a government-in-exile. I had Swedish and Finnish visas. About 270,000 people collected to demonstrate between one and two o'clock down by the Daugava and some deputies organized building barricades round Riga. Then I left for Tallinn.' To rally support, Ivāns went to Stockholm, Washington and Montreal, and finally to a meeting of émigrés in Hanover. He singles out James Baker and Robert Gates, a senior CIA official who had become deputy National Security Adviser, for their positive attitudes. It is his impression that in the White House those who had no faith in Gorbachev at this moment acquired the upper hand over those who supported him.

After the high drama of that January, the coup six months later appeared almost an anticlimax. Still, while he was chairing a meeting to discuss the text of yet another declaration emphasizing independence, the sound of equipment rumbling into Doma Square could be heard. OMON troops fired tear gas and bursts of automatic fire into the air. Ivāns went to General Kuzmin to demand the withdrawal of these troops. By the evening they were gone. The monument to Lenin was then demolished.

Ivars Kezbers was the last Ideological Secretary of the Latvian party. Between the March 1990 election and the declaration of independence on 4 May, the party split – at a stormy congress on 7 May, to be precise. Rubiks the hardliner took over and purged his predecessor Vagris, as well as Kezbers. In theory, the Ideological Secretary should have provided Marxist justification for retaining power in the name of the proletariat. Lively and English-speaking, Kezbers depicts himself as one of the younger perestroikists, well-informed, too modern for primitive methods. He is now a businessman in Riga.

Originally a protégé of Pugo's, Kezbers was seconded in 1987 to Moscow, to be deputy Minister of Television and Radio. His office was at the Ostankino broadcasting centre, with other branches in Berlin and Havana. He had responsibility for all Soviet programmes sponsored abroad, as well as for jamming Western radio stations. Glasnost put an end to that. He reported directly to Yakovlev. Along with others like Valentin Falin and Vitali Korotich, the editor of the magazine *Ogonyok*, he was also in the Ligachev entourage. He received material monitored from all over the world as well as classified information, though not from KGB tapping of telephones. Every morning his first task was to prepare an analysis of news for Gorbachev, Shevardnadze and Yakovlev.

Gorbachev paid close attention to radio and television, and on a personal line used to ring up Kezbers four or five times a month. Prepared to accept critical comment of his own speeches or policies, he lost his temper over personal issues. The least criticism of Raisa infuriated him. After a report that she had telephoned Yeltsin to ask for the streets of Moscow to be cleaned for a VIP visit, for instance, Gorbachev got on the line to complain to Yeltsin about the city's dirtiness.

Gorbachev realized that democratic countries functioned better, Kezbers says. 'We understood that we had lost the fight. The question was how to retreat. That was difficult. It concerned our personal fates. Frank discussion of reversing policy brought us face to face with the KGB and the army, the state within the state. In the autumn of 1987 we discussed thoroughly a confederation along the lines of the British Commonwealth. The collapse of Eastern Europe was no surprise. I began to have very considerable doubts about what sort of future we could have, and how to operate in that future. In villages a thousand kilometres from Moscow they had probably never heard

171

of Gorbachev. That was one reason why I came to think that reform of communism was not possible.'

When Pugo was summoned to Moscow by Gorbachev, he sent Kezbers back to be one of four men trying to hold Latvia together. The others were the new First Secretary, Jānis Vagris, the chairman of the Supreme Soviet, Anatolijs Gorbunovs, and the Prime Minister Vilnis Bresis.

'The situation was terrible. We knew that the Baltic countries would be free but we had anticipated that it would take ten years. We could not call on the KGB or the army, we had only a few activists and the remains of a party structure to help us. We used to sit together and drink coffee and a little vodka, and try to plan our work. Vagris would say frankly that he was old and not too bright, but would stay first secretary for a few years. Anatolijs, he said to Gorunovs, you will be President – which in those days had no real function. Bresis, you are Prime Minister, and Ivars, you are Chief of Staff, you organize the programme. That's how I came to be Ideological Secretary. Let me repeat that from the first day the four of us knew that we would be losers.

'We participated in the process known as the Popular Front. Many of their prominent personalities discussed their plans with me though they may not tell you that now. They came to me in Moscow and asked me to find out what Gorbachev and Yakovlev were thinking. I received the answer from Yakovlev that he had discussed the matter with Gorbachev and confirmed that the Popular Fronts could proceed. Gorbachev thought that this would lead to a version of the DDR or Czechoslovakia where the party had enrolled half a dozen tame factions or organizations. Anyway, Vagris, Gorbunovs, Bresis and I authorized the Popular Front. I was elected a delegate to the Popular Front organizational congress. Only I sat in the twentieth row in the hall, you understand. After that organizational meeting, we realized that the Popular Front was a real force with which we should co-ordinate our activities. It was only according to the normal procedures of politics that after two or three months the organizers of the Popular Front began to fight us. This was a mistake. Together we would have made more progress.

'We tried to hold the ground between the army with its large concentrations including special units, and the Popular Front. We began and ended our working day with the slogan "No bloodshed in Latvia". Vagris left it to me to decide what was to be done with information from the KGB that some particular person in the inner circle of the Popular Front was actually working for the KGB. They infiltrated and operated more or less effectively. They could control organizations or factions, but not the whole people. Gorbachev and his advisers had not perceived that they were ruling people quite different from what they had been before. After glasnost, it was another country.'

Did the Soviet army want to use force?

'*Yes, yes!* I worked together with the two commanders, Generals Kuzmin and Grishin. We had no private contacts, only official and political discussions. Our telephone calls were maybe twice a day, two angry dogs barking at one another. Many officers whom I knew personally here had been trained to attack Scandinavia. They could have surrounded the Danish Royal Palace in Copenhagen but had no idea where to find Gorbunovs in Riga. A week or two before the August coup Kuzmin asked Moscow to send howitzers to the Baltic as if he was intending to strike out for Paris.'

Could the army have stopped the declaration of independence?

'Vagris, Gorbunovs, Bresis, we all supported it. Rubiks was against it, he considered Gorbachev a traitor and he had the army with him, and half the KGB, the internal forces and the party. I think he also had Pugo's support. In December 1990 in Moscow we had multi-level talks about the Baltic future. Gorbachev said to us, Yes, you will be free, but through economic and other ties you will stay with the Soviet Union on the same status as Russia. He tried to find people to stand against Rubiks here. The climax came on 2 April at a very tough Politburo meeting in Moscow. Gorbunovs was ill so Vagris and I had gone together. I understood that this would be my last trip to Moscow as the situation was so difficult. We went by army plane, we wondered if this was to be the Dubček treatment. A one-way trip. I proposed to Gorbachev that both Rubiks and I should be sent out of Latvia, but he did not agree. Five days later Rubiks was elected First Secretary and I and about 300 liberal communists were thrown out of the party.

'Personally I think that Gorbachev knew about the decision to use force in January 1991. He believed it was necessary to accept limited bloodshed in Vilnius and Riga in order to demonstrate what a real occupation might be like, and what was a true balance of forces. It was a mistake to think that tough measures could be used to support reform. They planned to surround the Ministry of Internal Affairs, to show that our freedom was nothing more than a sheet of paper. The situation went out of control. The nine-man detachment of Alpha Delta operating here had come from Moscow as *provocateurs*. They shot some people. They had precise instructions and they carried them out.

'Gorbachev is a clever and interesting person with his own way of thinking, and his place in history is fixed, but he was surrounded with second- or third-grade advisers. He repeated his mistake in August. He knew the scenario at large, he wanted his colleagues to reveal themselves at that moment, but it slipped out of his control.'

★   ★   ★

On a visit to Latvia in 1988 Gorbachev had inspected the Ādaži kolkhoz. Its chairman Alberts Kauls is a genial red-faced man, always bustling in the style of Soviet managers. Gorbachev seems to have had plans for him as would-be First Secretary, thus killing with one stone two very different birds, Vagris and the die-hard Rubiks. Searching in 1990 for a way to bypass Yeltsin and the Congress of the People's Deputies, Gorbachev set up a Presidential Council. Empowered neither to advise nor to legislate, this body was a typical Soviet improvization to test out where strength lay. Kauls was a member. He liked Gorbachev's charm and sincerity and makes a good defence: 'Nobody had any proposals for doing differently what he did.'

The Presidential Council met once a week in the Kremlin and Kauls flew in for it. 'We had a family feeling.' Gorbachev set the agenda and took the decisions, which were really *ukase* about how to invent a market economy. It would not be right, in Kauls's opinion, to say that Gorbachev was demoralized by developments. But he had probably taken the decision to attack in Riga and Vilnius as early as November 1990, by way of showing how dangerous the old regime was. It was a repeat of Gorbachev's Tbilisi tactics. 'Not very many people realized what sort of theatre this was, but it had the effect of mobilizing the whole nation. Hardliners had to give way. That was the monster's way of creating independence. Without some step of this kind on Gorbachev's part – given the Soviet military presence – Latvia would never have been free.'

Jānis Vagris succeeded Pugo as First Secretary on 4 October 1988. It was bad luck that a demonstration 100,000 strong took place in the centre of Riga just a fortnight later. The crowds started to chant for Vagris. Appearing at the microphone, he uttered just two sentences: 'I must say that I did not do harm to the Latvian nation. I will not do so in the future.' No communist First Secretary anywhere can ever have expressed himself so apologetically.

In 1940 Vagris was ten, a child of poor and landless peasants. The Soviets gave them land, although immediately collectivizing it. 'From my own experience,' he says, 'I considered the official version of events true. It is too strong to say that we were deceived but there was a lack of information.' Vulfsons's speech in June 1988 had shocked him. Vulfsons and Berklavs had been together in the Latvian division of the Red Army and he remembers how after that speech Berklavs had joked, 'Now I don't understand if I am an occupant or not.

'Hardliners immediately advocated the use of force. That is true. They did not say so openly at mass gatherings but in the Central Committee they argued for it. The First Secretary, the chairman of the Supreme Soviet and the Prime Minister had the duty to prevent the Central Committee from

accepting the hardliners' course and deploying force. The local army commanders were standing by for orders from the Central Committee. From
Kuzmin downwards, the generals were in favour of using force and they
insisted that if such an order arrived, they would obey it. None of us wanted
to be the official initiator of such a command. The whole time we were
pressured and harried into using force by the hardliners and by Interfront.'
Alfrēds Rubiks was a member of the Central Committee like any other but
in plenums he was the one to express the hardline position. Those who shared
his convictions were Russian settlers who had become factory directors and
the like. The greatest pressure came from the Central Committee of the Soviet
party.

'Whenever I met Gorbachev he never said that force had to be used. Nor
did Yakovlev or Medvedev. But lower-level functionaries did, hinting that we
knew where army headquarters were and we could put a stop to current
developments. You could talk to Gorbachev without any sense of being his
inferior. It was possible to say things you knew he would dislike and he would
disagree without taking offence. A public statement was quite another matter.
He could not accept that. It turned out that the goals of perestroika had been
unclear to him. In the last stages he was always changing his decision, not
sticking to a line.'

*The Central Committee declaration of 26 August 1989 threatened to remove the Baltics
from the map.*

'I was First Secretary by then and took this statement into account. There was
nothing concrete to it, only a general opposition, and intimidation. The
Central Committee attitude was that we would finish up under the heel of
the West. We could not deny close economic ties to the Soviet Union, which
probably prompted that sharp statement. The Popular Front was not proposing
complete independence outside of the Soviet Union. It was a question of
confederation and even that seemed unobtainable. Republican parties and
their Central Committees had no more than regional significance. What was
then called the Latvian Communist Party could not in fact take decisions for
Latvia.

'The idea of absolute independence developed slowly. Central Committee
plenums became more fraught, even dramatic, during 1989. It was the fourth
year of perestroika but no progress came with it. There were already decisions
within the Central Committee, as Yeltsin had started on his move to power.
The Baltic question was always raised, but discussions of it were confined to
the Politburo. The Baltic First Secretaries were very often summoned to
Moscow to meet Gorbachev.

'It was not permitted to argue with the Politburo. Gorbachev never asked my advice. But it seemed that he understood my point of view; he would calm down. In the Politburo by no means all the members supported him. Opposition might not be open but it could be felt. Ligachev was the real hardliner. I used to request personal meetings with Gorbachev and I was never refused. I never heard him make the slightest reference to the Russian army in Latvia and its possible unleashing against us. He stressed democratic procedures to solve the Baltic question.'

Vagris is haggard, with a bony face. He was sitting by a window as dusk fell in Riga, and his voice slowed down. Evidently a decent man, he seemed to find it difficult to come to terms with what had happened, as though in a state of shock. Asked about those two inadequate sentences which he had blurted out on his first appearance in his new post, he set his mouth in a pained expression. The Popular Front had brought him along as a courtesy. He had not been prepared. What else could he have done?

In the old days, committed to party work, he had known Konstantin Chernenko, who had neither the intellect, the experience nor the health to be First Secretary of the Soviet Union party. Demoralization began then. What with the nationalist movement and inner division at the top, the party had no future.

Did you try at that final congress on 7 April to hold the party together?

'I tried to do what I considered useful and necessary. Why was it necessary to hold the party together? Let it split, some said. The Lithuanians had the idea of making their party a parliamentary party and with hindsight we can say they succeeded. My policy was to prevent a split and also to transform ourselves into a parliamentary party.

'At that plenum of 7 April, a resolution was passed that the work of the Communist Party was considered unsatisfactory. In those circumstances, I said, I could not continue. This resolution was passed by the faction remaining within the party. The liberals had already split off and were no longer participating. So who was to lead the party? Pugo had come specially to attend as a representative of the Moscow Central Committee and he proposed Klausens. The delegates rejected this. Rubiks was then elected.'

As the new First Secretary, Rubiks was involved with the two violent episodes of January and August 1991. When I was in Riga he was in prison awaiting trial on a charge for being responsible for the deaths which had occurred.

'The court will give its verdict,' Vagris said, 'but nothing could have been done without his being involved in the decisions. The attack on the Press House in January was an attempt to threaten us, as in Lithuania, but co-ordinated from Moscow. Gorbachev may not have given the command but it is impossible to believe that he knew nothing about it. It might have been done without his authorization but it speaks for itself that no punishment has fallen on those who perpetrated it. Nobody has yet been brought to account in any republic.'

So Gorbachev avoided any mention to you of using force while in practice turning a blind eye to it, perhaps even deceiving you?

'Yes.'

18

'COMMUNISM HAD ROTTED
FROM WITHIN'

At the point when I was about to cross its border, Lithuania could not pay for the fuel which it was importing from Russia, and in ringing Gorbachevian terms President Yeltsin had declared an embargo. The driver laughed at proposals to stock jerrycans. There was nothing to worry about. Sure enough, at many if not most of the crossroads in Lithuania a tanker was selling petrol. The racket stretched back hundreds of miles across Belarus into Russia proper. Quartermasters of the army, perhaps the high command itself, were freelancing by placing vehicles and fuel on to the black market. A mind-boggling number of soldiers, customs and police officials, inspectors and politicians must have been on the take.

The vranyo culture, of which that embargo was such a good example, bleeds more or less invisibly into absolutism with its lies and self-deceptions. Lithuania has no democratic traditions. Traditionally it was a peasant society with a Polish aristocracy. Between the wars, emerging democracy was stifled. President Smetona took power in 1926 in a coup, somewhat Ruritanian to be sure, but ending first experiments in party politics and power-sharing. Under communism the Nomenklatura mimicked the dispossessed aristocracy, but grossly and without any of its style. Surviving intellectuals were too few to have much influence and they were in any case urbanized. With the show of stolid obedience instilled down the generations, the huge majority in the countryside continued to accept whatever was wished upon them from above.

Nothing remains of Sajudis now, except a bittersweet memory of a mass movement, democracy itself, which soared into the air exhilaratingly like a rocket, only to fall to earth extinguished in sparks. Soviet occupation had ended, but not the native absolutism which accommodated it so cosily. Liberation has proved sullen and precarious.

A large black car flanked with outriders and flying a national flag carries President Algirdas Brazauskas through Vilnius. In old days the same car would have carried party First Secretary Brazauskas, its sole differentiation being the red hammer-and-sickle flag. Every inch the Nomenklatura boss, he looks bullish and well-fed, the only healthy man in the country. Whenever he can, he gives the same interview and it is pointless to rehearse it. The old Communist Party had 3 per cent believers and 97 per cent members who worked for the country – his figures cannot possibly be substantiated but he loves to repeat them. To call them collaborators is slanderous, in his opinion. Old party hands like him should be pitied and admired for what they put themselves through. The cast of his face dares the listener to disbelieve him. Rüütel and Gorbunovs are in this mould, and so is President Leonid Kravchuk in neighbouring Ukraine; the latter also has the appearance of the one man in his country in good physical shape. Political skill is one prerequisite for the overnight transformation of communist one-man ruler into nationalist one-man ruler, for all the world a latter-day Smetona. Another prerequisite is the absence in society of any general comprehension of democracy.

In its declared aim of ending Soviet occupation Sajudis was a success. Its steering committee consisted of thirty-five members, and probably only one or two hundred people all told had any influence on its development. Most of these were careerists at least as concerned with what Sajudis could do for them as with what they could do for Sajudis. An old communist writer Vytautas Petkevičius might have become its leader, as might Romualdas Ozolas, a philosopher. Once elected, Landsbergis used Sajudis exclusively for the national end which absorbed his whole being. He kept it as a personal vehicle. Whether tempted by the taste of power or blind to the future, he made little attempt to convert the movement into a party and blocked others from doing so. As soon as independence became a reality, Sajudis therefore dissolved into a whirlpool of jealousies and rivalries, in which all drowned. Put another way, Brazauskas emerged on top by steering clear.

One depressing conversation tends to follow another. Paranoia and conspiracy theories flit over Vilnius. No policy decision was so firm that it did not have provocation deep within it. It is all the fault of the KGB, of the Poles, of the Jews, of the crooks, who often turn out to be one and the same. It is also all the fault of Vergilijus Čepaitis, once the organizing secretary of Sajudis, accused in print by Mrs Prunskienė and others of having been a KGB agent. Nobody seems to know the whereabouts of the old First Secretary, Ringaudas Songaila. Accusations are hair-raising as well as unverifiable. Landsbergis was manipulated by the KGB, Mrs Prunskienė was an outright KGB agent operating under the code name Shatria. I am shown a documentary film to that effect. In it Balys Gajauskias, a dissident who had been in Gulag for twenty-five years and received a sentence of fifteen more years for collecting archive material, asks for the Shatria evidence to be dispassionately reviewed. Those accused say that nothing can be proved from the archives: the material has been tampered with, or alternatively fabricated. Debate in parliament is venomous by any standard. The building, Soviet-made but handsome for once, is in an open space close to the River Nerys. In its corridors, a deputy said to me, 'I am helping you because I do not want you to show Lithuania as a banana republic.'

The last communist Prime Minister was Vytautas Sakalauskas. A bulky man, he has the no-nonsense demeanour of the apparatchik who during thirty years in the party learned how to make his way up the ladder. From the Kaunas Polytechnic, in his case, to factory foreman, chief engineer, manager, Lithuanian Central Committee, First Secretary for the City of Vilnius. In that post in 1980 he had first met Gorbachev, showing him round on an official visit. Songaila, then Agricultural Secretary, escorted Gorbachev through the countryside. Four years later Sakalauskas was sent to Moscow for eighteen months to be groomed in the party secretariat for the highest promotion. One of his colleagues took him to Gorbachev, who asked this man if he had ever been to Lithuania. The answer was no. 'The country had made a great impression on Gorbachev and he said to this man, You haven't seen their green fields. The impression that I had of him in Moscow in 1985 was that his way of thinking was rather intellectual. He likes to speak a lot.'

Perestroika to Sakalauskas signified that everyone should work harder and better. 'Discipline and work efficiency were at a very low level. That's a fact. The main mistake as I see it was lack of purpose or programme on the part of the Soviet government – now we can criticize it openly. It was based on slogans of improvement, and nothing more.'

Demonstrations built up in frequency and numbers during the course of 1988. The demonstration on 28 September was to mark the day of the signing of the secret protocols of the Ribbentrop–Molotov Pact. The militia broke it up. The authorities claimed that eighteen militiamen had been injured and forty-seven demonstrators were arrested. The facts remain uncertain. Sakalauskas, Songaila and Vytautas Astrauskas, the chairman of the Lithuanian Supreme Soviet, were all in Moscow at the time for a Soviet Central Committee session. As earlier in Estonia, the militia had introduced a sense of crisis. A commission was set up at once to investigate and on 17 October it reported that Songaila and Nikolai Mitkin, the Russian Second Secretary and effectively governor of Lithuania, had authorized the militia to use force. Songaila was dismissed and Mitkin replaced by Vladimir Beriozov, a Russian born in Lithuania.

Sakalauskas cannot say whether Songaila gave any order to use force. 'I participated in no conversations about it. There were different reports. Some said that he did give the order, others that it was given by Lisauskas, the Minister of the Interior. What the truth is I don't know, but this confrontation was stopped by Misiukonis, the deputy of Lisauskas, who ordered the army to withdraw.'

Would force have stopped Sajudis?

'No degree of force could have stopped Sajudis in 1988 and 1989. Even those of us who were leaders did not think of stopping Sajudis for the very good reason that their slogans and ideas were right. During the founding congress of Sajudis, they sent a telegram to Gorbachev. The text is irreproachable. Gorbachev's policy was approved, perestroika was to be pursued, and the telegram contained no mention of separation from the Soviet Union.

'Brazauskas replaced Songaila at that moment but I am not sure what the connection is to the aborted use of force. All of us in the leadership saw that Songaila could no longer do his work. He was a farmer, everyone has his limits, and he had reached his. Brazauskas replaced him just before the founding congress of Sajudis, where he spoke to warm applause.

'I would not say that the Sajudis–party relation was complicated. Sajudis had its allotted television exposure, its own newspapers with which nobody interfered, and its premises. We tried jointly to resolve economic problems. For some, Sajudis was not pleasant. I think the 11 March declaration of independence was right. I want to make another point, that in February that year we had elections, and if the old Supreme Soviet had stayed in power, they would have adopted the same declaration of independence. The supremacy of Lithuanian law over Soviet law had already been established in the old Supreme Soviet, for instance, and so had the act declaring unlawful the 1940 decision of the Supreme Soviet of the day to join the Soviet Union. The national anthem and flag had already been restored. Unlike Sajudis, we members of the old Supreme Soviet did not think that everything had to be destroyed before something new could be formed.'

At the congress of 6 December, Sakalauskas was among the majority voting for the decision to separate the Lithuanian party from the parent Soviet party. Over-centralization had been one of the main mistakes of the Soviet party, in his view. 'Our special name for the hardliners who remained was the Night Party. I was not one of them either.' In fact he had seen that a dead end had been reached, and arranged to be posted to Mozambique as an economic adviser. Wisely he was abroad when Soviet forces moved into Vilnius on 11 January 1991. The tanks should have not been on the streets, he thinks, but then Landsbergis should not have exposed people to force. His reaction to the Sajudis government was that 'These were the first people who came to hand.' Under the wing of Brazauskas, Sakalauskas himself once more has a Nomenklatura post.

Perhaps no one in Lithuania has been more in the public eye than Algirdas Kauspėdas. With his Roko maršas, otherwise Rock March, he was certainly its most famous entertainer in glasnost days. Debonair and highly intelligent, he has film-star looks. An architect by profession, he lives in a complex which he designed in his home town of Kaunas. He still communicates the headiness of the days when everyone could flock to Sajudis, and nationalism appeared to mean liberation and freedom. His uncles and their families had been in Siberia for fifteen years. One was shot and all were damaged psychologically. Sometimes, he says, they speak in Russian like invalids.

A man with a strong sense of the absurd, Kaušpėdas gauged exactly how to subvert the authorities through mockery. He called his group Antis, which in Lithuanian means a homely quacking duck. The word is also a near anagram of *Tiesa*, the party daily whose name has since changed to *Diena* meaning day, and he borrowed its lettering for his group's logo. He and the other eight musicians made a point of wearing mock uniforms and outrageous make-up, but then posing laconically on stage and in publicity photographs as though they were completely ordinary, just a row of heads in the style of Politburo photographs and appearances. Soviet life, he stresses, was extremely boring. You could never be sure to what extent you were in the grip of Soviet aesthetics. 'It was something new to be rid of them. We never said anything directly but suggested ironies. Some songs had hidden meanings, others were blatant, such as "For comrade Tatatavičius", which is the Lithuanian way of saying comrade Bla-bla-bla. On stage this comrade was made to look like Lenin, and the song had a chorus with a monstrous roar of ha-ha.

'Glasnost was something big and powerful. Before it, things were clear for the bureaucrats but after it they felt ashamed. We were acquainted with all the rules and all the tricks, but in your inner self it was difficult to play this game. All the time my house was under KGB surveillance. They sat out there in cars. I was very popular. Concerts were free of charge to start with as I might have faced accusations if I had taken money.'

After a concert early in June 1988, Romualdas Ozolas and Alvydas Medalinskas, already two of the Sajudis leaders, asked for his help. 'So on stage I asked the audience, Can I? Must I? They roared back, Yes!'

As secretary of the Association of Architects, Kaušpėdas had the run of its headquarters, a big building with a hall. There he organized the Kaunas Sajudis group, with a council of twenty. The first meeting had two hundred enthusiasts. Communists were admitted so long as they shared the Sajudis outlook. At the founding congress of Sajudis that October, he was elected to the main board.

'In 1988 we were thinking about human rights for Lithuania within the Soviet Union. We wanted economic concessions and some form of separation, but it was almost a joke to entertain such hopes. Brezhnev had centralized everything, he had seemed eternal, an endless drag. You don't find the word independence in the programme either, only sovereignty. The next big step was the separation of the Communist Party from the Soviet party and the nomination of Brazauskas to the Congress of People's Deputies. He was very careful whenever he reached a crossroad. Mrs Prunskienė was more courageous.' He values Landsbergis for his stand that independence had to be achieved no matter what the cost. But he thinks it was mistaken to try to draw so harsh a line between Sajudis and the party. It was unnecessarily divisive, especially where Russians and Poles were concerned.

Two days after the 11 March 1990 declaration of independence, Kaušpėdas received a telephone call from Česlovas Stankevičius, Vice-President to the new President Landsbergis, to propose that he become head of national television. By happy coincidence his predecessor had been editor of *Tiesa*. Actual nomination took six months to come through. So he had not been long installed when the Soviets mounted their January 1991 attack.

When, suddenly, he heard them coming upstairs he locked the door to his office. 'I was at my desk when they began to shoot the door open. I jumped to one side where I couldn't be hit. Seven shots were fired with dumdum bullets. They were a select Alpha team, professionals with flak jackets and special equipment, pure James Bond stuff. Once they were in, they pushed the gun into my back and I was kicked out, hands up, into the street. They switched off the television broadcasting. The second group were ordinary soldiers and they stole everything, from the videos and television equipment down to the chairs and tables. One man was killed in our office, and twelve near the tower (the fourteenth was a Russian soldier, crushed by one of the tanks). Many more were injured. They shot directly at the crowd from the tanks with blanks – eardrums burst and started to bleed. The psychological effects were dreadful. They blew the glass out of the windows. I went straight from the street where I was thrown out to parliament to inform Landsbergis. Everyone in Lithuania saw the Russian soldiers entering the building on television. Landsbergis went to the radio to say that it seemed we were losing our television. My wife called and I said I would try to come home. Then the television screens went blank. My mother's hair turned grey. This was worse than Antis for her.'

For reasons that have never been explained, the Russians did not occupy the transmitter in Kaunas. Kaušpėdas continued working from there. On the day of the August coup they finally closed it down and so for twenty-four hours Lithuania had no broadcasting of any kind. By the time the Russian army pulled out, his office had been occupied for 222 days.

A political theorist, as well as a medallist for swimming in the 1976 Olympic Games, Arvydas Juozaitis is an all-rounder. In democratic circles he is regarded as his country's white hope. Since the age of twelve, he says, he knew that Lithuania would recover its independence. On 20 April 1988 he gave a lecture in the Artists' Union to an audience of several hundred. 'Lithuania and the Problem of Political Culture' is somewhat academic in presentation, though not in its implications. The lecture's theme is that the continuity of Lithuanian history had been interrupted by the Soviet interlude. A law-based sovereign state should be created. He declared, 'It is impossible to wait any longer because a sense of helplessness has brought us to the edge of doom.' Glasnost had found an outlet leading towards nationalism, just as it had done with Vulfsons's speech in Riga at about the same moment. A video taken at the time registers the shock on the faces of those listening to him.

Never a party member, Juozaitis was also no dissident but in case the KGB took him into custody, he had distributed a dozen copies of the speech to friends. He took the precaution of hiding his papers. Written out by hand, the lecture spread immediately in thousands more copies. Within a week it was in America, translated into English.

Why did you make such a speech just then?

'It was my reaction to the very aggressive pro-Soviet celebration on 16 February, marking the seventieth anniversary of Lithuanian independence. I was so angry that I thought out what measures would be the most influential, and hit on this form. What came out of it was the need to organize.' Sajudis was then started by a founding group thirty-five strong, including Landsbergis, Ozolas and Čepaitis, sometimes referred to as the Charter group. Supporters from the Academy of Sciences prepared a draft constitution to expand Lithuanian sovereign rights within the Soviet Union.

'At the beginning we had no problems, everyone understood we were not dissidents, but they might crack down on us unless we had in our ranks national communists. These were more national than they were communist. Because we admitted them in our ranks, the popularity of Sajudis spread fast. From the beginning we thought sovereignty would translate into independence. As a word sovereignty was deceptive, just a manoeuvre because we had no wider choice at that time. We were in accord with Gorbachev but also going that extra step.'

That was their moment to round you all up and suppress the movement.

'Yes. Two months later, it was already too late for that. We used that summer for very active propaganda. Nobody really knows why Songaila didn't strangle the movement. He kept Moscow informed but he hesitated on 28 September, he could not bring himself to take responsibility because he knew his colleagues had no respect for him. His deputy, Mitkin, a hardliner, was a newcomer who had no perception of our culture or language. Perhaps Gorbachev did not react seriously on account of Mitkin's lack of experience and anyway was obliged to allow local initiatives to get under way in each republic at the time.

'In spite of the activities of my friends and colleagues, and with all respect to Sajudis, I am convinced that our achievements were possible only because communism had weakened. In terms of a value system, as a method of interpreting history and human society, communism had been dead for a decade. Its inner death had allowed people like Brazauskas to rise to the top, as oriented towards nationalism as communism. To belong to the Nomenklatura had become an end in itself. Their children, the second generation of the Nomenklatura, only desired the best possible material life. The profound reason why Sajudis and all of us were not repressed was that they had no belief in the ideals they were supposed to stand for.'

Lionginas Šepetys had been the Ideological Secretary. His denigration in 1988 of Lithuanian independence had been the last straw for Juozaitis, pushing him to deliver his breakaway lecture. Just a year later Šepetys was himself celebrating independence, in what was still an occupied country. 'Around the middle of 1989 the communists were already moving towards the decision to secede from the Soviet party as a pressure group. Sajudis evidently had become the whole nation.'

During the weeks between the founding congress of Sajudis and the declaration of independence due to be made on 18 November, the party and Sajudis had worked harmoniously together. But thanks to Brazauskas, the declaration of 18 November was not voted through. In an atmosphere of crisis, confrontation replaced co-operation. On the grounds that it was prudent to side with Brazauskas, some Sajudis members looked like backtracking. A Sajudis leader had to be found to prevent the possibility of splits and factions. 'Everything was very confused and mixed, based on personal feelings and contacts. You had to have twenty-four votes out of the thirty-five in the Charter group, and Landsbergis got twenty-one, so he was elected without a quorum. But we had to have a formal leader.'

Brazauskas has subsequently deplored his mistake in obstructing that November declaration of independence. It made him seem a hardliner, perhaps in conspiracy with Moscow or with the Russian Interfront now starting in Lithuania. A rationalist through and through, Juozaitis prefers to give him the benefit of the doubt, in the belief that Brazauskas was a second-rank party leader without ideology or serviceable experience. In a rare act of abnegation he surrendered to Brazauskas his own chance to be a deputy in the Soviet Congress of People's Deputies. That too was rational. 'Brazauskas was more important in Moscow for Lithuania than someone like me. I was more popular, he had the right influence. The Lithuanian delegation remained solid. That was Sajudis's chance.'

At the time of his visit to Lithuania in January 1990, Juozaitis says, Gorbachev was in a panic, in spite of behaving in his traditional manner as the First Secretary who had everything under control. Six weeks before the election, the visit was poorly timed. Sajudis used the period for intense activity and duly swept the field. 'There might have been a crackdown then. Brazauskas was saying there was a danger of bloodshed and I had a sense that the Russians might try such measures. But what would have been the objective of physical assault? The party, Sajudis, administrative structures? Tanks, a state of emergency, the deportation of Brazauskas, the wholesale arrest of Sajudis, would have been the minimum programme but that was too expensive in every sense. And the Congress of People's Deputies was an obstacle to Gorbachev. Yeltsin was restraining his freedom of action. Yeltsin played the Baltic card. Gorbachev tried to, so that to some extent their quarrel took place over us. We were lucky in this. But they had not realized what a mistake it had been to swallow the Baltics after the war.'

Sajudis's great achievement came to a head in the declaration of independence of 11 March. Underneath, Juozaitis explains, democratic tendencies were already fraying. As Prime Minister, Mrs Prunskienė was one centre of power, Landsbergis as President was another. After the January 1991 attack, Landsbergis offered no condolences to those who had been killed, no word of grievance beyond saying that they had sacrificed their lives for their country and its freedom. It offered a chilling insight into the inner man that he could be so adamant and single-minded of purpose.

On the night of the capture of the television tower, Juozaitis had gone to sleep at one thirty in the morning, when he heard shooting. Having once more hidden his papers and his computer, he went to parliament. Chaos reigned. 'There were a lot of young people with rifles, barricades were thrown up. Some fanatic said to me that if the Soviets attacked the parliament, they would shoot every communist in sight, that was the mood. It would have been a tragedy.'

On Doma Square, in one of the old buildings which have seen better days, are the offices of *Respublika*, reputedly the best of the new democratic newspapers. Its editor-in-chief, Vitas Tomkus, is in his late thirties. Representing Sajudis, he was elected to the Congress of People's Deputies in Moscow. He was therefore present when the Latvian Tolpeznikov pulled off the procedural trick of obliging the Congress to stand in silence in honour of the victims of the Tbilisi massacre. A resolution was then passed in Congress to set up an investigatory commission under Anatoly Sobchak, the mayor of

Leningrad, as it still was. Allowed to nominate a member, the Lithuanian delegation of deputies chose Tomkus. He was among those who flew three times to Tbilisi, to Stepanakert and to Yerevan.

The local commander, General Vladimir Rodionov, had been held responsible for sending in paratroopers with the sharpened spades which they used to kill people. But the commission discovered an essential document which laid down categorically that military assault was prohibited without a chain of orders duly proceeding from the top. The conclusion was inescapable, Tomkus says, that Gorbachev was ultimately responsible for this bloodshed. 'There was a meeting with Gorbachev. It was very polite. Sobchak proposed to speak with him tête-à-tête, but this was unacceptable. The commission members were all together. The Congress of People's Deputies then quibbled about the meaning of responsibility. Rodionov was posted away from Tbilisi to the Frunze Military Academy but otherwise there were no consequences. *Izvestia* carried a report and Sobchak spoke in his individual capacity on a Leningrad television programme. When I saw how the whole thing was swept under the carpet, I published the report in my newspaper here.'

With these brave words in my ears, I walked out into Doma Square and bought that very morning's *Baltic Observer*. On its front page the leaders of the Jewish community had published an appeal to the intellectuals of Lithuania to come to their defence. *Respublika* had carried a full-page article by a prominent Lithuanian journalist, blaming the country's plight on the Jews. An insignificant number, perhaps 6000, now live in Lithuania, 254,000, or 95 per cent of the community, were murdered after 1941 but no Lithuanians have requested a minute's silence or an investigatory commission for them.

Like Marju Lauristin in Estonia, Justas Paleckis was born into the communist aristocracy. In 1940 his father succeeded Antanas Smetona as the Moscow-imposed President of the new People's Government. For many years he was chairman of the Chamber of Nationalities, a second house of the Supreme Soviet for Potemkin purposes. A journalist to begin with, Paleckis worked on the Komsomol newspaper in Vilnius. Then he transferred to the Higher Diplomatic School in Moscow, a sure sign that he was being groomed for a Nomenklatura future at the highest level. As a young diplomat he worked in one of the European departments of the Foreign Ministry under Valentin Falin and Alexander Bondarenko, concentrating on Germany. For a Lithuanian this was exceptional. In 1989 he became what was to be the last Ideological Secretary of the Lithuanian party. He is generally credited with masterminding the split of the party from the parent Soviet party, as well as smoothing the way for Brazauskas to the top.

To listen to him, Paleckis always believed in Lithuanian independence and had even heard his father saying that this was correct and progressive. The example of Dubček in 1968 had fired him, and he remembers how his father had warned him not to talk openly on the telephone about it, for fear of KGB eavesdropping. Within the Foreign Ministry, he found himself in a minority arguing that the division of Germany was an indefensible punishment of a whole nation. In early glasnost days a friend of his, the poet Alfonsas Maldonis, had been present when hardliners warned Gorbachev to his face that he would destroy socialism and the Soviet Union. Gorbachev had apparently answered that they could shout and even bring him down but he would pursue a policy towards democracy without resorting to force. 'Perhaps naïvely, I believe he was sincere in following the line that democracy was the panacea for all problems.'

Yakovlev visited Vilnius in August 1988. 'He gave a huge boost to Sajudis and the reformist wing of the party. Mitkin was a very powerful Second Secretary, trying to suppress the national rebirth. He was confident that a member of the Politburo was certain to support him, and the confrontation between the two men was glaring. For Mitkin the shock was enormous.' Yakovlev's main purpose was to recruit allies in the struggle against Ligachev and the hardliners.

Songaila's attempt forcibly to suppress Sajudis came in the wake of Yakovlev's visit. 'Brazauskas was already famous for addressing the first mass rallies of Sajudis, when Songaila did not dare do so, and was not able to. He was a disgrace. It was obvious that Brazauskas had to take his place. Some elements in Sajudis recognized that he might be too strong one day – which proved the case. But for the first time in its history the Lithuanian party appointed its First Secretary in the teeth of influential departments in Moscow, and Ligachev and other hardliners. Gorbachev's role was decisive. He and Brazauskas were on the same wavelength. I can swear that the Department for Organizational Party Work did everything in its power to prevent Brazauskas from becoming First Secretary.'

With consummate timing, that autumn Paleckis attended a gathering of Lithuanian refugees and exiles on the Baltic island of Gotland. He had just been appointed Ideological Secretary. There he and Landsbergis and the representatives of Lithuanians abroad signed a short communiqué declaring that all Lithuanians shared the goal of independence. A shocked Ligachev demanded his punishment and exclusion from the party for this act. But Brazauskas supported Paleckis. In Starad Ploshchad, the party office complex near the Kremlin, he had a two-hour conversation with Yakovlev. That evening, at around seven o'clock, Yakovlev returned from a meeting with Gorbachev, to report their conclusion that the Lithuanians could do whatever seemed to them to be reasonable. But not at the expense of the army, the party or Russian settlers.

'I interpreted this as a signal that in Moscow the struggle between progressives and hardliners was hard, and the tension immense. If we were too insistent, then we would play into the hands of the hardliners. A typical Russian, Yakovlev could not sympathize with the concerns of small nations but I trusted him personally, believing that so long as men like Gorbachev, Shevardnadze and him were in power, step by step Lithuania would achieve independence.' The party and Sajudis needed one another against the common enemy of pro-Soviet hardliners, and Paleckis's role, as he presents it, was to ensure their collaboration. In any case, half of the thirty-five members of the Sajudis founding group were party members. Even if factionalism and a split followed, hardliners could never accept any surrender of their absolute power. A decision was taken in the late summer of 1989 to convene a special party conference to put them on the spot. Gorbachev tried to convince Brazauskas of the dangers involved. The Central Committee Department for Organizational Work again tried to intervene. 'They sent a lot of people with proposals and promises of career advantages for whoever supported Moscow's position. But it was obvious that the main wing of the party would support splitting away.'

Brazauskas was summoned to a meeting with Gorbachev on 16 November. Presumably Gorbachev told him to stop in his tracks.

'Yes. Our whole Politburo of twelve or fourteen members was at that discussion. It was difficult for Brazauskas. Yazov, Kryuchkov and Ryzhkov spoke harshly. Ryzhkov spelled it out that secession would be a decisive step in destroying the party, and that meant destroying the Soviet Union. He was right. Gorbachev played the role of peacemaker, so to speak, but he also condemned secession. He was the first General Secretary without experience of working in the republics. He had even less understanding than Yakovlev of small nations and their hopes.'

So by the time the party congress occurred on 6 December, a split was inevitable?

'It had been prepared in such a way that the delegates selected were people in favour of reforms and sovereignty, and would move cautiously towards independence. We manipulated these words. It was easy to be even more radical than Sajudis, but that would have been unreasonable. The atmosphere was very tense. We hoped not to have a direct split with the pro-Moscow groups but to give them some sort of special status. They rejected this proposal, maybe through pressure from Moscow hardliners. Nobody knew how Moscow would react.

'My personal opinion was that the worst thing would be if a hardliner replaced Gorbachev as a result of our activities. In February 1990 I was a guest of the plenum of the Soviet party when one of the main issues was the secession of the Lithuanian party. The weakness of Gorbachev's position was evident. His report received no applause, but Ligachev was applauded after almost every sentence. Ambassador Brovikov from Warsaw made an anti-Gorbachev tirade and was applauded a great deal.'

Gorbachev's fiasco of a visit to Vilnius at the beginning of 1990 was imposed on him by his enemies, Paleckis thinks, to expose and humiliate him. He tried to salvage what he could through media exposure, showing other republics the dangerous consequences of following the Lithuanian example. The tour had the opposite effect.

Why did Gorbachev declare a blockade instead of using force massively?

'They did not realize that the Baltic peoples would pay whatever price was necessary if only they could be independent. At prices below the world market for oil and minerals, we were receiving a subsidy of $300 per capita. The average salary today is $15 a month. I am sure Gorbachev was ready to use everything except force to keep Lithuania within the Soviet Union. He was so confident that the Baltic republics could not exist without the Soviet Union that he dismissed the idea of secession as unrealistic.'

The dispute between Landsbergis as President after his declaration of independence and his Prime Minister Kazimiera Prunskienė lay in their opposing attitudes to Gorbachev's blockade. To Landsbergis, negotiation under the circumstances was an insult to independence and therefore not to be entertained. Lithuania was in no position to resist the Soviet Union, Mrs Prunskienė argued, and therefore had no choice but to negotiate. They disempowered one another, and Sajudis too, through this profound contradiction. As long as the Soviet Union lasted, bloodshed might have proved one or the other tragically wrong. In the light of events, the question became academic. I interviewed Mrs Prunskienė in her apartment on Blindžiai Street in Vilnius, at the heart of a Nomenklatura district. I found myself sitting opposite a large framed photograph of her and President Bush at the White House. She spoke in long bursts but the gusto did not hide the raw wounds of yesterday's battle. Her line remains that independence and Gorbachev were not necessarily two immovable and irreconcilable objects. That was also what President Bush, Mrs Thatcher, Kohl, Mitterrand, had been trying to rub in during her whistle-stop tour of high places in the summer of 1990, when she was in the headlines day after day.

The immediate past weighs on Landsbergis too. Stouter now, grey, he would be almost unrecognizable from the old Sajudis figurehead were it not for the same professorial spectacles and a beard which seems to fit him for one of the roles in Puccini's *La Bohème*. As a member of parliament and a would-be leader of the conservative block, he seems to have forsaken his earlier career as a musicologist.

On 19 September 1989 Gorbachev said that the Baltic republics had joined the Soviet Union voluntarily. I asked whether Gorbachev could really have believed this.

'Of course not. He knew very well of the Ribbentrop–Molotov Pact, the documents are preserved in the Soviet archives. He denied their existence but this was not true. The evidence has recently been published that he did indeed receive the relevant information. He was a liar many times over.'

Did you treat him as someone who was manipulating you and telling you lies?

'I didn't express myself so directly. In my discussions perhaps I was too polite. When Gorbachev was still chairman of the Congress of People's Deputies, one of our deputies said in a plenary session that Gorbachev was lying. It caused a scandal. It was the first time that anyone had said that.'

The timing of the 11 March declaration of independence was critical. Landsbergis explains, 'I was elected President, on the 11th at midday. That same afternoon we debated and passed a chain of laws and acts. That day was not limited to passing the act of independence. We did everything possible to gather deputies in a constitutional manner – some had yet to be elected – but we had a legal constitutional quorum already gathered the previous afternoon of 10 March, as a preliminary. The 11th was specially reserved for taking the decisions and votes. Because on 12 March, the Congress of People's Deputies was resuming in Moscow. If Gorbachev was elected President as expected, he could obtain special authorization to fight us, as he had done before.

'We had to act quickly. Whether or not to go to Moscow was a further problem. Having won our own election, and gone into session to claim our restored independence, it was absurd to go to Moscow to elect another President. That would have contradicted our independence and was unacceptable. So we created our state as a barrier, and not a single deputy of ours went to Moscow as a deputy of the Soviet Union. We authorized some of them to go on 12 March as a delegation conveying our decisions to Gorbachev, and asking for negotiations to begin with a view to the peaceful resolution of our relations. It was not a secession from the Soviet Union because we have never consented to be a legal part of the Soviet Union. We had been annexed and incorporated. We were restoring the legal situation.'

The blockade was only one among other pressures on Landsbergis to back down. In those March days Soviet tanks and armoured cars circled around the Vilnius parliament in a form of psychological warfare. 'Generals visited me with ultimatums to annul our decision of independence and our law forbidding our citizens to serve in a foreign army. They wanted to draft our young men. That was impossible, of course. We had initiated our own law for the country's defence forces. Those conscripted by the Soviets hid but they were rounded up, beaten and even kidnapped in a few cases. This was violence. Western democracies did not react strongly. We had to fight politically for world opinion. Gorbachev was limited by world opinion, he was warned against using military force. If a decision had been made in Moscow to resort to violence, they would have undoubtedly put it into effect.'

As the head of what the Soviets still perceived as one of their republics, Landsbergis was qualified to attend the Presidential Council, which included *ex officio* each republic's President. As the head of what he perceived as an independent state, Landsbergis always rejected invitations to this Council as a matter of principle. As chairmen of their republics' Supreme Soviet and therefore the equivalent of President, both Rüütel and Gorbunovs sometimes participated. In justification, they argued that their countries were in a transitional period, which would lead to independence eventually. Rüütel and Gorbunovs added their pressure to Landsbergis to attend one of these Presidential Council meetings on the grounds that the Baltic republics could make common cause. Inflexibility came naturally to Landsbergis but for once he consented.

The Presidential Council was held on 12 June 1990. The clash with Gorbachev was now personalized as Landsbergis, followed by Rüütel and Gorbunovs, made their case for independence and lifting the blockade. Landsbergis was surprised to be supported by the Presidents of republics such as Kazakhstan and Georgia. Afterwards, Gorbachev kept a promise to adjourn to another room for private discussions. There he proposed a moratorium of the blockade. Landsbergis could not agree.

'That was the first of the meetings between Gorbachev and me. The next occurred shortly afterwards. Gorbachev proposed that I returned to Moscow for further discussion of the blockade and the conditions for a moratorium.' So Landsbergis, his Vice-President and the Lithuanian chargé d'affaires in Moscow talked to Gorbachev and Lukyanov. 'The next day Gorbachev invited us once more to come to his dacha outside Moscow as a group with Mrs Prunskienė and three deputies. On his side were Lukyanov, Yakovlev and Ryzhkov. We had another exchange of opinion without results. Ryzhkov pressed me on our plans for surviving without Soviet supplies and without the Soviet markets. That was not an object for discussion. Since 11 March we had proposed normalization of our interstate relations. Gorbachev rejected this unhesitatingly. He would never discuss with Lithuania, he said, because it was not a state.'

So there was nothing for it except to maintain his principled position, and hope not to be battered or terrorized into submission. On both sides it was a game of bluff, as Landsbergis refused to give an inch and Gorbachev consented to the limited attack on the television centre. Sajudis activity, so constitutional and peaceful, was only a function of Soviet passivity. Even Landsbergis says, 'Communism had rotted from within. The situation was ripe for a collapse, but this could have been implemented in very different ways.'

19

SOLIDARITY AND THE GENERAL

To the leaders of the satellite parties of Eastern and Central Europe, glasnost and perestroika meant belt-tightening and hard work, yet again. After eighteen months or so it became evident that the Soviet leadership was parting company with its own ideology and introducing political and economic changes which were destabilizing party control. Deceived by unfolding events, the satellite leaders and their parties were brought to face the brute fact of their collaboration. Without unqualified Soviet support, these collaborators were helpless. By the time they realized that they had been ditched it was too late to contrive some tightrope course midway between wholesale repression and surrender of power.

Consternation swept them, then panic and in a few cases anger. In every party, a minority vehemently advocated the tried and tested methods of mass repression. Of these, probably only a few hundred were ideologists with a genuine belief in the enforcement of the dictatorship of the proletariat. The majority knew that they were rightly perceived by the population as criminals – and not plain gangsters either, but men who had sold their country. Since they had gleefully participated or connived in the destruction of the previous society, they now feared that it was their turn for equally barbarous reprisals. Quite simply, they saw themselves in the mind's eye hunted down, lynched, hanging on lamp-posts.

Nothing in recent experience had given these regimes grounds for supposing that they might so soon be exposed for what they were. On the contrary, they had appeared reasonably stable on their own terms. The calendar rotated as usual around congresses and Central Committee plenums, communist anniversaries and parades and the visits of fraternal dignitaries, all under the guidance of counterparts and colleagues in Moscow and the KGB. With one exception, the First Secretaries were all in their seventies, veterans with recollections and reflexes going back to Stalin and the post-war takeover of their countries. Taking office, Gorbachev appeared a novice to men who had held uncontested power for at least twenty years, and in the cases of Todor

Zhivkov in Bulgaria and János Kádár in Hungary, over thirty years.

Poland alone in the bloc gave cause for concern. Legnica was the vital headquarters in Silesia from which Soviet military operations would be conducted in the event of war with Nato. The country had to be secured but since 1948 it had been in a state of imminent and sometimes actual insurrection. Gomulka, Gierek and Kania as successive First Secretaries had failed to convince the Poles that communism offered much more than submission to the Russians, and that was rejected by the entire thrust of Polish history.

A strike against arbitrary price-rises in the summer of 1980 led to a nationwide protest. The country came to a standstill. Out of this strike, Lech Wałęsa, at the time a discharged shipyard electrician, together with a score of diverse colleagues and advisers, built an independent trade union, Solidarity. As though by spontaneous combustion, a democratic alternative to the party coalesced. By the end of that year, Solidarity had 10 million members including a third of the 3 million people registered as belonging to the Communist Party. Almost as much of an instant celebrity as Wałęsa, Adam Michnik, hitherto an obscure dissident, judged that in 1980 Poland was 'a compromise between a non-sovereign government and a sovereign society'. That October, hurrying towards the crowd about to lynch a policeman in Otwock, Michnik, a slight figure in a leather jacket, saved the day by shouting out, 'I am an anti-socialist force!' The chief of the police station, no less, shook his hand.

Born in 1923, General Wojciech Jaruzelski was a stripling compared to the other First Secretaries in the bloc. In his memoirs he has described the family manor house at Trzeciny where he grew up, in a world of ponies, shooting game, oil-lamps and sledges in winter. Fleeing from the Germans to Lithuania in 1939, he was then deported by the Soviets with his mother and sister in a train of Balts on their way to exile, crossing the Urals to a place called Turatchak at the back of beyond in the Siberian taiga. Deported separately, his father was able to join them there but soon died. Far from arousing indignation, this unjust and arbitrary experience had the contrary result of impressing the young Jaruzelski with the power of communism. As the slave is said to love his galley chains, so he came to believe that persecution of people like him was only proper. Hatefulness lay in him and not in the Russians. His subconscious, he says, was always whispering to him that he had had an advantageous start in life. This led to 'a sort of submerged complex' towards workers and peasants. All over the world, men and women of his generation were converting this sense of unfocused guilt into abstract passion for the communist cause. Like all such fellow-travellers, Jaruzelski failed to see how condescending it was to treat workers and peasants not as human beings in their own right but as objects through whom he could complete his personality in a manner satisfactory to himself. Besides, as a communist of his background, he was still the one giving orders.

A commissar, or political soldier, Jaruzelski became Chief of Staff, and then Minister of Defence in 1968, going on to become Prime Minister, First Secretary and finally President, thus having in his hands the party, the army and the government. Repression of actual workers and peasants proved to be easily compatible with his idealization of them. On 13 December 1981 he declared a state of emergency and martial law. Equipped with crowbars and threatening to break down doors, secret police patrols dragged people out of bed and interned them. That same day the French Foreign Minister, Claude Cheysson, blurted out what most Western politicians preferred to keep to themselves, as though feeding on the shame of it: 'Of course we'll do nothing.' On a visit to the DDR that day, German Chancellor Helmut Schmidt was privately assuring Honecker that he would understand if the Polish regime were to repress Solidarity. In fascinating contrast to these attitudes, Soviet propaganda was blaming the crisis on Nato warmongering and German revanchist designs on Poland.

A twofold threat had arisen, according to Jaruzelski. An extremist Solidarity leadership was about to take over the state, and to head off such a coup Soviet military intervention was already on the road. Even now, in his memoirs, he likes to harp on rumours of the stockpiling of arms, plots, and secret agents with rendezvous in the dark of night: 'The spectre of civil war was arising.' Melodramatically he writes that on several occasions of the greatest strain he opened the drawer of his desk to look at his revolver. The Soviet army did indeed mobilize for manoeuvres on the Russian side of the border and Soviet notables flew in menacingly to Warsaw. Whether the threat of invasion and another wave of Soviet repression in Poland was genuine may well never be established. To most Poles, it appeared a vranyo-scare to enable Jaruzelski to clamp down on them. In his determination to keep Poland subjected to the Soviet Union, Jaruzelski slipped across the tenuous line dividing collaboration from outright betrayal. Thirteen thousand army officers were purged from the party. Dissolved and banned, Solidarity could no longer operate.

'The shock was enormous,' writes one authority, Aleksander Smolar. 'The multimillion mass movement was crushed, pushed off the public stage, with amazing ease. At the same time, a modicum of efficiency returned to the traditional political system.' To repeat official figures, by March 1982 6905 people had been interned by means of a variety of summary procedures. According to Andrzej Swidlicki, the historian of this repression, 732,042 cases were heard before petty tribunals, of which 196,596 involved violations of martial law including offences such as curfew violation. Several Solidarity activists were murdered, for example, Ryszard Kowalski and the Catholic priest Father Jerzy Popiełuszko. The secret police contemptuously dumped the corpses of their victims in rivers and drainage pits. Wałeşa was placed under house arrest. The Solidarity leadership, including dissidents such as Michnik and Jacek Kuroń, were imprisoned, and only one or two managed to go underground and keep the trade union alive. To Gorbachev, Jaruzelski was 'a man of high morality, of huge intellectual capacities'. Poland was at any rate cowed as never before. The Soviets had no need to invade.

No movement comparable to Solidarity existed in the other satellites. In Czechoslovakia, something like a thousand intellectuals signed Charter 77, a petition for human rights to be recognized in the light of the Helsinki Final Act. Václav Havel, the playwright who inspired Charter 77, was imprisoned three times. Following the Soviet example of expelling Solzhenitsyn and Bukovsky and others, the local parties exiled persistent troublemakers, like Wolf Biermann from the DDR or Paul Goma from Romania. On the streets of London the Bulgarian secret police murdered Georgi Markov by sticking into his leg the ferrule of an umbrella treated with deadly poison. Only after 1989 was the grip of the secret police in the satellites fully exposed. State resources had been entirely at the disposal of the various secret police forces. Probably about a third of available manpower had been diverted to the sole and unproductive purpose of maintaining party control by police methods.

Another revelation was that the West, through a series of loans, had artificially extended the power and the duration of the local Communist Parties. Far the greater proportion of the satellites' trade had been with the Soviet Union, and to that extent the communist bloc was an economic as well as a political reality. Soviet oil and natural gas at subsidized prices helped the satellites but at the cost of further dependency. It used to be held that their economies were performing adequately, in some cases well. The DDR was placed tenth or eleventh on a table of industrialized countries. The statistics on which this putative performance was based have been shown to have been fabricated. A reckoning would have occurred sooner if these countries had been left to bear the full brunt of the command–administrative economy.

During the 1960s the Soviet bloc obtained very few Western credits. The oil crises of the 1970s caused a flood of petrodollars. Western governments and banks hastened to loan these petrodollars to the Soviet bloc. It was in its way another outcome of the Helsinki Final Act, confirming the permanence of these regimes. A bloc debt of $13 billion in 1974 had risen to $50 billion four years later, and about $90 billion and still increasing fast by the time Gorbachev became First Secretary. By 1989 Hungary and Poland alone owed $20 and $40 billion respectively and could no longer meet interest payments. Romania owed $10 billion by 1981, and in squeezing the country dry to repay this sum, Ceauşescu forced his fellow countrymen to go without food, electricity or heating fuel year after year in a deprivation not known in peacetime Europe since the Middle Ages.

Apologists liked to argue that loans tied the satellites into the West's economy in so tight a manner that finally they had to be integrated politically as well. This is specious. Dubious creditors on this scale had never before existed. Used for consumption rather than investment, the money was no longer available for repayment. Bankers and diplomats have been engaged ever since in complex negotiations to write the debts off. Through this funding, leaders of Western democracies prolonged the misery of people whom they were officially proclaiming that they wished to see set free. Greed, callousness, indifference and frivolity compounded this contradiction.

Every satellite had its equivalent of Article Six of the Soviet Constitution, guaranteeing the 'leading role' of the party. Other political parties had long been suppressed. Neither dissidents nor the Christian Churches nor even Solidarity had the means to mount a political challenge to the party. The intellectual and psychological opposition of society to the party could find neither a legal nor a practical form of representation; the machinery of guaranteed rights of assembly and free speech and free election did not exist. National liberation movements on the post-1945 African or Asian model were certain to provoke a devastating Soviet military response. Since conventional political theory offered no blueprint for escape from closed totalitarian systems, the party as sole institution seemed destined to go on indefinitely.

It was in Poland that the concept of the Round Table was formulated. Agreeing in turn to other Round Tables, party leaders elsewhere did not foresee that surrender of the monopoly of power was implicit in the process. Taking their cue from Gorbachev and the Popular Fronts, they imagined almost to the end that they were co-opting their adversaries into Potemkin parliaments and institutions which they would continue to control as before. During 1989 Gorbachev and his advisers heard reports coming in regularly from the empire about Popular Fronts and the Round Tables, and deluded themselves that new bottles must improve the old wine.

By the time the Round Tables were under way, the party leaders had discovered that the balance of power had changed and the Soviet Union could no longer rescue or even help them. Communism and collaboration were finally bankrupt. In Romania, Ceauşescu clung to the monopoly of power and it cost him and others their lives. Everywhere else, the hardliners failed to convince the party to defend itself by force. At one Round Table after another, the party instead agreed to elections which were the prelude to surrendering the monopoly of power. It was a bargain: no violence from the party in return for forgiveness from the people. In one perspective, it was elegant and a triumph of common sense and democracy. In another perspective, it was flawed and unjust. Unlike Nazis, communists managed to avoid being brought to account through due processes of law for the crimes they had committed.

20

THE ROUND TABLE

No relation of the First Secretary of that name, Stanislas Gomułka was one of a small group of Warsaw university students in the early 1960s who drafted an anti-communist manifesto. Among them were future prominent dissidents like Jacek Kuroń. Influenced by the writings of Milovan Djilas as well as by the Hungarian Revolution of 1956, they advocated a multi-party system. The workers' unrest of 1970 was of course on a far wider scale but Gomułka makes the point that intellectuals and workers were uniting, as they would do in Solidarity. Leaving Poland, he became a professor at the London School of Economics. After 1989 he was economic adviser to the new Polish government.

Western loans had produced expectations of a rapid improvement in the standard of living, in Gomułka's opinion, and these were abruptly disappointed when the debt could not be serviced. The gap between expectations and reality contributed to a sense of crisis. As First Secretary throughout the 1970s, Edward Gierek agreed to the principle of borrowing, taking the view that reform financed by the West would strengthen the system. Here was a byproduct of the détente promoted by Nixon and Kissinger. Professor Gomułka wonders whether the Chinese may now have found a way that eluded other communists to combine monopoly of power with a largely private economy. 'In Eastern Europe and Russia at any rate the leadership was unable to adopt far-reaching reform without a change of the entire political system.'

Gierek's chaos foreshadowed Gorbachev's. In the best communist tradition Gorbachev wanted to preserve the monopoly of power while attracting younger talented people into the party. Both Gierek and Gorbachev were naïve in their belief that imported Western technology and westernization could build successful socialism.

Determined to be a practical ideologue, Jaruzelski was also in this mould. Once Gorbachev weakened overall Soviet control, Jaruzelski faced a dilemma: either he had to strengthen dictatorship or introduce some form of government by consent, with a popular mandate for reforms which were urgent but costly. Demoralization set in. 'Many communists were concluding that the failure of the whole historic politico-social experiment was imminent. As the old myth of certainty in a superior economic system collapsed, everything else collapsed with it. There wasn't the option to go back. Russia had the military power to confront us but it would have meant mass terror and I am not sure that a First Secretary would have found a sufficient number of people to help with that kind of thing. You would have had internal and international tensions. Crisis was necessary for reform, so anyone who contributed to crisis was also contributing towards the success of reform.'

In November 1987 Jaruzelski invited the nation to approve perestroikist reform through a referendum. Astonishingly in a party–army dictatorship, the vote went against him. Here was a first popular rebuff. In June 1988 Gorbachev visited Poland. A memorandum had been presented to him by the foreign-policy makers, Eduard Shevardnadze, Valentin Falin and Vladimir Kryuchkov of the KGB. Time was not on their side, this memorandum concluded, and it would be better to explain the Katyn massacre, and thereby close that issue. 'The costs of this course of action would be lower, in the final analysis, than the damage caused by our inaction.'

Gorbachev instead remained silent. In one speech in Cracow, he ludicrously advised Poles to find a model in 'Lenin's life and struggle'. Poles would evidently have to take responsibility for their own future. No sooner had Gorbachev left than feelers went out from Jaruzelski and his new Prime Minister Mieczysław Rakowski to Wałeşa and other Solidarity leaders. That December, over a hundred members of the old Solidarity leadership re-formed as a so-called Citizens' Committee. The Central Committee had to give its approval to open negotiations with this Citizens' Committee, who were in fact still outlaws. Hardliners made their last stand. Opposing and defeating them at a dramatic Central Committee plenum on 6 January 1989, Jaruzelski signalled that nationalism had won priority over collaboration with the Soviets. Reintegrating himself into Polish society, he may have saved his own and other lives.

The Round Table duly began a month later on 6 February 1989 at a government guesthouse at Magdalenka on the outskirts of Warsaw, and it lasted until 5 April. The following day Solidarity was once more legalized.

In the course of these talks, elections to the Congress of People's Deputies had occurred in Moscow, which Gorbachev and the leadership firmly believed would provide the hand-picked parliament needed to make their version of perestroika come true. Jaruzelski aspired to a Polish duplicate; like Gorbachev, he intended to be President and First Secretary as well, and believed that he had made the necessary prearrangements for his elections on 4 June.

The electoral procedure was 'truly confusing' in the words of one specialist, Jan T. Gross. In the parliament, known as the Sejm, the party and Solidarity divided the seats on a percentage basis, 65 and 35 respectively. Communist nominees ran unopposed on what was called a National List but they failed to reach the requisite minimum level set for the vote. In the second chamber, the Senate, Solidarity won 99 of the 100 seats, the odd-man-out being an independent. Tadeusz Mazowiecki, a lawyer and Solidarity adviser and a committed Catholic, became Prime Minister on 24 August. Four communists, including General Czesław Kiszczak, the Minister of the Interior, were in this government, although they were replaced within a short time. The party monopoly had been pulverized. That November, Jaruzelski shortened his term of office as President and Lech Wałęsa was elected in his stead. At a final congress in January 1990 the party formally abrogated its 'leading role', reconstituting itself as a social democratic and parliamentary party. In fresh elections in 1993, however, these neo-communists returned to office. By no means a complete democratization, the Round Table process had brought Poles together, and unity was enough to gain independence once again from their overbearing neighbour.

Long since vanished in recrimination and infighting, Solidarity is only a memory of that historic moment of Polish unity. With the advantages of an open manner and idiomatic English, Janusz Onyszkiewicz had been the Solidarity spokesman. He is married to the granddaughter of Marshal Piłsudski, President of Poland between the wars. On the day that I interviewed him he had a few more hours left before handing his post as Minister of Defence over to his successor in the newly elected government of Aleksander Kwaśniewski. Sloughing off its Soviet skin, the party was returning in its new guise.

As soon as martial law was declared in December 1981, Onyszkiewicz was arrested. By 1986 all political prisoners were released. Leniency implied full party control. Onyszkiewicz thinks that Jaruzelski was also motivated by what he calls a cultural factor, namely the hope for recognition in the West. Realization that the Soviet Union would no longer bail the party out had led to concessions to Solidarity. Jaruzelski and his Prime Minister, Rakowski, had previously shown themselves adept at stick-and-carrot games to split Solidarity. A constant aim had been to extract Wałęsa from Solidarity and treat him as a special case. Solidarity faint-hearts, the soft opposition, they believed, might be brought into the decision-making process.

A special Consultative Council, and a body known by its initials as PRON, were party fronts for such purpose. Jaruzelski even tried to substitute the Church for Solidarity as a partner. Up to the summer of 1988 he made his final efforts to isolate what he saw as hard-core Solidarity. Then, on 26 August, the Minister of the Interior General Kiszczak made a speech to raise the prospect of flexibility. He proposed a meeting without specifying who should participate or what they should discuss. He said, 'I still believe that day will come when we will sit down together at the same table and come to an understanding about what is best for Poland.'

Between the Central Committee meeting on 6 January 1989 and the opening of the Round Table talks, there were bitter negotiations about who would be present and in what capacity. Onyszkiewicz, Michnik and Kuroń were objected to by name on the grounds that they supported the legitimacy of the long-lost Polish government-in-exile. It was bizarre, he says, to belong to an illegal organization and yet to be negotiating formally with those who had made it illegal.

In the end the Round Table consisted of three separate discussion groups, political, economic and cultural. Subgroups were appointed for ecology, the media, youth and other issues, involving several hundred politicians, specialists and advisers.

'They thought they had cooked it and we worried that we might indeed legitimize their power. We saw ourselves putting a foot in at the door, to force it wider open afterwards. Controlling the media, they were convinced the election was in their pocket. Their worry was not about winning but about winning too convincingly. On many occasions we could see that they were captive of their propaganda. They believed that Solidarity had been hijacked by a group of extremists. Remove the extremists and there would be a bona-fide workers' movement which obviously could be a partner. Elections were not due for a couple of years. Consenting to immediate elections was a mistake from which they could not recover. But without the prior Round Table, we would have had elections in which their dream would have come true, of having an opposition hand-picked by them.'

Among technicalities to be decided was the exact constitutional power of the presidency, which Jaruzelski assumed would still be his. The communists had first offered Solidarity 30 per cent of the seats in the Sejm. This would have left them able to alter the Constitution at will. Solidarity insisted on raising the proportion to 35 per cent, since in that case the communists could make constitutional changes only if some of the opposition voted with them.

Why did the hardliners not attempt to annul the elections?

'There was a danger. They could argue that their National List had collapsed and therefore the electoral bargain had not been kept. The thing was this: out of their 65 per cent they selected seats which would not be contested in constituencies but on a nationwide basis. Their candidates for these seats were nationally known people like the Minister of Defence, General Florian Siwicki, and most of the hardliners. At the Round Table we asked them, What if this list were to be rejected? They said that was a purely theoretical question. It proved reality. I was immediately confronted by the media and put my head on the chopping block, saying, We will stick to the agreement. All hell broke loose. Still, they then had no grounds to claim that our part of the deal had not been fulfilled and the elections could be considered void. I think that was their last chance.'

As for force, there were only two Soviet divisions, though there were four more in both Hungary and Czechoslovakia. Jaruzelski could count only on the riot police, known as ZOMO, about 6,000 strong. Three or four times as many riot police would have been needed to control simultaneous troubles in the major cities. The army and the secret police were no longer reliable. Onyszkiewicz recalls how on one of the numerous occasions when he was arrested, the secret policeman holding him in custody asked, 'What will you do with us later?', a hint that secret policemen are indispensable to all regimes. On another occasion, the policeman who had arrested a colleague of his insisted on showing him that the offices of his bosses were behind the third and fourth windows on the first floor of the building, 'so that you know where to shoot, it's them, not us, we are just following orders'.

The country's regular upheavals had imposed a degree of decency on the communists. As he puts it, 'If you were a total swine, you would be ostracized socially, and in a moment of crisis under very heavy fire. In Russia or Czechoslovakia it paid off to be a total swine.'

General Kiszczak's speech of 26 August launched a free-for-all scramble for power. Some people were bound to be hurt, and one of them was Jarosław Kaczyński. One of the handful around Wałeşa in the Gdansk shipyard during the strike that August, he recalls a meeting there at which the concept of the Round Table was discussed. At this meeting were Wałeşa whose word was final, Professor Andrzej Stelmachowski who was delegated to negotiate with the party, Kaczynski and his brother. Proposals along Round Table lines were generally viewed as a trick to curb Solidarity from setting the pace for reform.

'The Rakowski government was a final attempt to transform society without taking Solidarity into partnership. In that framework they wanted to close down Gdansk shipyard, so provoking a strike. They would then have tried to portray Solidarity as basically anti-reform. Although the leadership was illegal it functioned openly. After intense debate, we refused to take up the strike. Next they staged a television debate between Wałeşa and Alfred Miodowicz, leader of the official trade union. They believed that Wałeşa would compromise himself but instead he won hands down. That was the end of the road for them.' Without Russian military intervention, a general confrontation with society was impossible. 'But even those like me who were most hardline did not grasp the full extent of their weakness.'

Why did Jaruzelski take six more months to set up the Round Table?

Tentative and secret meetings were held between the party and Solidarity. At one of these in a church in Gdansk, Solidarity agreed to the Round Table. 'We wanted to create a defined transition period to democracy while the communists wanted to co-opt a constructive opposition into the framework of their continuing rule.' How much of the communist structure was to survive, and how long a period of time would be needed to achieve democracy, at once became divisive issues within Solidarity. All the elements of Polish opposition had met in Solidarity in unanimity against Soviet imperialism. But between themselves, the various dissidents and their followers had competing visions of ultimate democracy: whether it was to be presidential or parliamentary; and Catholic or nationalist or even socialist in the values it embodied.

A Catholic and a nationalist, Kaczyński became a member of parliament and tried to form a party to represent his views, but with little success. To him, Solidarity representatives were more often than not children of old party members, or at least their heirs, with a conviction that they were better equipped than the actual Nomenklatura to put collective values into practice. Held mostly in Warsaw palaces, the actual Round Table sessions were in the form of seminars rather than negotiations. It was at Magdalenka that conflicts were resolved in small and intimate gatherings of both sides. It was not conspiracy, according to Kaczyński, but a meeting of like minds. Why did Solidarity agree to the communist proposal for a fixed share of seats in the election? In Hungary, in contrast, the elections were to be free, without any such mutual arrangements.

'Most of the opposition élite thought that Solidarity had to take over the government after the election, although Mazowiecki wrote a very powerful article in the summer to argue that this would be a mistake. I remember Professor Stelmachowski telling my brother and me right up to the end, "If this works you deserve a medal but I think we are all going to be arrested tomorrow." When we got into parliament and were walking around in a big group with Wałęsa, we had to pinch ourselves to check we weren't dreaming.'

Masowiecki's nomination as Prime Minister, and Jaruzelski's replacement by Wałęsa as President, in Kaczyński's view, were examples of horse-trading owing more to the old system than to democracy. 'There was no clear break with the past, and this weighs on people today. The Round Table was a process of fraternization.'

★   ★   ★

Bronisław Geremek was cultural attaché at the Polish Embassy in Paris in the early 1950s, and therefore in a Nomenklatura post. By profession he is a medieval historian. Slowly detaching himself from the party, he became a friend of Wałęsa's, and is generally held to have been the chief tactician of the opposition. He was Solidarity's negotiator at the Round Table political group. Mazowiecki was with him, and either man might have become Prime Minister. Geremek repudiates all suggestion of tacit understandings, let alone secret agreements. The few restricted high-level meetings at Magdalenka or elsewhere in Warsaw had the single purpose of overcoming obstacles which seemed vital enough to disrupt the talks.

The Round Table took shape from a confidential meeting early in 1988 between the party and Catholic bishops. Party representatives had frankly explained that they could not hold elections which they might lose, although delaying elections might be explosive and not in the national interest. That was the party's problem, the bishops replied, but they recommended negotiation with Solidarity. Geremek says, 'The aim of the party was not to surrender power but to preserve it. At our meetings, our interlocutors spoke frankly, that they had absolute power in their hands. To which we could only answer, Don't forget we are the people, and that is the reason why you have come to find us.

'We insisted in our discussion that we would accept limited elections this time, but never again. The communists refused to sign that paragraph. At one of the Magdalenka meetings we told them, There will be no agreement in that case. This kind of contract between us violates democratic principles, and we can accept it only under these exceptional circumstances for the sake of transition to democracy. At the end of that meeting, they accepted our point of view but it remained a difficulty right to the end. In the Sejm they voted through the new electoral law giving themselves the privileged percentage of seats, and they violated our agreement by omitting the article specifying that this law and its privileged percentage would apply only in 1989. So there was never any question of holding free elections. We knew we were living under a totalitarian regime. We hoped that we would win the 35 per cent allotted to us, and enough of their 65 per cent to begin the decomposition of communism. They played a double game. They told us they were intending to become a party adapted to democracy, while actually fashioning some sort of safety valve to last as long as necessary, so that they could return to the situation as before.'

Solidarity gambled, Geremek says, but it paid off. Unprepared, without access to the mass media, they did not expect such a clean sweep. He had not intended to stand for election himself, he explains, but Lech Wałęsa urged him to do so at the last moment when the only seat available was in the agricultural region along the western border. The secretary of the Central Committee told him that this region was completely under party control and that Geremek stood no chance. Like Solidarity candidates elsewhere, he won.

Did Solidarity shut out personalities or embryo parties who might prove uncongenial politically?

Some, Mazowiecki among them, thought that Solidarity should share its 35 per cent but Geremek and the majority in the opposition believed that any sharing out of seats at that stage would weaken the attack on the party. He recalls how he and Mazowiecki had visited the Pope, and told him that they would not be standing for election. Also present at this audience, Wałęsa had frowned, and on returning to Warsaw he had ordered them both to stand. Geremek had accepted on the assumption that Mazowiecki would do the same. No conspiracy here either, he says, just the stuff of politics.

Jaruzelski in 1989 atoned for his earlier declaration of martial law. There had been a danger of civil war, in Geremek's opinion, and the Round Table had averted it. Towards the end of that year, when already elected to parliament, he met Jaruzelski for the first time. Jaruzelski had told him how the Soviet Union had become his second homeland and communism his religion. Now that the Soviet Union and communism no longer existed, he felt abandoned. That, Geremek says, went for the whole party. 'Nothing was left except power, without the least moral or ideological justification.'

Mild and soft-spoken, Janusz Reykowski was chosen to head the party's delegation to the Round Table, the opposite number to Geremek. The two had long known each other. A professor of psychology, and a bridge-builder by inclination, he also wrote political articles whose gist was the need for reconciliation and reform. Reform required social approval. The results of the 1987 referendum were therefore disappointing. Jaruzelski had virtually wasted six or seven years, so that major changes had to be envisaged, although exclusively within the system. His fear was that Solidarity policy might lead not to an independent Poland but to destabilization and civil war. Elected to the Politburo in December 1988, Reykowski was immediately picked to be chairman of the political Round Table. His colleagues thought that the talks were bound to fail, he believes, and they protected themselves by avoiding association with them, pushing the newcomer into the hot spot.

Was there a sense of crisis at Politburo meetings?

'Every now and then someone would voice anxiety that we were going in the wrong direction. But agreement with Solidarity was regarded as the remedy for crisis, rather than the crisis itself. The typical Politburo meeting lasted from ten o'clock in the morning to ten or even eleven at night. In spite of prearrangements and cabals, things were discussed intensively.' After the very first meeting with Geremek at the Round Table, he received a note from one of the members of his group, to the effect that Solidarity was not interested in any agreement but only in obtaining power and destroying socialism. Further negotiations must open the road to such plans. This note was circulated in the leadership, and then debated fiercely. 'People concluded that the author may well be right, but the alternative to negotiations was a major political upheaval, leading to government by means of drastic force. And if power was going to be given to other hands, at least they were Polish hands.'

Were you given a brief by Jaruzelski?

'No. As things developed, I had a growing freedom of action. In order to make agreement viable I had to negotiate its elements with various sectors of the system, like the army and the police and other power structures. There was a great asymmetry between my situation and Geremek's. After a meeting, he was ready for the next stage in a couple of days. I needed ten days, to take into account all those who could undermine what I was doing.'

Technicalities almost scuppered the negotiations right to the last moment. Some were substantial, others piquant illustrations of human vanity. 'The main idea of power-sharing changed into the transformation of power. I and my colleagues assumed we should have a transition period of power-sharing, we didn't think Solidarity was prepared for the task of running the country. People don't generally understand that democracy isn't just a question of election but needs a well-developed infrastructure. Perhaps I was not realistic, but then we hadn't expected a chain reaction in the whole region. The tendency for ever more radical change became self-reinforcing.'

Once the party began to speak with more than one voice, decentralization and loss of control were self-accelerating. Improvization replaced ideology. People started to do what they thought was in their interest. Reykowski has a telling anecdote. At Magdalenka, in mid-March, Kwaśniewski on his own initiative suddenly asked Solidarity if they would agree to free elections to the Senate. This proposition could be discussed, Geremek replied. 'Next day was a Sunday, most people weren't around, and only a small group met with Jaruzelski for very intensive argument about free elections to the Senate. Those of us in favour said that the time when the party could protect its powerbase by force was over. Either it would fight politically for its survival or it didn't deserve to survive. For many hours it was hard to predict the outcome of this discussion. Jaruzelski finally intervened in favour. This small group had taken a decision which had to be ratified by the Politburo, which was due to meet on the Tuesday. But that evening the official spokesman Jerzy

Urban announced our decision, and so by Tuesday when the question was on the Politburo agenda it was very difficult to see how we could cancel it.'

Apprehension over the Round Table agreement turned to outright horror at the election results. Reykowski says, 'You can imagine what it was for Jaruzelski!' Some of the party almost mutinied.

Was there any real prospect of force?

'Not from the top level. But influential people argued that the failure of the National List justified invalidating the election. That would have been regarded as manipulation. Violence would have been almost inevitable. Jaruzelski's authority as the man who had declared martial law protected those politicians who wanted reform. But I always took care to see to the interests of the security police. You could never be sure of full control of the colonels and majors.'

As for the Russians, their involvement was only indirect. Presumably people from his side of the Round Table were reporting to them but he has no knowledge of it. Hardliners were in contact with sympathizers in Moscow.

From 1958 to 1982 Mieczysław Rakowski was editor of the party's main journal, *Polityka*, and he became a full member of the Central Committee in 1975. As he says of himself, he was 'well-trained in a political school'. In 1981 he took part in discussions with the rest of the leadership to introduce martial law. Two years later he appeared on television to rant against Wałeşa, and clips of this film were relayed around the world to fix an unflattering image of the man. Shortly afterwards, Wałeşa was to receive the Nobel Prize. Falling out with Jaruzelski, Rakowski was shunted to the post of deputy Speaker in the Sejm. Looking back, he thinks that communism was in evident need of reform as early as the 1960s, but dogma had blinkered them all. Arrogance brought down the party. Michnik once asked him why the Round Table had not been introduced in 1986 when Solidarity had been marginalized. A good question, he concedes. By his own account, he perceived in 1987 that perestroika would leave every satellite in the lurch and that September he presented a sixty-page memorandum to this effect to Jaruzelski. Nothing came of it. Discussion in the Politburo was perfunctory.

General Kiszczak's speech on 26 August 1988 came out of a Central Committee plenum held that day. During the session, Jaruzelski drafted a short motion that the Central Committee propose to open the way to a Round Table meeting, and Rakowski thinks the phrase may well have been invented then and there. Today considering himself to have been naïve, he believed at the time that it would be possible to form a government incorporating people from Solidarity. 'That is why we proposed the Round Table.'

Six months were wasted because Jaruzelski thought he could carry out reform on his own, and he also flatly rejected any accommodation with Michnik and Kuroń, whom he demonized. 'The wave of strikes put an end to that. We came to the Round Table without any arguments.'

Rakowski became Prime Minister in the autumn of 1988. 'At the plenum of the Central Committee on 15 December I made a speech to put a proposal, either we should accept Solidarity or fight it. Half an hour before I took the floor, I gave a copy of that speech to Jaruzelski. I didn't expect an answer, I told them, until a month later. Party members wanted to end a policy based on struggle. Even hardliners had had enough of it. They were also impressed by events in the Soviet Union. So at the subsequent meeting on 6 January 1989 they voted to treat with Solidarity.'

Reflection over the Christmas period between these two meetings, he says, led him to conclude that his government was acceptable to the voters, and elections should be held. On New Year's Eve he put this proposition to Jaruzelski. The electoral arrangements were supposed to suit the party and the opposition. 'We were partly blind, no doubt. At the end of May opinion polls gave us 14 per cent and 34 per cent to the opposition. The rest were Don't Knows whom we thought would vote for us. Again, arrogance. The Round Table will be judged as a historic step towards compromise. It was an unpleasant surprise to lose in June 1989 but I had realized that we had embarked on a process leading in that direction. I remember Wałęsa saying one evening in January 1989 that my government was working well and Solidarity wasn't ready to govern but by the end of the century would have 10 per cent of the power. Not much anticipation of events there.'

Rakowski first met Gorbachev in Warsaw in June 1988. As Prime Minister, he followed the old custom of going to Moscow to bow the knee, so to speak. Giving way as Prime Minister after the elections to Mazowiecki, Rakowski in August 1989 became the party's last First Secretary, succeeding Jaruzelski whose sole office was President. While Mazowiecki was forming his government, Rakowski proposed another visit to Moscow. Gorbachev put him off on the grounds that it might seem like political intervention on his part in Polish affairs. A story has arisen that Gorbachev told Rakowski that the party was now in opposition and would therefore have to co-operate with Mazowiecki. Rakowski denies this.

'Four communists were ministers in Mazowiecki's government and the concept of the party's "leading role" was still in Gorbachev's mind. Photographs in the papers of Wałęsa with leaders of parties who used to be our allies made him ask, Mieczysław, what's happened? He told me of his difficulties, how he had two wings, the cavalry who wanted to go too fast and the artillery who did not want to move at all. He said to me, You have to look for younger men, because you can do nothing with the old-timers.'

Gorbachev let Poland and all Eastern Europe go for nothing in return.

'Why, and what kind of thinking led him to retreat from empire, are still open questions. Shevardnadze wrote in his book that in 1986 Gorbachev and he had come to the conclusion that the status quo could not be maintained. We do not really know what was happening. Mrs Thatcher argued against German reunification when she was here in Warsaw, she told me outright that she was against it. I was in Moscow for the Warsaw Pact summit on 4 and 5 December 1989. Gorbachev wanted to report on his meetings with Bush in Malta, and with the Pope in the Vatican. New party leaderships were there, for instance, Modrow and Krenz from the DDR, Urbánek from Czechoslovakia, Mazow-iecki and myself. Even then Gorbachev said that Chancellor Kohl was speaking of a German confederation, and that he and President Bush had come to the conclusion that there would be no border changes. And now he and Shevardnadze tell us that they had already taken these decisions three years before. I asked him in 1989 why he did not give the Baltic republics their independence. He replied, I know they will achieve it but it has to be based on constitutional law. So as a matter of fact, he had some hope that they would stay within the Soviet Union. It is difficult to find the answer to what happened but I think that he had lost control. In 1989 and 1990 he still believed that he could take events over as they were overtaking him. Arrogance.'

In time to carry his share of responsibility for martial law, Marian Orzechowski joined the Central Committee secretariat in September 1981, and then the Politburo in 1983, and he was effectively the party's last Foreign Minister. The Russians had been prepared to invade in 1980 and 1981, he says, but they preferred the Poles to do the dirty work. 'Time and again they told us that Jaruzelski might have to be replaced and they had an alternative team of leaders waiting, with associations and journals and so on ready to act in their name.' Through the 1980s the Russians applied pressure for harsh measures to replace what they considered a cat-and-mouse game of interning Solidarity opponents only to release them. Why was Geremek still at liberty, for instance? Martial law did not keep the Church at bay, and only postponed the Pope's visit. 'How many talks I had about that in Moscow!' he says with a sigh.

With Jaruzelski's approval he first raised the issue of Katyn with Ligachev in Moscow in 1984. 'It was a dramatic conversation. I told him I had come specially to clarify this massacre. Ligachev asked, Why should we return to this matter? That was always the answer.'

A member of the political committee of the Warsaw Pact, Orzechowski met Gorbachev in Poland in June 1985 and found him highly cautious. His first confidential meeting with Gorbachev in February 1988 lasted for ninety minutes. Already Gorbachev had made up his mind that without perestroika everything would collapse. 'I could also sense that he was between the hammer and the anvil, between those like Yeltsin, whom he called neo-bolshevik in their haste to advance perestroika, and the military–industrial and party complex.'

A mixed Soviet–Polish commission was investigating Katyn. 'I think that in February 1988 Gorbachev was not yet aware of the secret dossiers although it is difficult to be sure. We discussed the Ribbentrop–Molotov Pact as well as Katyn, and he realized that without explanation of these matters it would be impossible to have good relations with Poland or the Baltic republics either. But if he was to give way anywhere he feared he would provoke a chain reaction everywhere. To recognize the Pact as invalid from the beginning also meant the beginning of the end of the Soviet Union and that is what he feared most of all. He had an obsession with the balance of forces in the world. If really existing socialism were to disappear then Pax Americana would be established, which he thought was not in the world's true interests. At all costs he wanted to maintain the Soviet Union, albeit as a federation or con-federation, and transformed in the direction of the market and pluralism. He wanted to have Katyn out in the open but he told me that the KGB opposed all inquiry into it. My friends from the Soviet–Polish commission on the contrary often told me that the Katyn dossier was on the desk of Mikhail Sergeyevich, and it lay there for months.'

Gorbachev had been expected to make amends for Katyn during his visit. At a meeting with intellectuals in the royal castle in Warsaw, he had his chance but did not take it. 'He lost much in the eyes of the Poles.' To draw attention to 'blank spots' in history but then not to fill them in truthfully left Gorbachev without the old cover of lies and without the credit for telling the truth.

'Gorbachev did not want to divest himself of influence in Central Europe but to be rid of the dependency of the satellites. Economic ties could not be easily severed. He felt that he could arrange relations on the Finnish model, where influence would be maintained. We can say it was not realistic because things have worked out as they have. When in February 1988 I told him that the position of Jaruzelski was under attack, he was very worried. In spite of his lack of resolution, his playing Hamlet, Jaruzelski was head and shoulders above the gerontocrats in the other satellites. Gorbachev realized that if economic reforms in Poland were to collapse, his hardliners could argue that deviation from the principles of socialism must lead to catastrophe. He came to Poland in June 1988 to provide moral support. At every meeting with Jaruzelski, Gorbachev approved of what was happening in Poland. Of course neither he nor any of us foresaw that the end of really existing socialism was so close. When control was slipping from their hands, the KGB here, with its resident General Pavlov, started to look for contacts with the opposition.'

On vacation in Bulgaria that August, Orzechowski concluded that the socialist experiment had run its course. Society did not want the party. 'It's a simplification but basically true to say that the division arose between those who agreed that the party could not maintain its leading role by force and by fraud, and those who thought that surrender of this monopoly would loose apocalypse on us.'

Force could only have been used, in his opinion, in the event of Gorbachev's overthrow in Moscow. Local hardliners could then have acted. 'But I have to tell you that I personally feel that 13 December 1981 had been a hugely negative experience for the army and police. I had discussions with General Kiszczak and General Siwicki that martial law could work only once. The army and riot police could not be mobilized against society. Most of the party leadership realized this, and that was why they consented to the Round Table and the election. You couldn't rerun martial law.'

What were discussions like in the party leadership between January and May 1989?

'Every day the party was disintegrating more and more. Contrary instructions caused havoc outside Warsaw. I saw internal documents and they were highly pessimistic. Of course if you read the party newspaper *Trybuna Ludu*, the picture looked different but this was propaganda. Ninety per cent of the members were waiting to see what would happen. But as a united and centralized organization, the way everyone imagined it, the party no longer really existed. A good example is free election to the Senate. Geremek supposed that this election would also be subject to contractual arrangement. Completely free election was the invention of Kwaśniewski. The Politburo could do nothing but accept it. Nobody was in control of events.

'Before the Round Table, the party leadership wrongly assessed the balance of forces within Solidarity. Geremek, Michnik, Onyszkiewicz, Kuroń, had been regarded as extremists but they turned out to be completely realistic and they did not want revenge on the communists. For Jaruzelski this came as a great surprise. The relief was even greater when they realized they were passing power to moderates.'

How did Gorbachev react to the Round Table and the June election?

'After the famous television debate between Wałęsa and Miodowicz in the autumn of 1988 the Russians lost touch with what was happening. The last official task I had was to attend the Portuguese party's congress, with Cunhal, one of the oldest Stalinists. There I met Yakovlev and Medvedev. I gave my word of honour that the Politburo hadn't authorized Miodowicz to appear on television with Wałeşa but they didn't want to believe it. And even if they had understood, things had gone too far and too fast for them. The election completely destroyed the party. When that blow came, everyone gave up. By force of inertia it lasted another six months till the January 1990 congress. The apparatus was not big, about 20,000 people, much less than the Solidarity apparatus which by then was 44,000. The party had simply ceased to believe that its existence was still meaningful.'

Except for Ceauşescu, General Jaruzelski was the last communist leader in the bloc to use force against his own people. In power for almost nine years, he had struck a most peculiar figure, slight in stature, seemingly dwarfed by the outsize peaked cap of the military uniform he always wore in public, inscrutable behind dark glasses, speaking in a dreary tone of menace. Down the years he has carefully thought out the defence of his actions. The lesser evil of cracking down on his own country had prevented the greater evil of the Soviets doing so. To a minority of Poles he was a saviour and patriot, to the majority he was a hateful traitor. No final judgement is possible. What was morally indefensible may have ameliorated a desperate plight. It is the classic stance of the collaborator throughout history. The closest parallel to him is Pierre Laval who in occupied France pleaded that it was better for him to persecute fellow Frenchmen partially rather than let the Germans do it thoroughly.

The office where I met Jaruzelski was in Aleje Jerozolimskie, one of Warsaw's thoroughfares rebuilt after the war in utilitarian style. He was in a brown suit, with the familiar dark glasses. When a lady entered the room at one point, he rose and kissed her hand with rather cramped courtliness. Through his delivery or perhaps his upright posture of attentiveness, he conveyed some sense of inner bewilderment that ideological certainties had after all been so fragile.

I asked him about Soviet pressure to declare martial law and he replied, 'I am heartily sick of the topic.' The Soviets had given an ultimatum: either the internal situation had to be brought under control by the beginning of 1982 or they would cut off supplies of oil, gas and other raw materials. In 1980 and 1981 he was summoned three times to the Soviet Union. On the last occasion, in September 1981, he witnessed army manoeuvres along the Polish border from Ukraine up to the Baltic. Marshal Ustinov informed him that what was happening in Poland was intolerable. 'Each of these conversations and meetings was very fraught, politically and psychologically. We had to convince our allies that we would not undermine the Warsaw Pact or allow the state to be destabilized. This was a duel, thankfully a verbal duel. The introduction of martial law allowed us to avoid other forms of duelling.'

Recent documents from the Soviet archives, I said, indicate from Politburo discussions that the Soviets were not intending to invade. Was he then the victim of a piece of theatre?

Familiar with these documents in detail, Jaruzelski had a number of objections. Basically, 'They were testing how far we were ready to introduce martial law and pressuring us, while we were testing them to see how far they were ready to intervene.' To spare themselves the costs of intervention in every sense, the Soviets preferred the Poles to solve their own problem. 'It would be beneath my dignity as an officer to say that, yes, they planned it for us, they forced us. It was our sovereign decision. I am proud that we were able to push through this painful but necessary act. Being on both sides of the barricade, Poles were unable to find a compromise. I may speak critically about myself at that point but I feel that an even greater responsibility is held by extremists in Solidarity who pushed the moderates to the margin.'

Solidarity had no influence by 1986. 'I won't try to beautify my position by saying that I realized that really existing socialism was flawed. We felt the system required deep reform, especially at its economic base. Sixty per cent of society was closer to the party than to Solidarity and we wanted them to see us as the source of revolution. We also realized that reforms required the support of the West and this would be greater if Solidarity were legalized.' To prove his reformist intentions, he pointed to PRON, the Consultative Council and the unsuccessful referendum of 1987.

'Gorbachev on many occasions said that Polish changes were an impulse to perestroika and that he closely analysed our experiences and drew his conclusions. He often requested material about what we had tried and tested, but of course here and in the Soviet Union the aim was deep reform, not change leading to collapse. That was something carried on later by life itself.

'I was closely linked to Gorbachev. We spoke to one another without reserve, saying that old men like Zhivkov and Honecker did not understand a thing. That was clear in Berlin, though the course of events was difficult to foresee. I was there for the fortieth anniversary of the DDR, standing next to Krenz for the torchlight demonstration with the crowd chanting Gorbi, Gorbi. We were saying, This is the beginning of the end of Honecker, but he has not yet understood it. I spoke to Gorbachev about this. He believed that a confrontation between East and West, or within the Warsaw Pact, had to be avoided. For this reason each country had to go its own way. He could perhaps have done more to delay the process but that is debatable.

'Before I agreed to the Round Table, I too had doubts, mostly of an economic character. I still remember how in 1981 Solidarity caused the collapse of the Polish economy through calling constant strikes. My greatest fear was that a reconstituted Solidarity would be able to undermine the economy in transformation. Despite that, I came to the conclusion that the risk had to be run and we had to find a common platform. If we were to jump the hurdle of reform, we had to mobilize everyone. In the first stage, most of the Central Committee did not agree. In the first part of the plenum in December 1988, Rakowski's speech played an important role in asking whether it was worthwhile to legalize Solidarity or not.

'At the second half of that plenum in January, the discussion moved against legalization. I was criticized sharply for failing to strengthen the party and socialism. I could see no way out other than a sort of blackmail. I demanded a break. I asked the Minister of Defence, General Siwicki, and the Minister of the Interior, General Kiszczak, to come to my office. I told them that I intended to resign because I could not go along with the line of this discussion and I asked if they were ready to do the same. The generals said yes. Together we represented a real force. Then I informed Rakowski, and he said he would also resign. We returned to the room and declared our resignation. Several Politburo members stood up and joined us. We then won a vote of confidence. This had been a genuine blackmail. Events moved quickly afterwards.'

You didn't appreciate that the party had so little popular support?

'The scale of the victory was a surprise for us as well as for Solidarity. Some felt that we would defeat Solidarity handsomely but I was more cautious. Opinion polls did not predict the result. So we have to accept that we were overconfident, we lacked understanding of how isolated we were. We couldn't judge the explosion of euphoria in people that a Solidarity victory would rain dollars on Poland. This was partly the fault of the Western media.'

Hardliners wanted to overturn the election results.

'There was always a chance of reversing the process after June 1989. There was even a legal basis to nullify the elections because at the Round Table it had been agreed that the campaign should not be confrontational. Unfortunately it was, from the Solidarity side. What we had visualized was power-sharing, while maintaining the key levers of power. We still had those levers in our hand, but it is difficult to say what might then have happened. It could have gone off smoothly but you might have had some sort of revolution. I remember a meeting of the secretariat of the Central Committee immediately after the results were declared, and I said straight away, We have to recognize this.'

Jaruzelski surrendered power in the didactic and unsmiling style with which he had exercised it. Because of this consistency, many Poles are inclined to give him the benefit of the doubt. The few mistakes to which he admits are revealing. He promoted people who were intellectually incapable of carrying through reform, he says, and he made what he calls an 'inadequate interpretation' of the likes of Kuroń and Michnik. A prisoner of the information he received about them, as he puts it, he did indeed demonize them. The secret police prepared extracts from their statements out of context, to show them at their most contentious. Knowing these former dissidents personally now, he says that he has come to respect them. And vice versa apparently. At the end of his memoirs, Jaruzelski prints a thirty-page dialogue with Michnik, whom he calls Adam to his face, while the latter assures him that victory was shared and both of them can remain faithful to their past.

Tadeusz Mazowiecki will be remembered as the first democratic Prime Minister ever to be appointed within the communist system. An inconceivable hybrid. Neither charismatic nor a compromiser, he is somewhat ponderous, known to be a stickler for detail. As an adviser to Wałeşa, he had held talks before the Round Table with party leaders as well as with Catholic bishops. The party had placed itself on one side of a chasm, in his phrase, with the population on the other side. After deceptive and artificial attempts to close the chasm they had themselves opened, the party leaders had no choice except to recognize Solidarity. The fact remains that they did so only as a last resort.

Without the Round Table there would have been no elections, and without elections Mazowiecki could not have formed his government. 'Those were the three decisive steps. Neither the party nor us thought things would turn out as they did, but history goes faster than we do, doesn't it? I decided not to stand for election because I thought that we should have more broad-based support than through the Citizens' Committee, taking in other groups and parties. I also didn't think parliament would be so important. It could have been a rebuff for me, but within a few days I became Prime Minister. I was rather detached from the games then being played, and was actually abroad. I ran the trade union Round Table, and was seen as someone with more of a prospect of reaching consensus. The decision lay with Wałeşa. My response was that he should fill the post himself but he did not want to.'

Why did you take the communist Generals Kiszczak and Siwicki into the government?

'The question is always, Is it more dangerous to have a communist general in your house or to leave him out-of-doors? It was clear to me that if the party was not represented one way or another in the government the reforms could not be carried through in a peaceful manner. The party still had at its disposal the means of using force. The generals had participated in the Round Table. In principle they behaved correctly, although the destruction of files and Politburo protocols from the Ministry of State Security created a problem. I do not know if Kiszczak himself or his people were responsible.'

As President, Jaruzelski still had constitutional powers to block you.

'Only in certain circumstances. He remained passive, loyal, in the period until Wałęsa took his place as President, but he had little choice. It made no sense for him to accept the fact of reform only to try to sabotage its practice.

'It was a matter of principle to keep the portfolio of Foreign Minister out of the hands of the party. I wanted to show the Russians that a sovereign Poland would conduct a peaceful foreign policy.' As Prime Minister, Mazowiecki was expected to visit Moscow on his first foreign trip but he broke with tradition by paying his respects that October to the Pope. The subsequent meeting with Gorbachev in November caused a protocol awkwardness because he refused to lay the customary wreath on Lenin's tomb.

It must have been a shock to Gorbachev to receive a Polish Catholic independent Prime Minister?

'Naturally, and a painful one at that. But I found him an open-minded man, ready for dialogue on all subjects with the exception of Germany. On this he spoke in the old style, so that I was amazed when he accepted its reunification so quickly.'

Why did he let Poland go free so lightly?

'He could do nothing about it, first of all. Secondly, the Round Table process was in a sense consistent with perestroika and he could not object to changes to which he had so evidently committed himself. Those over there who believed they could stop it all through sabotage were themselves against Gorbachev. So an open opponent of these changes had to built an alliance between Gorbachev and his enemies. That was too complicated. The Russians accept hard facts. It was a question of strength.'

21

THE IRON CURTAIN OPENS

The history of human infamy reserves a perpetual place in it for János Kádár. In October 1956 he joined the government of Imre Nagy, ostensibly in agreement with the mild reform proposed within Hungary and in relation to the Soviet Union. A few days later he calculated that the Soviets would put a violent end to this whole experiment and he therefore defected to them without informing anyone. When the Soviets duly crushed the Nagy government and the freedom fighters who defended it, they made Kádár First Secretary. Imre Nagy and his leading colleagues were tricked by a guarantee of safe passage to leave their refuge in the Yugoslav Embassy. Hijacked, they were then put before a tribunal and hanged in total secrecy. If the country had experienced a national uprising, Kádár was evidently a quisling without legitimacy, and therefore it was essential party dogma to claim that he and the Soviets had suppressed a counter-revolution. To be on the safe side, the Soviets until 1989 were still maintaining 170 military bases for their forces in Hungary.

György Krassó, one of the most eminent Hungarian intellectuals, was himself imprisoned at the time along with Nagy, and he has recorded how a Major Kovács and his assistant Karácsony used to carry out daily hangings of Nagy supporters. His measured conclusion is that although the final death sentence was passed in the Kremlin, Kádár might have used the threat of resignation to bargain for the lives of his former friends and colleagues. 'It remains a fact that with the execution of Imre Nagy he got rid of his most dangerous rival.' More than a collaborator, Kádár carried on him the mark of Cain.

The Soviet ambassador, Andropov, the future General Secretary of the party, orchestrated this repression. On his staff was Kryuchkov, later Gorbachev's KGB chief, and a Hungarian speaker. Like them, other hardliners including Ligachev took a special interest in Hungary,. Local food and wine, gypsy music and Magyar exoticism, drew them, and with it a dark urge to stalk the scene of their crime, and persuade themselves that vice was really virtue.

A Hungarian specialist, first in the Soviet Embassy and then in the Central Committee secretariat, was Valeri Muszatov. He speaks the language. He admired Kádár as 'a statesman'. In an interview he explained how Kádár used to make a point of spending time with Andropov whenever he visited Moscow. From personal knowledge, he can affirm that among satellite leaders Gorbachev respected only Jaruzelski and Kádár. Muszatov also says, 'Kádár had 1956 on his conscience at all times.' Nagy's corpse was dug up on 16 June 1989 and reburied in Budapest at a state funeral which served as rehabilitation. It was poetic justice that a disgraced Kádár died at that very moment. A circle was completed when Kryuchkov then made a statement which may or may not be true, that as an émigré in Moscow during the Stalinist terror Nagy had been a Soviet secret police agent and denouncer.

Krassó was persecuted and exiled to London, and his work was published only in *samizdat*. An exposé like his might have spread, enlarging into a public event which Kádár could not survive. Kádár and the party aimed to strike a tacit bargain with the population whereby in return for the monopoly of power they would create prosperity, famously touted as 'goulash communism'. The Kremlin licensed private enterprise in Hungary which was denied elsewhere in the bloc. The shortcomings of the command-administrative economy were revealed all the more starkly. Between 1948 and 1988, just 101 communists ruled the country. The sociologist András Nyírö has described how the economy was run in those years by just five Politburo members, 'a mechanic (Jenö Fock), a sixth-grade dropout (Sándor Gáspár), a typesetter (Rezsö Nyers), a butcher (Károly Németh), and a bricklayer (Ferenc Havasi)'. Another dissenting political scientist, Mihály Bihari, noted that these 101 Politburo members had spent enough years in prison to total several centuries, and most of the sentences they had inflicted upon each other. Captives of their own system, they had fought a murderous struggle for power.

The privileges and wealth of the pre-war aristocracy and clergy were at least visible, and within a legal framework, however inequitable. Between 1957 and 1989, the Politburo issued thirteen secret directives on the management in its favour of the Nomenklatura system. There was much to hide. Subsidized by the state, the party employed 4000 officials and owned property worth hundreds of millions of dollars, including 3000 buildings, four holiday resorts, and the printing and publishing industries. Privileged access to wealth was draining the meaning out of ideology. Elémer Hankiss, a philosopher and later head of Hungarian television, summarized the process: 'The characteristic oligarchic family in the mid-1980s was the father or the grandfather, a party apparatchik, a high-level party or state official; his son a manager of a British/Hungarian joint venture; his son-in-law with a boutique in Váci Street; his daughter an editor for Hungarian television; his nephew studying at Cambridge or Oxford; his mother-in-law having a small hotel or boarding house on Lake Balaton.' These diversified oligarchic families kept their businesses 'absolutely top secret'.

The last political prisoner in the country was Miklós Haraszti, released before Gorbachev's glasnost. His book *The Velvet Prison* analyses the subtle temptations and threats by means of which the party converted a free-thinker into a collaborator and Homo sovieticus. Brilliantly conveyed, the pessimism proved unfounded. The party still had three-quarters of a million members, but it had become a freemasonry in pursuit of self-help.

The ageing Kádár was not amenable to argument. Isolated yet still casting the aura of his crime, he kept in touch with colleagues through a favourite henchman and old Stalinist, György Aczél. Like his master, Aczél was to die as communism disappeared around him. Another hardliner supporting Kádár was the Ideological Secretary János Berecz, styled the Hungarian Ligachev. The Workers' Militia, 60,000 strong and armed, was generally considered to have the will and capacity to defend the party to the last.

A meeting in September 1987 of party intellectuals and some independents at Lakitelék, a tourist village near Budapest, marked the introduction of perestroika. The most prominent man present was Imre Pozsgay, who for some years had worked to build credentials as the representative of the up-and-coming generation of party leaders. He stuck exactly to Gorbachev's line. Reform did not mean a multi-party system but only socialism under a new leader like himself, and still within the Soviet bloc. Overweight and ungainly, Pozsgay was all things to all men. In his memoirs he indicates that his role was to link dissatisfied intellectuals and the majority or reformist wing of the party, and he suggests that without his efforts there might have been bloodshed. Had he instead, Yeltsin-like, committed himself to multi-party democracy and independence, he might have fulfilled his overriding aim of coming to power.

In alarm, the party élite decided that Kádár was no longer capable of heading off Pozsgay's bid for power. After the usual subterranean soundings, Károly Grosz was chosen as First Secretary and Prime Minister as well. The manoeuvre was formalized at a special party conference in May 1988. Apparently not even the State Security had warned Kádár in advance. As a sop to his feelings, a new post of President was created for him. Most of the old Politburo was purged though not Aczél, whose speech swayed the conference to give him another chance.

Grosz's dour and devious personality was the product of a lifetime in the party bureaucracy. He says that he was elected because he was known to be a Marxist who would never change: 'I always express my opinions in a very disciplined way within the structures and in accordance with the regulations of the party.' So strong was the party, in his view, that it could exploit the opposition by co-opting it into a coalition with a pretence of national unity.

It so happens that Grosz lives at Gödöllö, half an hour from Budapest. In the town centre is the castle where the Empress Elisabeth retreated while her husband Franz-Josef tried to hold together the failing Austro-Hungarian Empire. It is largely a gutted ruin, and the garden a wilderness. Grosz's comfortable modern villa lies set back behind an iron security fence, and on the day I went there gardeners and maids were busy at work in a Nomenklatura paradise. The choice of such a man as First Secretary is evidence of the party's intellectual and moral void.

On 29 November 1988 Grosz made a speech to hardliners in which he warned them emotively of the impending 'White Terror'. This allowed Pozsgay further to demarcate his opposition, and he did so early in the following January. A commission had been appointed to investigate the events of 1956. Pozsgay now declared its findings. This had been a popular and national uprising after all, not a counter-revolution. Reformers and hardliners were cutting the ground away under each others' feet, by mutual discreditation. An increasingly helpless Grosz conceded by slow degrees, first resigning as Prime Minister in favour of Miklós Németh, known to be a practising Catholic, and then consenting to a Round Table.

The Round Table opened six days after Solidarity had swept the Polish elections. A week later, the reburial of Imre Nagy dramatized the urgency of reaching consensus. Over 100,000 people gathered to pay their respects and to listen to eulogies that were almost inflammatory. Grosz took his next step in surrendering. There was to be an interim four-man presidency of Nyers, Pozsgay, Németh and himself.

The Round Table, in the expression of one academic witness, László Bruszt, was like wrestling in mud. Its overall president was Mátyás Szürös. József Antall, soon to be Prime Minister, led the opposition. A thousand politicians and experts participated in a plenary group, two technical committees and twelve more working groups. It was agreed to hold parliamentary elections in March 1990. The procedure for choosing the President to succeed the four-man improvization was another crucial issue. Pozsgay anticipated that he would emerge from the Round Table as President. To the opposition this looked like communist quick-change artistry for survival, and they obtained a referendum. As a result, the newly elected democratic parliament would vote for the President. At an angry congress that October, the party surrendered its 'leading role', changed its name and split into a social democratic majority and hardline rump.

Communism vanished from Hungary like air from a pricked balloon. The fabric was insubstantial. Borrowing the Polish compromise, Hungary nonetheless had a unique contribution to make. A treaty specified that East Germans who had entered Hungary illegally were to be returned, usually to serve long prison sentences. Early in 1989 the Government took a series of linked decisions all the more remarkable because they were autonomous. Like the rest of the world, the Soviets were taken by surprise. Hungary dismantled the obstacles along its border with Austria, restructured its units of border guards and decided that it was no longer appropriate to return illegal visitors. Quick to grasp that they now had an escape route, East Germans poured into the country. Unable and unwilling to deal with the numbers, the Government on 11 September opened its borders without restriction. The satellite bloc evaporated at a stroke. Pozsgay in his memoirs credits the whole Government with taking the decision. Gyula Horn, then Foreign Minister, has also written a book, in contrast emphasizing his role in dealing with both Germanys. Informed by Horn of his government's proposals to open the border, the East German Foreign Minister Oskar Fischer went as white as chalk and said, 'That wouldn't be very nice of you!' In his fury, Honecker unconsciously revealed the instinct to collaborate: 'We trusted them, but they betrayed us and did not inform anyone, not even the Soviet Union.'

The symbolic power of this decision was as great as its impact. The lifting of the Iron Curtain was the revenge of 1956.

As a prominent member of the Academy of Sciences, Kálmán Kulcsár was Minister of Justice in Grosz's government, and drafted Hungary's new Constitution. He had been in contact with Kádár and Grosz for a number of years. He had been invited to the May 1988 party conference. 'I used to leave my seat to talk to the people in the corridors, mostly representatives of the rural party organizations. Very much against Kádár, they wanted to change the top personnel. Kádár and Grosz had an understanding that some of the Politburo and Central Committee had to go, but it was a revolt of the rank and file. They were located in different hotels according to their counties, and Grosz and his friends visited them and convinced them that Kádár was an obstacle. Kádár was taken by surprise. He became very nervous, reacting irrationally. At the end of the conference, he cut a tragic figure, alone in the room waiting for his wife to arrive and take him away.'

The Nineteenth Soviet Party Conference was then taking place in Moscow, and they concluded from its proceedings that Soviet intervention was more or less inconceivable. Before and after Kulcsár's own election, Grosz visited Gorbachev: 'My impression is that he was given a free hand by Gorbachev.' As Minister of Justice, Kulcsár's first task was to prepare regulatory principles for a multi-party system and a free market. He soon found himself in the midst of the power struggle between Grosz, Miklós Németh who became

Prime Minister in 1989, and the hardliners. As Kulcsár sees it, Németh and behind him Pozsgay pulled power away from the party into the parliament. But parliament was itself a party institution, and the more representative Round Table then pulled power towards itself, in effect acting as an unofficial but nonetheless more legitimate parliament.

Into his brief came an overall review of the sentences passed against innocent people since the communist takeover, about 200,000 cases altogether. When Kulcsár presented this issue to the Central Committee, he found himself facing people who had themselves been in prison or consented to the wrongful imprisonment of others. 'Aczél recalled his arrest, and how he had been forced into confessions incriminating others besides himself. The mental and physical pressures of the secret police compelled these betrayals. And now all this would be published without taking the circumstances into account. But Grosz supported it. He could accept a lot, though not the disappearance of the socialist regime. He was unable to step over his own shadow.

'In the summer of 1989, the Government faced crucial decisions and wanted to be sure of the obedience of the armed forces. Some generals informed Grosz that they would accept party orders, so we restructured the army command system. Instead of the Minister of Defence, the Prime Minister became commander-in-chief and General Kálmán Lörincz was appointed Chief of Staff. We organized a manoeuvre at the same time, whereby parliament would legislate to dissolve the Workers' Militia and the army would disarm them. The soldiers went round and confiscated the Militia arsenals.

'Everybody in the leadership accepted that the party should be able to risk a free election, but because of the Kádár regime they had illusions about its outcome. People are also unwilling to believe that we did not inform the Soviet Union beforehand of our decision to open the border, but I have to emphasize that this was the case.' An inner cabinet of Németh, Horn, the Minister of Defence General Kárpáti and the Minister of the Interior General István Horváth, Pozsgay and himself took the decision. His particular task was to present this decision as in accord with various treaties and he drily says, 'We found a completely acceptable legal gateway leading to this path. After that, it was a matter of a few days to put it through the Government.'

Why did you do it?

'Another question is, Why didn't we first ask for financial assistance from West Germany? The answer is that we wanted to show that we meant what we were doing and saying. Poland and Hungary were then the only two countries on the road to reform and it was by no means excluded that others in the Warsaw Pact would try something against us. We were pretty sure that if hundreds of thousands of East Germans went to the West, the East German regime would fall, and in that case Czechoslovakia was also out. We were not too concerned about Romania, the only danger to us came from the DDR. We took the step for our own sakes. Very few people guessed that the DDR and Czechoslovakia would then collapse. Our internal situation changed completely. Suddenly conscious of the strength of its position, the opposition was able to advance the date of the elections, and that was the end of the party.'

The Hungarian parliament is an architectural masterpiece from the last century, a neo-Gothic splendour of stone and statuary. Mátyás Szürös has an imposing suite of offices there. In March 1989 he became Speaker and he was also a member of the interim four-man presidency. He had been Secretary for International Affairs on the Central Committee. Kádár, he says, himself chose Grosz as his successor, but he had had little forewarning of his ouster at the May party conference. Aczél may have given him some idea of Grosz's conspiracy behind his back. A month before the conference, the Politburo had held a stormy session behind closed doors.

'Grosz kept on thinking in the old ways, while a circle of reformed politicians was forming to destroy him. In June 1989 I made a speech in the Central Committee that he should resign or be forced to step down. We had already realized that really existing socialism was unreformable but many believed it could convert into democratic socialism. Historically we were in a dead end. Pozsgay and that whole group were tempted to experiment with democratic socialism but we did not have enough information about the possible Soviet reaction. The Warsaw Pact still functioned. Without Gorbachev, the process of reform might be reversible. After the Malta summit Gorbachev did not inform us that he and Bush had agreed to the free flow of events.'

The old parliament, in Szürös's opinion, had passed the vital laws affecting the transition by means of a new constitution and a new electoral law. Hastening this process, the Round Table firmly established the parliamentary framework. It was a process in which everyone except Grosz came out a winner.

Szürös suggested to the Soviet ambassador that Pozsgay and Németh should be invited to official talks in Moscow. 'At the Italian Communist Party Conference, Yakovlev met Pozsgay and advised him to support Grosz. That was their line as late as the summer of 1989. Gorbachev and all of them were so fully occupied with internal affairs that events were slipping out of their control.'

Reszö Nyers is a survivor. Pliant, humorous, he tells stories as old men should.

Wizened, his skin seems to have the texture of a walnut. After decades of delicate fencing with Kádár, he saw him one last time after the party conference. 'Everything disappointed him. He was looking back at what he had done and could not swallow the Imre Nagy case. It caused him mental anguish.'

As Nyers describes it, the Central Committee by the mid-1980s split down the middle on the question of what sort of changes were appropriate to deal with the economic crisis. Kádár was sceptical about Gorbachev's capacity to transform the Soviet Union. 'He didn't want reform but he didn't want to block it either, and he couldn't be budged. So events had to happen without his participation. Grosz couldn't impose himself either. Trying to stabilize the system, Grosz found himself in opposition to Pozsgay and the reformers.'

The decisive factor, Nyers thinks, was anti-Russian sentiment. That is why the party lost so heavily and unexpectedly in the elections. 'We did not demonstrate the fact that it was us who had reached agreement with the Soviets to withdraw their garrisons. Gorbachev himself took the credit for it, and the opposition was able to make the most of that.'

Why did the party enter the Round Table process?

'We wanted reconciliation, not national unity but a national compromise. By then we recognized that we couldn't maintain our position, so we had moved towards the nationalist forces which had gathered at Lakitelék, as well as towards the liberal opposition. We didn't count on winning but on compromising. We were prepared step by step to withdraw party cells from the factories and to negotiate the future of the Workers' Militia.'

As he describes it, personality disputes and raw ambition had already dissolved the party. Grosz was unwilling to resign. Pozsgay commanded little loyalty. Németh saw himself as a white knight. The collective four-man presidency, of which Nyers was titular head, evinced the party's psychological unwillingness to continue in power.

Counter-Revolution in Hungary by János Berecz was the standard propaganda work on the 1956 revolution. In today's light it stands exposed as pitiful, but when first published in 1969 with the party's imprimatur it was the received truth. Imre Nagy's views, Berecz wrote, 'were essentially identical with the programme suggested and transmitted by the organs of international imperialism'. The West had plotted to discredit communism, while the party should have given more united leadership, a euphemism for repression. A nugget of reality could still be mined out of the mendacity. Between 1952 and 1955, he wrote, 1,126,434 people had been investigated, and sentences passed on 45 per cent of them. The final chapter with its subtitle 'Shoulder to

Shoulder with the Working Masses for Socialist Consolidation' conveyed the authentic party flavour of menace and sentimentality.

In the early 1960s Berecz had studied social sciences for four years at the Humanities Academy of the party in Moscow. A candidate member of the Central Committee in 1971, he became a full member in 1980, and then took over the editorship of the party newspaper *Népszabadság*. With his excellent Soviet connections, he was billed as a future First Secretary. A *bête noire* to dissidents, he aroused fear to the end.

Berecz's house in the Buda hills is a decorative retreat, built by some nineteenth-century industrialist with a sense of pleasure. Pet cats and dogs have their bowls on the wide horseshoe stone steps. In a panelled conservatory full of birdcages, I find myself staring at a blown-up photograph of a Brigitte Bardot lookalike. It is his wife, a famous Hungarian actress. In Hungarian lore, a *honvéd* was a dashing and fearless soldier, and Berecz with his ginger moustache and broad shoulders corresponds physically to this ideal.

As a young man in 1956, he says, his first wife's unpunctuality alone saved him from being caught inside a party building which a crowd was surrounding and storming. The uprising, he now says with a chastened air, was lawful. 'I have given up my one-sided approach to it.'

A Kádár loyalist, Berecz became Ideological Secretary in March 1985, responsible for Agitprop, or indoctrination. In 1972 Kádár had proposed to resign on grounds of age. The Central Committee entreated him to stay. Ten years later in a speech in Stockholm he stated that he was negotiating his pension. 'I had to censor his speeches and supervise their consequences. I cut that paragraph out. It was his habit on a Monday to review the press with me. And now he asked why the bit about his pension had not been published. I told him that messages to the Hungarian people should be delivered here, not in Stockholm. Thank you, he said, I just wanted to know whether you did it deliberately. Which means that he did not really want to retire. But that summer he started asking others for their opinion about his retirement. For four months he made trips around the country and he recognized that the time had come.

'Otherwise in the voting at the party conference his name would have been crossed off the list of the Central Committee, as happened to six other Politburo members of the older generation, and he wouldn't have been elected President. The crossing-out of those names gave these proceedings the air of a putsch. In his own opinion, Kádár was a reformer and he thought that Gorbachev was following where he had led.'

Could someone else have done better than Grosz?

As Prime Minister, Grosz in September 1987 had gathered a following which

THE WAR THAT NEVER WAS

disappeared only after the party conference. A tactician, Grosz had no strategic conceptions, according to Berecz. 'The system itself was no longer tenable. We had to proclaim that clearly. The question was whether we would find a radical or a peaceful way out. The party faithful later accused me repeatedly of allowing things to happen as they did. Pozsgay and Horn, they say, are traitors. I used to tell them that the change of the system was an objective process which nobody could halt. We could have used force, but there was no body or institution in which those who believed in this solution dared to say so. So change was obviously unavoidable. We had to decide how, and with what aim. Pozsgay, Grosz and myself shared a belief in compromise and reconciliation, and in particular that nobody should be hurt physically, that private property was acceptable and that peasants could choose to leave collectives. If the three of us had been able to work together, the outcome might well have been different.' Central Committee meetings by 1989 'were like funeral sessions. We were gathering just because we existed, but that's all'.

Grosz scaremongered about 'White Terror'.

'Grosz's speech was not broadcast and I caught it only through a recording in the TV centre. It was done without me, I was not a member of the committee dealing with party affairs where this speech was agreed. I knew the immediate reaction because the next day I was in Tatabánya to make a speech of my own in a sports hall to three thousand people. I did not react to Grosz's comment but I knew the first question after my speech would be, What is your opinion about the danger of White Terror? I replied that extremes can arise in any crisis but I saw no such present danger. Hardly had I arrived back in Budapest before Grosz was summoning me to say that he had expected solidarity. We worked in the same building, and I gave him a personal response, namely that for my part I would have expected him to have consulted with me before mentioning White Terror. So all the time the threads were being pulled apart.'

The party controlled the armed Workers' Militia.

'I never heard a proposal to deploy it but people may have had such an idea. Grosz told me that he went to Czechoslovakia to go shooting with Jakeš, who offered military help if we asked for it. When I went to Czechoslovakia, my opposite number Jan Fojtík also told me that we should behave in a more forceful manner. I replied that the basic lesson to be drawn from the history of socialism is that the military solution is no solution. The Polish army was the best in the bloc, and we were glad when Jaruzelski introduced martial law but even he was unable to consolidate.'

The Soviet Union, he thinks, let Hungary go because Gorbachev could not maintain either the empire or himself. Granted ethnic divisions, reform could only be self-destructive.

Your job was to defend Marxist ideology. What convinced you that the system had to change?

'It did not happen from one day to the next. In 1983, there was an academic conference on capitalism. I said that capitalism could renew itself in a crisis, so that political science did not have to be exclusively Marxist. In the following year I began to see 1956 as a revolution, but by 1986 I had become a hardliner again, falling back on Marxism. At another conference, this time in Szeged in January 1987, I was asked about pluralism. I was prepared to admit it at the level of ideology and interests, while rejecting a multi-party system. But once you admit that state-owned property is not the highest good you have set off on the path which leads unavoidably to multi-party elections. When we were going to have elections, an interviewer from French television asked me suddenly in the corridors of parliament, What happens if you don't win? Then the winners will form the Government, I answered. He went on, Does that mean you are willing to renounce power? No, I told him, just that people are taking it back from us. Had I been asked that question two short years earlier, I would have answered him that we would defend the power of the working class.'

You must have felt your own character changing.

'Of course. I made many notes at the time and I am quite surprised at the contradictions in myself. Pozsgay writes in his book that he knew everything in advance. That was not my case.'

Grosz believed that the party could allow pluralism but still keep control.

'Until the moment round about June or July 1989, when he had to recognize that he could no longer influence events. The party had two wings – reformers at whose head the party itself had placed Pozsgay and Nyers, whatever they may now claim, and the hardliners of the so-called Marxist Platform of Unity. My point of view was that we should split in a civilized manner. I calculated that the reformers would take 45,000 members with them, and the Marxist Platform of Unity would form a new Communist Party with 60,000 members. Behind the scenes there was an unwritten agreement that Pozsgay would be President of the republic. He carried on all the time with his plans, and was unable to form alliances. We couldn't agree with the reformers, they wanted to abolish the whole party.'

A long-standing member of the Central Committee, István Horváth was

Minister of the Interior from 1980 to 1985, and again from December 1987 to January 1990. Responsibility for law and order, as well as for the Hungarian section of the Iron Curtain, therefore lay with him. The police force including the secret police, he says, numbered 35,000 and the border guards another 13,000. There were 'some hundreds' of informers. The State Security formed a separate department within the Ministry of the Interior but operated only down to county level. In small towns and rural areas the local police doubled as security agents.

Slight in person, with rapid gestures and a diffident manner, colouring easily, Horváth does not fit the stereotype of a secret police general. Since leaving university, he had been a friend of Pozsgay; they lived in the same building, and their wives were also friends. He was on good terms with Grosz. Another friend was Kryuchkov, who always called on him in Budapest. 'There were many in the Soviet party and the KGB who walked around as though the world ought to be glad that they were stepping on it. Not Kryuchkov. He may not have had the statesmanship of Andropov but he read a lot and saw things for himself, including Soviet weaknesses. Grosz had the courage to tell Kádár to his face that he ought to resign. I agreed but I wouldn't have dared say it. Kryuchkov was here at the time and asked me why I wasn't as courageous as Grosz. I said, Did you dare to tell Brezhnev to go? No? So that is the end of that subject.'

The KGB co-ordinated with Horváth and State Security, exchanging information and maintaining contact 'in case we had to carry out any action together. Just as we had representation in Moscow too.' Soon after entering his second period in office, Horváth relocated the KGB offices away from his building. 'I laid it down that if there was something important then the chief had free access to me. Equally I would call him up if I wanted to speak to him.'

He makes the point that dissidents were Nomenklatura children, or disillusioned communists; Haraszti, for instance, had been a Maoist. The State Security had been skilful in separating legal opposition from illegal, permitting or tolerating meetings and *samizdat* publications in order to woo moderates and isolate extremists. 'Political considerations dictated that we should cause them discomfort and inconvenience but we wanted to avoid putting them on trial.' Violence was used against demonstrators in 1988, Horváth concedes, especially at the ceremony to rebury Nagy. One of the speakers that day, Gáspár Miklós Tamás, a political theorist with an international reputation, was beaten to the ground. Tamás and Krassó and a few others – forty-two in all, he says – were deprived of their passports in order to impress upon them who held power.

On the afternoon of the day when Grosz delivered his White Terror speech,

Horváth happened to see him. He was in a position to know that there was no prospect of White Terror. Significantly, Grosz did not then raise the subject with him. 'We had two types of threat. Revenge, let's say. And then the hardliners, grouped in the Ferenc Münnich Society (named after a Stalinist who, like Kádár, had turned against Nagy in 1956). We wanted to exclude both extremes from having any real role. For example, Ferenc Kulin came to see me in June 1989 with a warning that people were planning an armed provocation during the funeral of Imre Nagy. State Security had to turn its attention to that, if only to exclude it.'

A Defence Committee had contingency plans for a general state of emergency. Sometimes Grosz spoke of introducing a state of emergency but the party leadership did not support him in this. Horváth says that the possible use of the Workers' Militia was not discussed in the party leadership, in the Government or in the police. Although he himself wanted to keep the party in a position of power, he anticipated that there would be a multi-party system in which the police and State Security would have to be accountable.

'The KGB chief never came to me about the opening of the border but I know it for a fact that the KGB did not think it would be of such consequence.' Nor did Horváth himself.

Six million Hungarians went abroad every year and 25 million tourists entered. 'Every year we also had between 200 and 250 cases of foreigners trying to cross illegally, while the maximum number of Hungarians was ten. These were drunks, children with bad school reports and husbands sneaking away from their wives. With such a huge legal traffic, what was the point of catching this handful?' A modern professional corps, Horváth also argued, should replace the conscripts forming the border guards.

What he calls the signalling mechanism along the border consisted of barbed wire, electrified with a low-tension current. 'It was a very imperfect Russian mechanism. Setting it off, a rabbit or a roebuck would start the guards running in that direction. The whole system was due to be renovated in 1995 at a cost of hundreds of millions of forints, and in 1988 I concluded that we had better deal with this problem right away. It was no longer in our interests to incur these costs for such results. This proposition was accepted, and in the following spring we began to dismantle the signalling system, proceeding faster than expected, so that the job was completed within a few months.

'At the beginning of that summer I put a stop to the earlier practice, whereby if we captured a German trying to cross the border we transferred him back there. This was a minor technical question. But of course the Germans noticed, first that we were no longer transferring them back, and secondly that we had got rid of the signalling system. They began to settle down here. By the end of July we calculated that there were already over

20,000 – 150 of them occupied the West German Embassy, as others did in Prague, creating a scandal. They could sleep out on Margaret Island (in a bend in the Danube in central Budapest) or down at Lake Balaton. But what would happen to them by the autumn? We had the same number of Hungarians coming from Romania and the refugee camps were overflowing. Once we had 40,000, it was clear that we would be compelled to let them go.

'We decided that we had no standing in the matter. This was a problem for East and West Germany to negotiate as best they could. The East Germans had set up a channel of communications with the West Germans via an attorney, Vogel, who may have been a Stasi officer or a West German spy, or both for all I know. The West German response came first. They were willing to give a document to all these people, asking us to treat them as West Germans. We replied that they had to negotiate with the DDR. Time had elapsed, it was about the middle of August, and we saw things were stalemated. Németh then proposed that Horn and I should go to East Germany and tell them that our patience was finite. I refused, on the grounds that if they had any problems then they should approach us. It was decided that Horn should go, accompanied by my deputy. If there was still no agreement by a certain date, Horn told them, then we would act unilaterally. We were no longer prepared to be their gendarmes.

'Honecker was ill and played no part in these proceedings. Egon Krenz took his place. He had been my colleague in youth organization days. They became very upset, they called it treason. Erich Mielke used this word. When Horn returned, we gave them another deadline, and this deadline also expired, and that is how we arrived at 11 September.'

The step was unprecedented, Horváth says, but neither he nor anyone else realized that the Berlin Wall thereby also became redundant and communism could no longer be insulated from the rest of the world. Who could have imagined the irony that communism would be at the mercy of a strictly capitalist-type decision not to incur the costs of renewing the Iron Curtain which alone had kept in place the ideology and the empire?

22

'WHOEVER ACTS TOO LATE
IS PUNISHED'

East Germany was a dismal country. Unbroken Nazi and then Soviet dictatorship had squeezed life and colour into a static social paste. Unrepaired war damage, communal housing, the exhaust fumes of the local tinbox Trabant cars, pollution from plants and power stations burning lignite, utility furniture and standardized cheap clothing, the eerie silence of ill-lit streets after dusk, and the dead end of the Berlin Wall, combined into a physical and spiritual claustrophobia.

An unintended museum to this claustrophobia is to be found in the Normannenstrasse, in East Berlin, where the Stasi or secret police had its headquarters. This hideous redbrick building, eight storeys high, was the centre of an apparatus holding the whole country in its grip. At its head was Erich Mielke, born in 1907 and titled for no good reason a general. He had risen from rigging show trials to run the Stasi in 1957, staying in office ever since. Thuggish and greedy, he was also vain. The list which he drew up of his 250 medals and orders covered eighteen pages of foolscap, in an echo of Hermann Goering. A little cabinet now displays equipment for physical and psychological torture. Mielke's own office is inexpressibly bleak, with its dingy brown colours, lace curtains, and bulky furniture. Here is a portrait of Felix Dzerzhinsky, Lenin's policeman and killer-in-chief, a death mask of Lenin, an old-fashioned telephone switchboard, as well as a document shredder. A safe and poorly made cupboards hid the daily work.

The 86,000 official Stasi agents were reinforced by over 100,000 unofficial agents and an unknown number of informers as well as regular employees, reaching into every factory, military unit, university department and housing estate. Files were kept on nearly 6 million of the 16 million population, and on half a million foreigners too. These files are said to extend for some 200 kilometres. A mysterious episode occurred on 15 January 1990 when a crowd suddenly rushed into the Normannenstrasse building, setting a small fire and destroying or stealing some files. Perhaps it was part of a Stasi campaign to cover its tracks. Most files survive to provide an X-ray of the DDR's totalitarian corpse. This stew of denunciation, rumour, blackmail and slander will be poisonous for years to come. Politicians, intellectuals and even former dissidents have already had their lives ruined by revelations that in one form or another they worked for the Stasi. Foreign operations were the task of the Hauptverwaltung Aufklärung, or HVA, under the spymaster General Markus Wolf, lionized in the West which he did more than anyone to undermine with his cold and brilliant enmity. These archives were destroyed late in 1989 on orders from the party leadership.

Whether the party controlled its security apparatus, or vice versa, is one of those scholastic arguments impossible to resolve. Power, the outward control and the inner claustrophobia, all derived from the knot tightened out of these two elements of the communist state. The size of this repressive instrument may reflect awareness of criminality on the part of the SED leaders and to some extent was therefore evidence of insecurity. But repression had its justification in doctrine.

According to this doctrine, there was a single German nation but two distinctive German states, the one a virtuous anti-Nazi dictatorship of the proletariat, and the other a vicious, warmongering capitalist slum. One day these two states were historically destined to unite under socialism. Until then, the Berlin Wall usefully symbolized and maximized doctrinal division. To a certain extent this fanciful depiction did capture the minds of East Germans, particularly the intellectuals and writers whose party task was to propagate it. Judged even against the standards of Hitler's generation, this willingness to serve tyranny and to accept its material rewards was abject. In contrast to official doctrine, however, it speaks for itself that something like 15 per cent of the population fled to the economic miracle of West Germany, which looked so enticing across the forbidden border. Every year still more tried to leave legally or illegally. After 1963, at a cost of 3.5 billion deutschmarks, 33,000 pensioners and children were bought out, and a quarter of a million families united, in what was a pioneering traffic in human beings; 1,094 political prisoners were ransomed by West Germany. By 1989 the cost of a scientist or a doctor was around $50,000. That year almost a quarter of a million people fled the DDR and public opinion polls showed that one in three of the entire population was prepared to leave. Only Cuba among the communist countries had a higher percentage of people fleeing from the regime.

Doctrine further encouraged the DDR to destabilize West Germany in order to hasten the socialist unity of a divided nation. In concert, the HVA and the Stasi mounted a campaign of violence, espionage, penetration and subversion in what was really clandestine warfare between two states nominally at peace. For the purpose, the Red Brigade and other terrorists were financed and armed to kill. A number of publications and businesses turned out to be DDR fronts. West German politicians were often caught in complex plots or compromising deals; some, like Franz-Josef Strauss, probably through an inflated sense of his own merit, others, like Herbert Wehner, Brandt's deputy and rival in the SDP, planted by Moscow as undercover operators. Thousands of agents and their local recruits, sometimes tragic but still destructive figures, were infiltrated into positions reaching as high as the Chancellor's office and Nato headquarters. The full extent has yet to be revealed.

This onslaught was meekly accepted. For reasons springing from the Nazi past, outrage was considered inappropriate and retaliation inconceivable. The press magnate Axel Springer, for instance, who directed his many publications to polemicize against the DDR, was thought to have placed himself outside polite society. Tending to defer to the moral and political superiority of their communist counterparts, many West German intellectuals mercilessly attacked their own society, creating a climate in which there were no absolute values worth fighting for. The SED was therefore helped to do as it pleased.

One of the most influential West German newspapers, *Die Zeit*, was for long the past master of this appeasement. In the end, appeasers were describing a state of mind with no attachment to the real world. In 1986 the editor-in-chief of the paper, Theo Sommer, approached the East Germans to set up a tour of the DDR for himself and a delegation of fellow commentators, including Gräfin Marion Dönhoff and Rudolf Walter Leonhardt. No ordinary reporters, these were nationally known opinion-makers. The East German files provide a case-study of how to handle people of this type, who have set themselves up to be led by the nose. Sardonic humour can be detected in the inter-ministry correspondence at the naïveté of the questions and proposals of this delegation.

From 24 May to 3 June the party was conducted around showplaces and introduced to leading personalities. Everything passed off without a hitch. At a farewell party Sommer thanked Politburo members for allowing him to perceive that DDR politicians, unlike those at home, meant what they said. The series of articles which *Die Zeit* ran from the end of July to mid-August was ecstatic. For Leonhardt, a new state had arisen, 'with a new self-awareness all its own, which is sovereign and internationally recognized'. Sommer rhapsodized about the lack of anxiety which he had detected, the plentiful supply of goods, growing rates of production, the protection of the environment and the fresh scope for artists. East Germans, he thought, rendered something like silent homage to Honecker. What was the public to make of this tragicomic farago? Fifty deceptive years had to elapse before the prewar fellow-travellers were exposed. The reality which they had been so embarrassingly unable or unwilling to see was to be rammed in the face of Sommer and his colleagues only three short years later.

This internalization in West Germany of the underdog and heroic image which the DDR sought to project of itself, was a major prop to its otherwise unlikely success. Adenauer's original view that the DDR was an illegitimate entity to be ostracized had softened over the years. The SDP under Willy Brandt evolved the new approach of Ostpolitik. Once the DDR had obtained the recognition it sought, the argument ran, it would become less aggressive, then less communist, finally tractable and civilized. Until then, the question of unity would lie like a Sleeping Beauty, constantly in mind but not to be awoken for fear of consequences.

Treaties in 1970 confirmed that the two German states and the Polish–German border were now finalized in their existing forms. These treaties and then the Helsinki Final Act certified that what had seemed like dangerous hangovers from the war had become political fixities. The conceivable reunification of the two Germanys, and the possible modalities of such an eventuality, remained questions of national import. Ostpolitik became an inextricable feature of political skirmishing. The question is now academic but years will have to pass before it can be established whether Ostpolitik delayed or advanced reunification. Like all appeasement, it did not at the time buy off aggression and subversion as intended. To have won international recognition for the DDR was a cause of jubilation to the party leadership. Safe themselves, they exploited what they perceived as a major defeat for the rival German state, on the one hand extracting credits and loans and family payments, on the other hand stealing industrial secrets and conspiring against Nato.

The principal beneficiary was Erich Honecker. The son of a coal-miner, he had been born in 1912 in Saarland. For ten years, in the Hitler era, he was imprisoned as a communist. In 1971, by means of a cleverly contrived putsch, he succeeded Walter Ulbricht, to become the second and almost the last First Secretary of the SED. Humourless and narrow, he invariably expressed himself in party parlance devoid of real feelings, more like a robot than a human being. His wife, Margot, a shrill fanatic nicknamed 'the Witch' or 'the Lilac Dragon', was in charge of education.

In one of his books, Honecker described how in Moscow in 1970 he visited Brezhnev to whom he attached himself like an understudy. Brezhnev said to him, 'Never forget that the DDR cannot exist without us; without the Soviet Union, its power and its strength, without us there is no DDR. The existence of the DDR corresponds to our interests, the interests of all socialist states. That is the consequence of our victory over Hitler's Germany. There is no more Germany, which is to the good, there is a socialist DDR and a Federal Republic.' These were exactly Honecker's guiding principles.

The culmination of Honecker's career came in September 1987 when he was received as Head of State on the official visit to Bonn for which he had long pressed but which was hard for a West German chancellor to swallow. Anyone who had then forecast that Honecker within five years would be on trial, accused of the deaths of East Germans fleeing westward, would have been written off as out of his mind.

Then and until the moment of collapse, the majority of informed observers and historians accepted at face value evidence which in other circumstances they would have scrutinized thoroughly. One such, David Childs, was writing in 1988 that the DDR had continued to make economic progress and 'it is apparently one of the world's most stable regimes'. Another, Mike Dennis, wrote at the same time that the DDR 'is often held up as a model for its particular brand of socialism'. Actually the budget deficit was $34 billion, a fact concealed because Günter Mittag, in charge of the economy, kept the figure strictly to himself, not even divulging it to Honecker. Local elections early in May 1989 threw up an almost 100 per cent vote for the SED. The count was manipulated at the level of *Stadtbezirk*, or city council, as explained eventually by Günter Schabowski of the Politburo, allowing in nice party parlance that this was the acme of political formalism. 'If the results did not suit them, the electoral officer of the Bezirk changed them.' Falsification on this scale was counterproductive.

Still, a shrewd and highly experienced observer like Melvin Lasky, editor of the monthly magazine *Encounter*, could visit the DDR in the summer of 1989 and sense nothing of the insurgence that was imminent. No Theo Sommer in outlook, he found a country radiating peace and confidence. The following year, the Allenbach Institute polled a broad sample of East Germans to ask whether a year ago they had expected their peaceful revolution. Three-quarters expressed total surprise and only 5 per cent answered yes.

Gorbachev's Soviet Union was less prepared than Kohl's West Germany to be so tolerant of the DDR. Honecker and Gorbachev had known one another since the 1960s, and between 1985 and 1989 they held ten lengthy private discussions, in addition to meeting on several public occasions. Stressing his achievements as much as to rub in that the old Stalinist methods were best, Honecker grated more and more on Gorbachev's nerves as the very type of sclerotic hardliner who was obstructing him at home. Employing his pet phrase of the 'Common European Home', Gorbachev raised in Honecker the suspicion that he might be forging some alliance with West Germany at the expense of the DDR, sacrificing the years of patient exploitation of Ostpolitik. 'In 1987 we received information from Washington which maintained that the DDR was to be the "price" paid for the common European home,' he writes in his memoirs. One side or the other had to lose in this deadlock.

Those around Honecker were equally incapable of adapting to perestroika; Mielke, Prime Minister Willi Stoph, Defence Minister Heinz Kessler, Politburo members Joachim Herrmann, Hermann Axen, Kurt Hager and others were well into their seventies. Not much younger, Günter Mittag was chronically ill, both legs amputated as a result of diabetes. Tactful promptings to reform were wasted on such men.

Another obstacle was their corruption. The élite huddled together in Wandlitz, a suburb of East Berlin nicknamed Volvograd. According to Fritz Müller, head of the party organization department of the Central Committee, in 1981 the Nomenklatura was 339,000 strong, enriching themselves through party positions. One of the most extraordinary agencies ever set up by any government was the Bereich Kommerzielle Koordinierung, familiarized as KoKo, for the express purposes of swindling. Completely secret, it was 'the most important industrial power of the DDR', according to an East German lawyer Peter Przybylski who has published the results of his investigation into it. In 1965 Hermann Matern, a Moscow KGB man on the East German Politburo, appointed Alexander Schalck-Golodkowski to run KoKo. It was an inspired choice. Freed from the laws and regulations of the capitalist market, Schalck gave rein to a true freebooting instinct. Writing back to Matern, he proposed stock-market deals, switch operations, speculation in gold and commodities, all to be carried out on condition that the Ministry of Foreign and Internal Trade was given unlimited power, and the Stasi co-operated strictly. Such help was necessary 'because a series of operations, such as illegal transport of goods and insurance frauds among measures to be kept strictly secret, should be known only in an exceptionally small circle – not more than two or three colleagues – and put into practice by you'.

In twenty-two years of illegal operations, KoKo amassed 27.8 billion Valuta Marks, the DDR currency, so Schalck stated in November 1989. Soon afterwards, during the night of 2 December, Schalck himself fled to West Germany with three files, which 'If they were made public would be revealed as highly explosive not only for the DDR but also for leading politicians of the West German Republic,' in the words of Przybylski.

Fritz Löwenthal had long ago described how the party 'inherited' estates confiscated from previous owners, and how these estates finished up in privileged hands. KoKo ran fictitious firms in both Germanys, with shares in twenty-five companies and six joint ventures abroad; and it operated secret accounts for Honecker and Mielke – the latter's Konto 0528 alone had 38 million marks in it. KoKo invented a technique of classifying pictures and ceramics in state museums as not worth holding, therefore to be sold illicitly –

668 paintings are missing from the Dresden collection alone. When KoKo was brought within the law, twenty tons of gold were found deposited in the office cellars in Berlin. Under investigation, Manfred Seidel, who had powers of signature for KoKo, wrote in January 1990, 'It was my task to employ all available means to create foreign currency for the DDR. To that end no legal restrictions were to be taken into account. That was the case at home and abroad.'

Mielke's salary was 6277 marks a month. Besides his KoKo accounts, he had Giro accounts containing 950,000 marks, a savings account with 42,000 marks in it, his house in Wandlitz and a shooting estate, Wolletz, in the Angermünde district. Arrested for misappropriation on 7 December, Mielke said, 'I shan't survive this. I shall die. You will be responsible for that.' How many of his victims had expressed themselves like that, but in their cases justly and truthfully? As chief of the trade union organization, Harry Tisch was accused of unauthorized spending of more than 100 million marks. Günther Kleiber of the Politburo built himself a house in secret in Marzahn. A Politburo candidate member, Gerd Müller, was accused of building a hunting lodge in the Thuringian forest with an asphalt road to it. He denied it but then at a press conference revealed that this property, worth between 700,000 and 800,000 marks, had been built on state funds. The full extent of the gravy train is unknown, its foreign penetration still a mystery. The ramifications of party institutionalized thieving are likely to provide scandals for years to come. Insidious corruption rather than Marxist doctrine was actually the implement by which the DDR was projecting itself and its purposes. A court order eventually obliged the Austrian Communist Party to hand over assets worth £138 million which had come from the SED. 'Our comrades went with great packets of money to Düsseldorf and returned home with fraternal encouragements for the struggle', in a caustic revelation of Günter Mittag's. Whether these great packets were bribes, hush money, smuggled bank deposits, or terror subsidies, he did not clarify.

On 6 October 1989 the DDR was due to celebrate the fortieth anniversary of its founding by Stalin. This turned out to be a final imperial jamboree, attended by satraps from the empire like Ceauşescu, Miloš Jakeš, Zhivkov, General Jaruzelski who had already lost his elections, and hangers-on like Yasser Arafat. That evening a huge crowd marched in a *Fackelzug*, the traditional torchlight procession, past a saluting stand in Berlin, chanting 'Gorbi, Gorbi'. It was a scene to which only Verdi grand opera could do justice. The loyalist demonstration which Honecker had laid on was actually his death knell, while these were plaudits Gorbachev could not survive. On the morning of the 7th, Gorbachev and Honecker had their last private meeting. In a corridor afterwards Gorbachev first let drop the sentence which reverberated around the world: 'Whoever acts too late is punished by life.' Then he gave a lengthy address to the assembled Central Committee. Ostensibly criticizing his own country for its dilatory reforming, he was evidently aiming at the DDR. Responding, Honecker gave no indication that he had heard, let alone properly interpreted, Gorbachev. Schabowski has recorded that Gorbachev gave a sound of 'Tsss' and his facial expression conveyed, 'Well, comrades, this is the end of the road.'

'I had long been convinced of the inevitability of German reunification. Already in 1986,' Shevardnadze said in an interview in *Stern* on 4 April 1991, repeating similar observations made in his memoirs. 'A nation, and a great one at that, cannot accept division over a long period. Gorbachev used to stress that it was a case of a "historical process". And any attempt to influence that process with force could have had catastrophic consequences. We took the decision not to disturb that process, not to be involved in it.'

This fatalistic *laissez-aller* is at odds with Gorbachev's conviction that at the Malta summit he and President Bush had agreed that European borders were not to change; and it appears to be an attempt to throw the best possible light on events. In the Soviet republics and satellites, Gorbachev was busy purging the old guard in favour of like-minded perestroikists, and the DDR was to be no exception. Suffering from gall-bladder troubles and an operation that summer, Honecker had been unable to decide whether Günter Mittag was to deputize for him, or Egon Krenz, the latter in theory his successor. Born in 1937, Krenz had risen through the youth movement and liked to project his image as a representative of the new generation. An associate of his was Günter Schabowski, a Politburo member with press responsibilities. The Dresden party First Secretary, Hans Modrow, was a possible rival. Markus Wolf's resignation from the HVA for no very obvious reason may have been a response to Gorbachev's aspiration to see him promoted to First Secretary.

Both Krenz and Schabowski have published their versions of events. Not claiming to have been present himself, Krenz reports that at the airfield the departing Gorbachev said to some bystanders, 'Act!' To Schabowski, this is a sentimental tale. Whatever the case, Krenz began his bid for power as from 7 October. Schabowski has depicted himself as the man who put in the legwork, enrolling one by one those Politburo members whom they had reason to trust. Sure enough, at a Politburo meeting on the 17th, Honecker was removed 'on his own wish' and thanked for his services. Mittag and Herrmann were also voted out. In just such a conspiracy, Honecker had levered out his own predecessor, Walter Ulbricht.

Rising tension throughout the country fuelled upheaval within the élite. As early as the beginning of September, the first of several voluntary associations, Neue Forum, held a founding meeting. Its activists were mostly well-known dissidents. Its manifesto – signed within a few weeks by 200,000 supporters – stated that communication between state and society had clearly broken down, and the broadest public participation must now be sought. 'We are therefore willing to form a political platform for the whole DDR.' Its monopoly of power under threat, the party on 22 September decreed that Neue Forum was 'an enemy of the People'. Once the party had taken the position that Neue Forum could not be co-opted, it set into play the logic of force.

The Volkspolizei, known as Vopo, consisted of approximately 100,000 men, split into a number of forces, all under the control of General Friedrich Dickel, Minister of the Interior. Of these, 73,000 were allotted the usual police duties but the system itself conceived policing as the defence of communism, not as the enforcement of human or property rights. The Volkspolizei was armed and equipped to the level of operational infantry. Behind them was the Volksarmee, the National Army, 167,000 strong, with 1500 tanks and an air force flying almost 400 Soviet combat aircraft. And further behind was the Soviet garrison, of 300,000 soldiers and over 200,000 civilian ancillaries. Few countries were so militarized. Something of the Prussian military tradition remained as a guarantee of steady performance.

Already in June Margot Honecker had declared, 'We have to defend socialism with all means. With words, deeds and, yes, with weapons if necessary.' This was also Honecker's attitude. Open signatories of manifestos, individuals with addresses and consciences, tapped telephones and bulging Stasi files, the dissidents of Neue Forum were not likely to be able to mobilize the masses. As from that autumn the weekly Peace Prayers at the Nikolaikirche in Leipzig provided an arena for such mobilization and therefore one where the logic of force would finally play itself out. Every Monday, thousands of protesters were in the habit of assembling in the old and winding streets around the church.

To ensure that nobody and nothing marred Gorbachev's visit, 1000 people were arrested on 6 October. During his visit, another 3456 were arrested and proceedings were taken against them. 'Give those pigs a sound beating!' Mielke instructed. The understated reports of the visit in the party press were a virtual announcement that Gorbachev had indeed decided to ditch Honecker. As his unsatisfactory guest and obviously false protector flew off to Moscow, Honecker found himself in a quandary. The weekend was over. On 9 October, a further Monday Peace Prayer would draw another crowd into the centre of Leipzig to capitalize on the First Secretary's weakness. It will be a long time, if ever, before Honecker's responses can be exactly reconstituted. Emotionally ready to authorize whatever degree of repression would be required, he was at pains to have his colleagues cover his tracks. On the 8th, Mielke placed the special forces on alert. Police in huge numbers, and ambulance and hospital services, were at hand in Leipzig on the 9th. Bloodshed was averted at the last moment by a combination of civic spirit, luck and the failure of the party chain of command. A massacre that day would have brought communism to a very different end in the DDR and the rest of the bloc.

Had Honecker had wind of the Krenz–Schabowski conspiracy, he could at once have taken steps to remove them from their party function and to arrest them. Already on the 8th, Krenz had a meeting with Mielke, although this is said to have been routine. But Gorbachev's speech to the Central Committee could only be interpreted by its members as authorization to choose another First Secretary. Orders from Honecker had therefore lost their imperative, and could be prudently delayed or even mislaid. Gorbachev seems not to have realized that in dooming Honecker, he was also entering a course of action which led straight to the loss of the DDR, an outcome he might not himself survive. Another General Secretary could have declared a state of emergency, or even martial law, closed the borders and ruled by decree. Or he might have whipped up an international nuclear-exchange scare. The fact that Gorbachev was sufficiently relaxed to encourage Krenz to plot, with Markus Wolf up his sleeve, indicates that he was still a believer in the absolute efficacy of centralized party power. If so, he was mistaking his own will for reality.

In the Politburo, Krenz raised his standard by declaring that a crisis was at hand and on the 13th he flew to Leipzig hoping that the avoidance of violence that Monday would somehow be placed to his credit. On the 17th, Willi Stoph proposed that Honecker should resign. Ratification the following morning at the Central Committee meeting was a formality. Krenz writes in approved party parlance, 'I knew that people in whom I had confidence had worked actively in preparing the ninth plenum in order to have a majority of votes.' Honecker read out his resignation and appointed Krenz in his place. Apostolic succession was the kiss of death. Krenz was never able to prove himself his own man.

The Leipzig demonstration on Monday 16 October had almost doubled in size. On 4 November a million people took to the streets in East Berlin. One more push – and it was given by Schabowski at a press conference on the evening of 9 November, when he dropped a bolt out of the blue, that the border to the West was now open. In a drama as emotive and historic as the storming of the Bastille two hundred years earlier, people in their hundreds of thousands broke open the Berlin Wall, demolishing some sections by hand, then bringing up heavy equipment. 'We did not suspect,' Schabowski wrote, 'that the opening of the Wall was the beginning of the end of the Republic.' In the shortest possible span, Krenz wrote, 'something happened which nobody had foreseen'. He still believed that unification of the two German states was not on the agenda.

A week after the Wall had fallen, Hans Modrow succeeded Willi Stoph as Prime Minister. 'A sincere communist', Krenz rightly called Modrow but none the less party and state were separating. Krenz and Modrow were a mirror image of Grosz and Pozsgay in Hungary. The party-state rivals cancelled each other out. At a crisis meeting early in December, the party abdicated its leading role, purged its Politburo one last time and obliged Krenz to resign. He had been First Secretary for just fifty days. The Round Table process was more comprehensive here than in any other country, set up at state and local levels. Neue Forum and other opposition groups did not manage to bring either the party or the Stasi to account, but obtained the necessary agreement to holding the elections of 18 March 1990. Chancellor Kohl's CDU then almost emulated Solidarity in Poland in the unexpectedness of its electoral victory.

23

FLASHPOINTS

The Nikolaikirche is the baroque style at its best. Its magnificent plaster-work, with entertaining details of palm fronds and dates, is picked out in delicate pink and green. The Lutheran Church has a hierarchy of bishops and superintendents, but on theological grounds leaves the local pastor fully responsible for his church and congregation. For the last fifteen years the driving force here was Pastor Christian Führer, who might almost have been allegorically named. Slight in build, and pale, he has close-cropped grey hair and a nervous intensity. The Lutheran Church has been in the forefront of evolving alternative forms of worship and service, supposedly more relevant to the age. Pastor Führer delights in describing how he attracted the alienated, dropouts and rowdies as they are known locally, incongruous as they squatted on the marble floors of the decorative side-chapels, playing guitars. Grudgingly the Stasi tolerated what it saw as social work in the lower depths rather than semiorganized opposition.

The 1980s, Pastor Führer decided, should be a peace decade. His 'Swords into Ploughshares' campaign was officially approved as swelling the propaganda chorus directed against Nato's introduction of Cruise missiles. A group in 1982 started Peace Prayers every Monday at five o'clock. The missiles were introduced, the campaign was laid aside and the group dwindled to six and might have vanished altogether, had not a woman said to him, 'If we in the Church stop, then there is no hope left for this country.' New impetus came from taking up the cause of those who had lost jobs and homes because they had applied to emigrate. He saw the Olaf Palme peace march to Prague in 1987 as a pilgrimage; he protested against the arrest of dissidents who had demonstrated at the monument to Rosa Luxemburg and Karl Liebknecht, patron saints of communism. When in February 1988 under the catchphrase 'To live and stay in the DDR' he decided to do what he could for those left behind by the emigrants, 800 people rallied to his church, few of them Christians.

Nobody was deceived by the local elections of 7 May 1989 and the next day, a Monday, police surrounded the church during the Peace Prayers. That had the effect of popularizing the occasion. Each Monday people continued to arrive from all over the country, and the police closed the motorway and searched trains and made arrests. A spiral of opposition and repression had become self-propelling. By Monday 2 October, the church was overflowing and four other Leipzig churches also held Peace Prayers. Each person attending, Pastor Führer likes to emphasize, had overcome inner fears. On 9 October the worst was to be expected. 'Schoolchildren were sent home, the university closed, shoppers could no longer enter the city centre, the army was standing to, tanks were in place, special units, police, an unbelievable pool of several thousand men in uniform. Riot squads in full gear started beating those who were making their way to the Nikolaikirche. And they could think of nothing better to do than send a thousand SED members to pack the Nikolaikirche. Six hundred arrived to sit stony-faced. By half past three the church was full. The Peace Prayer was held in an atmosphere that was truly frightening.' The quasi-compulsory presence of party members in the church was 'a tactic of God's', he says earnestly, and he took advantage of the situation to give them a lengthy sermon. 'Someone told us that Professor Masur of the Gewandhaus was supporting our appeal not to use force. Dr Hempel, the bishop, came and gave his blessing. And when we wanted to leave, we couldn't. I shall never forget the first sight of the crowd, the largest demonstration there had ever been in the DDR. We emerged slowly from the church, and the miracle occurred that people moved on without use of force, and the police were simply absorbed into the throng. People had been prepared for everything except candles and prayers.'

Ingolf Rackwitz worked as a radio journalist for a Berlin station, DT64, catering to youth. On the morning of 9 October, he heard rumours of a demonstration in Leipzig, his home town, and he asked to cover it. His chief editor, a man named Klaus Schmalfuss, decided against this but Rackwitz drove off in one of the radio station's cars on the offchance. With him went Hanno Harnisch, now the press officer of the reconstituted Communist Party. No Western journalists were in Leipzig that day. On the motorway they saw a convoy of Rapid Deployment Forces. Roadblocks had been set up at the entrance to the city. First they called on the local radio station, and then on the party district offices, to find Roland Wötzel the district secretary, and Jochen Pommert the secretary for Agitprop. The latter had to authorize their press passes. Much of the credit that the day passed off without bloodshed goes to this middle-rank official, who has since vanished without trace. Said to be seriously ill, the Leipzig party chairman, Horst Schumann, was prudently unavailable all day. It was clear from the instructions that Pommert and Wötzel were having to steer between pressures from the party above in Leipzig and in Berlin and the urgencies of the demonstration already unfolding on the streets. 'In the circumstances they could not have carried out orders from Berlin, and no doubt that was why they subscribed to the appeal for no violence. To say that they ignored orders is too much, they had no other choice. Pommert was in an unprecedented situation, he was under great stress and he was panicking, answering the telephone ceaselessly, with journalists swarming in. Anything was possible, including the Chinese solution which had recently taken place. Pommert promised to hold a dialogue with the city authorities.' On behalf of the party Pommert, Wötzel and Dr Kurt Meier signed a joint declaration with Kurt Masur, Pastor Peter Zimmermann and an actor, Bernd-Lutz Lange: 'We all need a free exchange of opinion over the further course of socialism in our country . . . We urgently ask for restraint so that peaceful dialogue is possible.'

From Pommert's office, Rackwitz drove north into the city centre past combat units armed with heavy truncheons. The Rapid Deployment Forces were conscripts doing their national service, 'visibly shaking with anxiety, showing not the least interest in injuring their neighbours or being themselves injured. Each was plainly asking himself what he was going to do when he received orders to attack the demonstrators.' He called in at a police station on Ritterstrasse, parallel to the Nikolaistrasse and 200 yards from the church. The press officer there was a Major Heilmann and he had invaluable equipment for broadcasting out of Leipzig. 'By then, the Nikolaikirche was already packed with party members. Thousands of people were in the small square round the church, and I started to do some interviewing. I was thunderstruck to realize for the first time that these people no longer believed what they were told. However sincere my approach and tactful my presentation, I wouldn't be believed. Then the masses poured out of what was Karl Marx Platz, and is now Augustusplatz again, and nobody had the least idea where they were heading for, nor why, they were simply circulating. I often had the impression that I was actually leading the march. They went past the station and the footbridges, where one half of the crowd went on in the direction of the Friedrich-Ludwig-Jahn-Allee, and the other half around the Ring.

'Microphone in hand, I went past the fire station, but the doors were closed and I never saw the tanks supposed to be inside. On the next corner the column stopped facing the Stasi building and next to it was another new building, whether belonging to the Stasi or regular police. Between six and seven o'clock our station carried live broadcasts. Here was our chance for a scoop, so we went in and announced ourselves, to find that by coincidence Major Heilmann had an office there as well. There was a microphone and a transmission line, and we were connected with our chief editor in Berlin. He said that unfortunately we could not be transmitted live, but only taped and played afterwards. So we recounted our experiences. Then Major Heilmann entered the room and asked if we had been broadcast. We listened but some ordinary programme was being run. Next morning the chief editor was to say that the quality of the tapes had not been good enough, but we retrieved our tapes and they were all right. That was panic too.

'Then we went on the rounds again and heard this appeal over the radio from Masur, Wötzel and Pommert. We called on Pastor Führer who had stayed in his church rather than go on the demonstrations. When we left him round about eight o'clock the demonstration was as good as over. We were infuriated to discover that *Tagesschau*, a West German television programme, was reporting the day's events, carrying a telephone interview while we had tried to do just that and hadn't been broadcast.' In fact their report ran the next day, when the chief editor Klaus Schmalfuss also announced that he would be taking a week's holiday, and did not know if he would be in the same job on his return. You most certainly won't be, Harnisch had replied, accurately, as it turned out.'

Did you think there was going to be shooting?

'Anything was possible, Everything had been prepared for all eventualities. The fascinating thing was that on the one side the state offered no violence and on the other side the hatred felt by the population was not expressed. You could have imagined that the crowd would have burned down the Stasi office as happened in Berlin on 15 January.'

We now know that Honecker gave instructions that law and order had to be maintained by all necessary means.

'For me the outstanding feature is that Wötzel and Pommert decided to disregard those instructions. Party discipline gave them no leeway to do this, they risked their own skins. But nobody had ever imagined that things could come to this in Leipzig.'

Director of the Leipzig Gewandhaus Orchestra, Kurt Masur is a conductor of world renown. Few people in the DDR were more eminent. In the state's closing period he refused an invitation to be President. A musician through and through, Masur is tall and somewhat forbidding, with a direct blue-eyed gaze. The Gewandhaus Orchestra marked its bicentenary in 1981 and Honecker consented to the building of its new hall for this occasion. Otherwise Masur and Honecker had met only formally, for instance, at Leipzig trade fairs.

The party-state liked to take credit for talents and achievements like his, but in return it had to allow scope to operate. A small area thus opened up for bargaining, which was privileged, though for the wrong reasons. Dissidence or active church membership carried less influence than a word in the right ear: stealth was part and parcel of the relationship of such a man to the party-state. The insider might succeed where the outright oppositionist would land in prison. Perestroika delighted Masur. Musicians whom he knew in the Soviet Union persuaded him that Gorbachev would deliver what he had promised. It appeared clear to him that Honecker feared that Gorbachev's failure in the Soviet Union would kill off the DDR, and he chose to bury himself under Stalinist communism. Masur's direct involvement in politics began on 11 June 1989 when he received a letter from a doctor with the news that the previous day the police had taken into custody some street musicians who had sung unauthorized protest songs. He turned to Dr Kurt Meier, the official responsible for cultural affairs. Permission was given for a large meeting to be held in the Gewandhaus. Masur acted as moderator for 650 street musicians and the party and the Stasi. 'I asked them about their fines and imprisonments. It was completely open. They started to talk. They were brave. It was the first open discussion of its kind ever held in the country. A good friend was also making a live radio broadcast. It was a breakthrough, a dress rehearsal for what was to come.

'Everyone understood Gorbachev's remark, Whoever comes too late will be punished by life. On the morning of the 9th, we noticed that military and police vehicles were surrounding the city and taking up positions in the centre. I got word from the Nikolaikirche and members of Neue Forum that the regime would repress the evening's Peace Prayers. The German word *niederschlagen* supposes that all means are permissible.'

Who gave orders for these troops to be deployed?

'Nobody wants to be known as the man who gave the order, everyone would prefer to be known as the one who rescinded it. The order to repress had already been aired the previous Friday, the 6th, in the party paper *Die Volkszeitung*, with a sentence which I shall never forget: "We will fight these enemies of our country, if necessary with arms." Live ammunition had been issued. The commanders of the special squads were at action stations. None of those young officers ever received an order to withdraw. That was done by the Leipzig people.'

The rehearsal for that evening's concert finished at noon. Masur then telephoned Dr Meier, who professed to be in the dark. Two hours later Dr Meier rang back to propose a meeting between three of the Leipzig party's leaders and Masur, Pastor Zimmermann and Bernd-Lutz Lange representing civilian society. 'The three party members told me that there were no strict orders. They agreed that we had to avoid bloodshed at all costs. They really did not want to unleash violence in Leipzig. We fought hard amongst ourselves about the wording of the declaration because the party members did not want to run the risk of signing a statement that could be interpreted as telling Honecker to step down. So we compromised, all six of us agreeing to a call for non-violence and negotiation. The miracle of Leipzig consisted in the fact that people on both sides discovered that violence is not the solution.'

It is not clear, but Honecker seems to have been ready to use force.

'Yes. And General Kessler. And Mielke and the Stasi because they knew that if they failed at that point, their regime was over. And so it was. Only we still did not realize it. We had challenged the regime to put down the demonstration and it backed away. People went round the city chanting *Wir sind das Volk*, meaning, We are not criminals or terrorists or whatever you want us to be, we are trying to have the right to a life of our own, to express an opinion, to travel. They went round the Ring which in old days used to be the defensive moat. Round about seven o'clock I got another telephone call to say that the crowd was passing the Stasi building and there was the danger of a confrontation. About half an hour later, people had completed the circle and were arriving back at the Gewandhaus. I was resting just before the concert. I could hear that the demonstration was peaceful. I went on the radio and everyone could listen to what I was saying, and they came round outside shouting Thank you. It was a very moving moment for me. It was just about eight o'clock, the house was full and we started to play *Till Eulenspiegel*.'

In communist theory, it was an impossible contradiction that the people should rise against their own regime. By definition, anyone attempting to do so was a counter-revolutionary who deserved to meet a bloody end. Sudden discovery of hundreds of thousands of counter-revolutionaries was a doctrinal heresy paralysing to the party. Logic indicated that those demonstrating against the regime had to be repressed. Failure to repress, according to this logic, meant that the people were not counter-revolutionaries and therefore that the party had no legitimacy. Replacing force with negotiation on 9 October, the party in fact scrapped the flywheel central to the entire mechanism of its rule.

Within a month events in Berlin, quite as accidental as those in Leipzig, proved yet more unmistakably that communism was either the rule of force or it was nothing. Faced with flight out of the country via Hungary, the Politburo had decided to relax the absolute ban on travel, but time was required for the administrative details. Schabowski's abrupt and obliquely worded announcement of the decision was premature, lending an air of conspiracy to the regime's incompetence. Nobody in East or West had

anticipated that people could take their future into their own hands. Chancellor Kohl himself happened to be away in Poland. With hindsight, the
outcome in Leipzig can be seen to have raised the costs of defending the
Berlin Wall unimaginably. Rushing to test for themselves the meaning of
Schabowski's statement, people found that the Wall had in fact become
notional.

At the age of thirty-six, Lieutenant Colonel Jürgen Surkau was unusually
young to have been promoted in August 1989 deputy commander of the
Berlin Wehrbezirkskommando, or military district. Broad-shouldered and
energetic, he looks every inch the self-confident professional soldier. A missile
specialist, as well as a convinced communist, he was marked for the top. In
his eyes communism was not impaired by the DDR's inability to realize it.
'We had lived in a continuous war-psychosis,' he says, 'and that was something
which we younger officers used to make fun of.' When offered the choice of
enrolling in the German army unified from both states in 1990, he refused to
do so for doctrinal reasons.

His superior in Berlin was Major General Franz Erdmann, commanding
the crack 9th Panzer division in Eggesin, in Mecklenburg-Vorpommern. That
autumn, Erdmann was ill so that Surkau was effectively the senior military
officer in Berlin. His office was at Am Kupfergraben, near the Friedrichstrasse
station.

For Gorbachev's visit the army was placed on alert, with eighty per cent of
troops confined to barracks, and all units prepared with weaponry and
munitions for action. This was only one level short of full emergency. By
international treaty, no troops could be stationed in Berlin itself, but the
regiments of the First Motorized Division were stationed around the city in
nearby Oranienberg, Lenetz and Stansdorf. By the beginning of November a
full state of emergency had been declared.

In Surkau's view, Schabowski acted with deliberate intent. Neither warnings
nor instructions had been given to Surkau. Soldiers on duty had shrugged
their shoulders as the crowds streamed by. That night Surkau himself was at
home. His wife, a senior air hostess with Interflug, returned in the small hours
from Peking. Giving instructions to the taxi-driver, she heard him ask if she
wanted to go the long way round or the short-cut through West Berlin. She
supposed the man was drunk. Back at his desk on Friday 10 November,
Surkau learned what was happening from watching television. This showed
youths from West Germany trying to clamber up the Wall at the point where
it reached the Brandenburger Tor, the official crossing-point, familiar for
decades as Checkpoint Charlie. Many metres thick, the Wall there rose to a
summit wide enough for a car to drive on and border guards were positioned
on top in an extended defensive chain. Hitherto any attempt to reach the top

of the wall meant certain death. 'It was incomprehensible to see the border guards there,' Surkau says, 'as meanwhile people were crossing the border everywhere else. Five hundred yards away on the Potsdamerplatz they were coming and going as they liked. It made no sense. For some reason which I don't understand, they were not supposed to climb up on the wall at that point by the Brandenburger Tor. Up there, the border guards were standing one next to the other. Water cannons were employed to drive the climbers back down.' During that Friday night Surkau received a telephone call from the duty officer, with orders to report at four o'clock in the morning to Straussberg in south-east Berlin, to a hotel there which belonged to the Ministry of Defence. Checking, he rang a colleague in the military district of Schwerin, to learn that all senior officers at divisional level in the army, navy and air force as well as the military district officers, had been summoned. 'We expected something would happen, that we would be told what was up and what to do about it.'

In the middle of this newly built hotel gushed an incongruous fountain of heated water. The officers took their seats in a conference room. 'The whole military leadership was there, General Kessler, Defence Minister Streletz, all their deputies, and General Klaus-Dieter Baumgarten, commander of the border guards since 1988. I recognized other generals like the commander of the First Mechanized Division, the commander of the fourth naval flotilla, and a good friend of mine Kapitän zur See Schirmer. I asked him, What's up? Everyone could feel that this wasn't some passing tension but a crisis, in some way the end of the DDR. You didn't need much imagination because all around us this whole socialist experiment had run out of steam. Only a fool could have believed that we were an island which could continue to function on its own. But that night the dimensions of the chaos became clear to me.

'Kessler began, and I shall never forget his opening sentence. He could say, on that 11 November, "The situation in the DDR is characterized through and through by the fact that there is a certain loss of confidence in the party here and there." All hell broke out. I was shocked, I thought it must be a military coup or something of the sort. Others jumped to their feet, to shout, Keep quiet, don't say anything more, sit down! One colonel actually ordered the Minister to stop. Kessler could get out only a few more words, saying, "The depth of the crisis has not yet been plumbed but there are grounds for optimism." That was another mistake. Next to speak was my friend Schirmer and on behalf of the officers of his flotilla he asked for the resignation of Kessler, Brunner who was the top military political adviser, Streletz and Baumgarten, on account of the actions of the border guards. Then there entered an adjutant of the border guards, who hurried up to General

Baumgarten and whispered in his ear. Baumgarten stood up to say, Comrades, we are facing the outbreak of war.

'In the tumult officers rose to their feet. The commander of the First Mechanized Division had had enough, he told Baumgarten not to play with our patriotic feelings, as he could detect no danger of war. He said, You have not understood that the game is over, but it is, there is no war, everything is over and done with. This meeting never came to an orderly conclusion, as more and more officers began pulling out of their pockets letters which had evidently been prepared in advance for asking for these resignations.'

Around six o'clock, Surkau with his friend Schirmer and Colonel Gerhard Filon from the First Mechanized Division in Schwerin had a cup of coffee before returning to their units to stand-down the state of emergency. Going home himself, he went to bed, telling his wife that if his duty officer telephoned the only instruction was to keep the armoury locked. The next day, he decided that the right course of action was to contact the West German Bundeswehr. In civilian clothes he and Colonel Filon duly crossed over to West Berlin, looked up addresses in the telephone book, and found a veterans' association which put them in touch with an Oberstleutnant Dr Horst Roder. A number of further meetings ensued on both sides of the border. 'I am convinced we weren't the only ones to set up such contacts, information must have been exchanged at other levels, to ensure that from the army's point of view nothing went wrong. That night convinced me that I had to act. It was such a shock for a soldier to realize that the army was in effect leaderless.'

So Honecker and later Krenz could not have used force even if they had wanted to?

The Stasi had a special force of between 1000 and 2000 troops, the Wachregiment Felix Dzerzhinsky, stationed in Berlin for the express purpose of defending the party. In the event, it played no part. 'From my position I cannot speak of the security organs but I consider that any deployment of the army was out of the question.'

Joachim Gauck is a Lutheran pastor from Rostock, where in the autumn of 1989 he became a Neue Forum activist. He participated in the Round Table dealing with German unity. After reunification, the Government made him responsible for the Stasi archives. Who should have access to these archives, and under what conditions, were explosive issues, gnawing guilty consciences but perhaps laying false trails for some who might be innocent. The office of the Gauckbehörde, or administrative body, in East Berlin, is a huge white-washed Kafkaesque cavern of paperwork and researchers. Gauck insists that the task is to bring criminal activity within the law. Justice has to be distinguished from revenge. Quiet-spoken and reflective, he has an impressive personality. The Soviets in a secret tribunal in 1950 condemned his father, a naval officer, to two sentences of twenty-five years in prison, and he was deported to Siberia, released when Adenauer opened diplomatic relations with the Soviet Union.

The impulse to open the Stasi files, Gauck says, derives from the former mass demonstrations on the streets which focused on Stasi headquarters. The cry was '*Stasi in die Produktion!*' or 'Put the Stasi to productive work!', which as he points out is very different from 'Stasi to the gallows!' Around the beginning of December, citizens' rights movements heard reports that the Stasi were destroying their files, eliminating the evidence of their crimes and misdeeds. Demonstrations began at local Stasi offices throughout the country, culminating in the episode at the Normannenstrasse on 15 January. The initiative for this, he maintains, came from Neue Forum but 'It is possible that certain interest-groups within the Stasi managed to remove some material.

'We found mountains of material destined for destruction, and there are still sackfuls in the Normannenstrasse, because by and large we picked up this scrap. What had already been shredded is lost. The people in Berlin had been slow to act and they allowed the Stasi six weeks to destroy what they could.' An order has been discovered, dated in November and signed by General Schwanitz: 'In the event of citizens establishing control, we must destroy material. A proportion should be shown to them but a proportion has to be eliminated.' Files covering agents, and in particular unofficial informers, are indeed missing. What survived and what was lost was often a matter of luck, then, a consequence of occupation of the Stasi offices, sometimes prematurely but more usually too late. 'All activity within the country had been duly reported to the Stasi; information was so detailed that its processing for the Politburo could only be far from thorough.'

As for the HVA, 'Everything for which Wolf was responsible is no longer at our disposal. This is a huge problem in conducting research.' The archives were destroyed with due process so that nobody can be prosecuted for it. As Prime Minister at the time of this destruction, Modrow was a better communist bureaucrat than his predecessors, in Gauck's words, but a communist bureaucrat none the less, with respect for the party and security rather than public opinion. 'Modrow's imagination did not stretch far enough to grasp that one could make a move against the interests of the secret police.'

Still, evidence exists to show not only how the HVA and Stasi acted in tandem but also how the HVA co-ordinated with the KGB. A central computer in Moscow, known by its Russian acronym as SOOD, contained dossiers of foreigners considered to be Cold War opponents, gathered from the secret services of the satellites, with the exception of Romania. The Stasi had contributed 75,000 such personal dossiers to SOOD.

The Stasi had learned its trade from Stalin's secret police but the extent to which latterly it was a Soviet instrument is not yet clear. In general terms, what strikes Gauck is how westerners used to conceptualize communism upon information provided by the communists themselves. A look into these extensive files shows that 'Researchers and commentators who used to describe communism without mentioning the Stasi or the KGB were not just insufficiently informed but intellectually defective.'

24

LITTLE BROTHERS

Here is Gerhard Schürer, in appearance like a sprightly gnome, doing his best to master resentment after a short spell in prison which he considered unjust, and living now on a pension he finds inadequate. Since 1965, he had been chief of the State Planning Commission with a staff of 2000 experts, and without a doubt he was one of the most able men in the DDR. For sixteen years he was also a candidate member of the Politburo. His relationship with Honecker was not close. 'I was always subordinate to Mittag,' he says. 'Mittag has been the trauma of my life.' Hugely ambitious, far from stupid, Günter Mittag believed that party-type mobilization produced the required results. This was simply unreal, but Honecker had absolute confidence in the man.

Marxists are not alone in making mistakes, Schürer points out. The system's inherent and fatal flaws consisted in the belief that decision-taking presumed achievement, and the inability to remove those at the top who were exhausted or inadequate. Planning in the DDR involved striking 600 'balances' in the supply and demand of major raw materials and consumer products; the Soviet Union had 3000 such 'balances'. Once drafted, his plan would be referred to Mittag, and might be returned two or even three times before it was finalized. Political considerations invariably had priority over economics. Two-thirds of DDR trade was with the Soviet Union.

Credit from the West, and Japan and West Germany in particular, Schürer says, can be considered to have prolonged the DDR's existence, with the proviso that until its very last day the country retained its credit-worthiness. Venezuela or Brazil, for example, were far more heavily in debt. But as much as 60 per cent of the loans were spent on consumption, where investment in productive capacity of up to 90 per cent of that money would have been the right policy.

In February 1989 he tried to come to an understanding with Krenz that Honecker should step down for the good of the country. But when Krenz tested the waters, the Soviets replied that they had too much on their hands at home to contemplate removing Honecker.

So what happened between February and 6 October to change this approach?

'Gorbachev came to see that he could use the DDR as a pawn to be sacrificed to developing friendly relations with West Germany. That this would bring down the Soviet Union he did not foresee. But Honecker sensed it, and from his point of view he was right.' Schürer heard Gorbachev say that life would punish whoever came too late, and he had been astonished to hear Honecker's meandering reply about electronic chips, as though holding quite another discourse.

What with Honecker's illness, and Mittag's prevarication, the Politburo during the summer and autumn of 1989 became 'truly incapable of conducting business'. The Politburo must take the blame, he says, 'but the DDR could never have survived the decline and fall of the Soviet Union'.

In old age, Werner Eberlein still seems to have stepped out of a party propaganda poster of the 1930s, the idealized worker. Even his hands are those of a manual labourer's. He lives in what was the Karl Marx Allee, the one example of bloated Stalinist town-planning likely to survive in Berlin. His father, Hugo Eberlein, before the war a member of the Central Committee, had fled to the Soviet Union with his two brothers. All three were shot in 1937, and the fourteen-year-old Werner was exiled to Siberia where he worked in a saw-mill for twelve hours every day without a break for seven years. When I asked him, indeed pressed him, to explain how in spite of these horrors he could have devoted his life sincerely to the party, his reply was that he had been too busy surviving to dwell on grievances. And besides, Stalin had been a god on high, supernatural, someone whom it had been inconceivable to criticize. After attending the Party Higher School in Moscow, he worked in the party organization department, became First Secretary in Magdeburg in 1983 and was a member of the Politburo. The Soviet Army corps in Magdeburg, he says, played no part at all. Fluent in Russian, he interpreted at the highest level, and he attended eight Soviet party conferences. The system may have failed, he says, but he remains as loyal as ever to the idea of communism.

Honecker's man, Werner Eberlein none the less speaks of the 'helplessness and silence' that afflicted the Politburo by 1989. Honecker took the crowds shouting 'Gorbi, Gorbi' as a personal insult, but reform was the issue, not personalities, and Honecker had set himself against the course of reform. 'He used to stake his claim on our social and material situation, which was better than in Moscow or Ulan Bator. But people were making comparisons with Cologne and Hanover. It's my theory that round about the end of 1988 one of us should have stood up in the Politburo and objected to this or that policy. Honecker would have found himself alone. But in our tradition there was rigid discipline and then fear of being accused of factionalism. He wanted to keep all the levers of power in his hands but it is still hard to explain why everyone around that table kept his trap shut, to put it crudely. Perestroika was fine in word and thought, but it had no programme for resolving our social problems.'

More by hints than anything else, Harry Tisch and Schabowski solicited his vote against Honecker in the Politburo, but he is contemptuous of what he calls 'the politics of the bush', meaning conspiracy as practised in Wandlitz among the élite. Contemptuous too of colleagues whom he sees as turncoats.

Even Magdeburg witnessed mass demonstrations. Neue Forum was a strong presence there. The Church took protesters under its wing. One day in early October, the bishop rang him up to ask if force would be used. No ammunition had been issued to the police. When the bishop further requested that the protesters should be self-policing, Eberlein rang the chief of police to authorize him to leave the demonstration well alone. 'There is no point in going against 50,000. Even 30,000 is enough for a hands-off policy.' None the less, talk of a general implosion is exaggerated. Between December 1988 and August 1989, he says, 900 members left the party in Magdeburg and 330 were expelled, but 2000 new members joined. 'The comrades were waiting for some signal of what to do, and how to do it, but no signal came.

'Gorbachev plugged this Common European Home but basically there was no room in it for the DDR. I can't imagine that when he spoke in this vein he simply overlooked the DDR. He set off to reform without a backward glance, writing off the DDR. The question is, How is the change in Gorbachev to be explained? It is as though when he was putting the case for the DDR, he was not being honest. I believe that when he was here for the fortieth anniversary he wasn't sincere with us.'

How did the Politburo meeting go of 9 November, concerning the opening of the Wall?

'We were unanimous that people had to be allowed to go to West Germany as they wished. We had to pass the enabling law. This had been in the works for weeks before it reached the Politburo. At that meeting it was decided that every citizen could go to the police and receive a stamp on his papers. There was no mention of opening the border. But instead of going to the police for a stamp people went straight across the border, which had not been the intention. And there was Schabowski who may or may not have known what he was doing – that's his secret – saying that he had found this piece of paper on the table, and he had read it and so on.'

Had the border guards or customs officers been warned?

'Not at all. They knew nothing. They were certainly aware of the instructions given in Leipzig not to resort to arms, and they had enough political sense not to grab their weapons now. In the Politburo we sat down and said, We took a decision, this has now happened of its own accord, we have to accept it, there is no going back.'

Squat and burly, with a growl in his voice, Wolfgang Herger had risen with Krenz in the early 1960s through the ranks of the Freie Deutsche Jugend, the local Komsomol. On Krenz's recommendation, in March 1985 he became head of the Security Department of the Central Committee. In this position he had responsibility for internal and external security, including military, although disarmament policy naturally ran in tandem with that of the Soviet Union. He makes the point that he was accountable only to the party, not to Mielke and the Stasi, who at least nominally were part of the state apparatus. His role amounted to keeping the party in power.

Like Schabowski and Siegfried Lorenz, Herger lobbied for his friend Krenz to succeed as First Secretary. But he was frustrated by Honecker's continuous tactic of playing Krenz off against Mittag. It became evident that if Honecker could not be persuaded to change policy, then he had to step down. Almost to the end, Herger believed that Honecker could be brought to see reason. 'For me the most depressing experience with Honecker was his speech on 6 October at the anniversary celebrations in the People's Palace. Between two and three thousand were in the hall and we all knew a huge social crisis was in the offing, if we weren't already in it. In the last few days 10,000 emigrants had left and we all hoped that he would have the courage to say that the Politburo or the Central Committee would address this matter, literally the very next day. But he stuck to his views that there was no better socialism in the world than in the DDR, and the emigrants had been seduced by Western propaganda. For me, there was nothing more to be said. I told Krenz that if we didn't act, we would all be swept away by events. As was indeed the case. So far removed was Honecker from reality that he proposed to stand again as First Secretary at the Twelfth Party Conference in May 1990.' But then the leadership, himself included, took it for granted that three-quarters of the population consciously identified with the DDR, and therefore there was no danger of being overwhelmed peacefully by West Germany. This was an absolute illusion.

The disastrous end of the country and its political system, Herger went on, was too comprehensive a phenomenon to be ascribed to any one individual. But the succession of Krenz marked 'some sort of inner liberation of the DDR itself'. Alternative scenarios could then be envisaged. Either a special party conference had to be called in order to elect a brand-new Politburo to put into practice a unique DDR variety of independent socialism, or the Stasi and the army had to defend the party through use of force. 'Either politics or police methods.' The political alternative was botched and half-hearted. The police alternative, otherwise known as the Chinese solution after the Tiananmen Square massacre that June, was ruled out and he gives particular credit for that to Krenz. Secret information, he says, had convinced them that internal violence would have been treated by Nato as a pretext to invade.

Even to a man in Herger's position, Honecker's intentions were obscure. Two telexes signed by Honecker, one in September and the other dated 8 October, have wording open to more than one interpretation, though the general sense indicates negotiation rather than shooting. Herger himself was one of those who drafted the telex of 8 October and he says, 'I assume that it is wrong to impute that Honecker may have played with a violent solution or thought of imposing a state of emergency.' A third telex was drafted on Friday 13 October by Krenz, Streletz, General Dickel and himself because the Peace Prayers demonstration planned for the 16th was expected to outdo even the previous week's. As head of the army Honecker signed this telex which expressly forbade the resort to weapons under any circumstances. But as to what Honecker was inwardly thinking, 'That is his secret.'

Born in 1929, Günter Schabowski had been an outstanding journalist. Appointed in 1978 editor-in-chief of the party paper *Neues Deutschland*, he writes, and speaks, in a lively idiom. Not only was he secretary of the Berlin party organization but also a Politburo member from 1985. Through his Russian wife, he had good connections with Moscow, and he knows the language too. After reunification, he took up a job with a local newspaper in West Germany, in a small and old-fashioned town where every house and garden looks perfectly maintained. SED personalities of comparable stature tend to have clung to whatever they could salvage by way of Nomenklatura privilege and pension, and they carp somewhat enviously about Schabowski and his new start. His book, *Das Politbüro*, is often unsparing of the old-timers but loyal to Krenz and his own contemporaries.

'It was completely unimaginable that the DDR could be so quickly scrubbed from the picture. The DDR could only disappear if there was no Soviet Union. That was simply not Realpolitik. The nuclear weapon held the bloc together.' In Gorbachev's eyes, he adds, the DDR was an especially robust component of the bloc. In 1986, when the SED was holding its Eleventh Party Conference Gorbachev was the guest of honour. Acting as his coach and guide, Mittag had then impressed on him the country's industrial and economic performance.

The next party conference was planned for 1990. Reform, as instigated from Moscow, could wait until then. Urgency was obscured by the fact that nobody had grasped the change in Soviet policy towards its satellites. During Gorbachev's 1989 visit, he had the chance at dinner to tell Gennady Gerasimov, Gorbachev's spokesman, that a shake-up was coming. Not even confidences of this kind brought Soviet responses, never mind guidance.

To Schabowski, much of what went wrong derived from stupidity or hardening of the mental arteries. He loves to describe dramatic Politburo sessions at which he asked long-standing fogies like Alfred Neumann or Horst Sindermann to resign, much to their indignation. Up to the May local elections, everything had appeared normal. By definition, communist elections involve mass manipulation, but fraud openly impugned the party's goodwill. It marked the beginning of a series of concessions which the party was obliged to make, each time discrediting itself further. The most glaring example was the confusion leading to the opening of the border in Hungary, which in effect signified the ending of the bloc. The removal of Honecker led to the dismantling of the former political structure. The 'leading role' of the party was easily laid aside because there was no longer a social basis for it.

Did Krenz have any chance to keep the DDR in existence?

Schabowski believes so. Krenz and he, Lorenz and a few others saw themselves as reformers who would grant certain human rights, for instance to travel, while sticking to socialist principles in the hope that some confederative arrangement with West Germany would evolve. 'We were not experienced in this kind of conspiracy,' he says. 'You can't train for it. We were limited by the Politburo meeting on the 17th. If you spoke to someone too soon, he might accuse you and telephone Honecker and reveal the plot. So we had only about twelve hours to influence the Central Committee. I told Krenz that Honecker himself had to declare his resignation to the Central Committee, on grounds of ill-health, and I drafted this declaration without writing in the name of his successor. It was a trick when he recommended Krenz, as though voluntarily, and the Central Committee could see no reason to refuse. Perhaps he thought that he could exert influence on Krenz, although he was startled and hurt by the fact that Krenz had intrigued against him.'

Had there been a debate on using force to maintain the party's position?

'On the Thursday after the Leipzig event, a few people were standing around at the end of the Politburo meeting, their dossiers under their arms, and Honecker was among them. Someone mentioned that a demonstration was in preparation for the following Monday in Leipzig. Honecker was depressed in general, and to be airing such a theme was completely unacceptable in the SED, an enormity so to speak. He made the passing comment that perhaps the tanks ought to be rolled out. I said to Krenz afterwards that we couldn't dawdle for a fortnight. There were too many imponderables. Someone throws a stone and the man who's sitting in the turret of his tank receives a blow on the forehead and the shooting starts. When that happens we can all say goodbye, there's a bloody uprising and sooner or later the SED big shots are hanging from lampposts. The day before the crucial Politburo meeting, Harry Tisch went to Moscow to meet his trade union colleagues there. On arrival he said that he had a very important matter to discuss with Gorbachev, and a short meeting was arranged. Tisch told Gorbachev that the next day Honecker would resign. Gorbachev seemed to be surprised and unsure, as if to query who Tisch was, and why he was telling him this, but he finished saying, Good luck to you. It was astonishing that he did not pursue it more deeply.'

One question still unanswered, in Schabowski's view, is the role of Mielke whom he visualized in close contact with the KGB. Why did Mielke so unresistingly allow events to take their course? Another question concerns the attitude of Hans Modrow, until October a member only of the Central Committee, with a reputation for standing up to Honecker. Schabowski claims that he and Krenz drew up lists of potential allies, and they appointed Modrow to the Politburo, also ensuring his promotion as Prime Minister. He is convinced that some undeclared alliance existed between Modrow and Markus Wolf, to supersede Krenz and to take power with the approval of the KGB. So Modrow used his office as Prime Minister to destroy Krenz? I asked. 'I would say so, absolutely. There was a dual power, typical in a revolutionary situation, with no clear division between them.' Modrow used his influence to prepare his rule through government and parliament without the party and the Politburo. Schabowski also holds Modrow responsible for the disappearance of the missing Stasi and HVA files.

As for Schabowski's hour under the spotlight of history as the Wall opened, he insists that he had not foreseen how it might develop. 'We did it because we were convinced that it was the immediate step necessary to gain acceptance at home and abroad. Either we opened the border or we didn't. The calculation was simple. To open the border meant that people could go out and then come back. Their Tante Anna might have them to stay for a fortnight but that was all the old lady could do. Their homes, employment, their little car, were all here. They could hope that if we gave them permission to travel like everyone else, to and fro, then other things might improve as well. We agreed to it in the belief that it would bring some relief – and it did.'

If you had put a future date on it, you would have had the necessary time to prepare for orderly change.

'Yes, of course it would have been better but we were up against the fact that there was no time. You must understand that we had overthrown Honecker, and we new men were disappointing, people were asking what we intended to do. To open the Wall was a proof of our intentions.'

Was Gorbachev shocked?

'I believe not. He showed no particular excitement. He and his advisers assumed that it would happen one day. By then, he thought it was better that we should do things on our own than under Soviet duress. Some complaint did arrive from Moscow, I recall, but it was not substantial, to do with the Four-Power Agreement over Berlin, where the DDR had no standing.

'Put yourself in Gorbachev's position, head of an empire with countries dancing to your tune. He starts reforms, and these reforms have consequences affecting the countries of the empire. But the DDR is a useful lever against West Germany, and it also produces a high proportion of the better consumer goods available in the Soviet Union. He wants to prolong this relationship. This means destabilizing the leadership for the sake of stabilizing the country – that was the concept. As long as Krenz was there Gorbachev could still back out of it. The KGB had told him that he would be receiving Modrow, but meanwhile here was Krenz, and he could do business with him. He could say, Egon, the DDR will survive, the Soviet Union will support it. But then the leadership in the DDR loses more and more of its authority, and now it is Modrow's turn, and people are clamouring more and more loudly for reunification, and the advisers are telling him that the line can't be held indefinitely. He has got to look to his own position. So he strikes a deal, reunification in return for billions of dollars from the West. It is another quite simple calculation: the line can't be held, so let's have the billions rather than stage some piece of theatre. Since he no longer had the military or political strength to pluck the DDR like a flower by the stalk, he might as well take whatever reward was going.'

25

GÖTTERDÄMMERUNG

It was customary that a First Secretary newly appointed in a satellite country should fly to Moscow as soon as convenient to pay homage, and Egon Krenz did so on 31 October. After their meeting on the following day, Gorbachev and Krenz declared that German reunification was not on the agenda. Five short weeks later, just as his tenure as First Secretary had expired chaotically, and the party was about to lose its 'leading role', and after Schalck with his files and his incriminating secrets had fled to the West, Krenz flew again to Moscow. This time he was accompanied by Prime Minister Modrow, to be briefed with other satellite leaders about the Malta summit that had just ended. Borders were not to be changed in Europe, it had been agreed with President Bush, an evident reference to the German situation. In the new year, on 30 January 1990, Modrow was again in Moscow, where in contrast he told a press conference, 'The reunification of the two German states is the perspective lying before us.' Some sort of confederation in stages was envisaged whereby the two Germanys would keep their separate identities for the foreseeable future.

Within three months, then, Gorbachev had reversed his position on Germany. Until then, Chancellor Kohl had been laying down a barrage of qualifications and Ten-Point Programmes, with vague assertions of unity over a ten- or fifteen-year period. Now he was quick to seize his opportunity. On 10 February, a westerner come to petition, he visited Gorbachev, and there occurred what his adviser Horst Teltschik called a miracle. Gorbachev gave his assent in principle to reunification. On a second visit, on 14 July, starting in Moscow and flying on to Stavropol and the Caucasus, Kohl achieved what for Teltschik was yet another miracle, namely consent to reunification within Nato. The modalities for this were then hurried through. Elections provided internal legitimacy and the awkwardly named Two-Plus-Four Treaty added an international certificate of approval, on behalf of the four wartime occupying powers. With a couple of giant bounds, Germany had unexpectedly broken out of what had been a straitjacket. With scarcely a demur, its every demand had been met in a way which none of its post-war leaders had dared to dream in their most extravagant moods of optimism.

During his October visit, Gorbachev had given one of his addresses in Schloss Niederschönhaus, a charming and unpretentious eighteenth-century building in Pankow, East Berlin, a celebrated Nomenklatura district. A few hundred yards away across the adjoining open park with its trees stands the house of Egon Krenz, a smart modern villa in a garden, protected by an iron security fence. For some time the youngest member of the Politburo, Krenz was fifty-two in 1989. Sports and the Komsomol and security had been his specialities. If his former colleagues are to be believed, he had reached his position through time-serving rather than brain power. In the mockery of his arch-enemy Günter Mittag, he was 'Der Mann ohne Konzeption', best translated loosely as 'the man without a clue'. Long in the face, with a tendency to roll somewhat mournful eyes, Krenz is polite and patient though a stratum of bitterness is now and then perceptible, especially when there is mention of the trials for criminal offences of former DDR personalities.

An attempt was made to bring to justice those responsible for falsifying the May local elections. Krenz maintained that he knew nothing about it at the time and he appears to believe that since communist elections were anyhow meaningless, a little cooking of the results showed keen party spirit rather than criminality.

In the political situation of 1989, he says, even the most capable men in the world would have been wrong in whatever measures they had undertaken. Individuals counted for very little. 'At that moment I did not recognize that the DDR had reached the end of the road. I reckoned that shoulder to shoulder with Gorbachev and the Soviet Union we could pull ourselves out of the deep political crisis. If you like, I was intoxicated with Gorbachev, and by the time I came round, it was too late. His approach to reform was right, I still believe, but it was hard to put into practice above the level of slogans, especially in the economy.' Personally, he had known Gorbachev since 1986, and his wife had then accompanied Raisa on her tour around the country.

A number of factors governed the DDR's collapse. 'Firstly, the internal situation, which was only one aspect of the worldwide crisis of communism, and secondly, the tangled political and economic plight of the Soviet Union. We had always pushed social and economic rights into the background, unfortunately we hadn't granted the right to travel.' But the economic base of the West had proved stronger in the Cold War. Military parity had squandered immense sums which could have been invested elsewhere: 'On our side we made a false analysis. You could say that the Americans forced us to arm ourselves to death. For decades the Western world had tried to marginalize the DDR. Of course their secret service had a hand in the matter.'

While in the Politburo, Krenz received a true picture of the economy, its debts and deficits, from Schalck, with whom he says that he had a friendly and open relationship. In the driest of understatements he adds, 'He was a man with an extraordinary capacity for business, and an economist with a political mind.' To reveal in the Politburo the information he used to receive from Schalck would have compromised his source. In the end, Schalck had fled because 'he felt himself deceived and he was fighting for his life'. Those who possessed full details of his activities all of a sudden pretended to ignorance.

The mere fact of Gorbachev's visit, he confirms, was interpreted as the green light to remove Honecker although no words were directly exchanged on the subject. Krenz himself had arranged for Harry Tisch to speak to Gorbachev on the eve of the decisive Politburo meeting. So Gorbachev had twenty-four hours' advance warning.

Was Honecker aware of what was about to happen?

'Hard to say but I think not. Had he been in better health, he might have realized, because we had a Politburo session lasting two whole days in which we attempted to draft some statement to put an end to the loss of communication.' He plays down Schabowski's version of the conspiracy, and also his meeting on 8 October with Mielke, apparently an insignificant discussion about seeing the VIPs safely on their way home. Mielke, he says somewhat contradictorily, was a complex personality with one single idea, that the DDR had always to travel the Soviet road. Willi Stoph, not Honecker, actually proposed him as next First Secretary, but there were procedural reasons for telling a lie at the time. It would have been better not to start his regime off with this particular lie but he thinks today that it had little significance.

Do you believe you could have saved the DDR?

'If I hadn't believed it, I would not have taken up my position. I started from the point of view that the DDR would remain communist and sovereign. Gorbachev wrote to me, and we also had a friendly telephone conversation. For better or for worse the DDR was highly centralized, and once Honecker stood down, people were drawn into public affairs. Suddenly everything turned emotional. The citizens' groups took to the streets, they saw the change as working to their advantage, and the SED leadership only crawled behind the campaign which had just started against abuse of office and corruption. Compared to corruption in the new Germany, we were relatively modest. But the popular movement grew still more highly emotional.'

What did you expect from your visit to Gorbachev on 31 October?

'Solid support for our common advance. My clear impression was that he wanted to help the DDR. The relationship between us was good, I felt. At the time he said that our people were second only to the Soviets in their wish for renewal. On my part I wanted clarification of the Common European Home in regard to the two Germanys, and whether he still accepted paternity for the DDR. He replied that there could be no question of a single Germany, and he affirmed that neither Margaret Thatcher, Mitterrand nor Bush, nor indeed any responsible statesman in the world, envisaged German unity. That was on 1 November. If he was already expecting that the path to German unity lay clear ahead, then of course I would have found it only honest if he had said, Listen, we can no longer entertain the prospect of renewal, and the two of us must make a proposal to the United States, Britain, France and West Germany for reunification. But that was not his view. He started to say so only later, when he had chosen that path.'

Gorbachev could give the DDR either full support or none. He had decided on the first, Krenz thinks, until the opening of the borders took the issue out of his hands. Whatever Shevardnadze might write in self-justification, in fact in October and November he was telephoning the West German Foreign Minister, Hans-Dietrich Genscher, to warn him to keep his hands off the DDR sovereign state. Krenz himself believes that the country could have survived with open borders, as it did from 1949 to 1961. In December and the following January, when the party had lost its 'leading role' and the survival of communism was in doubt, events deprived Gorbachev of any further element of choice. Two capitalist German states would evidently merge. 'Gorbachev understood that an official claim to restore private ownership rendered the division of Germany superfluous. We had tried to build an alternative to West Germany. That we failed is a tragedy, in my opinion, but that's the case.'

Did you talk to him about any possible opening of the Berlin Wall?

'No. We did speak about finding means to allow travel, there were no differences in opinion, but the ways and means of what happened on 9 November were not co-ordinated with Gorbachev. President Bush was the first to congratulate me and then Thatcher and Mitterrand sent goodwill telegrams. When Gorbachev saw how the other powers had welcomed this step, he came out openly to say so too. On 10 November he had a message sent through the Soviet ambassador to congratulate us on this courageous measure. But we alone were responsible for it.'

In common with his friend and confidant Wolfgang Herger, Krenz believes that it was a cardinal error not to have convened a special party conference as early as possible in October, in order to choose a new Central Committee, and so a new Politburo. Even so the course of events would probably not have been halted. Communism itself was foundering. Losing the overall political system, the other satellites nevertheless remained countries in their own right. Like the Soviet Union itself, the DDR was only a political system, and once that no longer existed, everything else disappeared with it too. 'Everything held together. The bloc could last only so long as the Soviet Union remained strong enough to hold it together. Once the Soviet Union could no longer maintain its own power structure, the Warsaw Pact disintegrated.'

On the damage done by Modrow's skilful use of parliament and the Government to wrest power away from the party and the Politburo, he remained circumspect. He emphasized that he and not Gorbachev had appointed Modrow Prime Minister. Why then did he feel that he had to resign on 3 December? Basically because there were alternative power centres. The long-postponed special party conference was due to be held a week later, and that was Krenz's responsibility. But in the run-up, all fifteen of the district First Secretaries and other notables put pressure on him to make a clean sweep of the party including the Politburo and Central Committee. In asking him to resign, they assured him that it was not a personality dispute, but it was clear to him that in fact it was. 'Since they were all in favour of my resignation, I saw no point in continuing to struggle on, so I took this step although it was unworthy, they could have waited out that one week to the special party conference. What we did was exceeded only by Gorbachev who dissolved his Central Committee without even convening it.'

Did you sense that events in October and November were slipping out of control?

'At the time when I was able to be politically active, perhaps not, but looking back I realized that this was the case.' Krenz's career and party rule effectively ended simultaneously. The apparent beneficiary, Modrow, found himself trying to govern through the *Volkskammer*, the official party-derived parliament, while the Round Table acted as a sort of unofficial or alternative parliament. 'Much was discussed', as Krenz observes, 'but little was done'. Unlike Round Tables in the other satellites, this one was not so much a mechanism for power-sharing with the opposition as an agency for paralysis which justified the ultimate West German takeover.

Are you disappointed with Gorbachev?

'My disillusion began when he returned from the Crimea after the August coup and said he was no longer a communist. [Actually he did his utmost to restore the party's power.] It was as if the Pope had dissolved the Vatican, on the grounds that there is no God. Another charge I bring against him is that when his old comrades Honecker, Stoph, Kessler and others were brought to trial and some of them imprisoned, he allowed himself to be fêted as an honorary citizen of Berlin.'

I met Hans Modrow in the East Berlin offices of the reconstituted Communist Party, near the Volksbühne Theatre. Gritty and dingy, the ground floor was occupied by the party bookshop, with its array of literature apparently trapped in a time-warp. A socialist with a human face, Modrow wore an open shirt and a leather jacket. While we were speaking, he was called away to learn that General Kessler and Streletz had that morning been sentenced to prison terms for abuse of human rights, a verdict which shook him.

Aged seventeen in 1945, Modrow had been drafted into the army, captured, and imprisoned by the Russians for four years. Soon after his release, he returned to Moscow for a two-year course in the Komsomol Higher School. He is on record as saying that the Soviet Union was his second homeland. First Secretary of the Dresden party since 1973, he was clearly an ideal man to put perestroika into practice.

A crisis broke out in Dresden on the eve of Gorbachev's October visit. Emigrants had sought refuge in Prague, and by consent of all the governments concerned, they had been allowed to transit the DDR in three trainloads, with consular officials aboard, and then to disembark in West Germany. Broadcasts had announced the times of departure of the trains from Prague and their arrival in Dresden. Instead of three trains, four or even five would have been preferable: people had been packed in. To prevent more emigrants flooding out of the DDR, the Czech frontier was closed, and Modrow telephoned the Minister of Transport with the request that the trains bypass Dresden. People in their thousands were already rushing to the main station there in the hope of squeezing on board, in what they saw as a last chance to escape to the West. Modrow spoke to Kessler and learned that the army would be called out to reinforce the police. There was never any intention to go out and beat people up, Modrow says, but only to block off the approaches to the station. This chaos lasted for three days. A number of people were hurt but nobody was killed, which to Modrow is justification for his preventive action.

Another danger of violence occurred shortly before that Christmas, he says, when the Leipzig demonstrators modified their chant of 'Wir sind das Volk' into 'Wir sind ein Volk', a neat and exemplary switch from a class response into nationalism. A proposal to suspend temporarily the Monday Peace Prayers almost brought into confrontation those who wanted to safeguard the DDR and those who now wished to bring it to an end. The latter, Modrow says, were too small a minority to overpower the majority at that point. Finally, he is himself among those who believe there was no Stasi manipulation behind the storming of the Normannenstrasse headquarters on 15 January 1990. 'It was a day on which the Round Table was in session, but there was no appeal from the Round Table for this attack; on the contrary, it was an initiative of Neue Forum. I was holding a conversation with the Yugoslav Foreign Minister when I heard the news, so I cut this short and hurried to the Normannenstrasse, driving my car through quite a crowd, thinking that this was a situation which could only be resolved politically and not by police methods. If we had introduced the police, there would have been violence. I spoke to the assembled crowd, not without anxiety, I must admit, mainly in case I was booed and the Government lost authority. After I had spoken for about ten minutes and was listened to, it was as if a heavy stone had fallen off my chest. The meeting broke up. Afterwards there was a greater commitment to keeping the internal situation calm.'

Honecker, he confirms, believed that his version of communism was incomparably superior to Gorbachev's. In spoken and written word, Honecker went on the assumption that Gorbachev would fail. 'Up to the present Gorbachev's treason is a phrase uttered more and more often, and with hindsight the whole thing is far more difficult to judge than it was in the simple perspective of someone who wanted to reshape the DDR in 1985 or 1986. And Gorbachev makes it essentially much harder because he has set up a situation now in which he makes pronouncements which cannot be reconciled with what he thought and said at the time.'

The removal of Honecker provoked a clash of personalities and a jockeying for power from which the SED never really recovered. Old and young, hardliners and reformers, were either ceaselessly demanding one another's resignations or scheming to those ends. The political details are as tedious as they are unedifying, but, politician that he is, Modrow has forgotten nothing and plainly is glad to be guiding me through a web of who's-in-who's-out intrigue. In brief, Willi Stoph's role in overthrowing Honecker hid neither his own advanced age nor his hardline outlook, and on 7 November he had to resign, to be succeeded as Prime Minister by Modrow after eleven days of bewildering ego clashes. Having outmanoeuvred the gerontocrats, the young perestroikists imagined themselves saving the DDR for communism. In reality, it was only a benign version of the traditional procedure of change through purging, though without the clear-cut splitting of other Communist Parties in this predicament elsewhere in the empire. 'Anarchy,' I commented, and he nodded in assent.

The Schalck scandal broke over Modrow's head in the first three days of December. As he tells it, he saw no alternative to keeping in office someone of Schalck's technical skills and involvement with West Germany. But his midnight flit was a setback, and had the further result of obliging the country's highest legal official, Peter Wendland, to resign. On 3 December the Central Committee held its final session, Krenz resigned, the party ceased to exist in its old form. Without respite, the very next day Modrow along with the leadership of the rest of the satellite bloc was due in Moscow. No longer First Secretary, Krenz still remained president of the State Council for a few more days and in that capacity he accompanied Modrow.

'I met Gorbachev for the first time on 4 December,' Modrow says. 'Right until the end, whenever Gorbachev and I met, he always made it clear to me that the DDR had to continue existing and that for its part the Soviet Union would support the DDR. Today he behaves as though for years he had seen things differently. So when did he change his conception?

'On that first visit I was expecting Gorbachev to impart the results of the Malta conference. That was the whole purpose. At one of the breaks, I took the opportunity to ask Gorbachev for a private discussion of the DDR's problems. It was evident that in this conversation, the Soviet side, meaning Gorbachev, was scarcely at all preoccupied with the immediate DDR question, and Gorbachev revealed how uninformed he was. But if there were to be any results of this discussion, then we had to hold our meeting very soon. My concern was to convince Gorbachev that the two of us should meet with the shortest possible delay. The load in his diary postponed the date until the end of January. Neither he nor I at that point foresaw the urgency of the changes about to occur in the DDR. The Round Table had not yet been constituted, it met only three days later, on the 7th. I had not wanted a confederation, at the outset I hoped for something less, a treaty of association (*Vertragsgemeinschaft*). The Soviet side also envisaged that as the best option.'

The Round Table followed the Polish model. Leading churchmen played a significant part. Although the Round Table could not legislate, and it failed to establish any powers of veto over the Government, it resembled a miniature parliament in its composition of five communist-affiliated parties and nine new parties or citizens' movements. 'Of course the Round Table was an important element in the collapse. The question is, Does the political attitude which became established after the elections on 18 March derive from the work which started in December? The Round Table certainly did not sit down on 7 December to demand the elimination of the DDR. I believe that the citizens' movements at the Round Table were equally taken by surprise, they had wanted to change the DDR but not at that time to join West Germany.'

By the time Gorbachev was ready for the meeting arranged on 30 January, Modrow was being pressed hard to share power with a coalition of Round Table parties and citizens' movements, and to hold the elections which would confirm this power-sharing. On the day before he flew to Moscow he had talks with all the Round Table parties on the composition of a Government of National Responsibility and actually settled the election date. And that, Modrow supposes, is why Gorbachev came to change his mind at this second meeting of theirs. Conditions had evolved so rapidly that the main topic of consultation with Gorbachev was now no longer confederation but what practical steps could be taken to complete unity.

In Modrow's opinion, the Two-Plus-Four Treaty was agreed with a speed and an inattention harmful to the half-million Soviet troops and citizens in the DDR, as well as damaging to Gorbachev. The July meetings between Gorbachev and Kohl at which this was settled in principle were 'mysterious'. Gorbachev had imagined that 'he would negotiate his own strong bilateral agreement with Germany. Apart from promises of credit, in fact he obtained nothing.'

26

THE LAST AMBASSADOR

In the sitting room of his Moscow flat, Vyacheslav Kochemasov has hung over the sofa the framed front cover of an illustrated East German magazine, showing him in diplomatic uniform. His involvement with Germany goes back to 1947. A year later in Berlin he first met Honecker, then head of the local Komsomol. Having been an adviser in the Soviet Embassy in the 1950s, he was appointed ambassador by Andropov in 1983 and stayed until the East Berlin Embassy was shut down on the day of reunification. For over twenty years he was a deputy Prime Minister, specializing in international and especially German affairs. Retired now but still the formal diplomat, he had a courteous manner which did not quite conceal that this probing into a still painful past was not really to his taste.

Wild rumours had spread as a result of a lightning visit by Ligachev to the DDR on 21 September 1989. To many at the time, and afterwards, this had appeared a sinister portent. Ligachev took the view that the DDR was legitimate war booty, never to be surrendered. In no sense a warning of imminent crackdown, according to Kochemasov, the visit had long been scheduled. Ligachev had come to familiarize himself with agriculture and he did not meet Honecker, who was still convalescing from his gall-bladder operation. Nothing threatening had been premeditated. 'Coincidences of the kind sometimes do happen.'

His own personal relationship with Honecker was good. Modest to begin with, Kochemasov says, capable of teamwork, an organizer and a speaker who could ignite the emotions of his audience, Honecker had made the DDR a force to be reckoned with. 'It was difficult to convince Honecker of something, but once convinced he would reliably perform what he had promised.' But then the man changed, seeing in himself the personification of the country's achievements, concentrating power in his hands and ignoring advisers. Finally, even in trivial matters, no decision could be taken without his permission.

Propaganda linked to perestroika had been widely disseminated in the DDR press. Honecker at first had accepted the recommendations of the

Soviet Party Congress in 1986 but his attitude soon veered and hardened. Kochemasov sensed which way the wind was blowing. Then, in January 1988, Honecker invited all ambassadors to a traditional annual event, a shoot. 'It was a terribly cold day. During the interval for lunch I was invited by Honecker into a hut with a large room where there were other members of the leadership. We thawed out, we had something to eat and drink, and then he said he would like a word in private. We sat by ourselves at a small table. I want to tell you, he said, that from now on we are not going to use the word perestroika any more and I want you to understand why, and then you are welcome to tell anyone who needs to hear it in the Soviet Union. Perestroika is a step back from Leninism, and in the DDR we are categorically opposed to this kind of revisionism in the way we interpret Soviet history. We are against blackening and undermining the achievements of the Soviet people. We are against destroying everything that hundreds of millions of people, including those in the DDR, have believed in over many years. If you are telling us that Soviet history is nothing but an unbroken chain of mistakes then our people are bound to ask, How can this be? How are we to explain that the Soviet Union became a great power? We cannot find an answer. That is the reasoning whereby we will no longer be referring to perestroika in any documents or in the press.

'In the Brezhnev era, relations had been dominated by the so-called principle of "limited sovereignty". We had forced a single model of development upon all socialist countries. Gorbachev developed a different policy whereby these countries had to take responsibility for their own actions, bearing in mind their requirements and their history. Honecker had to be allowed to go his own way.'

Did this conversation seal his fate?

'I concluded that if Honecker was not prepared to respond more positively to the pressures of the age, then it would end badly for him. We were well aware how rapidly discontent was rising in all layers of society, especially among the intelligentsia. Honecker was deaf to demands for democratization of the state and its organs, and for greater information. He kept on repeating his principle, which could be encapsulated in the notion that you should improve only what you could improve. Centralized control was becoming increasingly incompatible with reform, and people would read in the press what was actually happening.'

Like everyone, including Honecker, Kochemasov was caught by surprise when the refugees started to stampede out of the country. 'That August I was on holiday in Russia, and heard for the first time through Deutsche Welle and the BBC about this great flood of DDR citizens haemorrhaging away through

Hungary. I went to Moscow and approached Gorbachev, Yakovlev and Shevardnadze, to say that I felt that I should return to Berlin immediately. They said, Aren't you overdramatizing? Why spoil your holiday? Eventually they conceded that I was probably right and I flew to Berlin immediately. Then Hungary opened its borders with Austria.'

Did you have any influence over the Hungarian decision?

'The DDR leadership tried to persuade the Hungarians that it was a violation of their agreement but they wouldn't listen. All that summer Honecker had been ill and I met him again only on 6 October. He was fairly calm but he said, What the Hungarian leaders have done to us is nothing short of treachery. From the tone of that conversation, I understood that he was still hoping that somehow or other a halt could be brought to the process. Given the access I had to numerous sources of information, I was convinced that this was the beginning of the end. Minute by minute the Western media were broadcasting heart-rending scenes of euphoria. And then later that same day Gorbachev flew in.

'I was present at both meetings between Gorbachev and Honecker on the 7th. The first meeting was enough to convince me that Honecker's replacement was inevitable. It was a one-to-one meeting. Honecker did not listen to what he was being told. But Gorbachev was insufficiently firm and specific in describing what would happen to the DDR if Honecker did not accept the advice he was being offered.'

What was the tone of this discussion?

'One of friendly persuasion that Honecker needed to reflect on the best interests of his people and the stabilization of the situation. But to whatever was said to him, Honecker's response was invariable, that he had settled on the policies he wished to pursue, and he would pursue them, and continue to treat his enemies as enemies. When this conversation came to an end I accompanied Gorbachev as he walked down the corridor in the People's Palace, and he stopped and raised his hands in despair, and used a Russian expression, Everything is falling like peas off a wall, meaning, What are we to do? When he walked out of the building, the press and various people were hanging around and that was when he first tossed out this phrase about life not forgiving those who come too late. It is hard to know whom exactly he was addressing, bearing in mind what had happened to us. In contrast to the praise accorded to him in the West, in Russia Gorbachev is now held totally responsible for the destruction and awful failures of the last few years.

'I knew that Honecker had this unwelcome habit of meeting Gorbachev and then transmitting to his leadership what Gorbachev had said in a distorted and even perverted form. So I had insisted on a second meeting at which Gorbachev would address the whole leadership. I was also aware of the group within this leadership convinced that Honecker had to go. But of course at any open or general meeting nobody could raise that subject. Krenz and Stoph headed this group, setting in motion the initiative to oust Honecker. As First Secretary, Krenz did everything in his power to avoid bloodshed. Having been responsible for State security, his tragedy was that he was working in an atmosphere of great distrust.'

Did you encourage Krenz?

'I cannot say that. After perestroika, it was no longer good form for an ambassador to dictate who was going to be First Secretary in another country. On the eve of Honecker's own election as First Secretary, the entire Politburo had been invited to the Embassy and told whom to appoint. Times had changed. But the decision to elect Krenz did correspond to Soviet wishes.'

Was there any discussion of closing the frontiers and declaring a state of emergency?

'There were no discussions of that sort at any level. That is categorical. Neither with the Soviet leadership, nor with me. Before the second of the big demonstrations which took place in Leipzig, I was telephoned by Krenz who said that Honecker had ordered him to go to Leipzig, accompanied by the Minister of Defence and representatives of state security, to decide what measures to take. I said to Krenz, This is extremely brave, but my advice is on no account to use force. If you do, there is no telling what the consequences may be. I continued, I am informing you categorically that when I put down the phone, the first thing I am going to do is to ring the commander of the Soviet forces in the DDR and give him the order that Soviet armed forces are not to become involved in these events in any circumstances. Krenz's reaction was to say, Fine, I agree, I will act accordingly in the spirit of what you have said. I reiterated what I had said, emphasizing that bloodshed had to be avoided.

'As I had said I would, I telephoned the military commander immediately. At that stage I had not talked to Moscow, but was using my ambassadorial right to give the order as chief representative of the state. I ordered him to confine all Soviet troops to barracks and to suspend all training and troop movements. Air-force operations were also to be stopped. Even in the case of extreme provocation, there was to be no reaction. He replied that he understood the order and would act upon it. The following day Moscow repeated these orders.'

Had the Soviet army intervened, the West might have complained but as usual it would have sat on its hands.

'An army of half a million men could have done as it pleased, but any move towards military control would have led to nuclear war. I was sitting there; I knew. I was in regular contact with the American, British and French ambassadors.'

Did the opening of the Wall effectively end any prospect for a perestroika regime in the DDR?

'Everything was open already. It made no difference. It had become inevitable. What was essential was working out a way to do it without dealing a fatal economic and political blow to the DDR. That was not properly thought through, leading to distortion and the collapse of the reform process. Society became literally ungovernable and reunification was the consequence.'

Modrow, in Kochemasov's opinion, did whatever was possible to establish a framework of stability. His coalition government of representatives from the leading parties and citizens' movements was 'honourable and worthy'.

What happened when Modrow met Gorbachev on 31 January 1990?

'The conversation was in two main parts. First, the question of regularizing the situation in the DDR, and second, what help the Soviet Union could provide. The economic condition into which the country had fallen after the opening of its borders called for Soviet aid. Goods and industrial products were flooding out into neighbouring countries, where they could take advantage of exchange rates to sell them cheaply and profitably. The DDR requested oil and natural gas and other raw materials and some machinery. Unfortunately, Gorbachev did not respond positively.

'Modrow raised the possibility of an initial bilateral treaty with the Federal Republic, to be followed by confederation. To begin with, Kohl was in accord with this. I met Modrow immediately after his return and he told me that he was happy with this conversation, and the atmosphere had been one of trust. Nothing came out of it. Shortly after, it became evident that Gorbachev was prepared to dance completely to Kohl's tune. Had Gorbachev been prepared to give greater support to the idea of confederation, and added some practical measures, I believe he would have been able to avoid the total disappearance of the DDR. Where the DDR was concerned, Gorbachev unilaterally conceded everything.'

Until the March elections, it was unimaginable that Germany would be united within Nato.

'Keeping the DDR outside Nato was one of the prime conditions set by Modrow. And by me. But the leadership just gave up on it.'

Why?

'Our society had no idea what Gorbachev was doing. Following the publication of Teltschik's book in Russian, it became clear to all that at the February meeting with Kohl, Gorbachev gave him *carte blanche* to do what he wanted. Kohl could hardly contain his delight, he had never expected such a turnaround. That's how politics sometimes works!' Neither at that February meeting nor later in July in the Caucasus did Gorbachev pay attention to his advisers. 'He made no use at all of the briefing notes and documents that had been prepared for him by Falin and others.'

How is this to be explained?

'God knows, it was such an extraordinary transformation within an individual. During his visit in October 1989, he organized a supper party for his closest friends. My wife and I were invited. The conversation was relaxed, Gorbachev was in a good mood. But in the course of this pleasant dinner party, Gorbachev let drop a sentiment which turned out to be significant, saying, Things are getting very serious. If anything bad were to happen to the DDR, then we in the Soviet Union will not be forgiven. And then in December he repeated himself in even stronger terms to the Central Committee. Why was he saying one thing but doing something completely different?'

To Kochemasov, this is all the more inexplicable because he could sense from his meetings with the Western ambassadors the reservations of their governments. 'Despite the fact that they were theoretically allies of the Federal Republic, it was very far from true to suppose that they were delighted at the prospect of a militarily and economically powerful Germany. It is no coincidence that Mitterrand himself flew to Berlin in March 1990 to have a close look at what was going on. He met Gorbachev in Kiev with a view to stopping reunification. Mrs Thatcher was also against it. American pressure in favour was not detectable.'

Within the Soviet Foreign Ministry, those officials who had been preparing documents were informed about what was happening, but the exact truth was known only in a very narrow circle. Temperamentally Shevardnadze was always prepared to make concessions, and he put his views across to Gorbachev successfully. But ultimately the right to take decisions was Gorbachev's; he was in a position where he did not have to listen to Shevardnadze, Kochemasov insists.

So it was a weakness of the Soviet system that policy came to depend upon the character of a single individual?

'Absolutely!' Kochemasov replied, repeating with emphasis unusual for him, 'absolutely!'

27

GERMAN REUNIFICATION

Until well into 1990 the foreign policy establishment in West Germany had no sense that a historic moment was at hand. It is hardly an exaggeration to say that everyone concerned sleepwalked into the reunification of Germany. The helplessness of men in the wake of the events that they have themselves set in motion but cannot then master endows this alteration to the European balance of power with that fatality in human affairs which the ancient Greeks called hubris and nemesis.

Few worked harder than Günter Gaus to propound the one-nation two-states theory. Conceivably reunification might one day be realized through Brussels and the European Union, but to keep the idea alive seemed to him in the 1970s and 1980s a distraction from the task incumbent on West Germans of reaching accommodation with the DDR. In his opinion, the majority of East Germans were indifferent to ideology but an unspoken consensus existed that if they were not to be communists, they would not revert to past social patterns either. Pre-1933 Germany was as truly extinct as Hitler's Germany. In a book published in 1983 Gaus maintained scornfully that the Kohl government based its policy towards the DDR on the core belief that everything could be bought, rather than devising peaceful coexistence. Wrong-headed as this was soon revealed to be, Gaus none the less was speaking for an influential segment of German public opinion.

As editor-in-chief of the weekly *Der Spiegel* and a promoter of this line of least resistance, Gaus had caught the eye of Willy Brandt in 1972. A child of suspect paternity and doubtful future, the newborn Ostpolitik needed articulate champions like Gaus. From 1974 to 1981 he was posted by Brandt as West German permanent representative in East Berlin, in effect ambassador in all but title. Personable and obliging, Gaus was everything that the East Germans could hope for in a West German diplomat.

Ostpolitik, he believes, neither shortened nor extended the existence of the DDR. Its concrete achievement was to simplify the bureaucratic obstacles to normal human relations for families divided by the Iron Curtain.

'Everything depended on Moscow. Without Gorbachev the Warsaw Pact would still exist and Kohl would not have been the Chancellor of reunification.'

Communist propaganda and projection was a bluff, as Gaus found out later in 1988, when invited to Moscow as the official guest of the Soviet government. He held lengthy talks with Falin, with Falin's assistant Nikolai Portugalov, with the Central Committee official responsible for the DDR, and with Yakovlev. 'Yakovlev told me that he had taken a holiday in the DDR and met Modrow during the course of it. An apparent step towards Honecker was actually a call on Modrow. By the time I returned, I had the impression that the Soviet Union might be a great power with a huge military presence, but on that far western frontier of its empire it was in fact completely helpless. They had noticed that something was happening but could neither analyse what this might be nor what to do about it. It became clear that they were clueless. They wanted to know if I had any suggestions but I didn't either.'

Egon Bahr was 'one of the most fertile and influential practitioners, strategists and ideologists of Ostpolitik', in the words of Timothy Garton Ash. As head of the planning staff in Brandt's Foreign Ministry and afterwards the negotiator of the treaties determining boundaries, he played a leading role in enabling the DDR to put down what had appeared its lasting roots in Europe. He coined the shorthand slogan '*Wandel durch Annährung*', or change through rapprochement. To some this was a realistic route towards that convergence which one day would supposedly allow the two German states to live together amicably, but to others it was a dangerous illusion, if not a sellout. The inherent contradictions, he wrote in 1988, would be 'historically resolved'. Whatever this might mean, the takeover by West Germany on its own terms of a morally and economically bankrupt DDR was certainly not what he had in mind.

Whatever Shevardnadze or anyone else might like to claim, Bahr says, 'In 1988 and 1989 there was absolutely no question of unification. Three weeks before the opening of the Wall, the Chancellor gave his famous Ten-Points declaration, one of which included the *Vertragsgemeinschaft* with Modrow, after which he would negotiate a confederal structure, and still later confederation itself. In other words it was absolutely clear that German unification was not on the agenda. In February 1990 the calculation was that conditions might deteriorate in the DDR. Elections were planned for the beginning of 1991 and the coalition might not win them. It might therefore be necessary to win them by clearing the foreign policy frame first and advancing the date of elections to the end of 1990. When I had a confidential conversation with Foreign Minister Genscher at that time, he said that he had not the slightest idea if the foreign policy preconsideration could be resolved. He raised the Two-Plus-Four idea and we wondered whether an agreement could be initiated by the end of the year. The date of 2 October for unification was still unknown.'

After the DDR elections on 18 March 1990, Lothar de Maizière replaced Modrow and formed a government. His Defence Minister was Rainer Eppelmann, a Lutheran pastor, former dissident and avowed pacifist. That April and May, Eppelmann was pressing Bahr to become his adviser, offering a two-year contract to start on 1 June. 'Even as a member of the de Maizière cabinet', as Bahr rubs in, 'he was absolutely unaware as late as June that the country would cease to be in existence by 2 October. Very strange. Reality was too strong.

'I was absolutely convinced that some day we would have unification, and I was also almost certain that I would never witness it. On the night of the opening of the Wall, I knew that this was the beginning of the end of the DDR because the process could not be stopped. But I envisaged a period of two to five years. Later I asked Krenz why he had not given Chancellor Kohl a private message, that he was prepared to open the Wall on condition that he gave him the money to stabilize the country. He would have received billions of Deutschmarks and he and Kohl would have been heroes. Krenz answered that the pressure was too intense for such an assessment in the heat of the moment, and besides, Kohl was in Poland, and after 9 November, it was too late.' In Bahr's opinion, the DDR leadership was psychologically too weak and demoralized to have dared to resort to force. Senior figures like Kessler and Heinz Hoffmann, the commander of the Volksarmee, had let Honecker know that the army would not open fire on the population. The moral aspect therefore remains obscure. Credit for refusing to use violence rests upon uncertainty whether the order to do so would have been obeyed.

When Modrow visited Gorbachev in January 1990, Bahr supposes, he convinced him that the Wall could not be resurrected, people were fleeing in ever larger numbers and the country could no longer be held together. 'Modrow came back with a formula, *Einig Vaterland* (a united country). A sensation. But even with this formula, a process of negotiations might have lasted up to five years. Gorbachev had his internal troubles, he had to ride the tiger. He must have seen a chance to control German developments long enough for him to be able to dominate his own problems. And from the Germans he would obtain more money than from the Americans. Some such mixed expectations must have arisen.'

Why not argue for a confederation and gain a reprieve of a few years in which to settle with Yeltsin and the Baltics?

'The Allied powers still possessed rights, Germany was not sovereign. It was extremely clever of Kohl to argue that he fully accepted these rights but that

281

they amounted to nothing because people were escaping in such large numbers and he could not build a wall on his side. Either you bring the goods to the people, or the people will go to the goods. Since this flight had the potential to destabilize the Federal Republic, unification was the only way out. Kohl could take a position that the West Germans were not particularly anxious for unity but the East Germans were forcing it upon them.'

With the skills deriving from years of negotiation and sophistry over fine points, Bahr keenly defends Ostpolitik and his lifelong conviction that the West built up extravagant defences through overestimating Soviet military capacity and thereby extended the Cold War. His version of European security, he claims, put to rest the Soviet fear concerning Germany and revisionism, to the point where 'they sniffed that peaceful co-operation with Germany and Western Europe might be in their interests'.

Be that as it may, even he goes on to concede that events were decided in Moscow by the Soviets, not in the West by westerners. 'I saw Gorbachev very often and observed how he shifted his position. At the outset he was the master of decision and development, he could put his stamp on what he wanted to do. Somewhere about 1987, 1988, he was no longer the master, but under compulsion, trying to balance forces beyond his control. By 1990 his policy had been reduced to improvisation.'

A member of the small Free Democratic Party, whose tactical switches between the Christian Democrats and the Social Democrats were such a decisive feature of German politics, Hans-Dietrich Genscher was Foreign Minister for eighteen years. Among Foreign Ministers, only Gromyko held office longer. Born in Halle, just old enough to have been in an anti-aircraft unit at the end of the war, Genscher fled to the West in 1952. His frequent returns to East Germany where his mother lived, coupled with his advocacy of détente, were seen outside his own country with dismay sometimes verging on suspicion. He appeared to make a point of being out of step with his colleagues. His relationship with Kohl was particularly tense. To be cordial with the one generally involved taking a distance from the other. Genscher is never less than circumspect.

After his first conversation with Gorbachev, says Genscher, he was convinced that here was someone to set in motion fundamental changes in Europe. In internal and external affairs, things could no longer continue as before, but although the exposition was impressive, Genscher concluded, that was the limit of Gorbachev's outlook: he knew less what he wanted than what he did not want. 'You know, there was a difference in the initial assessment of Gorbachev between the Chancellor and his staff, and me and my staff.' By 1987 at the latest, he thinks, Gorbachev and Shevardnadze had made up their minds to focus on two political relationships: with Germany in Europe and with the United States worldwide. This was evident throughout the negotiations concerning unification. 'Whenever the Russian leadership was in any doubt whether to move or not, whether to make concessions or not, it was crucial to them that the United States and Germany took the same line.'

Several very public statements by Gorbachev in 1988 affirmed that for the Soviet Union every country had the right of self-determination. According to a joint Soviet–West German declaration of June 1989, all peoples and states were free to decide their destiny for themselves. Gorbachev's purpose here was to overcome East–West tension. His officials recognized an implicit threat to the future of the bloc. In working over the declaration in detail, Genscher felt that Shevardnadze was going further in making concessions than his officials would have wanted.

Nor did Gorbachev anticipate that the change of regime would eventually destabilize the DDR. As early as September 1988 Genscher had discussed with Shevardnadze the possible use of force against demonstrations. 'I made it very clear that our reaction would be quite different to what it had been in June 1953. My concern was to convince the Russians that their troops had to stay in their barracks whatever might happen.' The Krenz–Modrow team stood no chance at all. When the two of them were in Moscow at the beginning of December 1989, Genscher also had a meeting with Gorbachev. Amusingly, Krenz and Modrow had to wait in their cars on the road to the airport, as the Russians insisted on separating the German delegations and giving Genscher priority.

In December Gorbachev was still critical of Kohl's Ten Points, and ignored the question of unification. The change in his attitude became apparent in January. There were three options, in Genscher's presentation: united Germany in the Warsaw Pact, united Germany neutral, united Germany in Nato. Membership of the Warsaw Pact was unacceptable, so the choice lay between neutrality and Nato. But since Germany could never drop Nato in favour of neutrality, success meant persuading the Soviets that they were better off with Germany inside Nato, and the Two-Plus-Four Treaty confirming that Nato troops would not be deployed in the former DDR. By July 1990 only two questions were outstanding: How many troops was the united Germany to have, and how much was it to pay?

Horst Teltschik was Chancellor Kohl's security and foreign affairs adviser, therefore the official dealing directly with the Soviets on the Chancellor's behalf. His opposite number was Anatoly Chernyayev. The period between the opening of the Berlin Wall until German unification lasted three hundred and twenty-nine days, and *329 Tage* is the appropriate title of the diary which he kept at that time and which he has since published. This absorbing glimpse of high politics is all the more vivid for Teltschik's ceaseless amazement at the pace and ease of events, as if he were having to rub his eyes at the immense reward looming ever more brilliantly in this treasure hunt. Setbacks, in particular turf disputes with Genscher and the Foreign Ministry, in retrospect seem insubstantial.

Change for the sake of change was Gorbachev's initial position. How to change, in which direction and for what purpose, were questions which would have to take care of themselves. An industrial country, Gorbachev had realized, could not be run by Stalinist methods. 'He stuck to the decision he made when first he took over power, no longer to interfere in the internal affairs of his allies. This is what he promised to President Bush and Helmut Kohl. The Hungarian Prime Minister Miklós Németh once told me that they were constantly testing how far they could go with their reforms because they were unsure what finally Gorbachev might do, and could only discover by experience. Gorbachev was ready to accept that with us, but in the belief that this did not imply reunification. Developments in the DDR were too swift for him. The Chancellor's Ten-Points speech raised the issue, and Gorbachev had to decide what to do. At the very end, he accepted the idea of reunification out of the hope that the new Germany, accepting some of his special conditions, would be his main ally economically in supporting reform of the Soviet Union. I had dinner privately with him last Sunday [this was June 1993] and he told me again that it had been his dream to create a strong liaison between Russia and Germany.'

In the summer of 1989 Teltschik gave an interview in the *Bonner Generalanzeiger* in which he stated that the German question would once again become an international issue. 'The concept of our government was not territorial integration in the first instance, but that the DDR had to carry out reforms similar to those in Poland and Hungary. Since Gorbachev was willing to allow that to happen, we had to push for it and direct it, supporting them towards liberalization as a first goal.'

So you thought Modrow could succeed?

'Yes. This was not tied to Modrow as a person but to anyone who might emerge as a perestroikist to democratize the DDR and develop a market system. Then people could decide for themselves whether they wanted to have a separate state or not. I am by no means sure that Modrow really was a perestroikist. Instead of reforming, he started modernizing the Stasi, and from the beginning he was manipulating the new electoral laws. Our impression was that by December people had already lost patience, and even more so by January when still nothing had happened. True, it was a short period but

Modrow was behaving in accordance with the same old communist system that had engaged him during his whole career. That's why they stormed the Stasi building on 15 January. More and more people were fleeing to the West. In February we received 100,000 East Germans and the figures were increasing daily. They were mostly young and adaptable, and if this continued the DDR could not survive. Another factor was that they were close to economic collapse through incapacity to repay their debt. And thirdly, Modrow told us at the end of January during his meeting with the Chancellor that he could decide whatever he liked but nobody then executed his orders. Those were the reasons why the Chancellor had to advance the date for free elections from May to March.'

Forming his government after the election, de Maizière supposed that he would be Prime Minister for two years or more, and could retain some of the 'successes' of the DDR. But irresistible momentum had been set up. 'At their February meeting in Moscow the Chancellor laid out to Gorbachev the economic and political deterioration of the DDR. That was the main issue. Who was then to be responsible for the DDR? Who would rule in the event of the DDR government failing? How would chaos affect us? Soviet interference was obviously not in our interests and there was always the danger that the military or security organs would cut loose.'

Is there any evidence of that?

'Yes and no. Nobody really knows. Border guards could have lost their nerve and started shooting. Later on we got hints that in January there had been discussions within the Soviet leadership whether to intervene. After he resigned, Shevardnadze told me that people like Falin were trying to convince the leadership in that direction.'

The February 1990 meeting was decisive?

'Absolutely. The miracle was that Gorbachev told the Chancellor that it was now up to the Germans to decide whether or not to unite, and when, and how fast, and so on. That's why on my return I said that the Chancellor now holds the key to German reunification. The greatness of Gorbachev was that he had decided that military intervention was no longer an instrument to stop developments. The question then became whether Gorbachev would accept membership of a united Germany within Nato and, if so, would he further accept the dissolution of the Four-Power regime.

'Our position in the Government was that he needed to be helped over the hurdle with a package containing a number of things. Some elements were critical to the success of such a package, for instance, the bilateral treaty of friendship and co-operation and the breakthrough in the relationship between

Gorbachev and Bush at the end of May in Washington. Later on Gorbachev used to repeat to us how fundamental it was to have begun a relationship of trust with the American President. Another important part of the package was the special Nato summit in early July, offering friendship to the Warsaw Pact. The European summit and the G7 summit promised the Soviet Union economic support. Governments cannot handle several conflicts simultaneously and it was truly helpful to us that the Gulf War did not erupt earlier. Everyone could concentrate on the German question. Part of the package was the party congress in Moscow where Gorbachev got rid of Ligachev. At the end of May I was negotiating in Moscow a credit of 5 billion Deutschmarks. Gorbachev had to be able to say, We have accepted reunification and this is what we got in return.'

The July days spent in Moscow, Stavropol and in the Caucasus were in the nature of a formality?

'Our hope was that with the package we could come close to a breakthrough. There were hints. At the Bush–Gorbachev joint press conference in Washington at the end of May, Bush publicly repeated that Germany had to be within Nato, and Gorbachev said nothing, neither denying nor repudiating it. But in the Caucasus, Gorbachev suddenly blurted out to the Chancellor that we could remain in Nato. We had only to settle the details: Would the DDR be integrated into Nato, how long would Soviet troops remain, what should be the size of the German army, and so on.'

How did you find Gorbachev during those three days?

'Neither excited nor angry. Once he had accepted the main premise, he liked to repeat, then he would have to accept the conclusions that followed logically. Everything stemmed from the first decision. It was a five- or six-hour discussion, in good spirits, with a lot of trust on both sides.'

All in all, the Soviet Union received from West Germany a sum of money in the order of 60 billion Deutschmarks. Seventeen billion were allocated to the construction of housing for returning Soviet troops. The 5 billion credit negotiated by Teltschik in May alone enabled the Soviet Union to make a debt repayment due on 30 June. Evidently German sensitivity to Soviet economic distress demonstrated a willingness to save the face both of the Soviet Union and of Gorbachev.

But it allows Ligachev and other hardliners to claim that Gorbachev sold East Germany.

'Sure, but what was the alternative? We were aware that we had to do something, and that meant paying for reunification. At the very end, in August, Gorbachev telephoned the Chancellor and asked him to raise our payments. So we did. But no sum could ever be enough for Gorbachev.'

He did not make much attempt at bargaining.

Teltschik agrees, but points out that in May 1990 an attempt was made to stretch the issue out when Shevardnadze raised a proposal to separate the internal processes of reunification from the Two-Plus-Four agreement. It might have led to a situation in which Germany was unified without having recovered its sovereignty. The Chancellor understood that danger and rejected Shevardnadze's proposal, but Teltschik wonders whether the German Foreign Ministry might not have been ready to accept it. He says that he never received the complete protocols of what transpired at that moment between Shevardnadze and Genscher. But however prominent Shevardnadze was in matters of procedure, Gorbachev actually took the decision.

The question always boils down to Gorbachev?

'That is why he is a historic figure.'

28

'THERE WERE NO STATESMEN'

Among Soviet officials dealing with Germany, few had the long experience of Valentin Falin. Born in 1923, he became a member of the Central Committee in the 1950s. His German is good, spoken in a light and sometimes almost countertenor voice. His collections of ceramics and books are well-known, and he affects the weary aristocratic air of someone who has seen it all.

Arkady Shevchenko, the diplomat who defected from the United Nations, related in his memoirs how Foreign Minister Gromyko in the summer of 1970 had invited him to meet Falin, 'to discuss a review of Soviet plans for Europe'. An intelligent man with a reasonable and logical approach, Shevchenko continued, Falin was riding high at the time because Gromyko valued his aide's knowledge of German affairs. By means of the 1970 treaty with Germany, Brandt was to be obliged to do what the Soviets wanted of him, acting as 'the lever to draw Europe away from American influence'. Imparting inside information from the KGB, Falin had smiled mysteriously and said, 'We have quite a net in West Germany, you know.' Following the treaty, Falin became Soviet ambassador in Bonn until 1978. Then he switched to run the Novosti news agency, usually considered a KGB outlet for information and disinformation alike. In 1988 he became head of the International Department of the Central Committee and, as such, highly influential in foreign affairs. Among other things, this position involved paying subventions and other hidden fundings to Communist Parties abroad. After the 1991 coup, $660,000 in cash was discovered in Falin's safe, a sum whose end purposes were not explained.

During the Gorbachev era, Falin liked to issue threatening pronouncements. He warned that the Soviet Union might plan its own retaliatory Star Wars programme. 'So what?' he asked of the secret protocols of the Ribbentrop–Molotov Pact, saying that these had nothing to do with present realities. He put the blame for starting the Cold War on America. In an interview in 1987 he asserted that two German states without any foreign troops stationed in them might eventually become a fact, which drew a rebuke from Honecker himself. But as late as February 1990 he said, 'If the Western alliance sticks to its demands for a Nato membership of all of Germany, then there won't be any reunification.'

Since 1979 Falin has treated Nikolai Portugalov as his *homme de confiance*. Thanks to a German governess, Portugalov speaks excellent German. Chain-smoking Gauloise cigarettes, Portugalov is often held to have had the rank of a KGB major general, which leads to an unresolved query about Falin's possible rank. The two of them are depicted in Teltschik's journal as somewhat of an act, and plainly they were held in some suspicion in Bonn. The political line designed by Falin and executed by Gorbachev, Portugalov says, was a continuation of the policies of Gromyko, who would certainly have not balked at sending in tanks. Succeeding him, Shevardnadze had no power base. The Soviet ambassador in Bonn, Yuli Kvitzinski, was an extreme reactionary who urged the use of force. Shevardnadze did not allow the Central Committee to have much influence, but from September to November 1989 the International Department of the Central Committee did play a role in establishing what should be done in respect to Germany. Portugalov himself published an article in the *New York Times* on 15 December 1989 to say that both Germanys would continue to exist as sovereign and equal states.

Falin's position, so he himself claimed, was that the military–feudal dictatorship installed in the Soviet Union after 1917 should more accurately have been described as counter-communism. At the outset of perestroika, he presented to Gorbachev a memorandum of twenty-three pages to argue that it was not enough to lay aside this counter-communism, or in shorthand, Stalinism. In the light of the outcome, the whole October Revolution had to be reassessed. Although Gorbachev appeared interested, nothing resulted from this memorandum. For Falin, the idea of changing counter-communism into communism was a 'circus trick', rather than realistic politics. To recognize as much would have required courage, sincerity and inner conviction, qualities which he judges were lacking. Stalin at least had carried everything in his head. 'Since his day, there has been no system in Soviet politics.' Conceding as a minimum the inhuman aspects of Stalinism, many hardliners like Falin defend the past in this oblique way.

Had Gorbachev in 1985 or 1986 proposed clear and practical aims, nine-tenths of the population, including a majority in the party, would have been behind him. Such was the confidence in him that he could even have gone successfully against the party apparatus which was undoubtedly hardline and ossified. But Gorbachev had no idea what he hoped to achieve ideologically, socially, economically or in terms of human rights. Instead, he took to improvizations and meaningless slogans and promises. Falin could never have imagined that a General Secretary could have a mind so devoid of substance. He was only one among many, he sighs, who had had no idea that Gorbachev would launch escapades, and even run amok. He makes no attempt to hide his disappointment.

The Soviet Empire in his view consisted of a Russian metropolis which developed and paid for a non-Russian periphery. Whatever the other malign consequences of Stalinism, at the national level it had created a party and an intelligentsia qualified for national leadership, as was proved in each republic when the Soviet Union split up. Accusing Gorbachev of reaching ill-considered decisions through lack of intellectual grasp, he somewhat contradictorily goes on to argue that the empire fell primarily 'because it collapsed economically'. The colonies were too costly. The Soviet Union asked them for high-quality goods for which it was willing to pay world prices. The colonies preferred the security which derived from mass-producing low-quality goods for the captive Soviet market. Mutual impoverishment ensued.

The DDR was a prime military and economic asset, and the Soviet Union furthermore had legally guaranteed rights there. The forty-year occupation was a history of lost opportunities. Public opinion polls taken in secret had thrown up results which were never published, revealing that support for the party never reached 30 per cent, and was often far less. A few well-placed Soviet advisers had warned in the late 1980s that the DDR's economic debts would soon translate into yet more onerous political burdens but they met with the sort of resistance which comes from breaking a taboo.

In the summer of 1989 Honecker had been invited as a guest of honour to the steel town of Magnitogorsk, in the steppes beyond the southern Urals. Fifty years earlier he had worked on this typically Stalinist project of constructing a heavy-industrial site in the middle of nowhere. At a stopover in Moscow on his way home, Honecker had another of his fruitless conversations with Gorbachev. After previous discussions, Gorbachev had been displeased to learn from other sources how Honecker criticized perestroika as revisionism. In the presence of Falin he now told Gorbachev that perestroika was a Soviet affair, not really relevant to the DDR. 'On that note the two of them took leave of each other. Some of us thought that it was necessary or at least advisable to reform the DDR, and we persuaded Gorbachev to do this. We had good reason to suppose that Honecker kept to himself his discussions with Gorbachev. That is why Gorbachev made the demand that if he were to go to the DDR, he had to have the opportunity to meet the entire leadership. It was clear that the situation would be difficult for him personally, and unexpected things could not be ruled out. The trip was therefore to be restricted to thirty-six hours.'

Falin was in Gorbachev's entourage on 6 October. Honecker and Gorbachev drove in the same car from the airport through streets lined with hundreds of thousands of people cheering for Gorbachev exclusively. As the motorcade approached Schloss Niederschönhaus, Falin noticed a man holding a placard with the wonderfully ambiguous and possibly ironic words, 'Erich, go on as you are!' Perceiving that Honecker was excluded by his own people from all the celebration, Gorbachev commented in an aside on his arrival at Niederschönhaus, 'What shall we do if it goes on like this?' About 40,000 people marched past the rostrum on Unter den Linden, rhythmically chanting 'Gorbi', but there were still no calls in honour of the DDR and its fortieth anniversary. 'Honecker was standing there, angry and so agitated that you can hardly imagine it. We went from that rostrum to the private discussions. Honecker, Günter Mittag and a translator were on their side, and on ours were Gorbachev, Shakhnazarov and myself. We said that the DDR had achieved a great deal and should not be painted black, and that this anniversary offered a pretext to begin wide-ranging reforms. Honecker repeated what he had previously said many times, that the DDR did not need to emulate the Soviet Union and the people supported the party and its policies. None of the present difficulties were overwhelming. It could even be that he believed what he was saying.'

By the end of this discussion, Falin says, Gorbachev's concentration was wandering. He went straight from the room to the hall where the Politburo and the entire party-state leadership had gathered. In the corridor he had first uttered the sentiment about life punishing whoever comes too late, and he now repeated it: the words were evidently running in his head. 'Gorbachev weighed it very carefully and politically, so as to create no impression that he would either protect the DDR or force anything on it. He wanted to present the issue as though it were a reflection of Soviet experience, and to articulate very clearly that reform was a necessity beyond questioning. In his reply, Honecker mentioned his recent visit to Magnitogorsk and how he and his comrades had inspected the shops and found a shortage of matches and soap. After an interval, there was a reception. The atmosphere was really awful. Margot Honecker in particular showed her feelings. This mood lasted until we drove to the airport. As we were leaving, they said, You have done everything, and he has understood nothing. In fact Gorbachev did more than a guest could have done.'

What were Gorbachev's ideas for the future of Germany?

'He had no idea, no definite scenario. He didn't understand how it really was; he thought it might be possible to keep relations between states frozen while trying to normalize them.' According to Falin, debate was restricted to a circle consisting only of Gorbachev, Shevardnadze, Yakovlev, Yazov, Chernyayev,

Shakhnazarov and himself, and it did not extend to the Central Committee or the Politburo. 'An initiative came about whereby we and Germany would not get involved militarily or with any forceful methods. Experience shows that political problems can be solved only by political means.' Instead of a turning point, the October visit was virtually a terminal. The opening of the border put paid to even remote prospects of association or confederation.

A crisis committee had been set up in the Kremlin to deal with the German question, and in his book Shevardnadze says that at a meeting of this committee he squashed a call for the military option. If any such call actually was made, says Falin, it was in his absence. He was unaware of anything of that kind. Gorbachev used to open meetings by asking those present for their thoughts. Not even Marshal Yazov dissented from the natural unfolding of the political process.

But it remains a mystery why the Soviet Union gave up its main front against the West after those years of massive military security.

'We are still waiting for the answer to that from Gorbachev. It could be that he had no understanding of his actions or the future of the country. He confided in no one. He spoke on the telephone directly to Kohl.' Taking decisions on his own, or at most as a duo with Shevardnadze, Gorbachev may have had some logic which he himself could not clarify. What sort of democracy is it, Falin asks rhetorically, in which one man decides in the name of 300 million people what is right and what is wrong?

Falin's International Department of the Central Committee was another arena in which to raise the German question. Opinion there, he says, was in favour of three preconditions before any change in the status quo could be considered. Reunification did not mean annexation, Nato membership with the installation of atomic weapons was excluded, and finally a treaty had to settle outstanding issues relating to redeployment and rehousing of Soviet troops. By then a pronounced opponent of Gorbachev's policy of unilateral withdrawal, Falin was not invited to the July 1990 meetings with Kohl in the Kremlin and then in the Caucasus. At around midnight, on the eve of Kohl's arrival, Falin had a lengthy telephone conversation in which he restated to Gorbachev his three preconditions and tried to advise him against the course he actually took. He would do his best, Gorbachev had answered, but he could not exclude the possibility that the train had already left the station. In the event, Gorbachev locked out all advisers except Shevardnadze and Chernyayev.

Without too strenuous an effort, Falin maintains, the party could have repudiated the Caucasus decision. The view was instead taken that this would have led to even worse political damage. Here was the classic choice between two evils. When Falin took the opportunity to criticize Gorbachev at a meeting of the Committee of International Relations, Gorbachev leaned heavily on him. Falin's voice grows reedy: 'You think these were pleasant conversations!' The matter is all the more inexplicable in the complete absence of American pressure. 'The Americans were prepared to co-operate with us in order that events in Europe should not be stormy. At least partial control of events could only help American interests, which is why they were very loyal. French and British interests were served by the continuation of two Germanys. The Swiss and the Austrians were among those trying to prevent outright annexation.'

Three conspiracy theories exist, I put it to him: that the West German government gave promises of further financial credits which have not yet been revealed; that an agreement on the lines of the Rapallo Treaty of 1922 has been reached about future German–Russian relations; and, most far-fetched of all, that Gorbachev himself was massively bought.

Falin points out that Kohl and Genscher haggled hard and publicly about the sums of money they were to pay, and that circumstances today are very different from those after the First World War when the Rapallo Treaty was drafted to the advantage of both Germany and Russia, though never actually ratified. As for bribery, 'I would like to believe this played no part,' and it is only a fiction expressing the widespread bewilderment at what occurred. 'One thing is certain: on the side of the Soviet Union there were no statesmen, but only *petit bourgeois* in the highest political positions who forgot everything that had existed in the past.'

29

'LET'S CALL IN THE TANKS'

Until the arrival of national independence in the second half of the nineteenth century Sofia was an Ottoman backwater. For the part they played in the 1878 liberation from Turkish rule, Russians were perceived afterwards as kindred spirits, fellow Slavs and Orthodox believers. New buildings like the royal palace built for a Saxe-Coburg recruited to be king, the Alexander Nevski Cathedral and the National Assembly provided the trappings of nationhood in accordance with the age of Garibaldi and Bismarck. Many streets in the capital's centre are still paved with attractive pale yellow tiles imported from *fin de siècle* Vienna.

Without an indigenous aristocracy or much of a professional middle class, Bulgaria remained a rural society. Everyone had their grandfather's clogs in the attic, as a local proverb has it. The historic absence of institutions suitable to introduce power-sharing meant that corruption and violence took precedence over law, perverting an egalitarianism which came naturally. As elsewhere in the Balkans, conspiracy and feuding were accepted means of fulfilling ambitions and obtaining rewards. From its inception the local Communist Party adopted Lenin's calculus that all means were legitimate in order to seize and hold undivided power. In a notorious outrage in 1923, party activists placed a bomb in the cathedral which killed over a hundred Ministers and generals, but not the King who happened to arrive two minutes late and so was a witness to the carnage rather than another victim. During the persecution which lasted throughout the inter-war years, about 3,000 party members sought refuge in the Soviet Union. Almost a third of these were later killed by Stalin. What had begun in 1878 as goodwill towards a liberating Russia became after 1944 a deferential cringe.

Several times on the point of being liquidated, Georgi Dimitrov was one of those who survived the Great Terror. As the man accused of setting fire to the Berlin Reichstag, and head of the pre-war Comintern which was the foreign arm of the KGB and the party, he had been as celebrated a communist as any in the world. In the course of completing the Soviet takeover of his country, Dimitrov died in 1949. Embalmed, he was buried in what had been the park in front of the royal palace, in a mausoleum all his own, a portentous and pillared Soviet-Athenian temple whose marble steps led up to a central enclosure with wooden folding doors behind which lay the body. Only Lenin and Stalin had been sacralized in this way.

The likeliest local candidate to lead the party at that point was Traicho Kostov but Stalin in his last years purged anyone and everyone he could not be sure of controlling. Conniving in Kostov's judicial murder, Vulko Chervenko became First Secretary. Moscow-trained, he was a faithful imitator of Stalin. Terror and the labour camps came into their own. The yet more ruthless Todor Zhivkov had the nerve to challenge Chervenko and he did so with mastery unusual even in these circles. A consummate opportunist and cynic, he used his instinct for manipulation to remove those in his way, where necessary killing them by means not directly traceable to him. Although unable fully to push Chervenko out of public life for some time, he became First Secretary in 1954, to remain in office for thirty-five years. In 1972 he and Brezhnev went so far as to agree to the outright annexation of Bulgaria as the sixteenth republic of the Soviet Union. Brezhnev, it appears, back-pedalled. At Soviet behest, two specifically Bulgarian letters were purged from the alphabet. Bulgaria had become a Soviet backwater.

Today many who are disaffected for one reason or another live in tents sprawling around the Dimitrov mausoleum. The mummy itself was removed in 1991 and buried nobody knows where. Fouled, the marble steps and enclosure stink; graffiti on every available surface and in every colour, almost invariably obscene in meaning, look like wild parodies of modern expressionist art.

And Todor Zhivkov, 'Uncle Tosho' in the phoney image of popularity which he cultivated, was sentenced by the Supreme Court to seven years' imprisonment for embezzling on behalf of his family and friends state funds of 21.5 million leva, or approximately $18 million. Weaving and dodging with his usual artistry, he contrived to remain under 'house arrest' with his granddaughter. As soon as it was safe to do so, a member of the National Assembly pointed out that whereas King Ferdinand and his son Boris had four residences, Zhivkov had no less than thirty. Another speaker explained that Zhivkov's many books had actually been written by a collective of hacks, and their expensive production paid for with hard currency.

Pravets, the village an hour or so east of Sofia where he was born, has been selectively enriched by market-garden greenhouses and non-polluting light industries. A street was named after his mother; the modest family house was rebuilt more than once into a museum, displaying the would-be heroic war and clandestine party role which the man invented for himself. Favouritism, the spoils of office, self-aggrandizement, were ends to be trumpeted about rather than concealed. Threadbare peasant imaginings of glory were fulfilled by warlord practices. In the main square, Ozymandias-like, the heavy rivets at ground level in a waste of tarmac alone bear testimony to what had been a great commemorative statue in his honour.

Properly, Zhivkov should have been tried for his responsibility for the existence until well into the 1960s of camps like Skravena, Lovetch and Belene, to which people were deported without any due process in their tens of thousands; for the forced assimilation or outright expulsion of up to 300,000 ethnic Turks, scores of whom were killed in deliberate acts of terror; and for the murder of dissidents of whom Georgi Markov was only the most conspicuous. It was Markov who, one day sailing down the Danube and passing close to Belene, recalled his friends: 'Vassil, who was kept bound with chains for two whole weeks in a boat stuck in the ice of the river during the coldest February; Stamen, confined for several days and nights in a solitary cell with water up to his neck; boys from the Polytechnic who were shot on the spot without reason or sentence.' Between 1946 and 1985 border guards shot dead 339 people attempting to flee the country, and after 1985 another 105, including 36 foreigners.

In time-honoured style, Zhivkov toyed with several possible successors, first Aleksander Lilov, and then Andrey Lukanov and Petar Mladenov, the Foreign Minister who emulated Hans-Dietrich Genscher by holding office for eighteen years. His own preference would have been dynastic, in favour of his daughter Liudmilla whom he appointed to the Politburo, giving her responsibility for culture and the arts. According to rumour, she ensured the promotion of Aleksander Lilov. She died unexpectedly in 1981. Reputed to be the family's funnel for ill-gotten gains, his son Vladimir was a member of the Central Committee, and so was his wife's nephew Hristo Maleev. Among other stalwarts promoted from Pravets was Milko Balev, a member of the Politburo. Zhivkov's brother-in-law Atanas Maleev was Deputy Minister of Public Health, a post with the most lucrative prospects, diverting on to the black market otherwise unobtainable Western drugs and medicine.

Unable either to accept or to denounce perestroika, Zhivkov was in a quandary. The party was not ready to rewrite history or to adopt a new programme, he declared in 1987, but instead there would be 'a new cultural revolution'. Insignificant verbiage of this sort only encouraged those who stood to gain from moving into the space opened for them by Gorbachev. The few dissidents who declared themselves could be treated with the customary police methods; the poet Petar Manolev, for instance, went on a month's hunger strike when his papers were seized in February 1989. That same month, Konstantin Trenchev, a party loyalist turning maverick, started

Podkrepa, a free trade union and evidently a tribute to Solidarity in Poland. Originally a forum for debate, the Club for the Support of Perestroika and Glasnost had picked a name which enabled it to hide underneath Gorbachev's skirts. Its leaders, Zhelyu Zhelev and Petko Simeonov, introduced branches of the club throughout the country. It was characteristically rich of Zhivkov to blacken democratic leaders and their groups as 'the defeated classes, that had not forgotten their privileges'. Ecological protests built up. Under the auspices of the Conference on Security and Co-operation in Europe, the World Eco-Forum had long arranged to hold its meeting in Sofia from 16 October to 3 November. This legitimized in turn the local Eco-Glasnost group, and 4,000 people demonstrated on its behalf on the 26th in central Sofia, in what is called the Crystal Garden. In the presence of foreign journalists and diplomats, this demonstration was broken up violently on the orders of the Minister of the Interior, Dimitar Stroyanov. Over twenty activists were arrested.

One of the small number of Western authorities on Bulgaria, R. J. Crampton, concluded in the final sentence of *A Short History of Modern Bulgaria*, a definitive work specially brought up to date for republication in 1989, that although the Zhivkov era might have almost run its course, the present power of the party 'is hardly likely to be challenged or to diminish'. This judgement was almost immediately proved to be horribly wrong, in another example of mistaking the appearance of communist politics for the reality. For months, ambitious perestroikists had in fact been planning the ousting of Zhivkov and the restructuring of the party under their control in accordance with Gorbachev's intentions. They represented far more of a danger to the future of both Zhivkov and the party than any ecological demonstrators.

Mladenov made the brute overt move on 24 October, when he wrote a letter of resignation to Zhivkov. This had been coordinated with Lukanov and the 74-year-old General Dobri Dzhurov who as Minister of Defence could bring in the armed forces. Ministry of the Interior troops had been merged with the border guards. The special forces which had terrorized the Turkish minority were said to number only 160.

On 9 November, in the Politburo, Mladenov confronted Zhivkov, pressing for his resignation. Evidently Zhivkov believed that he could prevaricate. Next day at the Central Committee meeting, Prime Minister Atanasev repeated the call to resign and the Central Committee voted to accept it. The scene was filmed, and Zhivkov was shown on the news that day looking shocked to the core at the outcome. As a face-saver, he was thanked for his services and allowed to continue as state President. The inevitable purges then started in the party. He and his family and cronies were dismissed from all their sinecures and legal proceedings were eventually instituted against them.

Experienced in political wiles, Mladenov and Lukanov fought a sustained rearguard action for almost a year in order to maintain the party in power, and they may be considered to have been more successful in this respect than perestroikists in other satellites. As new First Secretary until he promoted himself President, Mladenov displayed the same sort of unswerving obedience to Gorbachev that Chervenko and Zhivkov had shown to previous general secretaries. Reform, he declared, would remain within the framework of socialism. Introducing glasnost and abolishing Nomenklatura shops, as well as Article 273 of the Penal Code used to punish dissidents, he then deconstructed that framework, exactly as Gorbachev had done in the Soviet Union. In a snowball effect, reform rolled on a self-enlarging course.

Zhivkov had fallen on exactly the same day as the Berlin Wall. Throughout Europe the atmosphere of excitement and expectation heightened. In daily news reports on radio and television, the opposition appeared in one Soviet satellite after another to be pushing the party into a corner. Demonstrations became a daily feature in the centre of Sofia, sometimes involving crowds of up to a million. Naturally wishing to be on what appeared increasingly the winning side, people joined Podkrepa and the Clubs for the Support of Perestroika and Glasnost. Incipient democratic groups rallied around someone with charisma. On 7 December, sixteen such groups or organizations merged into the Union of Democratic Forces. Zhelyu Zhelev headed its council.

For Mladenov and the party, the issue then crystallized: the Union of Democratic Forces had to be either broken or co-opted. The largest demonstration to date occurred around the National Assembly on 14 December. The demonstrators were demanding the annulment of Article One of the Constitution, guaranteeing the party's 'leading role'. The party spokesman Emil Christov was booed. Wishing to speak, Mladenov appeared on the steps of the National Assembly and advanced towards a parked car with a loudspeaker. He began, 'Dear Bulgarians, brothers and sisters,' but he went on, 'You are patriots and citizens, you must realize your responsibilities. This extremism will destroy Bulgaria.'

Unfortunately for him a cameraman, Evgeni Mihailov, had been at his side, recording the event on film and soundtrack. Although the film was evidently shot under difficult conditions, in somewhat of a jostle and hubbub, it tells a clear story. Prolonged angry jeering greeted Mladenov after his speech, with roars of 'Resign!' Looking very shaken and frightened, he turned back towards the Assembly entrance, momentarily standing there, sideways on to General Dzhurov and two other party notables. On the film he can be heard saying, 'Let's call in the tanks.' An unidentified voice replies, 'It's a good idea.' Mladenov and others in the party leadership have tried to explain away this sequence, claiming that it was doctored, and anyhow irrelevant because no tanks arrived. The film is genuine, as Mihailov methodically showed me, detailing the precautions he had taken to keep safe his scoop. Arresting and detaining him for twenty hours, the police wanted him to sign false statements. A rumour was spread by the party that the film had been concocted in America. Only one odd element arises: this clip was not released for six months. On 14 June it burst like a bombshell between the two rounds of the general elections then taking place. Unable to brazen it out, Mladenov resigned. Whether out of demoralization or miscalculation, the party then offered no candidate to succeed him, with the result that Zhelev was elected President unopposed.

Whether 14 December really was a crucial moment when the party hesitated over the use of force may never be clarified. If there was to be no repression, the option of bringing the opposition into the political process alone remained. To make the point, Podkrepa was calling for a general strike. The party gave ground. The Round Table began in the National Palace of Culture in Sofia on 27 December, with Lukanov leading the party, and Zhelev and Simeonov representing the Union of Democratic Forces. The party's good faith was called into question by its flat refusal to remove its cells from factories or other workplaces, and the army. But an agreement signed by both sides on 12 March 1990 stated that there would be a peaceful transition to democracy. Elections were to be held in June.

Against all expectations, the party won those elections, which may go to show force of habit or quite the contrary, electoral volatility, or perhaps ballot-stuffing and other trickery. Lukanov had become Prime Minister in February and now he was to spend several arduous weeks trying to form his second administration that year. Between a communist government and a democratic President, the country was caught in dangerous contradictions. In this peculiar interim, there occurred one of those incidents characteristic of conspiratorial politics, in which elements of civil war jostle with farce. Party headquarters in Sofia was in a solid building a few hundred yards from the Royal Palace, and more or less opposite the President's office. As a matter of course, demonstrations passed this building on the way to or from the National Assembly. On 26 August arson destroyed much of the interior and contents of the party headquarters. Here was an echo of the attack on the Stasi building in East Berlin. Television film shows that spectators did nothing but gape at the blaze and cheer. Large numbers of police can be observed on this film loitering, as though instructed to do nothing. It seems certain that this was a provocation. Torching its own headquarters, the party was either instigating conditions for a crackdown or hoping for a violent reaction from the opposition which would permit the resort to superior force in the name of law and order. Party documents and archives could not have been removed without arousing suspicion and the fire may also have been a planned destruction of incriminating evidence.

A floundering Lukanov formed his government only on 21 September. His difficulties were compounded by the Thirty-ninth Congress of the party which started on his first full day as Prime Minister. Delegates decided to dispense with the old Politburo and Central Committee in favour of a new Supreme Council, and they constituted themselves as a new Bulgarian Socialist Party. Aleksander Lilov, once heir presumptive to Zhivkov, was chosen as its leader. Mladenov and Dzhurov failed to be elected to this Supreme Council. As the dust shook down, it was evident that these changes were cosmetic and that the hardliners were hoping to save themselves by blaming and ditching the perestroikists. Losing what little power base he had, Lukanov was unable to show that the party intended to respect the promises signed at the Round Table. At the end of November, politically paralysed, he resigned. President Zhelev then called on Dimitar Popov, a jurist and not a party member, to form a coalition government. Power-sharing was finally institutionalized.

Elegant in a tailored charcoal-grey suit, Petko Simeonov looked more like a successful young executive than a communist turned dissident. A philosopher by training, he is an academic at Sofia University. His father had been a cobbler, his mother a cook in a workers' canteen. An uncle and two other relations paid with their lives for being communist activists between the wars. His own communism was shaken by the Soviet invasion of Prague and then by reading in Russian a smuggled copy of Solzhenitsyn's *Gulag Archipelago*: 'I went into a deep depression. I needed a year or two before I could function again. I understand how millions now are experiencing a similar disillusion. I meet them, for instance university colleagues who once were in the party apparat, and I notice how they are trying to rewrite their entire biography in order not to be blamed for anything.' He quit the party only in 1990.

At the end of the 1960s, Simeonov says, there was a formula: Join the party in order to destroy it, and many in his age-group made careers in the party on that basis. It is one reason why there were so few dissidents. Glasnost and perestroika were propagated by Soviet radio and television broadcasting from the Moscow station of Ostankino, and by Soviet newspapers which were widely available and cheaper than Bulgarian. In about 1987 he and like-minded friends first held private discussions about organizing reform. One such friend was Zhelyu Zhelev, who told him that he too was taking initiatives of the kind involving a dozen other people. Informal groups appeared in the spring of 1988 in Sofia and other cities, to defend human rights or to protect the environment. Pollution from Giergovo on the Romanian shore of the Danube made life intolerable across the river at Ruse.

A National Environmental Committee for the Defence of Ruse had made a film with the title *Breath*. Most of the members of this committee were still in the party. 'I was the scientific secretary of the Institute of Sociology and we met in my office. We decided to show *Breath* in the film union and to publicize the establishment of this committee. This took place on 8 March 1988.' Among the group were Zhelev, Ivaylo Trifonov, Stefan Geitandjiev and others about to become democratic leaders. 'Pressure was exerted on all participants, some were expelled from the party. The Institute of Philosophy was closed down and so was the department headed by Zhelev within the Institute of Culture. There were between fifty and sixty people at the Institute of Sociology but I advised them not to sign on as members of the committee, I would be the only one to do that. When I was questioned, my response was, You are not against people breathing clean air, are you? Afterwards we discovered that the Politburo had made it a priority to dissolve the Institute but could hardly do so on the basis of my single signature. People on the Central Committee who had inner democratic convictions prevented extreme repressive measures against us, as had happened to the Institute of Philosophy.'

At a university party conference early in 1988, four professors severely criticized Zhivkov from an idealist standpoint. The next step was the formation of the Club for the Support of Perestroika and Glasnost in the summer and autumn of 1988. The Department for the Scientific Study of Communism was due to hold a discussion on some topic of its own. Eighty people were enrolled to pack out this occasion: 'The tactic was for everyone to attend and keep silent until it was over, when one of us would take the floor and say, Let's now continue with our proper work. The organizer of this was Goran Guranov, who was nothing less than Zhivkov's adviser. The secret service knew nothing about it. You would have to have lived in this society to appreciate what a feat this was. After a brief discussion of the rules and regulations, the club became an established fact.' The four chairmen were Zhelev, Nikola Vassiliev, Ivan Djadjev and Simeonov himself, in rotation, each a month at a time. 'The declaration which we put out had been carefully phrased to be immune from political attack. By supporting perestroika and glasnost we were turning Gorbachev's slogans back on him. One idea was actually to call it Gorbachev's Club.'

Why didn't the authorities arrest you all?

'On 19 January 1989 President Mitterrand was on a visit and he gave a breakfast for twelve intellectuals. The French Embassy contacted Zhelev for a guest list. So members of our club were among those invited. This breakfast was a recognition that we were a serious opposition group. But our club and its activities were now openly monitored by the secret police. The leadership met secretly in private homes. That April and May several of us were arrested and a number of houses were searched. But it was not as easy for them as it had been. One club member was the elderly Hristo Radevski, perhaps the most famous of Bulgarian communist poets. Another was Academician Alexei Sheludko, who during the Second World War had been one of the local KGB residents. There was no way that they could arrest men like these.'

Simeonov himself was arrested on 5 May 1989 and taken into custody from Zhelev's house, to make an example of him in order to frighten others. 'We had just sat down when they stormed the place. They took us to Razvigor, the main office for their investigations. Seven or eight other people had been rounded up from other houses besides Zhelev's. They held us from midday until half past ten at night. We had been preparing a declaration to the National Assembly in support of the Turks, and against the forcible changing of their names into Bulgarian. This was a major issue for the informal groups. The enforced changing of names was some kind of desperate step taken by a Head of State afraid of the future.'

He was in the Crystal Garden on 26 October. 'People from Eco-Glasnost had a petition against the diversion of two rivers for hydroelectric purposes but that was a pretext for protesting against the regime. A little table had been set up in the middle of the garden. Officials tried to block the garden off and stop the partition. Aleksander Karakachanov and others were detained. They were hit a couple of times, and then driven out into the countryside and dumped there, obliged to walk back to Sofia. One girl was punched in the stomach. Even this level of violence stirred everyone up. The Bulgarian pendulum can swing only very little. Western demonstrations, with stone-throwing and attacks on the police, would mean outright revolution here.'

The very next day, at an open party meeting in the Institute of Sociology, Svetlana Sharenkova introduced a resolution that Zhivkov and the Politburo should resign. A major row erupted. The downfall of Zhivkov and the system, as Simeonov put it, seemed to be materializing out of thin air. By 10 November it was as though things had reached a logical end. It is his belief that Zhivkov had long realized that communism was in terminal decline. 'In spite of the horrible things he did and the system he supported, Zhivkov was a subtle and consummate politician. I used to be disgusted by his stupid speeches – but I can now see that he was playing a political game rather than exposing his lack of education. Lukanov once said to me about him, He has the instinct for danger of a wild boar.'

From the fall of Zhivkov, and then all through the weeks of the Round Table over which he presided for the opposition, Simeonov was in close touch with the party leadership. For the June elections, he was campaign manager of the Union of Democratic Forces. The party still had in its hand the entire repressive mechanism. 'Had it wanted to keep power, it could have done so even if that meant a future of international isolation and industrial back-wardness. Someone at the top had only to give orders. The use of force against us remained a practical possibility right up to the end of May. We would have been unable to forestall it. The party could not have been replaced without goodwill on their part.'

The coup of 10 November was the first in the series of steps leading to the surrender of power. 'Mladenov was not a double-faced man. Talking about bringing in tanks, he had probably had a few drinks to calm his nerves. That day I had gone into the National Assembly in search of a megaphone. Then I was on the roof of the building opposite, with Zhelev and Trifonov, appealing to people to go home and promising that Article One would be struck out of the Constitution. Mladenov said that sentence, just like that, and no doubt he could have brought in the tanks. By the following April, I was speaking to him about the elections, and regularizing them, and so forth. You will have your elections, he assured me, and a new constitution, the President will be duly elected and one of you will be sitting here in this office.'

How did the Round Table get under way?

'After the establishment of the Union of Democratic Forces on 7 December, at a meeting once again in the Institute of Sociology, we suggested it to the party. Right after Christmas, Podkrepa declared a nationwide strike. That was crazy. They had no structure, they merely estimated that 30,000 people would respond. The communists answered that every day due to drunkenness more than that number failed to turn up for work. Such a strike would pass unnoticed. The communists then added that here was a good opportunity for everyone to get together and talk things out. Drawing on the Polish experi-ence, we felt that only a Round Table could break the deadlock.'

What was the atmosphere at the Round Table talks?

'To enter discussion meant that they were preparing to give up power. The sole genuine preoccupation concerned physical threats to them. They were afraid for themselves. There had to be no reprisals. Until the end of February we would call each other Comrade. Afterwards it became Mr and Mrs. I would not say that they were condescending although they were more pro-fessional and better informed about society than we were. Our invariable position was that we wanted democracy, not power. Never again should a single party take over and stay put. We presented ourselves as a political opposition, the beginning of a two-party model of politics. Decision had to be by consensus, meaning that the chairmen of the party and of the Union of Democratic Forces had to agree, which did not happen so very often.

'We advocated free and fair elections. Well aware that they had a political organization, the communists wanted these elections as soon as possible. James Baker came to Bulgaria on 12 and 13 February and we told him that we were not ready for elections but he replied, Why postpone? It was an illusion that elections would be the complete answer to everything. The communists then won. I am convinced that the American Embassy had been optimistic about the outcome. Even before winning the elections, Lukanov had come to ask us to join a coalition. We refused. We were at the start of a process of lengthy but real change. Once back in power, the communists had no idea what to do. They clung to their one fixed idea, that there had to be no physical reprisals. All of us had participated in that life, all of us are a little to blame for it. That is the mind-set in which the communists finally trapped themselves. Fear of retribution finally overruled their will to power.'

Zhelyu Zhelev is in the mould of Adam Michnik or Václav Havel, an intellectual sucked, as it were, from relative obscurity into prominence and power to fill the vacuum of retreating communism. Born in 1935, in a small country town, he had a career as an academic, with more downs than ups. Expelled from the party, he was unemployable for a long period. Written in 1967, his book *Fascism* was published only in 1982 and then withdrawn almost at once for the insights it provided into communism. Unassuming, slight in build, he has found himself carrying the responsibility for introducing democracy into a country which has known only despotism.

Under the influence of perestroika, Zhelev says, informal organizations were harbingers of democracy. A specific Bulgarian factor was the persecution of the Turks which might have resulted in violence against the regime. Events in the other satellites encouraged the opposition. The moment arrived when the Politburo decided to take the initiative in getting rid of Zhivkov, rather than wait until violence or strikes overwhelmed them. Even so, what he calls the inner party coup of 10 November came by surprise. 'As we later realized, it was a very well-kept secret. A ruler in the Soviet bloc had an unrivalled military and police apparatus but General Dzhurov settled the issue by siding with the plotters.'

Did you perceive 10 November as the beginning of the end of communism?

'In retrospect I can say that I had no expectations of overnight changes. It was a far more complicated question than the mere replacement of one dictator by another. But it was a signal for the opposition to rally and to act, as the way ahead was now open. We could set ourselves political goals. It was vital to organize, to acquire premises and cars and technical facilities. But we shared a common fear that there might be a restoration of the previous regime, to persecute those who had dared to raise their heads.' This fear persisted right through until August 1991, when Zhelev telephoned Yeltsin in the White House to express solidarity.

Proof of organizational capacity lay in the formation of the Union of Democratic Forces. But the party retained the presidency and the parliament, indeed total institutional powers. 'The only instrument in our hands was extra-parliamentary pressure, with demonstrations and rallies. Whenever there was a hitch in the Round Table discussions, we would call the nation out.' The period from 8 December until the run-up to the elections was one of mass protests on behalf of the opposition. Rallies which started in Sofia spread throughout the country and blended into the electoral campaign.

A long Euclidean debate, as Zhelev puts it, took place on the shape of the Round Table. The communists insisted that the table really be round, to accommodate representatives of state-sponsored organizations like the Konsomol. They envisaged a leisurely encounter, while the opposition's pressure for new legislation acquired the character of an ultimatum. 'The parliament rubber-stamped decisions taken at the Round Table. We decided on the amendments to the Constitution, on holding elections to the Grand National Assembly, and the electoral law with its mixed system of proportional representation and majority voting. It was a funny way of running the country. Whenever there was a hitch in our work, the crowds would gather and make a noise. Day and night there was an enthusiastic crowd around the National Place of Culture to boo the communists and acclaim us.'

The opposition made it a precondition that the Round Table proceedings were to be broadcast live on television and radio. This caused stoppages which interfered with the working day. It was a school for democracy. For the first time the party was publicly called to account for its crimes and this had the result of breaking all manner of taboos and stereotypes. It also legitimized the opposition.

'Then came the anticlimax. Despite our expectations, the communists won the election which showed that we were politically naïve. We had thought that the numbers of people going out on the streets was indicative of our strength. We underestimated the fact that the party structure was still intact, especially in rural areas, and that it had economic levers with which to pressure people into voting communist. But after those elections, the communists no longer had the will or stamina to rule. Two cabinets in succession collapsed. Lukanov did not introduce even the slightest reform during his months in office. They had no moral support from the active part of the population.

The burden of their political guilt also weighed on their conscience. Hence the incapacity to rule.'

At the time when I met Andrey Lukanov, he was about to face charges of diverting $60 million of state funds in donations or arms to Yemen, the PLO, Nicaragua, Chile and other Soviet-backed causes. With his connections to the Ministry of Foreign Trade, he is rumoured to have had a main share of responsibility for Bulgaria's external debt of $10 billion. In his early fifties, clean-cut, he shrugged off all such accusations as politicking. For much of the morning I spent with him, he insisted on detailing for me the eminent communist careers of his parents and grandparents. Between them, they had participated in the 1923 uprising, clandestine plots, the Comintern, the Spanish Civil War and Stalinism. Lily, his wife, was the daughter of Traicho Kostov. He sounded much like an Austro-Hungarian grandee of the old school instructing the uninitiated plebs in the quarterings of his coat of arms.

Born in Moscow, Lukanov speaks Russian like a native, and several other languages fluently. A visit which he made to the United States in 1973 opened up his career prospects. Although Zhivkov was then wooing Brezhnev, he was sceptical about Soviet conservatism and wanted to hear Lukanov's positive views about America. If Zhivkov was a Satan at least he was an interesting Satan, in Lukanov's eyes, and 'the last and best politician of the Byzantine type in Europe'. By way of an illustration, he recounts how in 1988 Zhivkov deflected pressure to resign. The full Politburo consisted of members, candidate members and secretaries, but for special policy decision Zhivkov called a smaller circle consisting of full members only, as he had the right to do. At a full Politburo meeting, he declared that he wanted to retire. Then he held confidential conversations with individual Politburo members, who naturally could only assure him that he was invaluable. 'Everybody knew that this was a provocation. If you had answered, Why not resign? you were finished. So having interviewed everyone, he convened the smaller Politburo to inform them that since everyone was in favour of his staying in office, he would defer to their wishes. This kind of theatre was then represented by him as a serious attempt to resign.'

Four men, in this version, played a decisive role in the palace revolution of 10 November: Mladenov, the Prime Minister, Georgi Atanasev, General Dzhurov and Lukanov himself. 'It was impossible for us to meet. We were living in a glasshouse, closely observed. I was actually the one to arrange meetings. Everyone knew that I was an old friend of Mladenov's. Then I was working with Atanasev, so that needed no explanation. Even so, we used to write notes and slip them across the desk. To meet Dzhurov was very dangerous but I knew his daughter and arranged a single casual visit to her at a time when Dzhurov was also there, ostensibly just as her father. It went unnoticed, I think. We could make no telephone calls.'

Mladenov's blunt letter of 24 October sparked in Zhivkov a sense of losing control. Alarmed, Zhivkov tried to persuade Mladenov to withdraw his resignation, inviting him for a drink and sending emissaries. Reconciliation was out of the question. When Mladenov addressed the same letter to the Politburo and the Central Committee, the coming clash could no longer be concealed. 'On top of that, I had a trip to Moscow and I took a copy of the letter out with me. I did not see Gorbachev but I found a way to pass it to him, by way of information. It was clear that nothing could be done before the Soviet position was neutralized. I also wanted to leave a record for history if something were to happen to us physically. People may laugh now when I say it was a risky thing to do, but it was.'

At the end of the month, Lukanov continued, Zhivkov was proposing a U-turn over his anti-Turkish policy, and he was also asking Gorbachev to receive him in Moscow, claiming an emergency. His hope was to gain support abroad. 'But Gorbachev refused on the grounds that he was too busy. Bulgarians had to sort themselves out, he said, if anything taking a neutral stand. Afterwards he congratulated us, saying, I am happy you have succeeded, I was just an onlooker and the risk was yours, and if you had failed I could have done nothing for you. It is not true that the Soviet Union pressured Zhivkov to step down.'

The refusal to meet Zhivkov indicated support for you and Mladenov?

'It was support for change. The refusal to intervene was certainly crucial. But Gorbachev did not directly use his or his ambassador's influence. He could not be sure of the outcome. Of course Zhivkov then became not just nervous but hysterical. A crisis was approaching with which he could not cope.'

A reception was held at the Soviet Embassy on 7 November, and General Dzhurov then asked Zhivkov for an appointment. Dzhurov went the next morning, accompanied by Mincho Yovchev of the Politburo and Dimitar Stanischev who had been the long-standing secretary of the International Department of the Central Committee. All three had been members of a wartime partisan brigade with which Zhivkov claimed to have been linked, although this 'is far from proven', in Lukanov's view. On the morning of the 8th, these three told Zhivkov that the time had come for him to resign. 'At which he replied, Well, I asked the Politburo a year ago and you all said no, but now you say yes. I will, but not yet. The point was that he needed time to prepare his counterattack.'

Mladenov happened to be away in China. Lukanov claims that the moment he heard how this confrontation had gone, he went to Atanasev and then to

Dzhurov, to say that postponement of the showdown would be suicidal. 'To mention resignation meant that it had to be now or never. If you gave him a week then everything would be finished, and we would be finished too.

'So Atanasev went back to Zhivkov on the 9th, at midday, to say that, for three years now Comrade Zhivkov had been working against Comrade Zhivkov: that was his phrase. At four o'clock, Dzhurov and Yovchev and Stanischev returned to the charge, to propose that the resignation come into effect immediately and it should be announced at the Politburo session due to start at five o'clock.

'When this session started, Zhivkov said that he was old and unwell and someone younger should replace him. He expressly stated that he wanted to resign as First Secretary but not as President of the State Council. As First Secretary to succeed him, he proposed Atanasev, in the hope of playing him off against Mladenov. Rising immediately, Atanasev declined, proposing Mladenov instead. I took the floor and said that we agreed to this resignation in the interests of the party and the country. A meeting of the Central Committee had been scheduled a month previously, and the decision was taken that there would be "an organizational idea" as one of the items on its agenda – this was a Bolshevik phrase which meant that someone might well be shot. It was thus decided to recommend to the Central Committee that Zhivkov should be thanked for his contribution and his resignation accepted. Reading out this proposal, Atanasev said that Zhivkov had resigned as First Secretary and as President of the State Council. To which Zhivkov reacted at once, saying, But we did not agree on that. The Central Committee plenary voted unanimously in support of Mladenov, with the exception of one vote for Lilov. So Zhivkov was ousted. Mladenov, Dzhurov and myself were the heroes of the nation at that moment.'

Why didn't Zhivkov resort to force?

'He couldn't. Actually he had at his disposal the special unit stationed at Vranya, where the King's summer palace was, trained as OMON forces with over sixty armoured vehicles including T-72 tanks and personnel carriers. The unit could have smashed Sofia, not to speak of the Central Committee, to pieces. The fact that Dzhurov stood firmly for a constitutional solution prevented Zhivkov as President of the State Council from abusing his powers. That was Dzhurov's great contribution.'

Why did Gorbachev take the neutral position you have described?

'He did not expect things to crumble. He thought reform communists could manage the situation and that changes in Eastern Europe would help the Soviet Union to reform in the way he envisaged. I saw him twice in 1990, for an hour on each occasion. He told me, I'm being pressured to act the strong man but I don't want to, I am not the person for that. Against me, there are 15 million party hardliners. Please tell me how I am to cope with that? By that time, he was as courageous as ever but his morale was ebbing.'

Was it your intention prior to the Round Table to come to an agreement?

In reply, Lukanov pours out stories of his approaches to the opposition as early as 13 November. By his own account, he seems to have sought out every dissident in the hope of enlisting allies. From his praise of democracy and the market economy, he appears now to have no conceivable linkage to the forebears whose Stalinist blood-shedding makes him so proud, and whose hideous privileges once served him so well.

Petar Mladenov lives in a Nomenklatura district within walking distance of the National Assembly. The drawing room in which we sat is spacious. Not in good health, he has now retired. He seemed to bulk large in his armchair. The heavy frames of his spectacles gave a benevolently owlish expression to his broad face. He had studied at the prestigious Moscow State Institute for International Relations. With his experience, status and outlook, he was the obvious choice to introduce perestroika faithfully. In his words, 'There was no practical difference between what we thought we should do in this country and what Gorbachev had in mind.'

The move to be rid of Zhivkov started in July 1989, he explains, at the Political Consultative Committee of the Warsaw Pact, which was holding a meeting in Bucharest. 'Ceauşescu, Honecker, Zhivkov, everybody was there. We were each sitting in our delegations. Gorbachev was at one end of the hall, and he crossed its whole length to come over to me. He said, I want to talk to you. So we went, the two of us, into a corner where there was nobody. In a totalitarian system it was inconceivable to have the Foreign Minister rather than the First Secretary talking to Gorbachev. I was not authorized to have private discussions with him. Of course we knew what Zhivkov was like and we had to hope that nobody was eavesdropping. If he had known what was going on between Gorbachev and myself, he would have acted pre-emptively. It was then that I told Gorbachev that we intended to carry out our change in early November. He did not advise me, he made no comment on the time-span, he did not say whether we were being too hasty or should move more slowly. This is entirely your business, he said, you have to sort it out by yourselves. Whether you sort it out now or later is for you alone to decide. Probably Zhivkov suspected what we might have been saying in that corner, he had very strong intuitions. But it is one thing to suspect, quite another to have proof.'

All Zhivkov had to do after that was utilize available intelligence; to note who entered Mladenov's office, how long he stayed there, whom Mladenov met, whether he had one or more companions. 'These were the signs to be read by anyone who cared.' The course of events only confirmed Mladenov to proceed with his palace coup. He emphasizes that he acted legally, meaning in accordance with the statutes of the party.

If Zhivkov had been able to rely on General Dzhurov, things would have been very different.

'Quite another scenario! But we had been working together for many years as two of the longest-serving members of the Central Committee and the Politburo. We had very clear ideas of what everyone was thinking, and we had complete confidence in one another. Dzhurov and I had a final talk in unusual circumstances. During that same visit in Bucharest, the two of us went out into the street where there was no fear of eavesdropping. It was not an easy discussion as General Dzhurov had to give his final consent. I realized that the outcome could have been very different.'

You obtained Zhivkov's resignation at the Politburo meeting at five o'clock on the 9th. What did he do between then and the Central Committee meeting next morning which confirmed the resignation?

'At the Politburo meeting he argued that his resignation should be deferred to another plenum. But we wanted the decision voted through without delay. Afterwards he went to his office and asked several of us to come there. We had a brief discussion, he was concerned about how he was going to live. We didn't discuss politics at all.'

Why didn't he take measures to defend himself?

'He did, until the very last moment, right up to the session of the Central Committee on 10 November. In the middle of that plenum, he asked for an interval, and sent some of those closest to him to lobby on his behalf among members of the Central Committee. After so many years in power, he had proposed and promoted all of them. He counted on that plenum to postpone voting on his removal and he expected that another plenum would be convened some time in the future. After he had been voted out and I had been elected in his place, he left the hall by himself. On television he was shown leaving, it was a lonely picture. I walked up to him at the elevator. Nobody else did. He then asked me for another meeting and there he raised several demands. One was to be allowed to continue to live in the official residence in Bankya, near Sofia. Since it was not cosy at Bankya, he next asked if he could move to a smaller state residence and I told him that he could do as he pleased. I wasn't interested in living in any of these places, but in my own home. Then his pension, which was 2600 leva a month if I remember correctly. I suggested that a decision be taken by the State Council to grant him this pension. One last request was to be allowed to work two or three days in his office with his aides and secretaries. Of course he had safes and documents to sift through on his own.'

At the plenum, you thanked Zhivkov for the work he had done, but at the next plenum on the 17th, these thanks were withdrawn.

That is absolutely right, Mladenov agrees, and it is to be explained away as one of the conventional lies arising from circumstances like these. 'On 10 November we proclaimed that we were starting perestroika. A day or two later we were obliged to reveal the true plight of the country. There had been persecution, violation of human rights, as everyone knew full well. Now it was for us, the new leadership, to explain how this had happened and try to find a way out. We had to tell the truth. We set up a group to prepare for a new plenum. We held Politburo sessions of twelve and even fifteen hours, and wrote policy documents so that in two or three weeks we could rectify the omissions of years. The question arose: ten days ago we extended gratitude to the ex-leader, and should it be left at that? It could not be. Against the background of this analysis, it was ridiculous, we would have been exposed as people without principles.'

But surely the ugly truth could only explode perestroika?

'At the time we did not believe so. We thought that was the right way to proceed. Nobody spoke of changing the system. Ours was simply the new generation, with others like Yakovlev and Shevardnadze speaking about their belief in improving socialism through perestroika. Of course the results came out quite differently, and the entire system had to be changed.

'I saw my role as bound up with the moment of change. I had to participate in the events of 10 November and assume state responsibility for a certain period,' Mladenov says, 'but I warned my colleagues that this period would be limited.' The situation evolved far too rapidly into a power struggle, and that explains the events of 14 December and his disastrous aside about the tanks. 'Of course I could have called out the tanks. I was the army commander-in-chief. They would have cleared the square in ten minutes. But I did not even issue the order to arm the police. When I had finished my speech, I started for the entrance to the National Assembly and someone standing on my left said that sentence. I just turned towards the group and repeated it. It's all recorded on the film. People take it out of context. The important thing is that I did not call for the tanks and never would have done. Nobody was hurt, nobody was coerced.'

To what extent did you anticipate violence?

'The question was constantly on my mind. I realized that reconciliation was almost impossible in a country which had been in a state of silent civil war for decades. One of my first addresses to the nation was aimed at reconciliation. We had no other way out. I suggested the Spanish or Greek model for transition to democracy. The totalitarian state is a monster. I proposed to establish a commission whose members would go together to the furnaces to burn the personal files of the KGB and all collaborators, informers and denouncers.'

A Round Table in itself implies annulling the party's 'leading role'?

'Yes. The decision was taken in the Politburo very soon after 10 November. We had no doubt whatsoever that there had to be pluralistic politics. We might have spoken about improving socialism but we believed that this would go hand-in-hand with a multi-party system. I do not want to underestimate the struggle of individuals from the opposition, but they were disorganized protesters.' The decision to allow live broadcasting of the talks, he says, was taken collectively, even though it was bound to enhance the opposition.

But the party obtained nothing from the Round Table?

'When I go nowadays to meetings with hardliners, they say, You are to blame, you surrendered power just like that. I can't think there were any specific advantages which the party could have obtained in its own interests. With this exception: it was laying the foundation for a new democratic society.'

It is hard to believe that the party packed up and went home like good little boys.

'Resistance was put up, for instance some people hoped to keep party organizations in workplaces. One plenum discussed "deformations" in the past. I can't recall a more difficult period in my entire life. Literally thousands of people came to lobby me. There was a real internal fight within the party to keep things as they had been.'

In *Anti-Memoirs*, one of his several books, Gorbachev has described a meeting on 5 December 1989 at which Mladenov reported that he had the situation in Bulgaria under control, the population welcomed perestroika, and Gorbachev's prestige was rising. In an exchange of compliments, Gorbachev appreciated the courage shown by Mladenov, and added in typical communist parlance, 'There exist in the party and in society forces which are ready to harness themselves to the task in hand.' Illusions so profound have a midnight, ghostly quality. The conversation took place exactly as recorded, Mladenov confirms. 'As far as Gorbachev's personal attitude towards me was concerned, I could not have wished for better. He told me everything that was in his mind. I was in close and regular contact with him, in Moscow and elsewhere.'

It is mysterious that Gorbachev allowed the whole Soviet bloc to evaporate without making any serious attempt to hold it together.

'A fundamental question indeed. I have my views but not *the* answer. When Gorbachev came here in 1985 he did not have a prepared plan. Glasnost, democracy, perestroika, a return to authentic Leninist themes – that was all a process as well as a way for him to accumulate experience. But which Head of State can tell how things will work out? I can guarantee that Gorbachev was not stupid, but an erudite man, and no traitor. It may have been an historic turning point. The world could not remain as it was. Secondly, the experiment of 1917 simply had not worked. Lenin says that the system which guaranteed higher productivity would prevail, and this proved to be capitalism.'

30

CIVIC FORUM

As an independent republic between the wars, Czechoslovakia was a centre of heavy industry equal to any in the world. Imposed in a police coup in 1948, communism systematically destroyed resources and prosperity. Created out of former Habsburg lands, its standard of living in 1938 had been higher than Austria's. Forty years later, Czechoslavak living standards were lower than Austria's by a third. The average unit price of its engineering goods had been the equal of the German price in 1948 but by the 1980s this had sunk to a quarter. Although telephones were manufactured locally, 400,000 Czechoslovaks were on the waiting list to have one installed. Soil erosion affected half the cultivable land of Bohemia and Moravia, and sulphur emission had killed a third of the forests. As in Kazakhstan, genetic deformities have been appearing in people and livestock.

As successive First Secretaries, Klement Gottwald and Antonín Novotný were conspicuously brutal and slavish collaborators of Stalinism. Gottwald's son-in-law and Minister of Defence, Alexey Čepička, left his particular stamp of cruelty and corruption, with a fortune estimated at millions of dollars. In his safe, according to the defector Jan Šejna, were found 'hundreds of letters from the condemned cells, pleading innocence and asking for the death sentence to be commuted. Each one carried the single word "execute", initialled by Čepička.' The chain of repression was dislocated when Alexander Dubček set in motion what the world immortalized as the Prague Spring of 1968.

With soft and melancholy features full of self-deprecation, Dubček was a First Secretary quite out of the common run. His intention was to co-opt rather than coerce the population. What at the time seemed like blind naïvety about the system in retrospect was a portent of the overall crisis which ensued when Gorbachev likewise renounced force.

At an impressionable age, Dubček had been in the Soviet Union, only to draw from his experience there the conclusion that the number and nature of its victims provided no sort of absolute moral judgement. Fault must lie in the self rather than in the party: here was the classic fellow-travelling illusion, working on him as it did upon General Jaruzelski, someone else formed in this particular mould.

A man 'searching for a dream', Dubček's father had been an unsuccessful immigrant to America before setting off with his wife and young family to Pishpek, lost in Central Asia, to be a star-struck volunteer in building communism. 'I remember dreadful scenes at the Frunze railroad station,' Dubček was to write in his memoirs as he recalled peasants deported as a result of collectivization. 'Some died en route, and those who survived, including children, looked like living corpses. They were so hungry that they ate fodder for pigs and poultry that was teaming with maggots. I can never forget the sight of a dead man with his belly blown out. I asked my mother what the man had died from, and she said, "From hunger" ... I don't remember anyone who understood what was causing this misery.' The same incomprehension gripped him at the sight of Kirghyz resistance fighters hanged by Soviet officials.

Once in office, Dubček tried to introduce competition into the Nomen-klatura and a degree of public debate, bravely though clumsily distinguishing the party from the state. Hardliners understood the danger. As early as May 1968 Brezhnev and his obedient cohorts, Ulbricht, Zhivkov, Gomułka and Kádár, were declaring that Czechoslovakia was threatened by counter-revolution. The next three months were to pass in a heightening tension of denunciation and plot. At one of the many hectic secret meetings of the time, General Jaruzelski ironically had 'a sad impression of fragility' as he listened to arguments of Dubček's which years later he was to repeat as his own.

On 29 July at Čierna-nad-Tisou, a Slovak railhead on the Soviet border, and then again on 3 August at Bratislava, Brezhnev and his Politburo sum-moned Dubček and browbeat him. At no point, Dubček was later to admit, did he believe that his country might suffer invasion. In fact, while the angry Brezhnev was hectoring in full spate, local stooges in the persons of Vasil Bilak, Alois Indra, Drahomír Kolder, Oldřich Svestka and Antonín Kapek were already requesting the Soviets 'for active support and help with all the means that you have'. The degree of Soviet collusion in their treason is not yet fully known. On 20 and 21 August 200,000 troops from the Soviet Union, Poland, Hungary, Bulgaria and the DDR crossed into Czechoslovakia and by mid-September the total was half a million. The DDR provided the smallest force, but there may have been some who under the Red Star were repeating their earlier invasion under the swastika. To an American communist Angela Davis, visiting Prague, Dubček and his associates were 'common criminals'.

Hijacked and in manacles, Dubček was flown to Moscow along with his colleagues. One of these was Zdeněk Mlynář, a friend and former roommate of Gorbachev since Moscow University days. Until that moment, like others of his generation, as Mlynář expresses it in his memoirs, he had been taught a black-and-white image of the world, 'the enemy on one side and its antagonist on the other'. Now Mlynář had to listen to Brezhnev, his voice quivering with regret as he reproached Dubček. 'I believed in you, and I stood up for you against the others . . . and you disappointed us all so terribly.' Cast aside, Dubček was to spend the rest of his life as a forester. 'I could not ever be anti-Soviet', he was pathetically lamenting in 1990, 'I feel whole-heartedly for that nation.'

Gustáv Husák, his successor as First Secretary, was every bit as damaged psychologically. Sour and fanatical, he had stalinized his native Slovakia after 1948, only to be imprisoned himself for a number of years in the 1950s. He described in 1968 how officials took it in turns to humiliate and beat him, using artfully designed tortures. 'The party had posted you here, the party had already decided your case. You must confess! Confess! . . . Every nervous system has a definite threshold of resistance to pressures; where this threshold is exceeded, the nervous system gives up.' Far from acquiring insight into the system from this experience, Husák became perversely intent on extending it further. Deputy Prime Minister in 1968, he proclaimed that he would 'stand and fall' with Dubček. In the manner of Kádár a few years earlier in Hungary, he then betrayed his colleagues, allowing himself to be promoted First Secretary to Brezhnev in 1969. Reformers and supports of Dubček's were then purged from the party and the Nomenklatura by Miloš Jakeš, Husák's hatchet man.

At the time of the 1948 takeover, Czech intellectuals by and large had proved party enthusiasts. The writer Pavel Kohout, for instance, could rhapsodize about the People's Militia marching in the coup with their arms linked. Later he was to apologize. 'I was stupid for about four or five years.' What had been a widespread acceptance of communism now drooped into glum apathy. Fatally setting fire to himself in a public square in Prague, the student Jan Palach terrifyingly symbolized the national plight.

Some sense of continuity was provided by individuals with great gifts, like the writer Bohumil Hrabal, and the philosopher Jan Patočka, and the magnificent Cardinal František Tomášek, the Primate, a man born in the last century. Imprisoned in a labour camp after 1948, forbidden to resume his episcopal function, fending off collaborationist bishops and priests appointed by the party, Tomášek represented far more than religious or sectarian values. Though few in number, younger dissidents with the courage to speak out were in the humanist tradition: Ludvík Vaculík, Milan Šimečka, the novelist Josef Škvorecky, Václav Havel, those who inspired and signed Charter 77. In the words of another of them, Vladimír Karbušický, 'A cultural regression is taking place.' The intellectual and moral consequences of communism were leading the human race backwards to a version of prehistory, with 'rituals, magic costumes in the form of uniforms, fetishism, taboo, the influence of medicine men, charms and curses in the form of slogans and petrified clichés, the totemistic worship of symbols'.

In April 1987 Gorbachev visited Prague and Bratislava. In a speech tailored for glasnost, he declared that the party's claim to omniscience was arrogant. But it was his spokesman Gennady Gerasimov who uttered a pronouncement as stupefying as any in the course of the empire's dissolution. Asked by Western journalists to clarify the difference between the Prague Spring and perestroika, Gerasimov replied, 'Nineteen years.' It was the equivalent of a death sentence, not only for Husák but for all satellite parties maintained in power by Soviet force. If Dubček had been justified as a premature perestroikist, then Husák had no legitimacy. That December he duly resigned, though remaining President of the state.

Approved by the party, and smoothly executed, the transition of power to Miloš Jakeš was pointless. Compromised by long association with Husák, his heart was not in perestroika. Those now appointed, for instance, Ladislav Adamec as federal Prime Minister or Rudolf Hegenbart as head of the Central Committee Department for State Administration and therefore the party official responsible for the secret police, shared his belief that changes had to be sufficient to satisfy Gorbachev but not enough to damage party control. Party real-estate and property was valued in 1990 at about $550 million. Large secret funds in hard currency were revealed to have been paid to Moscow to promote communism in democratic countries.

The Soviet garrison in the country consisted of 75,000 troops, providing four frontline divisions with the task of invading Germany in the event of war. The local security forces were in the order of 80,000. The informer network was several thousand strong with a continuous turnover which obliged people to play safe and keep quiet for fear of denunciation. The party had its own armed protection in the People's Militia of about 25,000. Its chief-of-staff, Miroslav Novák, was responsible only to Jakeš.

Anniversaries provided the occasion for demonstrations which raised the political temperature during the course of 1989: on 15 January, in commemoration of Jan Palach; on 20 August, against the invasion of 1968; on 17 November, in honour of another student, Jan Opletal, killed fifty years earlier by the Nazis, a counterpart to Palach. During January 800 people were arrested, among them Havel, who received another prison sentence, this time for nine months. Others, like Ján Čarnogurský, were arrested in August only to find themselves Ministers by the end of the year. Repression was an option available to the party right to the end.

November 17 was a Friday. Mystery still hangs about that day which set in motion the events which brought down the party and communism itself within less than four weeks. At a moment when the opening of the Berlin Wall was virtually bound to have a knock-on effect, the party obliviously organized the demonstration. Anti-Nazism slid straight into anti-communism. In the late afternoon, with darkness coming on, crowds estimated at 50,000 made their way from Vyšehrad to the National Theatre, past Havel's windows, along the river. Národní Třída is a street between the embankment and the bottom of Václavské náměstí, the central square. Agents led the demonstrators into an ambush there; the waiting police beat them up. 'All we have is bare hands!' people shouted. There were scores of injuries, some serious. Rumour spread that a student by the name of Martin Šmíd had been killed. *Agents provocateurs*, an ambulance carrying off the corpse of Šmíd who supposedly jumped up and ran off, KGB involvement, a statement by a well-known dissident Petr Uhl to Radio Free Europe, suddenly materialized into high drama; disinformation, whether deliberate or not, could not be sifted from truth.

On Saturday and Sunday, up to 200,000 demonstrators occupied more or less continuously the centre of the city. On the Sunday the Politburo met and called for the restoration of order 'by all possible means'. At the same time, the Charter 77 dissidents gathered in the Magic Lantern Theatre. Arriving late himself, Havel became ex-officio leader of the impromptu and somewhat amateurish group who then and there banded into the official opposition under the name of Civic Forum. Negotiations with the party were the objective. To emphasize popular support, Civic Forum also began calling for a general strike.

In fact the party on Tuesday 22 November was summoning the People's Militia to intervene. Confrontation with the crowds and Civic Forum could only have been violent. Among those implicated in issuing orders to the People's Militia are Jakeš and the Politburo, Hegenbart and Miroslav Štěpán, the head of the Prague Party Organization. No sooner had Militia units reached the city than they were ordered to return to barracks. Like the meteoric course of Martin Šmíd, this incident has been obscured.

The party leadership immediately plunged into confusion and panic. Having been put up by Moscow in 1968 to call in Soviet troops, Bilak, Indra and Kapek had been members of the Politburo ever since. Out of fear of reprisals, they are said to have advocated a resort to the army. But Jakeš and the entire Politburo resigned on 24 November, and Karel Urbánek became the last First Secretary. A pallid figure, he was once a railway worker and now represents a Czech business venture in Moscow. 'We are aware of the fact that we don't have the trust of the people. We simply lost it,' he was to moan later to Havel.

Ladislav Adamec, the ambitious not to say self-seeking federal Prime Minister, saw his chance to take advantage of the collapse of the Politburo. Contacting Havel and Civic Forum on his own initiative, he was splitting the state away from the party, though perhaps not intentionally. At Havel's invitation, Adamec addressed a meeting on the 25th at Letenska pláň, an open space on a hill overlooking much of the city. There he made the fatal mistake of all perestroikists, by promising to reform within a communist framework. He also condemned all ideas of a general strike. Had he instead announced himself a democrat, he could have been the local Yeltsin. From that moment onwards, nobody could have salvaged the party.

The next day, Adamec, still a one-man band, received a Civic Forum delegation; it marked the beginning of what was in effect a speeded-up Round Table. Havel presented his demands: Husak was to resign, and Adamec was to remain Prime Minister on the condition that he re-formed his government. Evidently Civic Forum did not yet feel capable of assuming power. Interrupting the informal negotiations, Adamec flew to Moscow on 3 December for the famous meeting at which Gorbachev debriefed those present about the recent Malta summit, bringing down the curtain, if only he had known it, on the Soviet bloc. After a private talk with Gorbachev, Adamec flew home and took everyone by surprise by resigning in favour of his deputy Prime Minister, Marián Čalfa. 'I took the job because Gorbachev asked me to do it,' Adamec was to say. 'Not because he is Gorbachev, but because he is carrying out a policy which the world needs. I took the risk.' Even Havel assumed that Gorbachev was backing Adamec, but this cannot have been the case. The changeover now moved as though by clockwork. Čalfa resigned from the party, and although he retained in the government a majority of communist ministers, he included known anti-communists like Čarnogurský and the economist Václav Klaus. In any case, free elections were to be held the following June. Husak resigned as President and, still in the manner of Kádár, he soon died. The old communist parliament also remained true to its rubber-stamp self by voting unanimously that Havel was to replace him as President.

In the second week of November 1989 the Ideological Secretary Jan Fojtík had knocked on doors in the Kremlin to explain to anyone who would listen that, as in 1968, the situation could best be retrieved by Soviet armed intervention. A noted hardliner, Fojtík had been talking in that vein for some time, for instance, to his Hungarian opposite number János Berecz. It so happened that he flew home on the 17th, to spend the rest of the weekend trying to find colleagues whom he could convince to use force. When I went to Fojtík's apartment to meet him as agreed, I found that he had gone to ground. According to the neighbours, Fojtík behaves as though in hiding; he wears hats which he believes disguise him, he has grown a beard. The same evasiveness has gripped others, the hardliner Jozef Lenárt, Vasil Bilak now an old-age pensioner in Bratislava, Adamec licking his wounds, Lubomír Štrougal who allegedly in Gorbachev's view would have been preferable to Jakeš as the First Secretary to introduce perestroika. No doubt they have been alarmed by efforts to bring former party leaders to account for their crimes, and by the so-called lustration laws which forbid public employment to StB or security agents and policemen. Accusations of StB collaboration have already ruined a number of careers.

Zdeněk Urbánek is among the country's best-known literary figures, a translator of James Joyce and Walt Whitman. Born in 1917 as a subject of the Habsburg Emperor, he has spent his whole life in the same city but under seven different regimes. In his apartment is an almost historic object, the typewriter which he used to address the envelopes containing the text of Charter 77, due to be posted to the signatories. Instead, on the morning of 6 January 1977, he and Havel and Vaculík and the actor Landovský and others were detained by the StB.

Another dissident is Martin Palouš, a philosopher at the university. 'The important thing was to set an example. We compared ourselves to Poland where Solidarity was so massive, in contrast to dissidence here.' He recalled hearing from first-hand sources that even in the summer of 1989 Wałeşa believed that the Soviet bloc could be deconstructed only gradually, and he was advising the Czechs to hold back.

As for causal connections, 'A small development disturbed the whole system. At the very last moment there comes a crossroads, a choice is made and it catches everyone by surprise.' On the 17th Palouš had an appointment at midday with an American journalist on the Charles Bridge. The two went on to the demonstration. No confrontation had been expected because Vasil Mohorita, the secretary of the Komsomol, had arranged the event in conjunction with independent students, but still 'something was in the air'. Like everyone, he heard of the alleged death of Martin Šmíd, and how this rumour had been put about by a certain Mrs Dražská.

Palouš gives himself the credit for starting Civic Forum, proposing it on the following day. Twenty-four hours were to pass before Havel returned from his house in the country, and by the Saturday evening he found that all sorts of activists and representatives from different groups were already fore-gathering. On the Sunday, it was agreed, they were to meet in Havel's Prague apartment. A sort of growing caravan, they were to move from place to place, picking up incredulous journalists, to finish in the Magic Lantern Theatre. 'Nobody could guess that the party was so unsure of itself. There was an astonishing discrepancy between the party's low-level actions such as issuing statements, and its expectations. Civic Forum leaders were constantly shocked that their proposals, dreamlike, turned into reality. It gave everyone a false impression that they were marvellous politicians. The crossroads had been reached. The party structure of communication and power disintegrated. I was at the press conference when Čalfa, then still in Adamec's government, promised to repeal the "leading role" of the party. The parliament which then passed that law was composed of members voting against their own interests. This was the case when Havel was elected President – deputies made speeches against him but they all voted for him.'

The Round Table talks proved that Civic Forum was to be taken seriously. Adamec, Palouš says, had been perceived as someone a cut above the unpopular Jakeš, Kapek or Štěpán. 'When Adamec came to the microphone at Letenská pláň on the 25th to address at least half a million people, there were shouts of "Long live Adamec". He had a chance. When he opened his mouth, out came the stock phrases of a communist functionary who simply couldn't rise to the occasion. The blindness derived from ideology. They had transformed terror and enthusiasm into a social anaesthetic, and after working at it for so long they still thought of themselves as experts in the human soul.'

So fast and wide-ranging were the repercussions of the 17 November demonstration that a commission was set up almost at once to investigate whether conspiracy theories held water. This commission reported five months later that the StB had intended to change the party leadership in collusion with the KGB. The commission itself was then suspected of some secret agenda, and a second commission with wider powers to subpoena witnesses and examine documents was appointed. Its chairman, Jiří Ruml, was a post-1948 communist who had long since crossed over to the opposition. Tall and emaciated, his face a network of wrinkles, he has now retired. As Minister of the Interior in 1993, his son had the task of reforming the police.

Recent persecution had equipped Jiří Ruml to work on the commission. On 16 August he had been detained. His StB interrogators had then told him that at the end of October they and he would be jointly demonstrating. The secret police were by no means all of one mind. The more intelligent among them perceived how Gorbachev had sent Yakovlev and Shakhnazarov and emissaries to contact possible perestroikists and even future Civic Forum members. It is Ruml's impression that such ambitious secret policemen worked to depose Jakeš and other hardliners on the grounds that they could keep control of society and win Gorbachev's approval at the same time. He cites as evidence his questioning on behalf of the commission a Czech spy by the name of Minařík. This man described how during the course of that summer Soviet agents had reproached him for failure to take positive action. So this Minařík had drafted an article for *Izvestia* in favour of perestroika, and Hegenbart had signed it. But to see Hegenbart as a Soviet agent, he believes, is to overrate him. 'I think they detained Havel in January, and then Dubček, and Rudolf Zeman and me once again in November, to provoke a reaction, to make the opposition more visible.' Havel and others were soon free but Ruml was not released from prison until 26 November, with Čarnogurský among the very last political prisoners in the country.

On the 17th, the StB was under orders to monitor the demonstration but not to engage. The KGB were up in their villa in Prague, in Dejvice, with General Alojz Lorenc, who as federal deputy Minister of the Interior was the head of the StB. 'It seems they were doing the same as our StB, monitoring the situation.'

The role of Lorenc was critical. 'We hoped that in the Government appointed on 10 December, the post of Minister of the Interior would remain unoccupied. The former communists Čalfa and Valtr Komárek, together with Čarnogurský, shared the Ministry, which meant that effectively nobody was in charge and Lorenc could do as he pleased. He had time enough to plan the StB retreat, and to destroy files. In February 1990 Havel flew to Moscow with Richard Sacher, now adviser to the Ministry of the Interior, and they signed an agreement with the KGB. This agreement had been prepared by the deputy chief of the StB, General Karel Vykypěl, who was later imprisoned.' Officially much of the StB archives has been destroyed, but there is no proof that it was not secreted away. Lorenc, Ruml remarks, is a man with an analytical mind.

Having said that, the second commission of inquiry examined 279 witnesses and over 4000 statements as well as 20,000 pages of records from the Military Prosecutor's Office, to conclude unanimously that the events on 17 November did not suggest a preplanned attempt to overthrow the regime with Soviet or any other aid. It did however uncover the fact that four of the fifteen members of the first commission had been secret StB collaborators, and that instructions had been given to sabotage the opposition on the very day that the party's 'leading role' was annulled. A secret briefing ran: 'Use influential agents to intensively infiltrate opposition parties. Aim to disinform the opponent. Compromise the most radical members of the opposition and exacerbate divisions within the opposition. At the same time, create conditions for StB officers to obtain civil service positions and posts at selected companies. Upgrade conspiratorial activities throughout the StB.'

Where did the rumour of the dead student begin?

'It remains a mystery. We have no evidence that it was organized by the StB.

There was a secret police agent who behaved as reported, and was taken by ambulance to hospital, where he ran away. His name was Zifčák, with the alias Růžička, which he actually put up on his door-plate. Then Mrs Dražská, who spread the news to press correspondents, had been in contact with the StB some time previously, but she was clearly deranged, and there is no proof that she had been manipulated before the event. Investigation of the secret police revealed nothing concrete.'

Towards the end of November, a delegation arrived from the Soviet Central Committee, headed by the son of Bohumil Šmeral, a founder of the Slovak party after the First World War. The delegation hinted that in the event of force being used, the Soviet army would intervene. 'So they would liberate us for the third time', as Ruml puts it sarcastically. Regional party functionaries were afraid of reprisals. Hardliners like Bilak knew that once the Soviet invasion was admitted as a mistake, they would be exposed for inviting them in. The then Minister of Defence General Milán Václavík was among those at the Central Committee meeting on 24 November urging the deployment of the army. Tank units had been prepared. 'There was also a perverse idea that supersonic fighters should fly over Letenská pláň at low altitude and cause chaos for the big demonstrations held there.'

A businessman now, Vasil Mohorita has offices in a beautiful old manor house on the outskirts of Prague, once a property of the Schwarzenberg family, whose arms are still on the building. A large man, he sports a black beard and talks rather as though the past was long behind him. Rising through the Komsomol, he became a candidate member, then full member, of the Central Committee in 1987. On 26 November 1989 he was elected First Secretary of the Central Committee and in that capacity he had to wind up the old party during the course of 1990. He was to raise the estimated value of party property to $768 million. 'I fired over 12,000 people. We had to empty the former Lenin museum, we had to take Gottwald's pictures and busts away, and find a grave for his ashes which were removed from the National Memorial. Travelling around the country, I used to be asked, Why did the party finish like this? People couldn't believe it. All their lives they had toiled in factories and collectives and suddenly they were being cursed for having been in the party. The only answer I could give them was that the system had been unreformable. Husák had the best opportunity to reform after 1968 and I still don't know why he didn't take it.'

With Jakeš, Mohorita had attended the fortieth anniversary celebrations in the DDR. On the grandstand as the *Fackelzug* marched past, he sensed that here was a farewell. Friends from the Freie Deutsche Jugend told him that Honecker was finished. Returning two weeks later to Berlin, this time with

Čalfa, he found changes already under way with Krenz. Czechoslovak Central Committee meetings, he says, had become more realistic in their discussions, but nobody foresaw loss of control. They supposed themselves to be improving the system.

Throughout the Soviet bloc there had been huge demonstrations against the party. If you could not head them off, why not prepare to make them ineffective?

'It was impossible to prevent them. On 17 November we were co-organizers. I was there myself. But the party was not unanimous in its attitude, and that's why it ended up in Národní třída as it did. People don't like it when I say it, but 17 November was also a generational issue within the party. To call out the People's Militia was futile because the Militia themselves would not have obeyed orders to use force.' The illustrate the point, he describes how a party audit in 1990 discovered that helmets and truncheons issued by the Prague police to militiamen for Ústí had gone missing, in fact thrown into the river. The Ústí party organization had then to pay for these items.

The critical meeting of the Central Committee on 24 November, he says, was chaotic. Some leading functionaries were unaware of what was going on, others wanted to exploit the situation by resigning. 'Jakeš made an unfortunate speech, and then came the traditional debate, who's to blame? I was almost purged too. I proposed changes in the leadership, and a number of others joined me. We then pushed through the resolution that the entire Politburo resign summarily. My impression is that Jakeš didn't even defend himself. It was a complete decline and fall. Nobody was using their head, nobody was able to imagine what should be done next day or the day after. We had a new election, and as was the good old habit in the party when the going got rough, the man with the poorest capabilities won. As Havel says of Urbánek, he's a terribly nice man. The shake-out of the 24th was finalized at the subsequent meeting two days later. Although I was elected unanimously as secretary of the Central Committee and member of the Politburo, I knew that the whole structure of personal relations and relations with the state organs had broken up, a process which could not be stopped.'

The first contacts with the Civic Forum came via a rock musician Michael Kocáb and a journalist Michael Horáček, who called on him and on Adamec as well. Mohorita describes himself as negotiating for the party, while 'Adamec had his interests. I think his estimation of the situation was wrong. He lived in a dream of becoming President and General Secretary, the director of the process of democratization. He showed that he was one of a kind with Jakeš and the others in the old guard. I think that Gorbachev gave him his support. Adamec resigned, I suspect, because he thought that if he were no longer Prime Minister he could more easily be elected President. It became clear that this was impossible, the situation developed too quickly. If you did not do something at once, an hour later it was too late.'

One of the foremost communists of the younger generation, Miroslav Štěpán was chairman of the Prague City Party Organization, and in that capacity he was responsible for the Prague People's Militia. This consisted of 12,000 men with automatic weapons. He denied giving the Militia any order to move. He was chairman of the Defence Council, too, in his opinion an arena better adapted than the Militia to propose the use of force. Since 1988 he was also on the Politburo, far and away its youngest member. Seeing in him the heir and continuator of the post-1968 party, Jakeš allowed him his head. By the time I interviewed him, he had served a prison sentence for abuse of his powers in 1988, and has overcome, he says, 'any emotional residue'. Words pour out of him; he loves to chase hares, and to weave some stray encounter into a plot. For instance, Kryuchkov's first deputy, Colonel General Gruschkov of the KGB, was with General Lorenc on 17 November. For instance, Dubček was detained during the demonstrations for hours in the Palace of Culture. For instance, that same day he himself had given an order that nobody unauthorized was to enter Prague security headquarters, but two people did so, a Dr Grusík from Hegenbart's staff, and General Tashlenko, from the Soviet Ministry of the Interior and on the Embassy staff. For instance, that the Minister of the Interior had gone on vacation, but signed an emergency order for the 17th which delegated responsibility to General Lorenc. Not surprisingly, Štěpán finds the report of Jiří Ruml's commission incomplete, of temporary interest, even a piece of folklore. The report, however, exonerates him from calling in the People's Militia.

One special contact of his was Gennady Yanayev, Gorbachev's Vice-President and leader of the August coup. In October 1989 Yanayev told him that if Gorbachev had his way, then nothing would be left of the Kremlin except the flagpole. Recalling this in prison, Štěpán sent Yanayev a telegram at the time of the coup. 'Recently I met some Soviets who told me that if the Czechs had smashed the opposition, that could have saved Gorbachev and the former socialist countries. I was at least ready to defend everything positive from the past, but that was not enough. I see from our history that Czechs have not been left by other powers to take their own decisions. In 1989 it was the same. Had Moscow reformed, there would have been no problem here. But it didn't, and so the socialist countries all collapsed with it. It would be absurd and trivializing to say that all the socialist countries had incompetent First Secretaries at the same moment.'

However late in the day, practical steps could have been taken in 1989. 'All those sitting round the Politburo table with me had been appointed as a result of the conflict with Dubček.' That was an ideological dead weight. 'And I can assure you that the strength or weakness of dissidence played no part. A hundred kilometres from Prague nobody had heard of Havel or Charter 77. Civic Forum would have completed its mission the moment it was founded, had the party leadership not been prepared to make contact.'

On 17 November Štěpán had been in his office. He had authorized the demonstration. Like the overwhelming majority of people, dissidents included, he says, he had no idea what might develop. Next day, Saturday, he had driven sixty kilometres to Louny, to a flat where his mother was. His intention was to rest. Towards midday, the chief of security in Louny arrived to pass on a telephone call that he was to return urgently, as the situation was deteriorating. Back in Prague, he first heard the Šmíd story. 'I left for Jakeš's villa. He was sitting there, and he asked, What's going on? I was surprised that even he was quite so out of the picture. I proposed that he call a meeting of the Politburo or even the Central Committee. He accepted. So at 6 p.m. on that Sunday the Politburo met. We invited General Lorenc, who confirmed that no special forces had participated in the Národní třída attack. In various articles later on, he admitted that perhaps some troops in special clothing, even special forces, had duties there.' None of them knew of the initial meeting of Civic Forum in the Magic Lantern Theatre for the simple reason that neither the secret police nor anyone else had reported it.

On the Monday it might have been possible to save the party. 'The situation could have been serious if certain people had declared that a coup was taking place, and the population had to stay in their homes or do their duty in their workplaces. At that point we had nothing to lose because the Kremlin was against us, in practice had sacrificed us. Even on the Tuesday, possibilities still existed. We could have called an immediate party congress, made radical changes in the party and called a proper Round Table. We could have used strong measures, not to kill anyone but to be exemplary. Call out the army. Demonstrate power like a stage prop.'

Did anyone suggest it?

'Such measures are not usually discussed. In accordance with the Constitution, the Defence Council had the right to declare martial law. In view of the global context, I am convinced that our approach was right. And we were discovering that the party was very disturbed within itself, its leaders too weak even for a show of force.'

What about the army?

'I am aware only of the statement of the Minister of Defence, Václavík, during the plenary session of the Central Committee on the night of the 24th that the army was ready to defend socialist achievements in accordance with the statutes and the law. But in the political situation which had evolved by then, this meant next to nothing.'

A technocrat to his fingertips, Marián Čalfa has a laconic manner and an air of not suffering fools gladly. A bohemianized Slovak, he was twenty-six when he began to work for the Government in 1972, as a legal draughtsman. Encountering the political élite, he says that he mastered the mechanics of life at the top, and acquired insight in how to rule. 'But I didn't wake up in the morning with the conviction that the Communist Party had to be the ruling party.'

Was there anything, I asked him, that the party could have done which it did not do? 'The question should be rephrased, Did the Czechoslovak authorities do anything?' In his view, there was no revolution, merely an overdue splitting of state and party powers. As a member of the Government, he had listened to Obzina, the Minister of the Interior, lengthily explaining after 17 November that he was only taking measures such as closing down theatres. In fact, both Obzina and General Václavík were to stand trial afterwards for abuse of power. Čalfa claimed that he himself was insisting on contacts with students and dissidents.

On the 25th, Havel met Adamec for the first time in the centre of Prague, in the building known as the Obecní dům. Čalfa accompanied Adamec. Afterwards they all drove out to Letenská pláň, and he had the chance to listen to Adamec's speech and the jeering that followed. 'It was an expression of disgust. Had Adamec asked for everyone's help in deposing the party, he would have become leader of the whole crisis. When he asked people not to go on strike, his political career ended. We know today that the leaders of the opposition did not contemplate a complete change of the system, but only power-sharing, some kind of plurality.' So by the time Adamec formed his government on 3 December he had already missed whatever chance of success he might have had. 'Besides, the composition of the Government was impossible to understand. I was deputy prime minister but I would never have accepted some of my colleagues. Adamec was creating a new absolutism.'

What happened when Adamec saw Gorbachev?

'He has never revealed it, but he handed in his resignation right after his return. This surprised Havel who was negotiating with him on the assumption that Adamec would continue as head of the Government. I can only presume that Gorbachev would not back him. A party apparatchik from northern Moravia, Adamec became a reformer at the last minute. In Gorbachev's eyes, Adamec remained an unregenerate communist, not in his blood group.'

Taking over the Government, as laid down in the Constitution, Čalfa was also in the position of negotiating with Havel. 'It was a Round Table with political parties represented, in the Palace of Culture, opposite the Forum Hotel. My first task was to agree on the composition of the new government which would be acceptable to the opposition and to the general public. The general strike was in the air, the situation was ripe for a solution. It was possible to resolve it by means of force, and it is necessary to be explicit and clear about that. The whole police and security apparatus, and the army, stood at our disposal. The key factor was that nobody appeared with the guts, instinct, character, whatever you like to call it, to use force and to convince others that this was appropriate. Once we had the Government of National Reconciliation, with opposition members in it, the Round Table process became superfluous.'

My impression is that Jakeš and possibly Štěpán might have used force.

'The party had lost its influence on the instruments of the state. The seat of power had shifted from the Politburo to the Government, where nobody was ready to use such means. Voluntary concession of power was the approach of the Government.'

In your experience, did anyone suggest using the security forces or the army?

'Of course. Obzina and especially General Václavík were convinced that these means could be used, but neither could decide on his own. And nobody else could decide it for him. The party was by no means as united as it might appear to the external observer. There were several layers. At the regional level, the party lived its own life. Disintegration was quickest there, because contact with people was direct and resistance to the party was obvious. The party remained strongest in the provinces. In the centre, the emergence of a second seat of power in the form of a government was the major blow.'

Towards the end of the year, Čalfa paid his obligatory visit to Gorbachev and the Kremlin. 'Across the table he was studying me. He was straightforward, genial, he wanted a precise analysis of the situation, and his responses were logical, historical and right. He was intrigued by the mechanism of maintaining calm and orderliness. Apparently he did not think in geopolitical terms. His main principle was that each state should lay the grounding of parliamentary and pluralist democracy. The one thing he wasn't expecting was that at the mention of plurality, the whole bloc would reveal itself anti-Soviet. We do not overestimate ourselves, we are aware that our change was a function of Soviet change.'

Žd'ár is a lugubrious small town, a couple of hours east of Prague, down the country's sole motorway. Its old buildings, including a church designed by Santini, that most original of eighteenth-century architects, are mouldering, hemmed in and dwarfed by serried blocks of housing in jaundiced concrete. In a village beyond Žd'ár lives Rudolf Hegenbart in a chalet right at the edge of an overshadowing forest. On the day that I drove there, the landscape was bound in snow and ice.

'They are demonizing Hegenbart,' Miloš Jakeš had said to me. And that is what Hegenbart himself believes. Suffering from diabetes, he has long been in poor health. Suspicious and aggrieved, he sits in his armchair, face quivering with apparent righteous indignation. A student of politics and economics, he had done a course at the Academy of Social Sciences in Moscow in the early 1970s. Rising through the party, he had been a deputy Prime Minister in the Czech government, becoming important only in 1988 when Jakeš picked him to reshape the state administration, including the security services.

For this interview, Hegenbart has prepared a lengthy memorandum which he insists on elaborating aloud at great length: his travels in the Soviet bloc in 1988 and 1989 to learn about security, his lonely stands at this and that plenum, his memoranda in favour of reform. On 16 January 1989 he and the federal Minister of the Interior and the Prosecutor General had met in a restaurant from which they could watch the demonstration unfolding. 'The Ministry had reported that there would be punks and a few students, the underclass. What we saw wasn't nice. Dogs were used, and water cannons. Not degraded youngsters at all, these were protesters against the regime who wanted us all to resign. The Minister and the Prosecutor General condemned the violent action of the police. We raised our glasses in a toast in white Moravian wine for better times.' When this event came on the agenda for discussion, the Politburo instead congratulated the police and strengthened the law restraining assembly and freedom of speech.

Once in control of a structure which inspired fear and obedience, he has come to see himself somehow as a victim, in a self-serving distortion of memory typical of these party loyalists. After all, he had only been engaged in purging, the process without which there was no implementation of party policy. 'In agreement with Jakeš, I began to pull down the pillars which supported the Husák, Štrougal and Obzina clique. All the deputy ministers from the era of these people left. Some chiefs of the police department left. I had my own plan how to get rid of them all. We wanted to destroy this mafia, this interconnectedness of the Central Committee and the Ministries of the Interior and Defence. They were doing as they pleased. But along comes Jakeš and Hegenbart destroying the gang, so they wanted to get their own back.' The events from 17 November onwards were 'an intra-party putsch aimed at Jakeš and me, and organized by the Prague members of the Central

Committee'. This means Kapek, Štrougal, Mohorita, maybe Štěpán, among others. During the demonstration Hegenbart himself had been here at home, listening to the news on the radio and television.

When the Politburo met on the Sunday, why didn't it summon a whole Central Committee meeting?

'It is a mystery to me. It was the opinion of Kapek, Štrougal and others from Prague that the Central Committee should only be summoned on the 24th. I was ill. When Jakeš asked the doctors if I could attend, they said no. But doctors accompanied me there. Everything had been lost by then.'

Were the security organs keeping the party in touch with the reality of public opinion?

'It was clear, the leadership was receiving briefings. The hardline group around Fojtík did not believe them, and neither did Indra nor Husák. Jakeš received direct information but failed to pass it on, which helped to radicalize the situation. Indra would have liked to have used the army. Discussions to that effect went on within the army where the chain of command was between Husák and General Václavík. I was preparing new leadership there, and by January Václavík would have been replaced.'

'Everyone in Žd'ár,' he says bitterly, 'knows that Hegenbart invited in the People's Militia.' Here is his account of what happened. 'At 2 p.m. on the Tuesday, 21 November, Jakeš phoned me to say that I was to come round at four o'clock with Novák, the chief of staff of the People's Militia, to prepare political and organizational backing for the possible use of the People's Militia. Arriving at that appointment, we were informed that there was a threat of chaos in Prague. Jakeš was afraid of bloodshed. In the interest of keeping order, units of the Ministry of the Interior were to be reinforced by the People's Militia. He was very nervous, and did not look us in the eye. He was due to speak on television. Novák was told to prepare a plan. We were invited to the Politburo at six. The visit lasted twenty minutes, and during it Jakeš twice left the room. I felt something was wrong. I went to the doctor when I left, I wasn't feeling well. I called Jakeš to be excused from the Politburo session, I didn't say that I was ill but that I had a visitor. He accepted this. I went to my Prague apartment. On three separate occasions the telephone rang there but when I picked up the receiver there was nobody there. In the meantime the Politburo was in session and there was a question about my absence. They approved calling in the People's Militia.

'Before midnight I received a call from Kincl, at the Ministry of the Interior, asking me what he should do as Prague did not want the People's Militia. I told him that I had not been at the Politburo, and had nothing to do with the People's Militia, and that it had its own Chief of Staff, and I did not want to be dragged into this. Also that the People's Militia could be invited in only after a demand from the federal Minister of the Interior, namely him. If he had not been able to clarify this at the Politburo, he had only to call Jakeš. By midnight I had received a call from Novák, to ask me what he should do as Prague did not want to have in the Militia. I asked, Why call me? He should call Jakeš or Štěpán. I learned that Štěpán had not been present at the Politburo.

'In the morning the Politburo was again in session, and it immediately fired Novák for exceeding his powers. They gave him a task in the evening and fired him next morning. That was dirty business.'

Out in Dejvice, the smartest district of Prague, is the Bauhaus-style villa where Miloš Jakeš lives. The interior is spacious but colourless, a symphony in treacle-brown and grey. Jakeš himself has a white and almost papery face, and it takes a moment for any reaction visibly to percolate into it. His eyes are clear to the point of blankness and he seems to lack the musculature for a smile. Parlance about the restoration of capitalism or the strategy of imperialism comes naturally. Angry at the collapse of the party and his own position and ideology, he is evidently baffled and sometimes contradictory in his responses, especially where Gorbachev is concerned.

Jakeš used to take his holidays in Stavropol and has therefore known Gorbachev since 1977. 'He was different from other Soviet leaders. Not working in leading institutions, he did not have their experience. A debater, democratic-minded, he spoke openly about the problems of Soviet agriculture. With his wife he came to lunch, which was unheard-of in Soviet conditions. We talked about our families and struck up a friendly relationship. Over the years I often met him, especially after I became First Secretary. He developed. He was a bit of a dreamer, but otherwise had the right idea. The party had to be disconnected from the state, and its influence exercised by other means. The Soviets were the proper basis for the power of the people. We welcomed the course he had adopted at the party congress of 1986, and at the two plenary sessions of January and June 1987.'

Which leads him without a break into recrimination. 'His big mistake was to sully the past. That's the way to fall. Maybe it was an attempt to obtain support for perestroika. But everyone with a grievance at that moment tried to gain ground, they wanted revenge. The one feature they had in common was vengefulness, a serious shortcoming, for which they ought to be excluded from politics. The thousands of communists who had to leave the party here after 1968 also wanted satisfaction as the price of their humiliation. Gorbachev came from the provinces, and despite all his efforts he never mastered international politics. In good faith, he wanted to be rid of the burden of the arms race in order to raise the standard of living. It didn't work out that way. He did nothing but surrender unilaterally. And he had one more characteristic, which in the light of history will be called treason, a love of glory. It was a drug. Whoever provided this drug was his man. It wasn't the Soviet public but the anti-socialist powers who gave him what he craved.'

Did Gorbachev press to replace Husák with you?

'The very opposite. Many party leaders had concluded that Husák should go. He made great efforts to have Štrougal as his successor, and Štrougal started to behave as though he were already First Secretary. Then Gorbachev came here in 1987 and praised Husák's positive role, which froze everything. Towards the end of August a Politburo member told him openly that he had to step down. Husák was prepared to discuss it. He visited the Soviet Union where Gorbachev told him that this was his own business, refusing to say either yes or no.'

Jakeš himself had attended the Soviet Party Congress in 1986, along with Husák and the Czechoslovak delegation. They had all stayed in a villa. Out on a walk there, Štrougal told Jakeš that Husák was not in good health and, furthermore, was opposed to reform. 'He proposed that I should take over. I answered that he was better prepared for this than I was, and that was the end of it. He replied that in Husák we had had a Slovak leader for the past twenty years, that Bilak was excluded because he was another Slovak, and it was time for a Czech. The other members of the leadership told me that they considered it right to propose me. At the Politburo in November 1987 Bilak opened the question and over the next two sessions Husák came to agree that I should be his successor. There was no Soviet pressure. Husák may have called Gorbachev who would have said that he supported the choice. That is probable.'

A change of policy, Jakeš says, is invariably destabilizing, and perestroika proved no exception. It opened the path for anyone discontented. 'We had information that the opposition wanted to abuse the situation and they were paid from abroad. Without international support from Radio Free Europe and the Voice of America, they were nothing.'

The fact that the demonstration of 17 November was tolerated in his opinion is confirmation that liberalization was well under way. That Friday at around 6 p.m. he received a call from the deputy Ministry of the Interior, to say that the demonstration was over. So he left for the weekend at his country house about fifty kilometres away, arriving there after dark. At half past nine, the deputy minister telephoned again: there had been some shouting but order had been maintained, and it had not been necessary to summon ambulances. 'Two days later I hear all this mystification about a dead student. Parents were saying, They are beating our children. It was hysteria. After all, practically nothing had happened. I looked into it and summoned the

Politburo for that evening. Everyone present had arrived from the country, the deputy minister again confirmed that nothing had happened and that nobody was dead. Then Štěpán told us about the founding of the political movement, Civic Forum. So we began to deal with that in detail. We issued defensive orders to forbid security forces from attacking because we knew that the opposition wanted an escalation.'

So the Sunday evening Politburo took place in an atmosphere of calm, not crisis?

'In view of the reports of rough goings-on, we decided that the Prosecutor General would investigate. Pitra, the Czech Prime Minister, went on television to inform the public about that. The decisive moment came on Tuesday, when the employees of television switched to the opposition and began to broadcast live about nationwide demonstrations. There were none. But from then on people kept on demanding that the Government be deposed, and things started to slip out of control.'

'The Militia were supposed to come on Wednesday morning, the 22nd. That was in agreement with Štěpán. Many comrades told me that the Prague police had been without a break for days, and were exhausted, and in need of reinforcements. We agreed to invite the Militia but the Prague City Party then decided against it. Changing his mind, Štěpán now said that the city had enough forces as it was. At about 1 a.m. Novák came to this house, to inform me that the Prague City Party no longer approved of the presence of the Militia. I said, What can I do? Are they on their way? He answered, Some of them are. So I said, If they aren't here, stop them but those who have already arrived should be employed in keeping public order. When news spread that the Militia was coming, uproar broke out. Novák came to me again on the 24th, to report that people were beginning to attack the Militia. I told him, Let them go home.'

Were they armed?

'They had no ammunition.'

The 24th is the day you resigned. Did Novák come before your resignation?

'We sacked him for imperfect preparation of the action. If the Militia had come immediately, it would have turned out all right.'

A show of force at that point would have been effective?

'It would have undoubtedly contributed to the keeping of order. Events would not have developed like an avalanche. We could not repeat Jaruzelski's methods or the Chinese solution. That left only the political option. But we were not prepared for the fact that everything would begin to crumble around us. It is a godless lie to claim that here was a movement of the people against the party and socialism. Socialism in Czechoslovakia would never have fallen had it not been for the global process and for the support of the United States for anti-communist forces and for the de facto treason of Gorbachev.'

So what made you resign?

'First the dissidents, the opposition. They saw several leaders as obstacles, and were demanding that Husák, myself, Indra, Fojtík, Pavel Hoffman and others resigned. Štrougal quit of his own accord. I tried to persuade him not to. He was not persuaded. There was the question: Do we summon the Central Committee or not? I supported not doing so, but acting instead, by mobilizing the party and the apparat, searching out those in opposition who we could talk to on a basis of shared socialist values, and quickly publishing prepared documents, for instance, a draft of a new constitution omitting the leading role of the party, and bills on the right of assembly and freedom of the press.'

Why did the Politburo reject the proposal and all the members instead resign?

'Many members of the Central Committee, the Politburo and the Government had to leave.'

What does 'had to leave' mean?

'Because they were too old. We were recruiting younger members. It was all timed to the party congress due the following May. Those who were being forced out saw in the events of 17 November the chance for revenge by getting hold of the party leadership. Kapek, Štrougal, Milán Klusak the Minister of Culture and many other party secretaries hoped to negotiate their survival with the opposition. Only the outcome was different. They destabilized the party leadership. When Civic Forum and Havel heard that Jakeš had fallen, it was champagne all round.'

I want to be clear. You had been prepared to make a stand and modernize. Instead you were outmanoeuvred on the 24th by the old guard of the party?

'Yes. I believe that our renewal of socialism would have suited the people.'

You were First Secretary, you had only to purge the hardliners.

'The Politburo is a collective organ. I was one of them, not like Husák who always took his distance. I put the question, Should we resign? I warned that it would be a dangerous step. My mistake was to submit to pressure. One after another, with the exception of Husák, they said that we should resign. So after the evening intermission, I took the stand and announced our collective decision. The international context decided the overall issue, but this meant the end of the rule of the party. The new leadership was inexperienced, in a fearful panic, expelling us from the party as though to put all the blame on us. They made a more devastating critique of communism than an archenemy could have done.'

Adamec wanted your job?

'Certainly. But he was not as open about it as Štrougal. Kapek proposed Štrougal. Kapek later died, he hanged himself, I think it dawned on him what he had done.'

So you went into the Politburo meeting on the 24th with a policy of continuing, but came out realizing that everything was over?

'Unfortunately my close collaborators did not tell me that this conspiracy was being prepared. If I had known, I would have spoken in a totally different way. That would not have changed our relations to capitalism, or to events in Poland and Hungary and the DDR, but the party need not have become the object of destructive revenge and the lustration law and accusations of unlawfulness. I told them then and there that they should have supported me. Beforehand, they had been raising their hands to vote yes. Suddenly, everything was wrong. I could do nothing right.'

Did Gorbachev contact you after the 24th?

'No. I wrote him a letter that we were out, and asking him to support the work of the leadership, but he did not respond. I had seen him for the last time on 7 October in Berlin. He behaved very badly. All the First Secretaries of the European parties had been present. He refused to meet them. He treated Honecker as though he were not there. He had lost interest. He confirmed that he had opted for a policy of renouncing influence in this area. I blame him for not even trying to influence anything. He said that he wanted a thorough exchange of opinion. All the First Secretaries met, the meeting lasted ninety minutes, there were no preparations and no agenda, and half the time was taken up by his speech. Then he said that he had to leave. Without solidarity it was impossible to survive.'

31

'WE HAD IMPOSED OURSELVES'

A foreign correspondent of the old school, Archie Gibson of the London *Times* knew Romania well between the wars. As the country lay under the Nazi yoke he wrote an envoi. 'During the period 1924 to 1940, Romania made enormous progress: its railways, river and seagoing vessels, and airlines were without equal in South-East Europe ... There were wide boulevards, pollution-free lakes, elegant stores and modern cinemas ... there was a good telephone service, a growing capital with tree-lined streets, and industry which had managed to give Romania even heavy locomotives.'

Peaceful construction of the sort was not even a memory by the 1980s. The years under the Soviet yoke had reduced the country to a misery unparalleled in Europe, unless in Albania. Stalin's imperial power games confiscated territory in Moldavia and Bessarabia, but handed over Transylvania where some two million people of Hungarian descent naturally identified themselves with Hungary and so ensured the continuation of a historic enmity destructive to all parties. Prosecutor during the Great Terror, Andrei Vyshinsky was devoid of all scruple. Instructed to bring Romania into the Soviet Empire in 1945, he installed the Popular Democratic Front, a guise for the regime of collaboration which was to come. His threat to return Transylvania to Hungary was a successful blackmail. But the local communists were then to inflict far greater damage on the country. First Secretary from 1965 to 1989, Nicolae Ceauşescu derived from Marxism–Leninism the parlance and strong-arm methods to justify tyranny in his own name and on his own account. 'Giant of the Carpathians' was only one of the many high-flown epithets he lavished on himself. His collected works in twenty-seven volumes of ghost-written guff went under the rubric 'Romania on the Way of Building Up the Multilaterally Developed Socialist Society'. Socialism in theory and practice was unilateral profiteering. His Romania was a modern travesty of a despotism out of the Middle Ages.

Ceauşescu was born in 1918 into a large and poor peasant family. Politics for him was the fulfilment of a backwoods dream of self-aggrandizement through cunning, and where possible and if necessary, fraud and force. By the end of his career he owned no fewer than eighty-four palaces, hunting lodges, villas and retreats. Between fifty and sixty of his close relations held dominant and lucrative posts in the party-state. Coming from a similar background, his wife Elena shared his aspirations. Having left school at the age of eleven she seems to have wished to compensate for a sense of her own ignorance and inferiority by manufacturing an academic career. Scientists were hired to write papers published under her name. The title by which Romanians were to refer to her, she laid down, was 'Madame Comrade Academician Engineer of World Renown'. A shrew, suspicious and greedy and acquisitive, she exercised undue influence. Their son Nicu, notorious for debauchery, was party leader in Sibiu; their daughter Zoia became head of a small mathematical institute, and among other stolen property found in her house was $97,000 in cash.

Small in stature, with stiff and jerky movements, his face usually taut with a superior sneer, Ceauşescu was unattractive. Defecting in 1978, his chief of security Ion Pacepa was to paint an insider's portrait of the man, murdering enemies when he could not bribe or suborn them, holding the lowest opinion of everyone else except himself, foul-mouthed, corrupt, channelling secret funds into Swiss banks. He was 'the absolute proprietor of Romania', Pacepa wrote, whose will 'becomes law at the mere scrawl of his pen'.

Ceauşescu's lawlessness was deliberately elaborated on the grapevine to inspire the fear which underpinned his regime. Modelled on the KGB, the secret police or Securitate held society in its stranglehold. It was said by Pacepa to number 25,000 but in all likelihood was larger, perhaps 100,000. Every workplace, collective, institute, hospital or point of contact with foreigners had its informers whose numbers are also unknown, but were in the hundreds of thousands. Anti-terrorist forces and an élite bodyguard were also at Ceauşescu's disposal. Better armed, the army had been highly politicized. Some of its most professional units were seconded to the Securitate. In key military posts Ceauşescu appointed either relations or officers whom he could keep at his mercy. Commanding the Bucharest military district until 1978, General Nicolae Militaru, for instance, had been abruptly transferred out of the army for political unreliability, in his case exposed as a Soviet agent. Victor Stanculescu was a particular favourite at court, promoted to the rank of general.

A colleague in the early years of Ceauşescu's rule was Ion Iliescu. Born in 1930, an engineer by training, he had made the conventional rise through the Komsomol to become Ideological Secretary and heir apparent of Ceauşescu. In 1971 Ceauşescu and his wife had visited China and North Korea, where they had been favourably impressed by Kim Il-Sung and his son. The idea was born that they too could found a communist dynasty through grooming their son Nicu as eventual successor. Protesting, as he was bound to do, Iliescu was pushed aside into jobs of diminishing importance, to end up as a publisher of technical books and journals. Nobody and nothing except self-interest was to influence Ceauşescu.

Intuitive skill at cheating his way stood him in good stead internationally. Refusal to break off diplomatic relations with Israel on instructions from Moscow in 1967, and then open support of Dubček and the Prague Spring cost him nothing, but appeared to set a distance between the Soviet Union and himself. Soviet occupation forces had already withdrawn, if only to Moldavia. The split between the Soviet Union and China opened up another arena for profitable manipulation between antagonists. American and British policy-makers showered favours and rewards on to Ceauşescu in the vain misapprehension that he was a maverick through whom the break-up of the Soviet bloc might be implemented.

By the 1980s Ceauşescu's confidence was evolving into megalomania, and his police-state mentality into paranoia. Typewriters had to be registered and inspected annually in case the keys had been tampered with, the sure sign of a dissident engaged in underground publishing. Buying what were considered excessive quantities of food could earn a prison sentence of five years. Food was severely limited and finally rationed. By 1989, according to the economist P. Ronnas, Romanians were able to buy less than half as much meat, dairy products and rice as in 1980, with the percentages for milk and sugar only a little higher. In the effort to squeeze out the money with which to repay foreign debt of $10 billion, fuel supplies and electricity were suspended for long periods, so that people not only starved but froze to death. Supposedly in pursuit of status by means of a crude head count, contraception was forbidden and women were regularly inspected to account for failure to bear children. Infant mortality rose to such an extent that it was forbidden to register the death of a baby under the age of twelve months.

To build himself a pharaonic palace with a government centre and Nomen-klatura housing attached, Ceauşescu razed an ancient quarter of Bucharest, ejecting 40,000 residents and demolishing 15,000 buildings, including two historic monasteries and twenty-six churches. Not quite finished, the cranes rusting on the site, this House of the People as it was mendaciously known, is a monument to folly and waste. The Patriarch did not protest. Like Bishop Gyula Nagy and Bishop László Papp of the Hungarian Reformed Church or Rabbi Moshe Rosen, the higher Orthodox clergy were part of the security apparatus. In the manner of Honecker, Ceauşescu took to selling his citizens for sums of up to ten thousand dollars a head. As he gloated to Pacepa, 'Oil, Jews and Germans are our most important export commodities.' German spokesmen and Rabbi Rosen gladly collaborated in this human trade.

The programme of *Sistematizare*, or systemization, was social engineering yet more destructive in intention, and indeed more mad even than the earlier digging with slave labour of the Danube Canal. Romania consisted of 13,000 villages. Although land had already long been collectivized, farmers and villagers were to be uprooted and resettled in agro-towns, as yet existing only on the drawing board. Communal life would replace the family. Deprived of any last means of independence, Romanians were to be reduced to mere productive units. As David Turnock, a British specialist, wrote, '*Sistematizare* would have been the culmination of decades of struggle against individualism.' Perhaps so inhuman a concept could never have been realized but scores of villages were destroyed and thousands of lives ruined. Turnock gives an example from the commune of Snagov. 'The people were warned of the impending change in May 1988 and then forced to move at three days' notice the following August. All houses and vineyards were destroyed and the village converted into cereal fields. No compensation was paid for the houses destroyed and the people displaced became tenants in Ghermanesti where they found inadequate accommodation for the domestic animals (pigs and poultry) they took with them.'

Because Ceaușescu presented himself as a communist and a nationalist independent from the Soviet Union, Western fellow-travellers of every stripe homed in on him. From their books and articles it was impossible to learn that the country was an abject police-state. In 1977 coal-miners in the Jiu Valley went on strike, and in 1987 workers in Brașov rioted in protest against declining living standards. First attacked and beaten up, those who had participated in these events were then deported in internal exile. But epitomizing the fellow-traveller, the publisher and businessman Robert Maxwell interviewed Ceaușescu for an anonymous biography which his publishing house was to issue in 1983. Under the veneer of respectability and statesmanship, one international crook was addressing another, both presumably relishing the charade. 'Dear Mr President,' Maxwell gushed, 'You have been holding the highest political and state office in Romania for almost eighteen years, a fact for which we warmly congratulate you. What has – in your opinion – made you so popular with the Romanians?'

To be a dissident, like Doina Cornea of Cluj University or the poet Mircea Dinescu, required exceptional bravery. In the general absence of truthful Western reporting, the Securitate image of them pertained, as eccentric and possibly a bit touched, with only themselves to blame for being held in house arrest or prison. The poetry of Ana Blandiana is an unforgettable lament over the decline both in material conditions and moral values, conveying resignation and helplessness.

> Entire decades waiting for
> The turning of the key in the lock;
> More and more rusted,
> Lying in wait for entire decades
> Without words,
> Without a destiny.

Gorbachev shared what had come to be the habitual Soviet response to Ceauşescu, that the man was distasteful and should now and again be threatened and if possible disciplined, but that on balance he served as a useful example that the communist movement worldwide was not monolithic, as its capitalist critics insisted. In May 1987 Gorbachev, accompanied by Raisa, visited Bucharest and launched perestroika. In a broadcast speech, he uttered statements for which a Romanian would have been hauled in by the Securitate. 'We know that your country faces a number of difficult problems, that there are difficulties which affect daily life.' At their final meetings, in Bucharest in July 1989 for the Warsaw Pact, in Berlin for the DDR's fortieth anniversary, in the Kremlin after the Malta summit, Gorbachev and Ceauşescu did not hide from observers that they held one another in growing aversion and even scorn, each believing that the other's policies must lead to ruin. As though in defiance of all opinion, Ceauşescu staged on 20 November 1989 what proved to be the final party congress in the approved style. Sixty-seven standing ovations and over one hundred 'spontaneous' outbursts of clapping interrupted Ceauşescu's five-hour speech. Contributing to this circus were the very colleagues and generals who were to kill him on Christmas Day five weeks later.

The only people in Romania in a position to exploit perestroika were old hands, whose long and faithful record of party duty would cover the attempt now to return to high position and to be doing what Gorbachev wanted of them. One such was Silviu Brucan, an eager participant in the Stalinist takeover and purging after 1945, rewarded with the post of Romanian ambassador to Washington, and then acting editor of *Scînteia*, the party newspaper housed in the skyscraper presented by Stalin himself as a gift to Bucharest. Surviving every twist and turn, and somehow wheedling out the self-exculpatory phrases, Brucan is the local Ilya Ehrenburg. Anything he says needs confirmation. In his memoirs *The Wasted Generation* he describes a meeting towards the end of 1988 with Gorbachev in the Kremlin. Gorbachev agreed to a scenario to topple Ceauşescu, on condition that it was well-conceived and also that it maintained the party as the main political force. 'The party must remain upright,' he quotes Gorbachev as repeating, 'otherwise there will be chaos.'

Accordingly, early in March 1989, Brucan and five others with comparable careers mailed to Radio Free Europe in Munich an open letter to Ceauşescu, to protest against the destruction of villages and other abuses of human rights. Although this so-called Letter of Six was well within the limits set by Gorbachev, the Securitate moved. Brucan was kept under house arrest. In all likelihood the letter was no more than a marker put down on behalf of themselves by disgruntled men unwilling to renounce power, but in the hectic atmosphere of Romanian politics it has sometimes been construed as evidence of deep-laid conspiracy.

Two researchers, Katherine Verdery and Gail Kligman, writing in *Eastern Europe in Revolution*, a book edited by Ivo Banac, opened their account of the overthrow of Ceauşescu by stating that it is simply impossible to say what 'really happened' that December. In the political culture of the Balkans, the spoils go to the strong and the weak go to the wall. Even those who intend to have clean hands and a clear conscience find that compromise and conspiracy are irresistible. There is no tracing the subterranean ebb and flow of accusation and rumour back to source.

Timişoara has a population of 350,000, with a large Hungarian minority. One of its prominent leaders was Pastor László Tökes, the son of a deputy bishop and professor of theology already in trouble with the authorities. Several times that year, Pastor Tökes had spoken from the pulpit against the programme of *Sistematizare* and in defence of human rights for Romanians as well as Hungarians. His bishop, László Papp, no doubt on orders from the party, started legal moves to evict and dismiss him. On the 15th and 16th, larger and larger crowds gathered round his house. What began as a gesture of solidarity turned into anti-communism. Party headquarters were ransacked. Bonfires were built of placards and other propaganda material, as well as volumes of Ceauşescu's speeches. Pastor Tökes himself was afterwards to praise Romanians, Germans and Hungarians for acting together in spite of the regime's fostering of hatred between peoples. 'The revolution opened the way to reconciliation.'

December 17 was a Sunday. Early that morning the Politburo (here it was called the Political Executive Committee, or Polexco for short) met in Bucharest to discuss the situation. The transcript of the proceedings has been published. A furious Ceauşescu, backed by Elena, reproached the army commanders for issuing blank rather than live ammunition. 'I didn't think you would shoot with blanks; that is like a rain shower. Those who entered the party building should not leave the building alive ... They have got to kill hooligans not just beat them.' Elena added, 'You shoot them and throw them in the basement. Not even one should see the daylight again!'

To the Ceauşescus, this was not a protest or part of a general emancipation from tyranny, but a plot. 'Everything that happens and happened in Germany, in Czechoslovakia and Bulgaria now, and in Poland and Hungary in the past, are things organized by the Soviet Union with American and Western support ... What has happened in the last three countries, the German Democratic Republic, Czechoslovakia and Bulgaria were *coup d'état* organized with the help of the scum of society with foreign support. This is the only way of understanding these things.'

Listening submissively to the Ceauşescus at this meeting were the Ministers of Defence Colonel General Vasile Milea, the commander of the Securitate General Iulian Vlad, and the Minister of Internal Affairs General Tudor Postelnicu. 'Do you know what I am going to do with you?' Ceauşescu raged. 'Send you to the firing squad.' Apologizing for their misguided leniency, the generals promised to use live ammunition to clear Timişoara. Ceauşescu concluded, 'All right, shall we try once more, comrades?'

That evening Ceauşescu was due to fly to Tehran where the mullahs in the regime were courting and flattering him, much to their subsequent embarrassment. Elena, Emil Bobu and Manea Manescu were to run the country in his absence. On the eve of departure as planned, the Ceauşescus presumably congratulated themselves on the cleverness with which they had put the generals on the spot. They could take credit if the status quo was restored but blame the generals for anything that might go amiss.

Armoured columns started to advance in strength into Timişoara during that afternoon. Round about dusk the shooting began. In the next twenty-four hours somewhere between 100 and 200 people were killed, according to reliable estimates. Brucan seems to have been the source for 50,000 and then 60,000 dead, the figures which Western media took up, adding to confusion and consternation. Among those who arrived in Timişoara to conduct or supervise military operations in accordance with Ceauşescu's orders were General Victor Stanculescu, General Ştefan Guşe, the Prime Minister Constantin Dascalescu and Emil Bobu, the Central Committee Secretary for Party Organization.

Through the centre of Bucharest runs the main thoroughfare of Calei Victoriei. This leads into Palace Square, more an irregular and extensive open space than a square. Around it are monuments like the former Royal Palace which is the national art gallery, the majestic Athenaeum concert hall, the National Library, the Congress Hall, some of the ministries and two of the leading hotels, the Athénée Palace and the Intercontinental. In the north-east corner looms the forbidding Central Committee building, which was effectively the seat of the regime, and it was here that Ceauşescu bunkered himself after his return from Tehran late on the 19th. Somewhat set back, it has its own approach, a decorative tree or two, and shallow steps leading up to the main doors. At first-floor level is the kind of balcony designed for a dictator's triumphs. The vast and pilastered block projects brute power. Behind it is University Square, and Magheru Boulevard which runs parallel to Calei Victoriei.

When demonstrations broke out again in Timişoara on 20 December, crowds gathered in support throughout this central area of Bucharest. At 6 p.m. Ceauşescu held a meeting with the chiefs of the Securitate and the army. Afterwards he broadcast, using the hoary jargon that Hungarian and 'imperialist circles and foreign-espionage agencies' had fomented this unrest. True to form, he decided to stage a ceremony of mass applause, bussing in thousands of supposedly loyal workers to cheer as usual while he addressed them. On the morning of the 21st a crowd of eighty thousand densely packed the area in front of the Central Committee building. Ceauşescu appeared on the balcony. Before he launched into his speech, some unidentifiable noise close by startled him. All over the country, television viewers were then suddenly confronted by a momentarily blank screen. By the time that the picture was normal again, the crowd had taken the initiative with chants of the separate syllables of Timişoara and 'Down with the murderers!' Visibly at a loss in the face of angry barracking on this scale, Ceauşescu paused, and Elena, standing behind him, could be heard exhorting him to raise the cost of living allowances. Stuttering a few more sentences, he came to a halt. The realization finally dawned in all its implications that he was the object of general hatred and he stood there open-mouthed but reduced to speechlessness, psychologically collapsing in the face of reality. Capturing the man's inner thoughts as reflected in the facial expression, the television film sequence of this moment offers dramatic insight not only into this particular character but into the whole nature of tyranny.

Both sides now consolidated. That afternoon and evening, revolutionaries built barricades around the Intercontinental Hotel. Taking up positions around Palace Square, and blocking access to it, the army and Securitate cordoned off the Central Committee building with Ceauşescu still inside it. At about 7 p.m. they opened fire on the barricade. About another hundred people were killed. Exhorting the army to regain control of the streets, the Ceauşescus were to spend that night in the Central Committee building, within sound if not sight of the gunfire. Among close advisers with them were Bobu, Manescu and General Postelnicu. Recalled to Bucharest from Timişoara where he had been co-ordinating repression, General Stanculescu seems to have been the first to realize that life-and-death decisions were at hand. His movements are hard to reconstruct. According to one story, he too spent the night in the Central Committee building. In his own version he denies this but admits to returning home and calling for a doctor who as a stratagem put his leg into a plaster cast, whereupon he presented himself on the following morning to the Ceauşescus as someone more or less disabled.

Cleared off the square by the army the previous night, hundreds of thousands of people converged there on the morning of the 22nd. A bloody outcome seemed certain, when in mid-morning news broke that General Milea, the Minister of Defence, was dead; by his own hand according to first rumours, but on orders of Ceauşescu in later accounts. The army almost immediately went over to the revolution. The crowd surged towards the entrance of the Central Committee building. To escape the impending lynching, Stanculescu escorted the Ceauşescus up on to the roof, where he had summoned a helicopter. Accompanied only by Bobu and Manescu, faithful retainers to the end, the Ceauşescus flew off. Plaster cast and all, Stanculescu had timed his switch of sides with split-second accuracy.

Lasting several hours, the sudden power vacuum drew into it the political and intellectual establishment. Those with pretensions to power and office hurried to the three centres of action, the Central Committee building, the Ministry of Defence and the television centre, circulating between them according to the dictates of the minute. By car the journey between the Central Committee building and the television centre is a good half-hour. In a continuous scramble careers were determined then and there through combinations of transport, chance and acquaintanceship; the lucky man had to be in the right place at the right time. At five o'clock on the 22nd, the National Salvation Front met on the first floor of the Central Committee building. Its principal personalities were Iliescu as chairman, Dimitru Mazilu as vice-chairman, Petre Roman, Silviu Brucan, General Militaru, and General Guşe, now the Chief of Staff.

Much has been made of the conjuring out of nowhere of this phantom body, whose purpose seemed like a distant echo of the Popular Democratic Front of 1945 which had put paid to democratic hopes. Conspiracy theories notwithstanding, it appears certain that this handful of men with actual or prospective power constituted themselves only that afternoon into an impromptu committee, in order to have the mechanism for eventual taking or sharing of the posts of government.

In further response to the power vacuum, shooting broke out in the centre of Bucharest, in Palace Square where the monuments were damaged and the National Library was burnt out with the loss of its entire collection of incunabula and printed books. The television centre was also subjected to heavy firing. In the next forty-eight hours about 800 people were killed. Six months later Iliescu was to say that 1033 deaths had been verified, though the figures from several provincial cities were still to come. Who was doing this shooting, whether there were any concerted plans or orders behind it, remain riddles. Common sense indicates that the Securitate or special units were making a last-ditch stand. Military groups on the loose and trigger-happy revolutionaries may in addition have been mistaking each other for conspirators.

Like fugitives on the run, transferring from helicopter to hijacked car, the Ceauşescus were eventually cornered at about the same time that the National Salvation Front was holding its first meeting. They were escorted to a military barracks at Tirgovişte, only fifty miles from Bucharest. It is surprising that they had not prepared an escape route back to some capital like Tehran where they were welcome. Nicu and Zoia Ceauşescu were arrested that afternoon, as were the Minister of the Interior Tudor Postelnicu, Bobu and Manescu and a few others. Sure that the outbreak of firing was the work of Securitate sharpshooters, Brucan credits himself with cross-questioning the 'slippery' General Vlad, as he calls him, until he too was arrested.

The news of Ceauşescu's arrest was broadcast only on the evening of the 23rd. Random shooting still continued all over Bucharest. Next day Iliescu and his supporters on the National Salvation Front decided that the Ceauşescus should be put before a military tribunal, sentenced and summarily executed. Miraculously free from his plaster cast, General Stanculescu took charge of the arrangements at Tirgovişte. A film of these rigged proceedings reveals Ceauşescu and his wife rejecting all accusations against them in the spirit of outraged innocence. Misplaced as it was, their courage at such an hour was undeniable, fortified perhaps by the presence in the small courtroom of Stanculescu. He owed them everything, and they may have hoped that this favourite of theirs would devise some trick of a happy ending. In a classic drama of betrayal, the film shows Stanculescu going to great lengths to avoid catching the eye of either the Ceauşescus. Condemned, holding hands, they were led down into the courtyard of the barracks, where the firing squad shot them.

Ceauşescu was the one and only communist leader in 1989 with the will to order violence against his own people. His fate suggests that the others had been right to restrain the temptation to take a similar course. The political process everywhere else had split the state from the party, crippling the latter by removing its power base. In Romania, as a consequence of violence and the need to restore order, the military and security apparatus simply changed hands from Ceauşescu to Iliescu. So the man who had long been heir apparent succeeded after all, and he found it very little trouble to arrange the election necessary in order to ascribe to himself new-found democratic credentials.

Ion Caramitru has the good looks and easy manner of the famous actor that he is, and head of the National Theatre as well. The house on Rosetti Street

345

with his office on the ground floor had been presented by the party to Zoia and Nicu Ceauşescu. It is within walking distance of Palace Square. Set in a leafy garden, it is luxury itself by local standards. Under the old regime, members of his family had been imprisoned, but Caramitru was protected by his reputation, and had only been called in by the Securitate for interrogation.

At midday on 21 December he had flown in from Cluj, to hear Ceauşescu's last speech being relayed over the loudspeakers at the airport. The city was already full of buses bringing into the centre special forces and Securitate. The crisis was evidently mounting. Living behind Piaţa Romana to the north of Palace Square, he drove home, changed into a tracksuit and 'I went out and did not return for five days'. The area was blocked off, and further divided into two by armoured cars, to prevent approach to the Central Committee building or the University beyond it. Recognizing him, teenagers asked him to join them and the revolution, and he in turn began to recruit older people. Many of these were actually trying to persuade the young to leave this danger zone. He supposes them to have been Securitate agents in ordinary clothes. In his opinion, the order to open fire came from Ilie Ceauşescu, a brother of Nicolae who was a Securitate general.

'They started to shoot only at night. They arrived in lorries and large cars, running down some people. By one in the morning they blocked the other streets off the Palace Square. I believed then that they wanted to kill everybody, but after a couple of hours they disappeared. I spent that night roving around. Between six and seven on the following morning, the 22nd, people started arriving. The subway had never stopped running. They had prepared placards and started to take to the streets.

'I had promised my wife and my mother to call them every half an hour, on a public phone near the place where I was basing myself. I had lots of coins. I called my wife up between ten and half past and she said, Something strange is up, on television the speaker is saying that General Milea has committed suicide and that he is a traitor. She placed the receiver against the television set so that I could listen. I immediately realized that the army would join us. It was the key. I went straight up to a fat man bulging in his uniform, a major or colonel, with four or five armoured cars behind him blocking the street, and I told him, They've killed the army chief. That's not true, he replied. He got into the armoured car, he may have telephoned or found out somehow, but he then climbed out and reversed the machine gun saying, It is true. We have no other orders, I am at your disposal, what are we to do?'

Taking over these armoured cars, Caramitru and hangers-on drove straight down the boulevard to the television centre. On the way he spotted the helicopter flying out over the city, as well as another small aircraft which was scattering leaflets warning against foreign and Western agents. At the television centre, he took over Studio Four. 'Mine was the first voice to he heard on it – a romantic tale!' Into the studio came a highly nervous Mircea Dinescu. 'He was the only writer among us and I told him that he had to put together some words for the people. He did. It was a very simple declaration, to ask for a cease-fire, and that the army join the revolution.' That first declaration was about one o'clock in the afternoon. Hearing that heavy fire had broken out in front of the Royal Palace, Caramitru left the studio.

'After that, Iliescu, General Militaru, Petre Roman, Brucan and others gathered there in Studio Four to read the communiqué they had drafted in the Central Committee building where they had been until then. Iliescu had practically been taken out of his home, he wasn't on the street. It was our innocence, let's call it, that we did not say we were going to organize the Government and take power. Nobody had that sort of inspiration. I am an actor. I had no conception of myself as President or anything of the sort.' It is his conviction that Iliescu came to power with the support of the army and the Securitate and second-echelon party apparatchiks because he offered them a chance to survive. 'Mazilu had a Ten-Point Programme. They had been waiting for something to erupt although they could not have guessed Ceauşescu's stupid move in organizing the mass meeting around the Central Committee building a few days after Timişoara.'

Back in Palace Square, Caramitru saw about ten tanks around the Central Committee building firing their machine guns at the Royal Palace. There was little chance of killing any terrorists who might have been inside its thick walls. Meanwhile the National Library was on fire because Ceauşescu's bodyguard had its quarters in a building to its rear, and the exchange of shots had set alight adjacent buildings. 'Such a military mistake made me desperate. I went up to the balcony of the Central Committee building, where everything was as Ceauşescu had left it. The microphone was still set up, with a TV bus for outside broadcasting below. I took the microphone and spent twenty minutes trying to appeal to the army to stop firing. Then we organized a group of soldiers and volunteers. Late in the evening, about nine or ten, we managed to stop them.'

And who was firing at the army?

'That is the question. The evidence has been destroyed. Hundreds of terrorists were reported, but all of a sudden there is nobody at all.'

Going back to the television centre, he was to spend the night there. 'People kept arriving to announce that they were joining the revolution. Most of them were former Securitate people and church people. We tried to be selective. We could spot all sorts of lies as people made out that they had been dissidents for years when they had been at Ceauşescu's beck and call. But we

347

didn't identify them all and in the end we couldn't stop them. When Nicu Ceauşescu was brought in, I told him that he was guilty for not preventing his father's actions. Someone had stabbed him with a knife in the stomach but he was scared rather than hurt.'

The day was still not over. During that evening, Caramitru heard that he had been appointed to the National Salvation Front, one of the eleven members of the Executive Committee. 'I wanted the historical political parties to return to a new parliamentary system. I used to argue that the National Salvation Front was just an administration in the transition period until the May general elections. At the end of January they had a vote on whether to convert the Front into a political party. I was to be President of this new party. For me it was a moment of truth. I was the only one who had never been a member of the Communist Party. Now I understood, and I refused. On the 22nd they had needed me. I had been used as a screen.'

A burly genial figure, Octavian Andronic had been a cartoonist and then a news editor for *Informaţia*, a party newspaper. The offices are in a side-street off Palace Square. On the 21st he had left for a meeting at the television centre. 'I was thrilled and shocked at what I heard. Nobody could understand what was going on during Ceauşescu's address nor why transmission was interrupted. In fact a small cracker, a petard, had exploded. People wondered where the loudspeaker was, they scattered and dispersed in waves. The operator of the television camera was on a platform up at the level of the balcony, and when the crowd hit this platform he lost his footing. The camera was then turned towards the sky which was all that we could see for a few minutes. This whole accident followed from the little firework, which of course someone had exploded on purpose to create confusion. Ceauşescu did not know how to respond. Transmission returned after a couple of minutes. All the written slogans were disappearing as you looked. I think that to the end of his life Ceauşescu never understood what was going on.'

That night Andronic stayed at University Square until about two in the morning, and then he wrote up an account of the day's events. Around 8.30 a.m. on the 22nd, he was out again on Magheru Boulevard, watching people arriving in huge numbers. Youths had draped themselves in the national flag with the communist emblem cut out of its centre. 'Everything broke apart when they heard of the death of General Milea. Militia and soldiers melted away and everybody headed towards the Central Committee building. I saw how scared the soldiers were. Ceauşescu attempted once more to speak to the people, he shouted warnings on the loudspeaker, but the crowd was yelling accusations at him and he withdrew hurriedly to the roof, to his helicopter. My impression is that at that moment neither leaders nor the public could foresee the possibility of changing the system. I myself did not dare hope that we could do more than replace the head.

'At about half past twelve, I had the idea of rushing out the first free newspaper. We changed the name to *Libertatea*. I had not written my account of the previous day for publication but now I used it under the title "Jurnal Imediat!" It was all an unconscious action. We did not have time to reflect that if Ceauşescu were to return most of us would be shot. But some of the staff were afraid and slipped away. The press is on the premises and the printers were terrific, they did the best they could without a break. We got the paper out in just thirty minutes. Then I went to the television centre to publicize it.' Iliescu was there, already recognized as the leader, according to Andronic, and conducting himself as such.

I have a copy of this issue of *Libertatea*. Its headlines cover most of the front page: 'Citizens, Romanian Brothers! We won! The Dictator has been overthrown.'

Nicolae Dide is a deputy in parliament, leader of a splinter party. On the morning of the 21st, he had been in Braşov making a film set in 1944. The order came that their period weapons could not be taken out on location that day. Watching television, he decided to drive to Bucharest, arriving just in time to build barricades. The chairs and tables from the Dunarea restaurant in front of the Intercontinental had already been removed for that purpose. With others, he broke into Ministries around the square, seizing four or five vehicles to be incorporated into the barricades. Tanks then closed in from all directions. Water cannons and tear gas were finally followed by bullets. He also recalls lines of troops advancing on foot. The first line consisted of men with riot shields and sticks; among them were unarmed men grabbing and carrying off revolutionaries, as it turned out to Jilava prison. In the second line were the troops who fired, some of whom were in civilian clothes.

By three in the morning, everybody had gone home. Dide and his group from the Intercontinental reassembled towards 7 a.m. in front of the Ministry of Agriculture. He too recalls the moment around half past ten when the officer opposite him called him over to his armoured car to say that he wanted to withdraw. Dide was to organize safe passage for these troops by opening up a space ten metres wide between them and the crowd. 'It was about a quarter past eleven when people realized that no obstacle stood in front of them. We found in the Central Committee building arms and ammunition with which the guards could have stood a siege, but they did not try to prevent us storming in. On the contrary, they placed themselves at our disposal. Inside, there were troops from the Ministry of Defence. Room by room, we took control of the building.

'One soldier said, Come with me and I will show you where the Prime Minister is. Five of us went with him up to the sixth floor, into a room where four or five advisers were standing around a table with Dascalescu. That was his office and he was on the telephone, giving instructions to release political prisoners. One of us asked, Why so late in the day, Mr Dascalescu? Dascalescu was trembling. He answered, I never in my life agreed with Ceauşescu. He was arrested, with others then in the building, Constantin Dinca the deputy prime minister, General Postelnicu, and two of Ceauşescu's advisers, Silviu Curticeanu and Ion Nicolceoiu. Our group took only Dascalescu. We put him in a room until about four o'clock, when we forced him on to the balcony to announce that he and his government were resigning. I was surprised to see how scared he was to go out on that balcony. He kept shifting his eyes midway between the door and the balcony before being obliged to take the loudspeaker.

'All the prisoners were taken to the second floor and held in the library. Their hands were tied with wire, except for Dinca who had a weak heart and was allowed to lie on a bed in another room. The headquarters of the revolution was on the second floor, in Curticeanu's office. General Guşe and General Vlad were there, issuing and receiving orders. Supervising the two generals were a group of eight of us, Milionescu, Christina Chontea, Dan Robulescu, myself and the others. In the afternoon Iliescu arrived and that was the point when we lost the Revolution. We gave it to him not because we wanted to but because we were not good at revolution. For about two hours we had been an alternative government, the first government of the Revolution. When Iliescu and company entered the building, they spread out. Iliescu and Voican-Voiculescu went up to the second floor. At that moment we were on the first floor and General Gheorghe Voinea appeared. He said, I want to talk to the revolutionary political structure. All of us remained rooted on the spot. None of us had any conception of political structure. At that moment Petre Roman stepped up from behind us, to say, We are here. And he took General Voinea off to meet up with Iliescu and his friends to form the Committee of the National Salvation Front and then they went off to television. General Voinea was a part of it. And that's the way they did it.'

Prominent in the throng of place-seekers was Ilie Verdeţ, the husband of Ceauşescu's third sister, Reghina. In the old days he had been a member of the Central Committee and the Politburo, and Prime Minister. As a result of the usual personality conflicts, by 1984 he had been forced to resign from all these positions, remaining a member only of the party's Financial Control Commission. Chain-smoking, and punctuating his conversation with the up-and-down beats of a massive index finger, he is the epitome of the old-style communist, unregenerate in spite of everything. There was a popular movement but it was against totalitarianism which he maintains has nothing to do with communism. And naturally there were plots. Hungarians and other foreign infiltrators were at the bottom of it. Sixty bodies were never reclaimed in Timişoara, he asserts, while in Debrecen there is a monument glorifying those killed defending Pastor Tökes. Without foreign intrusion the change would not have been bloody.

People were admittedly discontented but it had been 'colossally stupid' of Ceauşescu to appear on that balcony. He should have offered political solutions not propaganda. 'He himself organized December the 21st but by the 22nd people had organized themselves and it was impossible to stop them. There was a period after midday on the 22nd without leadership. Around two o'clock individuals were promoting themselves on television and those who did so became leaders of the National Salvation Front.'

The Central Committee balcony was the alternative arena for self-projection into leadership. Verdeţ had his opportunity. Between midday and five o'clock, he says, 'I was just sitting there. Fortunately I knew many of the demonstrators, patriotic guards, workers and so on. During those hours, I talked to the crowd in the square, asking them to be rational and calm, to avoid bloodshed, which was no longer necessary now Ceauşescu had left. I met Iliescu and his team when they arrived. And then he addressed the masses and afterwards they all went into a room and organized this Front, which was announced on radio and television afterwards. The mass movement created the Front, not the Front the mass movement.' They did not invite him to join the Front and he claims that he did not request it.

'In the week I spent inside the Central Committee building, it did not seem like the unfolding of history but just a lot of people not doing anything very precise. Since General Guşe and General Vlad were there, in constant contact with their forces, they were able to guarantee a power base and take steps to avoid the spreading of conflict.'

But while they were co-ordinating their forces, the shooting was continuing?

'By uncontrolled forces. But who? The consensus inside the Central Committee building was that the shooting had to be stopped as a precondition to whatever political steps were to come. I was not afraid for myself. The fear felt by everyone with a political reputation was that a civil war threatened unless order was re-established.'

Except for Caramitru, members of the Front were old communists like himself, and disappointment that they elbowed him out is discernible. 'I don't want to defend Ceauşescu or justify him, he did what he did,' Verdeţ says, 'but without the army's support nothing could have happened. I cannot say even now if Milea was murdered or he killed himself. The facts are controversial. The National Salvation Front decided that he killed himself. That was the first version. That is why he was buried with such pomp and ceremony. The other version, that he was killed, implied a murderer, and the accusation requires proof.'

As for Ceauşescu's death, 'That was not a trial but a masquerade.' Verdeţ's proposal had been to annul the National Salvation Front, to call a special session of parliament to deprive Ceauşescu of his functions as Head of State and First Secretary of the party, and then arrest him and put him on trial. This put paid to any prospect he might have had of advancement through the National Salvation Front. Was he obliquely trying to save his brother-in-law? He assumes a judicious air. 'The haste with which he was dispatched suggests to me that some people, not only Romanian but foreign, had an interest in making him disappear. Ceauşescu's biggest mistake was to be against Moscow. If he had taken another stance towards Moscow he'd probably still be alive, in much the same position as Zhivkov.'

In the process of coming to power, Iliescu co-opted Petre Roman into the National Salvation Front, and then appointed him Prime Minister. The choice required no explanation. Aged forty-two, debonair and personable, Petre Roman was a professor at the Polytechnic. He knew Iliescu professionally. He knew everyone. It is said that Zoia Ceauşescu had been much taken with him. His father Valter Roman had held the rank of general in the International Brigades during the Spanish Civil War, becoming a communist celebrity as well as a member of the Romanian Central Committee. In his memoirs, Silviu Brucan says that through the father he had known the son since student days. Roman claims to have joined the Front by accident but Martyn Rady, in his masterly account *Romania in Turmoil*, considers this implausible. 'Roman was a close associate of Ion Iliescu and his inclusion at the inaugural meeting of the Front suggests the degree of influence which Iliescu had already succeeded in accumulating.' In a nutshell, such are Romanian politics.

By the time I met Roman, Iliescu had forced him out of office and ditched him. Roman has a political party of his own, its headquarters in a turn-of-the-century mansion within a walled park in an exclusive quarter of the city. Until recently it had been the Securitate document centre. Elegantly tailored clothes and handmade shoes seemed to match perfect English and French acquired as a student in France. In him, the Nomenklatura had slipped smoothly into the jet set.

At the beginning of December, he was carrying on with his job in the conviction that although communism was exhausted, its overthrow through popular uprising was inconceivable. The party's power was absolute. At the news of Timişoara he proposed that he and his colleagues sign a protest, but they refused. Although the Christmas break had begun, on the morning of the 22nd he went to the Polytechnic and from there set off with some students in the direction of the Central Committee building.

The movement of the crowd brought him to within a hundred metres of the entrance. From below he glimpsed the Ceauşescus appearing on the balcony, only to withdraw and then depart by helicopter. Fifteen minutes later he was pressing forward next to the bus with facilities for outside broadcasting. Inside it were several young men already relaying anti-Ceauşescu slogans. One of these was a former student of his, and he wanted Roman to speak. So in the very first wave, he was helped and pushed into the building. He went straight up to the balcony. Microphones there then had to be connected to the loudspeakers of the bus. After that, 'I uttered the few sentences which have become famous,' – these proclaimed that the dictatorship was dead and that the people had taken power. Those around him then led him to a room specially equipped for television broadcasting, and there he wrote a statement. But the equipment could not be made to work. Into that room came General Voinea, the senior officer of the military unit positioned in the square. Voinea provided a cameraman and then commandeered a car into which he and Roman and six others crammed, in order to deliver the tape in person to the television centre. Once in the studio, in fact, he read the statement live. Iliescu then made his entry and listened to Roman elaborating the statement.

General Voinea drove him on to the Ministry of Defence. It is said that as Ceauşescu climbed into his helicopter he had appointed Stanculescu as the Minister of Defence to succeed Milea. This has never been clarified. 'The fact is that we simply entered the Ministry as representatives of the revolution and there we found Stanculescu speaking with Ilie Ceauşescu. I ordered Stanculescu to arrest him on the spot. Knowing nothing about me, Stanculescu none the less obeyed. Ilie Ceauşescu immediately surrendered his side-arms. I later asked Stanculescu why he had obeyed me, and he answered, Because I saw you on the balcony.'

By the time that Roman had returned to the Central Committee building, he had earned the right to be in the inner circle. 'The former top bureaucrats of the communist system were gathered there and I remember how everybody was of the opinion that Iliescu should assume responsibility. Radio Free Europe had an important role in that, because for years it had been presenting him as open-minded and a reformer within the system. Among the old guard, Brucan, General Militaru and so on, I was the only one to have come from the street. General Militaru proposed that the National Salvation Front should be an institution of the state and of the party. When I objected, Brucan said,

What are you doing here? Probably I had been admitted because of my statement on television and because Iliescu knew me through my father, and he had published two scientific books of mine.'

That was the first mention in his hearing of the National Salvation Front. If it had existed earlier, it could only have amounted to some sort of tacit agreement between those involved. The night of the 22nd he spent working on a manifesto for the Front. Gunfire continued unabated. When Roman returned to the television centre the next morning to announce and read out the new manifesto, he himself came under fire. 'We were on the eleventh floor and the shooting was directed against that floor, so they must have known we were there. There was no real investigation into who they were.'

Once you were Prime Minister could you not have ordered one?

'The prosecutor was independent, I did everything I could but the results were completely inadequate. During the shooting we captured about 80 Securitate men from very different parts of the country. After the execution of Ceauşescu, about 800 more were brought in. The investigating prosecutors released them all. It is a real problem. This is the weakest spot in the entire sequence of events and gives rise to the suspicion that something lies hidden behind it.'

The supposition on the day was that those shooting could only be Ceauşescu's defenders. The initial decision had been to segregate the captive Ceauşescu for fear of some attempt to free and reinstate him. 'Stanculescu had contacts in the Ministry of Defence with the unit commander. They had a secret code, to frustrate Securitate bugging. The unit commander put Ceauşescu and his wife into an armoured car, and then continuously changed its position. Any attackers could only have killed the Ceauşescus.'

On the 24th the shooting intensified, but the military was not prepared to undertake an operation which might involve 80,000 soldiers in armoured units, calculating on a ratio of 100 soldiers to deal with each sniper. So a collective and unanimous decision was taken to put Ceauşescu before a military tribunal. Stanculescu and Gelu Voican-Voiculescu then took off by helicopter to attend the tribunal on behalf of the Front.

According to Ion Pacepa, General Militaru was 'one of Ceauşescu's favourite generals'. Trained at the Soviet Military Academy, he was a Soviet loyalist. With evident relish Pacepa goes on to describe how the general fell into a honey-trap, to use the term for seduction by an agent for purposes of espionage. In this case the lady's name is given as Olga. When shown the film shot in secret of Olga and the general, Ceauşescu left the room to vomit, and he tore up the decree he had just signed appointing Militaru to be Minister of Defence. A defecting security chief might have his reasons for unfolding such a tale, but it might also have been true.

Disgraced in 1978, when he was fifty-two, Militaru became Deputy Minister of Industrial Construction for the next six years. By 1989 he had retired, to live in a house between the Piaţa Romana and the busy Calea Dorobantilor. The strong silent type, with very blue eyes, he cross-questioned me at length about whom I was meeting and what they had said, painstakingly noting it down. General Guşe has died, and so has General Voinea; Generals Vlad and Postelnicu are in prison; and as for General Stanculescu, he never commanded troops at any level but was chief of the army budget department. How come Stanculescu is now somewhere in foreign banking? And Militaru plunges into the labyrinth of conspiracy which apparently was Ceauşescu's Romania. The first plot to come his way was in 1966 when he was commanding in Cluj, under General Milea. Ceauşescu was due to visit the city and the plan was simply to detain him. 'Milea was anti-Ceauşescu. You must be clear about that,' he says. But he claims to have argued Milea out of it. The arrest would have been misunderstood. 'Ceauşescu had two faces. To the Soviets he played anti-Western and to the West he played anti-Soviet. The Romanian people felt that he was on the right lines.'

Commanding Bucharest district, Militaru felt that he came to know Ceauşescu close up. Reducing the army's fighting capacity, and strengthening the Securitate at its expense, Ceauşescu antagonized the military leadership, in particular General Ion Ioniţa, then Chief of Staff. What with special forces, the Securitate came to be 150,000 strong, he says. A military plot under Ioniţa's leadership started in 1982, with a parallel civilian plot under Iliescu. 'I was the link between these two groups,' Militaru says. 'We were due to remove him through a *coup d'état* in 1984 when he was going to visit the Federal Republic of Germany. Someone betrayed us. Who, and how, is only supposition, but we started to be like belled cats.' None the less plans continued to be elaborated, the last of which would have involved smuggling weapons in from Ankara early in 1990.

While standing in a bread queue with General Ioniţa, Militaru first heard that Gorbachev had become General Secretary, which both of them interpreted as positive for Romania. By 1989 the level of hatred for Ceauşescu was as high internally as it was externally. The Letter of Six sent to Radio Free Europe, he says, was a warning from the Iliescu group of plotters. What Ceauşescu should have done was to take the opportunity of the party congress in November to stand down, and had he done so, he would still be alive.

If really there had been anything worthy of the name of conspiracy, it added up to very little. 'The revolution started absolutely spontaneously. In those first days in Timişoara we had no idea what was going on.' On the 16th, a

355

Securitate agent with whom Militaru was in contact arrived to say that if he left home, he would place his life in danger. He then telephoned a nephew who was an army officer in Tirgu Jiu, but the wife answered that he had been called to his unit because of the events in Timişoara. Guşe, Ioan Coman and Stanculescu heedlessly gave orders to repress a popular uprising. He makes the point that if the Hungarians had wanted to foment anti-Romanian violence they would have exploited cities and districts which had a far higher proportion of Hungarians than Timişoara.

'On 22 December I was listening to the radio. Milea was not the type of man to commit suicide, and from the very first report onwards I did not believe that he had. When I took over the army I checked the record. I did not find any order that he had given to open fire against the civilian population. On the contrary, he had opposed Ceauşescu on the grounds that no regulation allowed the army to take any such measures. The news on the radio had been falsified to put the whole blame on Milea and to provoke the army to take revenge on the radicals by plunging Romania into a blood bath.'

Putting on his uniform, he hurried to the television centre, which is close to his home. There he issued an appeal in emotional language, addressing generals by name, and ordering them to cease firing and withdraw their troops to barracks. After Milea's death, Guşe became senior officer: 'He did not exactly hesitate but he proved himself very weak. After what he had done in Timişoara, he felt guilty or scared. There was a real crisis of leadership in the army. From the night of the 22nd onwards, Guşe was not in the Ministry of Defence at the head of the army but with Iliescu in the Central Committee building. He did not take control. And please remember that Stanculescu had also been at Timişoara, he was very close to the Ceauşescus and in the good graces of the Securitate. Some authoritative people claimed that Stanculescu was sent to Timişoara as Ceauşescu's eyes and ears.'

Militaru says that Stanculescu returned from Timişoara during the night of the 21st to the 22nd and on arrival went to a military hospital where his leg was plastered. In the early hours he went home. A Securitate car came to drive him to the Central Committee building and Ceauşescu thereupon told him to take command of the army. He is curt: 'A soldier obeys orders and if not, he must be prepared to face the consequences. He does not bandage his foot.'

In a comparable procedure, Iliescu verbally nominated Militaru himself to be Minister of Defence during the afternoon of the 24th. That night there was a meeting in the Ministry at which Stanculescu proposed to organize everything for the trial of the Ceauşescus. 'They had it in mind to condemn and execute them. Nobody asked me if I agreed with the execution or not. I declared in public that a trial was absolutely necessary, but I would have condemned them to life imprisonment, to be shown to the public on film standing in line for their daily bread.

'After the trial and execution were seen on television, the intensity of the shooting halved. By New Year's Eve it was all over. Don't ask me who the terrorists were. Whether they were Arabs or Russians or who, God knows. And it doesn't matter because the Securitate were the organizers. I can give you a detail. On the night of the 23rd, the leaders of the Front were in the Ministry of Defence. It would have been enough to kill five of them to stop the revolution in its tracks. Two special armoured cars arrived at the entrance and did not respond when challenged. So the guards opened fire. A few escaped from the armoured cars and ran to seek refuge across the street. The Securitate made a number of such attempts.'

Stanculescu had the last laugh perhaps, when he became Minister of Defence after Militaru resigned on 16 February 1990, though it turned out to be only an interval before his new career as a financier.

Gelu Voican-Voiculescu catapulted himself out of nowhere into a leading role. A geologist by profession, he is well-read in several languages and the extensive library in his house is esoteric indeed, concentrating on Freemasons, Ros-icrucians, Aleister Crowley's black magic and the Zodiac. At one point he discoursed upon the relationship between Nazism, the Cliveden set and the occult. In old days he seems to have been sentenced three times to prison, serving a total of two years. One sentence was apparently passed and served in Hungary. 'I belonged to the passive resistance,' but he adds that his past was 'rather up-and-down'. It had suited prosecutors' purposes, as far as I could interpret it, to twist anti-communist politics into accusations of fraud.

A large man with a trim grey beard, he rolls his eyes while talking fast in a manner suggesting the many mysteries he knows but is not at liberty to reveal. He dearly loves a plot and releases much deep laughter at the uncovering of long-planned wickedness. A rumour that he was himself a Soviet agent pleases him. Once in power, he purged everyone he could with Soviet connections, for example General Militaru, whom he describes as 'the best military brain in the country but hopelessly deformed by a Soviet cast of mind'. Today he himself is ambassador to the PLO in Tunis.

In fact, in Romania there was no question of any clandestine movement. At best, people had hoped that Ceauşescu would soon die and that Iliescu would replace him. 'Many people now boast of conspiracy but that is idle talk. Under the pressure of the security police collective action was impossible. At the last party congress in November, Ceauşescu should have been removed statutorily. Out of fear that some such move might be attempted against him, Ceauşescu had ordered the Securitate to mop up every last opponent.' The flying visit to Tehran was a fatuous mistake. By means of the demonstration on 21 December, Ceauşescu foolishly and finally stage-managed his own downfall.

A few question marks hang in the air. Whoever set off the firework which disconcerted Ceauşescu at the start of his address has never made himself known. Some short circuit of the amplification system then made a din as though tanks were rushing towards the square. And as yet the terrorist phenomenon has no soundly-based explanation.

On the 21st Voican-Voiculescu was in his office close to Palace Square working on a project which had to be completed by the end of the year. Hearing the news on the radio, and then looking out of the window, he went down on to the street out of curiosity, to find that he was gripped by the frenzy of it. 'There were no instigators, only young people shouting like madmen.' In the evening he returned to the Intercontinental and was there as the tanks opened fire and moved in to crush the barricade. Having counted eight casualties taken on stretchers to hospital, he fled.

'Next morning I once more returned, and at about one o'clock I entered the television centre, just like that, someone off the street. By five o'clock I was one of Iliescu's team, and five days later I was deputy Prime Minister. It's almost unimaginable!'

At the television centre he ran into Dimitru Mazilu. He then spotted a cousin of his, who vouched for his spells in prison and allowed the two of them to proceed into the studio. With his Ten-Point Programme, Mazilu was making a bid for power. Winning the jostle for the microphone, Voican-Voiculescu had his chance to speak for a minute and a half, in which time he said that defence committees should be organized, and the Securitate archives taken over. 'Once the studio emptied, everything became completely disorganized, and I heard someone saying, Who is this Iliescu? There he stood. Pushing back a couple of men who escorted him there, I went to protect him. With another young man who had wavy hair and appears in all the photographs, I took Iliescu by the arm and ushered him up to the cameras. He had no idea who I was. It was about a quarter to three, and he told me that we had to keep an eye on the clock, because at five everyone who had a contribution to make to the launching of our revised political life was due to come to the Central Committee and form a National Salvation Front.

'After that, we moved through other rooms, meeting people who had arrived earlier from the Central Committee including Petre Roman and Brucan and Militaru and others whom I did not recognize. The role of the young man with wavy hair and myself was not defined but everyone assumed we were Iliescu's associates. By now it was past three o'clock and Iliescu was saying we had to go to the Ministry of Defence. So we accompanied him in his car. The driver turned out to be one of the two men I'd just pushed away, having no idea that I had never met Iliescu before. He began to apologize. Nobody knew what to expect.' Roman, Brucan and others also drove first to the Ministry and then to the Central Committee building, which they entered through a side-door.

'Inside there was Verdeţ, and with him General Vlad and other veteran communists aspiring to set up a government of their own. Our success lay in having been on television. Iliescu approached them as the master of the situation, and he spoke from the balcony. The crowd was delirious, but it was a shock for him to hear their cries of "No communists!", as he thought that a socialist regime would be replacing Ceauşescu's tyranny. It was painful for him to see his ideals vanish, but his hand was forced and he is an adaptable man. Verdeţ wanted to change nothing at all, arguing that we had a government and a National Assembly and a Central Committee, all of which should be maintained with himself in Ceauşescu's place. Surrounded by us, Iliescu was disposed to act, and thanks to that, Verdeţ could make little headway. It was absolute madness. Quick-witted, Iliescu said that we had to find some breathing space, so we backed away into another room, some sort of office. The young man with wavy hair stood sentry at the door. Everyone wanted to push in. Discussion started. They were all former communists. Petre Roman was the only one to come up with a proposal that all the institutions of the former regime had to be scrapped.

'Iliescu announced that he would be issuing a communiqué, and was going to find somewhere private where he could draft it. At that moment, about seven in the evening, shooting broke out along the corridor, shattering windows. Throughout the building Securitate men were mingling among us, which we couldn't know. It is true that from outside nobody shot at the façade of the Central Committee. People always ask why we were not shot at when we stood on the balcony. On the opposite side of the square, the Royal Palace was under heavy fire. What was this? Out of fear, soldiers were loosing off whole magazines in a single burst. In the corridors it was dark, there was no electricity, nobody knew who was shooting at who. I said to Iliescu, This is a rat-hole and we have to escape. With a leap here and a dive there, we reached the boulevard. I intended to telephone someone who could fetch us in a car. The young man with wavy hair then said that he was a taxi-driver so Iliescu and I got into the back of his car, to return to the Ministry of Defence. Roman, Brucan and the others followed in another car.

'At the Ministry of Defence I recognized General Stanculescu, and I raised with him the question of putting Ceauşescu to death. You understand, everyone there thought I was someone extremely close to Iliescu. The situation remained uncertain, I said, as long as Ceauşescu's whereabouts were unknown. Stanculescu said, They are up at Tirgovişte in a barracks, I am holding them safe. So I answered, Have them shot immediately. He dialled a number and spoke in code to the colonel of the regiment there. Then he turned to me and said, I have given orders. When you say the word, he will be killed. He gave me a three-figure number and I linked up to this colonel, to confirm with him, When I tell you, Resort to the Measure, you are to have Ceauşescu shot.

'We had no great confidence in the people at the Ministry, and we left a revolutionary to keep an eye on them. On the whole, however, they were rather frightened of us, believing us to be better organized than we were. Our success lay in this sort of confusion. So we left the Ministry to return to the television centre. Shedding the former communists, Iliescu was now surrounded by us and by young people, with the exception of Brucan and Mazilu still with his Ten-Point Programme. We issued a radical communiqué that the old institutions no longer existed, that the party and the Central Committee had been suspended, and power was exclusively in the hands of the National Salvation Front. Only at the moment when we signed this communiqué did we learn who all the other signatories actually were. The whole team then appeared on television. We did not appreciate properly that our success lay in the successful exploitation of television. Verdeţ did nothing of the kind.

'We were being chivvied between the television centre and the Ministry of Defence, though no longer the Central Committee building. The young man and I still stuck to Iliescu. I said, There is nothing else for it, we have to kill Ceauşescu. Iliescu replied, We cannot start a new regime of equality and democracy with an execution which has no legal standing, that would be a crime. I wanted to take sole responsibility, to pick up the telephone and give the order to Resort to the Measure. Instead I tested Iliescu out. Yes, I said, you don't want to start your reign with bloodshed. What do you mean, my reign? he asked. The others are afraid to kill him straight away, I said, but it is the right thing to do. Unknown people are shooting at us from all directions, and the army is responding. These people had fled but now they are counter-attacking to eliminate us, and I told Iliescu that the fate of Allende lay in store for him. He insisted that we had to have a Nuremberg trial and that anything else would be criminal. I had no such sentiments. Ceauşescu had set off from Bucharest in the hope of reaching a radio station. Under arrest in the barracks, he kept repeating that the army was with him and he intended to appeal to the nation. On the 24th, when we had almost lost, and the television was in danger of being captured, I finally made Iliescu realize that it was either us or them.

'That morning, someone proposed to hold a special military tribunal with an emergency procedure and a summary judgement. On condition that there was due sentencing, everyone agreed to Ceauşescu's execution. A short decree was then drafted to that end. I was delighted that my opinion had been accepted. Someone then proposed that an emissary be sent on our behalf, and everyone turned to me. I said I would go with General Stanculescu. We organized the technical details for the next day, choosing the prosecutor and the lawyers. We set off in a convoy of three helicopters with yellow markings to signal to anti-aircraft batteries not to fire. At Tirgovişte we went through with this make-believe of a trial. Whatever people in the West may say, from a formal point of view this was all to the good. I wanted everything to be over within a quarter of an hour, but proceedings lasted fifty-five minutes.

'Remaining coherent, Ceauşescu dominated everyone else there. Not Elena, she was wretched, stupid, she could not even speak grammatically. During the trial he was always giving her caresses, but her reactions were thoroughly crude. At least he had guts, I was even able to admire him; he was a tyrant, a Mussolini, not to be written off as a mere madman. Right to the end he believed that the presence of Stanculescu meant that the proceedings amounted to a *pièce montée*. Only when their hands were tied did they realize for certain that they were going to die. The officer in charge of the firing squad had been attending in the courtroom, and he waited for orders to draw up his men and go through the ceremony. The Ceauşescus were brought down the staircase and as soon as they emerged into the yard the men could not wait and they opened fire and the Ceauşescus were riddled with bullets. The film everyone saw is a fiasco because the cameraman was taken by surprise and could film only the last few bullets, by which time the Ceauşescus had already fallen to the ground. It led to speculation that the film had been faked, which is ludicrous. Unable to master themselves, the soldiers had simply fired point-blank. Next day when I stepped out on to the street, the firing had dwindled and I realized at last that we held power. Had Ceauşescu been dragged through house arrest and prison like Zhivkov or Honecker, the revolution might well have ended differently. We had imposed ourselves.'

32

'A LACK OF POLITICAL WILL'

A thriller writer could lift a good deal of significant detail straight from General Leonid Shebarshin. With his pipe and his Labrador and tweed jacket, and his virtually faultless English, not to mention Farsi learned as station chief in Tehran, he seems more like a British regimental buff than the spymaster he actually was. After a lifetime in the KGB, he was appointed head of its First Main Directorate in February 1989, surviving in the post until September 1991. He was therefore the official responsible for seeing that Gorbachev received intelligence from the Soviet republics and from abroad. In the aftermath of the August coup, he had to report to an outraged Gorbachev on his own boss Kryuchkov, suddenly held in prison as one of the plotters. For twenty-four hours, Shebarshin replaced Kryuchkov. When Vadim Bakatin then replaced him, he resigned.

The intelligence-gathering apparatus was formidable indeed. 'We looked at our country through a foreigner's eyes. We had our sources and suppliers of information outside the country, reporting on plans and personalities. Supplementary sources included the Chief Intelligence Directorate of the General Staff of the Armed Forces known as GRU, and then the Academy of Sciences and the institutes whose members were writing specialist papers. All the journalists of the Soviet press were controlled by the party. Through the International Department of the Central Committee we had feedback from all our communist friends abroad, and this went to Gorbachev. Very perceptive and far more experienced than Gorbachev, our communist friends were conscientiously watching developments. In the final stages of my career, I tried to be in touch with people in the know and I read reports from all over the world by very competent people. I must say that none of them could predict how things were going to develop but overall the picture was not favourable. Some premonition was in the air that unless a remedy was found – what kind of remedy I did not know – things would develop as they have.'

Influential as the KGB was, Shebarshin maintains, it was still only the party's auxiliary arm. Just as the role of the KGB is overestimated, so the military–industrial complex was underrated. 'If a KGB man became a member of the Politburo his standing there rose according to his place in the KGB. That is something that cannot be condensed into words.' Though not himself in the repressive directorates of the KGB he says bluntly that 'The element of fear never disappeared. Every year in my country can be 1937. Democracy is not irreversible. Authority is not respected but it is feared, and the purpose of authority is to put society under its control.'

In 1985 the country was indeed stagnating and reform was necessary. Economic, social and political reform. Education needed complete restructuring. The country could not compete with the West. A psychological attitude had developed since 1917 that the human will could mould nature and history into whatever shape was appropriate. 'I am a poor student of Marx, I am afraid,' he says, rather engagingly. Absolute belief in the supremacy of the human will seems to him to be a link between Soviet and American outlooks.

In a Pavlovian reaction after thirty years in the profession of espionage, Shebarshin cannot resist lashing out at the Western enemy. 'There are many things I do not like about the United States and Europe. It confirms my suspicions when I hear Americans say that without their efforts the Soviet Union would still be a superpower. I have grounds for knowing that they did everything possible to destroy the Soviet Union economically and politically. They were very conscious of the fact that destabilization would cause more bloodshed. Not cannibals, they are businesslike people, they did what was in their national interest.' Since war was never a realistic prospect in the nuclear age, the West skilfully picked trade as an arena of competition in which its superiority was assured.

Which factor counted for most in the collapse, systemic internal deficiencies or Western anti-Soviet policies? Eliding opinions which are sometimes contradictory in nuance and substance, he is as eager to blame as to analyse. 'The party in 1985 was almighty. It concentrated in its hands whatever power there was, without rivals or competition. Quite local and supported only by the West, the dissidents did not determine the agenda at all. No task was easy in the Soviet Union, you could not change the culture of so huge a country overnight.' He professes a respect for Sakharov and Solzhenitsyn. 'It should have been possible to jettison totalitarianism over a period of time through careful consideration of ways and means. I do not believe that Gorbachev thought his reforms were going to destroy communism. I accept that he was trying to resurrect it.'

By the time that Shebarshin took over the First Main Directorate, 'Anyone could see that things were not moving in the right direction. I was presiding over the disintegration of the empire.' His calm voice acquires a frozen sarcastic anger. Receiving the vital information from the KGB, Gorbachev did not study it and draw conclusions. Without proper interpretation, even the best information has its limits. 'I don't think that he took an overview, or that he cared very much. He was a party man, a functionary. His education was defective. He used to boast that he had two higher degrees, in law and agriculture. He might have made a very efficient Minister of Agriculture. And he may not be telling the truth, you wouldn't expect a politician like him to do so. He is a master of excuses. He and Yakovlev and a whole host of them proved to be not what they had seemed.'

Nationalism was the danger in 1989 and he warned Gorbachev of it. Since 1945, émigré organizations and the CIA had been fuelling its destructiveness. 'The formation of Popular Fronts in all the republics was definitely no coincidence. The KGB was trying to find out if there were any organizers.' Beginning to describe the KGB technique of setting up dummy organizations for purposes of control, as the Popular Fronts were intended to be, he caught himself up and stopped. 'I thought bloodshed would start in Georgia but before that came Karabakh, Azerbaijan and Tajikistan. Some of the Popular Front people obtained the posts and jobs they wanted but you cannot satisfy entire groups of educated people. Our society was never a very happy one, there were shortcomings in the Soviet Union and through nationalism you had a natural sounding board for them.'

Were your communist friends in the bloc warning you that reform would lead to their downfall?

'Definitely. Throughout Eastern Europe.'

What did you reply?

'Official hypocrisy, based on Gorbachev's circumstances and party statements. Zhivkov, Honecker, Husák, Ceauşescu, were all determined to find ways and means to make Gorbachev see the light: they sensed the approach of something terrible. This picture of perestroika with its common human values influenced public opinion. Any reasonable person hearing a government talking about values common to the whole of humanity must conclude that this government either intends to cheat the whole of humanity or else consists of bloody fools.'

A man for fieldwork, in office Shebarshin travelled to interview his contacts and monitor developments throughout the empire, reporting back to Gorbachev. In April 1989, for example, he headed the delegation of the First Main Directorate of the KGB to East Germany. Colleagues there included Erich Mielke and other correspondents. In January 1990 he visited the Baltic republics. 'I was sent there by Kryuchkov to look with a fresh eye. What I saw appalled me. On my return I predicted to Gorbachev that these liberals were hell-bent on separating from the Soviet Union and that the Russian population there was in for a hard time. The KGB could still have used political methods but my advice to do so was disregarded. I am convinced that those who took armed action in January 1991 did so with Gorbachev's consent. There is an apocryphal story but I can quite believe it, that Gorbachev telephoned Marshal Yazov at the time to ask what was happening. The poor old marshal dropped the handset. That was Gorbachev's style.'

Why did the Soviets give up Eastern Europe but obtain nothing in return?

'Simple. You have to see foreign policy in the context of Gorbachev's internal situation. The country's foundations were badly shaken, the economy was sliding downhill, the party had lost authority. How were you to put a foot down and stand firm? By way of rescuing himself, Gorbachev and his team forfeited their independence in international affairs. Whether in the field of disarmament or in Eastern Europe, they did not try to hold any position, squandering whatever had been accumulated in order to appease their Western partners. It was very easy to be popular. But a policy of compromise must evolve from a position of strength, not weakness. There was no real decision about it, only an escalation of indecision. Even in 1989 they were seriously discussing post-war frontiers and realities, and they were arguing that in the event of Germany uniting, it would have to get out of Nato. That shows how things were breaking down. They were pretending to control events when in fact they were following.' Nobody in the inner party, Shebarshin claims, advocated force. For practical reasons. Force had proved successful in Hungary and Czechoslovakia but its application had to be cyclical, on each occasion a swift interruption to what otherwise passed as normality. The invasion of Afghanistan and the imposition of martial law in Poland introduced continuous violence, which was then damagingly internationalized. Another General Secretary might have resorted to the Soviet troops in the DDR, but that would have run counter to Gorbachev's entire policy.

It is credible that Shebarshin and his directorate provided Gorbachev with the requisite information to make choices in the national interest. In the tradition of the KGB, the implication is also that force would have been acceptable so long as it was 'political', in other words surreptitious, not so flagrant as to arouse superior counter-force. 'The decisive factor,' he concludes, 'was a lack of political will at the centre.'

33

THE LEADING ROLE

Once the satellites had melted like ice in the sun, an ultimate and even existential question faced the Soviet leadership: What was the point of absolute centralized power if not to defend the party-state? With the outer ring of client countries now escaped irretrievably from central control, the inner ring queued untidily for the exit.

It was an article of faith to General Secretaries that their will was supreme. Gorbachev was prepared to consider the 'middle way'. Fixes of the sort encouraged those opposing him to go further. At the next stage in what had to be an escalation of politics, finding himself obstructed or opposed in a committee or at a plenum, instinctively he devised a parallel or substitute channel or institution whereby yes-men were appointed to legitimize his policy and serve his will. The political process became clogged as tests of strength were fought out in mutually exclusive institutions. 'Infantile ruses' poured out of Gorbachev's imagination in the belief that a benevolent central power and an intact Soviet Union were compatible. To the end, he believed the ideology of communism to be independent from the mechanism of force without which that ideology was only one among other theories about human nature and society. Law-based measures entailed the bankruptcy of communism; lawlessness entailed the bankruptcy of Gorbachev and his policies. Here was an either–or dilemma impervious to a middle way or any amount of deals and infantile ruses. Contradictory concepts of totalitarianism and reform were fusing into a single chaos.

By 1990 reform was manifest almost exclusively in economic decline and loss of authority. Gorbachev initially charged ahead energetically. First came the repeal in February of Article Six of the Constitution guaranteeing the party's 'leading role'. Many within the Soviet élite argued that since Gorbachev had encouraged such a measure in the satellites, he could hardly reject it at home but Anatoly Sobchak for one, the mayor of the city soon to revert to its original name of St Petersburg, judged it to be 'the most radical event in our country's life since October 1917'. Gorbachev then sidestepped the

Politburo and Central Committee, in the first case by creating an alternative known as the Presidential Council, and in the second case by purging from it all but 59 of the 412 members, including Ligachev whose career now came to an end, much to Gorbachev's relief. Whole departments of the Central Committee were closed down, and half the permanent staff fired. The Council of Ministers was relabelled a cabinet. Hitherto Chairman of the Supreme Soviet, in effect its Speaker and therefore in charge of the agenda, Gorbachev finally arranged to have himself elected unopposed to the new post of President of the Soviet Union, or Head of State. Into the vice-presidency he railroaded Gennadi Yanayev.

Taken together, these changes appeared to introduce a quite different country, modern and civilized, with a president and parliament, competition and representation. The reality was otherwise. Retaining the position of General Secretary, Gorbachev used the presidency to amass further legislative and executive power. The party-state machinery was still entirely in his hands. The party maintained its cells in the army and the KGB, which even acquired extra powers. Thanks to force of habit and absence of democratic alternative, the party could well survive without Article Six, and even prosper. Arranged democracy was easier to justify than monopoly. 'If we want things to stay as they are, everything will have to change,' says a character in Lampedusa's novel *The Leopard*, who could have been speaking for Gorbachev at this point.

Like Honecker or Ceauşescu, Gorbachev presided over one last party congress, in July. The majority of the 5000 delegates were resentful at the dislocation of the old system. If not they themselves, then colleagues very like them were being deprived of Nomenklatura status and privileges. To them, power-sharing and the market economy were surrenders to the capitalist enemy. At this party congress hardliners made it clear that they were determined to reverse perestroika and all its works. As though to confirm their worst fears, Gorbachev left the congress to greet Kohl and to fly him to the Caucasus to finalize in private their arrangement for the DDR.

Those who took positions against Gorbachev for reforming too fast were matched by those who urged him to reform yet faster. At the head of this group, Yeltsin mobilized what was known as Democratic Russia, a weak and loose coalition of oppositionists, followers of Sakharov, disaffected intellectuals, the young, all without power. Theirs was the politics of gesture, of speechifying and demonstrating. Gorbachev therefore found himself holding a centre against hardliners at one extreme, and Yeltsin and his supporters at the other. To one and all, it was a power struggle, in which the question of reform happened to be the instrument available for attack. A welter of technical and apparently legalistic detail, of debating points and tedious politickings, veiled the immense drama of the impending test of strength.

In old days, rivalry of ambition would have been handled in the Kremlin by conspiracy, leading to a show trial and a bullet. The public at large would have learned of the whole affair only after it was over and done with. In theory Gorbachev should still have been able to overcome what were essentially more challenges against him. Perestroika tied his hands in that he was obliged to allow the proceedings of the party congress to be televised, and millions of people had the unprecedented experience of seeing party leaders heckling and being heckled. In weakening and bypassing the party, Gorbachev had obviously undermined his natural power base but the factor which finally allowed the test of strength to emerge and to dominate everything else arose with the unexpectedness of a summer storm.

For imperial reasons, the distinction between Soviet and Russian had been carefully blurred. Rather than have to bow to Russian conquest, constituent peoples of the Union were supposed to feel liberated at joining the common Soviet cause. To foster the illusion that Russian nationalism had long ago converted into Soviet idealism, alone of all the republics Russia – more properly the Russian Federation of many peoples and ethnic groups – had no Communist Party. Now the transformation of the old rubber-stamp Soviet into the two-tier Congress of People's Deputies and a Supreme Soviet or standing parliament, had to be replicated at the republic's level of government. The election to the supposedly secondary or republic level of government was in March. Neither Gorbachev nor anybody else anticipated that such an election would restore Russia and its identity from the spectral Soviet limbo to which it had been so long confined.

Yeltsin had voted to retain Article Six, a move inconsistent with the democratization he was claiming to stand for. Gorbachev had only to oppose the Baltic States for Yeltsin to affirm his solidarity with them. To head off Yeltsin's campaigning, at the last moment Gorbachev sponsored a Russian Communist Party. Its head, Ivan Polozkov, ran against Yeltsin for the Russian presidency. His victory might well have saved Gorbachev, for the time being at least. But within the space of a few weeks of high political gambling, Yeltsin managed to secure a first walkover election as a deputy to the Russian Congress and then a hard-fought second election among new fellow deputies to become its President. In office, able to dispense patronage, he appointed Ivan Silayev as Russian Prime Minister, and Ruslan Khasbulatov as Speaker.

There were then two Presidents in one country and even in one capital, two parliaments, two governments. On 12 June 1990 Yeltsin used his Russian Congress to pass a declaration of sovereignty. Russian law now claimed supremacy over Soviet law. He was to follow it up by withholding two-thirds of the payments due to be contributed by Russia to the central Soviet budget. When Gorbachev rejected the Shatalin Plan for the Soviet Union, Yeltsin accepted it for Russia, an instant convert to the free market about which he had only the haziest notion. The 'war of laws', this whole ominous counterpoint, seemed like preliminaries to a rerun of 1917 and civil war.

The Baltic States had set a precedent in denying that they had a legitimate Soviet identity. Russia accounted for half the Soviet population and a far greater proportion of its natural resources. Building Russian identity at the expense of the Soviet Union, Yeltsin was prising the state away from the party with a strength not available to a Landsbergis or a Savisaar in their small republics. At the July congress he took the next step dictated by this logic and resigned from the party. 'The atmosphere was extremely tense', as he was to recall in his memoirs, 'and two-thirds of the 5000 people in the hall were feeling negative, but I did not respond to the booing, because everything was very serious by now. I spoke after having thought everything over beforehand, but when I descended from the podium I felt that the eyes of the people in the hall were following me: would I go back to my seat or leave? I left, and I think that put an end to it.' In more senses than one. Expressed another way, the stakes had risen so high that Yeltsin and Gorbachev were equally willing to rearrange the Soviet Union, Russia, the party, nationalism, communism, democracy, the free market and the Cold War and anything else that might advance their ambitions.

The observant Dieter Knötszch, the German schoolmaster resident in Moscow, noted in his diary on 13 October 1990 that unreliable food supplies and threatening rumours had produced impatience, anxiety and aggression. 'In the shop on Vernadskogo people stand in their hundreds, but the tables and shelves are empty. They are waiting for whatever may arrive. A counter is opened and packs of sausages are thrown down on to it. At the sight, people's patience and discipline no longer hold, they rush at the sausages, snatch and grab whatever they can carry off ... the strongest win in this struggle of bodies and elbows, which is waged recklessly but not yet brutally. People with armfuls of sausages arrange themselves in a new queue before the till, to pay. The feeling arises that things cannot go on like this.'

As with the struggle for sausages, so with politics. No institution or agreed structure existed to mediate an acceptable compromise. At least twice in the latter half of the year, Gorbachev and Yeltsin had lengthy private conversations in the Kremlin, in which each was weighing the other's intention, seeking to enforce error, playing for time, interpreting the chances of mobilizing supporters and neutralizing opponents in the same offensive and defensive strategies to tug power in the desired direction.

Yeltsin's brilliance in perceiving that the recovery of Russian identity was his opportunity for an open and popular faction fight was clouded by suspicion of his motives and character. Could a man with a command–administrative career like his carry conviction when he split the party by resigning and declared himself a democrat? Had he not simply colonized an available political space? As supporters rallied either to Yeltsin or to hardline opponents, so Gorbachev had his Democratic Platform, a last-moment attempt to strengthen those who believed that a reformed communism was a practical possibility. At its opening congress in May, one of its founders, Vyacheslav Shostakovsky, intoned the hoariest of formulas, 'We need to create a new kind of party.'

Shostakovsky was Rector of the Moscow Higher Party School, where the high ideological line was hammered out and taught. A writer of speeches and other material for Gorbachev, he has continued to work with him up to the present. 'Stalin used to say that personnel decided everything,' he began, and that had been Gorbachev's intention too. 'Perestroika was by no means aimed at diminishing the military–industrial complex or affecting the militarization of our economy. His talk about democratization was only a slight variation from orthodox communist perceptions. The novelty was to allow elements of election for party secretaries and managers of industrial enterprises. Concluding that old methods were ineffective, he had to use other levers of influence. That was when the hardliners panicked. They were clearly not going to implement Gorbachev's decisions as expressed at the party conference and congresses.'

He has an instructive account of a meeting of the Moscow City Party at which delegates were to be elected for the party conference. Gorbachev was present. People in the hall argued that the names of proposed delegates were well known and required no discussion. Gorbachev disagreed. 'Zaikov as Chairman of the Moscow City Party said, Let's discuss them in alphabetical order. Comrade Abalkin, who had a reputation as an iconoclastic economist, stood up and was questioned. Next Yuri Afanasiev, an even greater iconoclast, was questioned even harder on his attitude to Gorbachev. Then someone with the initial B, after which Zaikov said, That's enough, let's vote. The whole list was accepted unanimously.'

Although the party and the Congress of People's Deputies might seem locked in opposition, this was only the reflection of the more profound faction fight. 'Even after Article Six was removed, the Central Committee still ruled. When the first Congress of the Russian People's Deputies was about to begin, there was a conference of the Soviet Central Committee to which all the Russian deputies who were party members were invited. The first item for discussion was how to prevent Yeltsin being elected Russian President.' Shostakovsky is among those who thinks that the abolishing of Article Six was also a function of the faction fight. Furthermore, 'It was about four months too late as far as the political temperature of society went. Gorbachev and the Central Committee were trying to catch up with developments, for instance the election of Yeltsin and the formation of a new Union.'

Double-think, in George Orwell's famous phrase, helped to destroy the party, and he gives an illustration. Three weeks before Yeltsin's election as a deputy to the Soviet Congress, Shostakovsky spoke to a plenary meeting of the Moscow City Council. 'In the closed part of this session, those present said that we should call on all communists to vote against Yeltsin, this would be a test of communist strength. But this was proposed by people who deep inside realized perfectly well that such a decision would be impossible to implement, and that Yeltsin alone would benefit because those who had been pressured to vote against him would actually vote for him. Everyone was expressing staunch support for what they knew inwardly would never happen. When I spoke, I said that the party was entitled to 100 seats for which it was presenting 100 candidates, an obvious arrangement which must rebound against it. The chairman started to shout about the pass we had come to, if the Rector of the Moscow Higher Party School does not understand why this should be.'

To Shostakovsky, it is all a history of lost opportunities. If only those responsible for bloodshed in the republics had been brought to trial; if only Article Six had been repealed in 1989; if only the army and the KGB had been depoliticized; if only Gorbachev had resigned as General Secretary once he became President; if only there had been a civilized division of the party into its hardliners and Democratic Platform; if only this Democratic Platform had been able to build a bridge to Yeltsin.

Minister of the Interior Vadim Bakatin was another key member of the Democratic Platform. After the August coup, he was given the task of making the KGB accountable, and he has described in his memoirs how this proved impossible. He has assured and athletic looks that might be American. 'I don't claim to be a prophet or a genius, the only things I pride myself on is that earlier than Gorbachev I realized that we should abolish Article Six, and that we should replace the federal Union with something looser. If once and for all we had acknowledged private property, the outcome would have been very different. But it took me a period of two to three years to understand that. Like everybody else, I was saying that everything should be done through the party and by the party alone. Gorbachev never understood the relation between private property, freedom and the prosperity of the state.

'If you analyse Gorbachev's evolution, you see that he had not the slightest idea where perestroika would lead. In his opinion a strengthened party could deal with the economy. Almost every day he used to proclaim his conviction that socialism was the right option – it led to chaos. He concluded that he had to create a multi-party system only when he had to catch up with events.'

Centralized planning meant a constant issuing of decrees and orders whose translation into practice depended on the subjective reaction of party functionaries. 'The role of General Secretary was bound up with Article Six. Gorbachev wanted to compensate by being President, with a Presidential Council, which started its work without offices or staff. Procedure was erratic. The Politburo had rules, the Presidential Council did not. The Presidential Council was supposed to have functioned as the transitional mechanism whereby a presidency could take over the legal and political process of the communist system.

'Without the insistence on unity there would have been no party at all, but I experienced in person how deceptive unity was. My suggestion when we were preparing for the 1990 congress was to scrap a single party in favour of a union of republican parties. This meant consenting to the independence of the Georgian party for instance, or the Lithuanian party with Brazauskas. All the parties finally split as a direct result of the policy of the centre. The attempt at unity caused splintering. It was impossible to keep the Union together by force. The more we used force, the faster it would have fallen apart. True, the whole bloc was based on force. If force had been used, things could have dragged on but the end of it would have been much more explosive.'

During the course of 1991 Gorbachev devoted most of his time and energy to holding the Soviet centre together against Russia and the other republics. A referendum was held on 17 March on the question, 'Do you consider it necessary to preserve the Union of Soviet Socialist Republics as a renewed federation of equal sovereign republics, in which human rights and the freedom of people of all nationalities will be fully guaranteed?' The language was loaded. Yeltsin had a ruse of his own, adding a second question to the ballot, to ask if voters in Russia wanted direct elections for a Russian President. The result allowed both men to claim to have won approval, in an extension of the 'war of laws'. Six republics including the Baltics boycotted the whole process. But that April, Yeltsin and the leaders of the eight other republics met in a dacha at Novo-Ogarovo outside Moscow. In return for an independence whose exact scope was still to be negotiated, they would commit themselves to a treaty which would recognize the Soviet Union in a new form. 'We could have maintained the Soviet Union,' Bakatin now argues, 'if two or three years earlier Gorbachev had rejected the ideology of centralism just as he refused to use force in external affairs. Had he agreed from the beginning of the Novo-Ogarovo sessions to keep the Union structure but cede maximum power and rights to the republics, then he would still be President today.'

At the age of twenty-three, Yuri Prokofiev had been the youngest regional

Komsomol leader in the Soviet Union. The rest of his career was spent rising in the Moscow City Party, whose chairman he became, in the footsteps of Yeltsin and then Lev Zaikov. He was a member of the Central Committee and of the Politburo in the last two years of its existence. He and Ivan Polozkov seem to have aspired to power through the construction of the Russian Communist Party in 1990. It was not communist ideology which collapsed, he likes to think, but communist practice. Through no fault of its own the party became too incompetent and too paralysed to be able to continue administration. No state system could have survived Gorbachev's working method, 'which we called forward-and-backward'.

Pointedly rejecting the proposal which Bakatin among others had made in 1989 to remove Article Six, Gorbachev reversed himself a few months later and promoted it. He repudiated the use of force but ordered troops into the republics, in Vilnius for example. 'He would give an order and immediately step back from it. His policies were therefore unfathomable unless you knew the internal levers and springs. You are faced with a choice of seeing him either as stupid, incapable of drawing correct conclusions from previous mistakes, or alternatively as clever enough to pursue mysterious goals.

'Gorbachev set up a commission to investigate Yeltsin's past. This commission never met, but as a result of what looked like persecution 4 million Muscovites voted for Yeltsin. A wave of popular feeling swept him in. At the session of the Supreme Soviet Gorbachev stands up and denounces Yeltsin, and goes off to America, whereupon Yeltsin is instantly voted in as chairman of the Supreme Soviet. Just when there's a decision to hold presidential elections in Russia in March 1991, Gorbachev brings troops on to the streets, which again bolsters Yeltsin's position.' Since there was no legal or constitutional reality against which to measure words and deeds, the imagination runs riot. To Prokofiev, as to many of the party faithful, it appears that 'Gorbachev attempted to boost his own position by having violence done against himself.

'Gorbachev distanced himself more or less totally from the party, he made no use of advice from the Central Committee or the Politburo, he replaced his close circle of party advisers with his Presidential Council which had neither popular support nor a constitutional basis. The Central Committee found itself working partly under party authority, partly under presidential authority. This led to enormous confusion. There were no clear divisions after that.

'In the whole course of 1990 only two Politburo meetings had any significance. In September we discussed the political and economic situation. On 16 November, we met after the Supreme Soviet had called Gorbachev to account for what was happening and to take responsibility. He had made a most amorphous and unsatisfactory speech, and the question was raised of a vote of No Confidence. That same day he called the Politburo, and turned to us and said, What are we to do? We produced a series of ten-minute speeches detailing an Eight-Point Plan which he accepted and read out the following day in the Supreme Soviet, almost word for word as we had given it to him. All other Politburo meetings in 1991 were formalities.'

The publication back in March 1988 in a hardline newspaper of Nina And-reyeva's open letter in defence of Stalinism was a first portent of the coming test of strength against Gorbachev. A shaken Ivan Laptev, the editor of *Izvestia* which was bound to be involved, had then spoken for everyone when he warned his staff, 'The time to choose has arrived. Personally, I am for Gorbachev but I am getting ready to retire. The youngest of you must make your decision, knowing what the risks and the stakes are.' This was prescient, but somewhat premature. How was the decision to be made? The choosing depended upon whether you lived in fear of the future or in hope of improvement that it might bring; on whether you had something to lose or to gain, or belonged to the undifferentiated millions for whom politics was a Homeric contest out of sight above their heads. Like a malady with oppressive symptoms but uncertain diagnosis, the time to choose lingered unhealthily. All you could do was postpone work and commitment by means of masterly inactivity, in case some higher order arrived to invalidate or expose you. You had to watch television and read the press for what lay unspoken between the lines, developing a sixth sense for the dangers of provocations and traps. Who was behind what? You had to be a soothsayer. Huge demonstrations were held regularly in Manezh Square in central Moscow as from February 1990. 'Party Bureaucrats: Remember Romania', were the words of one banner. Then Gorbachev was publicly booed at the May Day rally. The Central Committee agreed to repeal Article Six but contradictorily put out a letter in which the party reserved the right to use force. Strikes broke out in the mines of Siberia and Ukraine. Miners were reduced to violence to obtain soap. That September, paratroopers from Ryazan filled the streets of Moscow and KGB troops were put on alert in what was evidently a show of force. Marshal Yazov brushed this away as regular manoeuvres. In the preface to a book about the Soviet army which was published that year, he wrote that force and the threat to use it must be excluded as an option, and people had an unconditional right to choose the course that their society would follow. Within months, he was authorizing force.

'Among us there are carriers of ideas and viewpoints alien or even wholly hostile to socialism,' said Viktor Chebrikov, the recent head of the KGB. The ambassador to Warsaw, V. V. Brovikov, addressed the Central Committee:

'Our country, the mother of us all, has been reduced to a sorry state. It has been turned from a power that was admired in the world into a state with a mistake-filled past, a joyless present and an uncertain future.' If proper measures were not taken, harangued Colonel Viktor Alksnis, a hardline deputy, 'people will arm themselves and take to the streets'. The state was collapsing, according to the writer Aleksander Prokhanov, as a result of deliberate actions by leaders who received their authority from structures devised by themselves. 'We probably deceived ourselves in thinking that we lived in the twentieth century,' wrote the philosopher Aleksander Tsipko with self-pity corresponding to the general mood. 'Maybe history just performed an experiment on us, freezing our brains, thoughts and feelings, compelling us to wander about the world asleep, committing a mass of idiocies, murdering one another, doing no end of atrocious things.' On the national television programme with the highest ratings, Yakovlev spoke of the destruction of the peasantry which had thrown the state into crisis: 'History has never known such a concentrated hatred towards man.'

One day Gorbachev was offering to resign: 'It turns out, we're going in the wrong direction. So we're mistaken. If that's the way you feel, comrades, you will have to elect a new Politburo and a new general secretary.' And another day he was red in the face as he raised his voice: 'Enough of defending ourselves. We must go on the offensive!' During the course of November and December 1990, he rid himself of his close advisers, Yavlinsky, Shatalin, Academician Petrakov, and the Minister of Finance Boris Fyodorov, and eventually even Yakovlev. He replaced Bakatin as Minister of the Interior with Boriss Pugo from Latvia, and Prime Minister Ryzhkov with Valentin Pavlov. Ryzhkov was given to weeping. 'There is now neither a plan nor a market,' was his parting shot. Gorbachev appointed Leonid Kravchenko to run television and broadcasting, in effect his chief propagandist. He abolished the Presidential Council which he had launched at the start of the year. Resigning as Foreign Minister that December, Shevardnadze said in the Soviet Congress, 'The reformers have gone into hiding. A dictatorship is approaching. No one knows what this dictatorship will be like ... as a man, as a citizen, as a communist, I cannot reconcile myself to what is happening in my country and to the trials which await our people.' Kryuchkov on 11 December accused the West of attempting to destroy the Soviet state. On the evening news programme he made a statement that plotters had a list of people whom they proposed to neutralize. An all-out struggle was being waged over property and power, which threatened the existence of the Soviet Union. 'We of the security forces have made our choice.' On the 22nd he spelled it out: 'The use of force may be necessary to restore law and order.'

Like so many leaves in autumn, they were one and all blown uncontrollably this way and that in the culmination of this test of strength. It was endemic. The system offered no alternative. Scaremongering was a party tactic, according to Yeltsin. 'I don't believe civil war is possible. No matter how much the President and his comrades are raising the level of tension, I have an absolute belief in the common sense of the people.' 'The important thing,' Gorbachev said in the Soviet Congress on 18 December, 'is not to smash each other's bones.'

34

MAFIAS OF THE WORLD UNITE!

Until the Gorbachev era, the newspapers had sometimes reported the execution or imprisonment of someone for 'economic crimes'. Too elastic to carry precise meaning, this term mostly indicated activities normal in a free market, or it could have been a code for a political mistake, or even for anti-Semitism. Every commercial, social or political transaction between people contained this element of favour, therefore subject to bargaining, therefore corruptible. In the myriad little tests of strength that made up Soviet daily life, nothing restrained the strong except an innate sense of what was an appropriate gain or else the danger that immoderate extortion would lead to reprisal. Denouncing to the party those who had taken advantage of them, the weak risked bringing about a confrontation which would formalize their inferiority. Rising towards the top, party-state officials, the entire Nomen-klatura, increasingly enriched themselves, obtaining goods and services and emoluments in ways which in a law-based society would have been incon-ceivable. Officials down to quite low ranks were exempt from customs inspec-tion, for instance, which was an open incitement to smuggling. Whenever someone embezzled grossly enough to be scandalous, his party colleagues usually managed to hush it up as an issue of internal discipline; they were motivated by their own vulnerability to similar accusations. Very few members of the Nomenklatura were ever demoted from their post and privileges.

In September 1988 Yuri Churbanov, Brezhnev's son-in-law who was also a colonel general and a candidate member of the Central Committee and a deputy to the Supreme Soviet, was charged with corruption. The indictment ran to 1500 pages. He was duly sentenced to prison. In media controlled by the party there could be no place for investigative journalism. After the Churbanov case, as perestroika burgeoned, reporters started to be able to describe in print examples of corruption too flagrant for the party to bury them. One reporter bursting through these blind-eye bounds was Vitali Vitaliev, who exposed a whole range of frauds from the siphoning of goods out of the official economy, faking products, price-rigging, down to prostitution. In his book, *Special Correspondent*, he records that he received a letter from the secretary of the Dnepropetrovsk party committee to say that after one of these articles 138 people had been sentenced to imprisonment and 75 militiamen punished, and all the chiefs of the regional and city militia and Prosecutor's Office had been sacked. These victims could reasonably believe that they had been unfairly singled out for practices long since standardized.

Another investigative reporter, Arkady Vaksberg of *Literaturnaya Gazeta*, gave currency to the 'Soviet mafia' and the coinage is now universally accepted. One among many of his wild examples of corruption reaching to and from the leadership of the Union and the republics concerned the one-time Minister of Railways, Ivan Grigorevich Pavlovsky. In an attempt to save some of the grain harvest in Kazakhstan, this Minister had located and employed thirty-four wagons. Hourly progress reports of the train arrived at his office. 'An hour ago,' the unfortunate Minister complained to Vaksberg, 'I was informed that there are no wagons. None at all. There never were any ... the whole thing is a mirage, fruit of a vivid imagination, a deception which I swallowed like an idiot.' Hustlers with more influence and money than the Minister had commandeered these wagons to harvest fruit in the Caucasus, and corrupt officials all along the line were trying to lie their way out. As Vaksberg concluded, 'The winners were infinitely more powerful than the people whose job it was to check railway movements.'

'Soviet mafia' as a phrase is somewhat misleading in that it suggests criminals in apposition to the honest segment of society. The entire society, each person in his degree, was obliged to cheat and bribe and cut corners in pursuit of desired goods and services, which in a democracy would have been acquired through straightforward trading and purchasing. The sovietologist Alain Besançon summed it up when he wrote that without corruption, not one factory would produce its raw materials or spare parts, cities would no longer be supplied, production would cease, famine reign, and nothing would remain except 'socialism', which is to say nothing. Losing its moral dimension, corruption had become functional; that was what was so destructive and frightening about it.

Most people are prepared to stretch their conscience only so far, and Russians are naturally no exception. Resigned ruefully to humdrum corruption, the huge majority balked at violence. The Nomenklatura of course had no need to be violent; they had only to pull their party rank in the effort to obtain whatever it was that they had in their sights. But for some careerists it was simpler and more efficient to satisfy their ambitions by force. These were the Soviet mafia. No proper, meaningful line can be drawn between the Nomenklatura and the mafia; it was all a blurred tangle of methods and urgencies. Abstaining from Marxist pieties, avowedly out for themselves, perhaps the mafia was less hypocritical. In any case, those concerned shared the essential outlook that they should have whatever they wanted, no matter what might happen to anybody else in the process. *Komsomolskaya Pravda* in July 1988 reported that in the previous three years 40,000 police officials were dismissed for illegalities, such as fabrication of cases and collusion in corruption.

Insiders as a rule were secretive about their manifold practices of exploitation and General Oleg Kalugin caused a sensation when he began to speak openly about them. Defectors apart, he was the first KGB officer to break ranks and complain of the unsavoury reality. Quickly becoming a favourite of Western reporters, he made a number of claims, for instance that he had worked professionally with Kim Philby. Whether unguarded or publicity-seeking, remarks of his about the murder of Georgi Markov were to lead to his temporary detention in London for interrogation.

After twenty-five years in the foreign arm of the KGB, Kalugin had received his first home posting in 1986, as first deputy of the Leningrad KGB under Colonel General Daniil Nozyrev. 'My tasks were to oversee the Leningrad police, economic affairs, fighting dissidents, and guarding the borders. I had known about crime from Western publications but I had never believed them. To learn at first hand the extent of this criminality, and to have the documents to prove it, was to look at things differently. I discovered corruption when I was posted to deal with internal affairs – how they protected the privileges of the Nomenklatura. Corruption meant bribe-taking by party officials. We had forty people arrested for taking bribes, wheeler-dealers who gave evidence against the party and the apparat. The first deputy chief of the Leningrad council was incriminated and there was evidence against party secretaries, dealing with economic or party affairs. The Prosecutor General in Leningrad said to me, You have forty under arrest, isn't that enough? I told him that people of that kind were undermining the whole system. I was summoned to the Leningrad Party Committee. Why rock the boat? they asked. Friends are friends. That's fine, I replied, this has nothing to do with friendship. Colonel General Nozyrev said that he would not intervene. Everyone agreed that this issue of corruption was of no concern to us.'

Kalugin tried to work within the system, he emphasizes. At that point he had confidence in Gorbachev and wrote him a letter about corruption, with a copy to the Procurator General. When nothing happened, he wrote a second letter. Chebrikov, Kryuchkov's predecessor at the KGB, summoned him to Moscow, to ask him what he was hoping to achieve. A commission then did arrive to investigate the charges, 'not against those who had been involved in bribery, but against *me*. What forces had driven me to act like that, who was behind me, and so on. Anyone who raised a finger against the system was suspected of undermining it, while I had been wanting to make it perfect.'

Recalled from Leningrad, Kalugin was first placed in the KGB reserve, and then promoted to the Ministry of Electronics, under a Minister directly accountable to the Sixth Directorate of the KGB. When he reached the age of fifty-five in 1989, he was immediately pensioned off. 'It takes several months before you actually leave. On the first day of my retirement in February 1990, I felt a free man. I walked into the offices of Yuri Afanasiev, I produced documents and declared that I was ready to fight for the democratic cause. He said, I knew people like you would come over to us. Korotich was editing *Ogonyok* and I wrote for him but he never dared publish it. Someone informed on me to him.

'The brother of Igor Chubais was prominent in the democratic movement, and I called him one day. It was after midnight. In June 1990 there was to be a conference of democratic forces, and I wanted to speak at it. This meeting was in the Oktyabr cinema in Moscow. My speech was announced five minutes before I actually spoke. When I was introduced as a general of the KGB who wanted to expose that organization, 2000 people gave me a standing ovation. I was immediately assaulted by hundreds of correspondents. Reprisals followed quickly. I had spoken on 16 June and on 30 June Gorbachev issued a decree stripping me of my rank and pension. The Prosecutor's Office started proceedings against me in July for leaking state secrets. Yakovlev told me that Gorbachev had read my letter but decided that it was premature. Now that I had gone public, he should have sympathized.'

There is no reason to doubt Kalugin's revulsion at the spectacle, close-up, of corruption. Another way to describe his transformation is that he was quick off the mark to perceive how to interpret perestroika. To choose for Yeltsin was also to stand clear of any KGB house-cleaning that might follow. His Russian visiting card carries the word 'expert' after his name. His American visiting card describes him as chairman of a company called Intercon, with an office in downtown Washington.

The standard work about the Soviet economy was by Professor Alec Nove and it ran into several editions. Any Soviet official would have approved the accuracy of the model portrayed, but since the book omits all mention of corruption and its guiding role, it had only a notional relationship to real life. For every Besançon who depicted Soviet moral and physical squalor, there were scores of Noves motivated by some obscure desire, whether driven by inner psychological pressures or by ideology, to rescue communism by concentrating on the theory proclaimed by its practitioners to the exclusion of their habitual practices.

A small handful of professional economists grew up and worked without illusion within the system; and among these invaluable witnesses were the Hungarian János Kornai and the Pole Jan Winiecki. Winiecki spoke of centrally-approved corruption, by which he meant not just the privileges of the Nomenklatura but their powers to intervene in the state's production and distribution systems. Intervention in the wealth creation programme was actually wealth appropriation. In an inversion of Marxism, each was receiving not according to his needs but according to his ability to take. The exercise of a Nomenklatura post as Politburo or Central Committee member, as First Secretary, as manager of a military–industrial plant or any factory, conveyed property rights in all but name and legal entitlement. It was Winiecki's startling suggestion, as early as 1988, that these property rights be acknowledged and bought out. To compensate the Nomenklatura for loss of putative but very real property rights would have proved a cheaper and more efficient transition to the free market than the chaotic stampede which actually occurred: a stampede into crime on the part of the Nomenklatura, the KGB and the party, indeed everyone who could read the writing on the wall.

Ilya Zemtsov is a Soviet academic who emigrated to Israel. Another witness, he has made specialist studies of Soviet corruption. Racketeers and black-market operators, he was writing in 1991, wielded enough power to dispense with the party. They had only to destroy the old communist fiction and fashion some new arrangement designed to provide their actual power with some legitimacy. This would mean communism's total collapse. Everybody was directly connected to public property at some level. Granted the cast of mind and ingenuity to lay hands on the property within reach, everybody could be a mafioso in his own right. To refrain, to be disgusted, was self-injuring and finally stupid, a gesture which might appease the conscience but actually made no practical difference. Or as Zemtsov put it: 'Every day thousands of Soviet people contribute to the Mafia by stealing from others' pockets or becoming dealers, gamblers or prostitutes. The most capable and dynamic of these, having sized up the situation, joined the world of crime. With luck, they will start climbing its ladder. Those who are intelligent, energetic and callous enough will end up managing the most crucial sectors of government administration: first the economy and then politics.'

After 1917, the party-state had plundered everything, public and private. As soon as the laws had changed to permit private employment and co-operative enterprises and joint ventures, a reverse process started, whereby individuals could regain what the state had grabbed. By 1989 there was a stock market, commercial banks and private companies whose exact legal status was as unclear as their operations. These mushrooming institutions were so many unauthorized compacts between entrepreneurs and party-state officials whereby public money could be diverted to them. Karamzin's 'thieving' does not quite cover the case. Capricious and ugly and unjust as the process was, enriching the undeserving few at the expense of the deserving many, it was in the broadest perspective an historic revenge.

The population at large had perceived that just as the leadership had not been prepared to use force in defence of its ideology in the former empire, so it would be reluctant to return to mass repression at home. Nothing less than the reactivation of the Gulag camps could have served after 1989. In its final eighteen months the Soviet Union became a paradise for the bold and the unscrupulous; its entire product and resources, its stores of wealth, were prised loose and torn from hand to hand. Another gigantic redistribution of the spoils took place. Here was the asset-stripping of a nation.

The armed forces disposed of probably the largest and most accessible depository of public goods for which there were immediate buyers. The first soldiers to have sold their weapons seem to have been those garrisoned in the DDR. Grenades, rifles, Kalashnikovs, fuel and radio sets and tanks, found their way on to the market. First arming themselves, mafia gangs sold weapons all over the world, not least in former Yugoslavia. Eventually the director of something called the Ukrainian–Siberian Commodities Exchange was to offer for sale the newest jet fighters. General Vladimir Rodionov commanding in the Far East on the China border was one among senior officers arrested, in his case for running a ferry service for passengers in combat transport aircraft. Two million roubles were found in his possession, according to the prosecution.

Vyacheslav Kebich, the Prime Minister of Belarus, was to read out to his cabinet the following statement, which gives an idea of what had become general practice.

'A first Deputy Minister of Belarus, Colonel General Anatoly Kostenko, is suspected of illegal trade in military property. When he was the commander of the Byelorussian [sic] military district he ordered that gasoline be distributed from army stocks among servicemen free of charge. The military procurator's office has also instituted criminal proceedings against several army commanders and their deputies. For instance, General Rumyantsev, commander of the anti-aircraft Fifth Tank Army, and Colonel General Ivanitsky, commander of the Seventh Tank Army, are accused of the construction of dachas for themselves by subordinate soldiers and illegitimate use for personal purposes of service transport ... Almost 100 general officers of the Armed Forces of Belarus are suspected of various illegitimate activities, mainly of co-operation with commercial organizations to the detriment of the state. Many civilian high-ranking officials turned out to be at variance with the law. For instance, Deputy Chairman of the State Committee for Oil Products

Zaryonok directly participated in a barter deal with Latvian businessmen, exchanging 250 tons of diesel fuel for half a ton of honey and a ton of sausage.'

According to available dossiers, this statement declared, 2000 state officials of various ranks had taken bribes.

Factory managers had long been accustomed to treating their concerns as private, with the happy proviso that they loaded on to the state the capitalist responsibilities for profit and loss, for the welfare of the workers, pensions and so on. Factories became corporate-like affairs, owning their suppliers, laboratories and depots, spawning subsidiaries to make components not accounted for by central planning, building sanatoriums and hotels and dachas, shading into all manner of fringe operations. Ownership of much of the accumulated property was unclear. One manager of a factory manufacturing aircraft was quoted in a Moscow newspaper: 'I personally have invested a lot in this factory, and I am determined to be its owner.' Nobody could stop him.

A wide range of stratagems conveyed these assets to those who already visualized themselves as effective owners. This was 'spontaneous' or 'director' privatization. Sometimes the manager set up a company of his own and sold to it at a giveaway price what he had been managing previously. Sometimes he authorized the issuing of shares or the disposal of assets to nominees, of which he was one. Or he might find some method of diverting to himself financial and material resources earmarked by the state to his factory according to a plan no longer operational. Mikhail Gurtovoi, chairman of a commission in the Yeltsin era to establish financial–legal controls, was to say, 'According to our information, a third of the Soviet debt accumulated under Gorbachev was simply stolen. For instance, hard currency was given for the building of a factory, but there is no factory and not even a trace of the millions of dollars that were allocated to it.' Those left behind could join the race later, like former Prime Minister Nikolai Ryzhkov, once head of one of the largest Soviet military engineering combines. Emerging as a director of a private bank, he was quoted as saying that he had decided he would no longer be humiliated by remaining poor.

Those within the bureaucracy, who had the power of signature authorizing any form of trade, sales or purchasing, were key to this transfer of wealth. At the founding congress in October 1990 of Democratic Russia, it was noted publicly for the first time that on the pretext of privatization members of the Nomenklatura were seizing state and party funds and property for themselves. Subterranean, undocumented, hidden behind banking secrecy, this process is largely immune to inspection. Only fleeting and dramatic glimpses appear of almost unimaginable fraud.

Among those quick to line their pockets were the managers of the oil industry. Oil siphoned off on to the black market began to arrive in quantities on the European spot-market. No less a man than Kryuchkov referred at the end of 1990 to unjustified losses in the oil market. Whereas 127 million tons had been sold at low prices in 1989, in 1990, when prices rose, only 101 million tons were exported. In 1991 this would drop to 61 million tons. The discrepancy between these figures points to the scale of the swindling. The *Sunday Times* in 1993 was to report that 'oil barons' had emerged from the Nomenklatura and the KGB. They appeared to earn fifty dollars a month but somehow possessed houses in Geneva.

Other extractive industries followed suit. One-third or even two-thirds of the entire Soviet production of rare minerals is estimated to have been illegally exported for private profit. Estonia has no copper but suddenly became one of the world's leading exporters of it. Central planning had ignored real supply and demand, and the ensuing gap between notional costs and world prices attracted a hoard of speculators, some of whom were in league with Western carpetbaggers. Furthermore, the obsession with fighting capitalism to the finish had led the authorities to create a variety of roubles, whether for internal use only or for foreign trade, transferable or not, paper or gold-backed, to be exchanged for hard currency at varying rates. Killings were to be made by manipulators of these anomalies.

By 1993, according to the Russian media, four in five of every joint venture was in the hands of the KGB. Former KGB officials were at the head of the major new financial institutions and private companies. Huge sums of money had been sent abroad by the KGB to subsidize foreign Communist Parties. Since the 1950s the French party had received $24 million, and the Italian party $47 million between 1971 and 1987. In 1987 subsidies of $2 million were paid to the French as well as to the American party. Final approval was given on 5 June 1990 by the Central Committee to a deal with Libya involving communications, repairs and spare parts, arms and ammunition, worth $1.58 billion to be repaid with oil.

In his interview, Ivars Kezbars, the last Ideological Secretary of the Latvian party, gave me a graphic account of transactions escaping bank transfers. 'The Soviet ambassador in some countries would receive an attaché case with a million dollars in it. Then he would invite to dinner the First Secretary of the local Communist Party, or the head of some left-wing organization which had hidden purposes. He would hand the money over, and they would not sign any document to that effect. The ambassador would simply say that the money was for agreed activities, and it was accepted that some who received the attaché cases were poor. If they chose to send their children to a Pioneer summer camp, or make some such use of the money, that was their business.' Quite what sort of terminal deals the KGB and its dependants cut is unknown, but its funds, completely unaccountable, appear to have been banked securely in Düsseldorf, in Zurich and in Danish banks, and no doubt elsewhere. Former senior KGB officials are now owners of villas on the Riviera. The true power structure remained largely intact in its new form of old–boy network. Vladimir Mukusev was the moderator of the most popular television talk show *Vzglyad*, and when he resigned in 1991 he said, 'One could not become a chief editor without having been a career officer in the KGB.'

The party-state itself completed its own looting. Kryuchkov in 1990 had stated in the Soviet Congress that twelve billion roubles had been smuggled out to Switzerland. That was an understatement. The Soviet television personality Vladimir Pozner, never someone to stick his neck out, wrote that he had learned from generally reliable sources that the party secretly transferred 200 billion roubles abroad at an exchange rate of 18 to the dollar. The party was said to have as many as 7000 foreign accounts. In 1990 at least three dubious westerners appeared with an offer to buy 140 billion roubles in return for dollars. This sum was equivalent to all the cash in circulation in the Soviet Union. It seemed nonsensical to part with hard currency for paper inflating worthlessly. The proposal has been investigated by Claire Sterling in her book *Crime Without Frontiers*. Among tangential facts, she reports an official from the Prosecutor General's Serious Crime Squad saying that 100,000 dummy rouble accounts had been used to export roubles through the banking system. She links the attempt to corner the rouble cash-market to the otherwise inexplicable decision of the then Prime Minister Valentin Pavlov to withdraw without warning all the 50- and 100-rouble notes.

In April and May 1991 shipments of Soviet gold variously reported at between 1000 and 2000 tons reached the West. More shipments just before the August coup showed evidence of having been packed in haste. The economist Grigori Yavlinsky had the delicate task in September of announcing that the Soviet gold reserve had dwindled to 240 tons. Investigators had traced Soviet flight capital to accounts in almost eighty banks worldwide, with investments in hotels and property and businesses. Police Captain A. V. Yastrebov from Moscow's Economic Crime Department has accused officials of complicity in the transfer of the gold reserve to Switzerland. None of it is likely to be recovered, nor will the truth emerge. *Izvestia* on 3 October 1991 commented bitterly that over the last three years the Government, with the approval of Gorbachev, had deflected for some unknown purposes gold worth $25 to $30 billion. In any normal country, the article went on, the President and his Prime Minister would have to account 'for such a fantastic embezzlement'.

So the very people who were listening to the increasingly tetchy and harassed Gorbachev appealing for perestroika, and to the ever more ebullient Yeltsin outflanking him by appealing for his different version of perestroika, were inwardly calculating that come what may, they needed a future safeguard above everything else. Whatever their public postures and mutual slagging and apocalyptic cries, hardliners and reformers alike hastened to make their dispositions, as prudent men might take out insurance policies in other societies.

A few days after the August coup, the party treasurer Nikolai Kruchina was found dead on the pavement below his highrise apartment. Sixty-two, he had been in the post since 1983, an Andropov protégé. He knew every detail of the party portfolio and its assets, estimated to be worth between 5 and 7.7 billion roubles with an income from all sources of about 2.7 billion roubles, its 114 publishing houses and 81 printing presses, its hotels and factories, sanatoriums and car-pools; he kept the record of who enjoyed which palaces and villas; and he possessed the numbers of secret accounts and he had the signature on them. Six weeks later, in October, his predecessor Georgy Pavlov was also discovered dead on the pavement below his highrise building. A few days after that, Dmitri Lissovolik, an official of the Central Committee's International Department responsible for channelling funds to foreign parties, met his death from a twelfth-floor window. Perhaps they had denounced these colossal frauds, and perhaps they were detected in committing them. Perhaps they jumped, perhaps they were thrown out.

The epic battle of the two titans at the top mattered very greatly because it would decide who in the future had signatures authorizing the distribution of wealth. But in another sense, granted the essential lawlessness, it was sham, the jousting at a pageant. The Nomenklatura, the élite, the mafia, entrepreneurs of every stripe who had hitherto been active but invisible, had correctly weighed the opportunity to obtain title to property which they had enjoyed only as beneficiaries and could therefore not legitimately bequeath to their descendants. Communism had made them what they were, a ruling class of merciless predators, indoctrinated to believe that fraudulence and mayhem were the ordinary tools of class interest. Once beyond the reach of a political process grinding down and turning in on itself, they picked the flesh off the bones of the Soviet Union, as their predecessors had done with Tsarist Russia.

35

'INITIATIVES'

A career diplomat, Alexander Bessmertnyk succeeded Shevardnadze as Foreign Minister though only for six months. Essentially a Gorbachev man, he misjudged the August coup, with the result that the Foreign Ministry sat on the fence. This ended his career. Perky in manner, well-meaning, a good English speaker, he now runs a Moscow think-tank.

Foreign policy had been carried out by means of speeches and 'initiatives'. Gorbachev's foreign policy speeches were drafted by the Ministry, where the Common European Home was devised as a slogan. Draft speeches were presented to Anatoly Chernyayev who 'was excellent at changing them stylistically to Gorbachevian language'. An 'initiative' involved picking some arena for a test of strength, pushing to see what rewards might be forthcoming in the event of a foreign state under pressure preferring appeasement to resistance. 'First use force, and then devise a policy. It was a peculiar way of presenting a foreign policy line but very often effective, if only through surprise.' For decades class war had provided the basic concept behind foreign policy. A just war was one which could be waged advantageously in the perceived interests of the Soviet proletariat. To accept that war should not be waged at all therefore dismantled what had been militarized aggression against all nations outside the Soviet Empire. Bessmertnyk attended all the summits of the Gorbachev era. 'At the Geneva meeting in 1985 we stated for the first time that there must not be a nuclear war as there would be no winners. Now it looks like a platitude but at the time it was quite a change! Until then both sides had their strategic notions of how to emerge with superiority from a nuclear war. At the Malta summit, the two leaders at last agreed that fundamental changes were occurring and in the difficult circumstances they should try to act as partners.' In fact, the Start I Treaty and the agreement on conventional arms were more or less stalemated. According to Bessmertnyk, the military suspected the Foreign Ministry of betraying Soviet interests. He gives an entertaining account of winning over military experts in order to influence Yazov and other senior officers, playing on their lack of mastery of technical detail in order to obtain concessions.

Did Gorbachev lose standing through the way he allowed German reunification to proceed?

'That is the sad story. After the unification of Germany he had crossed a critical line as far as the Soviet public was concerned. The same goes for Shevardnadze. What they did they did excellently. It was then up to me to see the ratification of the German treaty. Parliament and public opinion was very negative. We had to prove that there was no other option. I addressed a closed session of parliament because I sensed that an open session would be a catastrophe. Gorbachev had wanted an East Germany outside Nato. The West took so strong a stand that he couldn't have his way. They wouldn't accept ideas we proposed to make things easier for us. The army and the older generation which had gone through the war were angered.'

From the way you describe it, Gorbachev appears to have had little choice.

'It was definitely *force majeure*, but in that situation a leader can more easily make a mistake. Theoretically Gorbachev might have played it differently. If it hadn't been for his own vision of the world, for the Malta summit, and of course the domestic situation, he might well have yielded to military and other pressures and created a crisis throughout Europe. But he was sincere about not using force – some people did not trust him but that was the case. In the best sense of the term, he was a pacifist. Often when the use of force was considered, at home or abroad, he was instinctively prepared to vote it down even if it were warranted by the circumstances. This distinguished him from all previous General Secretaries.'

On 14 January 1991, at the moment of his appointment, Bessmertnyk happened to have been passing through London. He bought six or seven newspapers with stop-press photographs of the attacks on Vilnius and Riga. 'Next morning, when I went to see Gorbachev, I showed him these news-papers. He wanted to have them. I said, I am accepting your offer to become Foreign Minister, but if things like this are going to happen the Soviet Union can have no foreign policy. When we talked about the Vilnius event, he said, I just did not know about it and it makes me choke to hear that nobody is responsible, *someone* is.' That someone could only have been in the military or the KGB. He thinks that it is 'a strange story, whose truth has yet to be revealed. It looks as though everyone has decided to forget about it because other events overtook it. Had the operation been successful, I am sure that many would claim the credit.'

During the night of 16 January, during his first twenty-four hours in office,

Secretary of State Baker telephoned to say that the assault on Iraqi troops in Kuwait would begin one hour later. 'That was a sleepless night, and during it Gorbachev and Yazov summoned me over to the Kremlin. Lukyanov suggested that I should speak to parliament. I said that it was the first day of the war but he insisted and Gorbachev agreed. So I did, and the colonels there attacked me, saying that they would like to learn when I would stop defending the interests of the United States and start defending the interests of the Soviet Union.'

The demise of the Soviet Union, in Bessmertnyk's opinion, ran in a straight line from the inter-communal fighting in Nagorny-Karabakh to Tbilisi, and to Vilnius. Neither Gorbachev nor anyone else perceived that destiny might rest in a small trouble spot like Nagorny-Karabakh. Once other republics began to fear that they might be dealt with in the ruthless manner of Tbilisi and Vilnius, relationships with the centre broke down irretrievably. Nationalism spread like a forest fire. A Council of Federation was set up for the purpose of devising a new Union, and he participated in some of its discussions. 'My concept was that foreign policy had to belong to the federal centre, otherwise there would be no federation. The republics wanted to steal it away from Moscow. That was one of the testing grounds. Ukraine, Kazakh-stan and Uzbekistan were the main republics trying to obtain a greater share of foreign policy decision-making than I thought advisable.'

At the beginning of 1991 nobody could yet imagine the independence of a sovereign state of Ukraine.

'No. Absolutely not. Even in the discussions of the Council of Federation. It could easily be discerned that Ukraine was using the opportunity to obtain more for itself as a republic, but not even the most nationalistic Ukrainians were thinking that far ahead.'

The referendum of 17 March was Gorbachev's way of appealing for popular support, in order to influence the outcome of the Novo-Ogarovo process. 'For a while he was able to capitalize on the referendum but the potential disappeared quickly. The Ukrainian countermove of having their referendum leading to their declaration of independence was a fatal blow. The Baltic States at first would have accepted a special status within a future federation instead of complete independence. Our leaders believed that evacuation of the Baltic would start a chain reaction.

'Gorbachev could not jump over *faits accomplis* he had himself created. One of his mistakes was not recognizing immediately the importance of Russia. I remember that when the presidential elections to the Russian Federation were held, he did not pay much attention. He was thinking about how to manage it, how to present better candidates for the presidency, things like that. He was still wrapped up in the idea of Union power. I would call it Moscow-centred. Of course you respected the republics, but not much.

'Gorbachev underestimated the importance of Russia emerging as a second power base. He was often blinded by his dislike of Yeltsin. If Yeltsin was to achieve an independent Russia, he had to ensure that the other republics could go their own way too. I don't think Yeltsin and the leading democratic groups had fully realized the consequences, they were prepared for years of opposition in a future federation of perhaps eight or nine republics. In a political sense, they were not prepared to take power at all. Here was an intensely passionate group who wanted to change the system first and the Union a long way afterwards. A rebel type, Yeltsin had been ejected from power, he was on his own, not knowing quite what to do, I think he was pretty desperate. Then he met Sakharov and adopted his ideas. A man with leadership instincts and prospects had merged with a democratic movement. Yeltsin was sincere, I am sure, and he regrets that things happened the way they did with the Soviet Union. If Gorbachev and all of us had played a better game with the republics, giving them more freedom to develop the way they wanted, the outcome might have been different.

'Reform was not well thought-out. Gorbachev says he had a master-concept but it was not so. His initial ideas were very modest. He started to reform the party piecemeal, repairing the image of party leaders and the handling of party business. Even that was enough to precipitate events which ran out of control. Without the coup, Gorbachev would have had to take drastic measures with the economy. He wanted political reform, then economic reform, then Union reform, huge arms control endeavours, involving basic psychological and ideological shifts at the same time. It was too much for society to handle, so it broke down. Since the system could not yield to reality and bend, like steel it had to break. The coup occurred, power was lying in the streets and Yeltsin had only to pick it up.'

36

'WHO IS LYING, I DO NOT KNOW'

Alexander Yakovlev's face might be carved out of wood, so stern is it. The dark and deep-set eyes are expressionless. Within the first few minutes of our meeting he was sighing that the KGB was a 'state within a state', in that hackneyed but still justified phrase. Why did he do what he did? Did he realize that he was digging the grave of the party-state? 'Perestroika was the only possible way from Bolshevism to the future.' And that's that. 'Never apologize, never explain' is a motto which might have been coined for him.

Yet he likes to give the account of some incident in circumstantial detail; who telephoned when, with which proposal, and what the consequences were. He participated in events, he repeats, but still he does not know the truth. His stories sometimes conclude, 'And who was lying I cannot tell.' Making his way through the Kremlin with that stiff limp from his war wound, attending the Politburo, he must have been a formidable presence. So rigidly certain of himself, yet so enclosed, he seems more a throwback to the old communist stereotype than a reformer feeling his way forward. So much drafting and redrafting of articles and programmes and speeches; so many innuendoes and unspoken purposes, such jockeying on committees; this huge expenditure of energy in a restricted political circle while in the dangerous outside world authority was withering and decrees and orders so carefully pondered into the small hours came to nothing, mere in-tray paper.

At his fingertips he has the intricacies of each and every Central Committee plenum, party congress, or Politburo meeting. Delicate special commissions of inquiry were entrusted to him, not only concerning the Ribbentrop–Molotov Pact but also the murder in 1934 of Kirov. It is a virtual certainty that Stalin had this rival killed, but there are discrepancies in the evidence and a suspicious Yakovlev did not sign this commission's final report.

To begin at the beginning, he says, Gorbachev's very first plenum of the Central Committee in April 1985 mentioned reform. The January 1987 plenum was then devoted to 'the question of party cadres', parlance for the usual purging designed to leave power in hands obedient to the new General Secretary.

'There was a working group at Zavidova, a country house in the suburbs of Moscow with a hunting reservation for the military. It was the habitual practice that all party reports for plenums were prepared at Zavidova by the three or four men responsible for the first drafts, then the Politburo discussed them, then they were read out at the plenum. When the first version was written, it was evident that it was relevant only to the past, and a new version was needed on the theme of democratization. So the second version dealt with the democratization of the party, with elections, human rights and freedom of speech, and a questioning of long-ago earlier resolutions concerning factionalism. That was the first time the Nomenklatura saw the danger for them. From that time on, the apparat, including the organs of repression, began to resist perestroika.'

What motivated Gorbachev to start perestroika?

'He believed in it. But before that plenum, and not just afterwards, he saw the resistance to it and decided to brake a little. It was fortunate that at that time at the head of the process was a man able to make compromises. The psychology imposed by Lenin on the party involved an uncompromising and permanent struggle against enemies in and out of the party. Gorbachev was the first Soviet leader to introduce the element of compromise. That was positive; but on the other hand in the course of events he became not the master of compromise but the victim of it. That was the drama, actively exploited by all the players on the scene.'

Surprises were never sprung at Politburo meetings. 'Everything round the table proceeded smoothly. There was an ethic. If someone was planning to say something against someone else, at a plenum or elsewhere, or over some article, as a rule he would telephone prior to it, and express his disagreement quite personally. As a friend, he would advise you not to take some step under consideration. Demands and decrees of the Politburo were characterized by the absence of a whisper in the ear.' But were his confrontations with Ligachev not a recurrent feature of Politburo meetings? 'On some questions yes, on others no. Personal relations with Ligachev were normal. He too would whisper in the ear.' Yeltsin provided the conspicuous exception, crashing through the ethic and everything that supported it. 'Yeltsin says that he went to the October 1987 plenum and everybody attacked him in a way he had not expected. There are many aspects to this. I don't regard it as true that Yeltsin selected the right time and place to express his position. It has its prehistory.

'In August 1987 Gorbachev was on holiday. Ligachev chaired a Politburo meeting. Yeltsin was then a candidate member of the Politburo as well as First Secretary of the City Party, and one of the items on the agenda was his proposition to introduce regulations for public meetings in Izmailovo, on the lines of Hyde Park. Everybody attacked him on the grounds that public meetings could not possibly be licensed at all. Yeltsin justified himself with the argument that he was merely implementing the instructions of a previous Politburo meeting. Nobody could recollect this. Either he or the other Politburo members were telling a lie. The members all took it that Yeltsin was acting out of personal whim. Why is it that in his books and speeches Yeltsin never criticizes me, but always supports me? Very simple. I then said that this is no place to discuss Yeltsin himself, but his proposals merit discussion and should either be implemented or voted down. Yeltsin remembered this. He is very touchy. In frustration after the meeting, he wrote to Gorbachev. Gorbachev did not show the letter to anyone, I did not know about it. Gorbachev told me that he had called Yeltsin, who had proposed to return to these suggestions after the 7 November celebrations. Gorbachev affirms that Yeltsin had agreed.

'Around 29 October, Gorbachev was proposing that the Central Committee plenum approve his celebration speech in which for the first time Stalin was to be called a criminal. Suddenly at this plenum Yeltsin made a speech which was unplanned, not on the agenda, to say that perestroika was going slowly, and Ligachev was a brake on it. After that the row began. I spoke at that plenum. Firstly, I was sorry that Yeltsin had spoilt Gorbachev's 7 November celebrations. Secondly, I reminded Yeltsin that he may have thought his speech was democratic but actually it was conservative. Why? That speech would act as a provocation to the hardliners. Thirdly, I said that Yeltsin had violated the ethic of the whisper in the ear. There had been his previous agreement with Gorbachev to raise the question again only after the celebrations. I once asked Yeltsin why he had violated this agreement – by then it was December 1992 and he was President – and he replied that there was no such agreement. Who is telling the truth and who is lying, I do not know.

'At the time Gorbachev did not want to fire Yeltsin, but the pressure from the Politburo was too great to be resisted. Why? Everybody thought perestroika was going too fast, not too slowly. Through a campaign of smears and illegal actions, they tried to erase him. Gorbachev proposed to post him as an ambassador. I should emphasize that on three occasions Yeltsin asked to be rehabilitated. In a speech at the October plenum he said that he had made a mistake, his comrades had misunderstood him, and if he had said something insulting to Gorbachev he asked to be excused. But that was a plenum of fools. There was an opportunity to settle the matter there and then. Maybe everybody thought that it was all preplanned with Gorbachev. I don't know.

At the Nineteenth Party Conference he again asked to be rehabilitated politically. There was a third occasion too. When his pleas were not accepted by the party apparat, and he realized that he would not be forgiven, he began his campaign for democracy.

'There were attempts to exclude him from the party, at which Gorbachev protected him, instead creating another committee to investigate his activities. The chairman was Medvedev. Medvedev never reported his researches. At one Politburo meeting Ligachev and Ryzhkov asked for the conclusions of this committee, and Medvedev replied that so far nothing had been found in Yeltsin's conduct against the party or the constitutional programme. Ligachev said, You are researching badly. Medvedev said to Yeltsin in person that he had found nothing because there was nothing to find. Gradually the situation was reached when Yeltsin was able to create committees against everybody else. That's the trick of it! Democratic forces had been searching for quite a time for a leader, and in that role Yeltsin came to the fore. It was a good option. Yeltsin is decisive in character.'

Did you find Gorbachev open to advice?

'Sometimes yes, sometimes no. He listened when he considered that my advice was useful to him personally.'

Did he have a vision of where he was going?

'For a long time he had been speaking about the creation of a democratic and legal society. Can that be considered a plan or not? Everything depended upon the political situation.'

Did he fear a mass uprising during the years of perestroika?

'That idea was implanted in him every day by the KGB. He did not realize that this sort of information from the KGB and the army had the aim of leading to his replacement by the State Committee [the August plotters]. Their line against perestroika was a firm political principle, but on the other hand they were engaged in a fight for their own survival.'

In his opinion, the hardliners mounted a putsch in three stages: the publication of the Nina Andreyeva letter, the destruction of the Shatalin Plan, finally the August coup. Yakovlev had been away in Mongolia when the Nina Andreyeva letter was published. 'It was impossible for such a letter to have appeared in print without Politburo support. When I returned I told Gorbachev that this was a platform for anti-perestroika. He agreed. I prepared a political article in reply and two days later we discussed the issue in the Politburo. The rule was that you had fifteen minutes to speak in. Every Politburo member spoke against the Andreyeva letter. One minute against the letter, fourteen minutes against democratic forces. Ryzhkov alone spoke decisively against the letter. All the rest were on both sides. Ligachev had a three- or four-minute speech devoid of content. He claimed to have seen the letter only on the day after its publication, but this was not true. He had immediately gathered all editors of papers and the media to tell them that this was an example of how to fight for correct communist principles. After the Politburo meeting, we published my reply. Ligachev did not try to resign – he never would do so of his own free will. Even at the Twenty-eighth Party Congress he tried to stay on in power as a deputy General Secretary. In my presence Ligachev proposed himself as a successor to Yeltsin.

'After the autumn of 1990, after all the military preparations and attempts to break democracy, conservatives and revanchists killed the Shatalin 500-days programme. That was the putsch in the sphere of economics. The real putsch took place in September 1990 rather than in August 1991. The hardliners won it, pushing reformers aside from the management of the country. The Presidential Council had been Gorbachev's last democratic card, its real purpose was to block the Politburo. So the Politburo retaliated by displacing the Presidential Council. Gorbachev gave ground before the determination of the Politburo, and the Presidential Council began to lose power. The Politburo succeeded in re-establishing itself, and this marked the end of Gorbachev's policy. After this victory, the hardliners thought that the task of obtaining power remained merely technical.

'In the April 1991 plenum they tried to remove Gorbachev from the post of General Secretary. But there was strong opposition to this from seventy-two members of the Central Committee. So the hardliners became afraid of a split within the party. These seventy-two could have taken with them a great number of party members. After this April plenum, Gorbachev became conscious that something was wrong with his policy, that he was building a house on flimsy foundations. On 18 April I wrote a letter to him, which I am going to publish, to expose the real danger of a coup. I wrote that there was no place for Gorbachev with the hardliners, even physically, and as regards being received by the reformers, charms still existed but were diminishing. Gorbachev began to turn but it was too late.'

March 28 1991 was a day of rehearsal for the coup, when the army was called out in Moscow. Spurred on by rumour, perhaps as many as a quarter of a million people demonstrated in Pushkin Square and then at the White House, the seat of the Supreme Soviet and therefore the symbol of democracy. Among the demonstrators was Yakovlev's son, Anatoly, editor of a professional journal of philosophy and an admirer of Bertrand Russell. He was in the front line of a human chain around the White House, and says that those a few rows behind had guns. According to him, blood was in the air and he is at a loss to explain why the democratic movement was not crushed at that point.

Alexander Yakovlev described a flurry of telephone calls between himself, Gorbachev and Gavriil Popov, the mayor of Moscow. Gorbachev came to have information from the KGB that the demonstrators had weapons and scaling ladders and ropes for an assault on the Kremlin walls. A provocation by either side was all too likely, and someone might be shot. In that case, Gorbachev told Yakovlev, the organizers of the demonstration would be responsible. 'I said, Good, but can you imagine the way Moscow will bury anyone who is killed? Shocked by my question, he remained silent for two or three minutes; he understood the full implications of my remarks. The next day, in other words, there'd be a mass rebellion.' Further agitated telephoning between Gorbachev, Popov, Kryuchkov and Yazov ensured that the demonstration was peaceful. 'Two days later, the army and KGB organized a meeting of hardliners, communists and veterans in the very same place because they knew what had occurred behind the scenes. There was a placard of my enlarged photograph in the centre of a target, with the words, This time we will not miss. Bakatin discovered that these placards and slogans had been produced in KGB workshops.'

By that August, Yakovlev himself had been excluded from the party, and was in personal danger. 'I imagined that they would arrest me, but not that they intended to kill me, immediately. Eighteen people in all were on the death list, including Shevardnadze and myself.'

Every single General Secretary before Gorbachev would have used force.

'Certainly. It was his idea to avoid that mode, maybe in vain sometimes. In Karabakh, Sumgait and so on, force had to be used to keep the peace. In Vilnius and Riga in 1991 there is still no evidence that Gorbachev made the decision. It may have been a provocation.'

Does everything follow from the inner refusal to use force?

'I'd interpret it another way. You have to include the factor of compromise in such a consideration. The people surrounding him, and the hardliners as well, used his inclination to compromise for their own benefit. His soft and delicate scruples about introducing force created the impression that if hardliners were themselves to use force, he would indulge them.'

37

'CAUGHT IN A TRAP'

It was a snowy October when I called on Leonid Kravchenko in the offices of a specialist legal publication where he now works. There were 10 degrees of frost outside but the building was unheated. How are the mighty fallen – this large and despondent man once controlled Gorbachev's image. In the eyes of reformers, he was one of the faithful minions whom Gorbachev had levered into the office and then manipulated for his own purposes. To have carried out his duties, as Kravchenko sees it, was a course he could not avoid, and demotion and disgrace for conscientiousness must be unfair.

In the days of Andropov, he had been chief editor of *Trud*, the trade union paper, with a print run of 19 million. Readers sent in over 600,000 letters a year, the majority complaints about living conditions. It was clear to Kravchenko that society had been reduced to a pitiful level. On seven occasions he had been reprimanded by party or trade union organs. In August 1985 Yakovlev, as new head of the Ideological Department of the Central Committee, had appointed him first deputy chairman of the state broadcasting service Gosteleradio, with a special brief for its television centre at Ostankino on the outskirts of Moscow. At the time, television was extremely conservative, 'with an almost Arab style of supporting the regime. The main news programme consisted principally of quotes from the leadership in favour of policy, and hardly qualified at all as journalism.' Then he became director general of the party news agency Tass, and finally chairman of Gosteleradio in the final months of the Gorbachev era. That post carried automatic membership of the Central Committee.

Not one per cent of programmes went out live. Censorship necessitated prerecording. Within six months of taking office, Kravchenko claims, a third of programmes were live. He used his experience of *Trud* readers' letters to introduce political comment and analysis. *Focus on Perestroika* was a fifteen-minute programme he dreamed up with Yakovlev. It had the largest volume of viewers' response because it put under the microscope a particularly acute social problem of the moment. Another was *Vzglyad*, a flagship news programme which he was later accused of trying to close down. He also launched 'bridge' programmes which went out live to invited audiences in America and Russia simultaneously. 'At first, the Americans suspected that the studio had been packed with professional propagandists. They insisted on selecting the guests from passers-by on the streets or in cafés and they photographed them to make sure that the studio audience actually corresponded to their choice. Tough things were said on these programmes. When someone asked on one of them why the Berlin Wall could not be pulled down, I was hauled in and reprimanded. Western politicians performed live, for instance Franz-Josef Strauss and Mrs Thatcher who felt she wiped the floor with three Russian journalists during a discussion. We started live phone-ins on television with ministers and officials. The population was able to see for the first time the faces of those running the country.' Television, in his opinion, played 'the leading role in bursting through the new frontiers of glasnost. It had a colossal effect on public opinion. The mass media politicized previously passive people.'

Who took the decision to televise the Congress of People's Deputies?

'In 1985 nobody could have imagined televising it. But by the time it happened, they had already shown party congresses and conferences and it would have been unusual not to show the Congress. In the first hour of its first meeting, the Congress voted to have its proceedings televised, and Gorbachev supported the decision.' The 1988 law on the press and the mass media established freedom of speech to such a degree that attempts by Gorbachev and the Central Committee to crack down on state-controlled organs proved ineffective.

'At first Gorbachev did not understand the potential power of television and he refused to have his walkabouts and speeches televised. I arranged for him to be secretly filmed and then I showed him the video-cassettes and persuaded him to authorize their release. These performances confirmed him as a politician of a breed hitherto not seen in the country.'

Might it not have been wiser to carry through reforms before raising expectations of them by mere words?

'A good question. By about 1988 I already felt that glasnost would prove a dangerous toy to be playing with, one which could explode in everyone's face unless priority was given to economic reforms. Until then the economy seemed to be developing nicely but it was at the expense of the country's reserves. Ryzhkov now admits that it was a mistake not to accept price reform at that point. They were afraid that people would not accept the freeing of prices, but it would have been easier to do it while Gorbachev still had a degree of credibility. On the occasion when Ryzhkov raised the price of bread by a few kopecks, Yeltsin and the reformers were able to take advantage of it, saying that they would lie down on the railway tracks. Now prices have gone up a hundred times but nobody has threatened to lie on the railway tracks.'

Tass, the party news agency, received dispatches from correspondents in over 120 countries, as well as from a comprehensive network within the local Soviet media. Much of this amounted to intelligence, and could not be published. 'I supplied Gorbachev with a huge amount of private information, relating to Ligachev, Yeltsin and what the opposition was doing. Nobody else saw this material, and he was extremely grateful. As director general of Tass, I wrote and presented to Gorbachev a major report on Yugoslavia. I drew a parallel to our situation, saying that unless we took measures in time we would follow their example. He very plainly underestimated the potential for national conflict.'

Every week the directors general of Tass and Novosti, an alternative news agency otherwise serving the KGB, used to be summoned to the Central Committee secretariat for instruction. 'During these briefings Gorbachev took to telephoning me deliberately, to say, Why are you wasting your time in Central Committee meetings, you'd be better off running a television station. As a disciplined party member, receiving orders from the General Secretary, I stopped going to the meetings.

'During his last year in power, we would speak on the telephone several times a day. I felt it was an absolute duty to inform him of everything I knew. In the short time available to him, he did not always take notice, which was a pity. On several occasions I pointed out to him that the ultimate fate of politicians depended upon success in domestic and not foreign policy. I repeated this observation shortly before he was due to be handed his Nobel Prize. He had the sense not to collect the prize in person, it would have looked shameful, granted the distress in the country. That was the first time, I think, that it dawned on him that he had been wasting too much time on international back-slapping and handshaking. Obviously it was tempting to go abroad where people were waiting to receive him with open arms.

'I knew Gorbachev very well personally, and I think that psychologically he was hostage to his international popularity. He could never quite get down to dealing with the tough economic nut he had to crack at home. Each time that economic reform bogged him down, he would rush off on another bout of international peace-making, to feed his ego again. Encouraging him to postpone, Ryzhkov connived in this.

'The personalized confrontation with Yeltsin was a painful and excruciating experience to him. He became increasingly frightened that Yeltsin would want revenge. In the course of their struggle for supremacy, both men overstepped political norms, pursuing personal aims to the detriment of the state. Gorbachev had three planks for support: firstly the party which he badly needed; secondly parliament, which thanks to Lukyanov's general virtuosity as the Speaker remained a conservative force; and thirdly television and radio which he believed he should be able to depend on. There were strong opposition channels on television, however, in Leningrad and Moscow, and Gorbachev was always turning to me to say, Why can't you put your house in order and produce a station supporting the regime?

'The party got increasingly in his way and at times he reacted quite brutally with it. There were three occasions when he threatened to resign. He used to worry about Central Committee meetings to such an extent that beforehand he had severe headaches. He was unable to manage effectively the party's highly developed instinct for self-preservation, so that instead of exploiting it to his own advantage, he began to take power out of its hands.

'Whenever Yeltsin wanted to make a television appearance, he would write to ask me for a specific amount of time. That always led to wrangles. Gorbachev had to be informed, and the first reaction was that on no account was Yeltsin to be given any air-time at all. Yeltsin might be demanding an hour and Gorbachev would say, Give him ten minutes, no more. Whenever Yeltsin appeared on television, it was a black day for Gorbachev. It looked childish, like little boys battling for domination, but it was based of course on the instinctive fear that Yeltsin was acquiring an authority with the people which threatened Gorbachev's own survival.

'Yeltsin started demanding the opening of a second television channel for Russia, in other words, for his own personal use, more or less. Gorbachev refused. People like Mikhail Poltoranin and Khasbulatov pounced on me and said that in front of numerous witnesses Gorbachev had promised that Russia would have its separate channel. I dragged out the process of preparing this channel but after as much procrastination as possible it was launched on 13 May 1991, only five days before the Russian presidential elections. As it turned out, Russian television served the opposition very well, functioning as media support for Yeltsin, canonizing him. At the time Gorbachev lashed into me, saying, How dare you help my opponents like this? I answered that I was not going to be used as a pawn in these political games, telling him, You sort it out at your political level with your political opponents.'

What was Gorbachev's conception of democracy?

'In the first stage he had a very subjective and personal understanding of it – a kind of performing artist's delight in seeing himself as the initiator of reform and democratization, and in the plaudits that went with it. In the second and very important phase, he began to realize that there was a boomerang effect, that he had unleashed glasnost and democracy and they were coming back to hit him in the face. Thanks to freedom of speech, he was subjected to criticism every single day. A child of the Stalin period, he had the instinctive reaction to recapture control of the forces he had released, and crack down on them. Instead of a violent imposition of censorship, he sought to find people whom he thought he could trust, like me, to impose control on the media for him.'

Did you censor?

'There were occasions, particularly over the conflict in the Baltic States. Gorbachev insisted on the overall political line. I was obliged to prevent certain things from going out, I had to take responsibility for that, I had to be the public fall guy. It would not have been professional to explain that my behaviour followed from Gorbachev's orders. Gorbachev had already sensed that I was disappointed in him and didn't like what I was being asked to do. But he trusted and respected me, taking me everywhere as part of his delegation, to London for the G7 meeting, to Japan and Korea. At that point I wanted to resign. I was under enormous pressure from all sides. Raisa used to say, We can't let you resign, every day we talk about you in the family. I could not help feeling flattered and was not strong-minded enough to have got out of what I really knew was a political trap. I didn't manage to leave the sinking ship soon enough.'

In Kravchenko's opinion, Gorbachev remained in charge of the political process until towards the end of 1990. In spite of everything, the party and the army and the KGB still backed him. The usual Machiavellian manoeuvrings would have stood him in good stead, at least until he was obliged to submit to the direct election which so far he had skilfully managed to avoid. But he became trapped by the forces he had created. Fundamentally, 'He proved incapable of decisive actions. Just full of words. The Presidential Council gave him the excuse to offer some kind of power or consultancy role to cronies. What he ended up with was a multi-layer confusion, with the Presidential Council, and above that the Federation Council, and above that, in theory at least, the executive power of the Government, all of them constantly consulting and advising but none capable of taking a decision. He disbanded the Presidential Council at the end of the year with a view to satisfying those of his supporters who did not like it. His own friends had become more dangerous to him than the opposition.'

Gorbachev's indecision peaked at the moment of choosing between a form of confederation for the republics or saving the Soviet Union, however desperate the measures for that might have been. Gorbachev's friends made the choice for him. 'The action they took was mistaken; they should have stuck to parliamentary procedures, they could have done so because Lukyanov was skilled enough to orchestrate them. What they should not have done is exactly what they did, to take to the streets with tanks. People now say they were betraying Gorbachev but I think they were trying to come to his aid. A whole year before the putsch, Kryuchkov reported a meeting of most of the republics' presidents at which they had agreed among themselves how to arrange the carve-up of the Soviet Union once they were rid of Gorbachev. It did not come as a surprise to Gorbachev that they were trying to get rid of him.'

Kravchenko's own predicament was dire. Invited to an East–West conference on journalism in Edinburgh which coincided with the coup, he almost had a fortunate escape. Instead Gorbachev telephoned to forbid the Edinburgh trip because he wanted a five-hour live transmission of the ceremony of signing of the Union agreement due on 20 August. 'I telephoned his Chief of Staff, Valery Boldin, and said that this was going to be terribly dull, and I would work out something more lively. It was agreed that Gorbachev would come back from Foros in the Crimea in the evening of the 19th and look over this planned broadcast. I assume that Boldin knew that the coup was being prepared but he did not say anything about it.

'For me the whole thing started during the night of the 18th to the 19th. I was in my dacha out of town. A KGB car came for me at 1.30 a.m. and took me straight to the Central Committee. At 5 a.m. Oleg Shenin, standing in as General Secretary, handed me selected documents to be read out on the television and radio concerning the takeover. Huge numbers of people afterwards took me to task for broadcasting these instructions but I had no right to edit or change a single comma. By 6 a.m. all the television and radio stations had been surrounded by tanks and the KGB had taken control. I could not get into Ostankino until I was accompanied by KGB officers and parachute troops.'

In exemplary Soviet style, *Swan Lake* was broadcast twice that day. 'People have implied that the swans were supposed to symbolize the putschists come to save the country.' In fact the ballet had been scheduled to go out a second time for the benefit of night-workers, he says, and hours were thereby blocked off which might have been devoted to sustaining the coup. 'You needn't underestimate the number of people flocking to the television centre to broadcast their support for what had happened. The most interesting broadcast that went out that day was Yanayev's famous press conference during which the camera homed in on his trembling hands. Involuntarily they undermined their own positions. It was obvious that these were men not confident of their own success.'

The following day, television broadcast foreign reaction, predictably enthusiastic in the case of Soviet clients like Saddam Hussein, Yasser Arafat and Fidel Castro. Among democratic leaders President Mitterrand was alone in condoning the coup. 'Everything was going out under the gaze of Kryuchkov's people, constantly criticizing me for insufficient supervision. I tried to persuade the likes of Bessmertnyk and Lukyanov to give interviews but none of them were prepared to do so. I think that over the next few days television occupied a fairly ambiguous position.

'I had one final personal contact with Gorbachev. On the evening of the 21st, he telephoned with the text of an announcement to the nation which he wanted me to read out in person. I got a newsreader to do so. A week later I received two presidential decrees, one from Gorbachev and one from Yeltsin, relieving me of my duties. Yeltsin had not appointed me and as President of Russia he had no right to issue such a decree. Gorbachev had become like a little puppy dog doing whatever Yeltsin told him and signing every bit of paper put under his nose. During that last telephone call Gorbachev had said that on his return to Moscow he would sort out my problems, but he never did. And that is the reason why you find me in this little office.'

38

THE STATE COMMITTEE AND THE COUP

Novo-Ogaravo is an estate which had belonged to a pre-revolutionary Russian industrialist. It lies on a bend of the Moskva River. Khrushchev was among communist leaders who had lived in its Gothic-style stone mansion. Such relics convey a forlorn regret at the turn taken by history. A team of specialists assembled there early in 1991 to draft out a new treaty defining the Constitution of the Soviet Union for the future. The issue in question was the ultimate relationship of the Soviet centre to the republics. This could be expressed in other forms. For instance, since the party had lost the satellites without a fight, could it at the last gasp find the will and the capacity to hold earlier conquests? Or, did Russia still have the right to maintain non-Russian republics in subservience? Or again, could Gorbachev use Soviet rope to tie down Yeltsin promoting himself on the back of Russia?

By the time the specialists received their brief at Novo-Ogarovo, Gorbachev was facing the reality that the centre could hardly project its customary power at all. This was already a rearguard action. Fighting over Nagorny-Karabakh, Armenia and Azerbaijan resorted to Moscow only in the hope of some arbitration which would cut out the opponent. Having declared independence through due process, and fully aware that force alone could subdue them once more, the Baltic States no longer considered themselves within the Soviet Union. Georgia was turning in on itself as a power struggle developed between Shevardnadze, now out of office, and a former dissident Zviad Gamsakhurdia, elected President in the same 1990 republic elections which had brought Yeltsin to the presidency of Russia. Separatists were gaining the upper hand in Moldavia. Ukraine, Belarus, Kazakhstan and other Muslim republics were Gorbachev's surviving building blocks.

For him, the supremacy of the Soviet centre was a heritage as well as an article of faith. Five years of criticism, purging and experiment had sapped the party as the instrument of dictatorship upon which each General Secretary had hitherto relied to guarantee the centre's supremacy. Here was a contradiction entirely of his own making. Shredding his power and authority with apparent recklessness, he now had virtually no means of enforcing his way in a crisis in which force alone could prove effective. Complaining loudly that the republics were escaping control, he could not stop them militarily but only plead that decentralization must lead further to dissolution and anarchy.

Gorbachev likes to maintain that he had foreseen this predicament and was moving into the future, leaving the party stuck in the past. This has the air of wisdom after the event; a rationalization which sets him in a gratifyingly liberal and even noble perspective. No longer capable of enforcing his absolute will as General Secretary, he undoubtedly expected to be able to fall back on the other position he had prepared for himself as President of the Union. The United States was evidently his model. Following the American example, he visualized himself as a President who was also commander-in-chief of the armed forces, master of the nuclear weapon, in control of foreign policy and the budget, with an integrated system of such essentials as taxation and the law. On an analogy with American states, Soviet republics would have specific but limited rights and powers devolved to them. Where the lines were to be drawn was the subject for discussion at Novo-Ogarovo.

Dextrous in pursuit of Utopia, Gorbachev conceived yet another body, the Council of the Federation. He himself was its chairman, and the fifteen heads of the republics were *ex officio* members. Was its role advisory or was this a constitutional novelty? Quite what the relationship was to the Supreme Soviet was undefined. Gorbachev seems to have believed that by means of this Council of the Federation he had devised some final forum in which to have his way. It also seems to have been immaterial to him whether the republics signed a treaty of federation or confederation. He floated a refinement, whereby republics might be independent yet confederated. As with the unification of Germany and the loss of the satellites, the vagueness was more desperate than creative. Nor did he regard it as a doom that the Presidents of six republics cold-shouldered his brand-new Council. A document, more or less any document, would do so long as enough Presidents of republics put their signatures to the continuation of the Soviet centre in some form or shape. In any respite granted for consolidation, the missing republics might be rounded up like so many straying sheep.

On 23 April nine of the republic Presidents committed themselves at Novo-Ogarovo to the principle of a Union treaty, with elections for all Union posts to follow six months after the treaty had been finalized. The first meeting to thrash out the practical details was held on 23 May. For the next two months, the centre and the republics squabbled over the division of spoils. Autonomous Republics, among them Tatarstan and Bashkiria and Yakutia, presented their claim for independence too, in a further ripple of disintegration.

Already the determining political figure, Yeltsin agreed that the Soviet centre should continue to control foreign policy, defence and the budget, and he carried with him the other republic Presidents who were present. In spite of apparently falling in with Gorbachev's wishes, Yeltsin was temporizing, with almost daily displays of ill-grace. As President of Russia, he was taking quite contrary measures which had the effect of rendering the centre superfluous; for instance, he set limits on the amount of money that Russia would remit to the centre, he forbade party cells in the army and the KGB in units stationed within Russia, and he recognized the independence of Lithuania.

However acrimonious and personalized, the Novo-Ogarovo talks none the less presupposed a sharing of power and so were the Soviet equivalent to the Round Tables in the former satellites. No other peaceful resolution of the 'war of laws' was conceivable. Representing the party, Gorbachev was in the same position as the satellite First Secretaries of conceding to the opposition demands which had become irresistible. Like them, he hoped that the party – and therefore himself – would retain power duly masked by a mixture of concession and the new but still only token vocabulary of democratization. A crucial difference separated the Novo-Ogarovo talks from other Round Tables. Deprived deliberately of Soviet military backing, satellite First Secretaries had seen no alternative to a negotiated surrender of power, to be consummated in a general election. Gorbachev could speak for himself in renouncing the use of force and agreeing to elections, but he could not guarantee the passivity of the Soviet army. Here was an unknown factor. The soldiers might or might not obey orders; they could determine the test of strength, and the onus was on them to select extremely carefully between winners and losers. Councils, talks and what could pass at a pinch for constitutional procedures offered the army no pretext for intervening in politics; hence Gorbachev's willingness to concede so much in return for mere signatures.

Many of the professionals in the army and the KGB perceived Gorbachev and his reforms as unconditional surrender. Loss of the satellites, and the East German bases in particular, as well as the various arms limitation treaties, looked like self-conflicted injuries. Devolution of power from the centre to the republics threatened the very existence of the Red Army. Conscripts were already evading the annual draft, to enlist in embryonic units in their own national republics. If national republics were to have armies, who would man the Red Army? Without a centralized Soviet budget, military expenditure could only dwindle, perhaps cease. The military–industrial complex itself might splinter. Among the deputies in the Supreme Soviet were a number of senior officers and they took to angry rhetoric there, as well as signing menacing declarations in the press. One such, on 23 July, had the title, 'Our home is already burning to the ground'. Whatever the outcome of the Novo-Ogarovo talks might be, in the six months leading up to the coup both Gorbachev and Yeltsin were at great pains to tour barracks and other military installations, flattering officers and soldiers with promises and prospects if only they would prove loyal. One élite division was visited by the two contenders within the same twenty-four hours.

Rumours of the coup circulated on all sides after Shevardnadze's spectacular resignation. The press aired the idea openly. Familiar with their own system, people anticipated the clash that alone could distribute power decisively. Tension and fear settled loweringly over the whole society. On 17 June, Prime Minister Pavlov in the Supreme Soviet asked for an expansion of his powers. The Minister of Defence, Marshal Yazov, the Minister of the Interior, Boriss Pugo, and Kryuchkov all supported him. Had the request been granted, Pavlov would have usurped Gorbachev's prerogatives as President. Gorbachev advised the deputies not to be 'hysterical'.

Nobody knows exactly at what point the conspirators first came together either to express their dismay or to plan their coup. According to Boldin, his Chief of Staff and eventually one of the plotters, Gorbachev one Saturday in the summer of 1990 suspected the worst when he discovered that Bakatin, Yakovlev and Colonel General Mikhail Moiseyev, the Chief of Staff, were apparently all out together walking in the woods. 'They've got a few generals with them as well; they're obviously up to something.' In Boldin's eyes the hysteria was Gorbachev's, and the result of his chronic indecision.

Even at the highest level, nobody escaped KGB surveillance. Telephones were tapped, mail intercepted and cars followed as a matter of course. At the Novo-Ogarovo talks, Yeltsin behaved as though his private conversation was being bugged, as no doubt it was. Towards the end of 1990, Kryuchkov was to be heard scaremongering that the Soviet Union was in distress, that the West was undermining it by every possible trick, and that Gorbachev was responding 'inadequately'. Whether taking precautions or accommodating the hardliners, Gorbachev instructed his close advisers to prepare for a state of emergency.

Kryuchkov had the task of informing Gorbachev of all intrigues. His bespectacled face is devoid of expression which might reveal the inner man. Intelligent, much travelled and allegedly widely read, Vladimir Kryuchkov had the experience which was to make him the moving spirit of the coup. He was born in 1924. As Third Secretary in the Soviet Embassy in Budapest, he had participated in crushing the Hungarian revolution. The ambassador at the time, Andropov, had taken Kryuchkov with him on his own promotion to the top. Appointed head of the KGB in 1988, he became a full member of the Politburo in the following year.

A secret order from him that same year states that one of the KGB's main tasks would be to prevent and head off political opposition to the party. The KGB would do so by placing its own people as deputies in the newly elected parliaments. In the spring 1990 elections to republic and local Soviets, 2756 KGB officers are said to have been elected.

Himself a general in the KGB, committed to the Soviet Union, Boriss Pugo could no longer expect to have a career in his native Latvia, now in the hands of the Popular Front. Every inch a veteran general, out to maximize power for his own sake, Marshal Yazov assumed that loyalty to the party was identical to patriotism. Between them Kryuchkov, Pugo and Yazov had command of all the armed forces. If they were to act in concert, armed opposition could only be rebellion. To make the coup a clean sweep, they enlisted General Valentin Varennikov, commander of the ground forces, Oleg Baklanov, the leading representative of the military–industrial complex, Oleg Shenin to speak for the Politburo and the party, and Prime Minister Pavlov. Others, Vice President Yanayev, for instance, were figureheads. By the end of July the specialists and assorted presidents at Novo-Ogarovo had agreed on the text of a treaty by the simple expedient of watering down and generalizing its language to the point of meaninglessness. The technical details were, if anything, less defined than they had been in April. Leonid Kravchuk, President of Ukraine, now joined those already unwilling to sign. Several Presidents of Autonomous Republics also abstained because they had not obtained guarantees of independence. Only eight of the fifteen Union Presidents committed themselves to the formal ratification of this treaty. Lukyanov raised the objection that parliament had not been consulted, a startling prevarication in a party-state. But the end result was as usual in these tests, that by means of ambiguity and the imaginative acceptance of grey areas due to be explored another day, the important personalities were able to emerge claiming to have obtained what they wanted.

The first of four completely mysterious aspects of the coup is the fact that Gorbachev and his family took a fortnight's holiday starting on 4 August. Instead of remaining in Moscow to proffer blandishments to those friendly to the treaty, and to pressurize Yeltsin and Kravchuk and those hanging back, Gorbachev retired far away to the presidential seaside house at Foros, in the Crimea. Heedless behaviour of the sort is quite out of keeping, and suggests that he was leaving the field expressly to others.

Secondly, the conspirators were Gorbachev's men. He himself had put Kryuchkov into the place of Chebrikov, a calm personality and a loyalist unlikely to have betrayed him. He had ousted Ryzhkov to make way for Pavlov. He had brought in Pugo. Had the instinct for self-preservation become defective? Unsparingly, Yeltsin was to draw the obvious inference about

Gorbachev: 'You cannot absolve him of his guilt in the conspiracy. Who chose the officials? He did.'

The leading conspirators gathered the moment Gorbachev had flown off. All of them were subsequently to state that the plot aimed to prevent the ratification of the new Union treaty due two weeks later. When they were brought to trial in 1993 they further maintained that they had acted in the belief that they were carrying out Gorbachev's wishes. Here is the next mystery, in all likelihood too deep ever to be unravelled. Gorbachev's style was often oblique, oracular, a matter of nods and hints. In his projections of a state of emergency, he may well have raised an eyebrow or gestured with his arms to imply more than he meant. Perhaps he spoke loftily of duties to be performed; perhaps he hinted to them, as he had to Mladenov and Krenz, that he was aware of their plans and he would back success and disavow failure. Since nothing was written down, everything could be misconstrued. His word would have to be weighed against theirs.

At his trial Marshal Yazov was to tell the prosecutor that on the 17th, a Saturday, Kryuchkov had called them all to a meeting. 'At a point in Moscow at the end of Leninski Prospekt – a left turn near the police post, there is a road there.' But the serious business was done in Pavlov's office. There they had formed a self-styled State Committee. Lukyanov arrived. He too had been on holiday. For him at that moment, the choice was too difficult to make. The State Committee needed him to provide a fig leaf of legality but it was certain to have no long-term use for the Supreme Soviet of which he was the Speaker. Declining to join outright, Lukyanov wriggled; he would put out a statement against the coming treaty. And so he did, in flowery legalese.

On the evening of the 18th, selected conspirators arrived unannounced at Foros with an ultimatum. Gorbachev must either back them or stand down, at least for the time being. By his own account, which is supported by faithful advisers also present like Chernyayev, Gorbachev reacted with spirit. The conspirators had no standing; they had launched into a stricken adventure likely to lead to bloodshed. Deprived of telephones, relying for news upon an old radio set found in an attic and cobbled up by friendly guards, Gorbachev remained under house arrest for seventy-two hours. The toll exacted by the experience was certainly etched on his face, as on Raisa's, when at last they returned to Moscow.

The country learned in the small hours of the 19th of the existence of the State Committee. By dawn tanks were occupying key points in Moscow. A state of emergency was declared, 'with a view to overcoming the deep and multilateral crisis, the political, inter-ethnic, and civil confrontation, the chaos and anarchy that threatened the life and security of citizens of the Soviet

Union, the sovereignty, territorial integrity, freedom, and independence of our motherland'. Because Gorbachev was said to be ill, Yanayev was standing in for him.

Yeltsin was then in his dacha at Arkhangelskoye, a short hour's drive from the White House, the seat of the Supreme Soviet. His daughter woke him up with the news she had just heard on television. He seems to have recognized at once that he had to do or die. His wife and daughter, he says, never cried. Silayev and Khasbulatov were house guests. On his way home to Leningrad, soon to revert to its former name of St Petersburg, the mayor, Anatoly Sobchak, called hurriedly, leaving with the grim exclamation, 'May God help us!' Yeltsin put on a bullet-proof vest, and he and his friends took their various routes past the military vehicles in order to reach the White House. There he was to stay, besieged and detained more dramatically than Gorbachev.

In the woods around his dacha that morning, Yeltsin records in his book, *The View from the Kremlin*, lurked an arrest squad. Still according to Yeltsin, the leader drank a full glass of vodka, 'expecting an order to arrest or destroy us'. Once the test of strength reaches this ultimate stage, and the resort to force is open and declared, such an arrest or destruction becomes imperative. Yeltsin, on balance winner of the Novo-Ogarovo talks, was far more dangerous to the State Committee than Gorbachev, on balance the loser. Why the State Committee did not launch its bid for power by arresting Yeltsin in the middle of the night is the final mystery. Of all people, Kryuchkov knew that scruples had no place in lawless undertakings of this kind. The last communist to have masterminded such a coup was General Jaruzelski, and he carried it through in swift, Stalinist style. About these conspirators, he commented expertly, 'How is the extraordinary amateurism of their proceedings to be explained? I can find no redeeming logic in it'.

Inside the White House, a telephone line was still open to the outside world; more evidence of the State Committee's lack of thoroughness. Yeltsin was able to mobilize support worldwide. Demonstrators flocked to the building and erected ramshackle barricades around it. Probably there were no more than 20,000 although some estimates soar up to 100,000 and even more. Three of them were killed in the one fatal incident to have occurred. It is generally agreed, even by Yeltsin, that the storming of the White House would have been a relatively easy operation. In the event of an attack, Yeltsin's aide Sergei Stankevich warned the awaiting soldiers, 'You will be cursed', a rather feeble admission that solid means of defence were lacking.

Troops also moved into Leningrad, as well as the capitals of the three Baltic republics. In Riga, General Kuzmin declared himself the Governor of the Baltics. Railway junctions, border posts, television stations and the seat of the Council of Ministers in Riga were all occupied. Two demonstrators in Riga were shot dead, and others wounded. Several Presidents, especially in the Muslim republics, declared their backing for the State Committee. So did 70 per cent of the regional party leadership.

A precedent for this coup can be found in the plot of 20 July 1944 against Hitler. Detonating his bomb in headquarters Stauffenberg believed that he had achieved his objective of killing Hitler. Notified, a number of generals, some as far away as Paris and Brussels, then had to decide whether to join the conspiracy or betray it. Those who made the wrong choice paid for it with their lives. Soviet generals and unit commanders were now in a similar bind. Kryuchkov and Yazov were giving them orders. Implementation might carry a death warrant, but so might disobedience. To hedge one's bets was the prudent course.

Yeltsin gives a telling illustration. One of the units he had visited while drumming up support before the coup was a parachute division under the command of General Pavel Grachev. The man made a favourable impression. One of Yeltsin's first calls from his Arkhangelskoye dacha on the morning of the 19th was to Grachev, to ask for support. 'Grachev was disturbed, there was a long pause, and I could hear his laboured breathing on the other end of the line. Finally, he said that for him, for an officer, it was impossible to disobey an order. I said something to the effect that I didn't want to expose him to attack.' While Grachev was sighing into the receiver, Yeltsin concluded, 'He was deciding not only his fate but also mine. And the fate of millions of people. That's the way it goes.' With philosophical resignation about what is in effect an inherent and deadly gambling, the tone does perfect justice to these tests of strength. As payoff, Grachev afterwards became Minister of Defence.

In the course of the coup, Pavlov retired to hospital with a heart attack. Yanayev was more or less continually drunk. General Varennikov flew to Kiev, apparently to inveigle Kravchuk. Pugo and Yazov and Kryuchkov sat in the Kremlin appealing to senior officers who presumably sighed much like Grachev, but then prevaricated. Suspended animation could last only so long. When the lack of commitment significantly outweighed obedience in the welter of telephoning, the coup expired. Throwing their hand in, on the afternoon of the 21st, Kryuchkov and Yazov and two others flew down to Foros, where they were arrested on Yeltsin's orders. Yazov was alone in sounding contrite: what had happened 'brings shame on the armed forces'. To his wife he apparently said that he was an old fool. In an opening address at his trial, Kryuchkov in contrast regretted that he had not impeached Gorbachev and saved the Soviet Union from foreign domination as well as Yeltsin's 'totalitarianism'. Following his own eccentric course, Lukyanov also flew to Foros on the 21st in another aircraft, and was arrested some days later.

*   *   *

In the continuing absence of documentary or conclusive evidence, each person has to interpret these events as best may be. Hard facts are few. Boriss Pugo is thought to have killed his wife, and then shot himself, although there is speculation that they may have been murdered. Marshal Akhromeyev, though peripheral to the coup, also shot himself. In February 1994, parliament amnestied the conspirators. General Varennikov alone insisted on standing trial on the grounds that he would implicate Gorbachev. In the Supreme Court later that July, he referred to Gorbachev to his face as 'the accused'. Testifying, an outraged Gorbachev emphatically denied that he had encouraged the plotters.

Paranoia and conspiracy theories are the bastard offspring of these tests of strength. Common sense is the only map through the swamp of mystery. In Riga I had interviewed Jānis Vagris. A prosaic man by nature, inured to the party and its ways by a lifetime toiling for it, Vagris was in a position to observe the coup from a privileged position, although not an insider. At the highest level of the old Soviet party *apparat*, almost everyone speaks in like vein.

On 4 May, during the Novo-Ogarovo talks, Latvia had finally followed Lithuania in affirming its independence, but with a proviso that there would be a transition period in which it would co-operate with the centre in all matters not touching sovereignty. In reaction, three days later, the Latvian party split and Vagris was deposed at its First Secretary, in favour of Alfrēds Rubiks, who then passionately supported the coup and landed up in prison for it. But Vagris remained an elected member of the Supreme Soviet in Moscow, and the Latvian representative on its Presidium. An old-timer like him cannot acquire the habit of referring to the Supreme Soviet in the new parlance as the Congress of People's Deputies. As he puts it, 'The Soviet Union was now a foreign state. It was not acceptable for Gorbunovs as Chairman of the Latvian Supreme Soviet to go to Moscow in the role of a Soviet representative. He and the Latvian Supreme Soviet decided that I should remain on the Presidium in order to act as a channel of information. As I now had nothing to do here, I used to fly to Moscow on a Monday morning and come back on Friday evening. On one such Friday I came back normally but the coup started the following Monday, 19 August. Listening to the news on the radio, I stayed in Riga.'

A telegram arrived from Lukyanov to say that on the 21st the Presidium of the Supreme Soviet would convene. 'In fact the Supreme Soviet was not then in session. Gorbachev was on holiday. Gorbunovs said that it was my duty to attend. So I left on the Tuesday. The Moscow atmosphere was very heated. I was living in our Embassy. Not a hotel. Normally my journey to the Presidium was two stops on the metro, getting off at the Moskva Hotel, crossing Red Square, and so to the Kremlin. But now the secretary of the Supreme Soviet telephoned and told me not to take that route, but to order a car as was permitted, and to enter the Kremlin from the other side. The car came. I went to the Kremlin, which was full of tanks and soldiers in flak jackets. My first thought was that I could enter but nobody could tell me whether I should ever be able to leave again. The crowd on Red Square blocked all hope of getting out that way.

'The Supreme Soviet was supposed to start at three o'clock and we were handed a package of documents including the agenda, as if the Presidium had already decided to support the State Committee, and all we had to do was endorse it. Lukyanov was not there. We were informed that he had left for Foros to consult with Gorbachev. Before his departure, he had advised that no decisions were to be taken and that the meeting should be adjourned until his return the following day. The meeting was chaired by Laptev. We discussed the fact that there had already been three victims in Moscow and two in Riga. The full seriousness of the situation was staring us in the face. In spite of Lukyanov's request for postponement of any decision, the Presidium resolved not to support the State Committee and called for an immediate meeting of the Supreme Soviet.

'The session started in fact once Gorbachev had returned. When he explained how he had been isolated and had shot a home video of what had happened and how an old radio receiver had been found under the roof, I remained unconvinced. In a place like that, nothing of the sort could conceivably be left behind and overlooked. This was a piece of theatre, as the members of the State Committee say, and Gorbachev must have been fully aware of what was going to happen. Later he even intimated that they had come to the Crimea to concoct a story, and he said that he could have no part in it and simply sent them packing. How is it conceivable that they could come to him with such a proposal and all he could do was send them packing? As President, he could not act like that. Lukyanov gave an interview to explain how they had all schemed, and in my opinion that is the true version. They went there to propose this coup because they were unwilling to sign the new Union treaty. Gorbachev's response was characteristic, that if the scheme turned out advantageously he would support them, but if not, then they would carry responsibility for everything. Those who flew to Foros are accused of wanting to take power, but of course they already had all the power they could possibly want in the key positions.'

39

'A FRIENDLY LITTLE CHAT'

My interview with Valentin Pavlov was early in the morning because he was due to appear later on for another court hearing. He had not long been released from prison. Lawyers with large black cars gathered around in the front parking lot of the apartment block in which he lived. It is a choice Nomenklatura building. Pavlov, 'the obnoxious Pavlov' in Yeltsin's phrase, did not seem at all nervous. Still chubby and smiling, he looked younger than his years. Answering the telephone, he discussed in front of me a business deal involving property in central Moscow, levelly disputing the price in dollars per square metre.

Before becoming Prime Minister, he had been Minister of Finance, and he sees himself as a technician. Needless to say, the spectrum of views about his capacities is wide, as well as a mass of contradiction. The Soviet Union did not collapse because it had run out of resources, he insists. Available resources were completely sufficient for the levels of productivity and economic turnover projected into the indefinite future.

'The only reason for any appearance of insufficiency was the sudden demand for increased production to raise standards of living or technological innovation. Take the oil and gas industry. This had the resources necessary for exploration and extraction. Before August 1990 five and a half billion roubles had been allocated for the purpose, which at that time's exchange rate was equivalent to eight billion dollars. Plans were well advanced for laying a wide-diameter pipeline from the north to the European part of Russia.'

If resources were sufficient, why did the economy go to pieces in 1989, leading to crash plans like Shatalin's, and a huge state deficit?

'The key is that the Soviet economy was divided into two parts. The first part was servicing the immediate needs of human beings, food, clothing, consumer durables and so forth. The second part was linked less directly to production for human needs, machine tools, technology, real estate. Because there was no private ownership, the transfer of resources from the consumer-linked sector to the productive sector was blocked. The direct interests of individuals or groups of individuals were locked into the consumer sector. Like it or not, that put limitations on stimulating the productive part of the economy.'

In office, Pavlov appeared to be a traditional communist, loosening planning and price controls only with reluctance. He still wraps personal struggles and ambitions in abstract party parlance. Nobody was arguing about the ultimate goal of moving towards a mixed economy, he now says, but how this was to be done threw up fundamental differences of opinion. 'I was, and still am, by nature a fundamental opponent of all kinds of violent revolution. I favour evolutionary methods. You need to prepare innovations before you dismantle what already exists. That was the basis of my strong objection to the Shatalin 500-days plan, and all other such economic plans.'

By the time you became Prime Minister in January 1991, the economy and indeed the whole political process appears to have escaped control.

'Yes, that is close to the truth. As I would describe it, separatist forces, assisted by certain aspects of central leadership including Gorbachev, had acquired too much power. Gorbachev had cultivated those forces too fondly over a long period without paying attention to the fact that they were escaping his control. With considerable surprise, he then discovered that he was not managing these separatist forces but they were managing him. One practical phenomenon which brought him up with a sharp jerk was the wave of industrial strikes starting in mid-1990 with the coal-miners. This was extraordinarily destructive to the economy. Two weeks after I became Prime Minister, there was an almost general strike of miners. For over two months almost two-thirds of the mines stopped working. You can imagine the consequences of taking decisive steps towards the market economy and the freeing of prices at such a moment.'

Why choose that time for your currency reform?

'I had long been convinced that currency reform was essential. It had been in preparation since about 1985. As its chief architect, I had the opportunity to introduce it as Minister of Finance, but in practical terms I could not finalize preparation until I became Prime Minister. From the point of view of price-rises, currency reform was needed to stop a sudden burst of hyperinflation. It was crucial for me to remove the superfluous mass of currency then floating around the country.' By a compulsory exchange of old notes for new, and freezing deposits and savings, he explains, he removed 25 billion roubles from circulation. 'Add to that another 12 billion which people possessed so illegally that they did not even try to exchange them. That amounted altogether to a

415

third of the total currency supply and having taken it out of circulation, I was then on 2 April able to free prices of approximately a third of the goods in the consumer economy. This combination of cutting the money supply and subsequently freeing the prices at least to a limited degree kept inflation down to one per cent over the next six months.'

Well-placed people were taking advantage to secure private fortunes. One example was the vanishing of the gold reserves. Resources and money were being removed on an enormous scale.

'Once Yavlinsky got access to that information about the gold, he started shouting it to the four winds. I suspect it was an attempt to gain cheap popularity. In actual fact, almost nobody apart from myself knew precisely how much there was in the gold reserve. I never even informed Gorbachev about it. I did not trust him either. Obviously, there was an outflow of capital. It is worth remembering that those who were draining money away knew that I knew what they were doing, and that it would not be long before their channels of exit would be closed off. I knew exactly whom I needed to call into my office for a friendly little chat, in order to persuade them to return this money. We are talking about considerable sums – there is no secret about that, nor about the means used to transfer them. Capital resources were draining away, the primary exports from the country, namely gold, oil, timber and so forth. You just need to look at the people in charge of those particular export industries.'

Why did you ask the Supreme Soviet for extra powers on 17 June?

'A strange power situation had arisen. There was a conflict of interest between the executive and the legislative. The President had set himself up as head of the executive, instead of functioning as Head of State. That meant that in effect there was no genuine executive power in the country. What should have been the executive arm of government turned into a seat of highly talented orators, rather than genuinely practical politicians. In this context, Gorbachev can be described as an extremely talented actor, in the sense that actors can give a thoroughly convincing performance of understanding things about which they have no real conception. So there was neither legislative nor executive powers. What with chaos and confrontation, we needed a strong executive government as never before.

'Even if the Supreme Soviet had sat around the clock, day in and day out, in order to elaborate a proper legal base for the new economy we were supposed to be introducing, it would have taken no less than five years. The proper base was never introduced. The idea of imposing economic reforms from above was doomed to failure from the start. Had we waited for the necessary laws to be gradually introduced, and allowed the economy to change in line with those laws, we would have found people functioning at the same speed as the legal base. For that reason I was, and still am, in favour of giving the executive branch certain legislative powers in a period of transition. Practical decisions taken by the executive must become the basis for law. Once adopted, laws can then begin to function as permanent norms.'

Is your request for special powers linked to the formation of the State Committee?

'There were five points. The right to take certain legal initiatives; the right to organize via the KGB and the police a special nationwide unit to deal with organized crime; a nationwide federal tax inspectorate; the creation of a unified banking system; the right for ministers to take immediate decisions to control the economy, for instance in cases where reforms had an impact which did not correspond to existing legislation. It is for others to judge whether this was connected with what happened in August.'

What with the lawyers and the black cars assembling downstairs, he fended off questions about the coup. I asked when he joined the State Committee, and received the unlikely reply, 'Not until mid-August, the 18th.' He had already told the prosecutor that at the Kremlin on that day, 'most of those present did not understand what the whole thing was about. Emergency measures had been discussed before.' All he would add now was, 'Already in 1990 there had been discussions with Gorbachev about the establishment of an emergency government committee. Gorbachev had long been aware of the power vacuum and the inability to take genuine practical measures.'

40

THE SPEAKER

The coup and imprisonment have aged Anatoly Lukyanov and what little is left of his hair has turned white. In prison he wrote two volumes of verse, and published them. Not very good verse, to be sure, but intellectually he stands apart from the other plotters. Burly and assured, he has an emphatic way of talking. A career spent in these wearying tests of strength carved a rugged, brute personality. His brown eyes reveal humour but there is no doubt that he thinks himself abused. When the elder-statesman posture slips, he is unmistakably angry and frustrated. It is a party piece of his to proclaim that long before Gorbachev's day he had worked with Molotov, Khrushchev, Brezhnev, Kosygin, Andropov and Chernenko: he enjoys the roll call. Into his conversation he drops quotable nuggets he acquired from meeting in person the likes of General de Gaulle and Harry Hopkins, Roosevelt's dubious adviser, sometimes suspected of worse than fellow-travelling. In prison, he says, he received 400,000 letters, including friendly ones from Mrs Thatcher as well as John Major.

To the task of Speaker in the Congress of People's Deputies, he brought intimate experience of every kind of chicanery and pressure, legal and illegal. It was a living legend at the time that he used to switch off the microphone for deputies who failed to please, and dangle before those who had to be kept sweet privileges like a car at a knock-down price. 'I do not consider myself a professional politician but a lawyer.' This throwaway line offers insight into his attitude both to the law and to politics. 'The position of Speaker in the Russian Congress is very far removed from British parliamentary procedures. My work as Speaker involved constant games and manipulations with deputies, trying to organize them into blocs, trying to popularize certain kinds of opinions, joking with them. The Speaker is really the prime mover in co-operation and mutual linking between various factions. I had cause to meet more frequently with Sakharov than with the communist faction. I recalled talking to a group of sovietologists in Oxford and they were incapable of understanding why it was necessary for me as Speaker to operate as this kind of parliamentary manipulator.'

A friend of Gorbachev's in his student days was one Andrei Lukyanov, whom the Soviet historian Roy Medvedev mistook for Anatoly. The result has been a widely repeated exaggeration of his early closeness to Gorbachev. 'I was two years ahead of him in college, though we did live in the same student hostel. So to some degree I knew the young Gorbachev and also his future wife. That was in 1950. When he arrived at Moscow's university, he had already been awarded a Banner of Red Labour for his agricultural work helping his father with the harvest. In the Komsomol he was very active, highly devoted to Marxist ideology, that is to say the Stalinist version of it then current. When Stalin died, Gorbachev took it hard, as a personal blow. As far as his studies went, he was pretty good but not outstanding; a typical example of a politically active Komsomol student of the period. He was the kind of young enthusiast who wanted to smash up everything without thinking what was to replace it.'

Gorbachev then returned to Stavropol while Lukyanov prepared his doctorate in Moscow University and became head of its Komsomol section. In 1977 Brezhnev promulgated a new constitution which involved changes of personnel. Lukyanov was promoted head of the secretariat of the Supreme Soviet Presidium, in charge of the supposedly redesigned parliamentary apparatus. That same year, Gorbachev was elected a deputy to the Supreme Soviet and from then on the two men were 'in more or less constant contact'. The Supreme Soviet was not a formality, he claims, because its various standing committees met all year round and initiated legislation.

'In my presence Gorbachev never said anything about major changes in the country before 1985. On the contrary, he appeared to all intents and purposes highly devoted to Soviet socialism in its distinct form. He was an extremely loyal colleague of Brezhnev, Andropov and even Chernenko. If we look at his speeches and official reports to all the congresses, the Twenty-sixth and Twenty-seventh and Twenty-eighth, and to the Nineteenth Party Conference, we find him consistently insisting that perestroika was a modernizing and deepening of socialism, not its destruction. That is the only way you can understand perestroika. At no stage was there the least doubt that we were moving along a path towards perfecting socialism. When Gorbachev became General Secretary in 1985, I worked with him preparing the report for the April plenum of the Central Committee, which launched the whole perestroika process. We were proposing to accelerate the introduction of new technology. We had the slogan, "More democracy, more socialism".'

He and Yeltsin enjoyed parallel promotion. 'In 1985 we lived in the same house and knew each other extremely well. Both of us were Central

Committee secretaries, and the only difference was that I was responsible for legal questions while he was responsible for building and construction. When in 1986 Yeltsin became head of the Moscow Party Committee, he simultaneously became a candidate member of the Politburo. I became a candidate member slightly later, in 1988, when I was elected Gorbachev's first deputy. Yeltsin, Ligachev and people like me all supported perestroika. All the comrades including Gorbachev were operating under the impression that they were working towards a better, renewed socialism. Had Gorbachev announced that he was planning some kind of new and unknown society he would have been completely on his own. The one person who might have been on his side was Yakovlev. He is a quite different matter. As early as 1985 I had major arguments with him over his support for ideas which he had picked up in Canada like a multi-party system, sale and purchase of land, and private ownership. Back then, Gorbachev had no time at all for his ideas.

'We have all fixed in our minds the image of Gorbachev as a country boy from Stavropol who gradually abandons the idea of modernizing socialism and hands himself over to superior academic authority, Yakovlev first of all, then Shatalin, Aganbegyan, Abalkin, Petrakov, who all wielded intellectual influence over him at various times. Without any profound idea of his own as to where he was going and what he was doing, he wavered between one and the other. The more he wavered, the more he found himself isolated. First to leave were the party old guard, like Gromyko, Vladímir Dolgikh and Mikhail Solomentsev. Then colleagues from 1985, Ligachev and Ryzhkov. When their aspiration to take Gorbachev with them failed, people like Yakovlev and Shevardnadze created their own movement for democratic reform, moving away to one side. Last of all were those who had believed up to the final minute that he was right and had collaborated devotedly, Kryuchkov, Yazov, Baklanov, Shenin and myself.'

Although superficially merely lobbying writ large, these were real battles, and cliffhangers too, with the internecine potential that came to a head in August 1991. Smouldering memories impelled Lukyanov to fight them still. For the tactical purpose of dissolving Ligachev's power base, Gorbachev liquidated the Central Committee secretariat, never mind the loss of control to the party. That was a betrayal. Then it was Ryzhkov's turn. Again, the whole institution was scrapped in order to put down the individual whose power base it had been. 'Let's take the example of a single night, 16 to 17 November, when Gorbachev decided that he was going to part company with Ryzhkov. He telephoned me to tell me of his decision, late on the 16th. Early the following morning he informed Ryzhkov. He did it by means of turning the Council of Ministers into the Presidential Cabinet, thus depriving Ryzhkov of his position. There was no place for Ryzhkov in that cabinet. I replied to Gorbachev that Ryzhkov might be kicked out today but in six months' time we shall see the consequence through collapse and chaos in the Congress. Do not overlook the fact, I told him, that three months after the Congress breaks up, you will also cease to be President. I was only three days out in my calculations. On 5 September, the Union Congress was disbanded and on 8 December, Gorbachev stopped being President. I knew on what basis the opposition was working. I participated in the Novo-Ogarovo talks. Many of the things that Yeltsin, Kravchuk and Nazarbayev did not want to say directly to Gorbachev, they were prepared to say to me.

'He was constantly under the illusion that if he eliminated those branded as conservative, he would somehow manage to save his skin and stay in power. Brezhnev or Andropov had understood that without the support of the party, they were nobody. Sadly, God did not endow this former Komsomol worker Gorbachev with such understanding. There was nothing premeditated about it, nor do I ascribe any sinister motives or bad character to him, nor do I wish to detract from his many good qualities. He was deluded by the idea that the country and the people needed him as an individual. He did not take account of the fact that if he abandoned the party and socialism and loyal comrades, then he would ultimately find himself entirely superfluous.

'The left-wing radicals never needed him, except for the period of transfer of power. As soon as he had irretrievably leapt from his red horse on to a white horse, they got rid of him as ruthlessly as he had previously got rid of Ligachev and Ryzhkov. Yeltsin declared himself a supporter of capitalism only in 1990. What happened in August was foreseeable as a result of these processes.

'At the time of Yeltsin's expulsion from the Politburo in October 1987, I told Gorbachev that he was creating a monster. But he never really listened properly to incisive observations.'

Yeltsin's opening came through the decision of the Nineteenth Party Conference to create the new Congress of People's Deputies. Did Gorbachev not realize that this would provide an alternative power base where Yeltsin would be able to build up his following, with greater legitimacy as well?

'We must remember that when Yeltsin lost his job he was still a nobody. A technocrat, dogmatic in his views, he is not very highly educated. Gorbachev had offended him, and that was enough. But he could nothing on his own. His political career really took off when the anti-Gorbachev, anti-Soviet, anti-communist forces decided that he was someone they could use for their own purposes. Everything that has happened since then has been more or less the manipulation of Yeltsin by these anti-communist and pro-capitalist forces. I have witnessed this process unfolding. Before my very eyes, the Inter-regional Group of Deputies formed in Congress as anti-socialist. At the beginning, as

Sakharov himself told me, they were rather doubtful about Yeltsin's intellectual capacity. Gradually Afanasiev, Sakharov, Zaslavsky and others decided that they could draw him into their camp and exploit him.

'The Soviet press and literature blamed one man alone for the transformation of the old Supreme Soviet into the Congress of People's Deputies, namely me. And it is true. I presented this idea to Gorbachev and he was in favour of it. A first-past-the-post winner in an electoral system removed from the Supreme Soviet categories like peasants and workers and women, and automatically replaced them with young intellectuals and academics of the Sergei Stankevich type, who could obviously outmanoeuvre village post-mistresses in majority-based elections. The representative nature of this central organ of power had to be sustained. So the Congress was to be made up of a combination of deputies, some elected on a territorial basis and others on lists reserved for unions, kolkhozes, national autonomous regions, women's organizations, and so on. When people accuse me of creating the monster that the Congress of People's Deputies turned out to be, I respond by pointing out that people like Popov, Sakharov or Afanasiev were all selected from academic institutions, not elected by a majority. If the Congress had not come into existence, they would never have been in positions of power.'

We can put that vice versa: it was made easy for Yeltsin to play the democratic card.

'He was the yeast by which the radicals backing him rose politically. I was not such an idealist as to imagine that the Congress would be an obedient creature. I was hoping to draw on the Russian tradition of provincial rural councils which were usually more than 2000 strong. I realized that a group of such size is not suitable for drawing up legislation or for the minutiae of running the state, but it is useful in a period of transition for expressing and forming public opinion. A representative body of the kind is an important outlet of steam.'

When did Gorbachev realize that Yeltsin was dangerous to him?

'At the beginning of 1990. In March that year he got himself appointed President in order to ward off the increasing threat from Yeltsin. Even as late as May he was speaking out against Yeltsin in the Congress of People's Deputies, still unconscious of the fact that Yeltsin was about to become a leader, a leader now of Russia. Yeltsin was voted chairman of the Supreme Soviet of Russia by a majority of only four votes, and at that time I said plainly to Gorbachev, The destruction of the Soviet Union is now beginning. In fact the unravelling of the Soviet Union had begun two years earlier with Nagorny-Karabakh. There are many types of politicians. Those playing political chess are planning ten to fifteen moves ahead. Some think no more than three moves ahead and leave the rest to intuition. Gorbachev is not more than three moves ahead. He has often accused me of playing complicated chess games, tracing things backwards or forwards too far.'

Lukyanov's own parting of the ways with Gorbachev began at the very end of 1989. Newfangled institutions launched another very old-fashioned but characteristic test of strength. 'When Gorbachev began to moot the idea of using the Politburo to create a presidency, Ryzhkov and I spoke against it in the Politburo. In my view, the function of President was thoroughly alien and unnecessary to the Soviet system. It created a parallel stream of government. When Gorbachev became President and I was Speaker of the Congress, there began to be increasing conflict and distance, not between us as individuals but between the parliamentary and presidential structures. That gulf widened. Gorbachev was constantly trying to turn his back on parliament and ignore it. This conflict reached its climax in the spring of 1991, when Gorbachev called the presidents of the republics to the Novo-Ogarovo talks but bypassed the legislative branch altogether.

'Gorbachev was always trying to get me involved in the Novo-Ogarovo process and I sat through the meetings, but I was not allowed to express the opinion of Congress in my capacity as Speaker. If I had moved to adopt Gorbachev's position, I would have been crushed by Congress. I was able to express parliamentary opinion only by attempting to stand out against the various proposals being made by the various Presidents including Gorbachev. The Union treaty proposed by Yeltsin, Kravchuk and Nazarbayev, and to which Gorbachev was prepared to concur, introduced a confederation rather than a federation. This directly contradicted the Constitution, as well as the referendum whereby two-thirds wanted to maintain the Union. Not to mention the will of Congress.

'My open admission of the split between Gorbachev and myself was my speech at the plenum on 26 July 1991. In that speech I dealt with three main points. We could not turn our backs on modernizing socialism; we could not reject the Soviet form of state administration; and we had no right to turn this country into a confederation. So cutting and sharp was this speech that *Pravda* was too frightened to publish it in its entirety, and it appeared next day in *Sovetskaya Industriya*. The Central Committee plenum greeted the speech with enthusiastic applause. The only person in the room not to clap was the General Secretary. Various historians have since tried to prove that the plenum was hoping to set me up as an alternative party leader but that is not the case. Far from aspiring to such a post, I was on the contrary trying to defend Gorbachev's interests and make him realize in time the error of his ways. But the contradictions by then were already too great to be overcome. Many people have told me that I signed my death warrant with that speech.'

When you made that speech, what were the plans of the State Committee?

'It did not exist.'

Not even among themselves?

'I was not a member of the Committee. It did not really exist and I know about it only from the criminal proceedings against its members. The idea of declaring a state of emergency cropped up about ten days after my speech. On 3 August Gorbachev himself talked in the Cabinet of Ministers about the need for a state of emergency. I myself was out of Moscow on holiday near Novgorod. As far as I know, some of the members of the State Committee met around 6 August and decided among themselves that it was crucial to introduce a state of emergency in order to stop the ratification of the Novo-Ogarovo agreement, and so to save the country. They were sincerely convinced that they were acting in the best interests of the Soviet Union. At that point, it was only a matter of discussion. These were all people in Gorbachev's immediate circle, extremely close to him. On 18 August some of them went to see him in the Crimea, to gain his permission for a state of emergency. Granted his conflict with Yeltsin, they were very confident that he would agree to the proposal.

'I knew nothing about that trip to Gorbachev. I was summoned to Moscow only when the delegation returned. When I arrived there on the evening of the 18th, the eve of the coup, I told the newly forming State Committee that this plot was doomed to failure from the start. Their continued trust in Gorbachev, their indecisiveness and their determination to avoid bloodshed at all costs were the factors which sealed its fate. I tried to tell them that the steps they were taking were extremely ill-thought-out and would inevitably lead to the destruction of the Communist Party, which we have indeed seen. The party was bound to be implicated in the plot.'

Here, in sum, was an ultimate example of what the Soviets meant by a provocation. Those in favour of the proposed treaty had tempted, almost dared, those opposing it to do their worst. Nothing now could be achieved in antechambers. Their possibilities exhausted at that stage, speeches and articles and cabals had to yield to tanks. Tanks without the leadership's resolution to accept victims on whatever scale might be necessary for victory were worse than useless, theatrical and soon counterproductive. Where real force would be decisive, the mere show of it was laughable, almost at once redounding against the State Committee. Only three-move men, to borrow Lukyanov's withering language, the State Committee members had been trapped into the mistake which finally played into their enemies' hands.

'The plot would be used subsequently by separatist forces to destroy the

Soviet Union, to remove themselves from the centre on the grounds that the centre had tried to grab all the power. It would be used to justify the destruction of the armed forces and state security by implicating them in the plot too. The population proved indifferent. Not a single factory went on strike in the Moscow area. At a generous estimate, something like 20,000 people out of a possible 11 million gathered round the White House. One organization went on strike in Moscow, namely the Stock Exchange. The brokers and dealers organized a brigade of a hundred of their members to defend the White House. So up-and-coming businessmen sent food and vodka to the defenders of the White House, while at the Stock Exchange they stitched together a 100-metres-long Russian tricolour flag which was paraded through the streets. Very few realized that it was a pre-revolutionary trade flag and not the Russian flag at all. The actual Russian flag is black, yellow and white.'

How did the State Committee respond to your warning about the likely consequences of their actions?

'They said, Sorry but you are telling us all this too late. We have already spoken to Gorbachev and burned our bridges. That explains why I took a protective stance towards Congress, trying to keep it independent, out of the hands of the State Committee and of Yeltsin as well.

'You can see the August events as a blank cartridge fired from a starting pistol for the long and violent overturning of social structures and institutions. The form of capitalism being introduced here will not be able to take root in Russia. We are dealing with a Euro-Asian power, with its own social mores, attitudes to property and ways of doing things. We have a far greater level of collectivism and decision-making, as in China and India. What is the compensation for the loss of human rights? It is no secret that each individual used to feel he belonged to a large and powerful national and state entity. Now that has been snapped off in every Soviet citizen. Any political party which can key in to that sentiment will drum up enormous popular support. You can see Russia balanced on a tiny tightrope with on one side fascism and on the other civil war.'

41

'WHAT ARE YOU DOING AMONG THEM?'

In the annals of the mass media there is little or nothing to compare to the press conference held in the Kremlin on the evening of 19 August 1990. Before the whole astonished world, journalists exposed that the State Committee consisted of men who lacked the will to carry out their threats. Television cameras lingered on the hands of Yanayev shaking with uncontrollable fear while he was speaking. Disregard for the self-proclaimed saviours on the platform became visible. Among them was a virtual nonentity, entitled the chairman of the Peasants' Union, one Vasily Starodubtsev. In the audience was Alexander Bovin, a large and jovial man as well as one of the leading political commentators, with a special question for Starodubtsev: 'We can see why the others are here, but what are you doing among them?'

In order to meet Starodubtsev, I had to leave Moscow before dawn and drive four hours into the country, in the direction of Tula, to Novomoskovskoye. For thirty years he has been unchallenged chairman of the V. I. Lenin collective farm. Far and away the largest building is a central block in which he has his offices. A bottle of cognac was waiting on the table: this was firewater not to be drunk but chucked straight down the throat.

To Starodubtsev, Gorbachev had been 'a slippery, career building functionary'. As from 1989, he says, he had had several meetings of two and three hours in order to persuade him that 'these semi-spontaneous reforms should be replaced by a proper programme and above all a proper market theory and a legislative base. I used rather rude forms of address and Gorbachev returned the compliments. I am now convinced that Gorbachev betrayed the country. The arch-villain was Yakovlev who long ago had sold the pass to the West. If you beat Gorbachev over the head it would serve no purpose. He always tried to weave his way around problems.'

Yanayev, he continues, telephoned him on the morning of the 19th and he hurried round to the Kremlin to join the others. 'The State Committee were all members of the Government, up to and including the Vice-President. My conscience is clear. I was acting only in the interest of agricultural workers.

The State Committee could have used force had it wanted to but that was not the task it had set itself. It introduced a state of emergency without the use of force. It was completely unforeseeable that prostitutes, homosexuals, drug addicts and other such types would defend the White House. Yeltsin is also a traitor of the first order. In my view, Gorbachev knew well what was going on. As a weak and vacillating character prepared to sell out at every stage, he was not ready to take responsibility for a state of emergency. If we had been successful, he would have leapt to join us.'

Looking at the dark hangdog face and restless bloodshot eyes across the table, listening to the specious bombast, I seemed to have stepped straight into the pages of Gogol's *Dead Souls*, that work of genius. It was almost hallucinatory. He might have been one of Gogol's inimitable blackguard landlords in the last century defending privilege with a crassness and ignorance which he did not realize was utterly incriminating. Nothing distinguished Starodubtsev from a serf-owner. I asked him how the Gorbachev years had affected his peasants. 'They went on as before, reaping and sowing.' There are 1500 of them, and 'only one so far has expressed the wish to go private'. And had Gogol not also said the last word about Gorbachev and Yeltsin? 'For a long time I simply could not believe it. Ivan Ivanovich has quarrelled with Ivan Nikiforich! Such worthy men! After that, is there anything solid left in this world?'

I was handed over to two estate-managers. In a reserved dining room we were fed cold appetizers, *zakouski*, stuffed fish, chicken, Italian wine. This blowout was intended to serve as the purpose of the day, on the principle that a full stomach means an empty mind. Afterwards I was escorted on a conducted tour of the property. And there is the church, presumably once serving the local village, destroyed in the war because the Germans mounted a machine gun on top of the tower, and afterwards rebuilt. A baptism ceremony was taking place for between twenty and thirty children. A few were babies in arms, but most were solemn little schoolboys and girls. The parents looked embarrassed. A young beardless man, the priest was wearing a pale blue nylon work-coat, of the sort appropriate in a hardware store or a grocery. His trouser bottoms and his shoes showed incongruously. Someone whispered in my ear that until very recently he had been a railway worker. Evidently unfamiliar with the order of service, he kept on instructing everyone to face this way, and now that. He stammered out apologies. As the little congregation did its about-turns, the faces seemed to grow pinker.

The innocence and visible trust were profoundly moving. I also thought that here was a master-image of the new Russia, in which the Starodubtsevs and their ilk would at last have no place. But on the way back, we had to cross a bridge over the Oka River, whose salient features I had failed to observe in the half-light and emptiness of the early hours. Here was a rival master-image. The highway at that point reduces to two narrow lanes carried across a high viaduct. Much of the concrete of this bridge has flaked away, whole sections of the parapet are missing, and the rest is cracking and crumbling. It looks structurally unsafe. The road surface has also eroded, to reveal underlying gridded wire, now broken and sticking up here and there in sharp spikes. Having suffered punctures, several vehicles had to be repaired where they had come to a stop, with a result that only one car or lorry at a time could weave past these stationary obstructions. One driver after another was trying to force his way through, mounting verges and pavements, on whichever side he could create an opening. Pandemonium for some, resignation for others; hours of misery for all. 'What is the meaning of this terrifying motion?' runs a famous prophetic passage in *Dead Souls*. 'Russia, where are you flying to? Answer! She gives no answer.'

AFTERMATH

Transference of power within this system had previously been an arrangement between a few men conspiring together. In the obvious precedent, Brezhnev and his colleagues had dumped an unwanted Khrushchev. But Yeltsin's takeover was out in the open. Standing on a tank outside the White House, he had defied the State Committee for all to view. This demanded conspicuous bravery. Staking himself out as a democrat, he had appealed to Russians at large, and committed himself at least nominally to representative processes of election and a parliament. Speaking a language of rights and personal freedom, he had to carry this new logic through to the end. But it was still a surprise that victory over Gorbachev necessarily entailed the collapse of the two elements which had interlocked to make that society what it was, the party and the Soviet Union.

The party had maintained its hold on power through the commitment to it of the KGB and the army, those joint guardians of the secret police state. During the August coup Yeltsin was able to persuade a majority of the KGB and the army in Russia to side with him. He was therefore the winner in the great governing test of strength. But the organizations charged to enforce the party's will were now caught in an unbridgeable division of loyalty. Failing to use power decisively in its own interest, the party had forfeited its monopoly of enforcement. This was a complete repudiation of Marxist doctrine, and contrary to the very nature of the party.

Conversely, Gorbachev no longer had military or KGB loyalists to whom to turn. Potential allies among hardline generals and officials who clung to Soviet ideology and were prepared to enforce it, had openly rejected him when they obeyed Kryuchkov and Yazov. In addition, they were now discredited, with charges of treason hanging over ringleaders. By the end of the month, those who could compact with Yeltsin had done so, while those who were compromised either through supporting the State Committee or close association with Gorbachev were already being purged from public life. Times were changing: they received pensions instead of a bullet in the back of the head in the Lubyanka cellars, in the summary manner of so many army and KGB generals before them.

Returning from his Crimean experience, Gorbachev declared that he found himself in another country, so significantly and swiftly had the political landscape shifted as a result of the party's failure to enforce its will. He might have driven straight to the White House to make his compact with Yeltsin; he might further have tried to promote new generals in the army and the KGB, inveigling them away from Yeltsin. Instead he retired into the Kremlin, losing no opportunity to affirm that he was more than ever a convinced communist, looking to a revitalized party for great things in the future. But his promises, like his threats, were now mere words, vacuous because not backed by means of enforcement.

Rearranging personnel, committees and institutions and even the party-state itself to suit and project his new-found power, Yeltsin finalized what had become a one-sided contest. In the Congress, he instructed Gorbachev to do his bidding by reading aloud from one piece of paper or signing another. The masterful smile on his face contrasted with the pinched expression of his defeated rival. These Congress clashes were shown live on television. Gorbachev's tones of entreaty emphasized that his authority had dissipated beyond recall.

Trying to save himself, Gorbachev resigned as General Secretary, he nationalized the party's property, he suspended the Central Committee. This eroded what little power base was left to him, and further incited Yeltsin to go one better. Yeltsin incorporated as Russian Ministries what had previously been Soviet Ministries, he dissolved the Soviet Congress to leave the field clear for the Russian Congress, he abolished the central administration; he banned the party and took to describing communists as criminals. In his memories he exulted, 'Gorbachev was extremely pained by the decision to suppress the party!' Soon all that remained of the centre was Gorbachev pinned and desperate in the Kremlin, and the unfinished business of the Novo-Ogarovo talks.

When Yeltsin spoke of 'That feeling of fear which lives in every Soviet citizen', he knew the weight of his words. In his time, he had contributed to causing much Soviet fear. 'He will install gallows in the street,' Ryzhkov had said of him, in the context, to be sure, of siding with Gorbachev. To Gorbachev now he was 'a neo-Bolshevik' and sometimes even 'Czar Boris'. Even one of his new allies, Sobchak, could say that he had long seen Yeltsin 'as just another party hack'. Nobody could have been a more typical product of the party and the Soviet Union. Through and through, he was the Soviet *beau idéal* of a First Secretary, a command-administrative manager, maximizing and relishing power for its own sake.

It was his singular fate to be employing against the system all that system's peculiarities of arbitrariness and improvization, so extending methods which he was purporting to end. Even while bringing about the demise of the Soviet Union, Yeltsin evidently regretted the inevitable loss of power. There was no alternative. Having obtained absolute power himself through the contriving of a policy of independence and democratization for Russia, he had no grounds for denying that the Presidents of the Union's constituent republics could do likewise. Once again there was a discrepancy between the ruler's aspirations and his deeds. Vranyo accordingly bloomed.

An Estonian, Rein Müllerson was one of the rare international lawyers in the Soviet Union, head of the International Law Department in the Academy of Sciences. He had been on the Yakovlev commission investigating the Ribbentrop–Molotov Pact, and in March 1991 he was appointed deputy Foreign Minister of an Estonia still blocked by the Soviet Union. By then he had become critical of the draft treaties emerging from the Novo-Ogarovo talks, on the grounds that the sovereignty of the republics and the existence of the Soviet Union as a sovereign state were incompatible. The coup brought the issue to a head. Without it, in his opinion, independence might have been realized only after violent clashes of the kind that had already occurred in Tbilisi and Vilnius and elsewhere.

Müllerson's first task after the coup was to draft the letter from the Estonian government requesting admittance to the United Nations. At eleven o'clock on 24 August, he accompanied President Rüütel and Indrek Toome, the chairman of the Foreign Relations Committee in the Estonian parliament, to a meeting in Yeltsin's office. 'Yeltsin agreed that Russia would recognize the independence of Estonia, but there was nobody to draft the text. Yeltsin first proposed to sign a protocol between the deputy Foreign Minister of Russia and myself concerning mutual recognition. I replied, Of course we can do that, but your decree is what is really important for Estonians and the world community of states. At that moment Yeltsin was the most powerful man in the Soviet Union and maybe he was flattered. Anyhow he agreed. As there was nobody to write this text, I simply went into the next-door room and drafted it. Rüütel and Yeltsin left to attend the funeral of those three young men who had been killed during the coup. By the time they returned, my text had been typed and was ready, and Yeltsin signed it. Under normal circumstances such a thing was unimaginable.'

In short order, the other republics then declared their independence too, with such haste that they adopted the Estonian text as it stood. In the case of Turkmenistan, the name of the Baltic republic was even accidentally incorporated. In a tactic borrowed from Gorbachev, supportive referendums were arranged and they naturally threw up a vote everywhere of over 90 per cent. The last republic to hold its referendum was Ukraine, on 1 December. Here was the *coup de grâce*. Ukraine was second only to Russia in resources and population. A week later, Yeltsin and Leonid Kravchuk and Stanislas Shushkevich, as Presidents respectively of Russian, Ukraine and Belarus, met in a forest lodge near Minsk, where they signed a declaration that a Commonwealth of Independent States had replaced the Soviet Union. Other former republics could join the three Slav republics if they chose. It was a deft conclusion to the Novo-Ogarovo talks. Obsolete now, the 'war of laws' had served its purpose and could be allowed to evanesce.

Communist Parties in the satellites of Eastern Europe had arrived at power-sharing with the opposition. In the Soviet Union power was instead distributed at the level of nationality. The process could only be imperfect and incomplete; the old party leaders remained in office, without a blush relabelling themselves democrats and constitutionalists. A few weeks after Leonid Kravchuk had suddenly sloughed off the skin of a party apparatchik for rebirth as a brand-new nationalist President, a journalist was to reproach him. 'You were all Gorbachev's sons, and you killed him!' To which Kravchuk replied that Gorbachev had been incapable of preventing disintegration and chaos, 'and that is where his guilt lies'. All the same, he suavely interjected, 'I would also like to read, one day, that Kravchuk was one of those who did much to break up the empire, that Ukraine played an enormous role in that.'

Deprived of an entity of which to be President, on 25 December Gorbachev resigned. That same day, the Soviet Union's final official act was to restore diplomatic relations with Israel. In Jerusalem, in a building known as the Russian Compound, the hammer-and-sickle flag was raised and then lowered one last time before its international recognition was withdrawn. There was something symbolic in this act of deathbed reparation for long-term bullying which seemed to have stemmed straight from Tsarist prejudices and pogroms.

The United States and its European allies had a declared policy of armed resistance to the Soviet Union, but the persistent effort to find ways to negotiate and collaborate called their resolve into question. Many, perhaps most, westerners had been brought to a belief that Soviet collectivism might have flaws but was in all sorts of respects superior to their own individualism. The overthrow of communism in a general war could in any event never be considered seriously in the nuclear age. Revolution in the party-state stood not the slightest chance of success. Soviet inhumanity and terror had come to be perceived as a fact of international life about which nothing could be done. The Soviet Union might not have built an economy more productive than capitalism but it had imposed itself through raw strength and will. Soviet leaders up to and including Gorbachev were gratified by the odd mixture of resentment and deference which they received on all sides. Here was confirmation of superpower status. The Soviet Union could have continued unimpeded on its own rough course.

Vulnerability lay within the system. The Achilles heel was the factionalism against which Lenin had warned. By means of a highly improbable and utterly unrealistic series of decrees and measures railroaded in the usual arbitrary manner through the party, Gorbachev created unique conditions for a faction fight, and one which could not be stifled at origin behind closed doors. A growing number of ordinary people could observe it, and then participate. Once out in the open, this became a test of strength which completely paralysed the party. Nothing but force could have set limits to it, and called a halt. By the time force was actually used in the August coup, a political process had already developed sufficiently to negate the nature of totalitarianism, and so release the Soviet Union and the rest of the world from the Cold War, as though by accident.

A fascinated, almost bewitched, West applauded Gorbachev and his measures on the grounds that the Soviet Union now really could be taken at face value, internalized and accepted as a normal state. That applause was the West's unwitting contribution to the downfall of the man and the system he embodied. It was an irony worthy of the whole inverted phenomenon of fellow-travelling that those who delighted in their perception of Gorbachev perfecting communism were in fact his auxiliary grave-diggers. Just as he refused to defend the party's strength in Eastern Europe, so he did not crack down on the faction fight he had himself permitted to develop so that it engulfed him and all he stood for. Out of hesitation or good character, he made an anachronism of the party's will. In the last analysis, the party could never be law-based. Those who take a high view of human nature will judge him to have been a historic personality of lasting stature. Those who take a low view will write him off as a simpleton.

Yeltsin's heady triumph was short-lived. The new independent Russia was supposed to be a law-abiding society and state. To appeal for the desirable ends of democracy and privatization was very much simpler than realizing them in practice. The dissolution of the party deprived the state of the machinery essential for government and administration. Party leaders had worked their will through the parallel but interconnected channels of the executive, the legislative and the judiciary. Yeltsin himself had become the executive. His Vice-President, Alexander Rutskoi, a decorated hero of the Afghan campaign, had supported him in the White House during the coup. The communist-derived Russian Congress was a rump legislature from the Soviet past. Its speaker, Ruslan Khasbulatov, a Chechen and therefore a Muslim, had also thrown his lot in with Yeltsin at that moment. Legal officials such as the Prosecutor General or judges, and indeed the entire police force, had no objectives to enforce once they no longer received instructions from the party. Except in the unlikely event of eviction by some irresistible superior, members of the old Nomenklatura had only to assert themselves in their former position and exploit it for all it was worth. In the wreckage, the scramble for power was unbridled. Personality rather than principle was still decisive.

In the historic Russian tradition there was little trace of concepts such as representation, accountability, contract, agreed rights, equality before the law; and the Soviet party-state had naturally suppressed them altogether as hostile to communism. To the population at large, the values and behaviour inherent in such concepts were untried and outlandish. None of the requisite institutionalized structure existed in defence of the individual as citizen, as property owner, as consumer, as buyer or seller. Civic sense, voluntary compliance with the law, plain fellow feeling and good manners, had been so many handicaps to the individual under communism. Laying the foundation of a rewarding career, cynicism and violence were only habitual. There was now not even the party's social discipline, primitive and barbarous as that had been; there was nothing at all to demarcate liberty from licence.

Here were laboratory conditions, so to speak, for the cultivation of tests of strength in order to determine where real power lay. From top to bottom, Russia accordingly broke out with enterprise which was indistinguishable from lawlessness and anarchy. Everyone with the ambition for it made his bid for wealth and power in whichever walk of life he found himself. Almost overnight, the streets filled with fortune-hunters and traders on the one hand, the poor and destitute on the other, people who for whatever reason were defenceless in circumstances which offered a standing invitation to the strong and unscrupulous to help themselves. This type of capitalist commerce was Karamzin's thieving in its latest guise. Communist corruption converted instantaneously into civilian corruption. Suddenly markets flourished in which everything was available, not only pop music and pornography but icons from churches, museum pieces, weapons, factories, shares, the vouchers offered in privatization, as in some gold-rush fantasy.

Five thousand criminal gangs are thought to be operating in Russia. Nothing restrains them except the superior violence of another gang. Protection rackets and armed robbery are routine. Gangsters chuck hand grenades and shoot it out with each other in public places. Hundreds of thousands of cars stolen in Western Europe circulate freely in Russia. Smuggling by Russians and their associates of drugs and currency and natural resources now preoccupies the police forces of the world. Criminals pass more or less at will across the borders of Finland, Poland, Turkey and even China. Russian prostitutes are the star attraction of the Arabian Gulf, of all places. Profiteers with suitcases of cash are active in the West, speculating and buying property. Cyprus has become the main offshore base through which about 2000 Russian companies and a dozen banks siphon off huge capital sums. Couriers of plutonium 239 and other weapons-grade materials have been arrested in the West. Policemen have turned extortionists: it is commonplace to be stopped on some trumped-up matter for which the policeman demands $50 on the spot. And the colleague who spots him then insists on his $50 as well. Security guards of businesses and factories are usually former KGB men, willing to use whatever methods are needed to safeguard their employers and fend off competitors. Investors or depositors in businesses and banks are cheated either in simple fraud or in sophisticated computer-operated scams against which there is no defence.

According to Yeltsin, $2 billion went missing from the Russian trade balance in 1992 and 40 per cent of businessmen and two-thirds of commercial organizations were involved in bribery and illegal transactions. In order not to stir up panic, he was hugely underestimating these figures, but he concluded truthfully, 'Corruption within government literally corrodes the state structure'. Western sources estimate that slightly over half the $86 billion that Russia received from the West in one form or another has found its way illegally into private accounts in Western banks. Put another way, all the money that Gorbachev wheedled out in return for the reunification of Germany has been misappropriated. Without proper mechanisms to absorb it productively in this economy at the absolute mercy of every vicissitude, Western money only fuels corruption.

It was perhaps poetic justice that Yeltsin found himself in a plight so like Gorbachev's. Ostensibly a president with powers which made him an absolute ruler, in practice he had no means of enforcing his writ much beyond the edge of his desk or the reach of his telephone. During the eighteen months following the coup, he and the Russian Congress locked into a contest as each sought to wrest the other's powers. In the manner of Gorbachev, Yeltsin manoeuvred, he jettisoned advisers criticized by his opponents, he cajoled and propitiated, seeking to turn his titular position into effective authority. In vain: Khasbulatov had seen his opening for a supreme challenge. So did Rutskoi, his expedient ally for purposes of toppling Yeltsin. So did the Prosecutor General, Valentin Stepankov, who used the evidence he had assembled during official investigation of the State Committee members to publish a book, *Kremlin Plot*. 'The civilized world has not yet known such a mockery of justice,' was the comment of *Izvestia*. Yeltsin could not keep even Kryuchkov and Yazov behind bars. Valery Zorkin, head of the Constitutional Court, used his position to attack Yeltsin, even threatening him with impeachment in the end.

These were generalized tests of strength between personalities in the name of the institution they apparently embodied, and they came to a head on 21 September 1993. Yeltsin dissolved the Congress and called for elections under new rules which were supposed to ensure that the sitting members would not be returned. This was an 'infantile ruse' to eliminate Khasbulatov and Rutskoi. As Yeltsin had done before them in 1991, they barricaded themselves in the White House and appealed to the population to come to their defence.

In his memoirs Yeltsin asked if there was not a malicious irony of fate in this. The refusal to use force would condemn him to impotence and rejection, as had happened with Gorbachev. So he ordered tanks to fire on the very White House where he had staged his own defiance. The building was soon blasted and scorched. Like surrendering prisoners, their hands above their heads, Rutskoi and Khasbulatov walked out through smoke, to be hustled away to prison. 'Formally, the President was violating the Constitution,' Yeltsin writes rather heavily of himself and his actions, 'going the route of anti-democratic measures, and dispersing the parliament – all for the sake of establishing democracy and the rule of law in the country. The parliament was defending the Constitution – in order to overthrow the lawfully elected President and establish total Soviet rule. How had we found ourselves in such a fix?'

Though reformed and going under another name, the KGB was still not accountable to the law. This time, Yeltsin had the greatest difficulty persuading the KGB and the army to move against his rivals. Even the faithful General Grachev, now Minister of Defence, jibbed. And it was all to little purpose. The newly elected Congress passed an amnesty for these latest plotters. Alexei Kazannik, the Prosecutor General who had replaced the gossipmongering Stepankov, issued a statement that Khasbulatov and Rutskoi were responsible for the most shameful act, and had tainted themselves with murder. But, in a phrase crafted to extricate himself, he added 'I must be guided by the letter and the spirit of the law.' Professing not to have powers to suspend this amnesty passed in Congress, he therefore resigned his office. Freed from prison like the State Committee members before them, Khasbulatov and Rutskoi vowed to continue their struggle against Yeltsin. Everything, even a coup, is negotiable.

Resorting to force, Yeltsin revealed that he too had no choice but to obey the logic of absolutism, while covering his tracks with the usual self-justifying vranyo. In that spirit, like any Russian despot, he has sent troops under one pretext or another into Nagorny-Karabakh, Moldavia, Georgia and Tajikistan, and he exploits the presence of native Russians in Ukraine, and Russian colonials in the Baltic, to exert pressure on supposedly independent govern-ments. With the fate of Gorbachev and the Soviet Union vividly before him, he foresaw that the Russian Federation in its turn might unravel through another round of declarations of independence. Self-determination for non-Russian people could be permitted to go only so far, and he took his stand over the Chechens. Muslims from the Caucasus, the Chechens had a proud history of resistance to Russian supremacy, whether Tsarist or Stalinist. The status of a Soviet autonomous republic had been imposed on them, and after 1991 many Chechens saw the opportunity to convert this fiction into a genuine nation-state of their own. Neither law nor due process then prevailed. Yeltsin responded by invading the republic, flattening its capital of Grozny, killing thousands and scattering the population as refugees. With the possible exception of Gorbachev, previous rulers in the Kremlin would have approved. Parlance now in vogue about democracy and a 'civilized' Russia evidently had no substance. Other people intending to follow the Chechen example have been warned that relationships with Russia remain tests of strength. Former Soviet republics like the Baltic states and Ukraine, now menacingly referred to as 'the near abroad', and even the freed satellites, suffer from many of the same social and political weaknesses as Russia itself, and they are susceptible to being coaxed or bounced into a reconstituted sphere of influence, if not empire.

In spite of its Marxist pretensions, communism was not intrinsically different from historic Russian despotism, but a particularly vicious and destructive version of it. An extreme nationalist might extend a new incarnation of it into the future. So might a military dictator. Alternatively, if there is to be a law-based society, a modern Speransky is required to write a constitution with proper checks and balances, above all the separation of powers. More difficult still, such a reformer has then to devise the means for the peaceful enforcement of constitutionality. As things stand, there is no prospect of it. Russian nationhood and civilization depend upon the future establishment of the rule of law. Until such time, the communist legacy survives and mocks the death of the party.

U.S.S.R.

Olenek ●

Tazovskıy ●

Yenisey

Tunguska

Lena

Yakutsk ●

Yenisey

Lena

Irtysh

Omsk ●

Novosibirsk ●

Ob

Irkutsk ●   Lake Baikal

Lake Balkash

Ulan Bator ●

MONGOLIA

N. KOREA

Alma-Ata ●

Bishkek ●
KIRGHIZIA

Beijing ●

S. KOREA

IKISTAN

oul

CHINA

Islamabad ●

NEPAL

Thimphu ●
·
Kathmandu ●   BHUTAN

New Delhi ●

INDIA

TAIWAN

INDEX

Aare, Juhan, 152–3
Abalkin, Leonid, 17, 98, 370, 420
Abel, Genevieve, 145
Abkhaz people, 2
Aczél, György, 221, 224–5
Adamec, Ladislav, 317, 319–21, 324, 327, 335
Ādaži kolkhoz, Latvia, 174
Adenauer, Konrad, 13, 71, 236, 253
Adilet (Kazakh Popular Front), 139
Afanasiev, Yuri: in Sadovy Ring, 17; on people's indifference, 26; and collapse of communism, 31; and popular demonstrations, 84; and Balts under Nazi-Soviet Pact, 95; at Moscow City party meeting, 370; and Kalugin, 380; and Yeltsin, 422
Afghanistan: invaded (1979), 15, 20, 105, 138; Soviet offensives in, 82; Soviet aid for, 116
Africa: independence movements, 20; Soviet policy on, 115–16
African National Congress, 20
Aftomatika-Nauka-Tekhnicka, 53
Aganbegyan, Abel, 17, 98, 102, 420
Agitprop, 227, 245
Agzybirlik (Turkmen Popular Front), 139
Akcharin, Marat: *Red Odyssey*, 34–5
Akhromeyev, Marshal Sergei, 150, 153, 412
Albania: created, 64
alcohol: consumption of, 78–9
Alepino (village), 128
Alexander, Tania: *An Estonian Childhood*, 144
Aliev, Haidar, 138
Alksnis, Colonel Viktor, 375
Allenbach Institute, 237

Alma-Ata, 135
Alpha Delta (military unit), 173, 183
Alpha (specialist unit), 12
Althusser, Louis, 72
Amalrik, Andrei, *Will the Soviet Union Survive Until 1984?*, 21
Ames, Aldrich, 117
Amin, Hafizullah, 20
Amu-Darya river, 58
Andrei, Stefan, 14
Andreyeva, Nina, 89, 96, 374, 394–5
Andronic, Octavian, 348–9
Andropov, Yuri: as head of KGB, 12, 31; and repression in Hungary, 219–20, 407; qualities, 230; appoints Kochemasov, 272; Gorbachev serves, 419; dependence on party, 421
Angola, 20, 110
Anishchev, Vladimir, 139
Antall, József, 222
Antis (Lithuanian group), 182–3
Arafat, Yasser, 20, 239, 402
Aragon, Louis, 72
Aral Sea, 58, 135
Arbatov, Georgi, 83
Archangelsk, 30
archives: opened in Russia, 94
Argumenti y Fakti (journal), 80–1
Arjakas, Küllo, 155
Armenia: independence, 2; and Nagorny-Karabakh, 128–31, 140, 404; massacres in, 130, 142
arms *see* defence spending; weapons
arms control, 120–1, 387
army (Soviet) *see* Red Army
Aron, Raymond, 73
Article Six *see* USSR: Constitution
Ash, Timothy Garton, 280

Ashar (Kirghyz Popular Front), 139
Ashkhabad, 135
Åslund, Anders: *Gorbachev's Struggle for Economic Reform*, 103
Association of Former Political Prisoners of Romania, 66
Astrauskas, Vytautas, 180
Atanasev, Georgi, 297, 306–8
Atgimimas (Lithuanian newspaper), 147
Atmoda (Latvian newspaper), 147
August plot (1991), 394–5, 407–13, 417, 424–5
Austria: Hungary opens borders to, 223, 274
Austrian Communist Party: receives assets from SED, 239
Axen, Hermann, 238
Azerbaijan: independence, 2; conditions in, 34–5; racket in caviar, 53; and Nagorny-Karabakh, 128–31, 140, 364, 404
Azeris, 140

Bahr, Egon, 280–2
Bakatin, Vadim, 362, 371–3, 375, 396, 407
Baker, James, 109, 114, 120, 170, 304, 389
Baklanov, Oleg, 408, 420
Baku, 107; cultural life, 137
Balev, Milko, 296
Balkar people, 127
Baltic Observer (newspaper), 187
Baltic republics: independence from USSR, 1, 15, 119, 131–2, 139, 147, 188–90, 211, 369, 389, 401; resistance to Soviet rule, 37, 143, 147–9; rackets in, 53; Russian presence in, 64; disposition under Ribbentrop-

441